NIETZSCHE

The Arguments of
the Philosophers

EDITOR: TED HONDERICH
Reader in Philosophy, University College, London

The group of books of which this is one will include an
essentially analytic and critical account of each of the
considerable number of the great and the influential
philosophers. The group of books taken together will
comprise a contemporary assessment and history of the
entire course of philosophical thought.

Already published in the series
Plato   J. C. B. Gosling
Meinong   Reinhardt Grossman
Santayana   Timothy L. S. Sprigge
Wittgenstein   Robert J. Fogelin
Hume   Barry Stroud
Descartes   Margaret Dauler Wilson
Berkeley   George Pitcher
Kant   Ralph C. S. Walker
The Presocratic Philosophers (2 vols)   Jonathan Barnes
Russell   R. M. Sainsbury
Socrates   Gerasimos Xenophon Santas
Sartre   Peter Caws
Karl Popper   Anthony O'Hear
Gottlob Frege   Hans D. Sluga
Schopenhauer   D. W. Hamlyn
Karl Marx   Allen Wood

NIETZSCHE

Richard Schacht

Department of Philosophy
University of Illinois at Urbana–Champaign

Routledge & Kegan Paul
London, Boston, Melbourne and Henley

First published in 1983
First published as a paperback in 1985
by Routledge & Kegan Paul Plc
14 Leicester Square, London WC2H 7PH,
9 Park Street, Boston, Mass. 02108, USA,
464 St. Kilda Road, Melbourne, Victoria 3004, Australia, and
Broadway House, Newtown Road,
Henley-on-Thames, Oxon RG9 1EN
Set in 11/12pt Journal by
Cambrian Typesetters, Farnborough, Hants.
and printed in Great Britain by
Hartnoll Print, Bodmin, Cornwall
Copyright © Richard Schacht 1983

Library of Congress Cataloguing in Publication Data

Schacht, Richard, 1941—

Nietzsche.
(The Arguments of the philosophers)
Bibliography: p.
Includes index.
1. Nietzsche, Friedrich Wilhelm, 1844—1900.
I. Title. II. Series.
B3317.S36 1982   193   82—12228
ISBN 0—7100—9191—5 (C)
ISBN 0—7102—0544—9 (P)

For Eric and Marshall

Contents

Preface

Until rather recently, most philosophers in the English-speaking world have paid Nietzsche little heed. European philosophers of diverse orientations have considered him a thinker to be reckoned with throughout the course of this century; but he has seldom been taken seriously across the English Channel (and North Atlantic). Outside of what used to be the Continentally-inspired underworld, he for the most part has been either ignored altogether, or accorded only minor significance as a forerunner of existentialism, or else crudely caricatured, vilified, and cavalierly dismissed. Indeed, his long neglect was no doubt at least in part due to the fact that a great many people formed their impressions of him from the uses made of him by fascist and racist ideologues, and from the related scandalous treatment accorded him by such commentators as Bertrand Russel. Russell may be an extreme case; but it is worth noting some of the things he says about Nietzsche in his *History of Western Philosophy* (New York, Simon & Schuster, 1945, pp. 760–3, 766–7):

> Nietzsche, though a professor, was a literary rather than an academic philosopher. He invented no new technical theories in ontology or epistemology; his importance is primarily in ethics, and secondarily as an acute historical critic. . . . His general outlook . . . remained very similar to that of Wagner in the *Ring*; Nietzsche's superman is very like Siegried, except that he knows Greek. This may seem odd, but that is not my fault. . . .
>
> [Nietzsche] attempts to combine two sets of values which are not easily harmonized: on the one hand he likes ruthlessness, war, and aristocratic pride; on the other hand, he loves philosophy and literature and the arts, especially music. . . .

True virtue [for Nietzsche], as opposed to the conventional sort..., is not profitable or prudent; it isolates its possessor from other men; it is hostile to order, and does harm to inferiors. It is necessary for higher men to make war upon the masses, and resist the democratic tendencies of the age.... He prophesied with a certain glee an era of great wars; one wonders whether he would have been happy if he had lived to see the fulfillment of his prophecy....

He condemns Christian love because he thinks it is an outcome of fear. It does not occur to Neitzsche as possible that a man should genuinely feel universal love, obviously because he himself feels almost universal hatred and fear, which he would fain disguise as lordly indifference. His 'noble' man — who is himself in his day-dreams — is a being wholly devoid of sympathy, ruthless, cunning, cruel, concerned only with his own power. King Lear on the verge of madness, says: 'I will do such things — what they are yet I know not — but they shall be the terror of the earth.' This is Neitzsche's philosophy in a nutshell.

Happily, it is no longer necessary to fight the battle that had to be waged to discredit this absurd picture of Nietzsche — even if, in some quarters, its influence still lingers on. As his writings have become more widely available, in better translations, and as more discerning commentators have weighed in, a different picture of him has at least begun to emerge; and it has become possible not only to discuss him in polite intellectual society, but also to engage the interest of a growing number of philosophers in the bearing of his thought upon a variety of issues of concern to them. Such earlier and more recent studies as Morgan's *What Nietzsche Means* and Danto's *Nietzsche as Philosopher* (to mention only two of the more notable cases in point) have contributed to this transformation of the climate of opinion; but the greatest credit for it belongs to Walter Kaufmann (whose untimely death occurred just as this book was being finished). Through his many excellent translations of Nietzsche's writings, his useful commentaries and introductions to them, and his fine and widely-read *Nietzsche: Philosopher, Psychologist, Antichrist*, he did more than anyone else in our part of the world has done to rescue Nietzsche from both his unjust detractors and his ill-motivated abusers, and to gain for him the attention and appreciation he deserves. I have not attempted to write another book of the sort he wrote. His remains perhaps the best introduction to Nietzsche's life and intellectual development (although

Hollingdale's *Nietzsche: The Man and His Philosophy* and Hayman's recent *Nietzsche: A Critical Life* are also deserving of mention); I commend it to the reader both in its own right and as a very helpful background text for this study. My concerns and approach here, however, are rather different.

Nietzsche was a thinker, figure and influence about whom many sorts of books have been and can and should be written. This book is an instance of only one of them. He had many sides and moments, and has had many audiences with differing sensibilities and interests; and no single work can do justice to all of the former, or satisfy all of the latter. The 'perspectivism' of which he speaks is not without a certain application in this context. The vantage point from which — and the eyes with which — he is viewed in the present study may be complemented by others, as others are here, to good effect. And that which is thus viewed does not have a sharp and clear shape and structure, but rather acquires definiteness only in the course of interpretation. These circumstances, however, far from diminishing Nietzsche's interest, are elements of his greatness and importance, and are among the reasons why we never will (or in any event should) have done with him.

Nietzsche's productive life was relatively short, encompassing less than a score of years (beginning in the early 1870s, and ending with his collapse in 1889), the second half of which was of far greater importance than the first. In this brief period, however, he did a prodigious amount of writing, and dealt with as broad a range of matters as almost anyone ever has. In addition to the considerable number of works he published and prepared for publication, he left a great mass of notes, which scholars undoubtedly will be mining for generations, and which can neither be entirely ignored nor easily digested. And even the works he completed for the most part consist chiefly in assemblages of rather loosely connected notes rather than sustained arguments and systematic treatments of particular topics. He had a great deal to say, about a great many things; and no single study can take account of more than a part of it.

This is so even if attention is confined — as it is here — to what Nietzsche has to say on matters of a philosophical nature, passing over his interspersed reflections on other matters (which are many), and his excursions along literary lines. The present study is an examination of his philosophical thinking; and while this already makes it selective (as well as interpretive), it is of necessity selective in other ways as well. In deciding what in Neitzsche's philosophical thinking and writings to deal with, and how to do so, I have been guided by two basic intentions: first, to do at least something approaching justice to the range, manner and issue of his philosophical endeavours; and second, to render them accessible, intelligible and interesting to philosophers and philosophically-minded readers more generally in the English-speaking world, regardless of their particular philosophical orientations and prior acquaintance with him. I have considered it neither necessary nor desirable to deal with the extensive secondary literature on him; that either would have added considerably to the length of this book (which is long enough as it is), or would have required that less be said about Nietzsche himself (which would have worked against my chief aims).

On the other hand, I have found it necessary for my purposes to make extensive use of things Nietzsche wrote but had not incorporated into any of the works he published or prepared for publication up to the time of his collapse. These unpublished writings too exhibit his philosophical thinking, and indeed contain much more of his expressed thinking on certain important matters than do his finished works. Restricting attention to the latter alone, therefore, would have been both artificial and impoverishing. In any event, what this book is a study *of* is the philosophical thinking expressed in the things he wrote, including manuscripts and notes he left as well as works he completed. One may always question the commitment of a writer to things he writes but does not publish; but this is a worry of which too much can be made. And it is doubly desirable not to make too much of it in the case of someone like Nietzsche whose productive life ended abruptly and quite early, with major projects under way and in the offing, material for which he was accumulating in the notebooks from his later years. One cannot know what use he might have made of this material; but this, in my opinion, is no reason to ignore it.

My decision to draw upon it, however, has been conjoined with another: to confine my citations and explicit attention largely to works Nietzsche completed, together with his unpublished early essay *On Truth and Lie in an Extra-Moral Sense*, and the extensive and reasonably well organized selection of material from his notebooks from the last decade of his productive life published under the title of *The Will to Power*. The former essay is too important and interesting to be ignored; and the latter collection is sufficiently representative of the mass of material in his notebooks to serve my purposes. Although a more extensive selection from them has long been available in German in Karl Schlechta's three-volume edition of his writings, and the complete contents of these notebooks are now available in the definitive Colli-Montinari *Kritische Gesamtausgabe*, their utter lack of organization presents enormous difficulties, for which the collection entitled *The Will to Power* provides a partial remedy. It more than suffices to reveal the nature and substance of the philosophical thinking expressed in the notebooks, as I believe anyone who expends the time and effort to investigate their fuller contents will discover.

I have sought to direct the attention of readers to texts indicative of his philosophical thinking which they might reasonably be expected to have read or to be able to read themselves. I take *The Will to Power* to be such a text (or collection of texts). I leave to others with more narrowly scholarly interests the labor of considering what refinements of interpretation might be suggested by other material in his notebooks (and also in his correspondence). I have given quite enough prominence to his unpublished notes in this study; to have dealt with them more comprehensively would have been to accord them more significance than is their due in relation to his other writings. While those not to be found in *The Will to Power* are not explicitly utilized here, however, I have sought to interpret Nietzsche in a manner consonant with what I have found in them.

Nor is this the last limitation of the present study requiring to be acknowledged. While I have at various points (especially in the last two chapters) taken notice of things Nietzsche has to say in writings antedating *The Gay Science*, I have concentrated my attention upon his philosophical efforts in the second half of his productive life, beginning with this work. It is his thinking in this period of his philosophical maturity which interests me most, and to which I believe the greatest value for philosophers today attaches. It is only occasionally in his earlier writings that he shows the kind of philosophical power, insight and sensitivity characteristic of so much of his later work; and indeed it is only occasionally that he even addresses himself to significant philosophical issues and tasks in them. Prior to *The Gay Science* he was only on the way to becoming the important philosopher he came to be. It is for the most part only as certain of his earlier discussions are germane to positions he later developed, therefore, that I have made reference to them.

I also have largely passed over his literary-philosophical efforts, written though they for the most part were in this later period — including not only his many epigrams, 'songs' and poems, but also his most famous work, *Thus Spoke Zarathustra*. I have found it useful and illuminating at various points to refer to certain things he says and themes he develops in the latter work, and consider familiarity with it to be essential to the understanding of him. It does not readily lend itself, however, to the sort of analysis undertaken here; and since there is little of a philosophical nature in it that Nietzsche does not elsewhere work out in a more straightforwardly (or prosaically) philosophical manner, I have preferred to concentrate upon his other ways of putting his points, calling Zarathustra in to give evidence only on occasion.

In a systematic study of Nietzsche's works, *Zarathustra* would of course require extensive discussion — as would the books he published prior to *The Gay Science*, in their entirety and for what they are, no less than would the others he wrote (not all of which, or all parts of which, are of a philosophical nature). The present volume, however, is no such study, and is organized quite differently. Each chapter in it is devoted to one of his major philosophical concerns, and draws upon material to be found in many different things he wrote which is pertinent to his treatment of the issues these concerns subsume. It is only if one takes account of the various things he has to say about them in his widely scattered discussions of them that one can do something approaching justice to his thinking with respect to them, which is in many cases much more subtle and complex than one might gather if one considered only the remarks he makes in some one place. He does not devote separate works to the systematic treatment of each of the matters he deals with, but rather touches upon them and returns to them on many different occasions, seldom if ever setting down anything that might be considered his definitive position concerning any of them; and so it is incumbent upon one who would understand him to draw together the many strands of his dispersed and unsystematic reflections upon each of them, and to attempt to discern what they add up to.

I have been guided in my interpretation of Nietzsche not only by these considerations, but also by the further conviction that although he was not a systematic thinker, his thought is fundamentally coherent, both with respect to particular issues and in general; and that what he says on some occasions is best construed in the light of what he says on others, rather than in a manner that would saddle him with numerous basic inconsistencies (as many commentators and interpreters, both unsympathetic and sympathetic to him, have been all too quick and happy to do). It was undeniably part of his method to approach problems and issues from a variety of different angles, and to experiment with different formulations (often of a one-sided or over-simplified nature) in dealing with them, even though this might result in at least the appearance of confusion and even contradiction. I would contend, however, that it is both a legitimate way of reading him, and also a very fruitful one, to take him thus to have been working toward and working out a set of interconnected positions which his various remarks and reflections collectively serve to indicate and elaborate, qualifying and complementing each other.

To be sure, the later Nietzsche unquestionably abandoned some of the views he advances in his earlier writings and modified others, as shall be observed in due course; and it would not seem to be possible to read him in this way in all cases even if attention is confined to his writings from the latter half of his productive life. But in most cases this can be done; and the results may be argued both to do him a greater measure of justice than is done him otherwise, and to be of considerable interest. I leave the final assessment of these results in both respects to my readers, however, and mean to do no more at the moment than to announce my interpretive strategy.

I also have chosen simply to pass over Nietzsche's frequent rhetorical excesses, and the ill-considered shots he so often takes at various targets which catch his eye along his way. I do so not because I do not find them annoying, offensive, or embarrassing, and not because I do not deem him deserving of criticism for indulging himself in them, but rather because I feel that dwelling upon them gets in the way of coming to terms with the substance of his philosophical thought. They blemish and mar its surface; but one must school oneself to look past them, filtering them out as so much unfortunate static, if one is to be able to get down to matters of philosophical moment. It is almost as though Nietzsche wished to give readers all the excuses they could wish to be put off by him, in order that only those large-minded enough not to be would stay with him long enough to see what he was really driving at; and indeed he frequently suggests as much. But there is no denying that his own shortcomings and all-too-human tendencies are often on display here as well. Still, while much can be (and has been, and no doubt will continue to be) made of them, I consider it the better course — at least for my purposes — to cut through them and focus upon that in his thought which can and should be taken seriously, and which neither stands nor falls with them and the expressions he gives them.

In sum, I have written one kind of book on Nietzsche's philosophical thinking, which should at least have its uses. It is intended both to serve as a counterweight to certain common and inadequate construals of him (among which I number not only those echoing Russell's, but also those advanced and inspired by certain recent French writers, of which Allison's collection *The New Nietzsche* contains a fair sampling), and to give new impetus to the attempt to gain for him the attention he deserves in our part of the contemporary philosophical world. In any event, it is one philosopher's interpretation and analysis of a substantial slice of Nietzsche — a sustained and extensively developed examination of what is surely the most philosophical part of the writing he did. This examination is carried out in a spirit reflecting extensive exposure to philosophical currents of the past several centuries on both sides of the English Channel. I would hope that it will not be found idiosyncratic, and have cited Nietzsche extensively in an attempt to show that this is not the case.

I would also hope that today, a century after the initial publication of *The Gay Science*, the time has arrived when a sober assessment of the philosophical enterprise Nietzsche launched in earnest in it can begin to be made by heirs of both traditions, with the aid of studies of this kind. Indeed, it might not even be too much to hope for something more. Philosophy today is again — or perhaps still — in something like the condition Nietzsche discerned a century ago, as he reflected both upon it and upon our culture more generally; and he could well prove helpful in our attempt to reorient our thinking, with some version of his 'gay science' serving as our compass. For anything like this to become a real possibility, however, or even for him to have a more modestly fruitful impact upon current and future philosophical endeavor, Nietzsche the philosopher must be brought into focus. This is what I have attempted to do; and the limits, organization, and procedure of this book all flow directly from this intention.

On a much more mundane plane, a word about my citations from Nietzsche's writings and their identification is required here. Important and useful as Kaufmann's book on Nietzsche has been and continues to be, his greatest and most enduring contribution to Nietzsche studies in the English-speaking world may in the long run turn out to be his generally excellent translations of many of Nietzsche's writings, including not only all of his completed works from *The Gay Science* onward, but also *The Birth of Tragedy* and the collection of notes published as *The Will to Power*. Certain other translations of some of these works exist, and continue to be made; but it would seem fair to say that his are the standard ones, and deserve to be accorded this status (although those that have been made by his sometime collaborator R. J. Hollingdale stand out from the rest, and may generally be relied upon). For this reason, and also because I have seldom found that I could improve significantly upon Kaufmann's renderings, I have for the most part followed them in my citations from works he translated. I have considered this advisable in view of their reliability, their remarkable closeness to the spirit of Nietzsche's own language, their general availability, and the desirability of enabling readers to locate things I cite easily in the passages from which they are taken. In the cases of writings Kaufmann did not translate, on the other hand, I view the existing translations differently; and my citations from them accordingly are my own versions.

Nearly all of Nietzsche's writings cited are divided into numbered sections (usually of only modest length), and in some cases into larger parts (chapters or divisions) as well. In a few instances these sections and parts do not bear numbers, but may easily be supplied with them along obvious lines. Rather than giving page numbers referring to the location of passages cited in particular German or English editions, therefore, it has seemed to me to be far preferable to follow what is fairly standard practice, and to identify my citations wherever possible by means of these numberings. (To have supplied the page numbers in various volumes of the *Kritische Gesamtausgabe*, for example, would have been quite unhelpful to most readers; although in a few instances I have had no recourse but to do this.)

I have identified all works cited by the acronyms of their English titles (e.g.: *GS* = *The Gay Science*). A key to the acronyms I employ, as well as other pertinent information, is provided following the Acknowledgments. In the cases of works in which sections are supplied with numbers running consecutively from beginning to end, I have given only these numbers (e.g.: *GS* 353 = *The Gay Science*, section 353). In the cases of works in which the section numberings supplied begin again in each part of the work, on the other hand, I have given both part numbers (in Roman numerals) and section numbers (e.g.: *GM* II:24 = *On the Genealogy of Morals*, essay II, section 24). I have done the same thing in the case of *Thus Spoke Zarathustra*, in which the numbers of the sections of each of the four major parts have had to be provided. In the identification of some citations the letter 'P' appears; it indicates that the sections designated are to be found in the Preface (or, in the case of *Zarathustra*, the Prologue) to the work specified. In the few cases in which page numbers have had to be given, they refer to pages in the volumes of the *Kritische Gesamtausgabe* as indicated in the Reference Key. This description of my practice may seem confusing; but the practice itself should be found quite transparent, and is much more convenient than any other that might have been followed. It allows readers to locate the passages cited quickly, whatever English or German (or other) editions they might happen to use; and it is also very economical in terms of the space it requires. Should some readers have preferred a different practice, I beg their indulgence of mine.

Acknowledgments

Acknowledgment is gratefully made to the following:

To D. Reidel Publishing Company and H. E. Zoeteman, rights and permissions department, for permission to use a revised version of my paper 'Philosophy as Linguistic Analysis: A Nietzschean Critique,' which was first published in *Philosophical Studies*, volume 25, number 3 (April 1974), pp. 153–171. Copyright © 1974 by D. Reidel Publishing Company, Dordrecht, Holland. (This essay was extracted and fashioned from an earlier draft of the manuscript of this book, and was published in advance of it for certain reasons; but it was intended from the outset to be a part of the first chapter, where it here appears. The same applies to the following two essays, which were drawn from earlier drafts of the first and second halves of the final chapter.)

To St Martin's Press, Inc., and Thomas V. Broadbent, director of the college department, for permission to use a revised version of my paper 'Nietzsche on Art in *The Birth of Tragedy*,' which was first published in *Aesthetics: A Critical Anthology*, edited by George Dickie and Richard Sclafani (New York: St Martin's Press, 1977), pp. 269–312. Copyright © 1977 by St Martin's Press, Inc.

To the Hegeler Institute and Eugene Freeman, editor of *The Monist*, for permission to use a revised version of my paper 'Nietzsche's Second Thoughts About Art,' which was first published in *The Monist*. It is reprinted (as revised) from *The Monist*, volume 64, number 2 (April 1981), pp. 231–246, with the permission of the publisher. Copyright © 1981 by the Hegeler Institute.

To Viking Penguin Inc., and Shelley Slater, permissions editor, for permission to make use of the Walter Kaufmann translations of the writings of Nietzsche published in the volume *The Portable*

Nietzsche, in my citations from these writings. Copyright © 1954 by The Viking Press, Inc. Excerpts from the writings published in that volume are reprinted by permission of Viking Penguin Inc.

To Random House, Inc., and Gerald Summer, permissions department manager, for permission to make use of the Walter Kaufmann translations of the writings of Nietzsche published by Random House (Vintage Books), in my citations from these writings. The volumes in question are the following:

Beyond Good and Evil, translated by Walter Kaufmann (New York: Vintage, 1966). Copyright © 1966 by Random House, Inc.

The Birth of Tragedy and *The Case of Wagner*, translated by Walter Kaufmann (New York: Vintage, 1967). Copyright © 1967 by Random House, Inc.

On the Genealogy of Morals, translated by Walter Kaufmann and R. J. Hollingdale, and *Ecce Homo*, translated by Walter Kaufmann; edited by Walter Kaufmann (New York: Vintage, 1967). Copyright © 1967 by Random House, Inc.

The Gay Science, translated by Walter Kaufmann (New York: Vintage, 1974). Copyright © 1974 by Random House, Inc.

The Will to Power, translated by Walter Kaufmann and R. J. Hollingdale; edited by Walter Kaufmann (New York: Vintage, 1968). Copyright © 1967 by Walter Kaufmann. Courtesy of Random House, Inc.

I also wish to express my appreciation to the general editor of the series in which this book appears, Mr Ted Honderich, for the opportunity to contribute this study to it; and both to him and to the officers of Routledge & Kegan Paul for their patience with me, during the considerable period of time which passed beyond the date by which I had undertaken to deliver my manuscript to them. Many things delayed its completion, and its writing also proved to be a much more formidable task than I had anticipated it would be; and I am greatly in their debt for their understanding and forbearance.

I further owe a good deal to students and colleagues at my own university and others at which I have held visiting appointments and given talks, as well as to philosophers elsewhere in this country and abroad sharing my interest in Nietzsche. I have gained much from my discussions of him with them and from their reactions to what I have been trying to do with him, and am grateful for the encouragement they have so often given me. And here again I must make special mention of Walter Kaufmann, through whom I first became interested in Nietzsche some twenty years ago, and who was an inspiration and a help to me in my work on Nietzsche in many ways.

Finally, I would thank my family for learning how to live with someone so much of whose time for so long has had to be spent with Nietzsche, that this book might be written. My work on it has spanned a considerable portion of my children's early lives, and of my life with my wife Marsha as well; and they know better than anyone the extent of my investment of my own life in it. Their ability to accept this investment is one of the most important things which made its completion possible.

Reference Key

		Published	GA Volume
BT	= *The Birth of Tragedy (Die Geburt der Tragödie)*	1872	III:1
TL	= *On Truth and Lie in an Extra-Moral Sense (Über Wahrheit und Lüge im aussermoralischen Sinn)*	(written 1870–3)	III:2
PTA	= *Philosophy in the Tragic Age of the Greeks (Die Philosophie im tragischen Zeitalter der Griechen)*	(written 1870–3)	III:2
UAH	= *On the Use and Abuse of History for Life (Vom Nutzen und Nachteil der Historie für das Leben)*	1874	III:1
SE	= *Schopenhauer as Educator (Schopenhauer als Erzieher)*	1874	III:1
HH	= *Human, All-Too-Human (Menschliches, Allzumenschliches)*		
	Volume I	1878	IV:2
	Volume II	1879	IV:3
WS	= *The Wanderer and his Shadow (Der Wanderer und sein Schatten)*	1880	IV:3
D	= *Dawn (Morgenröthe)*	1881	V:1
GS	= *The Gay Science (Die Fröhliche Wissenschaft)*		
	Books I–IV	1882	V:2
	Book V	1887	

Z	=	*Thus Spoke Zarathustra (Also Sprach Zarathustra)*		VI:1
		Parts I—II	1883	
		Part III	1884	
		Part IV	1885	
BGE	=	*Beyond Good and Evil (Jenseits von Gut und Böse)*	1886	VI:2
GM	=	*On the Genealogy of Morals (Zur Genealogie der Moral)*	1887	VI:2
CW	=	*The Case of Wagner (Der Fall Wagner)*	1888	VI:3
TI	=	*Twilight of the Idols (Die Götzen-Dämmerung)*	1889	VI:3
A	=	*The Antichrist (Der Antichrist)*	1895*	VI:3
NCW	=	*Nietzsche contra Wagner (Nietzsche contra Wagner)*	1895*	VI:3
EH	=	*Ecce Homo (Ecce Homo)*	1908*	VI:3
WP	=	*The Will to Power (Der Wille zur Macht)*	(notes from 1883—8)	VII:1,2,3 VIII:1,2,3

*Works completed by Nietzsche but published after his collapse.

Citations from *TL, PTA, UAH, SE, HH, WS,* and *D* are my own translations. Citations from the rest follow Kaufmann's renderings.

My translations are based on the Colli-Montinari *Kritische Gesamtausgabe.* Where citations are identified by page numbers, they refer to the volumes in the *Gesamtausgabe* in which the writings in question appear (indicated at the right above).

Introduction

Nietzsche presents a problem to many English-speaking philosophers. Schooled in the tradition of Locke, Berkeley, Hume and Mill, and strongly influenced by the examples of Moore and Russell, Ayer and Quine, and Ryle and Austin, they commonly find it hard to know what to make of what they find when they open one of his books and begin to read. His prose is lucid and free of cumbersome phraseology and obscure terminology, quite unlike that of most German philosophers from Kant and Hegel to Husserl and Heidegger; but there are few extended, systematic discussions of particular topics and issues to be found in them. They consist instead for the most part in collections of relatively short reflections (often of an aphoristic nature), the drift of which is frequently unclear, and the connections between which are often loose if not simply non-existent.

Remarks which seem quite sensible and strike familiar chords are interspersed among others which appear outlandish or are utterly perplexing. At one moment, one encounters calm, cool, cautious, detached analysis; at the next, one is confronted with heatedly polemical or highly metaphorical rhetoric. On the attack, Nietzsche sometimes proceeds with the precision of a surgeon and the finesse of a fencer; while at other times he resorts to the tactics of a street fighter, lashing out with anything he can lay his hands on. And when setting forth a position of his own, he avails himself of considerations of any sort which serve his purpose, however unconventional they might be in terms of traditional philosophical procedure.

For the most part, Nietzsche resembles less a mathematician attempting to prove a theorem, or a scientist attempting to substantiate a theory, than a (rather fiery) courtroom lawyer

1

attempting to persuade a jury, or an unruly Socrates challenging the convictions of a miscellany of interlocutors — or even, sometimes, a pamphleteer promoting a cause, or an Old Testament prophet hurling accusations at a society gone astray. He does not hesitate to confront the reader with suggestions involving radical modifications of commonly accepted ways of thinking, either in the form of flat assertions expressing his insights, or supported only by general indications of the kinds of considerations which might be brought to bear in justification of them. It is often as if he were simply saying: 'You think of the matter that way, and it is quite understandable that you do; but why not think of it this way instead?' Where he can, he attempts to make a case for thinking of things as he proposes, and for ceasing to think of them in ways he suggests to be mistaken; but he does not consider it the better part of wisdom to withhold all such suggestions unless and until decisive reasons for doing so can be adduced. And whether for rhetorical purposes or simply because he is wont to do so, he frequently peppers his discussions with outbursts and tirades of a sort seldom encountered in philosophical literature, sometimes offering nothing more in support of the positions he takes than the force they generate.

These are some of the reasons why many English-speaking philosophers find it difficult to come to terms with Nietzsche, even if they are sufficiently sympathetic to or intrigued by some of the things he says to be interested in doing so. Thus it is commonly urged against him, and cited as a kind of justification of this relative neglect by many recent and contemporary philosophers on this side of the English Channel, that however interesting and even right some of the things he says may be, he does not provide enough by way of argument in support of what he says to make it possible to deal with him in a serious philosophical way.

As the foregoing remarks indicate, there is some justice in this observation, at least in certain areas of Nietzsche's thought. As a final verdict concerning his philosophical efforts generally, however, its justice depends upon the legitimacy of regarding a particular sort of philosophical argumentation as constituting the only procedure appropriate to philosophical inquiry, and of taking Nietzsche's way of addressing issues to deviate too greatly from this paradigm to constitute a legitimate form of philosophical endeavor. And this is a matter requiring serious consideration; for the consensus of opinion concerning it may at least be contested. There is perhaps no more fundamental philosophical question than that of what constitutes appropriate philosophical procedure. It is a question which many philosophers never stop to consider. One who would read Nietzsche as a philosopher, however, is compelled to confront it — indeed, he clearly would have it so — both by what he himself has to say about the nature of philosophy, and by what he does when he deals with various substantive philosophical issues.

I

Must a philosopher proceed rather as a geometer or a logician does when proving a theorem, or as a physicist or an economist does when putting forth a theory, in order to be said to be doing philosophy? Philosophers themselves often have thought so, and consequently have either addressed themselves to the task of producing such arguments, or have confined themselves to drawing critical or skeptical conclusions from the fact that the views advanced by others are not accompanied by arguments of comparable rigor. Neither enterprise, however, is very fruitful. Attempts along the former lines seem invariably either to issue in trivialities, or else to turn out to be vulnerable to attack; while such critical responses neither constitute any real advance toward the solution of substantive philosophical questions, nor establish that these in reality are mere pseudo-questions requiring no solution. Furthermore, it is difficult to ignore the challenge posed to this view by the efforts of certain writers from ancient times down to the present who are generally held in high esteem in the philosophical community. To mention only two examples: what is to be made of Plato's procedure in many of the Dialogues, and of that of Wittgenstein in such later writings as the *Investigations*? Rigorous, straightforward argumentation was hardly unknown to either of them; but both of them apparently became convinced that their purposes would best be served by the adoption of different procedures.

The case of Wittgenstein is particularly relevant to the understanding and evaluation of what Nietzsche does in the course of his attempts to deal with philosophical issues. His later writings contrast markedly with his *Tractatus*, not only substantively but also methodologically. In them his criticisms of views which he considers to be mistaken do not typically consist in attempts to refute them by convicting them of inconsistency, circularity and the like, or by demonstrating the invalidity of certain of the assumptions on which they are based. Rather, they generally take

3

the form of attempts to *undermine* them, by adducing a variety of considerations intended to bring to light and at the same time call into question the kind of thinking from which they issue. And his efforts in the direction of reorienting our thinking along different lines for the most part do not have the character of tight lines of reasoning from other and purportedly more plausible or self-evident first principles or putatively indisputable facts. They largely consist rather in tentative suggestions or considerations intended collectively to convince one of the preferability of some alternative picture of the general matter in connection with which the views criticized were advanced. Wittgenstein would have been the first to admit that philosophizing in this way is a very untidy affair; but he seems to have believed that this sort of approach is required if one is to be able to get to the bottom of fundamental philosophical issues and begin to deal with them at all adequately.

Something quite similar is encountered in the case of Nietzsche. Indeed, I would suggest that there is a stronger basic philosophical affinity (certainly with regard to procedure, and possibly where certain substantive questions are concerned as well) between Nietzsche and the later Wittgenstein, than there is between either of them and at least most other philosophers of note with whom each is usually associated. To be sure, it is undeniable that Nietzsche does not hesitate to venture onto ground (some would say thin ice) on which Wittgenstein would not have dreamed of treading. But the difficulty with which one is faced when one looks for 'arguments' in Nietzsche is very much like that which faces one in the case of Wittgenstein. And the problem here, if there is one, may not be a matter of shortcomings in the sort of procedure followed at all. Rather, it may pertain to a tendency on *our* part to take for granted and insist upon adherence to a style and standard of philosophical 'argument' that is unduly narrow and possibly ill-suited to some of the more fundamental issues with which it is at least part of the business of philosophy to deal.

At times Nietzsche does attempt to tackle what he takes to be a mistaken position head on, developing lines of reasoning meant to leave any reasonable person no alternative other than to acknowledge its untenability. And at times he attempts to provide equally conclusive grounds compelling assent to substantive views which he himself advances. Instances in which he offers arguments of these sorts, however, are relatively few and far between in his writings. If one were to confine one's attention to them alone, the result would be a very incomplete and inadequate picture of what he is trying to do, where both the critical and the constructive sides of his philosophical endeavor are concerned. This would be

4

comparable to confining one's attention to the bones of a creature most of whose structural matter is cartilage, in an investigation of the character of its bodily frame.

Much more frequently, Nietzsche's procedure in critical analysis is less to try to *disprove* than to *discredit*. And in advancing a position, rather than trying to *prove* his point he generally seeks first to establish its viability and then to urge its greater plausibility in relation to various alternatives to it, availing himself of many different sorts of considerations in doing so. Here the analogy of a lawyer attempting to *make a case* in court is both appropriate and instructive. A part of his case may involve probing the credibility of witnesses, frequently by focussing more upon their general trustworthiness and circumstances rendering the reliability of their testimony dubious, than upon the actual content of their testimony and their apparent or even genuine sincerity in giving it. Another part often involves the marshaling of circumstantial evidence, particularly when direct evidence is lacking or too insubstantial to be decisive. And perhaps the most important part involves considering the possibility of various different interpretations of the whole of the testimony and evidence brought forward in connection with the issue before the court, and attempting to show — to convince the judge or jury — that certain of these possible interpretations are to be discounted in favor of another (which may be very different from that which at first seemed to be the most plausible, or even obviously correct).

Nietzsche's procedure is often very similar. Implicit in it is the idea that the situation of the philosopher is often comparable to that of a lawyer who takes on hard cases which do not admit of quick and easy resolution. It is undeniable that justice is not always done in the courtroom. And there likewise is no guarantee that a case made by Nietzsche (or by anyone else who philosophizes as he does), however persuasively argued it may be, may be relied upon to establish the superiority (let alone the finality) of one position on some philosophical issue in relation to another. (Thus he remarks (*WP* 17): 'what convinces is not necessarily true — it is merely convincing — a note for asses.') But it is not unreasonable to suppose that in general the likelihood of reaching a just verdict concerning the relative merits of various philosophical positions — where this cannot be established beyond all question of doubt in any more straightforward way — will be greater if one proceeds in this sort of way than it is if one declines to do so, and opts instead for some tidier and simpler but less penetrating decision-procedure. Moreover, just as a courtroom verdict can be appealed, a case made by a philosopher can always be reconsidered;

only here the line of appeal is neither hierarchical nor limited. To proceed by making cases is to leave oneself forever open to the possibility of counter-cases. But Nietzsche sees no alternative, short of shunning most important issues.

Nietzsche's own preferred expression for this sort of procedure is not 'making a case,' but rather 'interpretation.' It is his conviction that interpretation has been the actual, if generally unacknowledged, enterprise of previous thinkers who have not been content merely to work within the framework of interpretations developed by others. And it is his further contention that a genuine philosopher (as opposed to all mere 'philosophical laborers') will not and should not abandon interpretation in favor of some more 'exact' form of thinking and reasoning, but rather must engage more self-consciously and deliberately and less dogmatically in it. (Both of these points will be developed in the first chapter below.) So he characterizes his own philosophical activity as interpretive, despite the fact that this would appear to place his own positions on a par with those he rejects and brands as 'lies,' 'errors,' and 'fictions.' 'Supposing that this also is only interpretation — and you will be eager enough to make this objection? — well, so much the better' (*BGE* 22).

This might lead one to wonder whether, by allowing and indeed insisting that 'interpretation' (or, more fully, the devising and making of cases for and against various 'interpretations') is at the heart of all genuine philosophical activity, Nietzsche does not in fact lower the latter to the level of the mere mongering of *Weltanschauungen*, thus reducing it to a kind of quasi-literary enterprise of little or no cognitive significance. Some interpreters and many readers have in fact taken this to be precisely his intention, or at any rate the upshot of his treatment of the matter; and they have then proceeded to praise or condemn him, as this conclusion agrees or conflicts with their own sentiments. This is especially common among those inclined to suppose that 'interpretation' is a very subjective sort of affair; and that, to the extent that it can be shown to be involved in the development of a position being advanced, its presence undermines any appearance the positions may have of credibility. Once something becomes a matter of one interpretation against another, the idea runs, 'it is all relative' — relative to the feelings and attitudes of those advancing the conflicting interpretations; and thus the discussion has left the ground on which serious argument can alone be based and cognitively significant conclusions reached. *Incipit Zarathustra, exit scientia.*

As I read him, however, this is not at all Nietzsche's view of the matter. 'Interpretation' as he understands it is by no means an affair so hopelessly 'relative' and 'subjective' that to construe philosophical activity in terms of it is tantamount to depriving it of all cognitive import. Indeed, it seems to me that he is on to something important in taking the enterprise of philosophy — properly understood and carried on — to be fundamentally (although perhaps not exclusively) a matter of engaging in the complementary activities of critically examining received or proposed interpretations and developing (and making cases for) others which might improve upon them. And if this is so, the question of what constitutes and counts as a philosophical argument largely becomes the question of what is involved in the establishment of the relative soundness and adequacy of such interpretations.

In order to deal with this issue, it is necessary to consider the question of whether some interpretations are or can be *better* than others — 'better' not merely in the sense of being more 'life-enhancing' or more agreeable psychologically to certain types of people than others are, but rather in the sense of being less distorting and more faithful to the nature of that which is interpreted than others. Nietzsche does take the *value* of different interpretations in most human contexts to be primarily a function of considerations of the former sorts. He also suggests that interpretations are of considerable *symptomatic* significance, serving to reveal a great deal about those who advance them. It by no means follows, however, that he holds the relative soundness or tenability of different interpretations to be conceivable only along one or both of these lines. Indeed, an attentive reading of him reveals that he not only allows but moreover insists that some interpretations may be better than others, where 'better' is construed not in terms of such cognitively neutral notions as that of 'value for life,' but rather in terms of soundness and adequacy.

In this connection notice should be taken of the language Nietzsche employs in remarks of the following sort: 'The sense of truthfulness . . . is nauseated by the falseness and mendaciousness of all Christian interpretations of the world and of history; rebound from "God is truth" to the fanatical faith "All is false"' (*WP* 1). And again: 'One interpretation has collapsed; but because it was considered *the* interpretation it now seems as if there were no meaning at all in existence' (*WP* 55). Here he both commits himself to the appropriateness of characterizing a *particular* interpretation as 'untenable,' 'false,' and 'mendacious,' and at the same time quite clearly suggests the illegitimacy of concluding, from the 'collapse' of one interpretation discovered to be thus

7

unworthy of acceptance, that any other must be equally objectionable. Indeed, his derisive reference to 'the fanatical faith "All is false"' shows that he is by no means disposed to lump all 'interpretations' together as equally 'false.'

Nietzsche employs similar language in speaking of certain other interpretations as well. Here I shall take note only of something he says with respect to one in particular. He questions

> the faith with which so many materialistic natural scientists rest content nowadays, the faith in a world that is supposed to have its equivalent and its measure in human thought and human valuations. . . . That the only justifiable interpretation of the world should be . . . an interpretation that permits counting, calculating, weighing, seeing, and touching, and nothing more — that it is a crudity and naiveté (GS 373).

Several points about Nietzsche's many remarks along these lines may be noted. One is that he considers the various interpretations he singles out for attention — from the 'Christian-moral' to the 'natural-scientific' — to have a definite utility, in the sense of performing a significant practical function in relation to the needs and limitations of various sorts of human beings. And the second is that, this utility notwithstanding, he expressly terms each of them not merely perspectival but *erroneous*, or at any rate naive and superficial. He does suggest that the practical value of an interpretation endows it with a certain sort of validity, and even that it may thus be accorded a kind of (pragmatic) 'truth.' The fact that he also considers it appropriate to characterize inter-pretations enjoying this status in these other ways, however, clearly indicates that he not only envisions the possibility of attaining a vantage point from which their contingency can be discerned, but moreover takes it to be one of his accomplish-ments to have reached a position from which the untenability or inadequacy of such interpretations may be grasped.

II

Nietzsche does take the general position that 'it is our needs that interpret the world; our drives and their For and Against' (WP 481). So his answer to the question, 'what interprets?,' is 'our affects' (WP 254). As shall be seen, moreover, he both considers the 'drives' and 'affects' finding expression in interpretations to be quite various, and denies that anything on the order of 'a "drive to knowledge"' numbers among them (BGE 6). And he further holds that, at least as a rule, the kinds of interpretations to which they give rise are strongly colored by them, and so have a more or less distortedly perspectival character. These general considerations do not, however, lead him to reject the very possibility of a kind of comprehension issuing from interpretation that would amount to something more than this, to which philosophers might (and ought to) aspire. That he countenances this possibility, and what he takes its realization to involve, may be seen in the following passage, which sheds considerable light on much of what he says and tries to do:

> But precisely because we seek knowledge, let us not be ungrateful to such resolute reversals of accustomed perspectives and valuations which the spirit has, with apparent mischievousness and futility, raged against itself for so long: to see differently in this way for once, to *want* to see differently, is no small discipline and preparation of the intellect for its future 'objectivity' — the latter understood not as 'contemplation without interest' (which is a nonsensical absurdity), but as the ability to *control* one's Pro and Con and to dispose of them, so that one knows how to employ a *variety* of perspectives and affective interpretations in the service of knowledge.
>
> Henceforth, my dear philosophers, let us be on guard against the dangerous old conceptual fiction that posited a 'pure, will-less, painless, timeless knowing subject'; let us guard against the snares of such contradictory concepts as 'pure reason,' 'absolute spirituality,' 'knowledge in itself': these always demand that we should think of an eye that is completely unthinkable, an eye turned in no particular direction, in which the active and interpreting forces, through which alone seeing becomes seeing *something*, are supposed to be lacking; these always demand of the eye an absurdity and a nonsense. There is *only* a perspective seeing, *only* a perspective 'knowing'; and the *more* affects we allow to speak about one thing, the *more* eyes, different eyes, we can use to observe one thing, the more complete will our 'concept' of this thing, our 'objectivity,' be (*GM* III:12).

Notwithstanding his insistence that there is '*only* a perspective "knowing"' (as opposed to a knowing that would be absolute and independent of all 'perspective seeing'), Nietzsche thus is concerned to distinguish 'knowledge' from 'perspectives and affective interpretations' merely as such, and suggests that it is something which can be sought and can in some measure be achieved. It, no less than that which is employed 'in the service' of its attainment, has the character of 'interpretation' — but it is 'interpretation'

9

with a difference. It has an 'objectivity' that is lacking in the cases of the various 'perspectives and affective interpretations' it employs and upon which it draws. For when the latter are played off against each other, one ceases to be locked into any one of them; and so it becomes possible to achieve a meta-level perspective, from which vantage point various lower-order interpretations may be superseded in favor of others less narrow and distorting than they.

Here it is further illuminating to consider something Nietzsche says concerning the emergence of 'scientific thinking,' and also the possibility of its supersession by a 'higher' form of thinking:

> So many things have to come together for scientific thinking to originate and all these necessary strengths had to be invented, practiced, and cultivated separately. As long as they were still separate, however, they frequently had an altogether different effect than they do now that they are integrated into scientific thinking and hold each other in check. . . . And even now the time seems remote when artistic energies and the practical wisdom of life will join with scientific thinking to form a higher organic system in relation to which scholars, physicians, artists, and legislators — as we know them at present — would have to look like paltry relics of ancient times (GS 113).

Nietzsche might well have added 'philosophers' to his list, and have gone on to say that the kind of thinking he envisions is the very sort of thing the 'new philosophers' he subsequently called for would engage in. It likewise is the sort of thing he himself undertook to attempt to practice. This possibility requires extended discussion, and will receive it in the first several chapters to follow.

10

I

Philosophers and Philosophy

Nietzsche began his career as a philologist; but his investigations in this field, and his subsequent independently undertaken efforts in social and cultural criticism and psychological analysis, came to converge upon philosophy, leading him to it and requiring it of him. At least for the last decade of his productive life he thought of himself primarily (if not exclusively) as a philosopher, devoting himself chiefly to philosophical endeavor. Yet his relation to philosophy even in this later period of his intellectual maturity is not easily or simply characterized. He tended to be as harshly critical of much of what philosophy traditionally had been and had become in his time as he was persuaded of the great importance of philosophy as he practiced it and would have it be; and he was frequently as severe with most of his generally esteemed philosophical predecessors as he was extravagent in his estimation of what he often called '*my* type of philosopher,' and in his expectations of such 'new philosophers.' In this chapter I shall attempt to sort out his views on these matters. They warrant attention in their own right; and they also require to be borne in mind when considering his specific philosophical efforts.

The philosophical enterprise

I

One way of approaching the question of Nietzsche's conception of philosophy is to consider the sorts of issues and problems with which he takes it to be the business of philosophy to deal. And the most obvious indications of his thinking along these lines are provided by his own choices of subjects in his various writings in

11

which he engages in what he expressly regards as philosophical inquiry. From *The Birth of Tragedy* onward, for example, he addresses himself repeatedly to the nature of art and its relation to life, as well as to larger questions pertaining to human nature and the character of reality more generally. Problems relating to the nature and significance of scientific and rational thought are also raised in this early work, and in the essay *On Truth and Lie* written at about the same time — from which point forth he concerns himself extensively with various epistemological matters. Religious thought and experience receive considerable attention in many of his writings, as do a broad range of social, cultural and political phenomena. Morality is dealt with at great length in several of his works (of which his *Genealogy of Morals* is but one instance), and quite centrally in almost everything else he wrote. And a concern with the nature of value and the status of a wide variety of 'values' looms very large indeed in his writings from first to last, finding expression in his notion of the project of a 'revaluation of all values.'

All of these issues and problems are familiar enough. They are basically those with which philosophers generally have long been concerned and continue to occupy themselves. If Nietzsche parts company with them here, he does so more in his manner of dealing with these matters and in the positions at which he arrives with respect to them than in his selection of them. In the first instance, in contrast with some philosophers though in company with others (and with most today), he holds that all of these are matters with which philosophy cannot even hope to deal satisfactorily if it approaches them aprioristically, attempting to ascertain self-evident first principles of some sort from which conclusions with respect to them may be deduced or inferred. Such a procedure may of course be followed, and may issue in a logically rigorous system; but neither the appearance of self-evidence of the first principles selected nor the logical rigor with which consequences are inferred from them establishes that the system is anything more than a description of a possible world.

Nietzsche further is far from being persuaded, on the other hand, that philosophers should content themselves merely to make explicit the ontological commitments inherent in our ordinary or scientific ways of thinking and speaking about ourselves and the world, to provide a rational reconstruction of our everyday and scientific modes of cognition, and to systematize our axiological intuitions and explore the intricacies of our ordinary uses of moral and evaluative terms. Analyses of these sorts have their uses, on his view, and constitute a part of the business of

12

philosophy, but they by no means exhaust it. They serve merely to set the stage for the raising of a further — and philosophically more significant — set of questions. For example: do our ordinary and scientific ways of thinking and speaking about reality (ourselves included) adequately represent it, or do they distort or fundamentally misrepresent it? What is to be made of our every-day and scientific modes of cognition, and of the 'knowledge' they yield? What is their actual place, function, and value in human life? How are our basic evaluative intuitions and normative attitudes to be regarded? What is the status of the moral theories propounded by various moral thinkers? What value do prevailing 'values' themselves possess?

It is above all to questions such as these that Nietzsche considers it imperative for philosophers to address themselves. And he takes this task to be complicated by the fact that there is nothing pertaining to the objects of inquiry in each case which may be considered unproblematical. It cannot be assumed in ontological inquiry, for example, that even the most basic categories of our thought reflect actual features of reality; or that there is a qualitative ontological difference between non-human reality and our own. It cannot be assumed, in epistemological inquiry, that either language or science or even logic is self-warranting, or stands in any particular relation to the world. And it cannot be assumed, in axiological and normative inquiry, that any moral principles or values are self-evidently or unconditionally valid.

Thus philosophers may not take for granted that reality consists of 'things' or 'substances' of various sorts, and merely inquire into their natures. They cannot take for granted that knowledge conceived as the correspondence of thought and reality is possible, and merely inquire into the conditions of its possibility and the limits of its scope. They cannot assume that reason and logical thought yield truths about reality, and merely inquire into the content of these truths. They further cannot assume that there are at least some moral principles which are binding upon all men, and merely inquire into what they and their consequences are. And they cannot proceed upon the assumption that anything commonly supposed to be of value possesses the value thus accorded to it, and merely inquire into the relations between such 'values' and into their implications for various specific practices.

It may be very well (and indeed necessary) to take many things along these lines for granted in the course of daily life, and even in the context of various fields of intellectual endeavor; but Nietzsche considers it highly objectionable if a philosopher does so

13

in his philosophizing. This is not because he is committed methodologically to some requirement of absolute certainty or presuppositionlessness in philosophical inquiry. It is rather because he is convinced of the genuinely problematical character of any and all such assumptions. Thus he regards it as one part of the task of philosophy to bring them to light and subject them to intensive critical scrutiny. And its next major order of business is to reconsider the matters indicated, and to seek to provide accounts of them doing them justice.

This enterprise, while large and important, does not exhaust the task of philosophy as Nietzsche conceives it. For it further includes the investigation of a broad range of forms of human activity and experience, from the social and the religious to the artistic and the scientific. Philosophy for him thus is social philosophy and the philosophy of religion, art and science (and of language, education, history, etc.), no less than it is epistemology, value theory and philosophical cosmology and anthropology. But while current designations of the former sort may appropriately be used here, his view of the business of philosophy with respect to these various spheres of human experience is rather broader than that of most philosophers at present. For he does not take it to consist solely in the investigation of what transpires in them, let alone in the mere analysis of the forms of language associated with them. It also, and more importantly, involves their interpretation in terms of their place in human life more generally, and their assessment in the light of certain basic evaluative considerations. It is only as this is done, on his view, that analyses of the various 'forms of life' mentioned acquire any real philosophical significance. On the other hand, however, he considers it necessary to undertake such inquiries both in order to work out a satisfactory philosophical anthropology and in order to prepare the way for the 'revaluation of values' he regards as the culmination of the philosophical enterprise.

As a partial extension of this point, Nietzsche further considers it incumbent upon the philosopher to adopt a critical stance with respect to whatever might be the reigning 'ideal of today,' and indeed to stand 'in contradiction to his today.' Such philosophers find 'their task, their hard, unwanted, inescapable task, but eventually also the greatness of their task, in being the bad conscience of their time,' and in 'applying the knife vivisectionally to the chest of the very *virtues of their time*' (BGE 212). As has just been mentioned, it is part of their part, as he conceives it, to subject prevailing 'forms of life' to assessment; and he would not have such assessment understood as a purely theoretical exercise.

14

In contrast to Hegel, for whom philosophy is its age comprehended in thought and the discernment of what is 'rational' and 'necessary' in the way things have come to be, he holds that it is part of the task of the philosopher to *transcend* his age in thought, and to subject it to critical scrutiny.

Nietzsche recognizes that a philosopher, no less than anyone else, is at least initially a child of his age, and that therefore this task is a very difficult one. Indeed, he takes it to be further complicated by the fact that there is no philosophical method the employment of which enables one to achieve complete objectivity and a God's-eye view of things. But these difficulties do not add up to the impossibility of attaining to a standpoint beyond one's time from which it may be critically assessed, and the larger enterprise of philosophy carried on. Thus he asks: 'What does a philosopher demand of himself first and last?' and answers: 'To overcome his time in himself, to become "timeless." With what must he therefore engage in the hardest combat? With whatever marks him as a child of his time.' And this involves the development of a critical awareness of all that characterizes 'his time' as well, which is thus brought before the bar of judgment. It falls to him to be 'the bad conscience of his time,' to which end 'he needs to understand it best' (*CW* P).

By the same token Nietzsche rejects the Wittgensteinian view that philosophy has a merely analytic function to perform (except where its own house requires to be set in order by means of self-criticism), 'leaving everything as it is' where extra-philosophical 'forms of life' are concerned. He instead advocates what might be termed an 'interventionist' conception of the philosophical enterprise in its relation to the various domains of human life. 'My concept of the philosopher,' he writes, 'is worlds removed from any concept that would include even a Kant, not to speak of academic "ruminants" and other professors of philosophy.' For, he continues, 'I understand the philosopher as a terrible explosive, endangering everything' (*EH* III:2:3), through whom 'the highest self-examination' of humanity is undertaken and the course of human life is altered (*EH* III:4:2).

This sort of philosopher is far from 'leaving everything as it is' and merely subjecting it to analysis. Careful analysis, while highly prized by Nietzsche, is for him only preliminary to the main tasks of philosophy; and these likewise are not restricted to the forms of criticism he also calls for and himself undertakes. 'My style,' he says, 'is *affirmative*, and deals with contradiction and criticism only as a means' (*TI* VIII:6); and he conceives of philosophical thinking generally along the same lines. 'Critics,' on his view, 'are instruments of the philosopher and for that very reason . . . a long way from being philosophers themselves,' even though genuine philosophers will exhibit and insist upon 'critical discipline' of the highest order. One might with justice 'call them critics,' he allows; but they are further thinkers who 'employ experiments in a new, perhaps wider, perhaps more dangerous sense' (*BGE* 210), with a view not only to the attainment of a deeper and more adequate comprehension of what is the case than that for which mere 'philosophical laborers' settle, but moreover to the transformation of human life as they find it.

In short, Nietzsche holds that once it is recognized to what extent matters stand as they do in human life owing to 'the monstrous fortuity that has so far had its way and play,' and what 'might yet *be made of man*' under suitably altered conditions (*BGE* 203), the task confronting the philosopher becomes that of seeking out 'a new untrodden way to his enhancement' (*BGE* 212). Philosophy restricted to the analysis of established 'forms of life,' either resolutely or simply modestly 'leaving everything as it is,' like 'philosophy reduced to "theory of knowledge,"' is 'philosophy in its last throes,' blind to 'the masterly task and masterfulness of philosophy' as he would have it understood (*BGE* 204).

II

This characterization of the enterprise of philosophy is still incomplete, however; for the most important part of it in Nietzsche's eyes has yet to be made explicit. Philosophy, he maintains, is an essentially *creative* affair, in a number of ways, pertaining not only to the interpretation of events but also to the direction they take. 'To introduce a meaning — this task still remains to be done.' It can be accomplished only through the determination of some sort of 'goal'; and this must take the form of a 'creative positing,' a 'forming, shaping, overcoming, willing, such as is of the essence of philosophy' (*WP* 605). Thus he writes that 'my kind of philosopher' is one in whom 'a *creative* mode of thought dominates. . . ; a mode of thought that prescribes laws for the future' (*WP* 464). And in this connection he suggests that 'one can conceive philosophers as those who make the most extreme efforts to *test* how far man could *elevate* himself' (*WP* 973), by means of such legislative and prescriptive undertakings.

Nietzsche commonly puts this point in terms of the 'creation,' 'determination' or 'legislation' of *values*. 'There are two distinct kinds of philosopher,' he contends: 'those who want to ascertain

16

a complex fact of evaluations' and 'those who are *legislators* of such evaluations' (*WP* 972).

> I insist that people should finally stop confounding philo-
> sophical laborers, and scientific men generally, with philo-
> sophers. . . . Those philosophical laborers after the noble
> model of Kant and Hegel have to determine and press into
> formulas, whether in the realm of *logic* or *political* (moral)
> thought or *art*, some great data of valuations — that is, former
> *positings* of values, creations of value which have become
> dominant and are for a time called 'truths'. . . . *Genuine philo-*
> *sophers, however, are commanders and legislators.* . . . They
> first determine the Whither and For What of man, and in doing
> so have at their disposal the preliminary labor of all
> philosophical laborers. . . . With a creative hand they reach
> for the future, and all that is and has been becomes a means
> for them, an instrument, a hammer (*BGE* 211).

What Nietzsche terms 'the education of the genuine philosopher' may require that 'he himself has also once stood on all those steps' on which philosophical laborers remain standing. He holds, how-ever, that these are 'merely preconditions of his task,' which 'itself demands something different — it demands that he create values' (ibid.). Nietzsche can conceive of no more awesome and difficult task than that of developing systems of values capable of structur-ing and rendering meaningful the lives of men. Yet nothing is more imperative than this, on his view, particularly at the present time. For the old systems of values by which people long have lived are collapsing; and he fears that without at least the possibility of others which might take their place being recognized, the chilling hand of nihilism will achieve a stranglehold upon human life.

This undoubtedly will not sit well with those accustomed to conceiving of philosophical thought primarily in terms of the marshaling of arguments for and against assertions and theories of certain kinds. But it is one of Nietzsche's basic intentions to challenge such a conception of philosophy — not only by contending that the creation of values is part of the task of philosophy, but by arguing that all genuine philosophical thinking is fundamentally and importantly creative. The latter, larger point is certainly to be distinguished from the former, and may perhaps be less reluctantly conceded. If it is granted, however, then a step at least has been taken in the direction of the broadening of the conception of philosophy along the former lines.

The development of novel interpretations of things, Nietzsche insists, is a genuinely innovative affair, by no means consisting

17

simply in reasoning straightforwardly from various facts, or in coming to see some feature of the world the way it actually is. And if, as he supposes, this is an important part of the philosophical enterprise, his contention that the creation of values is part of it as well begins to look somewhat less bizarre. For although there are differences between the two, there are significant similarities as well. If it is a part of the business of philosophy to shape our thinking about the world, it would not seem unreasonable to hold that it is also a part of that business to shape our manner of esteeming things and so orienting our lives in it. And if the task of the philosopher is not merely to reflect upon what is involved in making interpretations of reality but moreover to *make* interpretations of this sort, it might likewise seem plausible to suppose that it is not restricted to reflection upon what is involved in making determinations of values, but further extends to engaging in their determination. These considerations may not be decisive; but they should serve at least to render his insistence upon the value-creating function of philosophy intelligible.

Nietzsche further suggests that the 'philosophers of the future' he envisions may appropriately 'be called *attempters*' (*BGE* 42) or 'men of experiments' (*BGE* 210), and terms philosophy as he conceives and practices it 'experimental' (*WP* 1041). This point, noted previously, to some extent both clarifies and is clarified by his conception of the creative character of philosophy. 'Experimental' here is not to be understood in the sense of empirical research. It rather refers to trying out different ways of viewing things, and exploring the implications and consequences of different possible ways of structuring and living life, with a view to determining which of the former are most fruitful and illuminating, and which of the latter are most conducive to the general 'enhancement of life.' Nietzsche's 'new philosophers' will likewise be 'attempters' in that they will devote themselves to 'attempts' along these lines — but without losing sight of the 'experimental' character of their undertakings.

Their 'attempts' and 'experiments' will be creative, in that they will involve the development of new interpretations of things and unconventional models of human existence, and thus of new conceptual frameworks and systems of values. 'What dawns on philosophers last of all,' Nietzsche writes, is that 'they must no longer accept concepts as a gift, nor merely purify and polish them, but first *make* and *create* them, present them and make them convincing' (*WP* 409). And the same applies with respect to the larger interpretations in which such concepts figure. What is required of philosophers is 'active interpretation and not merely

18

conceptual translation' (*WP* 605), replacing established ways of thinking born of all-too-human limitations and motivations through the fashioning and rendering persuasive of more sophisticated and penetrating alternatives.

In doing so, and indeed in undertaking any part of the task of philosophy as this has been characterized above, Nietzsche holds that the philosopher must be prepared to draw upon considerations of any sort which bear upon the matters with which he is concerned. These considerations may be psychological, socio-logical, historical, linguistic, physiological, or natural-scientific. All are relevant to philosophical issues far more frequently than philosophers commonly suppose. Their relevance, moreover, is by no means merely peripheral; and they may be ignored only at the cost of superficiality and error in one's philosophical thinking. This holds true, on his view, both with regard to epistemological, ontological, and evaluative and normative questions, and also where existing and possible 'forms of life' are concerned. Thus, for example, he suggests that, in the case of moral concepts and issues, the efforts of 'professional philosophers' to deal with them require to be informed by the work of 'philologists and historians'; and that 'it is equally necessary to engage the interest of physiologists and doctors in these problems,' leaving 'academic philosophers to act as advocates and mediators,' and 'transforming the originally so reserved and mistrustful relations between philosophy, physiology and medicine into the most amicable and fruitful exchange' (*GM* I:17n.).

To say this is not to say that (reversing the traditional relation of dependence) philosophy must be built upon the various special sciences, the testimony of which is beyond any question or doubt. On the contrary, philosophy has an indispensable function to perform in the analysis and criticism of their basic concepts and principles, in the interpretation of their findings, and in the resolution of problems arising as they thereby are recast and more adequately grasped. It is rather to say that neither philosophy nor the various special sciences should be conceived and treated as an absolute foundation for the other; and that they must depend upon each other in order for either to be capable of treating satisfactorily the kinds of issues with which it falls to them to deal. In the end, however, Nietzsche is quite emphatic with respect to their standing in relation to each other: 'I venture to speak out against an unseemly and harmful shift in the respective ranks of science and philosophy,' he writes, holding it to be objectionable that the former 'now aims with an excess of high spirits and a lack of understanding to lay down laws for philosophy and to play the

19

"master" herself,' and that philosophers all too commonly accede to its pretentions (*BGE* 204). Against this tendency on both sides, he urges that '*all* the sciences have from now on to prepare the way for the future task of the philosophers,' which he takes to culminate in 'the solution of the *problem of value*' (*GM* I:17n).

Problems with philosophers

III

Nietzsche's repeated reference to the need for 'new philosophers' reflects his judgment that philosophers previously have commonly fallen far short of satisfying his conception of the genuine philosopher. The latter may be further illuminated by considering in some detail his views concerning philosophy as it has long been carried on. He has a good deal to say in this connection, above all with respect to a number of widespread tendencies and short-comings which he takes to be characteristic of philosophers from the Greeks to his own day. In setting out his main charges against them, I would suggest at the outset that one would do well not to attach too much importance to the existence of exceptions to his many sweeping generalizations, if the exceptions are only that. His generalizations are to be taken simply as such, rather than as applying with equal force in all cases. The more important question is that of whether or not his observations and criticisms have the general validity he supposes them to have, and point to failings which in fact have been widespread in the course of the history of philosophy.

First, he contends that philosophers for the most part have not properly understood the nature of philosophical activity, and have been far too prone to dogmatism. They have generally failed to grasp the fact that genuinely philosophical activity is not only to be distinguished from the mere 'philosophical labor' of analyzing, explicating, systematizing and applying previously developed conceptual and evaluative schemes, but also does not consist exclusively in the apprehension and articulation of indubitable facts, the establishment of incontrovertible first principles, and the rigorous derivation of consequences from them. As has been previously observed, he considers it to be a fundamentally *interpretive* affair, involving the development of novel ways of thinking by means of which the comprehension of things and events and the course of human life may be reoriented.

This is not to say that philosophers have not in point of fact engaged in activity of this sort — although relatively few of them

20

have, in his opinion, while most (including even Kant and Hegel) have been mere 'philosophical laborers' in the above sense. But where they have, he contends, they have commonly misconstrued what they were doing. They have mistaken their 'creative positing' for purely objective 'ascertaining'; and, as a consequence, they have not been prepared to admit either the conditioning or the provisional and perspectival character of the frameworks they have developed. And, as a consequence of this, both they and the 'philosophical laborers' who operate within the context of these frameworks have tended to be excessively dogmatic, claiming (illegitimately) the status of absolute knowledge and truth for them. Nietzsche might call upon philosophers to be 'legislators' rather than mere caretakers and advocates of long-established conceptual schemes and modes of interpretation and evaluation; but he would not have them be dogmatists. Thus he never tires of inveighing against the dogmatic turn of mind and pretentions of his predecessors, and insists that one should

> . . .know that no philosopher so far as been proved right, and that there might be a more laudable truthfulness in every little question mark that you place after your special words and favorite doctrines (and occasionally after yourselves) than in all the solemn gestures and trumps before accusers and law courts (*BGE* 25).

Next, Nietzsche charges philosophers generally with something even more serious. 'Nothing is rarer among philosophers than *intellectual integrity*,' he writes, although 'perhaps they say the opposite, perhaps they even believe it' (*WP* 445). For their thinking tends to be strongly influenced by a variety of 'prejudices' of several different sorts, to which they are insufficiently sensitive, and which anyone of intelligence with a lively 'intellectual conscience' should be able to recognize as such and seek to put out of play.

In the first instance, he contends that they commonly are guilty of evaluative prejudices with respect to various features of human existence and experience. 'Philosophers are prejudiced against appearance, change, pain, death, the corporeal, the senses, fate and bondage, the aimless' (*WP* 407). And they further tend to be prejudicial in their treatments of a great many other matters, their positive and negative assessments of which are symptomatic of dispositions widely prevalent among them but seldom justified or even acknowledged. These include the transitory and the abiding, the developing and the permanent, the contingent and the necessary, the particular and the universal, the capricious and the

21

lawful, the chaotic and the orderly, complexity and simplicity, the irrational and the rational, the physical and the mental, the unconscious and the conscious, creation and cognition, conflict and concord, suffering and happiness, assertiveness and submission, egoism and altruism, and difference and equality.

It is not Nietzsche's intention to suggest that there is nothing to be said in support of any of the 'prejudices' of philosophers with respect to these things, let alone that they ought one and all to be reversed. He does in fact have strong reservations about many of them, and would reverse some, considering most to be 'merely foreground estimates,' made 'from some nook, perhaps from below, frog perspectives, as it were, to borrow an expression painters use' (*BGE* 2). But the point for present purposes is simply that, however understandable and even desirable it may be for most people to adhere unquestioningly to many of them, a philosopher has no right to do so. Indeed, *qua* philosopher, one has a positive obligation to set them aside, at least unless one can make a case for them. Otherwise they are mere prejudices, which often have far-reaching and important consequences in the schemes philosophers develop, but which render such schemes questionable to the extent that this is the case. And it is Nietzsche's contention that prejudices of this sort have been shared by so many philosophers that there is little in the history of philosophy that does not reflect their influence.

No less common and significant, in his eyes, are a variety of 'prejudices' of a somewhat different sort, consisting of certain things which philosophers have tended to presuppose or rely upon, but which ought to be the objects of the severest critical scrutiny. Here too, he has many things in mind, of which I shall mention only some. Philosophers, for example, are held to 'have trusted in concepts as completely as they have mistrusted the senses,' and 'have not stopped to consider that concepts and words are our inheritance from ages in which thinking was very modest and unclear' (*WP* 409). They also tend to take for granted the supreme importance and intrinsic value of 'knowledge for the sake of knowledge,' and in many cases the possibility of 'absolute knowledge' as well; and to regard as self-evident and unconditionally and universally binding 'moral definitions in which former cultural conditions are reflected' (*WP* 407). They commonly are naively disposed to 'believe that there are "immediate certainties"; for example, "I think," or as the superstition of Schopenhauer put it, "I will"' (*BGE* 16). So he observes that Schopenhauer 'only did what philosophers are in the habit of doing: he adopted a *popular prejudice* and exaggerated it' (*BGE* 19).

22

Philosophers also 'all are tyrannized by logic' (*HH* I:6), submitting unquestioningly to 'our subjective compulsion to believe in logic,' and 'imagining that this compulsion guarantees something connected with "truth,"' as though the machinery of logic 'enabled us to fix the *real world*' (*WP* 521). This too is a prejudice, on Nietzsche's view, and an erroneous one at that, as shall be seen. They likewise are held to be under the sway of 'the prejudice of reason,' which 'forces us to posit unity, identity, permanence, substance, cause, thinghood, being,' even though all are fictions. And they are purported to embrace all too readily the 'crude fetishism' involved in 'the basic presuppositions of the metaphysics of language,' which begins with a 'belief in the ego,' construes 'the ego as a substance,' and 'projects this faith in the ego-substance upon all things,' everywhere seeing 'a doer and a doing,' and interpreting all events in terms of this fictitious model (*TI* III:5).

Nietzsche further suggests that philosophers have commonly simply taken for granted such things as the basic rationality of reality; the nomological character of events; the existence of 'things in themselves'; the possibility of a correspondence between thought and being; the existence of non-natural values and absolute and universally binding moral principles; the preferability of knowledge and truth to ignorance and error under all circumstances, and of 'moral' to 'immoral' actions and intentions in all situations; the explicability of human actions in terms of reasons and intentions; the intrinsic worth of the human individual; the autonomy of the soul in relation to the body; the unsurpassability of humanity in its present form, man's limitations notwithstanding; the essential equality of all men; and the teleological character of human existence and human history.

Not all philosophers, of course, have taken all of these things for granted; but many of the latter have at least commonly been accepted as articles of faith. And since Nietzsche considers these assumptions in point of fact to be very questionable (and indeed largely untenable), he contends that the particular positions philosophers have gone on to develop on the basis of them are thereby rendered dubious at best. What he finds most objectionable, however, is simply the readiness of many philosophers to take things of this sort as 'given,' without considering and taking seriously the possibility that there might be good reasons for thinking them untenable, and recognizing that they are at least highly problematical. It may not be immediately apparent what these reasons might be; but even so, his basic point would seem to be well taken.

Nietzsche further considers philosophers often to be 'prejudiced' in an even deeper respect: they are committed in advance to certain positions and views, which they profess to arrive at by disinterested inquiry. Thus they act as 'wily spokesmen for their prejudices which they baptize "truths,"' though they may be '*very* far from having the courage of conscience that admits this, precisely this, to itself' (*BGE* 5). Among them 'only certain truths are admitted; they know what they *have* to prove; that they are at one over these "truths" is virtually their means of recognizing one another as philosophers' (*WP* 445). Those assumed 'truths' Nietzsche goes on to cite in this passage pertain to morality; and it would seem that, together with certain religious beliefs (notably with respect to God and the soul), various general moral views and evaluations are what he chiefly has in mind here. Determined to preserve or salvage as much as possible of the religion and morality to which they are committed, philosophers have frequently been prepared to go to any lengths to vindicate and justify their basic tenets, adopting whatever tactics they found to be necessary in order to be able to do so.

Thus he contends that the reason why 'all philosophical architects in Europe from Plato onward have built in vain' is that they 'have built under the seduction of morality.' 'Their intent seemingly was directed toward certainty and "truth," but actually it was toward "*majestic moral edifices*,"' as Kant had put it (*D* P: 3). And to this he adds the charge that, historically, one finds them 'always in the service of the nihilistic religions' — religions, that is, which, by promoting the view that the loci of all value are God and the soul while 'this world is good for nothing,' are covertly nihilistic (*WP* 401). To the extent that they have been mere 'philosophical laborers' on behalf of such basic interpretive and evaluative constructs 'which have become dominant and are for a time called "truths"' (*BGE* 211), committed to them from the outset and determined to preserve them in their essentials in the face of all challenges, they are ruled by prejudices rendering their thinking profoundly suspect.

It is not enough, however, simply to observe that this is frequently the case. It is further necessary to consider what is to be made of these sorts of prejudices and the fact that philosophers so often are subject to them. And what Nietzsche goes on to propose in this connection is that their thinking, no less than that of human beings generally, tends to be shaped by and reflect their basic needs, dispositions, and other influences of a very 'human' sort. Such factors require to be taken into consideration, on his view, in order to enable one to understand the adoption by various philosophers of similar or differing general orientations, basic

24

assumptions, points of departure and forms of procedure. And thus he undertakes a form of investigation which he terms his 'psychology of philosophers.' It may not by itself settle the question of what is to be made of what they have to say; but he contends that it is indispensable to a proper resolution of this question. 'Every philosophy is a foreground philosophy,' he remarks. 'Every philosophy also *conceals* a philosophy; every opinion is also a hideout, every word also a mask' (*BGE* 289).

IV

It is commonly held that, where such fundamental features of philosophical thinking are encountered, philosophical bedrock has been reached; and in a sense, Nietzsche would agree. He would grant, that is, that there may well be no answer to the question of what a philosopher's *reasons* might have been for settling upon certain possibilities on this level rather than others — since arguments can be mounted and justifications given only within contexts in which this has already occurred. It does not follow, however, that there is no answer to the question of *why* he does so. And Nietzsche suggests that the answer to this question is generally and largely to be sought along 'psychological' lines, broadly construed.

> Gradually it has become clear to me what every great
> philosophy so far has been: namely, the personal confession
> of its author and a kind of involuntary and unconscious
> memoir (*BGE* 6).

In this way, he writes, 'the *hidden* history of the philosophers, the psychology of the great names, came to light for me' (*EH* P:3). In the case of each of them, it sooner or later becomes appropriate to say: ' "There is something arbitrary in his stopping *here* to look back and look around, in his not digging deeper *here* but laying his spade aside; there is also something suspicious about it" ' (*BGE* 289). What on one level of consideration appears 'arbitrary,' however, is actually far from it. Thus he suggests that 'if one would explain how the abstrusest metaphysical claims of a philosopher really came about, it is always well (and wise) to ask first: at what morality does all this (does *he*) aim?' And he further contends that 'his morality bears decided and decisive witness to *who he is*,' and how 'the innermost drives of his nature stand in relation to each other' (*BGE* 6).

This does not mean that Nietzsche discounts the importance of cultural and intellectual-historical factors; on the contrary, he

25

places considerable emphasis upon them. He holds, however, that such factors seldom render a single orientation inevitable; and that psychological factors generally play a crucial role in determining which specific one is adopted. He further should not be taken to be advocating some form of strict determinism which would exclude the possibility of any real creativity and originality; from what has been said earlier, on the matter of creativity in the enterprise of philosophy, this should be obvious. But he maintains that philosophical thinking always occurs within a horizon which the basic needs and dispositions of the philosopher (modified by cultural and intellectual-historical factors) at least partly determine. All of 'the basic drives of man,' he remarks, 'have done philosophy at some time,' in various configurations and with different ones predominating in different cases. 'I do not believe that a "drive to knowledge" is the father of philosophy,' he writes; it is always some other 'drive' that 'has, here as elsewhere, employed understanding (and misunderstanding) as a mere instrument' (*BGE* 6).

It should be added at once that Nietzsche does not suppose that considerations of this sort are decisive in the evaluation of the merits of a philosophical scheme. Such a scheme may or may not prove fruitful and illuminating; the needs and dispositions of the philosopher which impelled him to develop it by no means settle this question. He does maintain, however, that there are many cases — particularly but not only when we are confronted with competing systems of values — in which considerations of this sort should serve at least to raise doubts. For example: if it can be shown that a certain sort of morality has been developed in response to various widespread but 'all too human' needs, or that a certain view of knowledge manifests a negative disposition toward the senses and the body, this will surely have some bearing upon their assessment. And in fact, Nietzsche argues, this sort of thing is to be found time and again in the history of philosophy. A variety of cases in point will be considered in due course.

It might seem that it would not be possible for Nietzsche to carry his 'psychology of philosophers' farther than this. In fact, however, he does so; and this brings us to the most fundamental charge he levels at them in this connection. If their thinking is commonly dominated and shaped by 'ulterior motives,' which more than anything else are held to have 'obstructed the course of philosophy' (*WP* 413), these 'ulterior motives' in turn are taken to reflect a basic and widespread disposition among philosophers throughout the history of philosophy, of hostility toward life and the conditions of life in this world.

If one wants a proof of how profoundly and thoroughly the actually barbarous needs of man seek satisfaction, even when he is tamed and 'civilized,' one should take a look at the 'leitmotifs' of the entire evolution of philosophy: — a sort of revenge on reality, a malicious destruction of the valuations by which men live. . . .

The history of philosophy is a secret raging against the preconditions of life, against the value feelings of life, against partisanship in favor of life. Philosophers have never hesitated to affirm a [metaphysical] world provided it contradicted this world and furnished them with a pretext for speaking ill of this world. It has been hitherto the grand school for slander (*WP* 461).

Thus motivated, he contends, they have been led to develop various metaphysical schemes involving a distinction between 'this world,' construed as a merely 'apparent world,' and another realm to which all honors are accorded. 'The latter has hitherto been called the "real world," "truth," "God."' For Nietzsche, however, it is a 'world invented by a lie,' which 'we have to abolish' — a 'lie' born of a lamentable disposition he seeks to diagnose, and to counter where it cannot be overcome (ibid.).

He often links the prevalence of this disposition to the general condition he calls 'decadence'; and he diagnoses the phenomenon of 'decadence' ultimately as a consequence of certain physiological deficiencies and psychological defects. He attributes some of the inadequacies of philosophers to the fact that they are too much children of their age, too naive and superficial, and ignorant of too many things; but he discerns this constitutional affliction at the root of the most fateful of their shortcomings. He speaks of their having been dominated by 'ulterior moral motives' in this connection, because the sort of morality he has in mind is one of the basic manifestations of 'decadence' (which he glosses in terms of exhaustion, weakness, hypersensitivity, and diminished vitality) through which a disposition of hostility toward life and the conditions of existence is both given a semblance of dignity and provided with an apparent justification. 'Concerning life,' he writes, 'the wisest men of all ages have judged alike: *it is no good.*' And rather than supposing that their general agreement on this matter 'evidences the truth,' he voices the suspicion that 'at least something must be *sick* here'; and that these seemingly 'wisest of men' have actually been 'decadents' (*TI* III:1), or '*types of decline,*' whose 'negative attitude to life' is a symptom of 'degeneration' (*TI* III:2).

It is the prevalence among them of this condition and the hostile disposition to which it gives rise, on Nietzsche's view, which accounts for many of the prejudices of philosophers, and for the steadfastness with which they cling to them. Their commitment to truth time and again has been overridden, and their thinking distorted, by a deep dissatisfaction with the conditions of human existence in this world, and a great longing for life to be other than it is. The inability to endure things as they are, he holds, has led philosophers to develop interpretations of reality which are more satisfying to them — philosophy 'always creates the world in its own image' (*BGE* 9) — and to make whatever assumptions are necessary to this end. At the same time, however, it has induced them to persuade themselves so completely of the reasonableness and self-evidence of their preferences and 'givens' that they suppose their conclusions to satisfy the high standards of rationality and rigorous argument they set for themselves as philosophers.

Seen in this light, the history of philosophy consists far less in a series of objective and disinterested attempts to ascertain 'the truth' than in a series of psychological case studies of flights from reality. In a sense, Nietzsche does not hold the failings of his predecessors along these lines against them, his charge that they have been lacking in 'intellectual integrity' notwithstanding; for he supposes that they would not have been driven to such lengths if the stakes for them personally had not been so great. Their attempts to construe reality in a manner more agreeable to them were not undertaken lightly, but rather with deadly seriousness: their very ability to find existence endurable hung in the balance. Nor does Nietzsche hold them in complete contempt for their inability to endure it on its own terms; for while he attributes this inability to weakness, he does not regard their weakness as any fault of their own, and considers the strength they have lacked to be rare indeed. In fact, he frequently expresses doubt that anyone is capable of confronting reality and enduring life entirely without illusion (cf. *BGE* 39). While philosophers whose schemes were developed in accordance with profound 'human' needs may be regarded with sympathy, however, this does not render such schemes immune to criticism. And it likewise does not remove the obligation of the philosopher to strive to resist this tendency, and to engage in continual self-scrutiny for indications that he has not been successful in doing so. Indeed, one who fails to do so is held by Nietzsche to be no genuine philosopher at all.

V

There remain to be mentioned several further, different sorts of criticisms which he levels at philosophers generally. One of them has been indicated in passing above: philosophers, he holds, have tended to attribute too much significance to, and to place too much trust in, certain forms and features of language. 'Words lie in our way,' as he remarks, tempting us to mistake labels merely constituting signposts of problems for their solutions, when they do not actually lead us astray (*D* 47). And it is not only particular words and concepts that seduce and mislead the unwary; for 'faith in grammar' does so as well, and even more profoundly. Thus he writes:

> Where there is affinity of language, it cannot fail . . . — owing
> to the unconscious domination and guidance by similar
> grammatical functions — that everything is prepared at the
> outset for a similar development and sequence of philosophical
> systems; just as the way seems barred against certain other
> possibilities of world-interpretation (*BGE* 20).

The most important example of this, which on Nietzsche's view has given rise to numerous philosophical errors, is the subject-predicate form of assertorial propositions. Philosophers have tended to suppose that it reflects the formal structure of reality, and have been led by it, for example, to think of both objects and the subject of experience and action on the model of substances modified by attributes. But this is by no means the only case in point. They also have been all too quick to draw substantive conclusions from the existence of certain linguistic conventions, often supposing, for example, that the conventional application of different sets of predicates to persons and to non-human things establishes the existence of an ontological difference between them; and that the unconditionality of the language of morals is indicative of the unconditionality of fundamental moral principles.

Philosophers further have frequently taken the practical indispensability of certain concepts and the existence of conceptual connections to yield information concerning ontological states of affairs. Thus they have inferred, for example, that reality consists of a multiplicity of discrete 'things' of some sort, from the indispensability of the notion of a 'thing' in our ordinary discourse about the world; and that human beings are free agents, from the fact that the language in which we describe their actions involves the attribution to them of responsibility for their actions, which in turn conceptually entails their freedom. In all such cases,

29

Nietzsche considers philosophers to have been extremely naive; and to have been led astray time and again by their blind 'faith in language.' For language, he observes, along with the entire stock of concepts embedded in it, is far from being a kind of Book of Revelation of ultimate truths or reliable guide to their discovery. Indeed, he takes it to be filled with crude oversimplifications, distortions, convenient misrepresentations, superstitions and remnants of our ancestors' ignorance (*WP* 409).

It is quite understandable that philosophers should have been slow to discern the problematic character of the very medium in which they operate. It seems to have all the marks of complete self-evidence, and to require no justification or critical scrutiny; and it easily escapes notice altogether, like the spectacles on one's nose. Nietzsche insists, however, that it is far from being a purely neutral medium, and that its specific characteristics and features — from its formal structure and its basic concepts to its conventions of usage and the descriptive and emotive meanings of its particular terms — tend in a variety of ways to be reflected in philosophical as well as ordinary thinking. Moreover, he contends, it is a *human* phenomenon; and the possibility must be reckoned with that the factors which have gone into making it what it is relate primarily to certain contingencies of human life. It is imperative, in this light, for the philosopher to treat linguistic data with the utmost caution. Thus Nietzsche exclaims: 'We really ought to free ourselves from the seduction of words!' (*BGE* 16). And he asks: 'Shouldn't philosophers be permitted to rise above faith in grammar? All due respect for governesses — but hasn't the time come for philosophy to renounce the faith of governesses?' (*BGE* 34).

Next, he contends that philosophers commonly have turned a blind eye to development. 'If one is a philosopher as men have always been philosophers, one cannot see what has been and becomes — one sees only what *is*,' he writes, adding that 'since nothing *is*,' i.e., since there is no immutable *being* but rather only the changing, 'all that was left to the philosopher as his "world" was the imaginary' (*WP* 570). Virtually everything about ourselves and about life and the world more generally has *come to be* as it is; but philosophers have been largely oblivious to this circumstance. And this, he holds, not only has led them to overlook the possibility of further change and development, but also has adversely affected their analyses of the nature and significance of things as they presently are constituted.

Nietzsche has a great many things in mind here. Among them are our (conventional) morality and values, our art, sciences, and religions, our language, conceptual schemes and logic, our perceptual and cognitive faculties, our social and political institutions and legal and economic systems, our patterns of inter-personal interaction, our emotional and spiritual life, our physiological nature, and the very world we live in and of which we are a part, with all of its animate and inanimate forms. Philosophers, he claims, have tended to confine themselves to descriptions of these things in their present states, and to regard the structures they describe as eternal and immutable. And in doing so, on his view, they have been profoundly mistaken. 'Everything has developed,' he contends; 'there are *no eternal facts*,' and thus 'no absolute truths' expressing them (*HH* I:2). He readily acknowledges the importance of that sort of analysis consisting in the careful description of what presently obtains. He argues, however, that an 'historical sense' is indispensable for the philosopher if he is to achieve any real understanding of the nature and significance of the phenomena whose present structures are thus described. And an 'historical sense' is something he considers most philosophers to have lacked almost completely.

> All philosophers have the common defect that they start out from present-day man and expect to reach their goal through an analysis of him. They reflexively think of 'man' as an *aeterna veritas*, as something unchanging amid all turmoil, as a steady standard of things. Everything the philosopher says about man, however, is basically nothing more than testimony about the man of a *very limited* time-frame. The lack of an historical sense is the hereditory defect of all philosophers. Indeed, many unthinkingly take the latest version of man — as it has emerged under the impress of specific religions, and even of specific political events — as the fixed form from which one must proceed. They are unwilling to learn that man has developed, and that his cognitive capacity likewise has developed (*HH* I:2).

Philosophers have been inclined (for reasons which Nietzsche thinks are partly cultural and partly psychological) to acknowledge 'becoming' and development only — if at all — in the form of accidental change, the Heraclitean flux, or at the most, the actualization of potentiality; and so they have tended to consider it irrelevant where most philosophical issues are concerned. For Nietzsche, on the other hand, it is 'becoming,' rather than 'being,' which ought to be foremost in the minds of philosophers, as they turn their attention to any of the matters indicated above. He thus maintains that a break with the traditional manner of philosophiz-

31

ing — which set its sights on 'being,' and in doing so gave short shrift to 'becoming' — is imperative; and that '*historical philosophizing* is henceforth necessary' (ibid.).

A further, related shortcoming of previous philosophers, according to Nietzsche, is that they have lacked a 'psychological sense,' which he holds to be no less necessary for the philosopher than an 'historical sense.' And here he has in mind much more than an appreciation of the need for the sort of 'psychology of philosophers' he advocates and undertakes. Philosophers also need an acute 'psychological sense,' on his view, in order to avoid serious errors and get very far in their inquiries into the nature and significance of many human phenomena. Thus he maintains that 'superficiality in psychological observation has set the most dangerous traps for human judgments and conclusions, and continues to set them' (*HH* I:37).

Many philosophers in the past have at least acknowledged that non-rational factors (e.g., 'appetites,' 'passions,' 'desires,' 'natural inclinations,' etc.) play an important role in human life. Nietzsche contends, however, that most have understood them in very simplistic terms, and have greatly underestimated their actual influence; and that few have taken them into account when they have turned to a consideration of the many spheres of human life in which the influence of such factors is not immediately apparent. If philosophers have been insensitive to the developmental character of such things as prevailing evaluations, moralities, modes of cognition, religions, institutions, and patterns of conduct, they have been even less appreciative of the extent to which psychological factors have shaped their development, and continue to affect people's involvement in and commitment to them. It is only if these factors are taken into consideration, on his view, that a proper assessment of such phenomena can be made. And because he finds most philosophers lacking in the psychological sensitivity required to discern and investigate their nature and effects, he considers their accounts of these matters to suffer accordingly. Thus he asks: 'Who among philosophers was a *psychologist* at all before me, and not rather the opposite, a "high swindler" and "idealist"?' (*EH* IV:6). And he holds that 'the mistakes of the greatest philosophers' commonly originate precisely in their deficiencies along these lines (*HH* I:37).

This shortcoming is related to the one mentioned before it, in that the latter consists in viewing things simply as they are, without regard to their underlying determinants. Either failing alone, on Nietzsche's view, is bad enough; but when the latter compounds the former, the consequences are likely to be very

32

serious indeed. Precisely this, however, is purported to be the general rule among his predecessors. And so also, in addition to maintaining that 'historical philosophizing' is henceforth necessary, he takes the position that 'psychology is now again the path to the fundamental problems' (*BGE* 23).

One further point Nietzsche makes remains to be mentioned. It is related to those just indicated, and stands to the latter somewhat as the latter does to the former. The psychological factors affecting the development of things human, he argues, must themselves be understood (at least in part) in terms of *physiological* factors; and he contends that philosophers generally have been, if anything, even more neglectful and ignorant of the role of such factors in the shaping of human life than they have been of the sorts of considerations indicated above. Thus, in answer to the question 'What do philosophers lack?', the first thing he mentions is 'an historical sense,' and the second is 'knowledge of physiology' (*WP* 408).

Nietzsche's thinking along these lines requires brief elaboration, in order to make clear his reasons for taking philosophers to task on this count. Human beings, he holds, are fundamentally natural organisms, all of whose faculties are ultimately grounded in physiological structures. The human mind consequently cannot be treated as a thing unto itself, which functions in a completely autonomous manner in relation to the human body in any of its operations. Our perceptual and cognitive abilities, the processes of thinking, feeling, evaluating and willing, and the wide range of experiences which constitute our spiritual and social life, all have their basis in our physiological nature. The latter is the condition of their possibility; and what is more, according to Nietzsche, it fundamentally conditions their character. This is not to say that it strictly and completely determines them; on the contrary, he maintains that through a process of sublimation, there can and does occur a qualitative transformation of physiological processes into mental and spiritual ones, which do not admit of explanation in purely physiological terms. It does mean, however, that the autonomy of the latter in relation to the former is never more than partial; and that attention to the physiological foundations of the various forms of human mental and spiritual life is necessary, if an adequate understanding of their natures, functions and limitations is to be achieved.

It is Nietzsche's contention, however, that previous philosophers typically have been heedless of physiological structures and processes, partly owing to their ignorance of them, and partly because they have erroneously assumed that the mind is not

33

significantly dependent upon factors of this sort in its various operations. And as a consequence, he maintains, the analyses they have given and the positions they have taken in their treatments of human nature, knowledge, religion, art, morality, and many other matters for the most part have been either profoundly mistaken or highly superficial. He recognizes that to admit and insist upon the relevance of physiological (and psychological) considerations to philosophical investigations of these matters is to abandon the ideal of philosophy as a discipline independent of the empirical sciences and untainted by the corrigibility attaching to all empirical knowledge. This is an ideal, however, which he considers it imperative to lay to rest. He is emphatic in his rejection of the view that philosophy can be no more than a handmaiden of the sciences, as has been observed; but he is equally insistent upon the erroneousness of supposing that philosophical questions are of such a nature that the sciences generally, and physiology in particular, can have no significant implications for them. Most philosophers, however, have on his view either supposed this to be so or proceeded as though it were the case; and this has seriously affected what they have gone on to say with respect to a broad range of issues.

One might well feel that, while Nietzsche may be justified in challenging the reverence in which those who have shaped the history of philosophy are so often held, his harsh treatment of them is carried too far, and does them considerable injustice. Yet while it may be that his criticisms are too sweeping, and that exceptions to his generalizations are more numerous than he recognizes, it must be allowed that he fastens upon some very real and fundamental shortcomings, which are common not only to many philosophers prior to him, but to many more recently as well. His critique has the further value of drawing attention to ways in which even the most able philosophical minds can go astray. And at the very least it serves to make clear the necessity of reconsidering the status and significance of many of the things philosophers are often disposed to assume or accept and rely upon, on the one hand, and to ignore or deem philosophically irrelevant, on the other.

Philosophy as linguistic analysis: a case in point

VI

In *Beyond Good and Evil*, Nietzsche proclaims that 'a new species of philosophers is coming up' (*BGE* 42) — philosophers who will differ greatly from those whose thought has dominated the history of philosophy, and also from his philosophical contemporaries. And in the course of the present century, 'new philosophers' have indeed arisen, both in Europe and in the English-speaking world, who have broken radically with the philosophical tradition of which he is so critical, and who have understood the enterprise of philosophy quite differently than earlier philosophers did. At least for the most part, however, they have not exactly been the kind of 'new philosophers' Nietzsche envisioned and called for. And while he can hardly be said to have undertaken to criticize conceptions of the nature of the enterprise of philosophy which have emerged and become predominant only in the present century, he does have a good deal to say that bears relatively directly on at least one such philosophical tendency. I refer to that recent variant (or family of variants) of analytic philosophy which might be called 'linguistic-analytic philosophy,' in virtue of its methodological emphasis and reliance upon one form or another of linguistic analysis in dealing with philosophical questions. This is a matter of no less interest and importance than Nietzsche's treatment of his predecessors; and so it is well worth considering how he stands in relation to this development.

It was not too long ago that most English-speaking philosophers were inclined to think of Nietzsche either as no real philosopher at all, or else as a philosopher whose only importance is historical, and who — as one who labored in the darkness before the dawn of the analytic era — could safely be ignored by those engaged in the ongoing enterprise of analytic philosophy. More recently, however, a very different view of him has come to enjoy some currency, according to which he is credited as having been a 'predecessor' of the 'analytic movement' in philosophy (cf. Arthur Danto, *Nietzsche as Philosopher*). There is an important element of truth in this view; and as a corrective, suggesting that analytic philosophers ought to take him more seriously, that what he has to say is by no means irrelevant to what they are doing, and that his contributions to certain of their concerns are considerable, its emergence has been a good thing.

To characterize Nietzsche in this way, however, is as misleading as the previously prevailing view of him was mistaken. To be sure, he anticipated many of the objections of analytic philosophers to earlier ways of philosophizing; and he dealt with many philosophical problems with an analytical rigor that is very much in keeping with the spirit of analytic philosophy. Yet he also was highly critical of the conception of philosophy as an enterprise to be restricted to or conducted exclusively on the basis of linguistic

35

analysis — or at any rate, of the presuppositions and self-limitations this conception involves. At one point Nietzsche speaks of himself as 'the first perfect nihilist of Europe who, however, has even now lived through the whole of nihilism, to the end, leaving it behind, outside himself' (WP P:3). He might with equal justice (and hyperbole) be styled 'the first perfect analytical philosopher of Europe,' who, however, perceived the limitations of mere linguistic analysis where the resolution of genuine philosophical problems is concerned; 'leaving it behind,' in the sense of seeing the necessity of going beyond it, and developing a mode of philosophizing which enabled him to do so.

Thus while Nietzsche may have been a predecessor of the analytic movement, he also is one of its severest critics, albeit *ante rem*. And in this latter capacity, he ought to be taken most seriously by analytic philosophers generally, and by linguistic-analytic philosophers in particular, even if they prefer not to avail themselves of his many positive contributions to the discussion of issues with which they themselves are concerned. For while they may safely go about their business without bothering to pay much attention to their predecessors, they cannot afford to fail to consider the merit of the arguments of their critics, where these apply. And Nietzsche is not just any critic, whose views may be dismissed lightly. Indeed, the very fact that he is sufficiently sympathetic to the aims and procedures of analytic philosophers to be legitimately ranked among their 'predecessors' (at the very least) suggests that his criticisms ought to be reckoned with; for he knew whereof he spoke, notwithstanding that 'the analytic movement' proper did not emerge for another generation.

VII

While it has become common in recent years to hear analytic philosophers claim philosophical descent from Socrates, their more immediate philosophical progenitors were men like Hume and Kant. Convinced that the reach of previous metaphysicians had exceeded their grasp, the latter were moved to place severe restrictions upon the knowledge to which philosophers (and human beings generally) could legitimately aspire, and to propose a fundamental modification of that conception of the business of philosophy which had prevailed previously. Proceeding from the premises that neither speculative reasoning nor experience can ever yield knowledge of ultimate reality, and that we have no other cognitive faculty by means of which certain knowledge of it might be gained, they argued that philosophers should abandon their metaphysical pretentions. We should restrict ourselves, they urged, to analyzing the nature and limits of our cognitive faculties and that kind of foreground knowledge of ourselves and the world which they can and do afford us, together with the basic values and moral principles which inform our evaluative and normative experience.

Analytic philosophy may be viewed as a development in this tradition. Its adherents observe the prescriptions and proscriptions mentioned quite religiously — a good deal more so, in fact, than Kant did himself. Kant labored to erect 'majestic moral edifices,' as has been observed, even though he renounced the attempt to raise speculative metaphysical ones; whereas analytic philosophers generally reject projects of either sort. Among them the main task of philosophy is usually understood to be the analysis of the concepts basic to the various areas of human thought and life, as opposed to the discovery of ultimate truths concerning the matters arising in each such area. They tend to regard the attempts of earlier philosophers and their non-analytic contemporaries to discover such truths as naive and quixotic; for the sorts of speculation they involve are held to be capable neither of logical demonstration, nor of empirical confirmation, nor of linguistic justification.

As heirs of a philosophical tradition further preoccupied with the desire to 'elevate' the status of philosophy from that of a mere handmaiden of theology to that of a discipline on all fours with mathematics (in some cases) and empirical science (in others) in terms of intellectual respectability, analytic philosophers generally feel obliged to renounce any endeavor that does not at least have the appearance of conforming to the highest standards of formal rigor and adherence to fact. The enterprise of analyzing conceptual schemes is seized upon by some, who feel that it meets this requirement, whereas the interpretation of reality and normative theorizing do not. Consequently, they are inclined to abandon metaphysics in favor of epistemology, ontology in favor of the philosophy of natural science, philosophical theology in favor of the philosophy of religion, philosophical psychology and anthropology and the philosophy of society and culture in favor of the philosophy of psychology and the social sciences, and normative ethics in favor of meta-ethics.

Philosophy for them is thus to be transformed from the attempt to give substantive answers to various kinds of fundamental questions in its own right, into the second-order analysis of the ways in which non-philosophers deal with these or related questions. The business of philosophy, as these philosophers understand it, is neither to discern the true nature of things, nor to indicate how we should or may best live our lives. Rather, it is to clarify and explicate the basic concepts employed by developers and employers of conceptual schemes of various sorts as they go about their non-philosophical affairs. Thus a well-known contemporary philosopher writes:

> Philosophy takes the conceptual systems developed by scientists, mathematicians, art critics, moralists, theologians, et al., as its subject matter and seeks to explain and clarify what has to be explained and clarified about such systems in order to render them fully comprehensible. (Jerrold Katz, *The Philosophy of Language* (New York: Harper & Row, 1966), p. 2.)

Philosophy so conceived cannot be held to consist merely in idle speculation about meaningless questions. It has its own special sort of relatively 'hard' data, and a useful task to perform in relation to them, involving the employment of analytical techniques which are at least as rigorous and 'scientific' in their own way as those of any other discipline, and more so than most. The respectability it thus acquires, however, is achieved at the cost of its effective relegation once again to the status of handmaiden: it is restricted to tidying up after others, and leaves the posing and answering of substantive questions entirely to 'scientists, mathematicians, art critics, moralists, theologians, et al.'

There is another group of analytic philosophers who do not envisage so purely subordinate a role for philosophy, at least in relation to the various special disciplines and interests of which the above are examples. They continue to be concerned (nominally, at any rate) with at least some of the sorts of substantive questions with which philosophers traditionally have attempted to deal, in such areas as ontology, the philosophy of mind, moral philosophy, and social philosophy. And they pursue them without constantly looking over their shoulders for guidance to the 'conceptual systems' constructed and employed by others. Yet they labor under self-imposed restraints of another sort, associated with their preferred alternative methodology of 'ordinary language analysis.' Finding the 'data' constituted by such 'systems' either too artificial, too constraining, or simply irrelevant to the questions with which they are concerned, and yet anxious to lay hold of relatively objective data of *some* sort by means of which to resolve disputes and maintain a degree of intellectual respectability, they seize upon the conventions governing the ordinary use of language (which in practice usually means the ordinary use of English).

Under the influence of philosophers like Moore, Wittgenstein, and Austin, these philosophers maintain that the proper way to evaluate a philosophical thesis is to determine whether it accurately reflects or does violence to the conventions of usage applying to the terms figuring in the statement of the thesis. They likewise suppose the proper way to determine whether or not a philosopher's treatment of a certain notion is sound is to consider whether it accurately reflects the way(s) in which the term in question is ordinarily employed in non-philosophical contexts. In general, they would have it that the proper way to approach substantive philosophical questions is to transform them into questions about the meanings and uses of terms, which then can be dealt with by a 'linguistic analysis' of the relevant features of the language making it possible to pose the questions in the first place. Conventions of linguistic usage may be explored with an empirical rigor that at least approximates the standards of scientific respectability; and they constitute an objective (or at least inter-subjective) criterion in terms of which arbitrary and idiosyncratic claims can be detected.

Their apparent concern with substantive philosophical questions notwithstanding, many philosophers favoring this approach are led ultimately to abandon the attempt to give substantive answers to such questions altogether. For some, it is replaced by an attempt to show that such questions only arise because philosophers violate conventions of usage and thereby become perplexed by problems which really are only pseudo-problems. For others, its place is taken by a program of analysis of the forms of language in which substantive assertions are made: thus moral philosophy is transformed into an analysis of the language of morals; ontology is transformed into an analysis of propositions with existential import and an examination of linguistic category-differences; and the philosophy of mind is transformed into an analysis of the language in which persons and their behavior are ordinarily described. Those who do remain concerned to deal substantively with at least some philosophical questions, on the other hand, tend to be led by their commitment to the method of 'ordinary language analysis' to regard linguistic conventions as decisive in delimiting the range of answers to these questions which warrant serious consideration, and in many cases as decisive in determining which of these answers is to be preferred as well.

Whatever their particular tendencies along these lines, these philosophers are implicitly or explicitly of the persuasion that linguistic conventions are not merely data, but philosophically important data; that the enterprise of philosophy depends for its respectability and success upon a close adherence to them, since none more informative and reliable are available to it, where questions for which the data of the various other disciplines are either irrelevant or indecisive are concerned; and that it is thus the business of philosophy, not to subject these conventions to critical scrutiny, but rather to deal with philosophical questions in the light of an investigation of them. Some hold, with Wittgenstein, that philosophers should leave them as they are. Others hold, with Austin, that a bit of rearranging may prove desirable now and then. One cannot go further than this, however, without seriously qualifying or abandoning altogether one's reliance upon the methodology in question, and thus departing from the philosophical orientation associated with it.

Conceived along these lines, philosophy is a much more autonomous discipline, and much less a handmaiden of other disciplines and interests, than it is when conceived along the lines suggested in the passage cited earlier. At the same time its close adherence to the body of data constituted by convention of linguistic usage may be argued with considerable force to elevate it well above the level of groundless and meaningless speculation, to the status of a genuine discipline on a par with at least some of the sciences. Yet, to repeat, a price is paid here as well, in the form of a relinquishment of autonomy in relation to conventions of linguistic usage. And it should be observed that any conclusions pertaining to substantive philosophical questions reached by means of 'linguistic analysis' — however correct they may be in terms of the relevant linguistic phenomena — depend for their validity upon an assumption the soundness of which is at least not immune to challenge: namely, the assumption that the language we speak and analyze is a reliable guide to the matters into which, as philosophers, we inquire.

The legitimacy of this assumption may, of course, be cheaply established, through the stipulation that, as philosophers, we may legitimately inquire only into those matters to which the language we speak and analyze is a reliable guide. If this move is made, however, it then becomes this stipulation the soundness of which may be questioned. And if this stipulation is defended on the ground that it is only if philosophers restrict their efforts in this way that philosophy can retain (or acquire) the status of a genuine discipline meriting the respect of the scientific community, the matter still is not settled, even assuming the truth of this claim. For it can still be questioned whether the end suggested is sufficiently desirable to justify the means required to achieve it, or indeed whether this end is desirable at all.

VIII

Nietzsche does not think it is. He writes: 'Permit me to say that the scholar and scientist. . .are fundamentally different from the philosopher. − What I desire is that the genuine concept of the philosopher should not utterly perish' (*WP* 420). He is fundamentally opposed to the cluster of philosophical tendencies whose more recent manifestations I have been discussing, in part because he feels that philosophy stops far short of performing its most important functions when philosophers take scholars and scientists as their models, or become too preoccupied with the conceptual systems of the latter. In the former case, they never become more than mere 'philosophical laborers,' who simply 'determine and press into formulas' previously established ways of thinking and speaking (*BGE* 211), and whose only accomplishment is thereby after a fashion 'to make previous events surveyable, comprehensible, graspable, and usable' (*WP* 972). In the latter case, they never become more than mere 'critics,' about whom Nietzsche has this to say, in the course of describing the characteristics of true philosophers as he conceives of them:

> Critical discipline and every habit that is conducive to
> cleanliness and severity in matters of spirit will be demanded
> by these philosophers, not only of themselves. . . − nevertheless
> they still do not want to be called critics on that account. They
> consider it no small disgrace for philosophy when people
> decree, as is popular nowadays: 'Philosophy itself is criticism
> and critical science − and nothing whatever besides.' This
> evaluation of philosophy may elicit applause from all the
> positivists of France and Germany. . . ; our new philosophers
> will say nevertheless: critics are instruments of the philosopher
> and for that very reason, being instruments, a long ways from
> being philosophers themselves (*BGE* 210).

In both cases, Nietzsche's complaint is that such philosophers never engage in the attempt to *go beyond* the explication, analysis and criticism of the efforts of others, and to develop interpretive and evaluative schemes which differ from (and perhaps improve upon) those previously fashioned and presently accepted. The same may be said of those who restrict themselves to either 'ordinary language' or 'special language' analysis. And since it is in terms of this attempt that he conceives the most important

41

function of philosophy, it follows that he would find the program of analytic philosophy — in so far as it consists merely in one or both of these kinds of analysis — to be seriously wanting. Commenting upon philosophers in the tradition of Hume and Kant, he writes:

> Philosophy reduced to 'theory of knowledge,' in fact no more than a timid epochism and doctrine of abstinence — a philosophy that never gets beyond the threshold and takes pains to *deny* itself the right to enter — that is philosophy in its last throes, an end, an agony, something inspiring pity (*BGE* 204).

His judgment undoubtedly would be no less harsh where 'philosophy reduced to "linguistic analysis"' is concerned. It is important to keep in mind, however, that his objection is not to 'critical discipline' and 'cleanliness and severity' of thought, which are philosophical virtues no less for him than for analytic philosophers. Indeed, he would find no fault with the most exacting projects of linguistic-analytical inquiry — as far as they go. In this respect, he sides with analytic philosophers and against their less cautious predecessors, as when he says, for example, with reference to earlier moral philosophers: 'How remote from their clumsy pride was that task they considered insignificant and left in dust and must — the task of description — although the subtlest fingers and senses can scarcely be subtle enough for it' (*BGE* 186). What he objects to is the notion that careful description and painstaking analysis of existing interpretive and evaluative systems and of linguistic conventions is the sole and entire business of philosophy, and that philosophers should concern themselves neither with the extra-systematic evaluation of these systems and usages nor with the development of new ones. It is here that he parts company with linguistic-analytic philosophy, in no uncertain terms.

The linguistic-analytic philosopher, seen in Nietzsche's perspective, is rather like 'the objective man' to whom he contrasts the genuine philosopher, and of whom he says he is 'an instrument, a precious, easily injured and clouded instrument for measuring and, as an arrangement of mirrors, an artistic triumph that deserves care and honor; but he is . . . only a delicate, carefully dusted, fine, mobile pot for forms that still has to wait for some content and substance in order to "shape" itself accordingly' (*BGE* 207). The 'content and substance' which give shape and direction to the reflections of linguistic-analytic philosophers are basically the two kinds of 'data' referred to above: in some cases, the 'conceptual systems of scientists. . . , moralists, theologians, et al.'; in others, conventions of ordinary linguistic usage.

To be sure, both do pertain, in Wittgenstein's terms, to 'language-games' which 'are played.' And it is undoubtedly true that the analysis of them can yield considerable insight into *how* they 'are played.' Such analyses are of great interest and importance, as Nietzsche himself was one of the first to see. For, on a general level, they can shed considerable light upon our nature and capacities as what he might call the 'language-game-playing animals' we are. And, on a more specific level, these analyses can reveal much about our practices, our institutions, the interpretive and normative frameworks in terms of which we tend to organize our experience and behavior, and the various other components of what Wittgenstein refers to as our 'form (or forms) of life.' Further, by bringing to light the implicit rules governing the playing of the language-games in question, they often show — more clearly and definitively than we may ordinarily be able to determine — how questions and problems arising in the course of playing them are to be dealt with.

Such analyses do not, however, establish either the impossibility or inferiority of other sets of language-games with different governing rules, or the reliability of the rules governing them where the resolution of philosophical issues is concerned. And the recognition that these games are played, and that philosophers no less than others tend to think and act in accordance with them, does not establish the meaninglessness or futility of any attempt to pose philosophical questions that transcend them, or to answer philosophical questions otherwise than in terms of the rules which govern them. Any general claims along these lines rest on assumptions the validity of which cannot in principle be demonstrated by the analysis either of the kinds of conceptual systems indicated, or of ordinary language. And on Nietzsche's view, there are reasons for doubting that any general claims along these lines are sound.

With regard to the first point, he would consider it extremely naive and parochial to suppose that the language-games which a certain group of people happen to play are the only ones which could be played, or are immutable, or represent the acme of perfection in spiritual development; and here, at least, most analytic philosophers would agree. Nietzsche further holds, however, that it is not only possible but moreover incumbent upon the true philosopher to take up a position outside of the language-games with which he finds himself confronted — ascending, as it were, to the meta-level in relation to them. And from this position he may undertake to criticize them as well as analyze them, develop alternatives to them as the results of his philosophical investigations and reflections suggest the desirability of doing so, and proceed to deal with philosophical issues independently of them. In other words, the true philosopher is not entirely a prisoner of whatever 'language games' happen to be played in the linguistic community and sub-groups with which he finds himself confronted (unlike most people — including mere 'philosophical laborers' — whose prison they are). If he were, his only alternatives to simply exploring his prison and making himself at home in it would be either silence or outbursts of protest against the absurdity of his situation. Nietzsche does not minimize the difficulty of escaping from this prison; nor is he unaware of the peculiarity of the attempt to do so when it is evaluated by ordinary standards:

> That one *wants* to go precisely out there, up there, may be a minor madness, a peculiar and unreasonable 'You must'. . . . The question is whether one really *can* get up there. This may depend on manifold conditions. In the main the question is how light or how heavy we are — the problem of our 'specific gravity.' One has to be *very light* to drive one's will to knowledge into such a distance and, as it were, beyond one's time, to create for oneself eyes to survey millennia and, moreover, clear skies in those eyes. One must have liberated oneself from many things that oppress, inhibit, hold down, and make heavy precisely us Europeans today (*GS* 380).

Few people are capable of doing this; but then Nietzsche never expected true philosophers to be very many. His argument that this sort of transcendence of the 'form of life' of one's own age is possible for at least a few is simply that from time to time men have appeared who have done it — who have hit upon ways of thinking which depart significantly from established patterns of thought. And in some cases, at least, these have marked genuine advances in relation to the latter in our understanding of ourselves and the world in which we live.

Such advances do occur, although it is difficult if not impossible to make them by simply deciding to do so, or to prove one is making one, or to lay down precise criteria for deciding when one has been made. They are made (although not by those who remain the unwilling or willing captives of received conceptual schemes and linguistic conventions); even though those who make them must draw upon existing ways of speaking and thinking in doing so. After all, Nietzsche does not mean to suggest that true

44

philosophers must invent whole new languages, or even new batteries of technical terms. Here his own example is instructive. He lifts certain terms *out of* 'the language games which are their original homes' (in Wittgenstein's phrase, but counter to his admonition); and, by linking them with other notions and suggesting new uses for them, while at the same time drawing upon certain of their original connotations, he employs these terms to work out novel interpretations. This sort of creative transformation of concepts may not be a very tidy affair; but that, for him, is no mark against it, since there is no tidier substitute for it. The fastidious may shun it; but without it, on his view, there can be no genuine advance in philosophical understanding — even though such advances may be the exception rather than the rule among attempts along these lines.

To be sure, it is one thing to recognize the possibility of breaking out of the confines of the conceptual framework initially structuring one's interpretive and evaluative thinking, and of developing another which differs significantly from it. It is something else to establish the possibility of developing another which not only differs from the first, but moreover places one in a position to offer legitimate criticisms of it, and to deal with philosophical issues in an arguably superior way. And it is crucial to Nietzsche's case that this second possibility should be established; for the philosophical desirability of making the attempt depends upon it. After all, if one could hope to do nothing more than develop *an alternative* to the initial conceptual framework, with nothing to recommend it over the latter other than the fact that it is different, nothing would be gained philosophically by the development of it.

The establishment of this second possibility, however, does not require that one actually succeed in producing an alternative that can be shown to be superior to the initial conceptual framework; although doing so would obviously clinch the case. It requires only (in addition to the first possibility) that one grant the essentially provisional character of all such frameworks; the conceivability of some being more adequate to what obtains and transpires than others (the measure of adequacy being explanatory power, subject to qualifications pertaining to the economy and non-arbitrariness of principles); and the supposition that for any conceptual framework that is merely relatively adequate in this respect, there could be another which would be more so. These assumptions are at least reasonable; and it is therefore with apparent justice that Nietzsche considers this second possibility to be a real one.

IX

Linguistic-analytic philosophers who confine themselves to the analysis of one or both of the sorts of 'data' discussed above, from which — when they are venturesome enough to do so — they draw their substantive philosophical conclusions, quite evidently do not attempt to go beyond the conceptual frameworks with which they are confronted and to develop new ones. As strictly 'analytic' philosophers, they analyze rather than devise. And, once again, Nietzsche parts company with them (and calls for a kind of conceptual innovation they shun) not over their projects of analysis as such, but rather over their restriction of themselves to such projects, and over their willingness to allow the resolution of substantial philosophical questions to be determined in accordance with them.

His reasons for doing so are connected with his reservations concerning the philosophical significance of both of these sorts of data. If either could reasonably be supposed to be the most reliable guides available — or even simply generally reliable guides — for the philosopher to follow in attempting to deal with any and all questions, he would have no good reason to hold that those who occupy themselves exclusively with the analysis of such data and their application to philosophical questions are not true philosophers, and that the real business of true philosophers lies elsewhere. It is his contention, however, that the status of data of both sorts is highly problematical, at least where their philosophical import is concerned.

Consider first 'the conceptual systems developed by scientists, mathematicians, art critics, moralists, theologians, et al.' The analysis of these conceptual systems will surely tell us a great deal about the terms in which those in question think, the kinds of judgments they make, and even the nature of the enterprises in which they engage. But the fact that a certain language-game is played does not settle the question of what is to be made of it; nor is this question settled by an examination of *how* it is played, what its rules are, what moves within it are and are not legitimate, and so forth. Likewise neither the fact that certain conceptual systems are developed by those who play them, nor the analysis of these 'systems,' settles the question of the status of the referents of the concepts employed. And thus the significance of such analyses for ontological, axiological and epistemological questions is far from clear. Nietzsche would consider it absurd to suppose that an analysis of the conceptual systems developed by theologians would settle a question such as that of the existence of God, or that an analysis of those developed by moralists would settle the question of whether or not there is some universal and unconditionally binding set of moral principles; and he clearly would be right. Similarly, the analysis of the conceptual systems of mathematicians and art critics does not by itself resolve issues pertaining to the reality of numbers and the status of aesthetic qualities. And it is only if one antecedently commits oneself to a certain philosophical position that one may feel oneself to be in a position to resolve ontological questions through the analysis of the conceptual systems developed by scientists.

More generally, Nietzsche holds that such conceptual systems are not to be relied upon by the philosopher for two reasons. First: *as* conceptual systems, they are no less provisional than are philosophical conceptual frameworks, and so constitute no secure foundation upon which to base philosophical inquiry. Indeed, because those who develop them often take things for granted that philosophers with any degree of critical awareness would find highly questionable and even untenable, philosophers would be foolish to repose any degree of confidence in them merely because those who develop them display a kind of expertise in the employment of them which philosophers are conscious that they lack.

Second, and equally important: Nietzsche is highly sensitive to the extent to which 'human, all-too-human' factors and other extraneous circumstances tend to influence the development of conceptual systems. He subjects scientists, moralists and religious thinkers as well as philosophers to a kind of extensive psychological analysis, with a view to showing that at the very least one must proceed very cautiously in dealing with the conceptual systems they develop, since it is quite commonly the case that these systems reflect either their own needs, interests and desires or certain deeply rooted errors and myths, rather than the actual state of affairs with respect to the matters with which they deal. If there is any reason to suspect that this may really be so in more than a few isolated cases — and Nietzsche's analyses would seem to establish at least this much — it follows that philosophers would indeed be well advised to refrain from treating the kinds of conceptual systems under consideration as data which may be relied upon in dealing with philosophical issues.

At this point one may be tempted to fall back upon ordinary language as a source of reliable data in philosophical inquiry; for it is not subject to difficulties of this sort. Nietzsche maintains, however, that it is subject to other difficulties of equal seriousness. To be sure, he is by no means of the opinion that the analysis of linguistic conventions is utterly irrelevant to philosophical inquiry. On the contrary, he argues that the language people speak exerts a profound influence upon the way they think, and that the analysis of language alone enables one to get to the bottom of many philosophical problems. For example, he poses the question, 'What light does linguistics, and especially the study of etymology, throw on the history of the evolution of moral concepts?' — and thereby also on the status of various moral concepts — and suggests that this light would be considerable (*GM* I:17n.). He contends that the ubiquitousness of certain metaphysical views — concerning, for example, the substantiality of both the self and whatever else there is — is related to the existence of basic grammatical forms which direct our thinking along these lines, quite independently of considerations of what is actually the case; and that therefore philosophers cannot afford to neglect the study of linguistic structures. Thus he speaks of our 'unconscious domination and guidance by similar grammatical functions,' which pave the way for some philosophical positions and tend to bar the way to others (*BGE* 20). And he constantly stresses the philosophical importance of exploring the subtle nuances, differing uses, and interrelationships of the terms in which philosophical positions are stated.

While thus insisting upon the importance of linguistic analysis in philosophical investigation, however, Nietzsche contends that the language we speak can hardly be taken to be a reliable guide in dealing in a positive way with issues of philosophical importance. Attending to deviations from conventional usage may occasionally reveal where and how some philosophers have gone astray; but if we take the language we speak as our guide, we only succeed in miring ourselves further in any confusions our language may happen to contain. And he suspects that it contains a great many of them. Thus he says, in a passage with the heading '*Words lie in our way!*'

> Whenever the ancients set down a word, they believed they had made a discovery. How different the truth of the matter was! — They had come across a problem; and while they supposed it to have been solved, they actually had obstructed its solution. — Now in all knowledge one stumbles over rock-solid eternalized words, and would sooner break a leg than a word in doing so (*D* 47).

Many linguistic-analytic philosophers would rather reject a philosophical thesis than depart from an established linguistic usage; and Nietzsche is in effect inviting us to reflect whether linguistic conventions warrant such deference. It may well be that one ought not to depart from them arbitrarily. When one considers the lack of philosophical sophistication of those among whom these conventions were established, however, it is difficult to see why they should be allowed to function as the ultimate arbiters of philosophical disputes. No one has ever produced a plausible argument to the effect that the conditions under which our language has developed guarantee that one has only to use the language non-deviantly in order correctly to represent reality; nor does it seem likely that any such argument could ever be produced.

In short: there will inevitably be many cases in which linguistic conventions reflect the prejudices, confusions, superstitions and plain ignorance of those to whom we owe them. We do not doubt that our ancestors had many such intellectual failings; and we should have to believe in something akin to Divine Inspiration in order to suppose that these failings did not affect the linguistic conventions they evolved. This reflection by itself does not enable us to determine precisely which conventions are to be abandoned; and it certainly does not establish that the entire lot of them constitute one great philosophical disaster area (although Nietzsche thinks that this is largely so). It does suggest, however, that a philosopher cannot safely suppose that the path to the satisfactory resolution of substantive philosophical questions is simply that of the analysis of ordinary language and the determination of its implications for these questions. Thus Nietzsche remarks, in a passage which could not bear more directly on the program of the form of linguistic-analytic philosophy presently under consideration:

> Philosophers. . .have trusted in concepts as completely as
> they have mistrusted the senses: they have not stopped to
> consider that concepts and words are our inheritance from ages
> in which thinking was very modest and unclear.
>
> What dawns on philosophers last of all: they must no longer
> accept concepts as a gift, not merely purify and polish them,
> but first *make* and *create* them, present and make them
> convincing. Hitherto one has generally trusted one's concepts
> as if they were a wonderful dowry from some sort of
> wonderland: but they are, after all, the inheritance from our
> most remote, most foolish as well as most intelligent
> ancestors. . . . What is needed above all is an absolute
> skepticism toward all inherited concepts (*WP* 409).

Nietzsche is far from oblivious to the dangers and difficulties

49

that beset the philosopher who ventures to break with established linguistic conventions, and attempts to develop a way of viewing things which is both different from and superior to that which these conventions dictate. For one thing, he observes, we tend 'no longer to observe precisely where words fail us, because it is hard then to think precisely' (*D* 115). For another, while the intersubjectivity of linguistic conventions is no guarantee of truth, it does endow them with a kind of objectivity that serves to check idiosyncratic interpretive tendencies on the part of those who observe them, which in most cases are of no philosophical significance whatsoever, and the indulgence of which is generally sheer folly. The philosopher who attempts to develop a new conceptual framework that departs from established linguistic conventions runs the risk of merely replacing commonly accepted errors with novel ones. And for a third, Nietzsche knew only too well that one who does so runs a further risk; for in breaking free from conventional patterns of thought, one is living very dangerously, as he explicitly observes. One thereby sets aside perhaps the single most important source of psychological security and stability in human life; and this is to risk more than the appearance of madness.

It is for reasons such as these that Nietzsche repeatedly states that those who have it in them to be true philosophers will never be many; that it would be most unfortunate for those who do not to try to follow the course he indicates; that nothing is more demanding and dangerous than genuine philosophizing; and that even in the case of those best able to undertake the task, the attempt to carry it out may well be their undoing, and may have the result (in the language of *Zarathustra*) that they 'go under.' Yet his conviction of the importance of the task, and his recognition that it cannot be carried out without breaking with established conventions of thought and linguistic usage wherever these are discovered to reflect errors, confusions, superstitions and the like (as they undoubtedly often actually do), led him to make the attempt, and to consign even the best of those who were unable or unwilling to do so to the category of mere 'critics' and 'philosophical laborers.' And it is to this category that he would (quite rightly, it would seem) consign those who restrict themselves to linguistic analysis and the application of results thereby obtained to philosophical questions.

'I do not wish to persuade anyone to philosophy,' Nietzsche writes; for 'it is inevitable, it is perhaps also desirable, that the philosopher should be a *rare* plant' (*WP* 420). The hazards of genuinely philosophical thinking constitute one of his reasons for taking this position; and his recognition of the fact that he has 'set up the most difficult ideal of the philosopher' ('Learning is not enough!') is another (*WP* 421). Few people possess the many qualities he takes to be required if one is to be able to measure up to the intellectual standard he sets forth. And fewer are capable of withstanding the rigors of philosophy as he 'understood and lived it.' For it involves 'living voluntarily among ice and high mountains — seeking out everything strange and questionable in existence' — and requires that one be able to 'dare' and 'endure' much more 'truth' than most people can (*EH* P:3).

Nietzsche's own philosophical practice may often fall short of or diverge from the standards and principles he advocates; and the picture of the genuine philosopher and philosophy he sets forth may strike many as uncongenial in various respects. But he would be neither surprised nor disconcerted in either event, and would take neither circumstance to count against the picture itself. Whether it admits of being more fully realized than it is in his own case, and what significance would attach to anything that might come of it should this transpire, are open questions. At the very least, however, both his critique of traditional and commonplace modes of philosophizing and his advocacy of alternatives to them make clear the need to reappraise much about philosophy that is all too often taken for granted among philosophers.

II

Truth and Knowledge

Perhaps no part of Nietzsche's philosophy is more confusing, even to the attentive reader, than what might broadly speaking be called his epistemology — that is, his treatment of knowledge, truth, and certain matters relating to them. Yet it also may well be that no other part of it is of greater contemporary interest and importance. The positions he takes in some cases turn out to accord closely with views currently enjoying considerable favor; while in others he in effect mounts a strong challenge to views equally widely held. This will already have become apparent to some extent in the course of the previous chapter. I shall now consider what he has to say along these lines more directly and systematically.

Toward a naturalistic epistemology

I

Two things must be recognized at the outset, if anything approaching a proper understanding of his epistemological views is to be achieved. First: when Nietzsche speaks of 'truth' and 'knowledge,' these terms do not have a single sense and reference in all of their occurrences. In some cases they are to be understood as they have traditionally been employed by philosophers with commitments to certain sorts of metaphysical positions of which he is highly critical. In other instances they are to be understood as referring to what ordinarily passes for 'truth' or 'knowledge' among non-philosophers (sometimes people generally, at other times specialists of various sorts such as scientists), and to the most that truth and knowledge can amount to in everyday or scientific affairs. And there are further occasions upon which he uses such terms to refer to the legitimate objectives of certain sorts of substantive philosophical inquiry which he himself advocates and undertakes.

Thus, for example, when Nietzsche says that something or other is true of the world, with respect to human nature, or concerning what ordinarily passes for truth, it should not be assumed that his observations about the nature of what ordinarily passes for truth are meant to apply without qualification to these assertions. And it likewise should not be supposed that he considers the latter to have the same sort of warrant that commonplace or scientific 'truths' are suggested to have. His various remarks in which terms like 'truth' and 'knowledge' figure can be rendered collectively coherent only if they are viewed as efforts on his part *both* to accept and analyze the ways in which such terms function in particular domains of discourse (without attempting to legislate an end to their employment in them), *and* to interpret and assess their employments in these contexts from several standpoints taken up external to and beyond them (from which standpoints the kinds of things which count as 'truth' and 'knowledge' within these domains often turn out to warrant characterization in different terms, and epistemic demotion). In examining any particular remark he makes along these lines, therefore, one must take care to consider precisely what sort of a remark it is intended to be, and how far and on what level of analysis it is to be taken to apply.

Next: Nietzsche's views on these matters cannot be properly understood unless one grasps the nature of his rather unconventional general approach to them. Like any philosopher concerned with them, he attempts to answer such questions as 'What is truth?' and 'What is knowledge?' And, as many others before and after him have done, he finds it advisable to begin by examining what are generally acknowledged (by people generally, by scientists, by most philosophers, etc.) to be typical examples or paradigm cases of 'truth' and 'knowledge,' with a view to seeing what they involve. But he is not content simply to try to understand what commonly pass as such on their own terms. Rather, he considers it imperative to view them in the light of other considerations pertaining to the character and circumstances of the kind of creature we are, in the setting of whose life all such forms of truth and knowledge are framed and attained.

This has the consequence for him that the longstanding idea of the autonomy and priority of epistemology in relation to other branches of inquiry must be abandoned. The results of inquiries into epistemological questions may have important implications for other forms and projects of inquiry; but the reverse is also true. The nature and scope of human knowledge, the cognitive significance of perceptual experience and scientific theorizing and logical reasoning, and the conditions under which various kinds of propositions may be considered true, are issues which cannot be settled prior to the consideration of all substantive questions. They can be dealt with properly only within the context of a general understanding of man's nature and his relation to the world, drawing upon their exploration from a variety of perspectives. Any such understanding, of course, will only be provisional, and may turn out to require to be revised or even fundamentally modified. But Nietzsche considers it incontrovertible that in dealing with epistemological issues one is dealing with certain sorts of *human affairs*, and that therefore one's conclusions concerning them will be either superficial or erroneous (as analyses of the knowledge we do or can have, etc.), if they are not interpreted accordingly.

II

The kind of approach he takes to them is often characterized as 'naturalistic.' This label has been used to refer to so many divergent philosophical orientations, however, that it signifies little more than a departure from both traditional empiricism and rationalism, and a disposition to interpret all things human in terms of the interactions of creatures of one distinctive but fundamentally natural kind with their environment and each other. Nietzsche's treatment of epistemological issues may be termed 'naturalistic' in this sense; but to characterize it in this general way is merely to indicate his approximate place on a very crude philosophical map. Its nature is suggested somewhat more concretely by such remarks as the following: 'To what extent even our intellect is a consequence of conditions of existence — : we would not have it if we did not *need* to have it, and we would not have it *as it is* if we did not need to have it *as it is*, if we could live *otherwise*' (WP 498). And, on the other hand: 'The way of knowing and of knowledge is itself already part of the conditions of [human] existence. . . : this actual condition of existence is perhaps only accidental and in no way necessary' (WP 496). Again: 'Behind all logic and its seeming sovereignty of movement there stand valuations or, more clearly, physiological demands for the preservation of a certain type of life' (BGE 4). And finally:

> There is no question of 'subject' and 'object,' but of a particular
> species of animal that can prosper only through a certain

relative rightness; above all, regularity of its perceptions (so that it can accumulate experience). . . .

The meaning of 'knowledge': here, as in the case of 'good' or 'beautiful,' the concept is to be regarded in a strict and narrow anthropocentric and biological sense. In order for a particular species to maintain itself and increase its power, its conception of reality must comprehend enough of the calculable and constant for it to base a scheme of behavior on it. The utility of preservation — not some abstract-theoretical need not to be deceived — stands as the motive behind the development of the organs of knowledge — they develop in such a way that their observations suffice for our preservation. In other words. . . : a species grasps a certain amount of reality in order to become master of it, in order to press it into service (*WP* 480).

Nietzsche observes that most previous philosophers, in dealing with epistemological and other philosophical questions, have tended to treat man and the elements of his conscious life as a being and a set of activities to be understood in terms altogether different from those appropriate to entities and processes occurring in the world of nature. And he regards this as a mistake, even though he does not think that there are no significant differences between ourselves and other things. He writes: 'To translate man back into nature. . . — that may be a strange and insane task, but it is a *task* — who would deny that? Why did we choose this insane task? Or, putting the matter differently: "Why have knowledge at all?"' (*BGE* 230). His answer to the question he raises here is indicated by the way in which he puts it: it is only if a man is 'translated back into nature,' at least initially, that we and our various activities can be properly understood.

To this it must immediately be added (lest one mistakenly conclude that he thereby opts for a merely 'biologistic' approach in these matters) that Nietzsche considers it no less important also to 'translate' ourselves back into *society*. For in this context, he holds, the human intellect is further shaped in important ways, and the means of all genuine thinking and possible cognition are acquired. This further 'translation back' likewise does not constitute his final move and last word where all truth and knowledge are concerned, however, but rather is only another part of his treatment of them, as shall be seen.

One of the points of departure of Nietzsche's discussion of epistemological questions is thus the assumption that man is a particular 'species of animal' with certain general capacities, which like those of other kinds of living creatures originated and

developed as 'means of life' (even if some of them may subsequently have come to be employed in ways standing in little or no
direct relation to this basic function). This, he contends, holds
true of our 'spiritual' faculties — including our cognitive powers —
no less than of our more basic functions. He does not present
direct arguments for this position; but he would appear to
consider at least something of the sort to be a consequence of the
supposition that there is no transcendent Deity. Once the
existence of such a Deity is dismissed, he takes the ground to be
cut out from under anyone who would give a non-naturalistic
account of the origin and nature of any of man's faculties. Or at
any rate, there then can be no 'religious sanction and guarantee of
our senses and rationality' of the sort to which Descartes and
others appealed; and this renders the idea 'that thinking is a
measure of actuality' a piece of 'moralistic trustfulness' which is
quite without warrant — 'a mad assumption, which experience
contradicts every moment' (*WP* 406). Thus he considers intellectual integrity to demand *not* that one *refrain* from presupposing
anything along the lines indicated above, but rather that one
make these presuppositions and not shrink from their consequences
for various further philosophical questions, such as those arising
in epistemology. His naturalistic epistemology represents his
attempt to work out these consequences.

Nietzsche is well aware of certain fundamental difficulties
which would at least seem to make it impossible to deal satisfactorily with epistemological questions. In particular, it is arguable
that a kind of knowledge we cannot have would be necessary for
us to be able to do so. Thus, for example, he writes: 'One would
have to know what *being* is, in order to decide. . .what *certainty*
is, what *knowledge* is, and the like'; and he goes on to suggest that,
'since we do not know this, a critique of the faculty of knowledge
is senseless: how should a tool be able to criticize itself when it
can use only itself for the critique?' (*WP* 486). In a similar vein,
he observes that 'the intellect cannot criticize itself,' at least as
philosophers have long set up the problem, because on the normal
view of the matter 'its capacity to know would be revealed only in
the presence of "true reality," i.e., because in order to criticize
the intellect we should have to be a higher being with "absolute
knowledge"' (*WP* 473).

Nietzsche is not deterred by these reflections, however, for he
finds that it is possible to say a good deal about epistemological
questions if they are approached in the manner he proposes. It
may be impossible for one who does not already 'know what
being is' to determine the status of what commonly passes for

56

'truth' and 'knowledge' *if* nothing whatever is presupposed about man's nature and circumstances. It does not follow, however, that this remains impossible even if certain presuppositions concerning them are made — although the conclusions one thereby reaches involve a severing of the conceptual link between these phenomena and 'what being is.'

The situation is further altered, moreover, if — as Nietzsche does — one repudiates the very notion of 'being' or 'true reality' as something transcending the world with which we find ourselves confronted in experience, and to which our thoughts or assertions must correspond if there is to be any 'truth' or 'knowledge' at all. For it then follows that we do not *have to* 'know what being is' before dealing with the question of what 'truth' and 'knowledge' are, since there is nothing of the kind to be known even in the ideal case. To be sure, one would be obliged to conclude that the latter notions, wherever they have a legitimate employment, must be analyzed in some way other than in terms of such a correspondence. This is a conclusion, however, which Nietzsche draws and embraces, leading him to attempt to understand them differently.

It is with their employment in connection with the idea of such a correspondence in mind that he at times says such things as that ' "knowing" itself is a contradictory idea' (*WP* 608), and that 'there is no "truth" ' (*WP* 616). It would be a great mistake, however, to infer from these and other similar assertions that he denies the legitimacy of these notions altogether. On the contrary: he does not merely mention them in the course of proclaiming them incoherent or empty, but also makes considerable use of them in connection with his own philosophical undertakings and achievements, as well as analyzing their uses (which he does not challenge) in a variety of non-philosophical contexts. Indeed, it is not even the case that he is unwilling to countenance anything like the correspondence theory of truth, and any associated conception of knowledge, as shall be seen.

A preliminary analysis of truth

III

It is somewhat artificial to consider Nietzsche's discussions of truth and knowledge separately. He frequently deals with them together; and his analysis of the former is very similar to his analysis of the latter. To talk about 'truth,' on his view, is to talk about 'truths'; and to talk about 'truths' is to talk about the contents of propositions asserted or beliefs held. And the same holds with regard to knowledge. Knowledge is usually taken to be something like 'justified true belief.' If the truth of a proposition is basically a matter of a certain sort of justification of its affirmation, however, as Nietzsche takes it to be, and if the justification required for a belief to count as knowledge is not different in nature from that in virtue of which the belief may be said to be true, as he also maintains, then the connection between 'truth' and 'knowledge' is quite close. Indeed, one might say that he is proposing something approaching an assimilation of the former to the latter, in that the operative notion in both cases — of something like 'warranted belief' — usually is associated more closely with the latter than with the former. Since what he has to say about truth has certain important implications for the question of what the nature and limits of knowledge are, however, I shall deal with the former before turning to the latter.

Nietzsche nowhere undertakes to give a thorough, systematic analysis of 'truth'; but he says a great many things about it in various places in his published and unpublished writings. Considered individually, many of his remarks are striking; while when juxtaposed, they collectively are both remarkable and bewildering. He is best known, in this connection, for remarks of the following sort: 'Truths are illusions, of which one has forgotten this is so' (*TL* p. 375: page numbers in references identifying citations from this work refer to the pages on which these passages are to be found in the Colli-Montinari *Kritische Gesamtausgabe* of Nietzsche's *Werke*, part III, vol. 2). And: 'What are man's truths ultimately? Merely his *irrefutable* errors' (*GS* 265). And: 'Truth is the kind of error without which a certain species of life could not live' (*WP* 493). And: 'There are many kinds of eyes. . . — and consequently there are many kinds of "truths," and consequently there is no truth' (*WP* 540).

Many commentators have seized upon his remarks along these lines, taking them to convey the main thrust and character of his position with respect to the nature of truth. It is less often recalled and taken into consideration, however, that the same Nietzsche who made these remarks also considered 'truthfulness' to be of the utmost importance (cf. *EH* IV:3), held 'the real measure of value' of a person's spirit to be 'how much truth' it can 'endure' and 'dare' (*EH* P:3), contemptuously attributed an 'absolute lack of intellectual integrity' to those who feel that 'it does not matter whether a thing is true, but only what effect it produces' (*WP* 172), and wrote: 'At every step one has to wrestle for truth; one has had to surrender for it almost everything to which the heart, to which our love, our trust in life, cling otherwise. That requires greatness of soul: the service of truth is the hardest service' (*A* 50).

This certainly raises problems of interpretation; and it must also be admitted that the language in which Nietzsche couches much of what he has to say about truth (as about most of the other matters he discusses) is often excessively metaphorical, unnecessarily hyperbolical, overly combative and provocative to a fault. If one takes seriously the variety of things he has to say and construes them as qualifying and complementing each other, however, one discovers that they collectively suggest and constitute elements of a comprehensive analysis that is not only coherent but also of considerable interest.

I thus shall take Nietzsche to have been proposing a number of different analyses, on a variety of levels, for several different kinds of 'truths.' Those things which he himself is prepared to affirm concerning matters of substance are instances of only one of them, and a very special and unusual one at that. Another embraces those garden-variety 'truths' of daily life and special human pursuits which he sometimes refers to as 'man's truths' — i.e., generally speaking, things pertaining to ordinary thought and experience and their more technical refinements and offshoots. More concretely, it consists in the kinds of things which commonly pass as 'truths' in ordinary descriptive and normative discourse, and also in such specialized forms of discourse as those of science and mathematics. (These are the 'truths' he usually has in mind when he uses such terms as 'errors' and 'illusions' to express his assessment of their ultimate status.) And a third consists in the putative 'truths' (which he takes actually to be 'lies' and 'deceptions') of other-worldly religious thinkers and metaphysically inclined philosophers for whom 'being' of some sort is taken to underlie all experienced reality. These broad distinctions must be recognized if one is to be able to get anywhere at all in sorting out the various things Nietzsche has to say about truth.

Broadly speaking, 'truth' for Nietzsche is primarily a kind of property of certain propositions; or rather, it is a property identifiable in the cases of each of a number of different sorts of propositions. Following long-established precedent, he sometimes also employs the term in referring to what these propositions are about; but he actually considers the notion to be only secondarily or derivatively applicable (if at all) to whatever this may be. The problem of the analyst of 'truth,' for him, is thus that of determining the conditions under which a proposition (or, more broadly, an interpretation) may be said to have the property of 'truth' — or of determining what that property is in the cases of the different sorts of propositions of which 'truth' may be predicated.

Several different kinds or levels of analysis of 'truth' may be discerned and should be distinguished in Nietzsche's writings. One is primarily descriptive. It consists in analyzing what might be termed the 'surface conditions,' or criteria employed within a particular type of discourse, in virtue of the satisfaction of which a particular proposition may be considered 'true.' (I shall refer to such analysis as 'first-order truth-analysis.') Another is also descriptive, or at any rate analytically interpretive, but on a deeper level. It consists in attempting to determine what is fundamentally involved — what is going on beneath the surface, conditioning the character of the surface — in the emergence of such forms of discourse and 'truth.' (I shall refer to this as 'second-order truth-analysis.') And a third is perhaps more prescriptive than merely descriptive or analytical; although none of these terms is really adequate to describe it. It consists in the development of an account of the conditions a proposition (or better, an interpretation) would have to satisfy, and might actually be able to satisfy, that would set it apart from both 'man's truths' and 'metaphysical truths,' and endow it with superior epistemic status. (I shall refer to this as 'third-order truth-analysis.') Since Nietzsche undertakes all three sorts of 'truth-analysis' at various points, one is bound to misunderstand him if one fails to heed their differences and their limits.

IV

His third-order analysis and his conception of the kind of 'truth' to which philosophers can and should aspire can only be properly appreciated in the light of his first- and second-order analyses of the other categories of 'truths' mentioned. Accordingly, I shall begin with the latter. Nietzsche is quite prepared to concede to the sorts of propositions in question eligibility for this designation, bowing to precedent and convention. He maintains, however, that the 'truth' of such 'truths' cannot be separated (other than very artificially and abstractly) from their being 'held true' or determined to qualify as true; and that it cannot be adequately understood independently of considerations pertaining to what this involves. 'Truth' may be a property of propositions; but it is a property of a rather complex relational sort, which propositions do not possess independently of their situation in a larger context. And this context is constituted not only by their relations to other propositions, but also by conditions pertaining to the standpoint and concerns of those by whom they are or might be asserted. Thus he considers it necessary to go further than analyses which

60

safely stop at the water's edge, and say no more than that the predication of 'truth' of a proposition is tantamount merely to the emphatic or deliberate assertion of that proposition, or that the truth of a proposition is simply a matter of what it asserts being so.

The broad category of 'man's truths' affords the analyst of 'truth' a wealth of types as well as innumerable particular cases, which should not be ignored. Indeed, this very wealth is well worth noting. There are many different kinds of such propositions; or rather, there are diverse sorts of ordinary and special (non-philosophical) discourse in which propositions are employed and adjudged to be true and untrue. It may be that one would be ill-advised immediately to conclude from the existence of this variety that 'truth' requires to be given a different analysis and has a different meaning in each case. It does suggest the possibility, however, that more might be involved here than a mere difference of particular truth-conditions in at least some such cases; and that what is called for may be a characterization of the nature of 'truth' in different terms where this is so, reflecting differences in the kinds of discourse in connection with which the notion has an established employment. Nietzsche takes this to be the case, at different times sounding conventionalist, coherence, correspondence, and pragmatic themes in dealing with the 'truth' of different sorts of 'man's truths.'

A fundamental idea underlying his analysis of all such 'truths' is that none of them can plausibly be regarded as holding true in virtue of standing in a relation of correspondence amounting to a picturing, representing or modeling of a reality which is as it is independently of our experience of it. They are inextricably bound up with the *domains of discourse* (and associated forms of life) in which they occur, and in terms of which the standards or conditions are set by reference to which they may qualify as 'truths.' This idea, of what I shall call their *D-relativity*, is at the heart of his celebrated doctrine of 'perspectivism,' according to which they may be considered to hold true only from some particular perspective, and thus only within the context of some particular 'language-game' played in accordance with rules more or less strongly conditioned by various contingent circumstances.

Nietzsche further holds the correspondence theory of truth (as traditionally understood) to be wanting in that, on his view, it *cannot* be the case that the 'truth' of any such propositions — and indeed of any propositions at all — is a matter of their standing in a correspondence-relation to a reality that has an intrinsic structural articulation and ordering, since there is no such reality

61

for propositions to correspond to. The world, as he conceives it, has the character of 'becoming' rather than of 'being,' of 'flux' rather than structure, and at bottom of 'chaos' in the sense of the absence of an inherent, immutable order of any sort. (His reasons for taking this position will be explored in the following chapters.) And if this is so, no version of the correspondence theory pre-supposing the existence of what he calls a ' "true world" of being' can stand.

To be sure, our *experience* always exhibits at least a degree of structural articulation and order; but to the extent that it does, Nietzsche contends, this is at least in large measure owing to the fact that such characteristics have been imposed upon it. Here his line of thinking is distinctly Kantian; and like Kant, he stops short of idealism, refusing to equate reality with the world as we experience it, but maintaining that our experience is as it is for us to a very great extent in consequence of the way in which we constitute it. He radicalizes Kant, however, naturalizing and relativizing him, and maintaining that it is chiefly practical con-siderations which account for our experience being ordered as it is.

If truth is conceived as a correspondence of thought and being, therefore, or of a structurally articulated proposition to a comparably ordered state of affairs the features of which are fixed independently of the process through which it becomes an object of experience, there is and can be nothing of the kind. When Nietzsche asserts that 'there is no truth,' his point is that no propositions are or can be true in this sense. And on the basis of considerations of this sort, he dismisses all 'truth-candidates' framed accordingly from further consideration, other than as oddities the persistent nomination of which is a phenomenon worthy of attention as such. Except in the case of metaphysical propositions, however, he does not consider this to be the end of the matter; for as has been observed, he finds it both possible and appropriate to construe other sorts of propositions and their 'truth' along different lines.

Indeed, having ruled out the idea of a correspondence of this nature, it can now be allowed that on the level of first-order analysis of certain sorts of 'truths' there *is* something to the intuition that 'truth' involves a correspondence of what is thought or asserted and what obtains. And far from conflicting with Nietzsche's conception of the perspectival or D-relative character of most 'truths,' this intuition actually squares with it not only readily but also significantly. To see how this is so, however, one must grasp one of the most important features of the domains of discourse or language-games in which his 'perspectives' consist.

62

They are not to be construed as mere vocabularies people somehow acquire and with which they articulate their experiences of
pre-linguistically determinate objects and events and states of
affairs of various kinds. Rather, they are 'forms of life' in the sense
of spheres of human experience and activity in which certain kinds
of objects and states of affairs are fixed and differentiated in
accordance with various sorts of linguistic apparatus. What counts
as an object, a difference between objects, and a relation between
them, is determined by the concepts and rules of particular
schemes of this sort, and has no standing or meaning independently
of them.

The 'truth' of a given proposition thus is a matter of its conformity to the linguistic-conceptual scheme within which it
functions, together with its appropriateness in relation to some
state of affairs holding among the objects that are fixed and
constituted in accordance with this scheme. Thus its 'truth' is
D-relative and may be given a 'coherence' characterization; but at
the same time it may more immediately (i.e., within the context
of the schematized experiential situation in which it is deemed
appropriate) be given a 'correspondence' analysis. Something does
occur to which a given proposition uttered may be said to
correspond, in many such cases; but this correspondence is made
possible and conditioned by the emergence of the form of life or
'perspective' which embraces and links what obtains in experience
and what is thought and said.

When Nietzsche proclaims 'man's truths' to be 'errors,' as he
does on numerous occasions, and says such things as, ' "Truth":
this. . .does not necessarily denote the antithesis of error, but in
the most fundamental cases only the posture of various errors in
relation to one another' (WP 535), on the other hand, he does so
to underscore the point that these correspondences should not be
thought to involve anything more than this. Such propositions
represent certain states of affairs as obtaining which do so only
for us, and cannot be supposed to obtain independently of the
'perspective' within which we happen to be operating. The terms
in which such propositions are cast cannot appropriately be
applied to the way the world is apart from our schematization of
it; and so, however things may actually stand with the world, in
relation to its nature such 'truths' turn out to be 'errors.'

This should not be taken, however, to preclude the possibility
of any 'true' assertions whatever except those the 'truth' of which
is strictly D-relative, and the ultimate 'erroneousness' of which is
as complete as (and of the same nature as) that of all such
propositions encountered within commonly played human

language-games. It has already been remarked that Nietzsche advances a number of claims of a substantive nature, which he would seem to regard as exceptions to this general rule. And he further is evidently committed to the possibility (and indeed the existence) of certain 'truths' that are neither 'true' nor 'erroneous' in the senses or respects in which the kinds of (strictly D-relative) propositions under consideration are: namely, those pertaining to the status of these propositions.

It may also be observed that, in pronouncing 'man's truths' generally to be 'erroneous,' Nietzsche is implicitly operating with something like a correspondence conception of 'truth' and 'error' after all — and one in which the notion of correspondence invoked is not simply a matter of the appropriateness of a D-relative proposition to an experienced or contemplated state of affairs, the relevant features of which are fixed by the discourse within which both occur. If he considered the latter correspondence to be the only sort conceivable and the sole and ultimate criterion of 'truth,' he would have no reason to term such 'truths' fundamentally *erroneous* rather than merely extra-systemically *meaningless*; nor would he if he took considerations of coherence or pragmatic value to be the last word where 'truth' is concerned. The elaboration of what he has in mind along these lines, however, must be postponed for the moment; for it pertains to third-order rather than first-order analysis.

Nietzsche's insistence upon the existence of very considerable differences among various sorts of commonplace 'truths' does not preclude the possibility of his giving any general formal characterization of what it is for at least most such propositions to be 'true,' which goes beyond the trivial analysis to the effect that ' "*p*" is true if and only if *p*.' And indeed more than this can be said. As a first approximation, the first-order analysis of such 'truths' he offers is this: to count as 'true,' a proposition must be stated in terms of the language of some domain of discourse; it must assert that some state of affairs of a sort articulatable in terms of the language of this domain obtains; and finally, this assertion must be warranted in terms of the criteria associated with this type of discourse governing the obtaining and non-obtaining of the kind of state of affairs in question.

If a proposition satisfies these conditions, it is true — though, of course, true only D-relatively. Or rather, the satisfaction of these conditions is for Nietzsche what the first-order truth of most classes of propositions amounts to. This formal characterization is not an adequate (complete) first-order analysis of their 'truth,' however, for the reason mentioned previously: 'being warranted'

64

in some linguistic-experiential contexts turns out upon examination to be quite different from what this involves in others. It is one of the virtues of Nietzsche's analysis that it compels attention to the detail which comes into view under such more fine-grained analysis, and to its importance for the understanding of both the status of such propositions and the nature of truth.

V

What then do the warrants of various kinds of propositions consist in, beyond the fact that they satisfy the minimal, formal conditions indicated above? Since Nietzsche is much more interested in the second-order analysis to be given of such 'truths,' he does little more than drop hints about how he would expand upon their first-order analysis along these lines. It is necessary to provide some indication of what he would seem to have in mind here, however, in order to set the stage for the discussion of his second-order analysis which follows.

In his scattered remarks along these lines, the principal types of propositions to which Nietzsche directs his attention may for purposes of convenience be designated as mathematical, semantic, empirical, scientific, logical, and normative. In the cases of some of the sorts of discourse in which such propositions are asserted, the criteria by reference to which their warrant may be determined are more clear-cut than they are in others. But it should not be difficult to see that they differ from case to case, in some instances very markedly, while in others more subtly but nonetheless significantly.

The warrant of a geometrical theorem (or other such mathematical proposition), for example, is relative to certain stipulated or tacitly assumed definitions, axioms and postulates fixing the specific character of the system in which it occurs. Moreover, it is a matter not merely of its consistency with the latter, but rather of a very tight connection with them (viz., entailment or derivability). These first principles of the system, on the other hand, are not warranted in this way. Indeed, they can hardly be said to be warranted at all, except where the selection of some such system for some practical purpose is the issue, in which event pragmatic considerations come into play. Such considerations play no essential role here, however, since the uses to which such systems may be put are incidental to their natures. On Nietzsche's view, therefore, one need say little more about the first-order truth of mathematical propositions than that it either is directly stipulative or else is a matter of derivability by specified procedures from stipulated principles.

The warrant of a semantic proposition (in which, e.g., the meaning of some expression is stated, or a conceptual relation between certain notions is indicated) is rather different. In the first place, while it may assert the existence of a kind of connection of elements, this connection is of another and much looser kind. And more importantly, the warrant of such a proposition is basically a matter of the conformity or correspondence of what it asserts about the meaning or use of an expression to the way in which the latter functions in the (natural or technical) linguistic context in which it characteristically occurs. This correspondence is what the (first-order) truth of such a proposition most immediately consists in; for its touchstone is the existence of an established specific practice among speakers of the language, rather than formal derivability from first principles. Such practices, however, are not discrete, monadic units. On the contrary, the very meaningfulness as well as the warrant of any assertion about any one of them depends not only upon its ties with the other or others which are explicitly mentioned, but moreover upon innumerable background ties with other linguistic practices which constitute the web of (that particular) language. This is a 'coherence' theme, which Nietzsche stresses in a variety of the contexts under consideration. And thus the more complete first-order analysis of the truth of semantic propositions he suggests is to be given in terms of a foreground correspondence and a background coherence.

Something of the same sort is also to be said, on his view, in connection with empirical propositions (here to be understood as assertions pertaining to the sorts of things, events and states of affairs figuring in ordinary human experience and admitting of description in ordinary language). Yet the warrant of an empirical proposition is to be analyzed in somewhat different terms. In the first place, it is a matter of the obtaining of a different sort of foreground correspondence. This is indicated in the common-sense observation, to which Nietzsche is quite willing to subscribe (as far as it goes) at the level of first-order analysis, that a proposition of this sort is true only if what is asserted squares with something which has been observed to transpire. As a first approximation, one might say that for Nietzsche the truth of such a proposition is to be cashed out in terms of its being an appropriate and accurate representation of some experiential phenomenon.

To say this much is not to say enough, however; for he considers it mistaken to suppose that truth here is a matter

66

exclusively of the obtaining of such a relation of correspondence. 'An isolated judgment is never "true," ' he observes; 'only in the connection and relation of many judgments is there any surety' (*WP* 530). What we are dealing with in the case of 'true' empirical propositions is something like an intricately woven tapestry of interlocking and mutually supporting threads. Moreover, the tapestry, while intricate, is loosely woven; and while it may be said to form a whole and hang together, all parts of it are not tightly linked with all others. To the extent that it does exhibit something approaching strict coherence, this coherence is a more or less local phenomenon. The warrant of an empirical proposition is in part a function of its coherence with other propositions held to be true which are in its immediate contextual vicinity; but it may and need stand in no discernable relation to others further removed from it.

Here the image may perhaps be shifted to that of the Wittgensteinian rope consisting of shorter, overlapping and intertwined strands; only it requires to be extended, by conceiving of each strand as itself being constituted as is the rope. The relation of a particular 'true' proposition to the entire domain of empirical discourse is not that of one of the larger strands of which the rope immediately consists to the rope itself, but rather of one of the smaller strands to one of the larger. A condition of the first-order truth of such a proposition — a part of its warrant — is that it can be woven in, at some point or other. If this coherence requirement is overlooked, on Nietzsche's view, the first-order truth of such propositions will be inadequately understood.

It would also be a mistake, however, to think that this sort of coherence is all that the first-order truth of such propositions involves. As has been observed, it also involves a relation to what might loosely be called experience, and more specifically to what transpires in experience. It is not a purely conceptual or linguistic affair, even if it is not a purely factual affair either. The form of discourse under consideration may roughly be characterized as discourse about the world as we encounter it; and while it may be naive to think that 'truth' here is simply a matter of the straightforward correspondence of propositions to extra-linguistically determinate states of affairs, this is something which must not be lost sight of. Such correspondence occurs (when it does) in a context set by a scheme which itself cannot be given a correspondence analysis; and even then it is not a sufficient condition of (first-order) truth, since a further 'coherence' condition must also be met, of the sort indicated above. It is, however, a kind of correspondence nonetheless, vindicating the widespread conviction that there is something too obviously right about the correspondence theory of truth to be denied or ignored.

VI

It is notoriously difficult to formulate some clear criterion enabling one to distinguish between empirical propositions in the above sense and those of a 'scientific' nature. Nietzsche suggests the warrant (and therefore the first-order 'truth') of assertions of the latter sort to be a more complicated and somewhat different affair than that indicated above, however, and to be very different indeed from that encountered in the case of mathematics. For propositions of this sort require a kind of justification that is neither necessary in the more ordinary cases, nor attainable merely by deductive reasoning or semantic analysis; while at the same time they are held to be *capable* of some further sort of justification and so to be either warranted or unwarranted, even if not 'true' in any ultimate or absolute sense. Claims of 'truth' are (and, according to Nietzsche, may reasonably be) advanced for such propositions, even if they may have to be retracted subsequently, and even if the possibility of this eventuality is recognized by those who advance them. What he is concerned with is the nature of the warrant which such propositions may have when they are sufficiently firmly established to gain the assent of the scientific community, *given* that this assent is hedged against the possibility referred to. This, he suggests, is what their first-order 'truth' amounts to; and he sees no reason to refuse to distinguish at all — even on the level of scientific inquiry — between 'truth' and 'falsity' merely because it does not amount to more.

The warrant of a scientific proposition, for Nietzsche, is to be conceived in terms of its connection with a theory redescribing some domain of phenomena in a manner facilitating generalization, quantification, explanation and prediction, of which theoretical model such a proposition may state some feature or consequence. Its warrant is thus a function of the warrant of the theory to which it is so related; and so his first-order 'truth' is fundamentally a matter of its coherence with a theory, which in turn stands in a more complex relation to what transpires in experience than that encountered in the case of empirical propositions and ordinary discourse. If it may be said to correspond to what transpires in experience, it does so only in a much broader and looser sense; and it is also subject to certain special systematic and pragmatic requirements. (More will be said in this connection later in this chapter.)

To be sure, Nietzsche would be the first to insist that ordinary languages in which 'empirical' propositions are formulated may also be said to be 'theory-laden'; that there are no simple, pre-linguistic (and therefore pre-theoretical) 'facts' or 'givens' about which such propositions are merely accurate or inaccurate reports; and that therefore there is an important sense in which the 'truth' of such propositions is no more a matter of a straightforward correspondence-relation of particular thoughts with particular segments of bare reality than is that of scientific propositions cast in theoretical terms. However, these observations only become appropriate *beyond* the level of their first-order truth-analysis. *At* this level, on the other hand, the conditions under which they are warranted are adequately characterizable much more simply. Thus the 'truth-conditions' of the two kinds of propositions may be seen to differ, and with them the nature of the first-order 'truth' associated with each.

'Logical' propositions (of the sort Nietzsche has in mind) differ markedly from both of these kinds of propositions; and while they have certain affinities with semantic propositions, their truth-conditions differ from those of the latter as well. They purportedly express facts of a certain sort about the ways in which our experience must be organized (if it is to be coherent), our thought must proceed (if it is to be rational), and our language must be employed (if it is to be intelligible), capturing basic presuppositions of our general way of perceiving and thinking and talking about the world.

At first glance, the warrant of such propositions might be thought to be essentially the same as that of semantic propositions; for a proposition of the former sort is not 'true' unless a kind of correspondence-relation obtains — unless, that is, what it asserts about the way our experience is organized, our thought proceeeds, or our language works, conforms to the way in which these things in point of fact happen to be. However, it actually involves more than this; for a logical 'truth' differs from a semantic 'truth' in that it purports to express not merely a purely contingent *fact* about the meaning or use of some expression, but rather a *necessity* of some sort.

Such necessities may ultimately turn out to be conditional rather than absolute (as Nietzsche in fact argues); but that is an issue arising only when one turns from their first- to their second-order analysis. At the level of first-order analysis it suffices to recognize that they have this character of necessity if they are logical truths at all, and to take account of the distinctiveness of status and nature which thus is theirs. Their 'truth' is not merely a matter of their correspondence to events or classes of events of the sort which may be encountered in the course of experience, nor yet again simply of the coherence of the principles they express with the kinds of experience, thought or speech to which these principles are held to apply. It is rather a matter of their warrant as expressions of fundamental constraints upon the latter, which structure and regulate (and so in a sense constitute) them in the manner of the rules of a game. 'Rational thought is interpretation according to a scheme that we cannot throw off,' Nietzsche writes (*WP* 522); logical truths are propositions expressing features of this scheme; and their truth is their warrant conceived in terms of the correctness of taking the principles they express to be partially constitutive of and inviolable within it.

Finally, mention must be made of normative propositions (here to be understood as assertions expressing moral and evaluative judgments or principles). It may seem odd to make reference to them here, at least to those who suppose that propositions of this sort are neither true nor false, but rather, for example, are to be regarded merely as covert recommendations or articulations of value-feelings. Nietzsche does have some sympathy with this view of them, as a possible *second*-order analysis of such propositions; and he is quite vehement in his denial that most such propositions which ordinarily pass for 'truths' have any genuine ultimate or universal validity. It seems to him, however, that propositions of this sort require to be included in any inventory of 'man's truths,' and analyzed along with the rest, because they represent a kind of 'holding true' that is as well established and as common as (if not more so than) any other. Indeed, he further suspects that other kinds of 'holding true' may well owe more than a little to it.

In speaking of such 'truths' (and in particular, of what he calls the 'moral "truths"' which he takes to have dominated the thought of philosophers as well as others for so long), Nietzsche does not have in mind any normative proposition which anyone at all might happen to assert. Rather, he is thinking of those which are expressions of what are sometimes called normative 'intuitions' and the principles which inform them — principles that members of a group or community take for granted, as beyond question, and as binding or valid quite independently of what they recognize to be merely their particular inclinations, needs, choices and wishes. Their immediate warrant is a matter of their being vouch- safed by the conscience or sensibility of those in question — when it accords with their 'sense' of right and wrong, good and bad, desirable and undesirable. Here the origin and status of these phenomena are not at issue. The only relevant considerations are that people commonly do make such determinations, and do so in this way. Thus for Nietzsche the proper first-order analysis to be given of the 'truths' of ordinary moral and evaluative discourse is something like an 'intuitionist' analysis; and consequently their 'truth' may be thought of as a matter of the correspondence of assertions made by those engaging in it to their normative 'intuitions.'

This requires some qualification, however; for it is a further feature of such discourse that the assent one may initially be inclined to give to such a proposition is subject to withdrawal if a loose sort of coherence condition is not also satisfied. Its status within normative discourse is to some extent problematic until it is seen whether it runs afoul of others of a like nature, and thus of the larger body of normative intuitions informing one's experience. The adjustment of the one to the other is a subtle and intricate process, rarely carried out either deliberately and rigorously or completely; but it does occur, and is a feature of ordinary normative discourse requiring to be taken into consideration in the analysis of what 'truth' amounts to in it. Such discourse is no more a completely disjointed affair than is empirical discourse; and thus here again one is confronted with a kind of foreground correspondence against a type of background coherence.

'Man's truths' and human life

VII

The foregoing remarks by no means constitute a complete first-order truth-analysis for the types of propositions and discourse mentioned; but they should serve at least to indicate the lines along which Nietzsche would have it carried out. On this level of analysis one's task is to discern and set forth the principles implicit in the making of various sorts of truth-determinations by those involved in forms of life in which such determinations are established practices, rather as one might try to discover and lay out the rules of a game as these are accepted and followed by those who play it. The kind of second-order analysis Nietzsche goes on to provide, on the other hand, involves stepping back from them, examining the nature of the games within which these rules are followed, and considering what is to be made of the kinds of 'truth-determinations' therein encountered, from what might be thought of as a general anthropological perspective.

Thus whereas his first-order analyses of 'truths' of various kinds center upon their contextual *warrant*, his second-order analyses focus upon the *functions* of truth-determinations of these kinds in the lives and activities of those who engage in the forms of discourse in which they are made. In place of the general theme of a foreground of some sort of correspondence against a background of coherence that runs through many of his first-order analyses, the dominant theme here is that of a foreground of convention against a background of pragmatic value, or what might perhaps better be termed instrumental significance. Here too, however, he discovers important differences, in degree and kind, of both conventionality and instrumentality.

In his early essay *On Truth and Lie*, Nietzsche suggests that 'the contrast between truth and lie' has its origin in the establishment of linguistic 'conventions,' involving the selection of a variety of 'metaphors' to serve as 'a uniformly valid and binding designation of things' (*TL* p. 371). He cites the existence of many different natural languages as reason enough for supposing that nothing more than convention is involved here. By virtue of such linguistic conventions, various 'sounds' and 'signs' are linked with each other as they are given specific uses and endowed with meanings. The truth of some propositions, termed 'semantic' above, is simply a matter of their accurately expressing the conventions governing the relations between certain of these 'metaphors.' The 'facts' or states of affairs they express are matters of convention. Thus in this sort of case, Nietzsche writes, comparing words to dice, ' "Truth" here means — to use every die just as it is marked. . . , and never to do violence to the order of castes and to the sequence of classes of rank' (*TL* p. 376).

More remains to be said about them than this, however; for a full appreciation of what the truth of such propositions amounts to requires that reference be made not only to the type of convention involved, but also to the general function of conventions of this type. It would of course be absurd to suppose that the truth of a particular semantic proposition or even the existence of a particular convention of language is a direct function of pragmatic or instrumental considerations of any sort. But when a broader view of the matter is taken, such considerations may be seen to loom very large indeed. We are here dealing with what might be thought of as a certain sort of linguistic *practice*. It is with the general *point* of such practices involving the identification of certain propositions as 'true' that second-order analysis is principally concerned. The practice under consideration is the maintenance of a network of linguistic conventions *within* which such propositions may be formulated (and to the perpetuation of which they contribute). And the purpose thereby served is twofold: it makes possible a form of communication without which we could not 'exist socially and in a disciplined manner,' as we perforce must do (*TL* p. 371); and it greatly facilitates the processing of our experience in ways lending themselves to effective action.

The linguistic conventions of which semantic 'truths' are expressions thus are not merely conventional but, moreover, are fundamentally anthropocentric in the sense of being geared to certain practical contingencies and requirements of our human existence. The purposes natural languages fundamentally serve, however, neither mandate the development of any one particular language (as is evident), nor place any premium on a strict and neutral reflection of reality. It is at most 'only the relations of things to man' that are registered in them, expressed in ways subject to no constraints other than the above-mentioned practical ones, and revealing everywhere the inventiveness of metaphorical thinking (*TL* p. 373). Thus Nietzsche writes:

> What therefore is truth? A flexible army of metaphors,
> metonymies, anthropomorphisms, in short, a sum of human
> relations, which have been poetically and rhetorically
> intensified, transformed, bejeweled, and which after long usage
> seem to a people to be fixed, canonical, and binding (*TL*
> p. 374).

This sort of account is taken by Nietzsche to be appropriate wherever the truth of a proposition is a matter of the linguistic conventions governing the use of the expressions figuring in it. Moreover, he regards it as at least a part of the story in all cases, owing to the fact that any intelligible proposition can only be stated by employing elements of some human language. He does not consider it to suffice, however, in the cases of various other sorts of 'truths,' for which he goes on to provide somewhat different second-order analyses.

Those he terms 'logical,' for example, are suggested to pertain to characteristics of human thought of a different and deeper order. They express rules which, while not conventional to the extent that semantic truths are, nonetheless have a kind of quasi-conventional status, and play a similar functional role, though on a more basic level. Rather than determining the meanings and governing the uses of particular expressions, they establish and relate the general categories into which such expressions fall, and set the formal conditions of their employment. They thus are not semantical but rather syntactical in character. They too are contingent; but while it is only 'the expediency of a certain race and species' that is reflected in them (*WP* 514), the formal features of our thought and experience to which such truths relate are 'conditions of life for us' which have become 'part of us' (*WP* 515). Their only necessity and universality pertain to the character and parameters of our human existence. This does endow them with a special status and significance, elevating them beyond the level of semantical variation and deliberate suspension or alteration. But that should not prevent us from recognizing that they are still only 'conditional truths,' owing their standing as such to the manner in which our species has developed.

Thus, according to Nietzsche, 'in the formation of reason, logic, the categories, it was *need* that was authoritative — the need, not to "know," but to subsume, to schematize, for the purpose of intelligibility and calculation' (*WP* 515). A proposition of logic, he contends, 'contains no *criterion of truth*, but an *imperative* concerning that which *should* count as true' (*WP* 516). Here both the proto-conventionality and also the fundamental instrumentality of the formal features of our thought and experience of which logical 'truths' are expressions are indicated. Nietzsche alternates between acceding to the employment of the term 'truth' in this context and seeking to clarify its nature in it, and insisting upon the point that if truth is construed in terms of some sort of adequacy relation between propositions and reality, the sort of thing encountered here should not be taken to exemplify it. For he holds that it is 'a sign that truth is not involved at all' in the latter sense if, as in the present case, it turns out that the basic operative consideration is the attainment of 'advantages' of a practical nature (*WP* 255).

On the other hand, it is by no means Nietzsche's intention to belittle the importance of devices which establish such advantages. On the contrary, he has a very lively appreciation of anything serving to do so. Indeed, he is concerned in part to free the notion of 'truth' from its exclusive association with the existence of such an adequacy relation. He would not have it reserved exclusively to cases in which some relation between propositions and reality might be supposed to obtain. He is prepared to allow its employment to stand in cases of the sort under consideration, and takes the position that 'truth' thus has an application and a meaning determined by the nature of the kind of relation and practice here encountered. When he says, 'The categories are "truths" only in the sense that they are conditions of life for us' (*WP* 516), he is attributing a conditional form of practical indispensability to them, and is further reconfirming their status as 'truths' precisely in virtue of this fact — though 'only in [a] sense,' only in *one* sense, and a limited one at that.

Allowing the application of the term 'truth' in this context to stand, analysis yields a sense differing from that in which he employs it when he says that 'truth is not involved at all' here. In the case of the former, though *not* in the case of the latter, 'the value for life is ultimately decisive' (*WP* 493). And where 'truth' is understood in this way, the fact that 'value for life' is relative to the particular 'conditions of life' of a type of creature, together with the fact that these 'conditions' are contingent and 'species-specific,' has the consequence that a radical 'perspectivism' obtains where such 'truths' are concerned. This is a point Nietzsche never tires of making.

VIII

His account of the 'truth' of what have been termed 'empirical propositions,' on this level of analysis, is closely connected (as might be expected) with that which he gives in the case of semantic propositions. A natural language, consisting of the 'flexible army of metaphors, metonymies, anthropomorphisms' that has become 'fixed, canonical and binding' for a linguistic community, fleshes out the syntactic and logical-categorial skeleton which structures our experience, articulating the world as we apprehend it. It is to the world of experience thus articulated that particular empirical propositions apply. And the truth of such propositions is a property they can be conceived of as possessing only within this relational context, in which only what has already been thus schematized can be an object of reference.

It is above all with this general situation in mind that Nietzsche says: 'The entire domain of "true—false" applies only to relations, not to an "in-itself"' (*WP* 625). And while from a first-order perspective it is quite legitimate to speak of truth as involving the obtaining of a correspondence-relation between what is asserted and some experiential state of affairs, from the standpoint of his second-order analysis he contends that ' "truth" is the will to be master over the multiplicity of sensations: to classify phenomena into definite categories' (*WP* 517). Such mastery through classification is in the highest degree useful, and indeed is imperative for creatures such as we are. But the facilitation of our dealings with the world, which function it performs, is the most that 'truth' here can be held ultimately to amount to. And the variable conditionality of such facilitation, together with the more radical contingency attaching to the selection of specific means of achieving it, has the consequence that Nietzsche draws in another of his 'perspectivist' pronouncements: 'There are many kinds of eyes. . . — and consequently there are many kinds of "truths," and consequently there is no truth' (*WP* 540).

Here again he adopts a double approach to such 'truths.' On the one hand, he repeatedly insists that since their 'truth' is ultimately merely a matter of the utility of the linguistic schematization of experience within which they figure, they have no epistemic status that could qualify them as 'truths' in any more significant sense. On the other hand, he is quite prepared to allow the term 'truth' a continued employment in this connection — with its sense adjusted accordingly. It would be an error to suppose that it is his intention to strip the term of all senses other than that with which he thus proceeds to supply it. But he does make much of it, and indeed makes use of it in a way that goes beyond the general context in which he initially identifies it, as when he writes: 'The criterion of truth resides in the enhancement of the feeling of power' (*WP* 534).

The basic idea here is still that of the facilitation of our dealings with our environing world. Something more than mere collective self-preservation and the mastery of the multiplicity of sensations and the complexity of processes it requires is indicated, however; and it is no longer simply the status of ordinary empirical propositions that he has in mind. The link between the two applications of this conception is nonetheless intelligible enough. We are, Nietzsche contends, 'a particular species of animal that can prosper' (that is, 'maintain itself and increase its power') only if there is a sufficient 'regularity of its perceptions' to enable it to 'accumulate experience,' and enough of 'the calculable and constant' in its schematization of 'reality' for it to develop a 'scheme of behavior.' In short, ours is a case in which 'a species grasps a certain amount of reality' — and also artfully transforms and schematizes it — 'in order to become master of it, in order to press it into service' (*WP* 480).

It is this basic picture, explicitly cast in 'anthropological and biological' terms, which Nietzsche takes to indicate 'the meaning of "knowledge"' and the character of 'truth' as they apply to the sorts of empirical propositions we employ in our ordinary affairs, on this level of analysis. And it is this line of thought that he extends in remarks like that cited previously on 'the criterion of truth.' The 'strict and narrow anthropological and biological sense' which he says these notions are to be regarded as having here (or rather, with which he here endows them) is on his view a very fundamental one, even if it is not the only one he is prepared to entertain. The fact that the general sort of facilitation in terms of which he explicates it is suggested to involve not only an artful, artificially regularizing and inventively articulating schematization of our relations to our environing world, but also a 'grasping' of 'a certain amount of reality,' is well worth noting. For while the latter is buried in the former in the ordinary case, it contains the germ of a development capable of transcending the confines of truth and knowledge as here realized and analyzed. In the present context, however, he passes over this possibility (to which I shall return), placing his main emphasis upon the former character of such 'truths.'

Thus, for example, Nietzsche chides 'the realists,' saying: 'that mountain there! That cloud there! What is "real" in that? Subtract the phantasm and every human *contribution* from it, my sober friends! If you can!' This contribution, he contends, is enormous and various: 'your descent, your past, your training − all of your humanity and animality' are involved (*GS* 57). As he had observed in *On Truth and Lie*, where ordinary discourse is concerned 'truth' in the sense of an 'adequate expression' of what exists and transpires independently of us 'is never the issue'; for language 'designates only the relations of things to man,' and expresses them in 'the most audacious metaphors' (*TL* p. 373). Only our general obliviousness to this circumstance enables us to 'imagine' that, in following the 'conventions of language' and their 'designations' of these relations, we 'possess a "truth"' consisting in 'the adequate expression of all realities' and the 'coinciding of designations and things' (*TL* p. 372). The 'laws of truth' which govern such discourse are of a different sort, deriving instead from 'the legislation of language' which operates along other lines altogether (*TL* p. 371). 'True' empirical propositions are thus more than the 'empty shells' Nietzsche takes mere 'tautologies' to be (*TL* p. 372); but what they capture are 'only the relations of things to man' metamorphosed and specified in particular contingent ways by 'artistically creating subjects' operating in concert (*TL* p. 377), along lines conditioned by the circumstances of their existence and their constitutional requirements and capacities.

This early second-order analysis of what the truth of empirical propositions amounts to is retained in its essentials by Nietzsche in his later writings, in which he repeatedly stresses the decisiveness of 'utility' in the framing of the experiential-linguistic context in which they have their place. Their truth, on his view, is ultimately a matter of the sort of truth he grants to 'the arranged and simplified world' of experience 'at which our practical instincts have been at work,' as when he writes: 'it is perfectly true for *us*; that is to say, we live, we are able to live in it. . .' (*WP* 568). The idea that anything more is involved here, along the lines of 'a sort of adequate relationship. . .between subject and object,' is 'a well-meant invention which, I think, has had its day' (*WP* 474). It may be appropriate to make use of the notion of such a relationship at the level of first-order analysis, along with the idea of coherence, in dealing with such 'truths.' On the present level of analysis of them, however, Nietzsche contends that 'the essence of "truth"' turns out to require to be understood and explicated in terms of 'valuations' expressive of 'conditions of preservation and growth' (*WP* 507). 'Our empirical world' is articulated along lines reflecting the operation of factors pertaining to the latter, and what we 'regard as true' follows suit (*WP* 583).

One further important part of Nietzsche's second-order analysis of such truths remains to be brought out. It relates to their social character, which is to be discerned not only in their conventionality but also in the kind of instrumental significance they possess. Given considerable prominence in *On Truth and Lie*, this point receives its most extended treatment in one of the central sections of the last part of *The Gay Science* (*GS* 354). Linking the emergence and character of 'consciousness' to the 'capacity of communication,' and this in turn to the 'need for communication,' Nietzsche argues that the 'strength and art of communication' are proportional to its practical necessity and utility, serving principally as a means of making possible and facilitating relations 'between human beings.' Thus 'the development of language and the development of consciousness. . .go hand in hand,' and both fundamentally do 'not really belong to man's individual existence but rather to his social or herd nature.' 'This is the essence of phenomenalism and perspectivism as *I* understand them,' he goes on to say: 'the world of which we can become conscious is only a surface- and sign-world, a world that is made common and meaner,' through a process in which what is *useful* in the interests of the human herd, the species,' is decisive in determining the character of experience and language. And this is held likewise to be the essence of the (only) sort of 'truth' that is here to be found.

To be sure, this second-order analysis of the truth of empirical propositions does not apply in any straightforward way to *particular* propositions of this kind. When the question before one is that of the conditions which must be satisfied in order for some such proposition to be considered true, nothing more than Nietzsche's first-order analysis in terms of correspondence and coherence is either called for or appropriate. While many philosophers might think that this is the end of the matter, however, and that nothing else remains to be said or can meaningfully be said about the status of truths of this kind, he demurs. For on his view it is only when one looks beyond this first-order analysis, taking a broader and deeper view of what is going on in the playing of this sort of language-game, that the matter becomes interesting, and one begins genuinely to comprehend rather than only superficially to understand it.

IX

Nietzsche takes a similar position with respect to 'truths' in science. His treatment of them differs in a number of respects from that considered above, however, owing to what he takes to be the differing character and status of scientific as opposed to empirical propositions and ordinary discourse. In *On Truth and Lie* he characterizes science as a latter-day successor to natural languages in the schematization of the world beyond the level of ordinary experience, building upon and also departing from the sort of articulation of it achieved by means of them: '*Language* is what originally worked at the construction of concepts; more recently *science* has done so.' And he goes on to observe that a difference of no little significance has thereby emerged, between the 'truths' at which science thus arrives and those life-sustaining 'errors' whose practical-social utility is the essence and limit of *their* 'truth' — suggesting further that the former are significantly privileged in relation to the latter:

> the inquirer builds his hut close to the tower-structure of science, in order to be able to cooperate with it and to find protection under its bulwark. And he needs protection: for there are fearsome powers which continuously press upon him, and which oppose 'truths' very differently fashioned and under many different banners to scientific truth (*TL* p. 380).

One of the general points Nietzsche is concerned to make with respect to the sort of truth under consideration here, however, is that what science comes up with is 'descriptions' rather than 'explanations,' and 'interpretations' rather than statements of sheer 'matters of fact,' even though it may purport and be thought to do otherwise. It redescribes and reinterprets phenomena in terms departing from those of ordinary discourse, schematizing them in ways reflecting a modified perspective upon events. This perspective, moreover, while modified, remains a fundamentally 'human' one, notwithstanding its greater subtlety, sophistication, and 'objectivity' in dispensing with many of the grosser anthropomorphisms of ordinary thought and discourse, and substituting for them a more abstract and quantitative conceptual scheme. Thus he remarks that 'physics, too, is only an interpretation and exegesis of the world (to suit us, if I may say so!) and *not* a world-explanation' (*BGE* 14). And he suggests that one might even go so far as to 'consider science as an attempt to humanize things as faithfully as possible,' in that the concepts devised and employed in it to 'describe things and their one-after-another' are more reflections of the character and requirements of our human intellect than appropriate designations of what actually exists and occurs. 'Our descriptions are better' than those given in 'older stages of knowledge and science,' he allows; but he qualifies this assessment by observing that 'we do not explain any more than our predecessors,' and 'operate only with things that do not exist: lines, planes, bodies, atoms, divisible time spans, divisible spaces' (*GS* 112).

To be sure, the sciences by no means have to do and present us with nothing more than complete fictions. Thus Nietzsche contrasts them with 'logic and that applied logic which is called mathematics,' in which 'reality is not encountered at all, not even as a problem' — as he thereby implies it is (at least to some extent and in certain respects) in them. But he considers it 'a crudity and naiveté' to suppose that 'an interpretation that permits, counting, calculating, weighing, seeing, and touching, and nothing more' is 'the only justifiable interpretation of the world,' and that the world has 'its equivalent and measure' in it. 'A "scientific" interpretation of the world' along these lines, he contends, 'would be one of the poorest in meaning,' in that what 'would be grasped first — and might even be the only thing that allowed itself to be grasped' through the kind of thinking it involves and by means of the concepts employed, is 'precisely the most superficial and external aspect of existence' — its roughest outlines and mere 'skin' (*GS* 373).

Like our ordinary, pre-scientific schematization of the world, 'the scientific view of the world' is linked in its development to our practical need to 'make comprehensible' and 'exploitable' (*WP* 677). It further manifests 'the intellect's dislike of chaos' and predilection for 'constancy' (*WP* 594). Its divergence from ordinary thinking is suggested by Nietzsche to have involved the impingement upon these requirements of a number of other impulses which 'had to come together for scientific thinking to originate,' such as 'the impulse to doubt, to negate, to wait, to collect, to dissolve' (*GS* 113). And the result has been a re-schematization of the world departing increasingly from the original embodied and perpetuated in ordinary discourse. The manner in which this is done, however, remains fundamentally linked to the basic human purposes of enhancing the fact or feeling of our mastery of the world with which we find ourselves confronted, and of rendering its aspect more agreeable to our intellect. 'Science,' he therefore maintains, ultimately 'belongs under the rubric "means"' (*WP* 610). And it is in terms of this understanding of it that he considers the 'truth' of scientific propositions and interpretations to require to be conceived on the level of second-order analysis.

Thus while scientific thought may wear the mask of disinterestedness, value-neutrality and 'objectivity,' it remains an expression of what Nietzsche terms our 'will to power' — a refined and subtle expression of it, but an expression of it nonetheless. It involves the establishment of new conventions of description, in the construction of models devised and the framing of concepts introduced in the elaboration of theories; but 'truth' here is not merely a matter of convention. For beyond such conventionality, scientific 'truths' have a further and more significant character, which he takes to constitute the fundamental sense of their 'truth.' It is to be construed, on his view, in terms of a twofold *effectiveness*, to which simplification, abstraction, the use of fictions, and even a kind of shrewd superficiality often contribute in important ways.

One face of this effectiveness relates to the extension of our capacity to control and exploit courses of events. The other pertains to the furthering of our ability to reduce the chaos and bewildering profusion of phenomena transpiring in our lives and encounters with the world to a semblance of order and simplicity. Such effectiveness is not tantamount to the achievement of an adequacy relation between interpretation and reality, as Nietzsche has been seen to insist; and thus scientific 'truth' is not to be conceived along the latter lines. If 'truth' *is* understood in that sense, which he not infrequently has in mind in speaking of it, then as he often observes, science yields but a modicum of 'truth' at most, and more 'error' than 'truth.' Indeed, he considers it to fall well short of affording us the most adequate and penetrating comprehension of life and reality that is humanly attainable.

Yet it does not merely falsify or fabricate. The effectiveness Nietzsche takes to be decisive here not only involves selectivity, oversimplification and artificiality, but also signifies the capturing of certain features of what obtains and transpires in the world.

81

The kind of 'error' encountered in this case is not that of 'lies' and 'illusions,' but rather that of distorting abstractions and convenient fictions, which engage with the world even as they misrepresent it — precisely through the way in which they do so. The sort of 'truth' which the issue of scientific endeavor possesses thus turns out, on this level of analysis, to be both distinct from those characteristic of other forms of discourse and a notable and significant human achievement — even if something rather different from what it is commonly and naively taken to be.

This discussion of Nietzsche's second-order truth-analysis is incomplete, in that normative discourse has not been dealt with. This omission will be made good, however, in later chapters dealing with values and morals, about which he has too much to say for justice to be done here to it. For the moment I shall simply observe that, in this case too, the analysis he offers is a further variation on the same general theme encountered in these other cases, of conventionality established in accordance with certain sorts of basic pragmatic or instrumental considerations, his usual blanket designation of which is 'conditions of life.'

Ordinary and scientific knowledge

X

At the conclusion of this chapter I shall explore Nietzsche's views concerning the possibility and nature of a sort of truth (and of a related form of knowledge) which would transcend those considered thus far, and which he takes to be exemplified by the issue of the kind of interpretation he undertakes and conceives genuinely philosophical thinking to involve. Before doing so, however, the foregoing discussion of his multi-level analysis of 'truths' of various sorts requires to be supplemented by an examination of his treatment of *knowledge* in its more common forms and as it has generally been construed. Much of what he has to say along the latter lines reflects his views with respect to the former, as one might expect from the nature of the case. It is only in his reflections on what various sorts of knowing and forms of knowledge (both putative and genuine) do and do not involve, however, that the general epistemological position associated with his analysis of truth fully emerges.

Certain basic features of Nietzsche's approach to the topic of human knowledge were indicated at the outset of this chapter. One should recall in particular his insistence upon the necessity of recognizing that *human life* is the context in which all forms of human knowledge arise; and that the intellectual operations they involve are developments of human powers which inescapably reflect various features of our human constitution and circumstances of our human existence, both biological and social. A proper orientation to the subject cannot be achieved, on his view, unless one dismisses the fiction of the mind as the seat of certain capacities with which we have somehow been endowed quite independently of our biological and social evolution, equipping us to do things having no connection with such mundane matters as our preservation, socialization, and basic dispositions.

This fiction is a variation of one of a brace of metaphysical hypotheses — the 'soul-hypothesis,' the 'God-hypothesis,' and the hypotheses of the existence of a world of 'true being' and of 'things in themselves' — all of which have some bearing upon the matter of knowledge and have long influenced its understanding, and all of which further are considered by Nietzsche to be untenable (as shall be seen in the next chapter). And when the problem of knowledge is confronted anew against a background of the recognition of their untenability, one is confronted with several radical alternatives, each wreaking a kind of havoc upon received views concerning it. One might choose to allow the traditional conception of knowledge framed along lines set by these hypotheses to stand. In this case, however, the idea of knowledge would then likewise have to be dismissed as a meaningless (or at any rate, empty) fiction. Alternatively, one might abandon this construal of it, and recast the notion along basically naturalistic lines. In this case it would retain a variety of legitimate applications, embracing a number of intellectual operations generally considered to be cognitive phenomena; but certain basic revisions in the understanding of what they involve would be required.

Nietzsche sometimes seems inclined simply to take the former course; but he actually opts for *both* alternatives. This is why some of the remarks he makes in this connection appear to be at such variance with others, and explains how he can say such things as 'our apparatus for acquiring knowledge is not *designed* for "knowledge"' (*WP* 496). On some occasions he confines himself to criticism of the possibility (attainability and meaningfulness) of the sort of thing the latter — 'knowledge' in scare-quotes — is supposed to involve. On others, however, he is concerned with the character of the products of the former — 'our apparatus for acquiring knowledge.' These he sometimes contrasts with the former in terms associated with it (e.g., as 'errors' in contrast to an imagined form of knowledge conceived in terms of the idea of truth as the exact correspondence of thought and being), and sometimes seeks to exhibit in more appropriate language, contrasting them only with each other. If this is not recognized, he is bound to be misunderstood.

Nietzsche's treatment of knowledge in effect proceeds in several stages. He is concerned both with what human 'knowing' generally amounts to and involves, and also with the possibility and status of further humanly attainable forms of cognition and comprehension. In conjunction with this twofold (analytical and constructive) undertaking, however, he also considers it imperative to lay to rest and rid ourselves of certain myths and illusions with respect to the nature of knowledge. We must recognize what our knowledge cannot be if we are to be able to grasp what it is and can be. Thus his theory of knowledge involves a critique of other theories of knowledge it is intended to replace.

One of the things our knowledge cannot be, he argues, is a non-perspectival, unconditioned apprehension of 'true being.' This is an ideal he considers to have seduced and misled a great many philosophers from Parmenides and Plato onward. On this notion of knowledge, 'knowledge and becoming exclude one another.' This is something upon which its proponents themselves have insisted, concluding that 'consequently, "knowledge" must be something else,' and must be *of* 'something else.' For Nietzsche, however, there *is* nothing else, the world being fundamentally 'in a state of becoming' rather than having the essential character of some sort of 'being.' And the recognition that ' "beings" are a part of our perspective' rather than ultimate constituents of reality — ontological fictions, as it were, with which we operate because we must do so 'in order to think and infer' — requires that the notion of knowledge framed in terms of their projection into reality be abandoned (*WP* 517). In short: if 'knowledge is possible only on the basis of belief in being' (*WP* 518), then the status of knowledge so conceived is the same as that of this belief; and its characterization as a mode of apprehension transcending our human condition and fastening upon the ultimate constitution of reality is seen to be without any substance.

Another sort of thing knowledge cannot be, Nietzsche contends, is the apprehension of various sorts of bare 'facts,' which when collected serve to make possible comparisons, generalizations and inferences. This empiricist picture of knowledge is as misguided in its own way as the rationalist model is ill-conceived. The latter rests upon the myths of 'being' and of the mind as a transcendent subject essentially attuned to its embrace in thought; the former, on the other hand, involves the myth of 'the given' and of thought

84

as its mirror and articulation. 'Against positivism, which halts at phenomena — "There are only *facts*" — I would say: No, facts are precisely what there is not, only interpretations. We cannot establish any fact "in itself": perhaps it is folly to want to do such a thing' (*WP* 481).

Whatever we experience is already schematized or structured in accordance with some mode of 'interpretation' informing our experience, for which some other may in certain circumstances be substituted, but from all modes of which we cannot abstract without eliminating an indispensable condition of the possibility of intelligible experience. There are 'facts' only in the context of interpretations which endow our experiences with whatever 'meaning' they have, and so are constitutive of whatever facts are available to us. Thus Nietzsche writes: 'There are no "facts-in-themselves," for a sense must always be projected into them before there can be "facts." ' The notion of 'a "sense-in-itself," a "meaning-in-itself," ' he contends, is simply 'perverse' and non-sensical (*WP* 556). Knowing, therefore, cannot be a matter of ascertaining and collecting any such ultimate particular facts which the distillation and reduction of our experience to its bare essentials might be supposed to yield.

XI

Abandoning empiricist as well as rationalist myths with respect to knowledge does not, however, leave us entirely empty-handed, and is not taken by Nietzsche to require that we abandon the notion of knowledge altogether. The quest for 'foundations' must indeed be abandoned, and the aspiration to 'absolute knowledge' relinquished; and the construal and criteria of knowledge must accordingly be cut loose from both. The effect of doing so, however, ought rather to be to reorient our approach to those actual and possible forms of thinking which have some legitimate claim to the title of knowledge — either because they have long and commonly been accorded it (and so have a *de facto* right to it), or because they may on other grounds be argued to be even more deserving of it. Nietzsche does insist that 'the biggest fable of all is the fable of knowledge,' insofar as it is supposed to deal with the unconditioned in an unconditioned manner; since 'there are no things-in-themselves,' and 'coming to know. . .is always "placing oneself in a conditional relation to something" ' (*WP* 555). On the other hand, however, he also is quite prepared to allow that there is such a thing as 'coming to know' if this is conceived in terms of the establishment of a certain sort of 'conditional relation,' as this passage itself indicates, and in which case the 'something' to which thought is thus related is no empty fiction.

What human knowledge generally amounts to and involves, on his view, is the assimilation of our relations to our environing world to a practically serviceable conceptual scheme, in the establishment and elaboration of which our needs are presumed to have played a dominant role. It is the comprehension of 'a world that we ourselves have made' (*WP* 495) — i.e., 'an arranged and simplified world, at which our practical instincts have been at work' (*WP* 568). Apart from mathematics, which Nietzsche regards as an altogether different matter (*WP* 530), 'there would be nothing that could be called knowledge if thought did not first re-form the world in this way into "things," into what is self-identical' (*WP* 574). This *has happened*, however; and consequently there *is* something that may be so designated — a type of belief which has this human 're-formation of the world' as its condition, and our human relations to our environing world as both its context and its content. So he writes:

> Coming to know means 'to place oneself in a conditional relation to something'; to feel oneself conditioned by some-thing and oneself to condition it — it is therefore under all circumstances establishing, denoting, and making-conscious of conditions (not forthcoming entities, things, what is 'in-itself') (*WP* 555).

That most common form of 'knowing' which consists in what is often called the 'understanding' of something is for Nietzsche fundamentally a matter of 'being able to express something new in the language of something old and familiar' (*WP* 479). This is what he has in mind when he suggests that ' "knowledge" is a referring back' (*WP* 575); its nature reflects the general fact that, 'in our thought, the essential feature is fitting new material into old schemas (= Procrustes' bed), *making* equal what is new' (*WP* 499). Such 'knowing' may not be the only sort of thing it is within our power to accomplish; but the modest achievement it represents is what passes for 'knowledge' most frequently — and not only in ordinary life:

> What is it that the common people take for knowledge?
> What do they want when they want 'knowledge'?
> Nothing more than this: Something strange is to be reduced to something *familiar*. And we philosophers — have we really meant *more* than this when we have spoken of knowledge? (*GS* 355).

To this a related point may be added, concerning another common practice which also is considered a form of coming to know something. This practice consists in *naming*. When something has been given a name, we feel that it has been brought within the compass of our knowledge. The name is thought to give us a handle on it, and so to enable us to grasp it in thought. As was earlier observed, Nietzsche recognizes that this may actually be a step in a process ultimately resulting in a substantial addition to the world of experience, and thus generating the possibility of new knowledge, since 'it is enough to create new names and estimations and probabilities in order to create in the long run new "things"' (*GS* 58). By itself, however, naming, as a way of rendering familiar what does not readily admit to the preferred strategy of reduction to something already familiar, does not amount to much. 'We set up a word at the point at which our ignorance begins,' but in doing so only mark 'the horizon of our knowledge,' rather than expand it in any significant way (*WP* 482). As long as our knowledge of something extends no further than the word for it, it is knowledge of a very minimal sort indeed.

If (as Nietzsche contends) the impetus to the schematization of the world of experience within the context of which human knowledge generally has its place originally was and continues to be of a fundamentally practical character, then the nature of such knowledge must be understood in functional terms relating to the basic requirements at work in it. These, he suggests, are several. We are held to be so constituted that, in order to live, we must be able both to 'reckon and calculate' and also to 'communicate.' A condition of the possibility of the former sort of operation is an 'adapted world' in which there is a 'continual recurrence' of 'identical, familiar, related things.' And by the same token, 'for there to be communication something has to be firm, simplified, capable of precision. . .' (*WP* 569). Both imperatives thus conspire to the same general effect. 'We "know" (or believe or imagine) just as much as may be *useful* in the interests of the human herd, the species' (*GS* 354). 'Knowing' here is a matter of applying elements of the conceptual scheme 'we have produced. . .in order to be able to live in a world' (*WP* 568), where this requires working out effective patterns of action and interaction.

'Knowing that' is thus a function of 'knowing how,' which relates to the attainment of practical objectives in our dealings with the world and each other, and in which efficacy takes precedence over all other considerations. 'Knowledge works as a tool of power,' not merely in the superficial sense that theoretical insight often can be turned to practical advantage, but also in a

87

more fundamental sense. For the character of 'knowing' reflects both a 'will to power' and the contingencies of our constitution on the one hand, and on the other the sorts of possibilities presented to us by the world. Such knowledge is essentially geared to the exploitation of circumstances rather than to their neutral ascertainment. It is 'not some abstract-theoretical need not to be deceived' that underlies and guides 'the development of the organs of knowledge,' Nietzsche writes, in commenting on 'the meaning of "knowledge"' here, but rather the need of 'a particular species to maintain itself and increase its power' (*WP* 480).

His reasoning here is that 'even our intellect is a consequence of conditions of [our] existence' (*WP* 498), and requires to be understood in light of the basic principle of evolutionary development to the effect that any salient traits possessed by forms of life are related to strategies of those forms of life serving to facilitate their dealings with the world. What is held to be more concretely 'at work here,' in the case presently under consideration, is 'the utilitarian fact that only when we see things coarsely and made equal do they become calculable and useful to us' (*WP* 515). Ours is a species that 'can prosper only through a certain relative rightness' in its apprehension of things, but also only on the condition that it develops and operates with a 'conception of reality' involving 'enough of the calculable and constant for it to base a scheme of behavior on it.' It 'grasps a certain amount of reality in order to become master of it, in order to press it into service'; but in order to do this it must 'grasp' selectively, and achieve a degree of 'regularity of its perceptions' which represents a simplifying and distorting imposition (*WP* 480).

Thus Nietzsche suggests that 'the entire apparatus of knowledge is an apparatus for abstraction and simplification,' geared to 'taking possession of things' (*WP* 503). 'The so-called drive for knowledge can be traced back to a drive to appropriate and conquer,' he writes; and its issue reflects the premium placed by the latter upon 'the quickest possible reduction of the phenomena, economy, the accumulation of the spoils of knowledge (i.e., of world appropriated and made manageable)' (*WP* 423). There is such a thing as human knowledge that is not only attainable but attained in considerable measure by human beings generally in the course of their lives. Its attainment is possible, however, only because things have first been 'made knowable,' through the creation of 'the deception of beings' (*WP* 517). In short:

> only to the extent that the 'comprehending' and 'knowing'
> intellect encounters a coarse, already-created world, fabricated

out of mere appearances but firm to the extent that this kind of appearance has preserved life — only to this extent is there anything like 'knowledge'; i.e., a measuring of earlier and later errors by one another (*WP* 520).

This, in any event, is the situation with respect to what most commonly passes for and counts as 'knowledge' in human life, which thus is obviously to be bracketed with the sort of 'truth' Nietzsche considers the greater part of 'man's truths' to possess. But this is by no means his last word on the entire subject, and requires to be qualified in the instances of certain more subtle, refined and modified forms of 'knowing,' in addition to those of a purely formal nature. One that he takes to be at least possible is linked to the philosophical enterprise he undertakes and has in mind in speaking of a 'philosophy of the future' and of 'new philosophers' capable of engaging in it. (I shall consider it subsequently.) Another is in certain respects related to it, though far from identical with it. I refer to what he takes to be the sort of 'knowing' encountered in the domain of 'scientific' thought, understood in the broad sense of *Wissenschaft* (and thus encompassing but not being restricted to the 'hard sciences'). It is to his discussion of such more refined and rigorous *wissenschaftlich* knowing (to which the term 'cognition' often is and may appropriately be applied) that I now turn.

XII

As has been seen, Nietzsche construes scientific inquiry as an interpretive affair, issuing in redescriptions whose 'truth' is fundamentally to be understood in terms of a foreground of convention against a background of effectiveness in the achievement of mastery, rather than in terms of anything on the order of an adequate depiction of reality. At the same time, however, he concedes to science a legitimate claim to the title of knowledge, and takes this claim it has established to supersede (although not entirely to cancel) the much older and persistingly strong claim to that title made by and on behalf of common sense. To be sure, he observes that there is an important respect in which the development of scientific thinking promotes the growth of an attitude of fundamental skepticism, at least concerning the attainability of anything on the order of a knowledge that would be 'absolute' and would have as its object 'true being.' In any event, it comes up with nothing of the sort. Its best confirmed conclusions are always provisional and subject to subsequent revision, and perspectival to boot. Its best efforts, moreover, never yield anything other than regularities, probabilities, and relative quantitative determinations, applied to theoretical constructs inseparable from the models in terms of which they are framed. Yet Nietzsche holds that, however modest it may be, and whatever might require to be said about its nature, a form of 'knowledge' *is* to be recognized as the issue of scientific inquiry.

He has been observed to allow that, 'in so far as the word "knowledge" has any meaning, the world is knowable,' even though he also goes on to say, 'but it is *interpretable* otherwise' (*WP* 481). The addition is important, but so is the initial point. And it is of science in particular that he is thinking when he makes this point. 'The word "knowledge"' *does* 'have meaning,' i.e., has both significant import and an appropriate application, in connection with it. There is a 'realm of knowledge' that may be and has been established; and although the domain of scientific thought is not coextensive with it, Nietzsche takes science to deserve much of the credit for its establishment, and to belong to it as well. Thus he writes:

> In science convictions have no rights of citizenship, as one says with good reason. Only when they decide to descend to the modesty of hypotheses, of a provisional experimental point of view, of a regulative fiction, may they be granted admission and even a certain value in the realm of knowledge — though always with the restriction that they remain under police supervision, under the police of mistrust (*GS* 344).

Entrance into this 'realm of knowledge' has as its condition the employment of 'scientific method'; and good standing within it is forfeited if fidelity to this method and the modesty appropriate to it are forgotten. This is a point on which Nietzsche lays great stress, even though he also recognizes that the development of this method was by no means entirely disinterested and devoid of ulterior motivation. Thus he remarks that 'truth, that is to say, the scientific method, was grasped and promoted by those who divined in it a weapon of war' (*WP* 457). It *opposed*, and thereby also aroused opposition: 'All the methods, all the presuppositions of our contemporary science,' he observes, have long been 'regarded with the profoundest contempt,' since 'the whole pathos of mankind' has been ranged against 'our objectivity, our method, our silent, cautious, mistrustful ways,' which gradually were learned and developed under its aegis (*WP* 469). A further and critical step in their development, however, beyond 'the victory of science,' is held to be of no lesser importance: 'the victory of the scientific method over science' (*WP* 466). For it is not to science as such that the last word with respect to knowledge of the world belongs.

Nietzsche suggests, in one of his aphorisms, that 'a thinker' is one who 'knows how to make things simpler than they are' (*GS* 189); and he considers those who think scientifically to be cases in point rather than exceptions to the rule (as the more enlightened of them recognize, even if their idolizers do not). This circumstance may importantly qualify the epistemic status of the knowledge they may be said to attain; but far from merely detracting from the status which such knowledge might be supposed to have, it is held to be one of the conditions of the very possibility of this sort of cognition. Similarly, while such thinking 'measures the world according to magnitudes posited by itself,' and schematizes it in terms of concepts and models of its own devising, 'there would be nothing that could be called knowledge if thought did not first re-form the world in this way. . .' (*WP* 574). This process does involve the use of 'fictions' and 'the invention of formulas and signs' by means of which 'confusing multiplicity' is 'reduced' to a 'manageable schema' (*WP* 584); but it does not follow that nothing at all is grasped thereby other than these thought-products themselves. Rather, as has been seen, Nietzsche is prepared to speak of such cognition as an affair in which one 'grasps a certain amount of reality' (*WP* 480).

Nietzsche makes much of the point that, in operating with such conceptions, and in refining and elaborating the models and accounts of the phenomena thereby designated, natural scientists achieve no more than a conditioned and perspectival understanding of certain features of reality. On his view, however, this understanding may nonetheless come to approximate to it sufficiently closely to warrant the ascription of limited epistemic status to it — in part precisely by virtue of the instrumental value it proves to have in facilitating our efforts to achieve practical 'mastery' of our environing world. Where models and hypotheses can be tested by experience, scientific knowledge is possible. And such testing does not simply function as a criterion in terms of the superior satisfaction of which something qualifies as a piece of scientific knowledge. It also can indicate that one has gotten hold of some feature of the world, however superficial and contingent that feature may be, and even if only in a rough and ready way.

It is characteristic of scientific thinking, Nietzsche observes, that it fixes particularly upon those features of things and our relation to them which admit of quantification (*WP* 710). Commenting upon the sort of knowledge presently under consideration, he writes: 'Our "knowing" limits itself to establishing quantities,' although in ordinary experience 'we cannot help feeling these differences in quantity as qualities' (*WP* 563). Our senses translate the former into the latter. In science, however, we learn to decipher this translation, and replace the latter with representations of the former. 'Qualities are an idiosyncrasy peculiar to man,' at least as we perceive them. 'But everything for which the word "knowledge" makes any sense refers to the domain of reckoning, weighing, measuring, to the domain of quantity.' Qualities are 'perspective "truths" which belong to us alone and can by no means be "known"' (*WP* 565). Quantities, on the other hand, are not thus so narrowly 'perspectival,' and admit of a form of cognition to which higher (and, as Nietzsche here suggests, more genuine) epistemic status may be accorded.

Such cognition is not so strongly colored by 'our human interpretations and values,' which pervade ordinary experience to the point that Nietzsche takes it to be inappropriate to employ the term 'knowledge' in a strict sense in connection with it. He does consider it important to recognize, however, that cognition of this sort too is connected with and bears the stamp of the fundamental practical human interests served by quantification ('reckoning, weighing, measuring,' and thus the mastery of the world with which we find ourselves confronted). And he further holds that it inevitably involves the employment of means of quantitative representation which are ultimately arbitrary and conventional. Such cognition, moreover, does not go very deep: 'It is an illusion that something is *known* when we possess a mathematical formula for an event: it is only designated, described; nothing more!' (*WP* 628).

In short: if 'knowing' is conceived as involving a full comprehension of something, then it cannot properly be said to be accomplished here, however greatly the employment of such representations might facilitate the obtaining of certain sorts of results. 'The calculability of the world, the expressibility of all events in formulas — is this really "comprehension"?' (*WP* 624). As Nietzsche allows in making this point, however, there *are* features of things and events which may thus be represented. The 'designation' of such features not only has its uses, but also constitutes at least a kind of limited apprehension of the realities possessing them. And knowledge *may* be said to be thereby attained if it is construed precisely as the 'reckoning up' of 'that which is calculable and can be reduced to formulas' in them. It is this sort of knowing, which is to be distinguished on the one hand from the 'understanding' that passes for knowledge in ordinary

92

life, and on the other from the fuller 'comprehension' that would surpass both, that Nietzsche regards as the main task and achievement of scientific thought.

Of greater importance, however, is a more basic feature of scientific thinking, which it has acquired along the way. Tied to no particular body of theory and no single way of rendering phenomena amenable to quantitative treatment, and subservient only to very general rather than highly specific human interests, it is characterized by a method and a conscience which render it capable of continual self-renewal. This not only enables it to develop, but moreover ultimately contributes to the establishment of the conditions of its own supersession. This, far more than the reduction of phenomena along quantitative lines, is what Nietzsche has in mind in lauding the victory of 'scientific method' over 'science.'

XIII

Nietzsche concedes the existence of 'something like a drive for knowledge' that is not merely a function and covert expression of 'the other drives of the scholar' in the scientific thinker: 'some small, independent clock-work that, once well wound, works on vigorously *without* any essential participation' of the latter (*BGE* 6). He also recognizes and appreciates the very considerable 'emancipation of science from moral and religious purposes' that has been achieved (*WP* 63). These points notwithstanding, however, he has doubts about 'the ultimate validity of the knowledge attained by the natural sciences' (*GS* 357), and considers the general orientation of scientific thinking and its characteristic manner of interpretation to be fundamentally suspect, even if not entirely misguided.

The fact that science continues to be sustained and motivated by the old metaphysical and religious faith 'that God is the truth, that truth is divine' (*GS* 344) is a circumstance which turns out not to be so very serious, since Nietzsche holds it to be capable of acquiring a new lease of life as an instrument of the 'will to power.' He contends, however, that it is tainted by a certain form of prejudice carrying over from this same traditional mode of thought. This is what he calls the 'prejudice of being,' which tends to the reification of processes, reduces difference to sameness, and elevates the contingent to the necessary and regularity to nomologicality. This prejudice accords ultimacy only to that which transcends change and ephemerality, assimilating to it (or

93

passing over and dismissing as insignificant or merely apparent) everything else that occurs and obtains.

Having abandoned the metaphysical and religious quest for a world of 'true being' beyond that in which we live, science is thus taken by Nietzsche to be generally characterized by a disposition to interpret 'this world' and all that transpires in it along lines which approximate as closely as possible to the outlines of this old ideal. He does not deny that a measure of comprehension of it may be thereby attainable, particularly insofar as the ability to arrive at quantitative determinations of things in relation to each other is developed. As has been seen, however, he considers such knowledge to be rather superficial; and thus he has reservations about science insofar as it not only concentrates upon those features of things which admit of quantitative determination, but also disregards others or treats them as derivative of and reducible to the quantitatively determinable. This is one respect in which he takes a 'critique of the psychological need for science' to be relevant to the assessment of 'the scientific view of the world': its accordance of primacy to 'what can be counted and calculated' is linked not only to 'the desire to make practical, useful, exploit-able,' but also to 'the desire to make comprehensible' (*WP* 677).

It is the latter motive in particular that Nietzsche associates with the above-mentioned prejudice. Quantification facilitates the subsumption of events under concepts and formulas by means of which we can represent the world to ourselves as constituted and ordered along lines answering to the demand of our reason for 'being' — or, failing that, for structure that at least approximates to the immutability and necessity of 'being.' Our reason is so constituted, as Kant had observed, that it is not satisfied until it fashions for itself an ontological scheme of constitutively rather than merely regulatively employed concepts and principles, in terms of which it can comprehend what transpires in experience. And this trait of reason, according to Nietzsche, lives on in science, even though overtly metaphysical and theological thinking might be repudiated.

The exaggerated significance attached to the quantitatively determinable in scientific thinking is to be viewed in this light. And the same holds with respect to the 'mechanism' and 'causalism' which he considers not merely to happen to charac-terize natural-scientific thought, but moreover to express tendencies very basic to it. (His critique of them will be considered in the next chapter.) It is drawn, in short, to that which most readily allows of treatment as forms (or at least approximations) of 'being' — to that, in other words, which admits of quantification, reification, logicization, classification. Nietzsche does not take this to render it devoid of epistemic significance; but he holds that it does severely limit it.

Truth and knowledge with a difference

XIV

Nietzsche conceives of the possibility of a further, somewhat related but importantly different way of thinking of significantly greater epistemic import, which he considers to find exemplification in his own thought with respect to such diverse matters as the world and life, our human nature and existence, and questions of value. It would be fair enough to call it philosophical rather than merely scientific; but this does not suffice to illuminate its character. To understand what he has in mind along these lines, it is necessary to examine the nature of the kind of knowledge, and the character of the related form of truth, which he associates with it and takes to transcend those considered up to this point.

Here he moves beyond his analysis and assessment of what generally passes for knowledge and truth in more commonplace human contexts, and in traditional philosophical and contemporary scientific thought. That he takes it to be possible to supersede them, at least in principle, is suggested by his repeated contention that in the final analysis propositions satisfying the conditions indicated in his first- and second-order analyses are not actually 'truths' at all, and that the various forms of knowledge considered above ultimately turn out to be of very modest or negligible epistemic significance.

This consideration, however, is not by itself decisive, since one might make these points and yet take a radically nihilistic epistemological position involving the denial of the possibility of doing any better. And it is a further circumstance to be reckoned with that Nietzsche not only repudiates the very idea of 'absolute knowledge' and of 'truth' as an exact correspondence of thought and reality, but also maintains that 'truth' is inescapably perspectival, and 'knowledge' essentially interpretive. Thus even in taking the positions he does on various substantive issues, he allows that they too are 'only interpretations' (*BGE* 22); and while contending that the 'new species of philosophers' he envisions (and to which he takes himself to belong) are assuredly 'friends of "truth,"'' he insists that they will not suppose that 'their truth' is or ought to be 'a truth for everyman,' let alone truth that is final and ultimate − for they are 'to be called

95

attempters,' and 'will certainly not be dogmatists' (*BGE* 42, 43).

One should not be too quick, however, to draw radical conclusions from such admissions and qualifications. In the latter case, for example, what Nietzsche says leaves open the possibility that the 'truths' arrived at by such philosophers might possess epistemic *superiority* to those of 'everyman,' from whose commonplace judgments they depart. Indeed, his point in this passage is by no means that all 'truths' are on an equal (and equally suspect) footing, but rather precisely the contrary. Thus he goes on to observe that 'great things remain for the great, abysses for the profound, nuances and shudders for the refined'; and his gloss on the 'new philosopher's' insistence that 'my judgment is *my* judgment' is that 'no one else is easily entitled to it' (*BGE* 43).

The force of his remarks concerning the interpretive character of all 'knowing' (his own thought and the efforts of such 'new philosophers' not excepted) likewise should not be misunderstood. It is one thing to hold, as he does, that 'there would be no life at all if not on the basis of perspective estimates and appearances' (*BGE* 34), that there is 'no limit to the ways in which the world can be interpreted,' and even that 'every interpretation [is] a symptom of growth or of decline' (*WP* 600). It is another, however, to take this to be the end of the matter. And that Nietzsche does not do so is indicated by his suggestion of the possibility that 'it might be a basic characteristic of existence that those who would know it completely would perish,' and that the amoral and discontented 'are more favored when it comes to the discovery of certain *parts* of truth' (*BGE* 39). This may also be seen, more concretely, in his proposal that one 'make the experiment' of considering whether all phenomena can be 'traced back' to 'the will to power, as *my* proposition has it' — and in his contention that, if so, 'one would have gained the right to determine *all* efficient force univocally as — *will to power*' (*BGE* 36). This might still be 'interpretation,' but it is clear that for Nietzsche it would be interpretation *with a difference*, having an epistemically favored status in relation to various others which have been and might be proposed.

What matters for the moment is not the specific content of this interpretation (which will be considered subsequently), but rather Nietzsche's commitment to the possibility of such an epistemic difference among rival interpretations, owing to which the notions of 'truth' and 'knowledge' acquire a force and meaning they lack in other contexts. And these remarks (together with many others to similar effect) make this commitment evident. Such an interpretation might *also* have 'symptomatic' significance, without its *only* significance being of this sort. Moreover, what it would be symptomatic *of* could be something which would not preclude according epistemic superiority to the interpretation, but rather might actually be at least indirectly relevant to the possibility of one's arriving at an interpretation having such favored status. So, for example, when Nietzsche suggests that 'the strength of a spirit should be measured according to how much of the "truth" one could still barely endure,' extraordinary 'strength' on the part of the interpreter (setting him apart from others who '*require* it to be thinned down, shrouded, sweetened, blunted, falsified') would seem to be the sort of trait he has in mind, of which such an interpretation could be regarded as a 'symptom' (*BGE* 39).

Nietzsche undeniably attaches the greatest significance to 'the enhancement of life,' and makes much of the point that 'lies,' 'errors,' 'illusions,' 'fictions' and the like always have been and will continue to be of the greatest utility with respect to it. Yet he also was possessed of a lively intellectual conscience, confirmed in his view of himself as a 'man of knowledge,' persistent in his attempts to arrive at a deeper and clearer comprehension of our human reality and the character of life and the world than others had attained, and committed to the pursuit of something he does not hesitate to call 'truth,' the status of which he takes to be quite different from that of 'man's truths.' He may be prepared to make large allowances where the flourishing and enhancement of life as it is and must be lived are concerned; but he is unflagging in his insistence upon 'truthfulness' in philosophy, contemptuously attributing an 'absolute lack of intellectual integrity' to those who suppose (as he clearly does not) that 'it does not matter whether a thing is true, but only what effect it produces' (*WP* 172). He may be unsure of the answer to the question, 'To what extent can truth endure embodiment?' But if, as he states, 'that is the question,' and that the fateful 'experiment' now underway as 'the impulse for truth' collides and clashes with our old 'life-preserving errors' (*GS* 110), this clearly commits him to the possibility of a sort of 'truth' and form of 'knowledge' differing from what generally passes as such but actually falls into the latter category.

In *Dawn*, Nietzsche characterizes our general human predicament in terms of the metaphor of being enclosed within a 'horizon, in which, as within prison walls, our senses confine us.' In it we 'live and move'; and from it we 'cannot escape.' He continues: 'We are in our webs, we spiders; and whatever we catch in them, we can catch nothing whatever other than what admits of being caught precisely in *our* webs' (*D* 117). Yet in the same work, reflecting on 'the thought of *self-sacrificing humanity*' and the possibility that it might come to 'supersede every other aspiration,' he writes: 'One may already swear that. . .the knowledge of truth would be the single great goal remaining to which such a sacrifice would be appropriate, because for it no sacrifice is too great' (*D* 45). If he subsequently came to have second thoughts on the matter, they pertain to the 'revaluation' of the 'value' of such knowledge than to the very possibility of attaining anything of the kind. As the previous passage suggests, he is well aware of the difficulty of getting very far; but he does not suppose that we are incapable of getting anywhere at all. Our 'imprisonment' notwithstanding, he holds that 'we seekers for knowledge' may yet attain something more than an awareness of it and an understanding of its particular features — although whether one actually succeeds in doing so will 'depend upon manifold conditions'.

> One has to be *very light* to drive one's will to knowledge into such a distance and, as it were, beyond one's time, to create for oneself eyes to survey millennia and, moreover, clear skies in those eyes (*GS* 380).

With the clearer sight thereby attainable, something approaching genuine comprehension becomes possible; and truths both large and small which escape those confined within narrower perspectives and conventional schemes of interpretation may be discerned. Here reference may be made to what Nietzsche says 'Zarathustra wants': namely, a certain 'type of man' who 'conceives reality *as it is*, being strong enough to do so,' and so 'is not estranged or removed from reality' either in his understanding of it or in his manner of existence. And he goes on to observe in this connection that 'when mendaciousness at any price monopolizes the word "truth" for its perspective,' as it does in ordinary thinking and religious thought (and has for so long in philosophy as well), 'the really truthful man is bound to be branded with the worst names' (*EH* III:6:5).

Nietzsche does consider it important to caution those who might aspire to number among his new 'philosophers and friends of knowledge' to 'beware of martyrdom' and of 'suffering "for the truth's sake,"' remarking upon both the detrimental effects and the needlessness of seeking to 'pose as protectors of truth upon earth.' It is significant, however, that he immediately adds: ' — as though "the truth" were such a weak and incompetent creature as to require protectors' (*BGE* 25). And neither of these cautions, nor yet again the employment of 'masks and subtlety' he here also recommends and himself frequently practices, signals any abandonment of his commitment to 'truthfulness,' or of the idea of a higher sort of 'truth' and superior form of 'knowledge' than those encountered elsewhere. On the contrary, he clearly means them to be reckoned among the 'manifold conditions' of the kind of thinking he associates with the attainment of such truth and knowledge.

XV

How, for Nietzsche, are these to be conceived? Very generally put, 'truth' here is to be understood as a matter of the *aptness* of a characterization in relation to that which it characterizes; and 'knowledge' is conceived in terms of the interpreting of something in a manner that does *justice* to it. Characterizations, like the metaphors employed in giving them, may be more or less (or not at all) apt. The justice done by interpretations to that which is interpreted may likewise vary greatly. On the other hand, there is no question of an exact correspondence in the case of the former, or of certainty and finality in the case of the latter. Some characteristizations may be seen to be inappropriate, and some interpretations found misguided, while others may be accorded superiority in relation to various alternatives; but in both cases the possibility can never be ruled out of further alternatives which might be superior in aptness and justice to them. While such superiority may be genuine, moreover, there is and can be no general set of rules for achieving it, or of criteria for assessing it. The idea of a rigorous decision-procedure has no place here, any more than it has in those disciplines dealing with human history, culture, art and literature, as well as the enterprise of psychology as Nietzsche understands it. Indeed, he regards the cases of these forms of inquiry as highly instructive in this matter, and is in effect extrapolating from them.

In conceiving of 'truth' and 'knowledge' along these lines, Nietzsche remains committed to the idea that they have a 'perspectival' character even here. He does not take this to be fatal to their epistemic significance; but he does consider it to affect their status. The language in which any state of affairs is characterized, he stresses, however apt the characterization may be, is never immaculately conceived. It always bears the stamp of human invention, whether it is of our own devising as conceptual innovators or originates in that more ancient and impersonal legislation through which words have acquired their conventional meanings. Indeed, what makes a characterization apt is not simply the relation of the proposition in question to the state of affairs to which it pertains, but also its relation to a specific sort of linguistic sensibility. The latter, in fact, is a condition of the very possibility of its aptness. The aptness of a metaphor in ordinary discourse obviously depends in no small measure upon its resonance for a group of users of a language, in abstraction from which its meaning is altered and impoverished. Its ability to articulate and convey something about that which is spoken of is a function of the exploitability of associations they are capable of appreciating; and this presupposes the existence or establishment of a discursive context or perspective.

It is no less important to observe, however, that this does not preclude the possibility of significant assertion by means of metaphor, or place all metaphors which might be used in some connection on an equal footing. Rather, it serves to render such assertion possible, and allows one to go on to consider the aptness of some metaphors relative to others, at which point it is their relative capacity to illuminate the state of affairs under consideration that becomes controlling. And the situation in which the philosopher finds himself, with respect to the basic status of the concepts figuring in the sorts of substantive assertion he may make and his task in arriving at them, is taken by Nietzsche to be similar. As was earlier observed, he urges that philosophers 'must no longer accept concepts as a gift, not merely purify and polish them, but first *make* and *create* them, present them and make them convincing' (*WP* 412). And what is at stake here is 'truth,' understood not merely in terms of useful fiction or inescapable illusion, but rather as a matter of the aptness of characterizations of what obtains and transpires.

Knowing likewise for Nietzsche is always and inescapably a perspectival knowing, because it involves a process of interpreting on the part of creatures whose relations to that which they interpret affect their interpretations — which relations are conditioned by their constitutions, histories and circumstances. We are not (and cannot transform ourselves into) pure spectators of all time and existence, whose apprehension would be independent of and uninfluenced by anything other than the nature of that which is contemplated. Indeed, even if we could, there would be much about our existence as human beings and the world of which our lives are a part which would escape our grasp, since the human relations which are largely or partially constitutive of their reality would become opaque to us. Nietzsche considers it an error to suppose that even if it were possible, a non-perspectival contemplation of things would yield a fuller and deeper comprehension of them than may be attained through perspectival interpretations of them. For he contends that the former would fail to capture anything of them, lacking any relation to them; whereas the latter affords at least the possibility of enabling something of them to be discerned. Their reality, on his view, is a relational affair; and their comprehension is possible, and indeed may meaningfully be spoken of, only by means and in terms of the adoption of standpoints attuned to the sorts of relations constitutive of them.

As shall be seen in the following chapter, Nietzsche rejects the notion that 'a thing freed from all relationships would still be a thing' (*WP* 560). '"Things that have a constitution in themselves,"' he writes, is 'a dogmatic idea with which one must break absolutely' (*WP* 559). This view has important implications for the nature and possibility of knowledge, as he indicates when he says: 'A thing would be defined once all creatures had asked "what is that?" and had answered their question' (*WP* 556). The possibility of differing perspectives, and the fact that 'coming to know. . .is always "placing oneself in a conditional relation to something"' (*WP* 555), take on a significance they might not have been suspected to have, if it is the case that things have no constitution other than that with which they are relationally endowed. For our multiply perspectival access to things and the world then turns out to accord with their fundamental character, and to be a condition of the possibility of − and a means of arriving at − a relatively comprehensive interpretation of them that would do something approaching justice to them. If the nature of something is a function of the various ways in which it admits of being encountered and the forms of interaction into which it is capable of entering, and if these are discernable only from a variety of specific standpoints, then to the extent (and only to the extent) that one is capable of making the appropriate shifts of perspective, that nature becomes accessible to one.

The unavoidability of 'placing oneself in a conditional relation to something' upon which Nietzsche insists in connection with 'coming to know,' therefore, does not deprive the latter notion of all save merely nominal application. Rather, it characterizes what 'coming to know' involves − 'it is under all circumstances establishing, denoting, and making conscious of conditions' − even as it rules out 'the fable of knowledge' conceived in terms of the 'unconditioned' apprehension of 'what is "in-itself"' (*WP* 555). What he understands by 'conditions' here are the 'conditional relations' of which he takes not only our 'coming to know something,' but also what there is to be known, to be a function. And thus what he seeks to do is not merely to lay this fable to rest, but moreover to resurrect the notion of the possibility of knowledge in modified form, as the conditioned apprehension of the conditioned.

XVI

Nietzsche makes much of the point that interpretation generally not only is at once reflective and determinative of the perspectives within and in terms of which we operate as we confront the world, but further is fundamentally bound up with our 'affects' (and so, ultimately, with the 'physiological conditions' in which they are held to be rooted). 'One may not ask: "who then interprets?"' he writes; 'for interpretation itself is a form of the will to power, exists (but not as a "being" but as a process, a becoming) as an affect' (*WP* 556). Or, if one *does* pose the question 'Who interprets?' his answer is: 'Our affects' (*WP* 254). We commonly attribute interpretations, as we attribute thoughts and intentions, to persons; and on a certain level of description, this is a reasonable and convenient way of speaking. But the postulation of a thinking subject whose nature it is to do such things as think, will, and interpret is for Nietzsche a piece of philosophical mythology. Thus he writes: 'Is it necessary to posit an interpreter behind the interpretation? Even this is invention, hypothesis.' It is a notion on a par with the idea of the 'subject,' which 'is not something given, it is something added and invented and projected behind what there is.' In place of this referring of interpretations to any such entity, he holds it to be 'our needs that interpret the world; our drives and their For and Against.' And he suggests that 'each one has its perspective that it would like to compel all the other drives to accept as a norm' (*WP* 481).

Here again, however, rather than taking this to rule out the possibility of the achievement of any sort of comprehension that might merit the name of 'knowledge,' Nietzsche draws the opposite conclusion, even while insisting upon the importance of not overestimating or misconstruing any results achieved or achievable along these lines. The very multiplicity and mutability of these 'drives' that is characteristic of our human constitution, on his view, lends itself to this purpose. Thus while suggesting that it may in a sense be considered to reflect a 'diseased condition in man, in contrast to animals in which existing instincts answer to quite definite tasks,' he goes on to observe: 'This contradictory creature has in its nature, however, a great method of acquiring knowledge: he feels many pros and cons, he raises himself to justice' (*WP* 259).

In short, Nietzsche considers it at least to be *possible* for us to 'raise ourselves to justice' in our thinking, or at any rate to something approaching 'justice,' through the development of more sophisticated interpretations, by drawing upon and yet transcending the narrower and more distorting perspectives attained under the influence of the various interpretation-engendering 'drives' at work within us. The latter may themselves be indifferent to such 'justice,' and indeed may perpetrate 'injustices' to the extent that they individually dominate our thinking. Collectively, however, they constitute the means of compensating for their particular 'injustices' sufficiently to bring the attainment of 'justice' and the acquisition of 'knowledge' so understood within the realm of possibility.

In a similar vein, addressing himself to the issue of 'the meaning of knowing' and reflecting upon Spinoza's view of it (*'Non ridere, non lugere, neque detestari, sed intelligere!'*), Nietzsche suggests that 'this *intelligere*' is ultimately a 'result of the different and mutually opposed desires' of the sort from which it is here distinguished. It *is* to be distinguished from them; but it does not develop and proceed entirely independently of them, for it is ultimately 'only *a certain behavior of the instincts toward one another*.' They are the conditions of its possibility: 'Before knowledge is possible each of these instincts must first have presented its one-sided view of the thing or event,' he writes; 'after this comes the fight of these one-sided views, and occasionally this results in a mean,' having the character of 'a kind of justice and contract' (*GS* 333). The qualification 'occasionally' is not to be overlooked; Nietzsche does not suppose that such 'justice' invariably arises. But it can do so; and when it does, it constitutes the attainment of an understanding transcending the 'one-sided views' of which he speaks which warrants designation as 'knowledge.'

It will be observed that the particular 'instincts' indicated here form a very short list, and stand at some remove from the sorts of things to which he often means to refer when he employs this and other such expressions. The shortness of the list is owing merely to the circumstance that these are the only ones of which mention is made in the line from Spinoza which is Nietzsche's point of departure. Elsewhere he mentions others, which, when they are 'integrated' and 'hold each other in check,' yield results very different from those in which they tend to issue: 'the impulse to doubt, to negate, to wait, to collect, to dissolve.' And these too are only cited as 'examples' (*GS* 113).

The fact that these are the sorts of things Nietzsche specifies, however, when he elaborates upon his contention that it is our 'drives' or 'affects' which are to be regarded as 'interpreting' here as well as in other cases in human life, is of considerable importance. For it shows that he does not mean that all interpretations are the immediate issue of rudimentary 'drives' linked directly to the basic constitutions and conditions of preservation and growth of those who develop and adhere to them. The kinds of 'impulses' he mentions may be reckoned ramifications and developments of the latter rather than dispositions of an altogether different origin. His insistence upon the rootedness of the former in the latter, however, is balanced by his recognition that the tendencies in terms of which our various particular patterns of thought and action are to be understood generally represent very considerable refinements and modifications of our more basic 'drives.' Thus he makes much of what he terms the 'spiritualization' of the latter, taking it to be crucial to our ability to turn to account our various forms of perspectival access to the world, and so to be able to lay legitimate claim to a measure of justice in its interpretation.

In this connection, I would refer again to an important passage from the *Genealogy*, in which Nietzsche writes: 'There is *only* a perspective seeing, *only* a perspective "knowing."' This is held to be owing to the impossibility of 'an eye turned in no particular direction, in which the active and interpreting forces, through which alone seeing becomes seeing *something*, are supposed to be lacking.' What he takes to follow, however, is not only the untenability of the idea of a 'pure knowing subject' and of 'knowledge in itself,' but also something more positive: 'the *more* affects we allow to speak about one thing, the more complete will our "concept" of this thing, our "objectivity" be.' By learning 'to see differently' and 'to *want* to see differently,' the necessary 'discipline and preparation of the intellect for its future "objectivity"' are acquired. This 'objectivity,' he continues, is to be understood as 'the ability to *control* one's Pro and Con and to dispose of them, so that one knows how to employ a *variety* of perspectives and affective interpretations in the service of knowledge.' It is 'precisely because we seek knowledge' that Nietzsche draws attention to the possibility of such 'objectivity' and to the role played by our 'affects' in its achievement (*GM* III:12).

One condition of the possibility of the higher-order 'knowledge' of which he here speaks is that there is something to be thus 'known,' which may or may not be comprehended at all adequately. And it should be obvious that he could not express himself as he does here (and frequently elsewhere) if he did not consider this condition to be satisfied, notwithstanding his repudiation of 'things-in-themselves,' 'true being,' and other such standard items of ontological inventories. Where both the world and life generally and also our human existence and nature are concerned, he supposes that there obtain and occur at least some things with respect to which it is meaningful to speak of the attainability of comprehension.

Another condition of the possibility of such 'knowledge' is that we be able to acquire the 'ability' Nietzsche here mentions, of 'knowing how to employ' certain resources in such a way that they serve its attainment. And here again, he clearly considers this condition to be at least satisfiable, even if not easily satisfied. Its satisfaction may be thought of as involving the achievement of skill at the art of interpretation, and indeed, at a special form of this art. Its immediate text, as it were, is the issue of various more narrowly perspectival and strongly conditioned ways of apprehending things (which themselves are interpretive rather than transparently revelatory). The greater this skill, and the richer the resources upon which it is able to draw and operate, the better are the prospects of its doing justice to that with which it is thereby brought into relations of both perspectival access and mediation.

Our capacity to do justice to things, moreover, will inevitably vary not only with the skill thus acquired, but also with the extent to which the perspectives we are capable of adopting embrace the range of relations constitutive of their reality. What we have made, therefore, and what we have brought about, and also what we have come to be, are for this reason more tractable matters of investigation than those where our involvement is more marginal. Even in cases of the latter sort, however, we are not entirely at a loss as long as all access capable of yielding some acquaintance is not precluded. Regardless of 'how far the perspective character of existence extends' (GS 374), our own existence and activity are not something entirely distinct from life and the world 'in themselves,' but rather instantiate and are of a piece with them. And this means that we are not debarred in principle from ever achieving any comprehension of the character of the reality they and we comprise.

XVII

Nietzsche makes a significant point in this general connection, by implication, in remarking that 'a "scientific" estimation of music'

105

restricted to 'how much of it could be counted, calculated, and expressed in formulas' would be 'absurd,' in that 'nothing, really nothing of what is "music" in it' would thereby be 'comprehended, understood, grasped' (*GS* 373). For it follows that he takes it to be possible, at least in this sort of case, to achieve a superior comprehension and estimation of that which is under consideration than this, by approaching it differently. And the fact that he cites this example in the context of a criticism of the adequacy of 'a "scientific" interpretation of the world' indicates that he takes something comparable to be possible in other sorts of cases as well. So he proclaims 'an interpretation that permits counting, calculating, weighing, seeing and touching and nothing more' to be 'a crudity and naiveté' approaching 'idiocy' (*GS* 373). And in doing so he clearly has in mind the possibility of improvements upon it. While remaining 'interpretations,' they would not merely be different, but moreover would be less 'naive' and superficial, and more adequate to their objects — whether these be pieces of music, human existence, or 'the world' more generally.

It is further instructive to consider certain remarks Nietzsche makes in connection with his contention that 'psychology is now again the path to the fundamental problems.' He calls upon others to join him in daring 'to descend into the depths,' and to explore the 'immense and almost new domain of dangerous insights' that is opened up when 'the power of moral prejudices' (which has 'operated in an injurious, inhibiting, blinding, and distorting manner' in previous interpretations of 'the spiritual world') is overcome. And he maintains that, if one who follows this course thus 'makes a sacrifice' of a hard and painful sort, 'it is *not* the *sacrifizio dell'intelletto*, on the contrary!' It is admittedly interpretation on his part to suggest that the 'spiritual world' which thus comes under scrutiny is to be construed in terms of 'the doctrine of the will to power'; and the same applies with respect to the 'hypotheses' he advances pertaining to various human phenomena and to 'the general economy of life' and its 'enhancement.' But it should be evident that he takes there to be features of human life calling for investigation and admitting of being both misconstrued and apprehended. And he clearly considers it to be not only legitimate but also important to distinguish between interpretations of them which are distorted by 'prejudices,' and others informed by 'insights' into them (*BGE* 23). It is not too much to speak of the attainment of knowledge in the latter case, notwithstanding the avowedly interpretive character of the enterprise and its issue. Indeed, Nietzsche's repeated references to himself as a 'man of knowledge' have no more common application than in this context, in connection with such 'self-interpretation.'

This moreover does not represent the limit of the domain in which he supposes it to be possible to develop interpretations that are more than merely fictitious (though possibly useful and life-enhancing) schematizations read into what obtains and transpires. As has been observed, he also takes it to be within our power to address ourselves to how matters stand with respect to life and the world more generally, and to develop accounts of them to which greater epistemic significance may be accorded. He styles himself 'an old philologist who cannot desist from the malice of putting his finger on bad modes of interpretation,' scientific as well as religious and metaphysical. And he further ventures to explore and devise alternatives, supposing it to be possible to improve upon such 'bad modes of interpretation'; even though he recognizes that whatever one might come up with would still be 'only interpretation' (*BGE* 22).

What goes on in the world may be easily and generally mis-interpreted, in ways which are more or less wide of the mark. Nietzsche is persuaded, however, that this world and what goes on in it have various characteristics in relation to which this may meaningfully be said — and what is more, that it is possible for us, even within the inescapable limits of our human perspective, to achieve some insight into them and interpret them in a manner more appropriate to them. So, for example, addressing himself to 'physicists' wedded to an interpretation involving the idea of 'nature's conformity to law,' he suggests that one 'could read out of the same "nature," and with regard to the same phenomena, rather the tyrannically inconsiderate and relentless enforcement of claims of power'; and thus one could (as he does) 'end by asserting the same about the world as you do, namely that it has a "necessary" and "calculable" course, *not* because laws obtain in it, but because they are absolutely *lacking*, and every power draws its ultimate consequences at every moment' (*BGE* 22). In both cases one is 'interpreting' what goes on in the world; but it does not follow that both 'modes of interpretation' have the same epistemic worth, or that it is meaningless to raise the question of what epistemic worth each has.

In speaking of 'bad modes of interpretation,' Nietzsche is posing this question and indicating his acceptance of the legitimacy and possibility of differentially answering it in particular cases. 'Bad modes of interpretation' might of course be worth retaining, if they prove to be of such convenience, utility, or other such practical value in certain contexts that they thereby more than

107

compensate for their want of fundamental epistemic significance. But this is a separate matter. If it were not possible for interpretations to be devised for which anything more could be said (either because, where life and the world are concerned, there were nothing to be grasped, or because we lacked any form of access to them), this would indeed be the only sort of thing to consider. No such interpretation would or could then have any positive epistemic significance. However we might interpret the world, there would be nothing about it of which any interpretation of it could ever be the comprehension.

But this, for Nietzsche, is not the case. On the contrary, he suggests that there are conditions under which one might 'gain the right' not only to deny the soundness of various characterizations of life and the world, but also to advance certain alternative hypotheses with respect to them, and indeed to regard these hypotheses as more or less justified and just, and so to allow for the attainability of a form of comprehension amounting to knowledge accordingly conceived (cf. *BGE* 36). And he likewise allows for the possibility of 'truth' construed in terms of the aptness of characterizations of states of affairs in the world, thereby preserving something of the basic idea underlying the correspondence account of truth. There may not be a great deal about the world (and ourselves) that admits of such comprehension and characterization; but that remains to be considered, and in any event is a different issue.

XVIII

One reason why Nietzsche has often been misunderstood on this matter relates to his repeated insistence that truth is something (requiring to be) *created*. It is supposed that this commits him to the rejection of the idea that truth has anything to do with an adequacy relation of the sort indicated, since it seems to reduce the establishment of truth to mere fabrication and invention. This view is mistaken; his actual position is a rather more complicated (and certainly more interesting) one. Before undertaking to correct this mistaken impression, however, I shall consider some of the points he makes in this connection which take him some distance in this direction.

Nietzsche does view most of what generally passes for 'truth' in something like this light, as has been seen in dealing with his various first-order truth-analyses. Moreover, if, as he maintains, 'it is enough to create new names and estimations and probabilities in order to create in the long run new "things"' (*GS* 58), then by the same token this process also suffices for the 'creation' of 'new truths' pertaining to the 'new "things"' thereby constituted. A further sort of case in point is indicated when he writes: 'Many ideas have come into the world as errors and fantasies, but have become truths, because men subsequently have provided them with a genuine foundation' (*HH* II:190). Here again the 'truths' in question may be considered to have been 'created,' coming to count as 'truths' precisely insofar as it has come about (or has been brought about) that there are events and situations answering to them.

In cases of these sorts, it may be noted, 'truth' has the sense of an adequacy-relation between propositions or concepts and states of affairs; and Nietzsche's insistence upon the 'created' character of such 'truths,' far from ruling out its construal in this manner, actually is but a corollary of the analysis of the status and circumstances of establishment of the states of affairs to which they pertain. To the extent that the world with which we deal and of which we are a part, in its particular features and contents, is the product of our transforming, constituting, fixing activity, 'truth' with respect to it (along with it itself) is our doing, and not merely something we may or may not discover. We bring it into existence as we fashion the reality we encounter and are in a determinate manner. We thus establish the conditions of the possibility of truth as an adequacy-relation, and in doing so 'create' it. It is at least in part along these lines that Nietzsche would appear to be thinking when he writes:

> 'Truth' is therefore not something there, that might be found or discovered — but something that must be created and that gives a name to a process, or rather to a will to overcome that has in itself no end — introducing truth, as a *processus in infinitum*, an active determining — not a becoming-conscious of something that is in itself firm and determined (*WP* 552).

But he has something more in mind as well, in stressing the created and creative character of 'truth' not only within such narrower contexts but also on the broader and higher plane of philosophical inquiry. This may be seen in his frequent recurrence to the idea that 'genuine philosophers' are not mere 'philosophical laborers,' content to operate with previously established concepts (*BGE* 211); and that they further are not simply 'critics,' who restrict themselves to the analysis and critique of concepts employed and views advanced by others (*BGE* 210). For both stop short of the *constructive* enterprise of reinterpretation and revaluation, which for him is the task of the genuine philosopher.

He is far from thinking that 'truth' here ceases to be a matter of any concern for such a philosopher. On the contrary, as has been observed, he maintains that 'these coming philosophers' are to be thought of as 'new friends of "truth"' (*BGE* 43). 'Truth' of the sort that concerns them is an adequacy-relation between characterizations of reality and the character of that reality on a more fundamental level than others are willing and able to reach. But in this case too it remains something requiring to be 'created' in an important sense, rather as even the most apt metaphor owes its existence to a creative act of formulation and is not merely read off from that to which it refers.

Nietzsche's point here is that all such truths are characterizations of states of affairs rather than the latter themselves; and that the former are not mental or linguistic copies of the latter, however well they convey something of their character. Rather, they are constructions in the different medium of concepts, which owe their status as much to the nature of the medium and what is done in and with it as to the states of affairs addressed. And just as even the most commonplace of characterizations (along with language itself) must be acknowledged to be human creations, any novel characterization departing from them and any endowment of terms with modified meanings and new uses is likewise creative. A philosopher who has something different to say, therefore, and who in saying it appropriates, adapts, extends and adds to existing forms of expression, is necessarily a 'creator' insofar as he does so. And such 'creativity,' far from being incompatible with the attainment and extension of comprehension, is indispensible to this end.

To be sure, not all conceptual and interpretive creativity issues in characterizations contrasting favorably with those of longstanding currency. On the contrary, this may be the exception rather than the rule. The history of philosophy, on Nietzsche's view, is replete with examples of failed attempts to devise interpretations doing more justice to things and events than is done by means of ordinary thought and language, even though their originality must often be conceded. But the frequent failure of such attempts does not warrant the conclusion that all efforts along these lines were better eschewed, in favor either of strict fidelity to established modes of conceptualization and expression, or of noncommittal analysis of them. And to ignore the element of creativity involved in all philosophical endeavor of an interpretive nature that ventures beyond these sterile limits is to fail to appreciate one of the essential conditions of the possibility of any enlargement of the bounds of truth and knowledge.

Another of Nietzsche's points with respect to truth and

110

knowledge, which is just as easily and commonly misunderstood, pertains to their inescapably 'human' character. As has been seen, he considers it meaningless (or at any rate profoundly misguided) to suppose that there is or could be any 'truth in itself' and 'knowledge in itself,' maintaining that it is meaningful to speak of 'truth' and 'knowledge' only in relation to the interpretive articulation of states of affairs in which we ourselves are implicated, by means of concepts of our devising. On his view all apprehending (whether or not it amounts to anything approaching genuine comprehension) involves interpreting; and 'truth' is a property which properly can be predicable of nothing other than propositions the assertability of which is warranted with reference to some interpretation. If this is so, and since moreover there are no 'interpretations in themselves' but rather only interpretations existing as a result of encounters on the part of creatures like ourselves with their environing world, it follows that truth and knowledge can exist only for interpreters. And more specifically, they can exist at all for us only as 'human truth' and 'human knowledge,' inseparable from the conditions and character of our human existence and interpretive situation.

It does not follow, however, that they are thereby radically invalidated in principle. On the contrary, it is a condition of the very possibility of truth and knowledge that there exist creatures having access to the world and with the capacity and means to address themselves to it. Indeed, there can be truth and knowledge only where there exists some medium in which states of affairs can be given expression; and in the absence of something on the order of human language and thought, this requirement would not be satisfied. Where nothing can be put into words because there is no such expressive medium at hand, and also in abstraction from the establishment and employment of any such interpretive schematization, the notions of truth and error, and of knowledge and ignorance, have no application. If the interpretive process renders everything that might be said or thought about the world by us a 'human' rather than absolute and unconditioned formulation, it also is our means of entry with respect to it.

In short, truth and knowledge may be held to be importantly 'human' without thereby being reduced completely to the *merely* human and denied all larger epistemic significance. It is simply a feature of what truth and knowledge *are* that they do not and cannot exist concretely except as bound up with some interpretive schematization of the sort exemplified by various human languages and conceptual schemes. If 'words lie in our way,' as Nietzsche suggests, so that we are constantly 'stumbling over

111

them' in every domain of inquiry (*D* 47), it also is only through the use of this medium that these obstacles to comprehension can be discovered and removed, and comprehension itself enhanced.

XIX

Truth and knowledge for Nietzsche must be dealt with together on this level of consideration; for while truth here may be given its third-order analysis in terms of a relative adequacy-relation between characterizations and states of affairs, the aptness of the former with respect to the latter is inseparable from the interpretation drawn upon in formulating it, and thus from what Nietzsche takes knowledge to involve. With this understood, however, I shall focus for the moment upon the former in abstraction from the latter, in order to bring out certain points relating to his third-order analysis of truth.

As has just been indicated, the requirement of some sort of relation of relative adequacy of something asserted of the world (our existence included) with respect to what happens to obtain and transpire in it is here regarded as essential. The basic consideration is that of how matters actually stand with the world and human life — whether there is anything in or about them which might and does answer to some assertion. And it is with this sort of consideration and conception of truth in mind that Nietzsche pronounces most of what we say and think to be 'false,' and the ways in which we tend to speak and think to be large-scale falsifications. Wherever reference is made to entities, properties and processes which owe their identity and reality principally or entirely to the manner in which we schematize the world, what is said is without positive truth-value of this sort; even though it may count as 'true' in terms of the appropriate criteria as brought out by first- and second-order analysis. And it acquires *negative* truth-value on this level of consideration (although its first- and second-order standing is not thereby affected) if it is elevated from its place within some domain of discourse and human experience, and is advanced to candidacy for inclusion in an account of the way the world is. It may apply well enough to what Nietzsche calls 'the world that concerns us,' which is real enough for what it is; but the reality of this 'world' is basically an experiential affair, the issue of our long-term collective encounter and interaction with an underlying reality with which it is far from agreeing.

Nietzsche thus takes virtually all of 'man's truths,' and even most 'truths' of science, to be fundamentally erroneous, in that they are cast in terms of notions which he considers to be subverted by a radical failure of reference when viewed in this larger context. His grounds for supposing this to be so in particular cases are not presently the issue. (They shall be considered subsequently.) What requires to be grasped here is the conception of 'truth' with which he is operating in arriving at this assessment of them, and which he is prepared to apply in connection with certain alternative characterizations of the world, life, and human existence. And the point of these remarks is that it is a necessary if not sufficient condition of the applicability of the notion of 'truth,' on this level of consideration, that anything of which essential mention is made must refer to (or be explicable in terms of) something that is not merely a fiction or peculiarity of the manner in which we may happen to schematize and experience the world, but rather actually is a part or feature of it.

There is more to the matter than this, however; for it is further only if (or to the extent that) the actual constituents or features of life and the world thereby indicated are *appropriately* construed and characterized, on Nietzsche's view, that propositions framed in terms of such notions may be considered to qualify as true. It is this further requirement which the idea of 'aptness' introduced above was meant to capture. What there is and goes on in the world, what life involves in general and in different sorts of cases, and what processes occur and transformations result under various circumstances in human life, are among the things he takes both to be commonly misrepresented, and to admit of more apt and revealing designation and articulation.

The terms of which Nietzsche avails himself in this connection — such as 'force,' 'system,' 'power,' 'master' and 'slave,' 'herd,' 'spirituality,' 'affect' and 'instinct' — are all borrowed from existing forms of discourse. They are transformed and refined in the course of his appropriation and employment of them, however, and are held to serve to bring out something important about the matters indicated. Unquestionably and indeed openly metaphorical at the outset, they are taken to be *illuminating* metaphors, admitting of development into concepts which are appropriate and revealing with respect to various features of the world, life and human existence. Characterizations of the latter cast in terms of them (or in terms of others which might be brought forward and developed in their stead) have as much truth to them as the diagnoses they provide are sound, and the interpretations they express do justice to the matters addressed. The metaphorical use of any such notions, however, will be fruitful in these respects only if it is restrained by what Nietzsche calls 'a

113

fundamental will of knowledge, pointing imperiously into the depths, speaking more and more precisely, demanding greater and greater precision. For this alone is fitting for a philosopher' (*GM* P:2). This is required if the potential for the more discerning articulation of events and states of affairs established by the emergence of language of sufficient richness and flexibility is to be realized.

It may not be possible to formulate any such account of events other than in the artificial medium of concepts; and no account may be free of perspectival distortion, or so exhaustive and accurate that it does not admit of being improved upon, and precludes the possibility of any differing but comparably illuminating alternatives. But Nietzsche does take it to be possible for language to be devised and employed in such a way that it captures and brings out features of what goes on in the world and life, and what human nature and existence involve. It need not invariably merely project artificial and fictitious constructions into them, or simply read out of our experience of them such constructions imposed upon them by the prior operation of our senses and intellect in accordance with their own characteristic structures and requirements.

More specifically, for Nietzsche, the processes they involve, the types of organization and relations to which they give rise, the kinds of development and change they exhibit, and even the basic tendencies at work within them, admit of diagnoses in conceptual formulations expressing something of their character. To be sure, this will be so only if it is the case that their character stands in at least some degree of homology to that of events of which we can and do have experience, and which language provides us means of designating and specifying. This is a condition, however, which he supposes to be satisfied. And if or where it is, then the language whose referential capacity in relation to such events is already established may be drawn upon, to fashion models and coin metaphors refinable into philosophical concepts and interpretations applicable to the phenomena in question.

Such refinement necessarily involves the generalization of such notions, in a manner required by reflection upon respects in which the homology may be suspected to be limited. Nietzsche's supposition that, while limited, this homology is nonetheless substantial, is of course problematic, as he is well aware. The fundamental homogeneity of all events, however, those constitutive of the basic features of human life included, is something he believes it to be not only reasonable to assume but also unreasonable (in the absence of countervailing evidence) to deny. In any event, its plausibility may be allowed. And this suffices to render coherent the notion of truth under consideration, construed in terms of the aptness of assertions with respect to how matters stand with reality, not merely as it is commonly apprehended in the course of our ordinary experience, but rather as it is more fundamentally constituted.

XX

The *value* of knowledge with respect to how matters thus stand with the world and life and our human existence is once again a separate matter for Nietzsche. It is truths of the sort presently under consideration that he has in mind, however, when he speaks of the possibility that 'something might be true while being harmful and dangerous to the highest degree' (*BGE* 39). And it is only in light of the third-order analysis of truth along the lines indicated above, which departs from and supersedes the first- and second-order analyses considered previously, that sense can be made of his frequent observations to this effect. The same holds with respect to the aspect which truths of this sort may be found to bear. They may be felt to be exhilarating, or harsh and ugly, or merely uninteresting, or all of these at different times and for different inquirers, depending on their states of mind, their fortitude and their chosen tasks; but this does not affect their nature and content, let alone their possibility. Thus Nietzsche speaks approvingly of those who are prepared 'to sacrifice all desirability to truth, *every* truth, even plain, harsh, ugly, repellent, unchristian, immoral truth. — For such truths do exist' (*GM* I:1). And he contends that the philosophers of the future he envisions, in whom 'the will to truth thus gains self-consciousness' and brooks no compromise with wishful thinking and 'moral' prejudice (*GM* III:27), 'will not dally with "truth" to be "pleased" or "elevated" or "inspired" by her. On the contrary, they will have little faith that *truth* of all things should be accompanied by such amusements for our feelings' (*BGE* 154).

The work in which the latter passage occurs opens with the famous rhetorical question: 'Supposing truth is a woman — what then?' The point Nietzsche seeks to make here is that 'truth' is something requiring to be *won*, by means quite other than the 'awkward and very improper methods' of those who think it something needing only to be seized to be possessed (or already theirs as a kind of gift). So he observes that 'what is certain is that she has not allowed herself to be won' by philosophical 'dogmatists' thus blundering and misguided (*BGE* P). He obviously

115

does not thereby mean to suggest that there is nothing deserving of the name that could in some different fashion be 'won,' nor yet again that what might be 'won' is in the end nothing more than a fantasized product of desire and imagination, the 'winning' of which is mere reappropriation. The force of his remarks is rather that, if we modify both our understanding of the status of the sort of 'truth' that is a possibility (along the lines of his third-order analysis) and our approach to its establishment (in accordance with his associated conception of knowing and coming to know), it is indeed something that may be won; even if it cannot be completely or entirely securely possessed, remains mutable and ambiguous in various respects, and will always be receptive to different, more attentive and persuasive suitors.

The road to knowledge for Nietzsche is no royal one, leading directly and easily to its goal by means of mechanical procedures, immediate intuitions or revelations. Indeed, it is not even a single road, but rather a variety of circuitous paths, enabling one to reach various vantage points from which different aspects of life and the world become discernable. Scientific inquiry, historical and genealogical investigation, psychological analysis, and reflection upon the character of differing forms of activity we may observe and experience all figure prominently among them. Each can afford some insight at certain junctures, and complements while informing the interpretation of the issue of the rest. The knowledge that is thereby attainable can only be 'discovered little by little, gradually and piecemeal.' And the same applies with respect to the emergence of 'the different means of knowledge,' which are manifold: 'imagination, inspiration, abstraction, de-sensualization, invention, educated guessing, induction, dialectic, deduction, criticism, material-collecting, impersonal thinking, contemplativeness, the ability to view things comprehensively, and not least, justice and love toward everything there is,' all play a part in it (D 43).

This relatively early statement of the 'many powers' needed by 'the thinker' anticipates Nietzsche's conception of philosophical thought as *fröhliche Wissenschaft* — an experimental, tentative and interpretive kind of thinking, 'hardened in the discipline of science' (BGE 230) and yet emancipated from the narrowness of its perspective; historically and linguistically informed, but resistant to longstanding intellectual prejudices and 'the seduction of words.' Creative and venturesome in the development of concepts and hypotheses, it is at the same time guided by the 'conscience of method,' which 'must be essentially economy of principles' (BGE 13). Prepared to avail itself of the results of any

116

narrower mode of inquiry capable of shedding light on matters to be dealt with, it is heedless of 'the siren songs of old metaphysical bird catchers.' (*BGE* 230). And, not least, it is characterized by 'that genuinely philosophical combination. . .of a bold and exuberant spirituality that runs *presto* and a dialectical severity and necessity that takes no false step' (*BGE* 213).

What may be attained thereby might not measure up to certain standards of knowledge reflecting the convictions or longings of some philosophers, or satisfy the criteria derived by others from their consideration of the way the notion functions in ordinary language or special domains of discourse and inquiry. Nietzsche attaches great importance to its attainment, however, even if not supreme importance or intrinsic value, as both his own dedication and his repeated accordance of high honors to it attest. And he takes it to surpass anything that might otherwise be achieved, in acuteness, penetration and profundity.

> And knowledge itself: let it be something else for others. . .
> — for me it is a world of dangers and victories in which heroic
> feelings, too, find places to dance and play. '*Life as a means
> to knowledge*' — with this principle in one's heart one can live
> not only boldly but even gaily, and laugh gaily too (*GS* 324).

There is a dialectic here that must be recognized, if Nietzsche is not to be misunderstood. The 'principle' he enunciates is not meant to stand unconditionally, as though knowledge were of intrinsic and supreme importance. Rather, on his view it derives its warrant from the fact that for someone like himself it is a recipe for living 'boldly' and 'gaily,' and so for living as well as it is possible for him to live. The strengthening and enhancement of life, which is what he takes in the final analysis to matter most, is not invariably or exclusively promoted in this particular way. He clearly supposes, however, that it can be.

III

Metaphysical Errors

As was observed in the first chapter, Nietzsche has a good deal to say about previous thinkers and their views, but finds there to be little to be said for them, and indeed is strongly and sweepingly critical of them. This is so not only where issues relating to morality and value are concerned (as shall be seen in due course), but also with respect to the interpretation of the world's and our own fundamental natures. He considers it to be his task not only to attempt to develop accounts of them which do something approaching justice to them, but also to subject the sorts of accounts which have long enjoyed favor to critical analysis, thereby clearing and setting the stage for his own.

Nietzsche focusses his fire in particular upon a variety of metaphysical hypotheses at the heart of certain traditionally and currently prevalent 'world-interpretations,' theological, philosophical, and natural-scientific; and it is with his treatment of them that I shall be concerned in the present chapter, before turning to what he proposes in place of them in the several chapters that follow. It is a crucial if only preliminary part of his philosophical enterprise to lay these interpretations decisively to rest (and not simply to seek to understand how they could have arisen, and to assess their 'human' significance and value for 'life'); and it is therefore of considerable importance to see how he undertakes to dispose of them. I shall begin with his critique of the hypothesis central to the world-interpretation which exercises him perhaps more than any other — the 'God-hypothesis' — and then shall turn to a number of others, which he takes to be rather closely bound up with it or akin to it.

God

I

For Nietzsche, it would be difficult to overestimate the importance (both practical and philosophical) of the question of whether or not there is a God. As he observes, with regard to belief in God, so much 'was built upon this faith, propped up by it,' that its abandonment has consequences beyond 'the multitude's capacity for comprehension' (*GS* 343). One could fairly characterize a good deal of his philosophizing as an attempt to draw out these consequences, for a whole range of issues: to show what positions are thereby rendered untenable, and to proceed to deal with these issues in the manner he takes to be indicated when both the very idea of God and the long 'shadow' cast by this idea over much of our ordinary and traditional philosophical thinking are banished. Thus he begins the third book of *The Gay Science* by remarking that the abandonment of belief in God is only the first step requiring to be taken: 'we still have to vanquish his shadow, too' (*GS* 108), and to carry out the 'de-deification of nature' and proceed to ' "*naturalize*" humanity' (*GS* 109). This lends particular importance to his treatment of the question of the existence of God. It is also of considerable interest in its own right, and in another respect as well: it constitutes a paradigm case of the kind of approach he takes to many other metaphysical hypotheses.

Nietzsche's most famous assertion concerning God is his proclamation that 'God is dead.' The death of God, he maintains, is 'the greatest recent event' (*GS* 343). He refers to this 'event' in a number of places, most notably in the well-known section of this same work bearing the heading 'The Madman':

> Have you not heard of that madman who lit a lantern in the bright morning hours, ran to the market place, and cried incessantly: 'I seek God! I seek God!'. . .'Whither is God?' he cried; 'I will tell you. *We have killed him* — you and I. All of us are his murderers. But how did we do this? . . . Who gave us the sponge to wipe away the entire horizon? . . . God is dead. God remains dead. And we have killed him. . . . There has never been a greater deed; and whoever is born after us — for the sake of this deed he will belong to a higher history than all history hitherto' (*GS* 125).

What Nietzsche is speaking of here, however, is the demise of belief in the existence of God, as a cultural event of profound significance for people who from time immemorial have been accustomed to thinking in terms of a theocentric interpretation of themselves, their lives, values, and reality. It is sometimes suggested that his concern with the question of the existence of God actually went no further than this — with the consequences of the decline of *belief in* a transcendent deity; that whether or not there really *is* a God was an issue of little or no importance to him; and that this is the sort of metaphysical question of which there can be no meaningful discussion, except in terms of the practical consequences of believing one thing or another. This construal of Nietzsche, however, is profoundly mistaken. He *is* very interested in the psychological (and cultural and social) consequences of 'the death of God' in this sense. But he is *also* intent upon establishing that, whatever these consequences might be, and however unprepared most people might be to deal with the fact, the supposition of the existence of a transcendent deity is philosophically unconscionable, and requires to be repudiated.

That Nietzsche denies the existence of a transcendent deity is sometimes questioned in light of the fact that he says such things as: 'The question of the mere "truth" of Christianity — whether in regard to the existence of its God or the historicity of the legend of its origin. . . — is a matter of secondary importance as long as the question of the value of Christian *morality* is not considered' (*WP* 251). And: 'That we find no God — either in history or in nature or behind nature — is not what differentiates *us*, but that we experience what has been revered as God, not as "godlike," but as miserable, as absurd, as harmful, not merely as an error but as a crime *against life*' (*A* 47). It is suggested that passages of this sort show his actual concern to be with something quite different from the question of whether or not God exists — namely, with the problem of what is to be made of the kind of morality and scale of values associated with belief in the existence of such a God.

While it is certainly true that Nietzsche was very much concerned with the latter issue, however, such a concern obviously does not preclude one's taking the question of the existence of God to be of great moment. Moreover, and more importantly, it should be observed that taking the position he does with respect to this morality and scale of values presupposes that one is prepared to answer this question, in the negative. For their tenability and significance obviously cannot be decided independently of it; and they come out very differently for one who thinks that the question is to be (or even might be) answered affirmatively. Nietzsche does say: 'The whole absurd residue of

Christian fable, conceptual cobweb-spinning and theologies does not concern us; it could be a thousand times more absurd and we would not lift a finger against it. But we do combat the ideal that. . .appeals to all the cowardices and vanities of wearied souls' (*WP* 252). Yet he also writes: '*Our* greatest *reproach* against existence was the *existence of God*,' belief in which 'turns life into a monstrosity.' And he goes on to remark that 'our greatest relief' is 'precisely that we have *eliminated*' this idea (*WP* 707).

The supposition of the non-existence of God thus underlies the condemnation of Judeo-Christian morality and values (and others of a like nature developed in association with similar other-worldly religious beliefs) to which Nietzsche gives such vigorous expression. The two issues, on his view, are intimately connected and cannot be completely separated. And the same holds where values are concerned. 'When we thus reject the Christian interpretation, and condemn its "significance" as a forgery, we are immediately confronted in a striking manner with the Schopenhauerian question: *Has existence then a significance at all?*' Nietzsche observes, with reference to Schopenhauer, that 'unconditional and honest atheism is simply the *presupposition* of the way he poses his problem,' asserting it to be 'a triumph achieved finally and with great difficulty by the European conscience, being the most fateful act of two thousand years of discipline for truth that in the end forbids itself the *lie* of faith in God' (*GS* 357). And the same is true for him.

That Nietzsche goes well beyond a cautious agnosticism, and shares Schopenhauer's 'unconditional and honest atheism,' is something he makes quite plain time and again. Thus, for example, he speaks of that which 'led to the positing of "another world" in primeval times' as 'an *error* in the interpretation of certain natural events, a failure of the intellect' (*GS* 151). He suggests that 'God himself' is 'our most enduring lie' (*GS* 344), and that 'God' is 'merely a mistake of man's' (*TI* I:7). He refers to the 'stupendous concept, "God," ' as the 'last, thinnest, and emptiest' of 'the brain afflictions of sick web-spinners,' which 'they place . . . in the beginning, *as* the beginning,' even though in fact it 'comes at the end — unfortunately! for it ought not to come at all!' (*TI* III:4). He regards 'God' and 'souls' as theological inventions which have no 'contact with reality'; they are said to be 'nothing but imaginary *causes*' and 'imaginary *beings*' (*A* 15). 'We deny God,' he states; 'only thereby do we redeem the world' (*TI* VI:8). In short, he takes the position that 'the belief in the Christian God has become unbelievable'; it is a belief we no longer may suppose to be tenable (*GS* 343).

In this light, it becomes clear what Nietzsche means in the passage cited earlier, in which he remarks: 'That we find no God — either in history or in nature or behind nature — is not what differentiates *us*' (*A* 47). His point is that to characterize him as an atheist is *not to say enough*, in that he does not *stop with* a denial of the existence of God, but moreover *goes on* to deny the 'divine' and estimable character of the qualities and traits generally associated with God and godliness.

> Who are we anyway? If we simply called ourselves, using an old expression, godless [ones], or unbelievers, or perhaps immoralists, we do not believe that this would even come close to designating us: *We are all three* in such an advanced stage that one — that you, my curious friends — could never comprehend how we feel at this point. Ours is no longer the bitterness and passion of the person who has torn himself away and still feels compelled to turn his unbelief into a new belief, a purpose, a martyrdom. We have become cold, hard, and tough in the realization that the way of this world is anything but divine. . . . We know it well, the world in which we live is ungodly, immoral, 'inhuman' (*GS* 346; emphasis added).

This passage is of considerable importance. It shows that what Nietzsche takes to set himself apart from atheists generally is not that he wishes to disassociate himself from their denial of the existence of God. Rather, he differs from them in that, while he no less than they makes this denial, he no longer shares the 'bitterness and passion' of those who find the non-existence of God distressing and remain preoccupied with this circumstance. His concern is not merely with the establishment and proclamation of God's non-existence; he is declaring himself to have gone further, addressing himself to the question which now emerges of how we are to reinterpret the world and ourselves and revalue our lives and our possibilities, given that we are no longer to think about them in relation to the existence of a transcendent deity.

II

This only serves to raise the question, however, of whether Nietzsche merely proposes to *assume* the untenability and erroneousness of what might be called 'the God-hypothesis,' or thinks there are compelling reasons for rejecting it. He does list 'No God' as one of his 'presuppositions' (*WP* 595); but this does not settle the matter, since one may obviously treat something

122

one has initially attempted to establish as a 'presupposition' of
one's subsequent reflections. He does seem to feel that it should
no longer be necessary to press the matter, in the sense that he
regards the non-existence of God as settled beyond any reasonable doubt; so he remarks that 'seriousness, the profound self-
overcoming of the spirit, no longer permits anybody *not* to know
about this' (*A* 38). In order not to leave his flank exposed,
however, he addresses himself to the issue on a number of
occasions, setting forth the considerations which he takes to
suffice to lay the 'God-hypothesis' to rest, apart from what he
supposes to be its harmful practical impact on human life.

'We deny God,' Nietzsche states; but for what reasons? 'The
belief in God is overthrown,' he claims; but how? The whole
answer to these questions is not to be found in his answer to his
rhetorical question, 'Why atheism today?', in *Beyond Good and
Evil*, where he writes: ' "The father" in God has been thoroughly
refuted; ditto, "the judge," "the rewarder." Also his "free will" '
(*BGE* 53). This is merely what he says he 'found to be causes for
the decline of European theism, on the basis of a great many
conversations, asking and listening.' The spread of atheism may be
attributable to the fact that such anthropomorphic conceptualizations of God as 'father,' 'judge,' 'rewarder' and the like cannot
survive the critical scrutiny of sophisticated thinkers alert to the
illegitimacy of construing God in human terms, and to the further
fact that for most people belief can no longer be commanded or
inspired in a being who is not thus readily comprehensible in any
such terms. But this does not suffice to show that a suitably de-
anthropomorphized and demythologized God is *no less* 'unbelievable,' and is likewise to be dismissed. The 'causes for the decline
of European theism' are not necessarily good reasons for the
complete rejection of the 'God-hypothesis'; and Nietzsche means
to do more than merely to suggest the untenability of belief in a
God conceived along crudely anthropomorphic lines.

Similarly, he does not wish to rest his case simply upon his
contention, with respect to the explanation of certain sorts of
events often taken to justify belief in the existence of a God, that
' "God" is far too extreme a hypothesis' (*WP* 114). For the fact
that other, less 'extreme' hypotheses are available, by means of
which the same things can be explained, would not by itself
suffice completely to discredit the 'God-hypothesis,' and to
warrant the contention that it is an 'error' and a 'lie' to be 'denied'
and 'repudiated.' A world-interpretation based upon this
hypothesis certainly has the virtues of explanatory power and
simplicity; for there is nothing the existence and occurrence of

which cannot be readily explained on the single assumption of the existence of an omnipotent and omniscient deity. Unless it can be argued that the 'God-hypothesis' is not only unnecessarily extravagant but also in some way fatally suspect, therefore, it can hardly be ruled out as categorically as Nietzsche evidently thinks it can be and intends it to be.

He likewise recognizes that the radical untenability of this hypothesis cannot be established merely by showing (as various earlier philosophers like Hume had attempted to do) that the kinds of arguments for the existence of God which are often taken to have considerable force in fact fail to accomplish their purpose. All that would follow from this is that the existence of God remains an open question; and while agnosticism might thus be indicated, it could not legitimately be inferred that there is no God of the sort these arguments purport to demonstrate. Under such circumstances intellectual integrity might require that one refrain from assenting to the 'God-hypothesis'; but it would also require that one refrain from denying it, unless there is more to be said concerning it than this. If none of the considerations mentioned up to this point are sufficiently relevant and decisive to warrant Nietzsche's claim that 'truthfulness' demands that the existence of God be regarded as a 'malignant counterfeit' (*A* 38), and that 'the falseness and mendaciousness' of world-interpretations based on it be recognized (*WP* 1), therefore, what other sort of consideration does he take to do so?

His thinking along these lines is indicated most clearly and explicitly in a relatively early work (*Dawn*) in a section bearing the heading 'The Historical Refutation as the Decisive One' (*D* 95). This section follows closely upon another in which he poses the rhetorical question: 'What if God were precisely *not* the truth, and precisely this were proven? And if he were but the vanity, the craving for power, the impatience, the terror, and the ecstatic and agonized madness of man?' (*D* 93). The sort of consideration he introduces admittedly does not *logically* rule out the possibility that the 'God-hypothesis' might be correct; but that he takes it to be both relevant and conclusive is evident from his use of the terms 'refutation' and 'decisive' in connection with it (or rather, with the case to be based upon it). He writes:

Previously one sought to prove that there is no God. — Today one shows how the belief that there is a God was able to *arise*, and in what way this belief has acquired its weight and importance: thereby the counter-proof that there is no God becomes superfluous. — When one previously had refuted the

124

proffered 'proofs of the existence of God,' there always remained the doubt whether there might not be better proofs to be discovered than those refuted: at that time atheists did not understand how to go about wiping the slate clean (*D* 95).

Much of what Nietzsche has to say about the notion of God consists precisely in discussion of 'how the belief that there is a God was able to arise, and in what way this belief has acquired its weight and importance.' He explores a number of possible explanations of both the origination and the development and 'weight and importance' of the belief. With regard to the former, he tends to oscillate between two rather different theories, which might be called his 'error' and 'projection' theories, appearing ultimately to favor the second over the first. The first itself has several versions, one of which has already been noted: namely, that the postulation of a God initially was the result of 'an *error* in the interpretation of certain natural events, a failure of the intellect' (*GS* 151). Another focusses upon the misinterpretation of the nature and significance of a different set of phenomena — namely, *linguistic* phenomena — which were thought to evince a rationality and to bespeak rational powers indicating a supernatural origin. It is in this connection that he remarks: ' "Reason" in language — oh, what an old deceptive female she is! I am afraid we are not rid of God because we still have faith in grammar' (*TI* III:5).

The second ('projection') theory also has several variants. According to one of them, 'one sets up one's own type as the measure of value in general; one projects it into things, behind things, behind the fate of things — as God' (*WP* 205). And according to another, each primitive community in *need* of a God to compensate for certain things it lacks is suggested to have '*created* its "God" according to its needs' (*A* 31). Here, therefore, Nietzsche is suggesting that the idea of a God may be the product either of strength or of weakness. Thus, on the one hand, he writes: 'A people that still believes in itself retains its own god. In him it reveres the conditions which let it prevail, its virtues: it projects its pleasure in itself, its feeling of power, into a being to whom one may offer thanks' (*A* 16). And, on the other, he speaks of 'the one God and the one Son of God' as 'both products of *ressentiment*' (*A* 40), suggests that 'one needed God as an unconditional sanction . . . , as a "categorical imperative" ' (*WP* 275), and remarks: 'It is a miserable story: man seeks a principle through which he can despise men — he invents a world so as to be able to slander and bespatter this world: in reality, he reaches every time for nothingness and construes nothingness as "God" ' (*WP* 461).

Nietzsche further contends that the tenacity with which people cling to the idea of God is in no small measure owing to the fact that they have in effect become addicted to it as a means of rendering their lives endurable. He writes: 'How many still reason: "Life would be unbearable if there were no God! . . . . Consequently there must be a God!"' But, he continues, 'the truth of the matter is simply that one who has accustomed himself to such ideas [as that of God] has no wish for a life without them: thus they may be ideas necessary for him and his preservation' (D 90). This tendency, on his view, is by no means characteristic of ordinary people alone. He also sees it at work in the thought of philosophers like Kant, who go to great lengths in an attempt to defend the legitimacy and preserve the cogency of the 'God-hypothesis.' Indeed, he takes it to be an indication of how strongly pronounced it can be among them that even their intelligence and commitment to intellectual integrity do not suffice to counter it. And behind this tendency he discerns a fundamental lack of self-confidence and of the strength to accept and affirm life in this world:

> Christianity, it seems to me, is still needed by most people in
> old Europe even today; therefore it still finds believers. For this
> is how man is: An article of faith could be refuted before him a
> thousand times — if he needed it, he would consider it 'true'
> again and again. . . . [It is an] *instinct of weakness* which, to be
> sure, does not create religions, metaphysical systems, and
> convictions of all kinds but — conserves them (GS 347).

These observations, however, pertain less to the tenability of the 'God-hypothesis' than to its appeal notwithstanding its dubiousness. The detection of such appeal does not count directly against it. It should serve to place one on one's guard, and to arouse one's suspicions about its tenability; but this only helps to set the stage for Nietzsche's 'historical refutation' of this hypothesis, or what might more aptly be termed his 'genealogical subversion' of it. His case against it does not stand or fall with the accuracy of the details of the account he offers of the origin and appeal of the idea; he regards it as sufficient for his purposes if it is conceded that some such specific treatment of these phenomena is capable of explaining them satisfactorily — as historical and psychological phenomena. One might be quite willing to grant this, however, and yet question whether the soundness of this sort of explanation is 'decisive' for the problem at hand. Does it warrant the conclusion that the God-hypothesis is unworthy of belief? Or is Nietzsche guilty of what is sometimes called the 'genetic fallacy' here, in supposing this to be so?

126

III

In undertaking to answer these questions, it should be observed that the reservations philosophers often have with respect to arguments of this sort are generally felt more strongly in some cases than in others. One need only substitute 'ghosts' for 'God,' for example, to appreciate this point. At the same time, it must immediately be granted that the possibility of providing this kind of analysis does not *by itself* suffice to 'wipe the slate clean' where the idea of the existence of an entity of some sort is concerned. If there are *independent* reasons for supposing that there may be something to the idea, then no matter how 'all-too-human' its origins and popular appeal might be, it cannot legitimately be written off straightaway as a fiction unworthy of serious consideration. A genealogical subversion of the sort Nietzsche attempts in connection with the God-hypothesis may fairly be taken to establish a strong presumption against the philosophical tenability of such an idea; but it is a presumption that *can* be overridden, at least in principle. Indeed, it is essential to his own purposes that this is so; for he is quite prepared to grant that an analysis of this sort can be given of any and every conception of what there is that has been or might be developed, his own included.

The crucial question for Nietzsche is that of whether and how any such conception can be resurrected from the ashes to which all of them are initially reduced by the consuming fire of genealogical analysis (and if so, which of them). He finds it inconceivable, however, that any such case might actually be made out in the instance of the idea of the existence of a transcendent deity. And it is because he takes the prospects for the philosophical revival of the 'God-hypothesis' on grounds independent of those tendencies exposed through genealogical analysis to be nil, that he considers this analysis to constitute a 'refutation' of it which is 'decisive.'

The strength of Nietzsche's case may perhaps be more clearly discerned by taking a somewhat different approach to the issue. Philosophy is not simply a matter of ascertaining what can be validly inferred and plausibly concluded from given sets of assumptions and data. It more fundamentally involves the attempt to decide what to make of various claims about the existence, natures, and interrelations of entities and events and states of affairs. At least for the most part, such decisions must be reached without benefit of self-evident first principles or incorrigible facts, and by lines of deliberation lacking the tight rigor of a logical deduction. There is not only a single question to be answered, namely: What can and cannot be proven and disproven beyond the possibility of doubt or challenge, i.e., proven and disproven *strictly speaking*? The answer to *that* question would be: virtually nothing. The more generally applicable and significant methodological question is this: Is there any way of settling the status of various claims clearly and decisively, at least to the extent of being able to distinguish those which deserve serious consideration from those which are completely untenable, given the *in*decisiveness of attempts to do so by rigorous methods?

Methods are useful in a field of inquiry only if they enable one to *settle questions* arising in that field. They are appropriately as well as clearly 'decisive' only if, in addition to enabling one to settle questions, they settle them in a way that is not arbitrary or philosophically suspect. It would be wrong to suppose, however, that a procedure is not reliable if it does not completely preclude the possibility of skeptical challenge either to the acceptability of the considerations upon which it draws or to the validity of the conclusions it yields. What a philosopher ought to be concerned to achieve is not certainty — at least where certainty is unattainable — but rather *understanding*; and understanding is not something the achievement of which depends essentially upon the development of lines of reasoning tight enough to eliminate the slightest possibility of doubt. It suffices for its attainment that one marshal considerations which serve to establish a point beyond a reasonable doubt, and which have sufficient force to warrant the judgment that it cannot *seriously* be disputed.

Nietzsche's claim, in connection with the God-hypothesis, is that the considerations pertaining to it to which he calls attention render it unreasonable to understand the idea of a transcendent deity as anything other than a fiction. And he regards it as frivolous (or worse) if one should continue to insist that it may be more than this merely because it cannot be demonstrated with logical rigor that there is no such entity. The strongest part of the case for the God-hypothesis — that is, the only thing that remains after one recognizes that it cannot be proven or supported by positive argument, and discounts the all-too-human motivations which have led people to embrace it — is the fact that it cannot be disproven. And that is hardly a sufficient reason to dispute the conclusion that it is untenable.

In sum: if we are ever to be able to settle the question of the existence of a transcendent deity, it is essential to begin by recognizing that what we are confronted with is an idea which people have conceived, and a belief which people have held; and that our basic problem is to decide what is to be made of this idea and this belief. The fact that philosophers have long felt themselves obliged to consider some such matter seriously is of no great importance, if considerations come to light which indicate that this fact itself is to be explained by reference to circumstances of an 'all-too-human' nature. Philosophers do not hesitate simply to dismiss the idea of the gods of the early Greeks (not to mention those of more primitive peoples) and the belief in their existence in this way; and it is Nietzsche's contention that nothing beyond what he terms 'the wishes of our reverence' and 'our *needs*' (*GS* 346), along with a reluctance to face up to the practical implications of doing so, stands in the way of our dealing with the idea of and belief in 'our' God in a similar way.

If the idea of God and belief in the existence of God are regarded as phenomena to be explained, genealogical considerations are clearly at least of potential relevance. If these phenomena can be explained in terms of such considerations, and if the only compelling arguments which can be brought forward on behalf of their conceptual and propositional content consist in demonstrations that they can be formulated or reformulated in such a way as to escape both logical and experiential objection, the view that such considerations are actually relevant and indeed of great significance with respect to the issue of their status becomes quite reasonable. It can hardly be denied that at the outset of their career in human thought their status was that of a fiction and a superstition. Modifications of their content serving merely to ward off objections made to various formulations of this content cannot as such be taken to alter this status. Their origins and motivations render them suspect; and the unavailability of any cogent arguments telling in favor of them must be conceded to tell strongly against them in light of this fact.

Nietzsche takes the upshot of these reflections to be that (in a manner of speaking) the 'God-*hypothesis*' is even more emphatically 'dead' (no longer a 'live' issue) than is belief in God as a cultural phenomenon. For while it may be that the non-existence of God has not strictly speaking been *proven*, the existence or non-existence of God is revealed to be a moot point. The very question is shown to fail to survive the preliminary screening which separates issues warranting serious consideration and hypotheses deserving to be reckoned with as genuine possibilities from those which do not. The 'God-hypothesis' requires to be laid to rest, and further debate concerning the existence of an entity of the sort indicated is pointless. And it is pointless not in the sense that the issue is one it is beyond our power to resolve (owing, e.g., to our own cognitive limitations), but rather in the sense that the genuineness of the possibility upon which the issue centers is to be discounted. Once a possibility has been recognized to be spurious, there ceases to be any point in continuing to discuss the issue it poses.

Nietzsche's emphatic repudiation of any suggestion that a transcendent deity does or might exist, and his often belittling and sometimes harsh treatment of those who fail to do likewise, are consequently neither unconsidered nor unreasoned. His claim to have provided an argument that has the force of a 'refutation' may be exaggerated. It is compelling enough, however, to render reasonable his contention that it is 'decisive'; and it must in any event be conceded to come closer to ruling out the God-hypothesis than could be done in any other way.

The soul

IV

Just as 'God,' for Nietzsche, can legitimately be conceived only as referring to something about the world, 'soul,' he has Zarathustra say, 'is only a word for something about the body' (Z I:4). And if there is anything which he takes to come at all close to rivaling the God-hypothesis in the importance of its philosophical and practical consequences — and also in the profundity of its erroneousness — it is what he correspondingly terms the 'soul-hypothesis.' What he has in mind here is the postulation of the existence of a peculiar entity distinguishable and distinct from the living human body, which however is supposed to be (identical with) that 'self' which each of us most fundamentally has or is. As he recognizes, this postulated entity is frequently denoted by a considerable number of names or labels other than the more traditional one of 'soul,' such as 'the ego,' 'the subject,' and also 'the mind' or 'spirit.' It does not greatly matter to him which of them one might prefer to use, what concerns him is the idea of the existence of any such entity.

It is Nietzsche's contention that this hypothesis not merely is sufficiently *problematical* to dictate a prudent suspension of philosophical judgment with respect to its validity, but moreover is quite as *untenable* as the 'God-hypothesis,' and so likewise requires to be abandoned. He is no more a mere skeptic where the existence of a soul-entity is concerned than he is a mere agnostic with reference to the existence of a transcendent deity. This should be clear to anyone who reflects upon the language he repeatedly uses to characterize the status of 'the soul,' 'the subject,' 'the ego,' etc., and of belief in the existence of some 'being' or 'substance' answering to these descriptions. The idea of the 'soul' as 'a "being," ' and as 'a something that is not process but enduring, substance,' he contends, is a piece of 'ancient mythology' (*WP* 631), and a 'fiction' that is 'of no use' (*WP* 480). He writes: 'To know, e.g., that one has a nervous system (− but no "soul" −) is still the privilege of the best informed' (*WP* 229). There are 'no subject "atoms" ' (*WP* 488), on his view. 'The "subject" is only a fiction' (*WP* 390). Again: 'The "subject" is not something given, it is something added and invented and projected behind what there is' (*WP* 481).

Likewise, with respect to 'the ego,' Nietzsche maintains that it 'does not exist at all' (*WP* 370). It is 'a fable, a fiction, a play on words' (*TI* IV: 3), 'only a conceptual synthesis' (*WP* 371); and a form of 'crude fetishism' is held to be involved in the belief that it actually exists and has the character of a 'being' (*TI* III:5). The 'I' too, conceived as a kind of spiritual entity, is termed 'only a synthesis which is *made* by thinking' (*BGE* 54). 'The word "I",' he suggests, is simply a word which 'we set up . . . at the point at which our ignorance begins' (*WP* 482), and which we erroneously take to refer to 'something that thinks' (*WP* 484) and is 'the given cause of thought' (*WP* 483).

These passages and others like them make plain that Nietzsche is a rather enthusiastic participant in what he terms the attempt 'to assassinate the old soul concept' (and its successor notions along with it), to which he considers many modern philosophers to have been party, albeit often unwittingly and even unwillingly (*BGE* 54). 'One must . . . give the finishing stroke,' he says, to that form of 'atomism which Christianity has taught best and longest, the *soul atomism*' (*BGE* 12). He thus is no less intent upon proclaiming 'the death of the soul' than he is upon proclaiming 'the death of God'; and it is no less crucial to his further purposes that he establish the former than it is that he establish the latter. For his own conception of man's nature presupposes that both notions are to be ruled out.

It may be observed, in this connection, that Nietzsche considers these two hypotheses to be intimately connected − the soul-hypothesis leaning upon the God-hypothesis for its philosophical and theological intelligibility, and the God-hypothesis leaning upon the soul-hypothesis for much of its evidence and intuitive appeal (and perhaps even being modeled upon it). He does not argue for the dismissal of the former, however, merely by contending that it presupposes the latter and therefore falls with it. Indeed, one of the more remarkable features of his discussion and critique of the notion of a soul-entity is his willingness to separate the two issues. Even though he does take 'the old soul concept' (and its latter-day variants along with it) to be incoherent once one abandons 'the old God' by reference to whom the purported existence and putative nature of such an entity could be explained, he does not push this line of argument. For he recognizes that the roots of belief in the latter go deeper than this, and thus that it requires to be dealt with in a manner better suited to the exposure of the sources of the idea and of the power it has over our thinking.

Before considering how he seeks to deal with it, however, it would be well to take note of what Nietzsche regards as some of the central features of the soul-hypothesis. On some occasions he stresses what might be called its purported *atomic* (i.e., substantial and unitary) character. Thus, for example, in the passage in which he speaks of giving 'the finishing stroke' to 'soul atomism,' he writes: 'Let it be permitted to designate by this expression the belief which regards the soul as something indestructible, eternal, indivisible, as a monad, as an *atomon*' (*BGE* 12). More generally, he has in mind 'our belief in the "ego" as a substance' (*WP* 487), and the notion of 'the "ego" as a being (— not affected by becoming and development)' (*WP* 517). The substantiality and unity of this entity are thus linked with the idea that it is essentially immutable, and thus 'ahistorical,' in the sense of having the status of something which has not and does not *become* what it is through some sort of contingent developmental process or processes. When Nietzsche states 'No subject "atoms". . . . No "substance" ' (*WP* 488), he is referring to the notion of an immaterial entity conceived as possessing these characteristics in particular.

On other occasions, he has something more in mind as well, calling attention to the imputed *causal* function in terms of which its nature is generally further specified. Thus he speaks of belief in a 'subject-substratum in which every act of thinking . . . has its origin' (*WP* 477), of the 'superstition' that 'the subject "I" ' is required as 'the condition of the predicate "think" ' (*BGE* 17), and of 'the subject' as 'the term for . . . the fiction that many similar states in us are the effect of one substratum' (*WP* 485). ' "The subject",,' he writes, is 'interpreted . . . so that the ego counts as a substance, as the cause of all deeds, as a doer' (*WP* 488). Its postulation involves not merely the sharp distinction of mind from body, but also a 'separation of the "deed" from the "doer" . . ., of the process from a something that is not process but enduring, substance . . . — the attempt to comprehend an event as a sort of shifting and place-changing on the part of a "being," of something constant' (*WP* 631).

Nietzsche's point here is that a certain (problematic) conception of what this entity is taken to *do* looms large in what it is taken to *be*; and that indeed the principal motivation of taking it to *be* something real is that the occurrence of certain sorts of events is construed as the performance of certain sorts of *acts*, which are supposed to be the *doings* of a special type of *doer*. Thinking, perceiving, imagining, knowing, willing, choosing and the like are regarded as activities having their seat and source in 'something that thinks,' etc.; and this 'something' is correspondingly conceived as a being whose nature it is to do such things. Against this view, he maintains that 'there is no such substratum; there is no "being" behind doing, effecting, becoming; "the doer" is merely a fiction added to the deed' (*GM* I:13).

V

The verdict Nietzsche renders with respect to this hypothesis is thus that it 'ought to be expelled from science' (*BGE* 12), and from philosophy as well, as a 'fabrication,' a 'fiction,' an 'illusion,' a piece of 'ancient mythology,' and 'merely a superstition.' The considerations he advances and takes to establish this conclusion are rather similar to those encountered above in connection with the God-hypothesis. While he observes (correctly enough) that 'our conception of the ego does not guarantee any actual unity' (*WP* 635), he recognizes that this does not suffice to make his case. Similarly, it may well be, as he observes, that the word 'I' which we have for so long and so glibly employed conceals more than it reveals, and is merely an opaque cipher introduced 'at the point at which our ignorance begins' (*WP* 482); but this by itself would not warrant the conclusion that the soul-hypothesis is to be rejected, and that interpretations of the 'I' as a 'substance' and a 'subject' are notions which 'have nothing to do with metaphysical truths,' as he maintains (*WP* 513).

Moreover, it does not suffice to establish this conclusion merely to point out that there is nothing we may discover through introspection that is anything like what this entity is supposed to be (as Hume remarks), and that the supposition of the existence of such an entity is not *required* for the explanation of certain features of our experience (*WP* 480). For all that follows from this is simply that the soul-hypothesis is philosophically *problematical*. Something more must be done if it is to be shown to be *untenable*, just as something more would be required to show that it is sound. And the mere absence of arguments strong enough to settle the issue along the latter lines is insufficient by itself to settle it along the former. Here again, his further case against it ultimately comes down primarily to an attack upon it of the sort which in the previous section was called genealogical subversion.

To begin with, Nietzsche suggests, one ought to ask oneself: ' "What gives me the right to speak of an ego, and even of an ego as a cause, and finally of an ego as the cause of thought?" ' (*BGE* 16). And he observes that the fact that doing so is 'habitual,' and may even be practically 'indispensable' for us, 'in itself proves nothing against [the notion's] imaginary origin' (*WP* 483). It may be the case that 'we need "unities" to be able to reckon'; but 'that does not mean we must suppose that such unities exist' (*WP* 635). Indeed, far from establishing our 'right' to affirm the 'soul-hypothesis,' the habituality, utility and indispensability of our belief in something like a 'soul-entity' is taken by Nietzsche to have the opposite significance, and to count *against* our having a philosophical 'right' to do so. For the 'necessity' of a belief not only is quite consistent with its having 'nothing to do with truth' (*WP* 478), but moreover — in light of the ubiquity of 'useful fictions' in human life and thought — creates a kind of *prima facie* presumption against any 'logical-metaphysical postulate' (such as this one) which accords closely with 'the fact of a very strong belief' (*WP* 484). So he remarks that 'it could be useful and important for one's activity to interpret oneself *falsely*' (*WP* 492).

To be sure, this presumption is one which *can* be defeated. It is of some importance, however, that the presumption established at the outset is this one, rather than the contrary one *in favor* of philosophical hypotheses according closely with habitual, useful or indispensable beliefs. For this has the consequence, on Nietzsche's view, that it is not necessary actually to disprove the hypothesis under consideration, or to show it to be internally inconsistent or incoherent, in order to discredit it sufficiently to warrant its dismissal. Rather, he supposes it to suffice for this purpose merely to show that the case for taking the notion of a soul-entity to be merely a useful fiction is strong, and that the considerations which have been taken to support the idea that something of the sort actually exists in point of fact do nothing of the kind.

One of the main points Nietzsche makes in this connection is that the habituality of our belief in a soul-entity is a consequence of what he terms a 'grammatical habit' or 'grammatical custom'; and that the strength of this belief is 'only owing to the seduction of language (and the fundamental errors of reason that are petrified in it) which conceives and misconceives all effects as conditioned by something that causes effects, by a "subject" ' (*GM* I:13). The

134

conclusion 'that when there is thought there has to be something "that thinks," ' he argues, is simply a reflection 'of our grammatical custom that adds a doer to every deed' (*WP* 484). So he writes:

> *It* thinks; but that this 'it' is precisely the famous old 'ego' is
> . . . only a superstition . . . and assuredly not an immediate
> certainty. . . . Even the 'it' contains an *interpretation* of the
> process, and does not belong to the process itself. One infers
> here according to the grammatical habit: 'thinking is an activity;
> every activity requires an agent; consequently − ' (*BGE* 17).

In short, Nietzsche is suggesting that our belief in the existence of a soul-entity, and indeed our very notion of such an entity, is rooted in an interpretation of a certain class of events as a kind of *act*, and of such acts as the operations of a kind of agent. This interpretation has long since 'found a firm form in the functions of language and grammar' (*WP* 631); and as a consequence of this fact it now appears to most people to be something intuitively obvious. It is one of the basic articles of what he terms 'the metaphysics of language' (*TI* III:5). Its centrality to the conceptual scheme built into the very foundations of our language, however, even if conjoined with the assumption that our language serves us quite well for most of the purposes for which we require it, does not warrant the conclusion that the interpretation of these events as 'deeds' of which some sort of soul-entity is the 'doer' is sound. On the contrary:

> The 'spirit,' something that thinks . . . − this conception is
> a second derivative of that false interpretation which believes
> in 'thinking': first an act is imagined which simply does not
> occur, 'thinking,' and secondly a subject-substratum in which
> every act of thinking . . . has its origin (*WP* 477).

Nietzsche is not here denying the existence of all events it is customary to conceive and refer to as mental acts of various kinds (thinking, perceiving, imagining, willing, etc.). Rather, he is maintaining that such events are misinterpreted when they are so conceived. And he is further suggesting that it is this misinterpretation which is at least immediately and most directly responsible for the further erroneous interpretation of the occurrence of these events as involving the existence of a mental entity whose nature it is (at least in part) to perform these putative 'acts.' This two-part interpretation, of course, is for the most part one that people neither work out step by step for themselves, nor even recognize that they employ. They simply assimilate it, as a single general 'doer-deed' model of conceputalization and self-interpretation, along with the structure of the language they learn.

VI

While Nietzsche makes much of considerations of the above sort, notice must be taken of a number of other, rather different points he raises in this same general connection, which he likewise considers to be relevant to both the understanding of the emergence of the soul-hypothesis and its assessment. One is that the emergence of 'belief in the soul' was associated with certain understandable errors made in man's first crude and fumbling attempts at self-understanding. So he surmises that it 'arose from unscientific reflection on . . . the body (something that leaves it. Belief in the truth of dreams −)' (*WP* 491). And in a passage with the heading 'Psychological history of the concept "subject," ' he suggests that primitive reflections upon the body as a ' "whole" construed by the eye,' and upon actions performed by this 'whole,' served to 'awaken the distinction between a deed and a doer; the doer, the cause of the deed, conceived ever more subtly, finally left behind the "subject" ' (*WP* 547). Attempts to understand what is involved in such experiences as seeing only served to reinforce this line of thought: 'To make a kind of perspective in seeing the cause of seeing; that was what happened in the invention of the "subject," the "I"!' (*WP* 548).

Thus this 'invention' is taken by Nietzsche to be the result of 'a simplification with the object of defining the force which posits, invents, thinks, as distinct from all individual positing, inventing, thinking as such . . . − fundamentally, action collectively considered with respect to all anticipated actions' (*WP* 556). Its occurrence may be quite understandable, in view of 'our needs, namely our need for security, for quick understanding on the basis of signs and sounds, for means of abbreviation' (*WP* 513); but it nonetheless must be recognized to represent nothing more than a kind of 'crude fetishism' (*TI* III:5). So Nietzsche speaks of 'our bad habit of taking a mnemonic, an abbreviative formula, to be an entity, finally as a cause, e.g., to say of lightning "it flashes." Or the little word "I" ' (*WP* 548).

There is more to the matter than this, however; for on his view, in this case as in many others, certain sorts of *social* factors have played roles of even greater importance. In particular, he argues that there is a close link between certain very fundamental requirements of human social existence and the notion of an atomic and agent 'soul-entity.' It is a virtual presupposition of the viability of social life among human beings, he contends, that they regard themselves and each other as accountable for their actions through time; for it is only thus that they may be deemed both liable to imputations of responsibility and guilt for actions performed in the past, and capable of making promises and undertaking commitment extending into the future. 'Man himself must first of all have become *calculable, regular, necessary,* even in his own image of himself,' for this development to occur (*GM* II:1). Under the influence of the idea that there is something about us which is constant and identical through time, and which renders us accountable for our actions through time in virtue of its being the source of our actions, our lives may actually come to exhibit a degree of regularity and calculability, which he supposes they otherwise would largely lack. The consent of the members of a society to the establishment of institutions designed to punish various forms of inconstancy and rule-infraction also is thereby more readily obtained; their operation further contributes to this development; and as they are internalized in moral or religious guise, it is carried further still.

This idea is thus of the greatest social utility, if indeed it is not socially indispensable. Far from providing support for the 'soul-hypothesis,' however, it seems to Nietzsche that this fact only serves to strengthen the case against it. For to the extent that acceptance of any notion may be seen to serve some practical purpose associated with contingent features of our manner of existence, the supposition that its actual status is merely that of a useful fiction is rendered more compelling. And if he is further right in suggesting that it was only as a consequence of a development (viz., the blocking and turning inward of certain basic drives) associated with the establishment of society that 'man first developed what was later called his "soul" ' (*GM* II:16), it would seem that the hypostatization of our resulting 'inner life' as a kind of mental entity does indeed 'have nothing to do with metaphysical truths' (*WP* 513), as he maintains. Taken together, these points suggest it to be but an artificial construct, fixed by the societal function performed by the notion in our social life, and by the nature of the changes brought about in us as a result of our socialization, the attendant 'internalization' of our natural impulses, and the influence of the notion itself upon us.

It may be observed that Nietzsche does not take it to follow from this analysis that we do not in fact exhibit anything like the kind and degree of 'calculability' and 'regularity' of which he speaks; nor does he conclude from it that we in fact are incapable of becoming accountable for our actions. His view is rather that, to whatever extent we may exhibit the former and be capable of the latter, we do not do so because an atomic and agent soul-entity actually exists in each of us and makes it possible. We do so owing rather to the fact that, under the above-mentioned conditions, we come to have much the sort of character we would have *if this were the case.* In short, Nietzsche is granting, and not denying, that we '*have become* calculable, regular, necessary'; but he is suggesting that we *are* this way (to the extent that we are) not because we are so by our very nature (as the 'soul-hypothesis' would have it), but rather because we have become this way. And it is his contention that our having become this way is to be explained primarily in terms of the social utility of our being this way — a circumstance which deprives our constancy and accountability of any metaphysical significance. Metaphysically considered, the notion of a soul-entity is a fiction; although it is a fiction which itself serves to help produce or reinforce this socially useful result. Or, insofar as it is anything more than that, it is simply a convenient way of designating (by hypostatizing) the result thereby produced — a result, however, which is no actual entity at all, but rather is properly understood as a functional characteristic of a socialized human being.

VII

Beyond observing that there would appear to be no other adducible reasons (different in nature from those which have been dealt with) by reference to which a compelling or even plausible case could be made for the existence of some sort of soul-entity, Nietzsche considers no further argument to be required to warrant the conclusion that the soul-hypothesis is not merely problematical but untenable philosophically. It may remain a useful — and perhaps even indispensable — fiction in a variety of contexts, both practical and theoretical, as he would be the first to admit; but that, for him, is quite beside the point. Here again, therefore, one finds him taking the position that a recognition of the 'human, all-too-human' genesis and appeal of an idea, conjoined with the fact that it has nothing else going for it, has the consequence not merely that he can no longer bring himself to take it seriously, but moreover that it *should* no longer be taken seriously philosophically (except as a profound and seductive metaphysical error).

In some respects, Nietzsche's treatment of the notion of a soul-entity (and its various philosophical refinements and modifications) is similar to Kant's, in the first *Critique.* Kant had argued that the notion is properly regarded as a 'regulative' rather than a 'constitutive' one, which it is natural of reason to produce and necessary for it to employ, but owing only to its own requirements rather than to the actual content of experience; and that consequently it is an error to take the notion to refer to a real entity the existence and nature of which might be matters of metaphysical inquiry and knowledge. Nietzsche in effect agrees, differing from Kant primarily in what might be termed his 'naturalization' of Kant's account. And it would seem that he is no more guilty of commiting a 'genetic fallacy' in his treatment of the matter than is Kant. What we are dealing with here, both contend, is the fact of an idea which plays a central role in our thinking and speaking and reasoning about ourselves; and thus the proper way to approach it is through a consideration of the nature of the role it plays. Once this role is understood, it becomes clear that the very reasons which explain its centrality are also reasons to regard it as being validly applicable only within the context of certain human enterprises, and as being legitimately understood only as a conceptual device facilitating these enterprises. It is erroneously applied and wrongly understood, on the other hand, when employed metaphysically, and construed in the manner of those who entertain and advance the kind of soul-hypothesis under consideration.

To be sure, Kant in the end allowed himself to postulate the existence of a noumenal self that is both atomic and morally agent after all, taking this to be justified in consequence of his reflections upon morality. Here he and Nietzsche part company — both in their interpretations of moral experience and in the inferences they draw from them — in no uncertain terms. Indeed, they part company even earlier, in that Nietzsche takes what Kant calls 'the transcendental unity of apperception' to derive exclusively from the functional unity of the body as the locus and instrument of perception and action, together with the ordering and integrating apparatus of language.

In rejecting the idea of a soul-entity as an atomic and agent substance or being, and the soul-hypothesis construed as the postulation of the existence of such an entity (whether in their traditional metaphysical and ordinary forms or in their Kantian guise), however, Nietzsche does not mean to be repudiating all talk of 'the soul' and all types of 'soul-hypotheses' in connection with the philosophical analysis of human experience and human nature. Thus, after asserting that it is imperative to 'give the finishing stroke to that . . . calamitous atomism which Christianity has taught best and longest, the *soul atomism*,' he makes the following remarks:

Between ourselves, it is not at all necessary to get rid of 'the soul' at the same time, and thus to renounce one of the most ancient and venerable hypotheses — as frequently happens to clumsy naturalists who can hardly touch on 'the soul' without immediately losing it. But the way is open for new versions and refinements of the soul-hypothesis; and such conceptions as 'mortal soul' and 'soul as subjective multiplicity,' and 'soul as social structure of the drives and affects,' want henceforth to have citizens' rights in science (*BGE* 12).

What Nietzsche has in mind here will be considered in detail in a later chapter. For the moment it is enough to observe that he is prepared to allow, and even to insist, that there is something important about our nature — and indeed about 'the body' — which it is legitimate (and perhaps even desirable and illuminating) to characterize in terms of 'soul.' It should be clear, however, both that and why he holds that the traditional and customary construal of 'the soul' and its near-relations ('the ego,' 'the subject,' etc.) as an atomic and agent substance and substratum requires to be branded an error and rejected philosophically, the 'naturalness,' utility and even indispensability of the notion notwithstanding.

Things

VIII

'When one has grasped that the "subject" is . . . only a fiction,' Nietzsche writes, 'much follows.' And one of the most important consequences is held to be that the 'object' too is a 'fiction,' and that belief in the existence of 'things' as 'substances' or 'beings' of a non-spiritual nature is no more tenable philosophically than belief in the existence of God and the soul. For he argues that 'it is only after the model of the subject that we have invented the reality of things and projected them into the medley of sensations.' The 'things' in question include not only the 'physical' or 'material objects' with which many philosophers suppose us to be surrounded, but also the 'effective atoms' of physical science, 'other hypothetical entities' of a 'material' nature, and indeed the very notion of a 'material' world: 'We have got rid of *materiality*' (*WP* 552). And they even include the 'things-in-themselves' of which philosophers like Kant are wont to speak.

Nietzsche thus does not maintain merely that it is necessary to modify the 'thing-ontology' with which philosophers usually and people generally operate, in such a way as to deny the status of reality to most kinds of purported 'things' and to grant it to a select few. His position is rather that it is necessary to abandon all forms of 'thing-ontology' (and to develop an altogether different way of thinking about the world).

He is no less emphatic on this point than he is with respect to the two hypotheses discussed above, employing much the same language here as he does in dealing with the notions of 'God' and 'soul.' 'There are no things (— they are fictions invented by us),' he writes (WP 634). 'At length we grasp that things — consequently atoms, too — effect nothing: because they do not exist at all . . .' (WP 551). 'It is we who created the "thing," the "identical thing," . . . after we had long pursued the process of making identical, coarse and simple' (WP 521). Among our many 'erroneous articles of faith,' on his view, 'are, for example, the following:— that there are enduring things, that there are equal things, that there are things, substances, bodies, that a thing is what it appears to be . . .' (GS 110). And in this connection he observes that 'it is enough to create new names and estimations and probabilities in order to create in the long run new "things" ' (GS 59). We may find it natural, useful and even indispensable and necessary to think in terms of the 'schematism' of things, and difficult to imagine that there is anything fictitious, artificial and invented about the 'things' we encounter in ordinary perceptual experience. As these remarks show, however, it is clearly Nietzsche's position that these circumstances are of no ontological significance, and that their apparent ontological implications are mistaken.

It is thus necessary to consider what he takes the notion of a 'thing' to involve, and the nature of the case he mounts against all versions of what might be termed the 'thing-hypothesis,' which he holds to be sufficiently compelling to warrant its rejection. In doing so, one must distinguish between 'thing' as an ontological category, which may or may not be a coherent notion and of which there may or may not exist actual instances; and 'thing' understood very prosaically, as a catch-all term appropriately applicable to all of the various items of ordinary experience designated by commonplace nouns ('tree,' 'rock,' 'house,' etc.), and subsuming whatever it is that they are conventionally used to specify. It is by no means Nietzsche's intention to deny that there is anything in the world of our experience to which they refer; and if a 'thing' is taken simply to be any such item of our life-world, he would be quite prepared to allow that there clearly *are* such 'things' — a great many of them, of many different kinds. The chair on which I am sitting is one, and the pen with which I am writing is another.

141

Nietzsche *is* concerned, however, to make it clear that the basic ontological status of these items of ordinary experience is quite problematical. Thus he considers philosophical inquiry into their ontological status to be called for — and he contends that such inquiry yields the conclusion that neither they nor anything else have the character of 'things' in the first sense of this term distinguished above. He does not take the notion so construed to be entirely unrelated to the way in which we tend (and are led by the grammatical structure of our language) to think of the contents of ordinary experience; on the contrary, he suggests that the former is modeled upon certain features of the latter. But he maintains that given the lines along which the former has been developed, and the kind of use to which it is put, it has no legitimate application either to the contents of ordinary experience or to anything else there is in the world.

It is also necessary to distinguish between the contents of our experience and the actual nature of the world in which we exist, in the context of our encounter with which such experience occurs. In principle, it is conceivable that the two should coincide; but as philosophers have long recognized, their coincidence cannot simply be assumed, and their divergence may be great. Nietzsche is highly critical of the ways in which most philosophers have conceived of the distinction between 'appearance' and 'reality,' and of the relation between them, as shall subsequently be seen. Despite his conviction that they are intimately related, however, he is by no means disposed to reject this distinction altogether. Indeed, he is no more prepared to subscribe to the view that the actual nature of reality and what there is in the world can be appropriately and accurately expressed in the language we use to specify the contents of our experience than he is to countenance the construal of the former in terms of the ontological schematism of 'things' commonly favored by philosophers persuaded of the merely 'phenomenal' character of the latter.

In short, Nietzsche contends that neither naive nor transcendental realism is a philosophically viable position; and that the kinds of entities to which reality is ascribed in each case have the ultimate status of 'fictions' and 'inventions.' They may be very useful fictions, and inventions the devising of which is understandable and even necessary for us; but even if this is so, the only inferences we are entitled to draw are inferences about ourselves. It is not his purpose, however, to try to persuade those who become convinced that he is right about their status that they ought to cease speaking and thinking in terms of them entirely, in all contexts of human life. Rather, he is intent only upon persuading us that we ought not to carry over this schematism into our philosophical reflections upon what there is in the world.

It is quite common for philosophers to regard 'thing' as a term so general and noncommittal that it may be used to refer to whatever there is, with the consequence that the existence of 'things' would seem to follow directly from the very minimal claim that the world does in fact exist. They may readily grant that at the outset of reflection the nature of what there is must be considered an open question; but it is very easy for this question to be turned into that of the nature of whatever things there are — and this restatement of the question is by no means entirely innocuous. Indeed, it is Nietzsche's contention that this in fact is a highly prejudicial way of orienting philosophical inquiry, which sets it on a most unfortunate course even while in a sense rendering it more manageable. It may facilitate thought as well as action to treat our environing world as though it were composed of a multiplicity of discrete entities (with various distinctive and common properties); but this is by no means merely to paraphrase the notion of 'that of which the world consists' in more precise but equally noncommittal terms.

The idea of a 'thing' thus is not neutral between all possible conceptualizations of what there is in the world, but rather only between alternative accounts of the general character of the entities of which the world is tacitly assumed to be the aggregate. This tacit assumption, far from being a self-evidently valid axiom requiring to be made explicit only in the interest of logical completeness, actually constitutes a substantive philosophical presupposition that is genuinely problematical at the very least. The idea that the world consists of *things* of some sort is no transparent truth, but rather an interpretation requiring to be analyzed and assessed. What we find ourselves as philosophers confronted with here is not the indisputable fact of a world of things, but rather a 'thing-hypothesis' (or a number of variants of it), the meaning and status of which must be explicated and determined. Nietzsche undertakes to show that this hypothesis is untenable, and that we err in our thinking about the world when 'we interpret it by means of the schematism of "things," etc.' (*WP* 479). Once the case is made and this interpretation is accordingly set aside, the way is opened for other, different interpretations, as will be seen in the next chapter.

IX

Turning now to Nietzsche's analysis of the notion of a 'thing,' the first point to be noted is that he considers it to be quite similar in certain fundamental respects to the idea of the 'soul,' as the latter was explicated in the preceding section. It is basically the notion of something having the character of a 'being,' which is both unitary (a single, persisting, self-identical, self-contained and independently existing whole), and agent (a substratum to which a variety of 'effects,' changes, activities and properties are traceable and attributable). Thus he speaks of 'the doctrine of being, of things, of all sorts of fixed unities' (*WP* 538). 'Things' are conceived as 'individuals' which 'are the same' through time (*WP* 520). A 'thing' is thus taken to be an 'object' with the characteristics of 'duration, identity with itself, being' (*WP* 552). It is further supposed that 'things possess a constitution in themselves quite apart from interpretation and subjectivity,' and that 'a thing freed from all relationships would still be a thing' (*WP* 560). A 'thing' is also thought to be something which can 'have' a variety of 'properties,' but which is not identical with any single one of them or with all of them taken together; thus 'the "thing" in which we believe' is construed as a unitary 'substance' which is 'a foundation for the various attributes' (*WP* 561).

A 'thing' supposedly not only 'is,' moreover, but also 'effects' (*WP* 561). It is construed as being capable of entering into relations with other 'things,' and of affecting them and being affected by them in the course of doing so. The conception of a 'thing' thus reflects the influence of 'the older, naive form of perception which granted energy to things' (*WP* 562). So Nietzsche speaks of 'things' as purported 'causal unities . . . whose effect remains constant' (*WP* 635). They are moreover taken not only to be the 'seat of a driving force' (*WP* 625) and thus to produce effects upon other 'things,' but also to 'behave regularly, according to a *rule*' (*WP* 634). This aspect of the notion of a 'thing' is given particular emphasis in that variant of the 'thing-hypothesis' Nietzsche calls 'materialistic atomism,' of which he observes that it 'sought, besides the operating "power," that lump of matter in which it resides and out of which it operates — the atom' (*BGE* 17). But it is characteristic of other variants of this hypothesis as well: 'Everywhere [language] sees a doer and doing' (*TI* III:5).

Nietzsche argues that the view that the world consists of 'things' of this sort is untenable for a variety of reasons. 'Ultimately,' he writes, 'man finds in things nothing but what he himself has imported into them' (*WP* 606). And this extends even to the notion that they *are* 'things.' Thus he insists that ' "constant causes," things, substances, something "unconditioned" ' have all been *'invented'* (*WP* 624).

At least a part of the motivation to advance and defend the 'thing-hypothesis' is removed, he suggests, when the identities of what he sometimes terms 'things-for-us' are recognized to have no ontological significance. Thus, he remarks:

> what things *are called* is incomparably more important than what they are. The reputation, name, and appearance, the usual measure and weight of a thing, what it counts for — originally almost always wrong and arbitrary, thrown over things like a dress and altogether foreign to their nature and even to their skin — all this grows from generation unto generation, merely because people believe in it, until it gradually grows to be part of the thing and turns into its very body. What at first was appearance becomes in the end, almost invariably, the essence and is effective as such (*GS* 58).

Nietzsche's own use of the term 'things' in this passage might appear to imply that he is here accepting the distinction between 'things-for-us' and 'things as they really are,' and thus that he is objecting only to 'naive realism' rather than to the 'thing-hypothesis' more generally. His point, however, is not merely that 'things-for-us' cannot be identified with 'things as they really are,' as the preceding section — entitled *'To the realists'* — makes clear. For in it he suggests that even if one could succeed in the impossible task of attempting to 'subtract the phantasm and every human contribution' from some familiar 'thing' and set aside 'your descent, your past, your training — all of your humanity and animality,' one would not then be able to catch sight of the 'reality' of the thing, for it would have ceased to be any 'thing' at all: 'There is no "reality" for us — not for you either, my sober [realist] friends' (*GS* 57). The implication seems clear: the only 'things' there are are 'things-for-us'; and what might be termed 'thinghood' is no less a part of the 'human contribution' to our experience of that which we take to be a 'mountain' or a 'cloud' (Nietzsche's examples here) than are the various particular qualities and characteristics we attribute to them. Thus he speaks of ' "beings," ' no less than sensuously perceptible properties, 'as appearance' (*WP* 617), and terms 'the concept of the thing' merely 'phenomenal' (*WP* 635). 'The origin of "things" is wholly the work of that which imagines, thinks, wills, feels. The concept "thing" itself just as much as all its qualities' (*WP* 556).

Nietzsche's case for the mere 'phenomenality' of 'thinghood' has several distinct parts. One of them consists in an attack upon the coherence of the notion of the 'thing's' purported self-subsistency

— that is, its self-identical, unitary substantiality underlying the multiplicity of what are taken to be its 'properties' and 'activities.' 'If I remove all the relationships, all the "properties," all the "activities" of a thing,' he writes, 'the thing does not remain over; because thingness has only been invented by us owning to the requirements of logic,' and so ultimately 'with the aim of defining, communication (to bind together the multiplicity of relationships, properties, activities)' (*WP* 558). Moreover, he argues that 'there is no thing without other things,' since 'the properties of a thing are effects on other "things": if one removes other "things," then a thing has no properties'; and thus 'there is no ' "thing-in-itself" ' (*WP* 557) — or, he might just as well have said, there is no 'thing-by-itself.' A 'thing' is supposed to be an entity the existence and nature of which are independent of those of other 'things'; but 'in the actual world,' Nietzsche maintains, 'everything is bound to and conditioned by everything else' (*WP* 584). The notion of 'things' each of which has the character of an 'in-itself' is not merely erroneous, but moreover 'is even an absurd conception; a "constitution-in-itself" is nonsense; we possess the concept "being," "thing," only as a relational concept — ' (*WP* 583A).

Nietzsche thus argues that the 'things' of ordinary experience have the properties and indeed the identities they do only by virtue of the relations in which they stand to other such 'things' and to us and our purposes (cf. *WP* 556); and that those who would maintain that there are any 'things' at all which differ in these respects from the 'things' of ordinary experience thus can derive no comfort from the common acknowledgment of the experiential reality of the latter. Indeed, he goes further. If the case for the existence of 'things' is made to rest upon the undeniability of the fact that the term has an established application to much of what we experience, he contends, what follows is not the plausibility but the absurdity of the 'thing-hypothesis,' quite apart from any considerations pertaining to a lack of correspondence between the world of our experience and the way the world actually is. For the 'things' of ordinary experience prove to lack the self-subsistency which 'things' are supposed to have. Consequently, the notion of a 'thing' must either be cut loose from its mooring in experience (in which event the case for the 'thing-hypothesis' based upon this connection collapses), or adjusted to take into consideration the results of this analysis (in which event the 'thing-hypothesis' itself is thereby in effect abandoned).

Nietzsche was not the first philosopher to recognize that, upon closer consideration, what we ordinarily take to be 'things' do not satisfy the description of a 'thing' indicated above. This recognition is almost as old as philosophy itself; and yet few of his predecessors were moved by it to abandon the 'thing-hypothesis.' One reason why they tended to cling to it so tenaciously, he suggests, is that they were determined to achieve a kind of *knowledge* the very possibility of which presupposes the existence of 'things' of some sort as its objects, through a process of thought which is capable of dealing effectively only with such 'things.' This disposition, moreover, is no mere philosophical idiosyncrasy; on the contrary, he considers it to be merely the most highly developed form of a fundamental characteristic of the human condition. We are creatures whose fate it is to have to deal consciously with our environment; and thus the requirements of expeditious thinking and the accumulation and communication of experience are among the basic conditions of our existence. This circumstance is reflected in the character and content of the conceptual scheme with which we generally operate, of which the idea of discrete 'things' is a central feature.

> We have arranged for ourselves a world in which we can live —
> by positing bodies, lines, planes, causes and effects, motion
> and rest, form and content; without these articles of faith
> nobody now could endure life. But that does not prove them.
> Life is no argument. The conditions of life might include
> error (*GS* 121).

More specifically, Nietzsche suggests that the conception of 'things' as 'unities' and as 'constant causes' is bound up in a fundamental way with the nature of rational thought, to the extent that the very 'process of reason' depends upon it; and that 'to let it go means: being no longer able to think' (*WP* 487) — or at least, to think clearly and precisely, to reason logically and to categorize, generalize and draw inferences. 'We need "unities" in order to be able to reckon: that does not mean we must suppose that such unities exist' (*WP* 635). That there are 'things that are the same' is only an 'apparent fact' (*WP* 520), the appearance of which is a consequence of the fact that rational thought is capable of dealing only with unities which preserve their identity.

The 'thing-hypothesis' is thus held by Nietzsche to require to be viewed and assessed in the light of the genealogy of the notion of 'things,' in which certain practical requirements of human life have been profoundly influential. 'Because we have to be stable in our beliefs if we are to prosper, we have made the "real" world a world not of change and becoming, but one of being' (*WP* 507).

147

The world in which we exist, he maintains, is one in which 'the "number" of beings is itself in flux,' and in which 'continual transition forbids us to speak of "individuals" ' (*WP* 520). As thinking beings, however, to deal with it effectively we are constrained to impose order upon it, through the 'apparatus of knowledge,' which is 'an apparatus for abstraction and simplification.' This 'entire apparatus,' on Nietzsche's view, is 'directed not at knowledge but at taking possession of things.' And it is only in a loose manner of speaking that it may be said to be 'things' of which we thus seek to 'take possession.' So he continues: 'With "end" and "means" one takes possession of the process (one invents a process that can be grasped); with "concepts," however, of the "things" that constitute the process' (*WP* 503).

The line of thought which runs through such passages as these would appear to be the following. What Nietzsche terms 'the schematism of "things" ' (*WP* 479) is not merely one of a variety of possible conceptual frameworks in terms of which we schematize our relations to our environment. Rather, it is one which (owing to the requirements of 'the process of reason' and to the indispensability of this process in human life) we are constrained to employ in order to get along in the world. Our belief in 'things' is, as a practical matter, one of the 'conditions of our existence.' 'But that a belief, however necessary it may be for the preservation of a species, has nothing to do with truth, one knows from the fact that, e.g., we have to believe in time, space and motion, without feeling compelled to grant them absolute reality' (*WP* 487). The practical utility and indispensability of 'the schematism of "things",' in short, neither guarantees that reality is in fact constituted accordingly, nor establishes any presumption to this effect which would stand unless defeated by independent argument.

It might seem that nothing more than an agnostic withholding of judgment with respect to the issue of whether reality does or does not consist (entirely or in part) of 'things' is warranted by the recognition that the 'thing-hypothesis' stands in this relation to the nature of our thought-processes and the conditions of our existence. Nietzsche, however, goes further. 'It is of the nature of thinking,' he writes, 'that it . . . measures the world according to magnitudes posited by itself — such fundamental fictions as . . . "things," "substances," logical laws, numbers and forms' (*WP* 574). His point in characterizing these 'magnitudes' as 'fictions' is that, as categories which 'thinking' has 'posited by itself,' they exist only for thought, or only for thinking beings like ourselves. There are 'things' (for us) only because there is thought; just as, for Kant, there is a spatially and temporally ordered experiential manifold (for us) only because there are minds whose sensibility has the forms of space and time.

'Thought' and 'things' thus go together; the former supplies the concepts in accordance with which our encounter with reality issues in the experience of specific instances and types of the latter. Eliminate thought from the picture, Nietzsche contends, and the schematism of 'things' ceases to be at all intelligible. 'Thing' is not only a category the *justifiability* of the employment of which is restricted to the world of experience which (as he puts it) 'we have arranged for ourselves' (*GS* 121). It is one the very *meaningfulness and legitimacy* of the employment of which likewise requires that it be confined to this domain. And so he concludes that the very 'concept of the thing,' and not merely various particular kinds of 'things,' is 'phenomenal,' i.e., it has application only to experiential phenomena, and not to the actual nature of reality (*WP* 635).

X

There is more to Nietzsche's case against the 'thing-hypothesis' than this, however. There might still seem to be another strategy of saving the hypothesis. It is reasonable to pose the question: what could have served as our model in our invention and development of this notion, if not something antecedently and persistingly present in our environment the character of which it reflects and at least fairly approximates? And if no other answer to this question is forthcoming, the 'thing-hypothesis' would appear to acquire a new lease on life.

Nietzsche has a different answer to this question; and it is one which he takes to complete his case. It represents a reversal of the more common view that this notion served as the model for the conception of the soul discussed in the previous section — a view he holds to be mistaken: 'The concept of substance is a consequence of the concept of the subject: not the reverse!' And it is his contention that 'if we relinquish the soul, "the subject," the precondition for "substance" in general disappears' (*WP* 485). In brief, he proposes that the origin of the notion of a 'thing' is to be found in the projection of the fictitious notion of a soul-entity into our environing world. And he argues that both the fictitiousness of the latter and the status of the former as a projection of the latter weigh heavily against the legitimacy of employing the former in giving an account of the nature of the world — and so against the tenability of the 'thing-hypothesis.' While 'the process of reason' may require the employment of 'the schematism of "things," ' both ultimately are based upon the soul-concept; and if the 'soul-hypothesis' is to be rejected, the 'thing-hypothesis' falls with it.

Thus Nietzsche rhetorically asks: 'Must all philosophy not ultimately bring to light the preconditions upon which the process of reason depends? − our belief in the "ego" as a substance, as the sole reality from which we ascribe reality to things in general?' (*WP* 487). And he goes even further: 'The logical-metaphysical postulates, the belief in substance, accident, attribute, etc., derive their convincing force from our habit of regarding all our deeds as consequences of our will . . . − But there is no such thing as will' (*WP* 488). It is with this thought in mind that he suggests that 'when one has grasped that the "subject" is . . . only a fiction, much follows,' and goes on to say:

> It is only after the model of the subject that we have invented the reality of things and projected them into the medley of sensations. If we no longer believe in the effective subject, then belief also disappears in effective things, in reciprocation, cause and effect between those phenomena that we call things. . . . If we give up the effective subject, we also give up the object upon which effects are produced. . . . If we give up the concept 'subject' and 'object,' then also the concept 'substance' − and as a consequence also the various modifications of it, e.g., 'matter,' 'spirit,' and other hypothetical entities, 'the eternity and immutability of matter,' etc. We have got rid of *materiality* (*WP* 552).

Nietzsche supposes it no longer to be necessary to argue for the idea that the perceptible qualities of what we ordinarily take to be 'things' are merely 'phenomenal.' Thus he places quotation marks around the following passage, to indicate the commonplace character of the thought it expresses: ' "In the development of thought a point had to be reached at which one realized that what one called the properties of things were sensations of the feeling subject: at this point the properties ceased to belong to the thing." ' Once this point was reached, he continues, all that remained of 'the thing' was the idea of 'the "thing-in-itself" ' conceived as a unitary substance having the power to produce various effects upon us and other things. Now, however, even this residual notion must be rejected; for 'analysis reveal[s] that even force was only projected into them, and likewise − substance. . . . Root of the idea of substance in language, not in beings outside us!' (*WP* 562).

Nietzsche speaks of 'language' here because he takes it to be the medium in which the 'psychological derivation of the belief in things' (*WP* 473) occurred, through the development of the soul-concept and its subsequent employment as a model for the elaboration of 'the schematism of "things".' 'Ultimately,' he writes, 'man finds in things nothing but what he himself has imported into them' (*WP* 606). And the source drawn upon in importing into them their most fundamental characteristics — those definitive of their very 'thinghood' itself — is in the last analysis our (erroneous) conception of ourselves as unitary and agent subject-entities, which produce effects and remain the same beings while doing so. 'We have borrowed the concept of unity from our "ego" concept — our oldest article of faith,' he contends. 'If we did not hold ourselves to be unities, we would never have formed the concept "thing." Now, somewhat later, we are firmly convinced that our conception of the ego does not guarantee any actual unity' (*WP* 635). And indeed, as has been seen, this for Nietzsche is an understatement of the matter, in that any such 'actual unity' not only is not thereby guaranteed, but moreover cannot be supposed to exist.

Nietzsche thus holds that man 'took the concept of being from the concept of the ego; he posited "things" as "being," in his image, in accordance with his concept of the ego as cause.' And so he concludes that 'the thing itself' or 'the concept of thing is a mere reflex of the faith in the ego as cause' (*TI* VI:3). We now tend not even to question the way of thinking which leads us to 'comprehend an event as a sort of shifting and place-changing on the part of a "being," of something constant,' because 'this ancient mythology' had 'found a firm form in the functions of language and grammar' (*WP* 631). Our thinking about ourselves and the world follows the lead of the language we speak; and, concerning the latter, Nietzsche writes:

> it projects this faith in the ego-substance upon all things —
> only thereby does it first *create* the concept of 'thing.'
> Everywhere 'being' is projected by thought, pushed under-
> neath, as the cause; the concept of being follows, and is a
> derivative of, the concept of ego. In the beginning there is
> that great calamity of error that the will is something which
> is effective, that will is a capacity. Today we know that it is
> only a word (*TI* III:5).

Nietzsche intends these remarks to apply not only to the 'things' of ordinary experience, but also to their conceptually refined logical and natural-scientific counterparts, insofar as they are to be conceived as having the same formal characteristics; for the latter, on his view, are merely derivatives of the former. Thus, for example, using the letter '*A*' in the manner of logicians of his day to stand

151

for the sort of logical object of which the principle of self-identity ('$A = A$') may be predicated and with which logical reasoning deals, he observes: 'The "thing" — that is the real substratum of "A"; *our belief in things* is the precondition of our belief in logic. The "A" of logic is, like the atom, a reconstruction of the thing' (*WP* 516). His basic point here is that the notion of a logical object is merely a reformulation of the notion of such a 'thing' in abstract terms lending themselves more readily to logical manipulation, which however is entirely parasitical upon the former with respect to the scope and limits of its applicability.

Similarly, Nietzsche contends that 'the atom [physicists] posit is inferred according to the logic of the perspectivism of consciousness — and is therefore itself a subjective fiction' (*WP* 636). He has in mind here 'the physical atom,' or the atom as construed in 'materialistic atomism,' which he takes to be 'one of the best refuted theories there are' (*BGE* 12). This 'older atomism,' he suggests, 'sought, besides the operating "power," that lump of matter in which it resides and out of which it operates — the atom. More rigorous minds, however, learned at last to get along without this "earth-residuum" ' (*BGE* 17). He thus locates 'the origin of atomism' in the following circumstances: 'To comprehend the world, we have to be able to calculate it; to be able to calculate it, we have to have constant causes; because we find no such constant causes in actuality, we invent them for ourselves — the atoms' (*WP* 624).

The notion of the atom as a kind of material entity is one which he feels it to be unnecessary to subject to sustained criticism, since he supposes that 'no one in the learned world is now so unscholarly as to attach serious significance to it, except for convenient household use (as an abbreviation of the means of expression).' For 'Boscovich has taught us to abjure the belief in the last part of the earth that "stood fast" — the belief in "substance," in "matter," in the earth-residuum and particle-atom' (*BGE* 12). This latter notion, he maintains, both is bound up with and succumbs along with what he calls the 'mechanistic' world-view, in which the world 'is imagined as only sight and touch imagine a world (as "moved") — so as to be calculable — thus causal unities are invented, "things" (atoms) whose effect remains constant (— transference of the false concept of subject to the concept of the atom)' (*WP* 635). (His critique of 'mechanism' will be discussed at length in a later section.)

In short, the substitution of material atoms for the 'things' of ordinary experience in the description of the world's constitution represents no real break (let alone a significant philosophical

152

advance) in relation to the conceptualization of the latter on the model of the fictitious subject-entity; for both are cast in the same mold. The rejection of the view that the world consists of such atoms is therefore another of the consequences Nietzsche takes to follow 'when one has grasped that the "subject" is . . . only a fiction.' Thus after observing that with this recognition 'belief also disappears in effective things,' he goes on to say: 'There also disappears, of course, the world of effective atoms: the assumption of which always depended on the supposition that one needed subjects' (*WP* 552). Here too we encounter but a variation on the theme of a fictionalizing projection onto the world in which we live of a fictitious conception of ourselves.

XI

Since Nietzsche thus makes much of what he terms 'the psychological derivation of the belief in things' (*WP* 473) in his critique of the 'thing-hypothesis,' it would be well briefly to review his reasons for supposing that we actually are confronted here with a case of projection. 'Analysis reveals,' he contends, that the ideas of unity, self-identity through time, and agency, and thus of substantiality and causal efficacy (in terms of which 'thinghood' is conceived) are not derived from 'beings outside us,' but rather are 'projected into' the world around us (*WP* 562) in accordance with our 'concept of the ego' (*TI* VI:3). A 'thing' is supposed to be a constant causal unit; but as Hume had observed, neither unity nor causality nor constancy may actually be observed to number among the perceptible features of the contents of our experience. To be sure, as he had also observed, they are not introspectively ascertainable features of what we call the 'self' either; nevertheless, it has come about (for reasons indicated in the previous section) that we do tend to think of ourselves in this manner. And so, Nietzsche contends, since an analysis of our experience reveals nothing else that might have been its source, the notion of a 'thing' as a constant causal unit must derive from the notion of ourselves as constant causal units — as 'doers' of extended sequences of 'deeds,' who are individual and remain the same individuals in the course of performing these sequences of actions notwithstanding their multiplicity, variety, and discontinuity.

Only our idea of our own agency, he argues, could have given rise to the idea of causally effective 'things'; for causal efficacy is nowhere to be found among the perceptible features of our experience of our environing world. Only our idea of our own unity underlying the diversity of our various characteristics and supposed capacities and susceptibilities could have suggested the idea of unitary 'things' which are one and indivisible beneath the multiplicity of qualities and putative interactive possibilities which are taken to be their 'properties'; for substantial unity is likewise nowhere encountered there, the only unity in evidence being what Nietzsche terms 'unity only as an organization,' which *'signifies* a unity but *is* not a unity' (*WP* 561). And only our idea of our own self-sameness through time as identical authors of different actions and as identical bearers of changing attributes could have led to the idea of constant 'things' which remain 'the same ones' despite significant alterations in their qualities and relationships; for constancy also is foreign to the contents of our experience, the configurations of and among which are continually changing, or persist only for relatively brief periods or only at a high level of abstraction.

In evaluating this line of thought (which evidently goes well beyond 'analysis' in any merely descriptive sense), it may be observed that Nietzsche would seem to be on solid ground in maintaining that apprehending the world in which we find ourselves as consisting of various sorts of discrete, enduring, unitary things, which affect each other and ourselves in a variety of ways, is something which human beings *learn* to do. He further would appear to be justified in maintaining that they learn to do it in the course of their acquisition of language, with its 'thing'-oriented grammatical structure and categorial vocabulary. And he also is surely right to insist that it would be rash to suppose that there must be a structural correspondence between language and the world, and that therefore the fact that our language has this character must be a reflection of the fact that the world is a world of 'things.'

If it is granted that the schematism of 'things' must be accounted for in a way that renders comprehensible its presence in our language (as well as its utility) independently of any assumptions concerning the tenability of the 'thing-hypothesis,' and moreover does so in terms which take into consideration the initial circumstances and resources available to human beings as they have evolved the way of apprehending and speaking and thinking about the world in which it figures so centrally, therefore, Nietzsche would seem to have a strong case for his view that it involves the sort of projection he has in mind. For the (naturalistic) restrictions he places upon admissible explanations of features of human thought are quite reasonable, especially in view of the persuasiveness of his critiques of the God- and soul-hypotheses. He has already been seen to render plausible the idea that what he terms 'our oldest article of faith,' namely 'our "ego" concept' (*WP* 635), could have been developed independently of and prior to 'our "thing" concept.' And it would be hard to fault his contention (linking him with a long philosophical tradition running from Heraclitus to Hume and Hegel and beyond) that the most fundamental features of the latter are not exhibited by or to be found among the various issues of our senses. If more would be required to make his case, it is difficult to see what that might be.

The case he makes must be allowed to be a fairly strong one. The utility — and even the indispensability for many purposes of a theoretical as well as a practical nature — of the 'schematism of "things" ' does not show that the transference of the notion of such an entity from our inward life to our environing world results in the attainment of a genuine comprehension of the nature of the latter; for its utility is explainable in quite different terms (the facilitation of calculation, classification, communication, etc.). The intimacy of the relationship between thought and 'things' renders the idea of unconceptualized 'things,' existing independently of a pattern of thought within which they acquire their natures as the 'things' they are, one to which no clear sense can be attached. What we identify as 'things' in ordinary experience, if allowed to stand as paradigm cases definitive of the nature of 'thinghood,' prove upon examination to require radical revision of the notion of 'things' which renders the idea of the world as consisting of such 'things' incoherent; while, if denied the status of 'things' in order to avoid this problem, they cease to constitute any compelling reason for supposing that there are 'things' at all. And there is much to be said for Nietzsche's view that it was the concept of the soul from which the basic lineaments of the very notion of a thing originally were drawn, and projected into the world.

It may be that none of these points suffices to establish beyond question that 'there are no things.' Collectively, however, they build a case against not only the validity but also the tenability of the 'thing-hypothesis,' which is at least as strong as Nietzsche's cases against the God- and soul-hypotheses. He may not have refuted it; but he might reasonably claim to have laid it to rest, showing it to be both unworthy of belief and undeserving of continuing serious consideration as a philosophical thesis. To be sure, he readily allows that for all practical (and even for many theoretical) purposes, 'things' are with us to stay. But this in no way affects his argument that the notion of 'things' has no application outside of the context of human experience and the human world which 'we have arranged for ourselves' (*GS* 121). Whatever

155

the fundamental nature of the world within which this world has been 'arranged' may be, he would seem to be entitled to his conclusion that it is no more to be construed in terms of this notion than it is to be understood in terms of those of 'God' and 'soul.'

A 'true world' of 'being'

XII

Belief in the existence of God, souls and things is much older than philosophy. Philosophers may have seized upon, developed and refined these notions, but cannot be held to have 'invented' them. Nietzsche takes the situation to have been rather different, however, in the case of another (although related) belief, which to a much greater extent is the issue of philosophical reflection. This is the belief in the existence of what he often terms a 'true world' of 'real world' or 'being,' transcending what concomitantly came to be characterized contrastingly as the 'apparent world' of change, becoming, creation and destruction, struggle and suffering, and birth and death.

Philosophers have long exhibited a strong attachment to this notion and distinction. Indeed, it seems to Nietzsche that what might be called the associated 'being-hypothesis' pervades much of the history of philosophy, from the Greeks to recent times. And he urges that 'it is of cardinal importance that one should abolish the *true* world' conceived in terms of it; for 'it is the great inspirer of doubt and devaluator in respect of the world *we are*: it has been our most dangerous attempt yet to assassinate life' (*WP* 583B). His strenuous opposition to this hypothesis, however, is by no means based solely on purely 'pragmatic' considerations, pertaining to the purportedly pernicious practical consequences of its acceptance for human life. He considers it to be fundamentally misguided and erroneous, and attempts to make out a case to this effect strong enough not only to show that it is too problematical to be confidently asserted, but moreover to establish that it is philosophically untenable.

Before turning directly to what Nietzsche has to say along these lines, it is important to take note of a fundamental ambiguity in his use of the terms 'real' and 'reality' and 'apparent' and 'appearance' (and related expressions), which runs throughout his discussion of it and related matters. On some occasions he allows these contrasting sets of terms to play the roles they have commonly been assigned by philosophers convinced of the existence of a 'metaphysical world' of 'true being,' which conforms not to the 'testimony of the senses' and to our experience of life but rather to the canons of logic and 'the categories of reason.' Here such expressions as 'real world,' 'reality,' 'true reality,' and 'true world' are used to refer to this postulated realm of 'being'; while expressions such as 'appearance,' 'apparent world,' and 'phenomenal world' are used in connection with '*this* world,' the world of human experience and action, and which is supposed by adherents of this metaphysical view to be *merely* apparent and *merely* phenomenal in relation to the 'other world' of 'true being.'

On other occasions, however, Nietzsche's use of these and related expressions is virtually the exact reverse of this. Here it is the latter 'world' which is held to be the 'actual world,' that world which alone exists, the 'real world,' 'reality'; while it is the former that is styled 'apparent,' an 'unreal world' which is erroneously and fictitiously juxtaposed to 'this world,' a world which is in reality 'nothing,' and which requires to be accorded the status of 'appearance' (for it is held to exist only as a product of philosophical invention and imagination.) Matters become even more complicated when one turns to Nietzsche's own account of the world, as shall be seen in the next chapter. It should already be clear, however, that one must proceed most cautiously in considering the meaning of what he says concerning the notion of a 'true world' of 'being.'

It is Nietzsche's contention that 'being is an empty fiction' (*TI* III:2), a category that is no more validly applicable to what there actually is than are those discussed in the preceding sections. The notion of a 'thing,' he was seen to argue in the previous section, is an 'invention' of the human intellect, which is projected into our experience of our environing world with the consequence that our 'world of appearance' is perceived and conceived under 'the schematism of "things".' He likewise takes the category 'being' to be a similar (and related) 'invention,' which philosophers have projected *beyond* our 'apparent world,' yielding the idea of another, higher or 'truer' reality, to which it may more appropriately be applied than it can be within the world of our experience. Different philosophers have conceived of this trans-phenomenal realm or order of 'being' in different ways. Nietzsche does not deal with them individually; for it seems to him that all such variations upon the 'being-hypothesis' involve the same general sort of philosophical move, and so may be dealt with collectively. If it can be established that 'the "apparent" world is the only one' while 'being is an empty fiction,' and that 'the "true" world is merely added by a lie' to our world of 'becoming, passing away, and change' (*TI* III:2), then on his view the differences between these notions cease to be of any real interest, and the question of their relative merit becomes moot.

Perhaps the earliest (and also the longest-enduring) instance of the supposition of the existence of something of this sort was belief in the existence of divine beings, and in particular in the existence of an eternal, immutable, transcendent God; and Nietzsche suggests that the idea of such a being has long served in certain respects as a kind of model for philosophers in their development of other versions of the 'being-hypothesis.' In contrast to the mutability and ephemerality observed to characterize all that is to be encountered 'in this world,' God has long been thought of by those convinced of his reality, if not as the only 'true being,' at least as the most perfect one, the 'being' *par excellence*, and even 'being itself.' And Nietzsche observes that while many philosophers have been willing to relinquish or forego belief in the existence of God, they have generally remained wedded to the idea that beyond the flux of 'appearance' there must exist some sort of reality answering to the same general description, in which 'the highest desiderata, the highest values, the highest perfection' are to be found. He continues:

> One has unlearned the habit of conceding to this posited idea the reality of a person; one has become atheistic. But has the ideal itself been renounced? — At bottom, the last metaphysicians still seek it in true 'reality,' the 'thing-in-itself' compared to which everything else is merely apparent. It is their dogma that our apparent world, being so plainly *not* the expression of this ideal, cannot be 'true' — and that, at bottom, it does not even lead us back to that metaphysical world as its cause (*WP* 17).

It is with this tendency of thought in mind that Nietzsche urges that we 'abolish the real world,' going on to say: 'The apparent world and the world invented by a lie — this is the antithesis. The latter has hitherto been called the "real world," "truth," "God," This is what we have to abolish' (*WP* 461). He suggests the necessity of a 'critique of the concept "true and apparent world",' in connection with which contrast he contends that 'of these, the first is a mere fiction, constructed of fictitious entities' (*WP* 568). He even goes so far as to refer to the notion of ' "absolute reality," "being-in-itself" ' as 'a contradiction' (*WP* 580). For, he argues, 'we possess the concept "being",' no less than the concept ' "thing," only as a relational concept — ' (*WP* 583A).

Thus, while Nietzsche maintains that 'whatever philosophical standpoint one may adopt today, from every point of view the *erroneousness* of the world in which we think we live is the surest and firmest fact that we can lay eyes on' (*BGE* 34), he urges 'war on all presuppositions on the basis of which one has invented a true world' (*WP* 583B). He does so in part because he believes that 'this hypothesis of beings is the source of all world-defamation,' the latter resulting from the idea that in the case of the former one has to do with a ' "better world," the "true world," the "world beyond," the "thing-in-itself" ' (*WP* 708). But he also does so because he considers this hypothesis in any form to be profoundly erroneous, and regards 'the "true" world' as 'an idea which is no longer good for anything.' It is, he continues, 'an idea which has become useless and superfluous — *consequently*, a refuted idea: let us abolish it!' (*TI* IV). So, in the section of *Twilight* prior to that in which this passage occurs, he writes:

> *First proposition.* The reasons for which 'this' world has been characterized as 'apparent' are the very reasons which indicate its reality; any other kind of reality is absolutely indemonstrable.
> *Second proposition.* The criteria which have been bestowed on the 'true being' of things are the criteria of not-being, of *naught*; the 'true world' has been constructed out of contradiction to the actual world: indeed [it itself is] an apparent world, insofar as it is merely a moral-optical illusion (*TI* III:6).

Whatever needs the idea of the existence of a 'true world' of 'being' transcending 'this world' of becoming and change may answer to, therefore, and however understandable its emergence in the course of the development of human thought may be, Nietzsche considers it to be completely untenable philosophically. We have 'absolutely no right to it' (*WP* 12A); intellectual integrity demands that we not only withhold assent to it but repudiate it altogether. The passages cited above give some indication of his reasons for taking this position; but his case against the 'being-hypothesis' requires to be spelled out more fully.

XIII

As in the instances of his critiques of the notions of 'God,' the 'soul' and 'things,' Nietzsche's procedure here is to marshal a variety of considerations which collectively are intended and held to undermine the philosophical legitimacy or credibility of this hypothesis. Certain of these considerations are derivative from or similar to points discussed in the previous section. Thus, for example, Nietzsche argues that 'the psychological derivation of

the belief in things forbids us to speak of "things-in-themselves" '
(*WP* 473). He contends that 'the antithesis "thing-in-itself" and
"appearance" is untenable,' on the grounds that 'the subject is a
fiction,' and that the former notion 'is fundamentally the conception of a "subject-in-itself",' a projection of this fictitious conception into and behind the world with which we find ourselves
confronted. Along with 'the subject' and 'things,' therefore, 'the
"thing-in-itself" also disappears' (*WP* 552). This notion is associated
above all with Kant; and Nietzsche joins many of Kant's critics in
attacking the use he made of it:

> Kant no longer has a right to his distinction 'appearance' and
> 'thing-in-itself' — he had deprived himself of the right to go on
> distinguishing in this old familiar way, in so far as he rejected
> as impermissible making inferences from phenomena to a cause
> of phenomena — in accordance with his conception of causality
> and its purely intra-phenomenal validity — which conception,
> on the other hand, already anticipates this distinction, as if the
> 'thing-in-itself' were not only inferred but *given* (*WP* 553).

More generally, he argues that 'questions [such as] what things
"in-themselves" may be like, apart from our sense receptivity and
the activity of our understanding, must be rebutted with the
question: how could we know that things exist? "Thingness" was
first created by us' (*WP* 569). He further maintains that 'the
"thing-in-itself" is nonsensical,' on the ground that 'If I remove
all the relationships, all the "properties," all the "activities" of a
thing, the thing does not remain over' (*WP* 558). Even if there
were to be a 'true world' of 'being,' therefore, he concludes that
it could not be supposed to be composed of entities of this sort.
While Nietzsche thus feels entitled to set aside this variant of
the 'being-hypothesis,' however, he recognizes that other variants
of it may be and have been proposed, which cannot be disposed
of this easily. In dealing with them he takes a number of different
tacks. One such line of criticism bears a certain similarity to
another part of his critique of the construal of the world's nature
in terms of 'the schematism of "things." ' He has been observed
to consider our development of and reliance upon this schematism
to be associated with the practical necessity of our having to be
able to categorize quickly, calculate readily and communicate
easily in order to be able to get along in the world and with each
other. He likewise takes the 'being-hypothesis' to answer to a
different but no less internal demand of the human intellect:
namely, the demand of our reason for a world more conform-
able to its nature than is the world of experience, even as the

160

latter is articulated by means of the imposition upon it of 'the schematism of "things." ' Thus, foremost among what he refers to as 'the places of origin of the notion of "another world," ' Nietzsche mentions 'the philosopher, who invents a world of reason, where reason and the logical functions are adequate: this is the origin of the "true" world' (*WP* 586C).

The difference between the two cases would appear to parallel Kant's distinction between the 'understanding,' which structures our experience in accordance with 'categories' it supplies (in the absence of which experience as we know it would be impossible and the 'sensible manifold' would be an unintelligible flux), and our 'reason,' which generates certain 'transcendent ideas' in accordance with its own nature and requirements, differing from the 'categories' in both form and function (serving as 'regulative principles' of purported utility in our theoretical endeavors to ascertain unity amid the diversity of our experience). For Nietzsche as for Kant, our utilization of 'the schematism of "things" ' is bound up with the character and operation of our 'understanding' as it structures our experience in such a way as to render it intelligible to us. And like Kant he gives a rather different account of the recurring postulation of a realm of 'true being' beyond the world of experience, linking it instead with the nature and requirements of our 'reason.' For it is taken to lead us to conceive of something unconditioned in contrast to the contents of our experience (none of which have this character), and to induce us to seek and suppose we may infer the existence of some sort of 'being' or 'beings' answering to this description beyond the phenomenal realm.

Nietzsche further follows Kant in maintaining that we err when we treat these conceptual products of both our 'understanding' and our 'reason' as notions which may be detached from the thought-processes from which they issue, and conceived as referring to something existing independently of these processes. For Kant, however, this is not the end of the matter; for he intends this criticism to apply only to metaphysical views insofar as they are considered solely with respect to what can and cannot be established by the use of our 'understanding' and our 'reason' in its 'pure *speculative* employment.' Thus he not only retains the notion of 'things-in-themselves,' but also concludes (on the basis of his reflections upon the nature and presuppositions of *morality*, and through the use of 'reason' in its 'pure *practical* employment'), that it is both meaningful and reasonable to suppose that there exists a 'noumenal world' in which notions closely paralleling the seemingly discredited 'ideas' of 'reason' have application, as 'constitutive' rather than merely 'regulative' principles. Nietzsche not only refuses to follow Kant in this, but also sees in Kant's reasons for making it one of the strongest reasons *he* can imagine for refusing to do so.

Before turning to this part of his case against the 'being-hypothesis,' however, that which focusses upon the relation between it and the demands of reason warrants further consideration. Ontological categories such as 'substance,' 'object' and 'being,' Nietzsche contends, 'have nothing to do with metaphysical truths'; for the 'inventive force that invented [all such] categories labored in the service of our needs,' rather than in the service of some impulse to apprehend the actual nature of the world (*WP* 513). Not only our 'senses,' he holds, but also 'our organs of knowledge' — our reason included — have 'developed only with regard to conditions of [our] preservation and growth.' He continues:

> 'The *real* and *apparent* world' — I have traced this antithesis back to *value* relations. We have projected the conditions of *our* preservation as predicates of being in general. Because we have to be stable in our beliefs if we are to prosper, we have made the 'real' world a world not of change and becoming, but one of being (*WP* 507).

Thus he holds that the 'categories' with which reason provides us, and in terms of which philosophers have been led to conceive of a 'true world' of 'being,' are to be regarded as ' "truths" only in the sense that they are conditions of life for us: as Euclidean space is a conditional "truth." ' And so, he goes on to observe, 'since no one would maintain that there is any necessity for men to exist, reason, as well as Euclidean space, is a mere idiosyncrasy of a certain species of animal' (*WP* 515). 'Logicizing, rationalizing, systematizing' are characteristic tendencies of human thought which developed initially 'as expedients of life' (*WP* 552), as a consequence of our having to cope with our environing world consciously rather than instinctively, and thus by learning 'to order, simplify, falsify, artificially distinguish' in order to facilitate observation and calculation. Once developed, however, these tendencies engendered a disposition to search for something in relation to which they could achieve greater satisfaction than they are capable of attaining in relation to the world of experience. Consequently, 'the fictitious world of subject, substance, "reason," etc., is needed,' in order to accommodate them (*WP* 517).

In other words: having come to accept the idea that these tendencies of mind alone are reliable guides in the search for knowledge, and finding that the process of rational thought in which they find expression does not meet with a comparably rational domain in the world of experience, philosophers concluded that this world must not be the 'true world,' and that there must exist a realm of 'being' beyond it so constituted as to answer to the criteria of 'knowledge' set by the nature of reason. The satisfaction of the requirements of logical reasoning is taken to be a necessary condition of the attainment of genuine knowledge. Such knowledge, it is further supposed, must be attainable, at least in principle — if not by us, then at least by an ideal 'knower' not subject to our limitations. The world with which we find ourselves confronted in experience is discovered to be such that it is not a suitable object of knowledge of this sort. Consequently, it is held, a realm of 'being' which would be a suitable object of it must exist as well. And such a realm, as the proper object of genuine knowledge, is thereby also most appropriately characterizable as the 'true world,' in relation to which the world of experience is 'merely apparent,' and less than truly or fully 'real.'

So Nietzsche writes: 'Man projects his drive to truth, his "goal" in a certain sense, outside himself as a world that has being, as a metaphysical world, as a "thing-in-itself," as a world already in existence.' But it is only 'his needs' which are reflected here, and which serve to 'invent the world upon which he works' (*WP* 552). In a note bearing the heading 'Psychology of Metaphysics,' Nietzsche draws together some of the considerations pertaining to the nature of *this* world (the world of human life and experience) which have led philosophers to conceive of such an 'other world':

> This world is apparent; consequently, there is a true world; —
> this world is conditional: consequently there is an uncon-
> ditioned world; — this world is full of contradiction; conse-
> quently there is a world free of contradiction; — this world
> is a world of becoming: consequently there is a world of
> being: — all false conclusions (blind trust in reason: if A
> exists, then the opposite concept B must also exist) (*WP* 579).

At least a part of the problem here, according to Nietzsche, is that it is a common tendency among philosophers to take a certain understanding of the criteria for the applicability of the notion of 'reality' for granted — namely, one according to which these criteria are assimilated to those of sound logical reasoning. It might appear eminently 'reasonable' to suppose that, in the principles of logic and the categories of reason, we find conditions which must be satisfied by any conception of the world warranting serious consideration where the issue is the fundamental nature of 'reality' (beyond and independently of our particular thoughts and feelings and perceptions as they occur in the stream of our experience, with which it is not to be identified). But the reason it is so 'reasonable' to suppose that nothing which does not conform to them can lay claim to this title — and indeed that what is most truly and fully rational must also be what is most truly and fully real — is that the notion of rationality has been employed in the determination of our conception of what it is 'reasonable' to suppose. And it is Nietzsche's contention that this wedding of the notions of 'reality' and 'rationality' has been most unfortunate:

> The aberration of philosophy is that, instead of seeing in logic and the categories of reason means toward the adjustment of the world for utilitarian calculation (basically, toward an expedient *falsification*), one believed one possessed in them the criterion of truth and *reality*. . . . And behold, suddenly the world fell apart into a 'true' world and an 'apparent' world: and precisely the world that man's reason had devised for him to live and settle in was discredited. Instead of employing the forms as a tool for making the world manageable and calculable, the madness of the philosophers divined that in these categories is presented the concept of that world to which the one in which man lives does not correspond (*WP* 584).

This ' "true" world,' in short, is a conceptualization of the underlying nature of reality developed in accordance with our most basic needs and the patterns of thought with which we feel ourselves to be most at home and best able to operate. Precisely because the character of this conceptualization is so conditioned, however, the supposition that the world in fact must be as it is thus conceived to be is at best a piece of naiveté. So Nietzsche speaks not only of the 'undemonstrability' of 'a "world-in-itself," ' but also of the more decisive attainment of 'an insight into the erroneous procedures by means of which this whole concept is arrived at' (*WP* 580).

XIV

If for Nietzsche the idea of a 'true world' of 'being' is itself a product of rational thought reflecting its own nature rather than that of the actual world, the pervasive philosophical attachment to the notion is a phenomenon which has yet another, psychologically deeper, root. And the analysis of this phenomenon he proposes constitutes the final part of his case against the 'being-hypothesis.' 'Finally,' he writes, 'one discovers of what material

164

one has built the "true world" ' (*WP* 37). And with this discovery, he holds, one can no longer in good conscience continue to attach any real significance to the fact that such a world has not been shown to be an outright logical impossibility. For 'as soon as man finds out how that world is fabricated solely from psychological needs,' it becomes clear that 'he has absolutely no right to it.' No alternative remains to 'disbelief in any metaphysical world,' which does not merely suspend judgment with reference to the 'being-hypothesis' but moreover 'forbids itself any belief in a *true* world' (*WP* 12A).

What Nietzsche calls his 'psychology of philosophers,' discussed at length in the first chapter, is given its most extensive application in this general context. As was there observed, the kind of insight such analysis is capable of affording admittedly does not constitute the kind of argument with which philosophers generally feel most at ease and are accustomed to regarding as capable of deciding issues conclusively. It must be granted, however, that if nothing more compelling can be offered in defense of the tenability of a hypothesis than the persistence among those who adhere to it of certain desires and dissatisfactions the 'human, all-too-human' nature of which becomes apparent once they are stripped of their philosophical camouflage and exposed to the light of day, Nietzsche is surely right to maintain that 'intellectual conscience' requires of us that we reject it.

Speaking of the construal of the notion of 'reality' in such a way that only a world of 'being' could merit this designation, Nietzsche asks: 'Whence does man here derive the concept *reality*? . . . Contempt, hatred for all that perishes, changes, varies — whence comes this valuation of that which remains constant?' He observes that, 'obviously, the will to truth is here merely the desire for a world of the constant.' And he then writes: 'What kind of man reflects in this way? An unproductive, suffering kind, a kind weary of life.' Such a man 'seeks . . . a world that is not self-contradictory, not deceptive, does not change,' and moreover, 'a world in which one does not suffer: contradiction, deception, change — causes of suffering!' (*WP* 585A). In the note entitled 'Psychology of Metaphysics' cited earlier, in which Nietzsche refers to the reasoning according to which, e.g., 'this world is a world of becoming: consequently there is a world of being,' he likewise suggests that 'it is suffering that inspires these conclusions: fundamentally they are *desires* that such a world should exist.' Indeed, he contends, 'to imagine another, more valuable world is an expression of hatred for a world that makes one suffer: the *ressentiment* of metaphysicians against actuality is here creative' (*WP* 579).

Thus Nietzsche discerns here a profound underlying dissatisfaction with life as we must live it. The interpretation of this world of change, struggle and suffering as merely apparent in relation to a 'true world' of 'being' is diagnosed as a response to a deep-seated antipathy to these and related features of life in this world, which he links to an inability to take them in stride. It serves to satisfy a compelling psychological need both to play down the significance of this inability — or to represent it as a virtue — and to substitute for this world a 'reality' with which those in question can feel more at ease. The 'being-hypothesis,' for Nietzsche, requires to be viewed in the light of this 'general insight' that 'it is the instinct of life-weariness, and not that of life, which has created the "other world" ' (*WP* 586C). And if this is so, it would indeed seem to place the hypothesis in serious doubt.

It is in *Twilight* that he sets out his thinking along these lines most directly and succinctly. In the section entitled ' "Reason" in Philosophy,' he develops his position in four 'propositions,' the first two of which have been cited in section XII above. In the first he simply insists upon the 'reality' of ' "this" world' and of it alone, maintaining that 'any other kind of reality is absolutely indemonstrable.' In the remaining three, however, he turns his attention to the issue of how the idea of a 'true world' contrasting with ' "this" world' could have arisen, given the indemonstrability of the former. In the 'second proposition' he alludes to the role of 'morality' in the motivation of its acceptance, characterizing it as 'a moral-optical illusion,' and contending that 'the "true world" has been constructed out of contradiction to the actual world.' He then proceeds to elaborate upon this suggestion and to analyze and diagnose the phenomenon of belief in the existence of such a 'true world' as follows:

> *Third proposition.* To invent fables about a world 'other' than this one has no meaning at all, unless an instinct of slander, detraction, and suspicion against life has gained the upper hand in us: in that case, we avenge ourselves against life with a phantasmagoria of 'another,' a 'better' life.
> *Fourth proposition.* Any distinction between a 'true' and an 'apparent' world — whether in the Christian manner or in the manner of Kant . . . — is only a suggestion of decadence, a symptom of the *decline of life* (*TI* III:6).

XV

Let us now review the case Nietzsche makes against the 'being-

166

hypothesis.' We are confronted with the problem of deciding what is to be made of the notion of the existence of a 'true world' of 'being' which has been advanced by many philosophers in one form or another, and which they have supposed to constitute the 'real world,' in relation to which ' "this" world' of human life and experience is contrastingly characterized as 'merely apparent.' We see upon reflection that the existence of such a world is indemonstrable, and moreover that there are no philosophically acceptable reasons which may be adduced in support of the supposition that anything of the kind exists. Indeed, we find that we cannot even meaningfully speak of it, once we recognize that the categories of reason themselves are of justifiable applicability only within the context of our dealings with ' "this" world,' and only by virtue of their pragmatic utility as means of facilitating our attempts to come to terms with it. Thus our task becomes that of deciding what is to be made of the fact of the emergence and persistence of the idea.

Some light is shed upon this phenomenon by a consideration of the way in which our language prompts us to think in terms of 'beings' whenever we seek to comprehend events. But this does not suffice to explain why philosophers have been so willing, and indeed so determined, to dismiss the entire world of human life and experience as 'merely apparent,' and to envision a 'true world' beyond it which contrasts markedly with it. No purely philosophical 'will to truth' can have been their dominant impulse. As long as one restricts oneself to a consideration of their views taken at face value, their commitment to the 'being-hypothesis' must appear to be something of an enigma. It loses its enigmatic character, however, if one takes seriously the idea that philosophers are not beyond the reach of very human needs and wants, and that in their thinking it is 'most often a desire of the heart that has been filtered and made abstract' which 'they defend with reasons they have sought after the fact' (*BGE* 5). Guided by the suspicion that we may be confronted here with a case in point, one may begin by reflecting upon the value judgments implicit in their framing and elaboration of the distinction under consideration, and then proceed to consider what could account for their commitment to these values.

Approached in this way, the notion of 'a world "other" than this one' ceases to have 'no meaning at all' and becomes quite intelligible — while at the same time losing whatever claim it might still have been supposed to have to philosophical respectability. For what renders it thus intelligible is its interpretation as an expression of a profound dissatisfaction with life in 'this world,' combined with a desperate determination to justify and assert oneself in the face of it. It becomes intelligible, in other words, just when viewed as a kind of compensatory device, defensive and reactive in nature, indicative of an inability to come to terms with and accept the reality of 'this world' and life in it as we must live it, and involving the wish-fulfilling projection beyond it of the opposites of those characteristics of it which are found most objectionable.

If this is what is to be made of the fact of the emergence and persistence of this notion, however, it is clear what is to be made of the 'being-hypothesis' as a philosophical thesis: it is a fiction with which we need and ought no longer to concern ourselves. 'This world' is the only one we have any reason and any right to suppose exists, and to regard as 'reality.' It is not to be dismissed as 'merely apparent' in relation to some 'other' or 'true world,' even if it is not to be characterized philosophically in the terms we ordinarily use to describe 'the world in which we think we live' either. But this only serves to raise anew — rather than to answer — the question of what we are left with when we arrive, with Nietzsche, at the end of the 'history of an error' which he sets forth in the section of *Twilight of the Idols* entitled 'How the "True World" Finally Became a Fable':

> 1. The true world — attainable for the sage, the pious, the virtuous man; he lives in it, *he is it*. . . .
> 2. The true world — unattainable for now, but promised for the sage, the pious, the virtuous man ('for the sinner who repents'). . . .
> 3. The true world — unattainable, indemonstrable, unpromisable; but the very thought of it — a consolation, an obligation, an imperative. . . .
> 4. The true world — unattainable? At any rate, unattained. And being unattained, also *unknown*. Consequently, not consoling, redeeming, or obligating: how could something unknown obligate us? . . .
> 5. The 'true' world — an idea which is no longer good for anything, not even obligating — an idea which has become useless and superfluous — *consequently*, a refuted idea: let us abolish it! . . .
> 6. The true world — we have abolished. What world has remained? The apparent one perhaps? But no! *With the true world we have also abolished the apparent one* (TI IV).

'*This* world' nonetheless remains; and in the following chapter it shall be seen what Nietzsche has to say about it. His critique of the main varieties of classical metaphysics, leading to the conclusion that the 'God-,' 'soul-,' 'thing-' and 'being-hypotheses' are all to be rejected, is intended to make an end of metaphysics-as-ontology generally. It by no means follows, however, that on his view there is nothing whatever to be said about the world that is both philosophically significant and any more tenable than these hypotheses. On the contrary, he has a good deal to say about it; and he is convinced that a strong enough case can be made for the account he develops to enable it to compete successfully for our philosophical allegiance with any rival interpretations on the horizon. Before turning to it, however, it is necessary to consider his treatment of one such rival, which he would appear to regard as its only serious one, once those considered up to this point have been dismissed.

Mechanism and causalism

XVI

'Of all the interpretations of the world attempted hitherto,' Nietzsche observes, 'the mechanistic one seems today to stand victorious in the foreground' (*WP* 618). This interpretation, which he associated with the science of his day, is at least in certain respects closer to his own than those framed in terms of the various religious and metaphysical hypotheses considered up to this point in this chapter. He parts company with it in no uncertain terms, however, finding much to object to in this leading 'naturalistic' alternative to his own avowedly 'anti-metaphysical' conception of the world's nature. It is his contention that 'mechanistic theory must be considered an imperfect and merely provisional hypothesis' at best (*WP* 1066), requiring to be superseded along with these older hypotheses and interpretations – to which, indeed, he takes it to be more closely related than its adherents generally recognize. He may borrow certain notions from it, and build upon it in certain ways; but in his hands what he appropriates of it is significantly transformed, and what he finds of value in it is modest in comparison with what he rejects.

It is a basic tenet of the 'mechanistic world view' as Nietzsche conceives of it that, very crudely put, the world is a collection of 'matter in motion' – a world consisting of material units, which have certain properties, are possessed of varying and perhaps also changing amounts and kinds of force, impinge upon and affect each other causally, and thus produce effects upon and are modified (either in their natures or their behavior) by each other, in accordance with general and immutable laws. One of his criticisms of this conception of the world relates to an implication of the Second Law of Thermodynamics deriving from mechanistic theory: a world constituted along these lines would sooner or later have to reach an inert final state of equilibrium, as a consequence of its 'running down' through the transformation of all of the potential energy of its constituent elements into kinetic energy, which eventually would be completely expended in the course of their interaction. '*Because* the world has not [already] reached this [state],' however, Nietzsche maintains that mechanism stands refuted.

In reaching this conclusion, he recognizes that it is necessary to assume certain things; but he takes his assumptions to be quite reasonable. They are, first, 'finite force' (*WP* 595) — that is, the fact that the amount of available energy in the universe is not unlimited. His second assumption is 'No God' (ibid.); i.e., there exists no power transcending this world which might be supposed to serve as the source of a continuing infusion of additional available energy into it replacing that which is expended. He further assumes 'the temporal infinity of the world in the past' (*WP* 1066), rejecting the supposition that the world could have 'had a beginning' (in the absence of a transcendent power which could at some point have created it). And finally, he makes the assumption that were the world ever to reach an inert state, it could not of itself emerge from this state, somehow replenishing its expended energy on its own. Given these assumptions, and the further point (which Nietzsche considers incontrovertible) that the world is not presently in such a final state of equilibrium or inertness, he takes it to follow that the world cannot be supposed to tend toward such a state. This, however, is required by the mechanistic theory under consideration. And so, he concludes, this theory must be rejected.

Thus Nietzsche observes that if the world 'were in any way capable of a pausing and becoming fixed . . ., then all becoming would long since have come to an end' (*WP* 1062). But it has not done so. 'That a state of equilibrium is never reached,' he therefore maintains, 'proves that it is not possible' (*WP* 1064). And he draws out the implications of these remarks for the mechanistic world view as follows:

If the world could in any way become rigid, dry, dead,
nothing, or if it could reach a state of equilibrium . . ., then
this state must have been reached. But it has not been reached:
from which it follows —
This is the sole certainty we have in our hands to serve as
a corrective to a great host of world hypotheses possible in

themselves. If, e.g., the mechanistic theory cannot avoid the consequence, drawn for it by William Thompson, of leading to a final state, then the mechanistic theory stands refuted (*WP* 1066).

This is only one of the further lines of argument Nietzsche advances, however. And while he believes it to be decisive even in the absence of any other considerations, he directs most of his criticisms to other features of mechanism. His most fundamental objections center upon the two notions involved in the conception of the world as 'matter in motion.' It must be recognized, he contends, that 'the theory of a mechanistic world' essentially involves 'employing two fictions: the concept of *motion* (taken from our sense language) and the concept of the *atom* (= unity, deriving from our psychical "experience"): the mechanistic theory presupposes a sense prejudice and a psychological prejudice' (*WP* 635). These two conceptions are closely connected with each other, and also with the notion of causality required by ready reckoning: 'The mechanistic world is imagined as only sight and touch imagine a world (as "moved") — so as to be calculable — thus causal unities are invented, "things" (atoms) whose effect remains constant (— transference of the false concept of subject to the concept of the atom)' (*WP* 635).

As has been seen, Nietzsche holds that 'the origin of atomism' is to be found in our need to be able to 'comprehend the world' in a way that both reduces it to the familiar and enables us 'to calculate it'; and 'to be able to calculate it, we have to have constant causes; because we find no such constant causes in actuality, we invent them for ourselves — the atoms' (*WP* 624). It is a mere 'prejudice' to suppose that science reveals to us the existence of any such constant units: 'We have *slipped in* the unchanging, my physicist friends, deriving it from metaphysics as always' (*WP* 623). The same observation applies here that applies to the 'thing-hypothesis' in any other form — the fate of which mechanism so conceived thus shares, as a readily recognizable form of it: 'We need "unities" in order to be able to reckon: that does not mean we must suppose that such unities exist' (*WP* 635).

Philosophically considered, therefore, mechanism as a world view formulated in the language of natural science does not differ as markedly from pre-scientific versions of this hypothesis and from the 'being-hypothesis' as might be supposed:

Physicists believe in a 'true world' in their own fashion: a firm systematization of atoms in necessary motion, the same for all beings. . . . But they are in error. The atom they posit is

171

inferred according to the logic of the perspectivism of consciousness — and is therefore itself a subjective fiction. This world picture they sketch differs in no essential way from the subjective world picture: it is only construed with more extended sense, but with *our* senses nonetheless — (*WP* 636).

Thus Nietzsche concludes that 'the concept "atom," the distinction between the "seat of a driving force and the force itself," is a sign language derived from our logical-psychical world.' And he makes essentially the same point with respect to the idea of 'motion,' even though it is one of his own most basic claims that the world is to be conceived dynamically, in terms of 'process': 'The mechanistic concept of "motion" is already a translation of the original process into the sign language of sight and touch' (*WP* 625). This concept, he argues, is merely a refinement of the inadequate understanding of what is involved in the occurrence of an event resulting from our tendency to approach it by asking, 'what was there to be perceived by sight and touch when this event took place?' It thus belongs in 'an inventory of human experiences,' in which it is to be included owing to the fact that 'man wants to arrange all events as events accessible to sight and touch' (*WP* 640). And it has its only legitimate application within the context of human sensibility and that perspectival and 'erroneous' construction of the world conditioned by our senses with which we are constrained to operate. So Nietzsche speaks of 'the conception of "motion" ' as involving 'a translation' of the world of processes and events in which we live 'into a visible world — a world for the eyes.' He continues:

This always carries the idea that *something* is moved — this always supposes, whether as the fiction of a little clump atom or even as the abstraction of this, the dynamic atom, a thing that produces effects — i.e., we have not got away from the habit into which our senses and language seduce us. Subject, object, a doer added to the doing, the doing separated from that which it does: let us not forget that this is mere semiotics and nothing real. Mechanistic theory as a theory of motion is already a translation into the sense language of man (*WP* 634).

XVII

The fact that we find the world more readily 'calculable' when we construe it mechanistically, Nietzsche contends, constitutes no argument in favor of the mechanistic world view as a philosophically

172

viable world interpretation. For, first, let it be supposed that when we thus render events capable of subsumption under 'formulas' and amenable to mathematical treatment, we do not misrepresent what actually occurs, but rather merely simplify their description and fix upon those of their features which admit of being dealt with in this way. It still would not follow that what we thereby come up with is an account of them enabling us either to explain or to understand what is happening. So Nietzsche remarks: 'It is an illusion that something is *known* when we possess a mathematical formula for an event: it is only designated, described, nothing more!' (*WP* 628). Moreover, he takes the status and significance of such descriptions to be philosophically problematical, in several respects. He asks: 'The calculability of the world, the expressibility of all events in formulas — is this really "comprehension"? How much of a piece of music has been understood when that in it which is calculable and can be reduced to formulas has been reckoned up?' (*WP* 624). And he is inclined to suppose that, in the case of the world and events generally as in the case of pieces of music and works of art, that about them which can thus be captured will seldom be of much importance in relation to what is missed.

Mechanistic theory does not simply involve the characterization of the world in terms of 'the sign language of sight and touch' and the 'sign language derived from our logical-psychical world.' It also endeavors to render experience thus characterized quantifiable — or, otherwise put, to reduce what is thus experienced to a form in which it is calculable in mathematical terms. For (as was observed in the previous chapter) this, on Nietzsche's view, is of the very nature of scientific thinking, thus serving more than anything else to distinguish 'science' from ordinary thought. Indeed, he suggests that on 'the *scientific* view of the world,' the 'only value' is 'what can be counted and calculated' (*WP* 677). He does not dispute the utility of this approach 'for the purpose of mastering nature' (*WP* 610), and is further prepared to allow that something of what transpires may thereby be grasped. The point upon which he insists, however, is that this does not amount to much. 'If I reduce a regular event to a formula, I have foreshortened, facilitated, etc., the description of the whole phenomena. But I have established no "law," I have [simply] raised the question how it happens that something here repeats itself' (*WP* 629).

More fundamentally, Nietzsche contends that the mechanistic characterization of the world in terms which lend themselves readily to quantitative treatment and thus enhance its calculability does not merely result in an overly simplified and superficial description

173

of it, but also 'falsifies' it in a way to which philosophical objection must be taken. 'Ultimately,' he says, 'man finds in things nothing but what he himself has imported into them: the finding is called science' (*WP* 606). And among the things which we erroneously 'import' into the world, in both our ordinary thinking and when we construe it mechanistically, is 'the concept of number.' This is no less merely 'phenomenal,' he maintains, than 'the concept of the thing' and 'the concept of motion.' These are notions mechanism borrows from ordinary experience and 'injects' into the world; and Nietzsche considers these 'additions' to require to be 'eliminated' (*WP* 635). It is we who establish the mathematical concepts in terms of which the events we experience become quantifiable and calculable; just as it is in the requirements of our thought rather than in the nature of reality that the principles of logic and the categories of reason have their origin. Precisely because it involves the characterization of the world and events in terms which maximize their calculability, the world view associated with mechanistic theory may be seen to be defective philosophically. For this requires the imposition upon them of a set of concepts which can be neither assumed nor even legitimately suggested to apply to them.

It further involves the attribution to them of a kind and degree of constancy and 'sameness' which they both fail to exhibit empirically and cannot be shown to have in any other way. It is only in the 'thought-objects' we create and invent for ourselves that we meet with these features. In experience we merely are confronted (at most) by similarities; and 'the "apparent fact" of things that are the same' (*WP* 520) is simply a result of our tendency to ignore differences and changes, and to treat the similar as the same. It may be natural, useful, and even necessary for us to do so; but that is only a fact about our nature and needs, rather than about the world with which we thus attempt to deal. So, in a note entitled 'Critique of the Mechanistic Theory,' Nietzsche observes: ' "Things" do not behave regularly, according to a *rule*; there are no things (− they are fictions invented by us); they behave just as little under the constraint of necessity' (*WP* 634).

Even if what is taken to answer to the notion of sameness or regularity (and to satisfy the demand for something about the world that is quantifiable and calculable) is not 'things' of some sort but rather simply the purported conformity of events to laws which govern them, according to Nietzsche, we only substitute one fiction for another. It is no more legitimate to conceive of the world in terms of the operation of 'laws,' he argues, than it is to conceive of it in terms of the behavior of 'things.'

'Regularity' in succession is only a metaphorical expression, *as if* a rule were being followed here; not a fact. In the same way 'conformity with a law.' We discover a formula by which to express an ever-recurring kind of result: we have therewith discovered no 'law,' even less a force that is the cause of the recurrence of a succession of results. That something always happens thus and thus is here interpreted as if a creature always acted thus and thus as a result of obedience to a law or a law-giver (*WP* 632).

Nietzsche readily grants that we find it convenient and useful, for purposes of 'our day-to-day calculations,' to characterize the successions of events we discern in terms of their 'obedience' to 'laws.' He contends, however, that in the world (or, as he allows himself to say here, 'in the "in-itself" '), 'there is no rule of law' (*BGE* 21). He detects the surreptitious influence of the picture of ourselves as moral agents subject to a moral 'law' in our adoption of this way of thinking about the world, and objects to the result-ing injection of a sort of anthropomorphic ' "morality" into the world by the fiction that it is obedient' (*WP* 634). Thus he writes: 'I beware of speaking of chemical "laws": that savors of morality'; and he goes on to observe that it is quite inappropriate to interpret events in the world as if they exhibited anything like 'a respect for "laws." ' (*WP* 630). We may 'reduce a regular event to a formula'; but 'it is mythology to think that forces here obey a law, so that, as a consequence of their obedience, we have the same phenomenon each time' (*WP* 629). Our belief in the 'lawfulness' of nature is held to involve a projection into the world of a notion deriving from certain purely conventional features of our social existence. And so, for Nietzsche, this belief cannot be regarded as anything more than a convenient fiction.

This is a point of some importance, warranting brief elaboration. Nietzsche's basic idea here is that the commonplace recognition of the ordering influence upon human behavior of men's acceptance of the idea that they are bound to obey various rules and edicts, issuing from some source having the authority to command things of them, has given rise to the view that whatever orderliness there is in nature is a consequence of the fact that natural events are similarly or analogously regulated. During most of the period in which this view has been embraced, the recognition that laws as we ordinarily understand them exist because they have been laid down by a lawgiver has inclined its adherents to complete the analogy (and thereby render it at least more coherent than it would otherwise be). Such 'laws of nature' were construed as edicts governing the natural world laid down by God; for God's relation to the world was conceived in such a way that he could quite plausibly be taken to fill the role of lawgiver.

A world in which there is no God, however, and which is not the creation of any such transcendent power, can no longer be interpreted as one in which events occur in accordance with divine decrees. The notion of 'laws of nature' has survived belief in the existence of God in the thinking of many. But Nietzsche contends that it is a mere 'residue' of such belief, an *'entr'acte'* (*WP* 69) which must give way to a different understanding of natural events now that the theological underpinnings of the use of the analogy have been removed. Without God, the world can no more be viewed as a world subject to 'laws' than it can be conceived as an artifact. Whatever order there may be in the world cannot be explained by means of the projection of our notion of 'law' into the world, because the very meaning of this notion renders its employment unintelligible once it is established that there exists no power beyond it capable of acting as a lawgiver in relation to it. And if the source of such 'laws' is taken to be, not God, but rather we ourselves, it becomes all the more evident that any world view involving reference to them is thereby rendered untenable insofar as it purports to be anything more than an anthropomorphically conditioned and distorted characterization of it.

Thus Nietzsche writes: 'Let us beware of saying that there are laws in nature. There are only necessities: there is nobody who commands, nobody who obeys, nobody who transgresses' (*GS* 109). In supposing that there are such laws, the 'error is made of giving a false reality to a fiction, as if events were in some way obedient to something.' To speak of events as determined in their occurrence by 'laws' is to construe them metaphorically, in terms of an analogy the use of which is understandable but insupportable. The conception of a world governed by such 'laws' is one which *'we* alone . . . have devised . . .; and when we project and mix this symbol world into things as if it existed "in itself"; we act once more as we have always acted — *mythologically'* (*BGE* 21). It may be that something more than mere human invention is involved in this notion, which can be brought to light through what might in similar language be termed a process of 'demythologizing' it. Whatever this process might yield, however, Nietzsche holds that it will in any event necessitate the abandonment of all talk of 'laws.'

Forgive me as an old philologist who cannot desist from the malice of putting his finger on bad modes of interpretation:

but 'nature's conformity to law,' of which you physicists talk so proudly, as though — why, it exists only owing to your interpretation and bad 'philology.' It is no matter of fact, no 'text,' but rather only a naively humanitarian emendation and perversion of meaning, with which you make abundant concessions to the democratic instincts of the modern soul! 'Everywhere equality before the law; nature is no different in that respect, no better off than we are' — (*BGE* 22).

He goes on to suggest an alternative interpretation, remarking that 'someone might come along' who would propose that the world does indeed have 'a "necessary" and "calculable" course, *not* because laws obtain in it, but because they are absolutely *lacking*, and every power draws its ultimate consequences at every moment' (ibid.). For the moment, however, I shall not elaborate upon his meaning, postponing discussion of this suggestion until the next chapter. Another matter remains to be dealt with here, related to but transcending that just considered: Nietzsche's treatment of the notion of causality. This notion figures centrally in the mechanistic world view, as well as in our ordinary way of thinking about the world. His critique of it constitutes another part of his case against mechanism, and also is of broader interest. It therefore warrants examination.

XVIII

Nietzsche is quite prepared to allow that this notion is one we constantly employ, and indeed could scarcely get along without. Indeed, he singles out 'the law of causality' as one of 'the most strongly believed a priori "truths," ' which not only is 'a very well acquired habit of belief,' but moreover is 'so much a part of us that not to believe in it would destroy the race.' He is by no means of the opinion, however, that such considerations suffice to establish the legitimacy and soundness of the supposition that the world is in fact to be conceived in terms of sequences of causally connected events. Thus he characterizes all such 'truths' as mere '*provisional assumptions*,' of which it requires to be asked, even after making such observations as these: 'But are they for that reason truths? What a conclusion! As if the preservation of man were a proof of truth!' (*WP* 497). As with all other such conceptual *modi operandi*, so also here: their needfulness 'does not prove them,' since 'life is no argument. The conditions of life might include error' (*GS* 121).

Nietzsche's discussion of causality is complicated by the fact that he frequently avails himself of the terminology of 'cause' and 'effect,' not only in passages in which he obviously is merely adopting it for purposes of convenience (as in his analysis of various psychological and social phenomena), but also in the course of many remarks pertaining to the world and our experience of it. The latter circumstance suggests that his objections to the notion are not intended to apply to every possible formulation or construal of it, but rather only to certain forms of it. Thus, for example, he writes: 'Cause and effect − a dangerous concept *so long as* one thinks of something that causes and something upon which an effect is produced' (*WP* 552; emphasis added). The nature and scope of his critical analysis of the notion and its uses must be considered, however, before the question of the sort of modification of it he is prepared to countenance can be dealt with.

To begin with, Nietzsche takes it to be significant that 'in our science . . ., the concept of cause and effect is reduced to the relationship of equivalence' of so-called 'causally' related states of affairs such that 'the same quantum of force is present on both sides' (*WP* 688); and thus that, in employing such a 'reduced' form of the notion, 'mechanistic theory can therefore only *describe* processes [in quantitative terms], not explain them' (*WP* 660). He considers it important to recognize both that 'the concept of *"causa"* is . . . a means of description' having some practical utility (rather than being either completely meaningless or entirely superfluous), and that it 'is only a means of expression' when cast in this form. The latter is something we tend to forget, owing to what he terms 'our bad habit of taking a mnemonic device, an abbreviative formula, to be an entity, finally a cause, e.g., to say of lightning, "it flashes" ' (*WP* 548). A part of the problem with the notion of causality, he suggests, is that it is generally construed in a way which reflects our tendency to hypostatize such convenient 'means of expression.' Thus he writes:

> One should not wrongly reify 'cause' and 'effect,' as the natural scientists do (and whoever, like them, now 'naturalizes' in his thinking), according to the prevailing mechanical doltishness which makes the cause press and push until it 'effects' its end; one should use 'cause' and 'effect' only as pure concepts, that is to say, as conventional fictions for the purpose of designation and communication − *not* for explanation (*BGE* 21).

It is only as he continues beyond this exhortation, however, that it becomes clear that Nietzsche is not merely side-stepping the question of the appropriateness of construing the world's nature causalistically by focusing instead upon the way in which these terms function and ought to be used. For he goes on to assert that 'in the "in-itself" there is nothing of "causal connections," ' contending that 'it is we alone who have devised [the idea of] cause,' and that we merely 'project' it into the world (*BGE* 21). It is his position that 'there is no such thing as "cause" ' (*WP* 551); and he argues that 'the belief in cause and effect,' which man 'applies wherever anything happens,' is 'an atavism of the most ancient origin,' and one of our most deeply rooted and most untenable myths (*GS* 127). At least in its more usual form, he holds, the notion is philosophically unacceptable and requires to be repudiated.

Nietzsche takes this position *both* with respect to the understanding of causation in terms of 'something that causes and something upon which an effect is produced' (*WP* 552), *and* with respect to its construal in terms of states of affairs one of which is taken to be the 'cause' of the other. Thus, concerning the former, he observes that 'the interpretation of an event either as an act or the suffering of an act . . . says: every change, every becoming-other, presupposes an author and someone upon whom "change" is effected' (*WP* 546). And against this way of thinking he argues that 'if we no longer believe in the effective subject, then belief also disappears in effective things, in reciprocation, cause and effect between those phenomena that we call things' (*WP* 552).

Concerning the latter version of the notion he writes: 'Two successive states, the one "cause," the other "effect": this is false. The first has nothing to effect, the second has been effected by nothing' (*WP* 633). This second, rather more sophisticated construal of causality is on Nietzsche's view little more than a refinement and modification of the first, developed as a successor to it by philosophers convinced of the necessity of describing changes in the language of sequences of events rather than in that of alterations of things. He realizes that the two require to be dealt with in somewhat different ways; and thus some of his remarks are directed at one and some at the other. In both cases, however, he considers the same basic impulse to be operative: 'Not "to know" but to schematize — to impose upon chaos as much regularity and form as our practical needs require' (*WP* 515).

XIX

In believing in causality construed in the first of the ways distinguished above, Nietzsche contends that we are seduced and misled by 'language (and . . . the fundamental errors of reason that are petrified in it) which conceives and misconceives all effects as

179

conditioned by something that causes effects, by a "subject".'
Actually, he maintains, 'the "doer" is merely a fiction added to
the deed — the deed is everything' (*GM* I:13). The reasoning underlying the above belief is that 'all changes are effects,' and that 'all
effects suppose an agent' (*WP* 136). And this reasoning suffers
from a twofold defect: 'To regard an event as an "effecting," and
this as a being, that is a double error, or interpretation, of which
we are guilty.' For here we merely reason 'in accordance with the
conclusion: "every change must have an author"; — but this
conclusion is already mythology: it separates that which effects
from the effecting' (*WP* 531).

Nietzsche's basic point here is that when we observe something
happening, we do not observe one entity producing a change of
some sort in another. That is an interpretation of the event in terms
of a picture — and an erroneous one at that — borrowed from our
customary way of viewing ourselves and our own behavior. Thus,
in a note bearing the heading 'Critique of the concept "cause," '
he remarks: 'We have absolutely no experience of a cause; psychologically considered, we derive the entire concept from the subjective conviction that *we* are causes,' as, e.g., when we suppose that,
in reaching for something, I bring it about 'that the arm moves.'
But, he continues, 'that is an error. We separate ourselves, the
doers, from the deed, and we make use of this pattern everywhere
— we seek a doer for every event.' So he goes on to argue that
'*causa* is a capacity to produce effects that has been super-added
to the events,' concluding that 'there is no such thing.' For the
introspective 'cases in which [causality] seemed to be given to us,
and in which we have projected it out of ourselves in order to
understand an event, have been shown to be self-deceptions'
(*WP* 551). This argument is set out most clearly and completely
in a section in *Twilight*, which warrants citing at length:

> People have believed at all times that they knew what a cause
> is; but whence did we take our knowledge — or more precisely,
> our faith that we had such knowledge? From the realm of the
> famous 'inner facts,' of which not a single one has so far proved
> to be factual. We believed ourselves to be causal in the act of
> willing: we thought that here at least we caught causality in
> the act. Nor did one doubt that all the antecedents of an act,
> its causes, were to be sought in consciousness and would be
> found there once sought — as 'motives': else one would not
> have been free and responsible for it. Finally, who would have
> denied that a thought is caused? that the ego causes the
> thought?

Of these three 'inward facts' which seem to guarantee causality, the first and most persuasive is that of the will as cause . . .: first the causality of the will was firmly accepted as given, as *empirical*. . . .

Today we no longer believe a word of all this. . . . The will no longer moves anything, hence does not explain anything either. . . . The so-called *motive*: another error. . . . And as for the *ego*! That has become a fable, a fiction, a play on words: it has altogether ceased to think, feel or will!

What follows from this? There are no mental causes at all. The whole of the allegedly empirical evidence for that has gone to the devil. . . . And what a fine abuse we had perpetrated with this 'empirical evidence'; we *created* the world on this basis as a world of causes. . . . The most ancient and enduring psychology was at work here and did not do anything else: all that happened was considered a doing, all doing the effect of a will; the world became to it a multiplicity of doers (*TI* VI:3).

In short, it is Nietzsche's contention that 'our faith in causality itself' is 'at bottom' our 'belief in the causality of the will' (*BGE* 36). In the absence of this belief, the notion of 'a world of causes' would never have suggested itself to us; for, as Hume had observed, our experience of mundane events nowhere presents us with an instance of anything answering to the idea. 'We have believed in the will to such an extent that we have from our personal experience' — which is itself misinterpreted — 'introduced a cause into events in general' (*WP* 488). So for Nietzsche 'the propositions, "no effect without a cause," "every effect in turn [implies] a cause" appear as generalizations of [a] much more limited proposition: "no effecting without willing." ' And thus, he goes on to remark, 'when Schopenhauer assumed that all that has being is only a willing, he enthroned a primeval mythology' (*GS* 127). At its core is the ancient 'error that the will is something which is effective, that will is a capacity.' But 'today we know that it is only a word' (*TI* III:5).

If these points are well taken, they have important and serious consequences for causalism. The idea of relations of 'cause and effect between those phenomena that we call things' is philosophically untenable, not only because the world cannot be supposed actually to consist of 'things' standing in such relations to each other, but also because this idea proves upon analysis to involve the projection into the world of a fictitious notion of the 'will' as 'something which is effective.' 'Only because we have introduced subjects, "doers," into things does it appear that all events are the consequences of compulsion exerted upon subjects — exerted by whom? again by a "doer" ' (*WP* 552). If this is so, and if 'the faith in the will as the cause of effects is the faith in magically effective forces' (*GS* 127), then the conception of causality under consideration must be acknowledged to be a fiction, however convenient and even indispensable it may be.

It is suggested that our attachment to this notion derives from our inability to comprehend events in terms differing radically from those in which we are accustomed to view ourselves and our behavior. 'The psychological necessity for a belief in causality lies in the inconceivability of an event divorced from an intent,' Nietzsche writes, adding pointedly: 'by which naturally nothing is said concerning truth or untruth (the justification of such a belief)!' (*WP* 627). Here he both follows Hume and then parts company with him:

> We have no 'sense for the *causa efficiens*': here Hume was right; habit (but not only that of the individual!) makes us expect that a certain often-observed occurrence will follow another: nothing more! That which gives the extraordinary firmness to our belief in causality is not the great habit of seeing one occurrence following another but our inability to interpret events otherwise than as events caused by intentions (*WP* 550).

Thus our employment of and reliance upon the notion of causality neither reflect some innate structure of the human mind, nor is prompted by the discernment of 'causes' and 'effects' with the aid of some special intellectual faculty. It can readily be explained along lines which do not necessitate the postulation of anything so *ad hoc*. The so-called 'sense of causality' is no genuine intuition (*WP* 551), but rather simply a deeply ingrained custom of interpreting events in accordance with the 'doer—deed' model transferred from our self-interpretation along these lines: 'it is only from this that we derive the feeling of causality' (*WP* 667). So Nietzsche writes: 'Critique of the concept: cause. — From a psychological point of view the concept "cause" is our feeling of power resulting from the so-called act of will — our concept "effect" the superstition that this feeling of power is the motive power itself' (*WP* 689).

This 'feeling of power' is held to be the psychological phenomenon upon which the notion of and belief in our own causality (and thereby also the notion of and belief in causality more generally) ultimately rests. And if, in turn, an analysis of the nature and origin of this feeling is sought, Nietzsche suggests that it is to be given in terms of a combination of the socially inculcated 'feeling of responsibility' we have with respect to our behavior, and a misconstrual of the actual relation between 'our intention to perform an act' and the occurrence of acts conforming to our intentions. Thus he not only argues that our generalized belief in causality derives from our belief in the will as causally effective, and that this belief is a myth, but also is able to back up this argument with a plausible explanation of the existence of this myth.

Nietzsche is equally convinced of the untenability of that variant of 'causalism' which departs from the 'doer—deed' model to the extent of abandoning the construal of 'cause and effect' in terms of 'things' acting and being changed by being acted upon, in favor of construing this pair of concepts in terms of sequences of events, some of which (the 'effects') are brought about as a consequence of the occurrence of others (the 'causes'). Supposing the notion of causality to be so conceived, he argues, its employment is either vacuous or illegitimate. For it is vacuous if it is understood to do no more than refer to the regular ordering of certain sequences of events; while it is illegitimate if it is supposed to convey anything more about the relationship between them than that they are so ordered. In short, if the notion is no longer used to refer to anything more than the regular ordering of certain sequences of events in our experience, it is 'saved' only at the cost of being lost to mechanism as a world view.

One of Nietzsche's objections to causality conceived as a relation between events pertains to the artificiality of the notion of an 'event' itself. He writes: 'Cause and effect: such a duality probably never exists; in truth we are confronted by a continuum out of which we isolate a couple of pieces.' Indeed, he goes on to suggest, 'an intellect that could see cause and effect as a continuum and a flux and not, as we do, in terms of an arbitrary division and dismemberment, would repudiate the concept of cause and effect and deny all conditionality.' It may be that we cannot alter our mode of perception in such a way as to apprehend the flow of processes with which we have to deal in experience as a 'continuum.' It is at least within our power, however, to grasp that, 'where the naive man and inquirer of older cultures saw only two separate things,' the one being termed the 'cause' and the other the 'effect,' there is actually 'a manifold one-after-another,' requiring to be conceived as a flow of 'becoming' rather than as a 'series of "causes." ' And even this conception itself leaves a good deal to be desired as it stands: 'we have merely perfected the image of becoming without reaching beyond the image or behind it' (GS 112).

Nietzsche also makes several further observations in this connection. First: 'From the fact that something ensues regularly and ensues calculably, it does not follow that it ensues necessarily' (*WP* 552). And second: even if the 'necessity' of some such sequence is supposed, 'a necessary sequence of states does not imply a causal relationship between them.' His point here is that 'an event is neither effected nor does it effect,' its calculability notwithstanding; for '*the calculability of an event* does not reside in the fact that a rule is adhered to, or that a necessity is obeyed, or that a law of causality has been projected by us into every event: it resides in the *recurrence of "identical cases"* ' (*WP* 551). He places the words 'identical cases' in scare-quotes because, far from being prepared to grant that there actually are such cases, he in fact holds that we merely find it convenient to *treat* as identical various cases of sequences of events which are at most similar, and which exhibit differences we choose to ignore. This is a circumstance he takes to render even more dubious the common supposition that the sequentially ordered events involved constitute a 'causal chain.'

It thus seems to Nietzsche that to construe causality as a relation between 'consecutive appearances,' which in turn are conceived 'semiotically, in terms of the senses and of psychology' (*WP* 635), is a course having little to recommend it. For it either results in an erroneous attribution of the relations of 'effecting' and 'being effected by' to events which in fact merely succeed each other; or else it leads to the abandonment of the very idea of efficacy (through the reduction of the notion of causality to the notion of constant conjunction), transforming 'the concept of "*causa*" ' into a mere 'means of expression, nothing more; a means of description' (*WP* 645).

XX

It might therefore appear that Nietzsche would have us abandon the notion of causality altogether (except, perhaps, as a convenient 'means of expression' in the context of extra-philosophical discourse). In fact, however, he considers there to be something to the notion of causality after all; and he holds that, if properly construed, it may appropriately be retained and employed in philosophical discourse about the world and human life. Thus, for example, in a section of *The Gay Science* bearing the heading 'Two kinds of causes that are often confounded,' he writes: 'This seems to me to be one of my most essential steps and advances: I have learned to distinguish the cause of acting from the cause of acting in a particular way, in a particular direction, with a particular goal.' And he goes on to spell out this distinction as follows:

> The first kind of cause is a quantum of dammed-up energy that is waiting to be used up somehow, for something; while the second is, compared to this energy, something quite insignificant, for the most part a little accident in accordance with which this quantum 'discharges' itself in one particular way — a match versus a ton of powder (*GS* 360).

In this connection it is worth recalling Nietzsche's qualification of one of the basic criticisms he levels at the idea of causality: 'Cause and effect — a dangerous concept *so long as* one thinks of something that causes and something upon which an effect is produced' (*WP* 552). While he rejects the idea construed in this way, he is very differently disposed toward a modification of it in terms of 'power relationships' and an 'interplay of forces.' So, for example, he writes: 'Supposing that the world had a certain quantum of force at its disposal, then it is obvious that every displacement of power at any point would affect the whole system'; and he goes on to observe that, in this case, 'together with sequential causality there would be a contiguous and concurrent dependence' (*WP* 638).

The 'kind of causality' he is prepared to countenance (cf. *BGE* 36) is not that represented in the model of 'doer' and 'deed,' or in that of discrete but connected events. It is rather to be construed in terms of an 'interplay of forces' constituting a 'continuum.' If it is understood in terms of such an interplay and consequent redistribution of forces, he considers it not only convenient but also legitimate to make use of the notion. The fundamental mistake philosophers have made in speaking of causality, on his view, is not that of supposing that what happens at one time and place is significantly affected by what has happened and is happening at others; this is something upon which he himself insists. *'The mistake lies in the fictitious insertion of a subject'* (*WP* 632). Otherwise put, the mistake that has so long and commonly been made lies neither in the introduction of the idea of force nor in the supposition of the existence of connections. It consists rather in the hypostatization of the former through a 'doubling of the deed' leading to the treatment of causes as entities exerting force upon others, and in the related construal of causal connections as changes wrought by such entities upon others.

It might appear that Nietzsche's revision of the notion of causality along purely dynamic lines is a move which is by no means as far removed from the 'mechanistic world view' as he seems to think. Indeed, it would seem to parallel closely what has happened to it in the course of the evolution of this world view in the present century, as variations on the theme of 'matter in motion' gradually have come to be replaced by the idea of fields of force in interrelation. It seems to him, however, that mechanistic theory is too intimately bound up with the empiricist tradition to be capable of coming up with conceptions of force and causation constituting anything more than a kind of useful conceptual shorthand for relationships observed to obtain between perceptible phenomena of various sorts. Thus he has been observed to hold that 'the mechanistic world is imagined as only sight and touch imagine a world'; it is articulated in terms of the contents and relationships of 'consecutive appearances,' which in no sense may be considered to constitute the 'forces' of which the world consists (*WP* 635). And no progress in the direction of their comprehension is made, on his view, when mechanistic theory redescribes these 'appearances' in quantitative terms, replacing semiotics with mathematics in the interest of achieving greater objectivity and calculability.

With the recasting of our experience in terms more amenable to quantitative expression than those of 'the senses and of psychology,' mechanistic theory reaches its limit. Farther than this it cannot go, without becoming a different sort of interpretation altogether. Its inadequacy thus stands revealed: 'Mechanistic theory can therefore only *describe* processes, not explain them' (*WP* 660). To explain them, it is necessary to conceive them neither semiotically nor mathematically, but rather in a different kind of way. And with this his critique of mechanism and causalism concludes, setting the stage for his elaboration of his own view of the world and life.

IV

The World and Life

If Nietzsche is concerned to establish that the world and life in this world (our own existence included) are not to be conceived in any of the ways considered in the previous chapter, he is no less intent upon arriving at a more adequate conception of them; and while he has relatively little to say about them in the works he published, his notes amply indicate both his confidence that his efforts along these lines were on the right track, and at least the outlines of their results. 'The victorious concept "force," ' he writes, 'by means of which our physicists have created God and the world, still needs to be completed: an inner will must be ascribed to it, which I designate as "will to power" ' (*WP* 619). Availing himself of the former notion, he argues that if it is modified along the latter lines, the result is an interpretation of life and the world which fares much better under critical scrutiny than do those he attacks. Thus he advances the hypothesis that 'the world defined and determined according to its "intelligible character," ' and all 'life' along with it, is 'the "will to power" and nothing else' (*BGE* 36). Characterizing 'this world' as 'a monster of energy' which 'does not expend itself but only transforms itself' and so is 'eternally self-creating' and 'eternally self-destroying,' his proffered '*solution for all its riddles*' is that '*this world is the will to power — and nothing besides*! And you yourselves are also this will to power — and nothing besides!' (*WP* 1067).

It admittedly is by no means clear, at least from these passages by themselves, just what Nietzsche's conception of the fundamental nature of the world and life comes to. It should be evident from them, however, that he is persuaded of the possibility of developing a philosophical cosmology (and biology) which not only differs from but also is more tenable than the interpretations of reality

187

(and our own existence) of which he has been seen to be so critical. In this chapter I shall consider what he proposes along these lines. And in doing so, it is necessary first of all to take up the question of the respects in which he is both critical of and committed to the distinction between 'appearance' and 'reality'.

Toward a philosophical cosmology

I

Nietzsche's position on this matter is not easily discerned; for on some occasions he appears to reject this distinction emphatically, while on others he avails himself of it in important ways; and on others still he argues for the inseparability of each from the other. The first of these strands of his thinking is easily illustrated, e.g. by his contention that 'we have no categories at all that permit us to distinguish a "world in itself" from a "world of appearance" ' (*WP* 488). Putting the point more strongly, he writes: 'The "apparent" world is the only one: the "true" world is merely added by a lie' (*TI* III:2). And at the conclusion of the section of *Twilight* entitled 'The History of an Error,' he states: 'The true world — we have abolished. What world has remained? The apparent one perhaps? But no! *With the true world we have also abolished the apparent one*' (*TI* IV).

In passages such as these, Nietzsche might seem to be taking the position that the only terms in which reality may meaningfully and properly be characterized are those appropriate to the description of the world of our experience. A somewhat different impression is gained, however, from a number of other passages rather similar in tone, but differing subtly in their implications, as well as in the fact that the language of 'appearance' is retained and coupled with the notion of the indispensability of 'appearance' for life. In a section of *The Gay Science* with the heading 'The consciousness of appearance,' for example, he writes: 'What is "appearance" for me now? Certainly not the opposite of some essence . . . . Certainly not a dead mask that one could place on an unknown *x* or remove from it.' Yet in this same connection he remarks: 'I suddenly woke up in the midst of this dream, but only to the consciousness that I am dreaming and that I must go on dreaming lest I perish' (*GS* 54). In a similar vein Nietzsche asks: 'Why couldn't the world *that concerns us* — be a fiction?' He goes on to say: 'Let at least this much be admitted: there would be no life at all if not on the basis of perspective estimates and appearances.' Yet he begins his discussion of this point with the observation that, 'whatever philosophical standpoint one may adopt today,

188

from every point of view the *erroneousness* of the world in which we think we live is the surest and firmest fact that we can lay eyes on' (*BGE* 34).

Further indications that Nietzsche does not wish to do away entirely with the distinction between 'appearance' and 'reality' are to be found in the many passages in which he reflects upon how it has come about that the world appears to us as it does. Thus, for example, he speaks of 'the world seen, felt, interpreted as thus and thus so that organic life may preserve itself in this perspective of interpretation' (*WP* 678); and he suggests that it may well have been the case that 'the true constitution of things was so hostile to the presuppositions of life, so opposed to them, that we needed appearance in order to be able to live' (*WP* 583A). The world as we ordinarily experience it, he contends, is at least a partial 'falsification' of the reality with which we attempt to deal by means of a pragmatic adjustment to it. 'Appearance is an arranged and simplified world, at which our practical instincts have been at work; it is perfectly true for *us*; that is to say, we live, we are able to live in it' (*WP* 568).

Nietzsche likewise contends that 'the perspective therefore decides the character of the "appearance." ' While he goes on to exclaim: 'As if a world would still remain over after one deducted the perspective!', however, he does not mean to suggest that there is nothing more to reality than *our* 'perspective,' *our* 'apparent world.' He does hold that 'there is no "other," no "true," no essential being,' and considers it appropriate to say that 'the antithesis of the apparent world and the true world is reduced to the antithesis "world" and "nothing." ' But he also suggests that the notion of an 'apparent world' is to be 'reduced' to the notion of 'a specific mode of action on the world, emanating from a center.' And while 'the world' as he conceives it is nothing apart from these 'modes of action,' it also is not to be identified with 'the apparent world' resulting from any one of them, but rather is to be conceived as 'the totality of these actions.' He continues: 'Reality consists precisely in this particular action and reaction of every individual part toward the whole' (*WP* 567). It may be far from clear precisely what he means in characterizing 'reality' in this way. It should be obvious, however, that its construal along these lines necessitates the retention of the distinction between the nature of reality and the constitution of the world of our experience.

Thus 'reality' for Nietzsche is not to be identified with the phenomena of which we are conscious, or with events as we encounter and apprehend them in the course of our conscious

189

experience. 'That which becomes conscious,' he argues, is a function of 'relations which are entirely withheld from us.' Our consciousness itself is a product of our encounter with the world, conditioned by certain practical requirements of human existence. 'It is our relation with the "outer world" that evolved it' (*WP* 524). And what transpires in our experience is at best a kind of sign language which transmogrifies rather than simply records what actually occurs, in a manner adjusted both to the particular character of our senses and to the demand that our experience be communicable.

With regard to the first point, Nietzsche takes it to be 'obvious that every creature different from us senses different qualities and consequently lives in a different world from that in which we live' (*WP* 565) — and thus that the world as we experience it exists only in relation to our sensibility. And with regard to the second, he holds that 'consciousness is really only a net of communication between human beings,' which 'has developed only under the pressure of the need for communication,' and thus may be supposed to have been shaped in accordance with an imperative of ready communicability, the consequence of which he sums up as follows:

> This is the essence of phenomenalism and perspectivism as
> I understand them: Owing to the nature of *animal
> consciousness*, the world of which we can become conscious
> is only a surface- and sign-world, a world that is made common
> and meaner; whatever becomes conscious *becomes* by the
> same token shallow, thin, relatively stupid, general, sign, herd
> signal; all becoming conscious involves a great and thorough
> corruption, falsification, reduction to superficialities, and
> generalization (*GS* 354).

If Nietzsche rejects what he takes to be the traditional way of drawing and spelling out the distinction between 'appearance' and 'reality,' therefore, he may also be seen to insist upon a different version of this distinction which precludes the identification of the world as we experience and generally conceive it with the nature of the world of which we are a part. In order properly to understand his conception of the relation between them, however, it is necessary to take into consideration yet another line of thought he develops in this connection. For on other occasions he argues that, while they require to be distinguished, the relation between them is a very intimate one, in that reference to the former must be made in characterizing the nature of the latter. Thus, for example, he maintains that ' "appearance" itself belongs to reality: it is a form of its being.' For since, on his view, 'the world, apart from our

190

condition of living in it,' is 'essentially a world of relationships,' he contends that 'it has a differing aspect from every point; its being is essentially different from every point' (*WP* 568).

Similarly, Nietzsche suggests that while reality is not to be equated with the world as we experience it, 'the antithesis of this phenomenal world is not "the true world," ' construed in some way such that all reference to anything like appearance is eliminated; for any such 'antithesis' or concrete contrast could only be *another kind* of phenomenal world, a kind "unknowable" for us' (*WP* 569). The world itself is not another world altogether, apart from the relations of which all such possible 'phenomenal worlds' are functions. It rather is essentially, in a sense, a world of appearance, the very nature of which is inseparable from the establishment of the conditions of their possibility. Appearance is not merely a matter of the apprehension (or misapprehension) of the world in consciousness. It is of the very nature of the processes and relationships in which the world's course and reality consist, for Nietzsche, that what transpires in it has at least in part the character of 'appearing,' which 'appearance' is bound up with the situation of each constituent element of this world in relation to the rest. And this results in what he terms 'the multiple ambiguity of the world' when these elements are considered collectively (concerning which more will be said shortly). Thus he can say that 'appearance is for me that which lives and is effective,' and that ultimately there is only 'appearance and will-o'-the-wisp and a dance of spirits and nothing more' (*GS* 54). For to eliminate all reference to 'appearance' would be to abstract from the relationships in terms of which the existence of everything in the world requires to be comprehended; and this would leave one, not with a 'world-in-itself,' but rather with nothing of which the term 'reality' could properly be predicated.

It is only if the whole range of these remarks concerning 'appearance' and 'reality' are taken into consideration that Nietzsche's rather complex conception of the relation between them can be at all adequately understood. When he asserts: 'The antithesis of the apparent world and the true world is reduced to the antithesis "world" and "nothing" ' (*WP* 567), his point is not that the only 'reality' of which it is possible and meaningful to speak is the world as we ordinarily perceive and conceive it. Rather, he means to suggest it to be an error to suppose that there exists some 'true world' of 'being-in-itself' or 'things-in-themselves' having a 'constitution-in-itself' to which the kinds of relationships and processes involved in the emergence of the world of our experience are related in a purely incidental way. Such a 'true world,' on his view, is 'a mere fiction, constructed of fictitious entities' (*WP* 568). Yet he also holds that there is an important sense in which the world of our experience — 'the world *that concerns us*' — is also 'a fiction' (*BGE* 34); it is likewise an error to suppose that *it* has the status of 'reality' unalloyed. For it bears the stamp of the special circumstances of our existence — our senses, our psychology, our social life, our conceptual apparatus, and, in general, both the 'conditions of our preservation and growth' and a variety of accidents of our development.

On the other hand, we are part of this 'reality'; and the world of our experience is no *mere* fiction, but rather is an expression of the complex of relationships with the remainder of it in which our lives consist. Indeed, to say this is not to say enough. As has been observed, the world, for Nietzsche, 'is essentially a world of relationships' (*WP* 568) in which there is an 'action and reaction of every individual part toward the whole' (*WP* 567). When we inquire philosophically into the world's nature, the world we must seek to understand is none other than that of which we are a part, and with which we collectively and individually must be able to deal if we are to survive and flourish. This world is the only one of which we can meaningfully speak, and to which we can legitimately accord the designation of 'reality.' Our philosophical task, however, is not merely to ascertain that 'this world' is the 'real world.' It also involves attempting to discern the respects in which its nature is distorted and even falsified by the ways in which we happen to perceive and conceive of it. And it further involves undertaking to identify those features of this world of appearing and appearance which are merely apparent, merely perspectival projections, additions or distortions of its actual nature, and on the other hand those which are indicative of its reality independently of the idiosyncrasies of our specific human perspective (or various particular perspectives) upon it.

Thus while Nietzsche at times speaks as though he holds that the distinction between 'appearance' and 'reality' requires to be abandoned, the point he actually wishes to make is that it requires to be redrawn. And he would have it redrawn in such a way that the latter is no longer associated with the idea of a world of being contrasting with the sort of world with which we are confronted in our experience, characterized as it is by 'becoming, passing away, and change' (*TI* III:2); while the former is no longer considered to constitute a realm of phenomena separate and distinct from the processes in which the latter consists. Many features of the world as we perceive and conceive of it are indeed 'merely apparent' in an invidious sense, as philosophers have long suggested;

192

only these are not those which philosophers often have had in mind when they have suggested something of this sort to be the case. And, on the other hand, not all of the features of this world are merely apparent, some rather being indicative of aspects of the world's actual nature. But these are for the most part features which philosophers have generally been inclined to overlook or dismiss, as characterizing only our experience rather than the world's fundamental nature.

So Nietzsche asserts, in what he terms his *'first proposition'* touching upon this matter, that 'the reasons for which "this" world has been characterized as "apparent" are the very reasons which indicate its reality' (*TI* III:6). More specifically, he contends that 'insofar as the senses show becoming, passing away, and change, they do not lie' (*TI* III:2). 'Becoming is not a merely *apparent state*,' he insists, going on to suggest that 'perhaps the world of beings is mere appearance' (*WP* 708). He considers it no less appropriate to characterize certain pervasive features of our 'apparent world' as merely phenomenal (and therefore as failing to apply to the world itself), than it is to insist upon the fact that this world is by no means merely phenomenal in its entirety and to be contrasted with some sort of transcendent reality. Thus he dismisses as 'phenomenal' such things as 'the concept of number, the concept of the thing . . . , the concept of activity . . . , [and] the concept of motion.' Yet he stops short of concluding that once these concepts (along with the various qualities which our senses enable us to perceive) are eliminated, no meaningful remainder is left either of our experience or of the idea of any sort of larger reality. For he continues: 'If we eliminate these additions, no things remain but only dynamic quanta, in a relation of tension to all other dynamic quanta: their essence lies in their relation to all other quanta, in their "effect" upon the same' (*WP* 635).

In short, while Nietzsche holds that 'the "apparent" world is the only one' (*TI* III:2), this identification of 'the "apparent" world' as the actual world does not obliterate the distinction between the 'merely apparent' and what actually is the case and transpires in the world. And it likewise does not settle the manner in which the question of the world's actual nature is to be answered, by simply directing us to consider the way in which we happen to perceive or conceive of it. Instead, it is but a new point of departure, from which we are obliged to go on to address ourselves to the question of how its nature is more appropriately and adequately to be construed.

II

It should be observed, in this connection, that while Nietzsche insists that 'we have no categories at all that permit us to distinguish a "world in itself" from a "world of appearance" ' (*WP* 488), this circumstance does not bar the way to the development of a philosophical cosmology. For the world the nature of which is at issue is not a 'world in itself' to which we lack any means of access. Our lives and experience do not unfold independently and apart from the course of this world; they may not constitute the whole of its reality, but neither are they separate and distinct from it. We may have nothing more to go on than our experience and our observations of human and natural phenomena, which admittedly are strongly conditioned in a variety of ways; but they nonetheless afford us the opportunity — however arduous the task of realizing it may be — of 'learning to know the course of the world' (*WP* 333), and thus of coming to understand at least something of its nature.

The understanding of it which we are capable of achieving may never amount to 'absolute knowledge' of it; it may never be entirely free of distortions and errors associated with our inability completely to free ourselves of our human perspective upon it; and it may always admit of being improved upon. Yet as Nietzsche's many assertions to the effect that he has discovered important 'truths' about it indicate, he considers it possible to achieve an understanding of it which stands in marked contrast — cognitively, and not merely in terms of its possibly greater 'utility for life' — to those ordinary and traditional interpretations of it which he brands 'mendacious' and fundamentally 'erroneous.' Thus he remarks: 'What is dawning is the opposition of the world we revere' — i.e., the 'world of true being' which requires to be repudiated — 'and the world we live and are' (*WP* 69n: this passage appears in a footnote to Note 69 in the Kaufmann edition of *WP*). In speaking of the latter, he does not hesitate to make reference to 'the properties that constitute its reality,' which are said to include 'change, becoming, multiplicity, opposition, contradiction, war' (*WP* 584); to claim that 'in the actual world,' contrary to what has often been maintained with respect to the 'true world' he pronounces a fiction, 'everything is bound to and conditioned by everything else' (*WP* 584); and, perhaps most notably of all, to proclaim: *'This world is the will to power — and nothing besides!'* (*WP* 1067).

What enables us thus to 'learn' at least certain fundamental aspects of 'the course of the world,' and so of its nature, is the fact that we are a part of it, and that its course and nature are thus discernable to one who knows how to interpret our experience as we live our lives in it and undergo our encounters with it. Such interpretation is a difficult and fallible affair; but it is neither a hopeless nor an arbitrary one. 'There is nothing for it: one is obliged to understand all motion, all "appearances," and "laws," only as symptoms of an inner event and to employ man as an analogy to this end' (*WP* 619). The soundness of this strategy of interpretation may be questioned; but the point, for the moment, is that Nietzsche thus shows himself to believe that it is possible to achieve at least some genuine understanding of the general character and basic constitution of the world by proceeding in this way.

Certain of Nietzsche's remarks might seem to suggest, however, that the results to be achieved along these lines are very meager indeed, owing to the circumstance that what we encounter, beyond everything that is merely phenomenal, is no 'cosmos' concerning which there is anything meaningful and significant to be said, but rather simply 'chaos.' So, for example, he asserts that 'the world is not an organism at all, but chaos' (*WP* 711). It is held to have no fixed and enduring structures, but rather to be 'in flux,' constantly 'in a state of becoming,' and 'always changing,' without ever achieving any sort of completion, goal, or final intelligible result which might be characterized in a Hegelian manner as its essential 'truth.' Thus it is said to be 'never getting near the truth,' as it continues to change; for, so construed, 'there is no "truth" ' (*WP* 616). This same theme is also sounded in both the earlier and later parts of *The Gay Science*. In these discussions, however, it becomes clear that Nietzsche has something rather less extreme in mind than the term 'chaos' might at first be taken to imply. 'The total character of the world,' he writes, 'is in all eternity chaos — in the sense not of a lack of necessity but of a lack of order, arrangement, form, beauty, wisdom, and whatever other names there are for our aesthetic anthropomorphisms' (*GS* 109). His point is even more clearly put in a later passage, in which he raises and then goes on to attempt to answer the question, 'Who are we anyway?'

> We have become cold, hard, and tough in the realization that
> the way of this world is anything but divine; even by human
> standards it is not rational, merciful, or just. We know it well,
> the world in which we live is ungodly, immoral, 'inhuman';
> we have interpreted it far too long in a false and mendacious
> way, in accordance with the wishes of our reverence, which
> is to say, according to our *needs* (*GS* 346).

To understand what Nietzsche means in speaking of the world as 'chaos,' it is necessary to take into consideration that to which he poses this term as a contrasting characterization. What he is thereby saying about the world is that it does not have the character of a fixed and immutable order of being, or of a moral order, or of a unified and coordinated organism, or of an orderly development unfolding in accordance with an inner or preordained purpose, or of a complex of processes and events occurring in accordance with a system of natural or rational laws, or of an organization answering to our idea of beauty, our logic and reason, or our needs and desires. In short, it neither constitutes nor manifests any of the sorts of order we are accustomed to think it has or are disposed to desire it to have — just as he elsewhere contends that life and the world do not have the sort of value and meaning we have long supposed them to have.

This parallel is instructive. Nietzsche is prepared to say, in the latter connection, that life and the world must be considered valueless and meaningless *if* value and meaning are conceived along the lines they traditionally have been. And in a similar vein, he is here suggesting that the world must be considered a 'chaos' *if* the only sorts of order one is prepared to recognize are those which traditionally have been associated with the world's nature (or with the nature of some 'higher,' 'truer' world of being).

This is only half of the story, however, in the latter case as well as in the former. If Nietzsche is persuaded of the untenability of any such religious or metaphysical conception of reality, he also is not prepared to halt with what he terms the nihilistic 'rebound from "God is truth" to the fanatical faith "All is false" . . . [and] "Everything lacks meaning" ' (*WP* 1). The world may be a meaningless chaos in relation to those ideals or standards of value and order associated with the sort of traditional world-interpretation he has in mind and considers to have been discredited; and from time to time he adopts this manner of speaking in order to make clear that he does indeed wish to repudiate the idea that the world constitutes the kind of meaningful cosmos it has long been purported to be by those who misguidedly accept this interpretation. But this should not be supposed to be his final word concerning it. Thus after observing that 'the world does not have the value we thought it had,' he goes on to suggest that 'the world might be far more valuable than we used to believe' (*WP* 32). And so also here: the world may be a 'chaos' in the sense that it does not have the kind of order, structure or essential nature people have thought it has; but it at least remains an open question whether both its general nature and what obtains and transpires in it might nonetheless admit of some sort of more positive characterization.

196

And in point of fact, Nietzsche is quite willing to grant, and indeed is prepared to insist, that there is a good deal of structure and organization in the world (and not only in our thought and experience), which while not eternal and immutable are of long duration. Moreover, he holds that beyond all such arrangements, that in which the world consists — both in its simplest form and in its most complex modifications — has certain fundamental characteristics which do not change in nature but only in expression; and that consequently the whole rich variety of processes to be found in the world at all times have certain common features. To be sure, if one abstracts from all established and ultimately transitory structure and organization, and seeks immutable substances with unchanging attributes and eternal laws inflexibly governing their interactions, one is left (or confronted) with nothing but an unintelligible flux of processes. In *this* sense, the world *is* a chaos. But it ceases to appear so chaotic if one ceases to approach it with expectations and concepts with which it does not accord, and begins to sift through this seeming flux with a view to discerning regularities, similarities and uniformities in its flow.

Nietzsche clearly does reject the idea that the world consists of a collection of 'beings' of some sort; for as has been observed, he argues that ' "beings" are part of our perspective' (*WP* 517), and are not to be accorded the status of reality. Yet he does not mean to deny that what might be called certain 'organizations' of the sort which we commonly consider to be 'beings' exhibit a degree of stability and persistence which others lack; thus he speaks of 'complexes of events apparently durable in comparison with other complexes — e.g., through the difference in tempo of the event.' Such 'duration' is 'inherent neither in that which is called subject nor in that which is called object' (*WP* 552). But it is a circumstance to be reckoned with and accounted for. It may be, as he suggests, that 'all unity,' including that which we discern in those 'complexes of events' which we ordinarily consider to be objects or beings of various kinds, is to be regarded as 'unity only as organization and co-operation . . . , as a pattern of domination that *signifies* a unity but *is* not a unity' (*WP* 561). This sort of 'organizational unity' too is a reality, however, no less than is the impermanence of all such unity, and likewise requires to be taken into consideration.

Further: at the same time that Nietzsche insists that 'there are no durable ultimate units, no atoms, no monads,' he makes reference to 'conditions of preservation and enhancement for complex forms of relative life-duration within the flux of becoming' (*WP* 715). It is thus not only particular 'organizational unities' in connection with which he considers it appropriate to speak of relative duration (rather than incessant and complete flux), but also 'forms' or types of such unities. They mark something significant: namely 'the fact that an abundance of similar creatures appear at the same time and that the tempo of their further growth and change is for a long time slowed down, so actual small continuations and increases are not very much noticed' (*WP* 521).

Similarly, while Nietzsche sometimes seems to be suggesting that it is only in our experience that the 'chaos' of the world is moderated by the presence of 'regularity and form,' and then only because it is a necessity of our existence 'to impose upon chaos as much regularity and form as our practical needs require' (*WP* 515), his actual position is rather different. This may be seen, for example, when one reflects upon the implications of such passages as the following:

> In order for a particular species to maintain itself and increase
> its power, its conception of reality must comprehend enough
> of the calculable and constant for it to base a scheme of
> behavior on it. . . . In other words . . .: a species grasps
> a certain amount of reality in order to become master of
> it, to press it into service (*WP* 480).

To be sure, the main point Nietzsche is making here is that our 'conception of reality' contains more 'of the calculable and constant' than reality itself does, in that it involves treating as regular and self-identical what in fact is only approximately or temporarily so. In making this point, however, he indirectly makes another: that the 'reality' with which we find ourselves confronted is by no means a complete chaos. For if it were, operation with such a 'conception of reality' could not have proven conducive to our preservation and development, and could not have facilitated our attempts to 'master' and 'press into service' even 'a certain amount of it.' Indeed, were this reality actually completely chaotic on his view, Nietzsche could not have spoken of 'a certain relative rightness,' and of the fact that our 'becoming master of' and 'pressing into service' various portions of reality involve 'grasping' it at least to some extent in the scheme on the basis of which we organize our actions in relation to it.

Considerations of this sort show that Nietzsche does not suppose the world to be as devoid of persisting features and organization as he suggests 'the formless unformulable world of the chaos of sensations' would be, if this is how one imagines 'the antithesis of this phenomenal world.' Reality can no more be regarded as comparable to (or identical with) the chaotic residue which would remain if our experience could be reduced to a succession of unconceptualized and unrelated Humean 'impressions,' than it can be identified with that 'true world of being' we are led to envision when we hypostatize the formal structure of our language and reason. Indeed, it is not to be conceived as antithetical to the world of our experience, and is not to be comprehended by attempting to imagine what the antithesis of this world would be. The way to think of it, according to Nietzsche, is rather as an interplay of forces and processes of which our efforts and experiences are instances, and in which our lives unfold, in a manner made both difficult and possible by the kinds of organization we and the elements of our environing world represent, and by the kinds of relationships obtaining within and among both.

III

There is a point Nietzsche makes much of, however, which at least at first glance might seem to block this endeavor on a deeper level, depriving most of the rest of what he himself has to say about the world of all claim to superiority, or even to anything approaching soundness. This point concerns what he terms the world's 'ambiguity.' Thus, for example, he speaks of 'the *multiple ambiguity* of the world' (*WP* 134); of its being 'knowable' but '*interpretable* otherwise,' with 'no meaning behind it, but countless meanings' (*WP* 481); and of the importance of refraining from wishing 'to divest existence of *its ambiguous character*' (*GS* 373). The question at issue here would appear to be that of whether the world (and what obtains and transpires in it) may be attributed any specific character; and the force of such remarks as these might look to be that it may not. Before concluding that this is his view, however, one would do well to consider more closely the nature of that 'ambiguity' and multi-interpretability of which he speaks. And when one does so, one discovers that, rather than cutting the ground from under his own feet here, subverting his own (along with every other) cosmological enterprise in principle, what he in fact is doing is getting on with it.

It should first of all be observed that the ambiguity of which he speaks is at least in part to be traced to the commonplace fact that the same thing can be seen and interpreted in very different ways when viewed from different perspectives. Thus, when he refers to 'the multiple ambiguity of the world,' he goes on to say that it is 'a question of *strength* that sees all things in the *perspective of its growth*' (*WP* 134). Here the ambiguity predicated of the world is at least in the first instance an ambiguity of the world-as-viewed, the source of which is identified as the differing perspectives of creatures with differing requirements and capacities. Each 'sees' the world in terms of those features which are relevant to its growth, and 'their worlds' differ accordingly; and, considered in this context, the world bears as many different aspects as there are 'growth-perspectives' upon it. But this does not mean that the world is to be understood exclusively and ultimately in terms of the multiplicity of aspects it thus happens to bear — even if it is nothing 'in itself' existing independently of that which develops and figures in these 'perspectives.'

Much the same thing also applies with respect to Nietzsche's contention that the world is variously interpretable, 'with no meaning behind it, but countless meanings.' After making this remark, he adds the word: ' "Perspectivism" ' (WP 481). The world has 'countless meanings' because there are indefinitely many different possible 'forms of life' which may come to exist, for each of which the world may be said to have a 'meaning' (or content and structure) determined by its own 'perspective' in the sense indicated above. Thus he also speaks here of the possibility of differing 'interpretations,' each involving a selective fashioning of a picture of the world in a manner prefigured in or prompted by the related perspective (and thus ultimately the conditions of preservation and growth) of the form of life in question. Such 'interpretations' can and typically do arise and function in a manner compelling our recognition both of the fact that their diversity is virtually inevitable, and of the circumstance that even though the world may be 'knowable, it is *interpretable* otherwise.' They are conditioned by the practical needs of the living creatures whose 'growth-perspectives' upon the rest of the world, as it vitally affects them, are reflected in them.

This does not mean, however, that the world's nature can only be intelligibly characterized in terms of the contents of such 'interpretations,' or beyond that, only in terms of the fact that it admits of such differing interpretations; and it likewise by no means follows that there is nothing in or about the world that admits of being comprehended. Nietzsche's contention that it 'is knowable,' even though 'interpretable otherwise,' clearly suggests that he is convinced of the contrary. And one should not read too much into the fact that he elsewhere is quite willing to allow that the conception of the world's nature he advocates is also an 'interpretation'; for that might only be a candid admission of the impossibility of achieving a kind of knowledge that would be absolute, final, rigorously demonstrable, and completely adequate to reality. It does not amount to a profession of the impossibility of ever advancing beyond the development of various interpretations whose sole claim to significance is their 'value for life.'

In speaking of the 'multiple ambiguity of the world,' however, Nietzsche has something more in mind, which he takes to pertain to its very nature; and it is necessary to consider carefully what further he does (and does not) mean to suggest here. Thus if he considers it 'a dictate of good taste' that 'one should not wish to divest existence of its *rich ambiguity*,' and if its 'ambiguity' is such that it warrants his admonition to the scientifically minded not to suppose that 'the only justifiable interpretation of the world should be one in which *you* are justified because one can continue to work and do research scientifically in *your* sense' (*GS* 373), one might wonder whether the sort of 'ambiguity' he insists upon precludes the possibility of anything other than alternative but comparably narrow, one-sided and superficial interpretation of it.

That Nietzsche does not take this to be the case, instead considering it at least to be possible to arrive at a conception of the world which takes account of the 'ambiguity' he attributes to it rather than merely laying hold of some further facet of it, is indicated by what he goes on to say in connection with the 'mechanistic' one to which he here refers. This way of thinking, he contends, involves seizing upon 'precisely the most superficial and external aspect of existence,' ignoring all else there is to it. This, he suggests, is comparable to considering 'a piece of music according to how much of it could be counted, calculated, and expressed in formulas.' And he continues: 'How absurd would such a "scientific" estimation of music be! What would one have comprehended, understood, grasped of it? Nothing, really nothing of what is "music" in it!' (*GS* 373).

This passage is significant for present purposes because of the light it sheds upon what Nietzsche means in speaking of the 'ambiguous character' of the world — and also, more generally, upon his conception of the world itself. If the world is analogous to a piece of music, we may surmise that the 'ambiguity' he attributes to the former is meant to be conceived analogously to that possessed by the latter, which in both cases would appear to be a matter of their having aspects other than (as well as including) that which is here singled out and seized upon. Each has a multiplicity of aspects, and thus a kind of 'multiple ambiguity,' which circumstance can give rise to a diversity of interpretations. The fact that some may be narrow and superficial, however, does not mean that all must be equally so; for others might be more comprehensive and penetrating, and do relatively greater justice to their various aspects. The fact that a piece of music has this sort of 'ambiguity,' moreover, obviously is quite compatible with the idea that it constitutes a kind of unity in which these aspects are interrelated. Indeed, this may plausibly be taken to be the case where music is concerned. And if the world is to be conceived analogously, the same may be true of it. In any event, taking Nietzsche's analogy as a guide to understanding his meaning, it is reasonable to conclude that so far we have no reason to suppose that the sort of 'ambiguity' he attributes to the world precludes any comprehensive account of the world's nature.

The world also has an 'ambiguous' character for Nietzsche, however, in the further sense that, being 'essentially a world of relationships,' with no absolute and fixed center of reference, 'its being is essentially different from every point,' and so it bears 'a differing aspect from every point.' Thus he suggests that the world itself has a 'perspectival' character. In this world 'where there is no being,' but rather only relationships which are thus specifiable only in terms of the manner in which the whole of the network they constitute is arranged in relation to some part of it, an inherent ambiguity is associated with the very notion of its having some definite character. For the network of relationships in which it consists has a definite character only relative to the manner in which it impinges upon some definite point or portion of it, which is thus variably specifiable.

Nietzsche's attribution of 'ambiguity' in this sense to the world, however, still does not necessitate the abandonment of the attempt to achieve any further understanding of its nature. For it remains at least conceivable that it has features which transcend or underlie the processes which establish these relationships, and which it may be possible to discern. In this connection, it is essential to distinguish between two different things one might mean in speaking of the world's nature: on the one hand, its nature in the sense of the manner in which it is constituted at any given time by this network of relationships; and, on the other, its nature in the sense of that which takes the form of some such network of relationships, and in terms of the basic features of which their emergence, transformation and dissolution are to be understood.

This is a distinction which Nietzsche considers it important to draw in philosophical inquiry concerning the world's nature, and which is not to be confused with the distinction he repudiates between a merely apparent world and a world of true being. Not everything about the world changes, even though everything in it does. And the importance of this distinction here is that the above sort of ambiguity he attributes to the world pertains to its nature in only one of these respects — to its existence as an actual (and gradually changing) network of relationships. In the other of these respects, it might not have this sort of 'ambiguous character.' The latter character derives from and pertains to the world as such a (changing) network; but is precisely for that reason a feature of the world only considered as such, rather than as it is more fundamentally to be understood. And thus, once again, we find that it does not preclude the possibility of arriving at a comprehension of the world's basic nature.

The same observations apply with respect to a further sort of ambiguity attributed by Nietzsche to the world, which is suggested by the analogy he draws between the world and a piece of music, and which might seem to present an even more serious difficulty. (It also brings to light something important about the world's nature as he understands it.) Here the analogy may be broadened, in keeping with the manner in which he frequently states it elsewhere, by substituting for 'a piece of music' the more general notion of *a work of art*. This broader analogy is already suggested in *The Birth of Tragedy*; and Nietzsche recurs to it frequently in his later writings. He means it to be taken seriously, despite the fact that it obviously cannot be taken literally (above all because, on his view, there is no transcendent 'artist' whose creation or work the world is). In place of the idea of the world as the free creation of God, he speaks of 'the world as a work of art which gives birth to itself' (*WP* 796). And it is with this analogy in mind that he writes of his conception of the world: 'An anti-metaphysical view of the world — yes, but an artistic one' (*WP* 1048).

A great deal of what Nietzsche has to say about the world is related to this way of thinking of it. For the moment, however, it is sufficient merely to take note of his employment of the analogy, and its implication that the world possesses the sort of ambiguity characteristic of works of art. One of their more significant features is that while they are by no means formless, they are commonly 'rich,' defying simple and univocal analysis. Their content is neither indeterminate nor definitely determinable in any conclusive, exhaustive way; it neither is anything at all that one may happen to read into them, nor is captured completely in any specific way of taking them. In a word, they are both determinate and ambiguous.

The same applies, on Nietzsche's view, with respect to the world, and to the network of relationships in terms of which its existence at this and every other time consists. This network is always some particular one, in contrast to others which may have existed or may come to be or might be conceivable; but *what it amounts to*, the specific character of the world and the concomitant status and significance of its parts, admits of differing construals. What it is, in a manner of speaking, is thus *left open* (even though not left *completely* open, but rather circumscribed) by the very nature of the network itself. It does not follow (any more than it follows in the case of a work of art) that all attempts to understand it are alike doomed to failure from the outset. But it does follow that an understanding of it must begin with a recognition of the fact of its essential ambiguity in this sense; and that further progress in understanding it can be made only if (as ought to be done in dealing with a work of art) it is approached in a manner calculated to elicit and take into account, not 'ambiguity' as such, but rather that specific ambiguity with which it confronts us.

The language Nietzsche employs in this connection suggests that the world for him is ambiguous in yet another respect, however, owing to an important *dis*analogy between the world and works of art. In the case of a work of art, it is commonly thought that the intentions of the artist who created it are, if not decisive with respect to the manner in which it is to be understood, at any rate relevant in this connection. Even when they are not known, the fact that the work can be assumed to have been created with intentions of *some* sort in mind is taken to contribute to some extent to our understanding of it, and to serve at least minimally to narrow the range of the ways in which it might otherwise seem possible to construe it. The configuration of the world, however, cannot be supposed to express any such artist's intention, if there is no God who created the world in accordance with something analogous to a human artistic (or other) intention. If this world is to be thought of as having 'given birth to itself,' and to have done so in the absence of anything like such an 'intention' of which its actual configuration may be taken to be the expression, we cannot hope to be able to simplify the task of comprehending it by somehow managing to gain access to the content of the former.

To be sure, in his notion of 'will to power,' Nietzsche does feel that he has succeeded in identifying a kind of fundamental disposition loosely analogous to an intention which both characterizes the very nature of that of which the world consists (however it might be configured), and also serves to explain both the emergence and development and the dissolution of all such configurations. But he does not take it to suffice to render intelligible the specific character of that configuration or network of relationships constituting the world as it now exists, or even to reduce the extent of its 'specific ambiguity' in the way in which the knowledge (or at least the presumption) of a more or less definite artistic intention does in the case of an ordinary work of art. Between the conception of a world in which 'will to power'

204

is the ultimate 'ground and character of all change' and the world conceived as the network of relationships with which we find ourselves confronted and of which we are a part — the world as *this* 'work of art' — there is a great gap; and there is, for Nietzsche, nothing like a specific artistic intention which fills it. And since no other sort of purpose or plan (or any kind of rational or nomological structure binding upon it) fills this gap either, we must be prepared to countenance the likelihood that the ambiguity of the latter is even greater than that which the analogy with a work of art suggests, owing precisely to one of the ways in which the analogy does not fit.

Yet the disanalogy is greater still, on Nietzsche's own account; and so also, for directly related reasons, is the sort of ambiguity he attributes to the world in this connection. For as he often suggests, the world may be better likened to many works of art rather than to one, and to indefinitely many at that: an enormous gallery, as it were, in which the lines of demarcation between work and work and indeed between works and gallery are indistinct. To the extent that such lines can be fixed at all, they may be fixed in different places and on different scales; they also may be eliminated altogether. There is no clear and single answer to the question of whether something in the world is itself analogous to a work of art, a group of such works, or only a part of one. The world is the entirety, which gives birth to itself as it is now or ever constituted; but if what is thus given birth may be regarded with equal legitimacy as one work or as a multiplicity of them, and if this multiplicity is likewise specifiable in an indefinite number of ways, the ambiguity to be reckoned with assumes dimensions vastly greater than those encountered within the domain of ordinary works of art.

If the world is thus 'ambiguous' in these respects, what can be said about it will obviously be limited, and will be subject to serious qualifications beyond the level of broad generalities. Yet it is no less important to observe that, on the other hand, this neither precludes all cosmological inquiry nor deprives efforts along these lines of any cognitive significance. At least in principle, it allows for a form of non-metaphysical cosmology; and this is a possibility Nietzsche seeks to realize, and thereby to demonstrate.

IV

Given that Nietzsche does not suppose the world to be so chaotic and ambiguous that nothing whatever may appropriately or aptly be said concerning it (beyond saying this about it, and saying what it is not), we now must consider what he does have to say about it.

As has already been indicated, the most basic and general point of consequence he makes concerning it is that it is a world of change, to which something like the notion of 'becoming' applies. Once it is recognized that 'any comprehensive unity in the plurality of events is lacking,' and that 'the categories "aim," "unity," "being" ' have merely been projected into the world and must be *'pulled out again'* if it is not to be misinterpreted, he argues that this leaves one with 'the reality of becoming as the *only* reality' (WP 12A). Thus he contends that 'becoming is not a merely *apparent state'* (WP 708). On the contrary: 'The world with which we are concerned' is 'something in a state of becoming' (WP 616); indeed, 'everything is becoming' (WP 518). So he writes: 'Insofar as the senses show becoming, passing away, and change, they do not lie' (TI III:2). Care must be taken, however, not to misunderstand his meaning here. His view of the world is not teleological; thus he insists that 'existence has no goal or end' (WP 12A). And the 'becoming' of which he speaks is not to be construed in the sense of a developmental process: 'Becoming does not aim at a *final state*, does not flow into "being" ' (WP 708).

Nietzsche's argument for this last point rests on two assumptions: first, that the world is finite; and second, that it cannot be supposed to have been created, and must therefore have already been in existence for an infinite period of time. He considers both of these assumptions to be beyond serious dispute, and thus argues as follows:

> If the world had a goal, it must have been reached. If there were for it some unintended final state, this also must have been reached. If it were in any way capable of pausing and becoming fixed, of 'being,' if in the whole course of its becoming it possessed even for a moment this capability of 'being,' then all becoming would long since have come to an end (WP 1062).

In short: 'If the motion of the world aimed at a final state, that state would [already] have been reached. The sole fundamental fact, however, is that it does not aim at a final state.' And, Nietzsche goes on to say, 'I seek a conception of the world that takes this fact into account' (WP 708). It must be admitted that this argument is far from unassailable, not least because the assumptions on which it rests are in fact more problematic than he allows. His commitment to its conclusion, however, is clear, and is at least not unreasonable; and for present purposes it suffices to take note of it, and to see where he goes from here.

It obviously is not very informative simply to characterize reality in terms of 'becoming.' More must be said by way of supplying this characterization with concrete content, if it is to be at all meaningful and to have any real interest. It is at this point that Nietzsche introduces a number of his more specific notions indicative of the way the world's nature requires to be conceived into the discussion. So, in the first instance, he argues for the construal of 'all events, all motion, all becoming, as a determination of degrees and relations of force, as a *struggle* —' (WP 552). The latter term, which he considers it necessary to add to bring out something important that is missing as long as the former is construed in a merely natural-scientific manner, obviously anticipates the related notion he goes on to develop of 'will to power.' Thus, as has already been observed, he holds that the concept of 'force' is inadequate in the form in which 'our physicists' employ it to characterize the world's course and nature; it 'still needs to be completed: an inner will must be ascribed to it, which I designate as "will to power" ' (WP 619).

Nietzsche considers this 'will to power' to be something so fundamental that even the phenomenon of 'becoming' is derivative in relation to it. Thus he suggests that 'the will to power [is] not a being, not a becoming, but a *pathos* — the most elemental fact from which a becoming and effecting first emerge — ' (WP 635). As a *pathos* (a fundamental disposition or tendency), however, this 'will to power' cannot be that of which the world itself consists. The former notion merely expresses what he takes to be the most basic characteristic of the latter, which requires to be specified in somewhat different terms: namely, as 'dynamic quanta.' He also speaks at times of 'quanta of force' and of 'power-quanta' in this connection, and on occasion even permits himself the use of the term 'will' here. Thus, for example, while insisting that 'there is no will' in Schopenhauer's sense, he goes on to say that 'there are *Willens-Punktationen* that are constantly increasing or losing their power' (WP 715); and he suggests that 'one has to risk the hypothesis whether will does not effect will wherever "effects" are recognized — and whether all mechanical occurrences are not, insofar as a force is active in them, will force, effects of will' (BGE 36). Here the term 'will' is used not merely to suggest the idea of a disposition, but moreover and at the same time to refer to that which is thus essentially disposed.

When Nietzsche speaks in this way, however, he is simply following the familiar practice of employing an expression singling out the salient feature of something to refer to it. Thus he should not be taken to be following Schopenhauer in actually conceiving of 'the world as will,' thereby hypostatizing the latter notion, let alone to be suggesting that reality fundamentally is the same sort of thing as is 'the will' of ordinary and traditional philosophical discourse. For as has been remarked, he repudiates the notion of 'the will' in the latter sense; and he also takes strong objection to Schopenhauer's impressment of it into metaphysical service, in which it becomes the name of that in which the world ultimately consists. He does consider Schopenhauer to have performed a useful service in so modifying the ordinary and traditional notion of 'will' (albeit unwittingly), through his novel applications of the term, that it is liberated from the confines of its conventional employment and so has come to be available for use in other ways. Thus he observes that in Schopenhauer's hands there occurs 'the reduction of will to reflexes, the denial of will as an "efficient cause"; finally — a real rechristening: one sees so little will that the word becomes free to designate something else' (WP 95). But that which Nietzsche considers the term to be most appropriately used to designate, at least strictly speaking, is the general disposition of one sort of dynamic reality or another (whether a human being, a society, an organism, or the 'quanta' of which all such organizations are configurations and the world in general ultimately consists), rather than that which manifests this disposition in its various relationships.

The world, for Nietzsche, ourselves and all else included, is to be conceived neither as some sort of substance or collection of material entities, nor as 'spirit' or 'will,' but rather as the totality of such dynamic quanta or fields of force, in a condition of internal tension and instability. Ultimately there exist 'only dynamic quanta, in a relation of tension to all other dynamic quanta' (WP 635); and 'reality consists precisely in this particular action and reaction of every individual part toward the whole' (WP 567) — although there are no discrete and self-contained parts, strictly speaking, since the 'essence' of these quanta 'lies in their relation to all other quanta' (WP 635). They form 'systems,' but in a manner reflecting no underlying world-order. For the state of the world at any time is strictly and solely a function of the specific nature of whatever systems or organizations of 'power-quanta' and relations among them happen temporarily to obtain — even though 'the name of the game,' as it were, remains ever the same. Nietzsche puts this point in the following way (availing himself for the moment of the convenience of employing the terminological shorthand of 'bodies' to refer to these dynamic 'organizational unities'):

My idea is that every specific body strives to become master over all space and to extend its force (— its will to power) and to thrust back all that resists its extension. But it continually encounters similar efforts on the part of other bodies and ends by coming to an arrangement ('union') with those of them that are sufficiently related to it: thus they conspire together for power. And the process goes on — (*WP* 636).

One consequence of this conception of what goes on in the world as 'the mutual struggle of that which becomes, often with the absorption of one's opponent,' is that 'the number of becoming elements [is] not constant' (*WP* 617). So Nietzsche observes that 'continual transition forbids us to speak of "individuals," etc.; the "number" of beings is itself in flux' (*WP* 520). It is only in a relative and approximate sense that it is appropriate to speak of 'specific bodies,' as he does in the above passage; for while they do represent arrangements which persist at least for a time with some semblance of continuity, they are only 'complexes of events apparently durable in comparison with other complexes' (*WP* 552).

The 'process' of which Nietzsche speaks in this passage is held to 'go on' throughout the whole of reality; but, although the same 'process' is everywhere to be found, this does not mean that the world constitutes a unity or system the constituent elements of which are integrated into a single overarching pattern of relationships. On the contrary, Nietzsche contends, 'a total process (considered as a system) does not exist at all' (*WP* 711). To be sure, he does speak of 'the world' in general as having 'a certain quantum of force at its disposal' (*WP* 638), and as itself consisting in 'a firm, iron magnitude of force that does not grow bigger or smaller, that does not expend itself but only transforms itself.' And he goes on to refer to it not only as 'a whole of unalterable size,' but also in language which clearly suggests a measure of integration: thus it is suggested to be 'a household without expenses or losses,' consisting in 'a play of forces and waves of forces, at the same time one and many' (*WP* 1067). Indeed, Nietzsche even goes so far as to speak of the world as a 'system' all of the constituent portions of which are interrelated: 'Supposing that the world had a certain quantum of force at its disposal, then it is obvious that every displacement of power at any point would affect the whole system — thus together with sequential causality there would be a contiguous and concurrent dependence' (*WP* 638).

What unites this 'system,' however, is only the web of power-relationships between its constituent quanta and fields of force, and not anything either substantial or nomological which stands above or lies beneath them and imposes unity upon them. They do not have the character of discrete monadic units existing independently of each other or only occasionally interacting; nor can there be any secession from this union. But this is only because their reality consists in the power-relationships between and within them (a distinction which involves an abstraction from what is in fact a single complex of relationships, 'internal' and 'external' being inseparable from one another here), and thus because they do and can exist only in relation to each other. For 'in the actual world,' there is no separate existence; 'everything is bound to and conditioned by everything else' (*WP* 584). Nietzsche tempers this view, however, with the observation that 'distant forces balance one another,' and that consequently it is only on a local level that this mutual conditioning of fields of force assumes any real significance, each being (as it were) 'concerned only with its neighborhood' (*WP* 637).

In short, what goes on in the world does not add up to 'a total process,' nor do the relations obtaining in it at any given time constitute aspects of an inherent systematic structure; yet it is no mere multiplicity, for Nietzsche, but — in the final analysis, at any rate — an interconnected totality as well. What he is intent upon repudiating is not the idea that the world is one, but rather any idea of its unity which postulates something over and above the power-relationships between the quanta and systems of force of which it consists as the source and principle of its unity. His reason for doing so is simply that the world cannot be conceived to have any other sort of unity if, as he contends, it is neither governed by laws nor subject to any transcendent power, nor has the character of any sort of (simple or complex) substance or 'being.' His reason for considering it to constitute the kind of unity indicated, on the other hand, is that he takes this to be entailed by the conception of the world in terms of quanta of force the existence and identity of which is a function of their relations to each other.

It has been observed that Nietzsche speaks of 'the world as a work of art that gives birth to itself' (*WP* 796). In doing so he makes two points, one of which has already been touched upon and should be recalled in this connection: namely, that the world is in a certain respect analogous to a work of art (or complex of works of art). I shall have more to say about what he means to convey by means of this analogy shortly. First, however, notice should be taken of a second point he also makes here: that in another respect the world is to be thought of as analogous to an artist. This point warrants brief elaboration.

Nietzsche holds (in a manner reminiscent of both Spinoza and Hegel) that the world is to be conceived as something which has made itself what it has been and is. And in availing himself of the analogy of an artist, he is suggesting that the course taken by the world as it thus proceeds to fashion itself is *creative* (and thereby also destructive), rather than merely mechanical or nomological or 'logical.' So he speaks of it as being 'eternally self-creating' (and 'self-destroying') (*WP* 1067). His point here, in availing himself of this language, is that it is not to be thought of as being governed either by laws or by purposes. Rather, it is to be regarded as involving a *development* of definite arrangements in which the only limiting and constraining conditions are a matter of the resources available to be drawn upon, the manner of their distribution and organization at the time, and whatever dispositions they may have either intrinsically or in consequence of this organization. And it is further to be thought of, not in terms of an increasing stabilization, 'rationalization,' or actualization of some inherent potentiality, but rather as a succession of such developments, which build to no conclusion.

Returning now to Nietzsche's first point, it may be observed that a work of art is no chaos, nor is the indwelling form of one identical with that of another. Moreover, the very nature of the source responsible for the kind of form which sets a work of art apart from a chaos and the product of a calculation or a machine is also responsible for the uniqueness of each such form. In characterizing the world as 'artistic,' Nietzsche is suggesting that reflection upon the world's general 'surface features' leads to a similar conclusion with respect to its fundamental nature. The fact that the world is *not* a chaos in the sense of being devoid of organization, is no less significant that it *is* a chaos in the sense of having no fixed and immutable structure. The fact of organization in the world (which he takes to *be* a fact) requires to be explained, but without invoking any transcendent agency, nor yet again by means of the projection of such notions as 'law' and 'reason' into the world. And it also requires to be accounted for in a way that will do justice to the variety, mutability, impermanence, and the developmental character of all such organization. The world cannot be adequately characterized merely in terms of the changing network of relationships in which its existence through time consists, let alone in terms of its configuration at any one time. And it also will not do merely to supplement this account through the introduction of the notion of force, and the suggestion that this network and its changes are to be understood as a matter of the shifting arrangement of quanta and fields of force and the interactions between them. For in the latter case as well as the former, the analysis given fails to account for the emergence as well as the impermanence of organization.

In short: it may be that no single type of organization is either necessary or eternal; but the tendency to organization (and to interaction that is not merely random and disruptive of organization, but rather is effective in the sense of being conducive to it) is so ubiquitous that Nietzsche feels it must evince some characteristic rooted in the specific nature of force itself. The emergence and development as well as the disintegration and dissolution of different types of organization, in the absence of pre-established purposes and of governing laws, requires to be explained in something like this way. The characteristic in question, on his view, must be a principle at least one of the issues of which is the 'creativity' exhibited by the world when considered through time and on a macrocosmic or semi-macrocosmic scale; but it need not (and perhaps cannot plausibly) be an impetus to creativity as such, especially when considered in its most rudimentary form and when the world is contemplated in a more microcosmic manner. The formula Nietzsche settles upon to designate its nature is 'will to power,' to the meaning of which I now turn.

The world and 'will to power'

V

Nietzsche terms it his 'purpose,' in this general connection, 'to demonstrate the absolute homogeneity of all events' (*WP* 272); and what he here has in mind is the idea that it is in terms of 'will to power' that the 'ground and character of all change' are to be understood (*WP* 685). In all events, he contends, this same fundamental tendency is at work. 'And do you know what "the world" is to me?' he asks; and after characterizing 'this world' as 'a monster of energy, without beginning, without end,' at once 'eternally self-creating' and 'eternally self-destroying,' he goes on to suggest that the '*solution* for all its riddles' is this: '*This world is the will to power — and nothing besides!*' (*WP* 1067). His reasons for taking this to be the case go beyond his reasons for supposing all events to be homogeneous in the sense of having the same general 'ground and character,' the latter being at least initially a hypothesis he feels compelled to entertain on methodological grounds alone. Thus he observes that it is a 'demand' of 'method, which must be essentially economy of principles,' that we 'beware of *superfluous* teleological principles' (*BGE* 13). And when he proceeds to advocate making the 'experiment' of conceiving '*all* efficient force univocally as — *will to power*,' he does so on the ground that 'conscience of method demands it,' once it is recognized that the fundamental character of some such 'force' requires to be conceived along these lines. 'Not to assume several kinds of causality until the experiment of making do with a single one has been pushed to its utmost limit (to the point of nonsense, if I may say so) — that is a moral of method which one may not shirk today' (*BGE* 36).

To be sure, there is more to Nietzsche's 'method' than this alone, as shall shortly be seen. Moreover, it is obvious that the acceptance of this methodological principle by itself neither entails the particular interpretation he goes on to develop, nor guarantees that all events will turn out to exhibit the sort of homogeneity he begins by postulating; since it is at least conceivable (as he here recognizes) that events might in the final analysis prove irreducibly heterogeneous. It is his contention, however, that they in point of fact are not; for he is able to satisfy himself that the results of this 'experiment' undertaken along the lines he indicates, far from leading either to clear-cut failure or to 'nonsense,' are sufficiently convincing to warrant the conclusion he here sets forth hypothetically: that 'the world viewed from inside, the world defined and determined according to its "intelligible character" — it would be "will to power" and nothing else' (*BGE* 36).

In taking this position, Nietzsche is neither setting aside nor relegating to a merely preliminary and superficial level of discourse his characterization of the world in terms of interacting quanta of force. Rather, he is adumbrating it by specifying their basic character, in a way which both distinguishes his interpretation from other 'dynamic' conceptions of the world's nature, and makes the important point that a quantum of force is not to be thought of as something of which 'will to power' is only a *property*. On his view, such a quantum is essentially to be conceived in terms of 'the effect it produces and that which it resists,' and thus 'is thought away if one thinks away this radiation of power-will.' So he goes on to say: 'that is why I call it a quantum of "will to power" ' (*WP* 634).

Nietzsche's notions of 'force' and 'quanta of force' thus are inseparable from his notion of 'will to power,' requiring the latter for their 'completion,' as was earlier observed (*WP* 619). Quanta of force are not something else, which happen (among other things) to 'have' this 'will,' or to 'want' power. Thus Nietzsche suggests that one should not ask: 'But *who* wants power?,' considering this

213

'an absurd question, if the essence itself is power-will' (*WP* 693). He considers the manner of their interactions to be definitive of such quanta; and since he takes these interactions to be fundamentally a matter of power-relationships, he holds that their nature must be understood accordingly. It is for this reason that he slips easily and frequently into speaking of them as 'quanta of will to power,' 'quanta of power,' 'quanta of will.' When he does so, however, he is not saying something different, but rather the same thing in different ways, which are intended to bring out what might be called the 'qualitative' character of 'force.' Here he avails himself of certain connotations of more familiar terms, which are drawn upon to give substance and the proper inflection to this otherwise rather uninformative notion; while the basic idea the latter serves to convey is utilized to set the general context within which such refinements are made, and to indicate at least in a general way how the meanings of the former are to be adjusted in order for them to be thus employed.

In going beyond hypothesizing the fundamental homogeneity of all events and of the forces at work in them, and proposing further that 'all driving force is will to power' and that 'there is no other physical, dynamic or psychic force except this' (*WP* 688), Nietzsche obviously is not guided by the methodological 'demand' of 'economy of principles' alone. There is another such requirement which he also accepts and to which he seeks to conform, as he moves in the direction of this conclusion. It too is a very familiar one, having long been employed by 'empiricists' in assessing the credentials and determining the meaning of notions purporting to have existential import. It consists in the idea that the meaningfulness and hence the legitimacy of such notions is established only upon the identification of something within the realm of actual experience to which they correspond; and further, that the nature of their referents requires to be explicated in terms of features identifiable in the latter.

While Nietzsche is in many respects critical of his empiricist predecessors (and of empiricism in general), he considers this principle to be sound, and to constitute a crucial check upon metaphysical speculation. It has immediate consequences, however, for the conception of the world in terms of quanta and fields of force. For as he observes, what we experience is never 'force' pure and simple, but rather 'only *effects* translated into a completely foreign language.' If this were the end of the matter, it would also be the effective end of the conception of the world in terms of force as a meaningful and significant one. Thus Nietzsche writes: 'A force we cannot imagine is an empty word and should be

214

allowed no rights of citizenship in science' — or in philosophy either, as he understands it (*WP* 621).

The reason he does *not* take this to be the end of the matter, however, is also the reason he conceives there to be so intimate a relation between the notion of 'force,' as he proceeds to employ it in his characterization of the world's nature, and the notion of 'will to power.' For he takes the latter expression to have application to a salient and basic feature of our experience, and so to have a meaningfulness which sanctions its use at least in the characterization of the nature of our human reality. And this is the opening wedge which he considers both to endow his employment of the notion of 'force' with legitimacy in going on to speak of that of which the world consists, and to suggest how this notion is to be more concretely understood. It is only in this way, he contends, that 'force' ceases to be 'an empty word,' and wins its 'rights of citizenship' in science and philosophy (*WP* 621) — even though the meaning and legitimacy it thus attains is rendered rather problematical at the same stroke, owing to the recourse made to a feature of human experience, to the identification and generalizability of which numerous objections are possible.

Nietzsche recognizes the vulnerability of his procedure here to criticism. He contends, however, that there is no other way in which it is possible for 'the victorious concept "force" ' to be both rescued from the fate of meaninglessness which would make its 'victory' a hollow one, and 'completed' in a way that renders it philosophically serviceable. It is for this reason that he argues that 'there is nothing for it: one is obliged to . . . employ man as an analogy' to the end of transforming this concept from an empty word into a significant notion in terms of which what goes on in the world becomes explicable (*WP* 619). And since it is after all the notion of *force* which he is concerned and which he thus undertakes to 'complete' and develop in this way, it is perhaps neither surprising nor objectionable that the human trait upon which he seizes for this purpose is a disposition clearly manifested in a variety of the interactions our lives involve which may quite plausibly be linked to it.

Nietzsche thus seeks to render the concept 'force' capable of satisfying the twofold requirement of being 'imaginable' (or meaningful in the sense of according with some discernable feature of our experience), and of being 'useful' (or illuminating in the sense of enabling us to explain the occurrence of a wide range of types of change). And it is in an attempt to do so that he contends that something like 'an inner will must be ascribed to it' which he proposes to conceive 'as "will to power," ' understood

215

along the lines of the sort of dispositional tendency indicated by such relatively intelligible (though also rather crude) notions as 'an insatiable desire to manifest power' and a drive to 'the employment and exercise of power' (*WP* 619). It is only with this supplementation that 'force' becomes a significant notion with explanatory power. 'The will to take possession of a thing or to defend oneself against or repel it — that we "understand": that would be an interpretation of which we could make use' (*WP* 627). And he further argues that this is really the *only* such 'interpretation' of force and change of which one can thus 'make use' and get somewhere, once one recognizes the untenability of any sort of thing-ontology and of any other construal of the basis and character of the notion of causality. 'If we translate the concept "cause" back to the only sphere known to us, from which we have derived it, we cannot imagine any change that does not involve a will to power.' We may initially be disposed to think otherwise; but on Nietzsche's view, no other way of thinking survives criticism. 'We do not know how to explain a change except as the encroachment of one power on another' (*WP* 689). It does remain open to us, however, to construe changes along these lines; and it is thus that he proposes to construe them, adjusting the general notion of 'force' accordingly.

VI

In order to understand the cosmological hypothesis Nietzsche expresses in terms of 'will to power,' it is necessary to observe that in his hands the ordinary meanings it and its constituent terms may be supposed to have are modified and transformed; and there is no surer way to misunderstand him than simply to take them to have the same import for him that they generally have. From the standpoint of established usage it will appear that this involves doing a certain violence to the language, or at least employing various terms and expressions metaphorically rather than literally. On Nietzsche's view, however, there is nothing wrong with this; indeed, it is precisely this that anyone who is a genuine philosopher rather than a mere 'philosophical laborer' must do, for there is no other way to devise interpretations departing from and improving upon conventional ways of thinking. This is something he does here; and the notion presently under consideration constitutes perhaps the clearest and most important case in point in his thought of his proposition that philosophers 'must no longer accept concepts as a gift, not merely purify and polish them, but first make and *create* them, present them and make them convincing' (*WP* 412).

216

The first point to be made is that in speaking of 'power' in this context, Nietzsche has in mind something both different from and more complex than 'force.' (As shall be seen, moreover, 'will to power' for him is identical with neither, and is a notion even more complex than 'power.') This point is an important one, and should be obvious; but it is frequently overlooked or given insufficient attention, with serious consequences for his interpretation. The 'power' a system *has* is not a direct function of the quantum of force or configuration of forces in which it *consists*. The former, as he construes it, is a matter of the system's ability to preserve itself from internal dissolution and external encroachment, and to transform itself and affect other systems; and as such it stands in no direct and necessary relation to the latter. Power is not even to be equated with the *disposable* force of a system, since it is much more a matter of *how* the latter is employed than merely of *how much* is available for employment. Thus Nietzsche speaks here of 'power-relationships,' which are essentially a matter of 'mastery' — of dominance and resistance, of relative autonomy attained and control exerted (*WP* 630). And while an interplay of forces may likewise involve a clash of distinct centers of force in which these same themes characterize their interaction, what is decisive for the establishment or modification of the associated power-relationships is not their relative quantity as such, but rather their *organization*.

To be sure, 'power' for Nietzsche is no more synonymous with 'organization' *per se* than it is with 'force.' There is 'power' as he conceives of it, however, only where there are 'power-relationships between two or more forces' (*WP* 631); and these power-relationships, as he understands them, are essentially a matter of the establishment of one sort of organization (between competing systems or centers of force) by means of another (within each system, in accordance with which the forces they each represent are marshaled). Similarly, an increase of 'power' is not taken by him to be merely a matter of quantitative enlargement; indeed, it need not even involve any such enlargement. It is rather to be thought of fundamentally as a certain sort of modification of a system, such that its ability is enhanced both to resist dissolution and encroachment or subjugation and to extend its influence in relation to other systems, either in scope or in the degree of dominance. Quantitative enlargement not only may bring no increase of power, but further may even result in its diminution, if it strains the ordering capacity of the system too greatly. Its sphere of influence 'constantly growing or decreasing,' Nietzsche writes,

the center of the system [is] constantly shifting; in cases
where it cannot organize the appropriate mass, it breaks into
two parts. On the other hand, it can transform a weaker
[system] into its functionary without destroying it, and to
a certain degree form a new unity with it (*WP* 448).

Thus Nietzsche suggests that 'becoming stronger involves an
ordering process' or 'organization' in which the enhancement of
the 'dominion' of a 'power' proceeds apace with its ability to
control lesser systems and incorporate them as 'functions' of it
(*WP* 552). What is essential, on his view, is above all the organization of mere 'force' in a manner lending itself to the consolidation
of a system and the extension of its sway in relation to others.

Likewise when Nietzsche speaks (as he often does) of 'growth'
in this general connection, it is essential to recognize that it is not
merely quantitative growth which he has in mind, but growth that
has a qualitative dimension (at least in this sense). The same also
applies with respect to such related notions as 'development' and
'enhancement.' In his hands they refer neither to the mere enlargement of the total amount of force present in a given system, nor
to an increase in the complexity of its organization as such. Rather,
they pertain to changes it may undergo which result in its achievement of greater effectiveness in resisting the attempts of other
systems to master it, and in achieving or furthering its mastery
over them. This kind of modification, moreover, may take different
forms, since under different external and internal conditions it
may require either quantitative enlargement or reduction through
the elimination of elements hindering such effectiveness, and
either the elaboration or the streamlining of the system's organization.

Thus power-relationships for Nietzsche involve an interplay of
forces; but they also characterize this interplay, in ways which are
not to be conceived merely in terms of quanta of force of differing
magnitudes impinging upon each other.

It is a question of a struggle between two different elements
of unequal power: a new arrangement of forces is achieved
according to the measure of power of each of them. The
second condition is something fundamentally different from
the first (not its effect): the essential thing is that the
factions emerge with different quanta of power (*WP* 633).

Next, it should be observed that Nietzsche's conception of 'will
to power' no more reduces to 'power' than the latter reduces to
'force.' In ordinary language, there is an obvious and important

218

difference between *having* power and *wanting* or *seeking* it; and this distinction is preserved in his adaptation of the two related but different notions. He does suggest that 'will to power' is characteristic of quanta and systems of force of whatever size and organization, i.e., of force as such. In doing so, however, he does not mean to suggest either that they all possess or enjoy the same measure of power itself, or that the 'will to power' characterizing all of them is proportional (either directly or inversely) to the extent of the power they actually enjoy. 'Power' refers to something about the relationships between them; 'will to power' refers to something about them which results in the fact that their relationships have this character. So he speaks of 'the will to power in every combination of forces, defending itself against the stronger, lunging at the weaker' (*WP* 655).

Nietzsche's basic idea, in speaking of 'will to power' as well as of 'power' here, is that the world is not to be thought of as a multitude of such forces which merely happen to be so arranged that some dominate others, and which happen further to change in ways resulting in a continuing modification of these power-relationships. It is his contention, rather, that it is of their very nature to attempt to acquire and extend their power in relation to others. The disposition he designates by the expression 'will to power' is proposed to explain why it is that the interplay of forces has the character of a changing network of power-relationships; why forces neither expend themselves randomly nor merely resist each other, but rather organize themselves into systems of greater or lesser effectiveness in achieving power in relation to others; and why the development of such systems does not cease with the emergence of simple and relatively durable forms capable of holding their own on a modest scale of interaction, but rather continues in a manner disruptive of order and issuing in the emergence of complex forms at once more powerful and less stable. If the possession of power presupposes or involves the organization of forces, he argues, the fact of such organization in turn presupposes a disposition to achieve power, and requires to be understood not as a mere accident in the interplay of forces but rather as the way in which this disposition is manifested.

'Will to power' for Nietzsche thus is neither a principle of mere adaptation or self-preservation, nor a 'will' to the mere 'accumulation' of force or its expenditure, nor yet again to its organization *per se*. It may involve all of these, but it is no more identical with them (individually or collectively) than it is identical with the possession of power. So he speaks of 'quanta of force the essence of which consists in exercising power against other quanta of force,' and among which 'the only reality is the will to grow stronger of every center of force — not self-preservation, but the will to appropriate, dominate, increase, grow stronger' (*WP* 689). This 'will to power' may be 'creative,' and may lead both to the establishment of order and to its dissolution; but it is not to be conceived as an impetus either to creativity or order or to destruction. Both the 'appropriation and assimilation' and also the 'forming, shaping and reshaping' in which it results are held ultimately to reflect something on the order of 'a desire to overwhelm . . . , until at length that which has been overwhelmed has entirely gone over into the power domain of the aggressor and has increased the same' (*WP* 656).

This disposition may surface in consciousness as an explicit intention, but it generally is not of this character at all. Indeed, the term 'will' in this expression functions in a way which departs radically from its ordinary and traditional philosophical uses, sharing with them little more than the idea of a directed impulsion. In its most general and rudimentary form, 'will to power' for Nietzsche is simply the basic tendency of all forces and configurations of forces to extend their influence and dominate others.

This is what he considers to be 'the one will that is inherent in all events,' in terms of which he proposes to analyze and 'explain' all phenomena as its multiform 'development and ramification' (*BGE* 36). Here he has in mind everything from the processes of inorganic nature to 'the organic functions' and even 'the spiritual functions,' interpreting them as neither more nor less than so many of its various 'modes of expression and metamorphoses' (*WP* 675). They collectively constitute the reality of the world as it actually exists, and require to be explicable in terms of the basic concepts of any adequate account of the world's nature. The concept of 'force' alone will not suffice for this purpose, Nietzsche argues, nor will its supplementation with the concept of 'power.' With the addition to them of the dispositional notion of 'will to power,' however, he holds that this requirement is met. It is for this reason that he attaches such importance to it, and gives it such prominence in his characterization of the world's nature, as when he suggests that 'the world defined and determined according to its "intelligible character" ' (i.e., its fundamental nature) is ' "will to power" and nothing else' (*BGE* 36).

Since what Nietzsche is concerned with here is the manner in which force generally is to be conceived as internally disposed or determined to express itself and operate, 'will to power' in this context emerges as a purely dispositional notion, in his formulation of which his use of the term 'will' is merely metaphorical. Once this is understood, it is possible to eliminate the latter entirely, and to reformulate what he has in mind (no less metaphorically, perhaps, but rather less misleadingly) in terms of a universal power-struggle among power-oriented quanta of force. It essentially and fundamentally determines the general character of their interactions and combinations, and remains the decisive feature of their interplay, even though it undergoes many and diverse modifications and transformations in the manner of its specific expression in the course of the emergence of different patterns and degrees of complexity in the relationships formed among them.

The notion of a power-struggle among myriad power-centers, resulting in a shifting array of power-relationships and in modifications of the constitution and changes in the very identity of these power-centers, is an intermediate one for Nietzsche. It is intended to bridge the conceptual gap between the basic but rather nebulous idea of an unspecified interplay of quanta of force, and the much more concrete but somewhat superficial conception of what there is in terms of the existence of a variety of inorganic, organic and 'spiritual' processes. It is meant to bring out the underlying homogeneity of the latter, and to indicate the nature of the more general process at work within them of which they are specific instances or expressions, while at the same time specifying the manner in which the interplay of forces unfolds and is to be conceived. The attribution of what Nietzsche calls 'will to power' to the quanta of force engaged in this interplay then serves to qualify the conception of the latter in such a way that the remaining conceptual gap between it and this intermediary notion of a power-struggle itself is bridged.

If it is the case that the world ultimately consists of dynamic quanta subject to no external law or constraint beyond that action upon each other, and if it is further the case that the interplay of such quanta (as manifested in the various specific processes in which natural phenomena, organic life and 'spiritual' activity consist) has the general character of a power-struggle, then it would seem entirely appropriate to construe these quanta as being essentially disposed accordingly. And the *pathos* Nietzsche thus ascribes to them, and characterizes as 'will to power,' has no further conceptual content here than this. Its meaning is specified and exhausted through its explication as the condition of the possibility and purported ubiquity of this power-struggle, given that this condition must be a matter of the basic character of these quanta themselves. Thus in considering the tenability of his conception of the world in terms of 'will to power,' one should proceed not by asking whether it is legitimate and warranted to speak of 'will' in this context, but rather by asking whether the idea that all processes consist fundamentally in such a power-struggle is as plausible and compelling as he takes it to be.

A word of caution is in order here with respect to the conception of power figuring in this hypothesis: it would be a mistake to take this notion too simply. In Nietzsche's hands it refers not merely to the more obvious forms of domination and control which most readily come to mind, but also to a whole range of much more subtle forms of the attainment of mastery and the assertion of supremacy. The forms of power are many, and the struggle for power of which he speaks is not to be thought of as a struggle for any one of them in particular. It is one of his main points that frustration in the attempt to achieve one sort of power commonly leads not to mere subjugation and assimilation but rather to the development of another — and not merely to the development of other means to the achievement of power of the same kind, but also to the development of alternate forms of competition, as it were, in which power is both differently won and differently measured.

Thus while Nietzsche does seek in one respect to establish 'the homogeneity of all events,' by arguing that the processes they involve are in all cases instances of the struggle for power, he also is concerned to make clear that they display a considerable degree of heterogeneity (even when conceived as instances of this struggle), owing to the proliferation of the forms it takes, and thus of the kinds of power which thereby become possible and contested. They cannot be collectively measured and assessed by reference to some further end or purpose to the attainment of which they all are directed and function as means; for he holds that nothing of this sort is prescribed by anything either in the nature of the world (or of force, or of life) or beyond it. It may be true that in this world, on his view, the name of the game (as it were) is power; but it is also the case that this game is by no means a single one, invariably played in the same manner. Moreover, 'power' for Nietzsche is neither the name of a single game nor that of a family changing through births and deaths, any more than is 'winning' in the domain of ordinary games. 'Winning' might be what games are all about (though this may of course be disputed); but what it is to win or play well at one may be very different from what it is to do so at another. And so also with respect to Nietzsche's understanding of power and his conception of the struggle for power.

Power further is not to be conceived as a means to some further end, survival included; just as the playing of games might be regarded as more than simply something one does to continue living or to enable one to do something else. Yet neither is power something in itself, apart from any specific context in terms of which its enjoyment can be distinguished from a relative lack of it, and which can be contested for as such. Thus in one sense the idea of a power-struggle is intended to provide a more fundamental and comprehensive characterization of a wide range of processes than that which consists in descriptions of the specific forms they take. In another, however, it is a rather formal, meta-level representation of them: a scheme under which these processes may be subsumed and to which they conform, but which itself is no such actual process.

Further, winning or excelling at a game is not something of which it is appropriate to speak with reference to everything done in the course of winning or playing or playing well at it. And it likewise should not be thought that Nietzsche holds that every event associated with the unfolding of each instance of processes of all kinds can be explained and is to be understood directly and simply in terms of 'will to power,' as an immediate manifestation of it. The elaboration of such processes is taken to be a multiplicity of developments, reflecting both the nature of the specific sorts of power-struggles already going on (as these have specifically evolved through prior developmental articulation), and also the impetus to establish new avenues along which this struggle may continue. It thus involves the continuing emergence of new and different complex arrangements, which only instrumentally and collectively contribute to the possibility and attainability of power in various forms.

It therefore is no valid objection to Nietzsche's view to observe that nothing like a power-struggle is immediately evident when one closely considers almost any sequence of particular events. It is not his contention that this is or should be so, or even that it is in principle appropriate to conceive of 'will to power' as manifest on this scale, except in the cases of the simplest of forces, in which the most rudimentary forms of power alone are possible. Beyond this level, where systems of greater complexity and forms of power of greater subtlety are concerned, the unit to be considered in speaking of the struggle for and attainment of power is not the ordered pair of events (an abstraction in any case) but rather the larger process. And in the case of systems as complex as living organisms (not to mention human beings), the magnitude of the processes requiring to be considered before it is possible to discern the nature of the power-struggles involved and the forms of power at issue is very considerable indeed.

223

Thus the 'will to violate and to defend oneself against violation,' of which Nietzsche speaks in stating what the 'will to power' amounts to 'essentially' (e.g., WP 634), is only the most basic form of this impulse, to which he does not mean to suggest all of its other forms in fact reduce. He conceives of it as undergoing radical modifications as it is sublimated again and again in the course of the emergence of more complex and differently organized types of systems of dynamic quanta. Once this is understood, it becomes apparent that the meanings of the terms he uses here are not adequately captured by the straightforward construal of them they may at first seem to invite. Indeed, they defy complete, definitive, precise explication — and it would seem to have been part of Nietzsche's intention in selecting them and using them as he does that this should be so. Like most of his other central notions, they are in the first instance metaphors, chosen owing to their utility in conveying or indicating certain things he wishes to suggest, but also with a view to rendering any ordinary way of interpreting them and the position they are used to express a virtual impossibility. As they stand, they do little more than serve as signs, which tell us two different things: first, that we should try to think in something like the direction in which they point — but second, that they are only pointers, and specify the direction to be taken only in a rather general way.

In Nietzsche's hands, to be sure, these notions of 'power' and 'will to power' do not remain the mere caveat-bearing road signs as which they begin. They subsequently acquire greater definiteness, in the light of what his further applications of them enable us to read back into them. Yet they retain a semi-metaphorical character even after ceasing to be merely metaphorical, in keeping with his view that we must relinquish the idea of attaining anything more by means of any cosmological concepts we might devise than the sort of truth which consists in a relative aptness. And they also are meant to preserve something of the imprecision, flexibility and openness to new extensions of metaphors which are living rather than petrified, without which Nietzsche takes all concepts to obstruct rather than facilitate the growth of understanding.

VII

There are several sorts of considerations which are highly relevant to the comprehension of the lines along which Nietzsche seeks to direct our thinking by means of these notions. One of them concerns certain associations of the German term he uses, which here and standardly is rendered as 'power': *Macht*. This term is closely related to another, which is among the richest and most suggestive basic verbs in the language; and its many meanings serve to endow the term *Macht* with a suggestiveness and implicit range no less significant than its more immediate connotations, upon both of which Nietzsche draws in his conception of 'power,' power-relationships, and the struggle for power.

The verb in question is *machen*. The English word 'make' derives directly from it, and conveys one of its most ordinary meanings; but it is just as commonly used in a way that would be rendered in English by the word 'do.' And it also can mean such things as 'to produce,' 'to form,' 'to construct,' 'to create,' 'to effect,' and much else besides. Without claiming that what Nietzsche means in speaking of 'the will to *Macht*' is actually 'the will to *machen*,' and that his notion of 'power' in general can or should be glossed completely in terms of *machen*, several observations may be made. First, all of these sorts of activity or process both presuppose and manifest force or energy in some form, involving both its accumulation and its expenditure. Second, they all have the significance of the establishment of a relation or sphere of dominance of some sort with respect to that which is acted upon, however temporary it might be. And third, the ways in which such activities afford the possibility of establishing dominance or supremacy are by no means limited to relationships involving the attainment of actual possession or the assertion of direct control, but rather also pertain to relationships of other kinds — e.g., of competition — in which cases the establishment of such more immediate relationships may be either merely instrumental or quite dispensable.

The same points all apply where Nietzsche's notion of *Macht* is concerned. There are thus significant connections between the manner in which he understands 'power' and 'will to power,' when he proceeds to employ these expressions in characterizing the world's nature, and the sorts of thing conveyed by the term *machen*. It may be that the right way to put the matter, for him, is not to say that it is because the world is one in which such processes go on that it is a world of power-struggles and power-relationships, but rather to say that the former is the case owing to the manner in which quanta of force are essentially disposed to behave. Even so, however, both the nature of this disposition and the manner in which the ensuing power-struggle develops, together with the content to be ascribed to the idea of power itself in this context, require to be explicated by invoking the range of the meanings of *machen*, if they are not to be oversimplified in a manner failing to accord with Nietzsche's account of the processes constituting life in general and human life in particular.

A second sort of consideration may also be brought into play here, which serves both to support this line of interpretation and to shed some further light on the notions in question. 'Will to power' stands as a successor-conception in Nietzsche's mature thought to two others figuring centrally in his early thinking, and more specifically in his first major work, *The Birth of Tragedy*. They too go beyond the idea of the nebulous Schopenhauerian 'life-will,' of which he there also speaks; and they likewise are conceived as impulses not only manifested in the domain of human psychology and 'spiritual' life, but also having the more fundamental status of 'energies which burst forth from nature herself.' These obviously are the two 'tendencies' which he calls 'the Apollinian and its opposite, the Dionysian' (*BT* 2), and which (as this reference to them as 'opposites' indicates) he construes as a 'duality' of very different principles (*BT* 1).

In *The Birth of Tragedy* both impulses are characterized as 'artistic,' albeit in different ways; and 'nature' itself, as the fundamental locus of these impulses, is likewise held to be 'artistic' in the ways they are, the human artist being but an 'imitator' or embodiment and vehicle of 'these *art impulses of nature*' (*BT* 2). The processes of which the world consists thus are understood along the lines of the forms of 'artistry' to which Nietzsche's expressions 'Apollinian' and 'Dionysian' refer. Both are conceived as creative, and at the same time as involving a kind of violation — but with a difference. The former is essentially an impulse to the creation of definite, enduring, limited, orderly and finely proportioned form. The creation of such form, however, is possible only by either imposing it upon a domain to which it is foreign, or by rejecting whatever resists such imposition in favor of a different medium developed along lines more amenable to it. The latter, on the other hand, consists in an artistry that is essentially a matter of the harmonious integration and blending of initially distinct, dispersed and discordant elements, introducing regularity into change rather than arresting it or stamping fixed structure upon it. Yet it disrupts established order and alters existing states of affairs, either imposing unity and regularity in a domain in which they were previously lacking (or different), or encroaching upon the domain of created form.

It is of little importance for present purposes that Nietzsche associates the former with 'dreams' and 'illusions,' and the latter with 'intoxication' and orgiastic excess. What is crucial is his conception of the former as an impulse to the establishment of form amid or beyond the flux of change, and his conception of the latter as an impulse to the attainment of harmonization within it through the regulation of 'transitoriness' by means of 'continual creation' which renders it more than mere chaos. (For a fuller discussion of these and related ideas, the reader may turn to the first part of Chapter VIII.) Even in *The Birth of Tragedy*, it is an error to infer that the Apollinian impulse has as little to do with reality as he contends its artistic (in the ordinary sense) and intellectual products have to do with truth; and that the Dionysian impulse is to be conceived exclusively in terms of the destructiveness, cruelty and chaos he remarks upon in contrasting it with the Apollinian. The world with which he there suggests we find ourselves confronted — of nature as well as society and culture — is one in which both are held to be creatively active, even if also (in different respects) destructively effective. And even at the end of his productive life one finds him employing these expressions in a similar way, to make the same sort of point (e.g., *WP* 1050).

To be sure, Nietzsche avails himself of this manner of expressing this distinction rather infrequently in his later writings, tending more often in them to employ the expression 'Dionysian' in connection with his view of the world as manifesting both of these tendencies. Both, however, remain central to his understanding of the course of the world. They are not merely superseded by but also preserved in his notion of 'will to power,' and inform his conception of the struggle for power and of the nature of the attainment, manifestation and enhancement of power. The dualism which seems to be implied in their initial formulation is overcome by means of his reformulation of his conception of reality in terms of the latter; but this reformulation involves no sacrifice of the richness of his earlier account. The process of imposing and establishing definite form and structure amid an undifferentiated and chaotic flux, and of merging dispersed elements into integrated and regular patterns of events, emerge as different expressions of a single more basic impulse. Each represents a transformative (creative-destructive) generation of order; and both constitute exemplifications of the tendency of which Nietzsche speaks, serving to flesh out the meaning of the associated conception of 'power' and such elaborative notions as 'domination' and 'mastery.'

When his idea of 'will to power' is viewed in this light, it is clear that it is only on the most rudimentary level that it is to be construed in terms of anything like a mere tendency to 'violation' and to 'defend oneself against violation.' While perhaps appropriate on this level, such language greatly oversimplifies what transpires

227

beyond it, where subtler relations between more complex systems of dynamic quanta are concerned. In a similar vein, one would do well to bear in mind his repeated warnings against thinking of power and power-relations too mechanistically, as though the interplay of forces involved in all actual processes were merely a matter of a kind of physical pushing and pulling. For this too indicates that he would not have power understood simply in terms of the strength of ability to repel and either destroy, incorporate or compel obedience; and that there is more to the struggle for power as he conceives it than a mere ceaseless trial of strength waged along these lines.

In point of fact, the leitmotiv Nietzsche discerns throughout the whole range of processes in the world is not violation and subordination or assimilation as such. Rather, it has the character of an *ordering transformation*, which under different circumstances takes such different forms as subjugation, regulation, structural articulation and fixation, and the functional integration and harmonization of constellations of forces. His contention that these processes constitute a power-struggle is to be understood along these lines. His notion of 'will to power' is to be interpreted as designating a tendency rooted in the very nature of force serving to impel all quanta and systems of quanta of force to some such manner of expression in their interplay. The 'power-relationships' of which he speaks are to be thought of in terms of the establishment and modification of relations among the latter which reflect the specific character of whatever transformations of this sort have occurred among them. And the 'power' Nietzsche refers to, which is thus variously indicated to be sought, contested, manifested and attained or diminished wherever change and becoming are to be found, is to be construed in the light of his identification of such transformation as their most fundamental general feature.

'Transformation' here is not tantamount to the idea of mere fortuitous change; but it also is not to be identified with *development*, conceived in relation either to the attainment of some goal, or to the realization of some ideal, or to the perfection of some ability — or even to the enhancement of the capacity to compete in the struggle for survival or supremacy. It further cannot be explicated in terms of 'power' somehow conceived independently of it; for reality on one scale or another is the concrete expression of the same thing of which the notion of 'power' is the abstract representation. The latter has no reality apart from the former, and no independently characterizable nature. Any ordering transformation of some portion of the world may be said to constitute a manifestation of power, because such transformations are what manifestations of power refer to and consist in. And the idea of an increase of power is to be understood in terms of the effecting of certain such transformations which render possible others of a more extensive or intensive nature.

In short, 'power' for Nietzsche is fundamentally a matter of transformation, involving the imposition of some new pattern of ordering relations upon forces not previously subject to them. The manifold power-struggle which is this world of 'becoming' is an endless and varying profusion of such transformations, each of which is strongly conditioned by certain others while occurring more or less independently of most, but all of which are ultimately bound up with the rest. And 'will to power' is but the expression he uses to convey the idea that the world consists of nothing other than force which is so constituted that the sole disposition attributable to it and operative in it, in terms of which all of its modifications are to be understood, is the impulse to such transformation.

VIII

Nietzsche takes it to count in favor of his supposition of the primordiality of this transformative impulse, and also to be one of its significant philosophical uses, that it enables one to explain something about the world with which any adequate cosmological theory must reckon: the fact that the world is not an undifferentiated unity, but rather a multiplicity. And he goes on to argue that the world cannot resolve itself into such a unity, if it has this basic character. His thinking here connects with his contention that the world not only is one in which change just happens to be both possible and actual, but moreover is *essentially* a world of change, in which 'becoming' neither will nor can ever give way to some final fixed state of 'being.'

It will be recalled that Nietzsche considers it necessary to conceive of the world in such a way that the 'permanence of change' can be accounted for. He takes the latter to be *established* by the argument that, supposing the world already to have existed through an infinite time, 'if it were in any way capable of a pausing and becoming fixed . . . , then all becoming would long since have come to an end' — whereas this evidently has not happened (*WP* 1062). This argument, however, provides no *explanation* of what it thus establishes. The desired explanation likewise is not provided merely by the introduction of the idea of 'force,' and the construal of the world in terms of it — especially in view of the fact that he speaks of the world in this passage as consisting in 'a finite, definite, unchangeable force' (*WP* 1062). As he elsewhere puts the point: ' "Change" belongs to the essence' (*WP* 1064). It would be a defect in a conception of the world's nature if it left this a mystery. And it does not suffice, to enable one to understand how it is that 'change' is an essential feature of the world, merely to propose that the latter is to be construed in terms of this notion of 'force.' For by itself this would be consistent with a conception of the world as a static equilibrium of forces, and also with its conception as a single, undifferentiated quantum of force the sole 'action' of which consisted in the preservation of its cohesion.

The existence of the world as a totality that is also a multiplicity of interacting forces (or as a multiplicity of forces that is also a finite, definite totality of interrelated elements), and moreover its existence as a multiplicity with respect to which 'change' is of the essence, are held by Nietzsche to be two basic features of the world. He both seeks to explain them in terms of the supplementary notion of 'will to power,' and takes them to constitute part of the justification of introducing this notion in providing a further characterization of the nature of 'force.' For all that the idea of 'force' itself implies, it could be essentially cohesive, and thus suppressive of both multiplicity and change. 'Force' of an essentially transformative nature, however, would inevitably issue in both. And conversely, the evident reality of both as features of the world, in conjunction with the argument establishing that change is a permanent as well as present feature of it, and the further argument that its permanence entails that of multiplicity as well, would seem to warrant the conclusion that the conception of the world in terms of force requires to be elaborated along something like the lines Nietzsche suggests.

These considerations may not by themselves show that the specific elaboration Nietzsche proposes (in terms of 'will to power') is the right one, but they do suggest that one is needed; and his would appear at least to be a tenable contender, for it provides the needed explanation at a minimal cost. 'The will to power can manifest itself only against resistances' (*WP* 656), he writes; and in a world supposed to consist of nothing other than force, such resistance can be provided only by this force being divided against itself. If it is of the very nature of force that it is disposed to manifest itself or operate transformatively, and if transformation requires that there be both distinction and access, the existence of a world of force as a world of differentiated if also interrelated forces (or fields, systems, centers, or quanta of force) is a necessity — as is the permanence of change in such a world.

Change, multiplicity, organization and disintegration, regulation and disruption all fundamentally characterize this 'world of becoming,' for Nietzsche; and all require to be taken into consideration and accounted for in terms of something about its ultimate nature. He takes himself to succeed in doing this through his 'completion' of the concept of 'force' by recasting and specifying it in terms of his notion of 'will to power.' In doing so, he not only embraces but also believes that he satisfies the general methodological requirements of sufficient explanatory power and economy of principles, together with the further empiricist stricture against the introduction and use of notions for which there is no experiential warrant (or a priori justification).

The parsimoniousness of Nietzsche's 'hypothesis' must be conceded. It further would seem adequate to perform the explanatory function required of it; for the impulse to ordering transformation it imputes to all quanta of force serves to render intelligible the existence of this world as an affair of ceaseless 'becoming,' which neither constitutes a complete chaos nor manifests or resolves itself into an order of fixed being, and the most pervasive basic features of which are the emergence of various sorts of order and their dissolution. It is not transparently clear, however, that the manner in which this hypothesis satisfies the third condition indicated suffices to endow it with genuine plausibility. A stronger case on behalf of its candidacy than has been set out so far thus requires to be made if its soundness is not to remain suspect. To this end, it is necessary to inquire more closely into Nietzsche's reasons for introducing the notion of 'will to power' into discussion of the world's nature in the first place.

Perhaps the best way to begin is to consider what Nietzsche supposes to be the right thing to take as one's point of departure in reflecting upon the world's nature, and what his point of departure in doing so actually is. This is a matter of no little importance, not only as it affects the lines along which he develops his world-interpretation, but in relation to the development of such interpretations generally. Different points of departure often serve to bring different fundamental themes to the fore, which suggest different models and thus affect the way in which phenomena considered subsequently are treated; and thus much depends upon the decision that is made at this juncture.

As has been seen, Nietzsche holds that 'there is nothing for it: one is obliged to employ man as an analogy' in interpreting 'all motion, all "appearances," ' and the world generally (WP 619). It is essential to observe, however, that this assertion is as ambiguous and potentially misleading as it is significant and revealing with respect to his thinking at this point. For while it indicates his commitment to the very important proposition that we can do no better — and indeed no other — than to take 'man' as our clue to the nature of the larger reality of which we are a part, it leaves unspecified the way in which 'man' is to be regarded when treated as such a guiding clue. And the idea of 'man' is one which is sufficiently vague that, as it stands, it scarcely even begins to give definite direction to the interpretation of the world's nature — or rather, it suggests a whole variety of different directions which might be taken, many of which alternatives Nietzsche emphatically repudiates.

Before it can be made to serve the function he suggests for it, therefore, it is necessary to give a general explication of it which lends it greater specificity and renders it amenable to this purpose without begging the question at issue. And the first point to be made here is that his thinking along these lines revolves around his broader conception of something that is not a 'being' at all but a *process*, of which human existence is a particular but illuminating complex form: namely, *life*. The idea of 'man,' on his view, requires to be recast in terms of the particular and general or composite character of the processes in which human life consists.

It is as one form of 'life' that Nietzsche proposes to draw upon 'man' in the elaboration of his interpretation of the world's nature, by means of a mediating reflection upon the phenomenon of life of which this form is a particular instance. The world, he contends, requires to be conceived not merely in terms which enable one to take note of the existence of life in its diversity and developmental capacity, but also in terms rendering it intelligible. And, more specifically, if the phenomenon of life should prove to exhibit some pervasive general tendency, the world's nature must be construed in such a way as to enable one to account for this fact. If, more concretely still, a case can be made out for its interpretation as 'the expression of forms of the growth of power' (*WP* 706), this will have implications for the understanding of the world in which it occurs.

Moreover, Nietzsche suggests that a proper understanding of so-called 'mechanical' and 'spiritual' occurrences and activities alike is attainable only by viewing them through what he calls 'the optics of life.' Indeed, he argues that there is an important sense in which the former constitute a domain characterizable as a kind of *'pre-form* of life.' They are allowed to have 'the same rank of reality' as that held even by such paradigms of life-processes as our 'affects'; but they are held to stand to them as 'expressions of lower states' of development, or as 'a more primitive form' of existence 'in which

232

everything still lies contained in a powerful unity' (*BGE* 36). The latter, on the other hand, are taken both to have as their basic function 'the enhancement of life,' and to constitute a special class of sublimated 'offshoots' of 'the basic animal functions' which have emerged as nature proceeds with 'the task of spinning on the chain of life' (*WP* 674). Yet while he considers reflection upon life in this way to afford one deeper insight into the world's nature than is attainable by starting with (and treating as paradigmatic) the ideas of either 'things' or 'thought,' 'matter' or 'reason', he stops well short of that metaphysical animism in which all processes are interpreted as life-processes, and 'life' is the most basic of all categories. Thus he does not allow this notion to stand as an undefined and undefinable primitive, but rather considers it imperative to ask: 'But *what is life?*' And he answers: 'My formula for it is: Life is will to power' (*WP* 254).

Nietzsche further issues the disclaimer that 'life is merely a special case of the will to power; — it is quite arbitrary to assert that everything strives to enter into *this* form of the will to power' (*WP* 692). He takes 'life' as his point of departure because it is that form of existence which is 'nearest' and thus most readily scrutinized and analyzed — 'the form of being most familiar to us.' And he further does so because he considers the middle-range processes basic to organic and human life to reveal the general character of reality more clearly than do the simpler interactions of inorganic nature and the more complex and artificially structured operations in which our linguistic and intellectual activities consist. So, upon arriving at the conclusion that life 'is specifically a will to the accumulation of force,' he goes on to frame a 'hypothesis based upon it' which is then 'applied to the total character' of reality: 'Should we not be permitted to assume this will as a motive in chemistry, too? — and in the cosmic order?' (*WP* 689).

This, however, is more a matter of procedure than an argument intended to be conclusive. Nietzsche commends and avails himself of 'the optics of life' in this context as a means to the end of developing an interpretation which transcends the peculiarities of the perspective making it possible, in the light of which these basic life-processes themselves (no less than the other processes indicated) are subsequently to be analyzed and reinterpreted. They are his point of departure, but they are only that. He does not consider them to be unproblematical or constitutive of the fundamental nature of reality as such. It is only provisionally that they may be taken for granted and drawn upon; ultimately they are to be accorded the status of derivative and emergent phenomena, and require to be redescribed accordingly. His reflections upon them afford Nietzsche his most compelling reasons for supposing and maintaining that 'the ground and character of all change' is to be conceived in terms of 'will to power,' understood as explicated above; but they are not thereby taken either to be definitive of it or to exhaust the range of its manifestations. Rather, once having suggested it, they are then reconstrued in terms of it, and are assigned places within a much wider range of processes all of which are understood to be expressions of its 'development and ramification' (*BGE* 36).

Life and 'will to power'

IX

Nietzsche readily acknowledges that the basic life-processes upon which he focuses are themselves rather diverse, and do not constitute a homogeneous group admitting of a single form of observation and analysis. This complicates his position considerably; but the different approaches he is accordingly led to take in dealing with them thus represent no objectionable vacillation in his treatment of them. Rather, they impart to it a fruitful tension that is one of its main strengths and chief sources of interest. This relates to a problem which will receive extended discussion in the following chapter: that of the relation between the mental or spiritual and the physiological, which here appears in the form of the relation between the biological and the psychological.

This is no distinction without a difference for Nietzsche, even though it is one of his most persistent concerns to show that it also is not a distinction which reflects an ultimate and impassable ontological gap. The basic life-processes to which he draws attention at times appear to be located in the domain of biology, and to require to be approached biologically and analyzed in biological terms. Yet at other times they seem to be selected from the realm of psychology, and to be approached and analyzed as a psychologist might deal with them. And the 'will to power' he discerns in these processes bears a correspondingly ambiguous aspect, which creates difficulties in its interpretation and in the evaluation of the broader hypotheses he frames in terms of it (even if this ambiguity is only apparent, or is resolvable on some higher level of discourse).

Neither 'life' regarded biologically-scientifically nor 'life' regarded experientially-psychologically is Nietzsche's exclusive point of departure. Rather, he directs his attention to both, reflecting now upon the one, now upon the other. In doing so he supposes that it is the same general phenomenon that is thus being regarded from different but complementary perspectives. For 'life,' on his view, happens to be something the nature of which can adequately (rather than one-sidedly and thus erroneously) be grasped only by approaching it alternately with the eyes of a biologist and with the eyes of a psychologist; and what is thus seen in each way requires to be drawn upon to aid in the interpretation of the other. (Actually, in dealing with our human nature more fully, his procedure is even more complicated than this, involving the incorporation of a variety of other — e.g., sociological, ethnological, linguistic, and intellectual-historical — perspectives as well; but this complication may be ignored for present purposes.)

For Nietzsche, therefore, any difficulty encountered here is specifically associated neither with his understanding of life nor with his particular manner of dealing with it. Rather, it arises from the awkwardness of thought and language when we are confronted with the task of conceiving and expressing something requiring to be grasped at once as drive and as action; and it further derives from the ill-situation of perception and understanding, which operate in such a manner as to prompt a schematic sundering of something existing as a unity into a bifurcated inwardness and outwardness, each represented very differently. The artificiality of this distinction of 'inward' and 'outward' with respect to life-processes must be grasped, he maintains, if their nature is ever to be properly understood; and he likewise considers their reaction in either direction to be profoundly misguided.

It is in an attempt to combat this error in either form that Nietzsche alternates between speaking of 'organisms' and 'organs,' and of 'instincts' and 'affects,' in his characterization of these processes. The reality of life as he conceives it does not consist in the existence and movements of entities whose nature is exhibited in the anatomical structures we perceptually apprehend and describe in the language of objects and attributes. It also does not consist in the upsurge and interplay of impulses to be conceived on the model of certain episodes in our conscious experience; nor, for that matter, is it to be construed in terms of some mere combination of the two. Instead it is held to be a matter of the mutually transforming interaction of certain arrangements of forces of differing dimensions and in various stages and forms of coordination and conflict, organization and disintegration. It exists as an array of types of such complex arrangements, which are characterized *generally* by their common disposition to ordering transformation and status as functional unities or systems capable of assimilation and elimination, intra-systematic modification and adaptation, and concerted and directed extrasystematic operation — and *specifically* by the relative distinctiveness and similarity of the manner in which these things occur in the case of each such type.

It is thus Nietzsche's preliminary understanding of life as an affair falling on neither side of the subject—object dichotomy (nor yet again as merely bridging it), possessing rather a unitary nature to which both dispositions and changes of manifest relational and organizational state are attributable, which leads him to avail himself of considerations drawn from the perspectives of both psychological analysis and biological observation. His apparent oscillation between the two is actually a calculated attempt to play them off against each other, in such a way as to benefit from each while moving beyond both. His immediate aim in doing so is to develop a comprehensive 'philosophy of life' that neither ignores the insights they afford, nor remains subject to the limitations and distortions of the orientations they represent. Experientially oriented psychological analysis and empirically oriented biological inquiry are both directly relevant to the philosophical understanding of the nature of life. (To this it must immediately be added, however, that while they jointly constitute the necessary points of departure for a 'philosophy of life,' they are not taken by Nietzsche to suffice to complete it.)

There is certain asymmetry between the domains of phenomena on which each focusses, which is often supposed to indicate that the latter (the biological) is of more fundamental importance than the former (the psychological) with respect to the comprehension of the nature of life generally — and indeed that the former must ultimately be reducible to it. Both are characteristic of *human* life; but *all* life falls within the compass of biological inquiry, whereas it is only with *human* life that an experientially oriented psychology has to do. Psychological analysis of course pertains to behavior; but it only does so (as Nietzsche conceives of and engages in it) in the context of reflection on experience. And since human experience is the only sort to which we have immediate access, it is this upon which such reflection of necessity must focus.

Nietzsche concedes the latter point, but rejects the inference drawn from it. It is with this point in mind that he contends, in the passage cited above, that 'there is nothing for it' but to 'employ man as an analogy' in seeking to achieve an understanding of the kind of 'inner event' which informs and directs the unfolding of all overtly ascertainable changes and interactions (*WP* 619). Yet as this remark also suggests, he is by no means persuaded of the

236

necessity of restricting the application of the insights attainable through psychological analysis in this narrower sense to human life alone; and of analyzing all other life-forms exclusively and completely in terms of the features they present to observation, interpreted in the light of the conception of the world as an interplay of quanta of force. To be sure, his misleading reference to an 'inner event' notwithstanding, he does not take the position that life in general is to be construed as a double-level affair, in which there is a reciprocal determination of distinct and discrete 'outer' and 'inner' events. He does, however, take all life to involve an internally operative determination to action and interaction, of which the particular domain of experientially oriented psychology is a specific and special instance. And he further supposes that the latter stands to other instances of it, associated with other forms of life, in a relation of similarity sufficient to warrant at least a cautious analogical use of insights derived from analysis of the former in interpreting the nature of the latter.

Whether or not it is deemed appropriate to speak of reflections along these lines as 'psychological' in some broader and extended sense, they represent an important line of Nietzsche's thought with respect to life that is at least continuous with the sort of psychological inquiry he begins by drawing upon. As in the case of his specifically psychological discussions, they are not to be regarded as having to do with something about life-forms that is actually distinct from the overt structural and behavioral features of various life-forms, but rather simply involve the adoption of a perspective upon them differing from that oriented primarily toward the latter. Viewing them in this way, however, is held to be necessary if an understanding of their nature is to be achieved that goes beyond the nebulousness of an unelaborated characterization of them simply in terms of 'forces,' and takes adequate account of the dispositions informing them.

Nietzsche's thinking here is guided by two basic (and very plausible) considerations. The first is that, while human life may differ in many particular and important respects from other forms of life, it cannot be supposed to be an affair entirely apart, differing so radically that little more than the word 'life' is common to them. We are, after all (as he never tires of observing), 'a species of animal.' If human life is 'no longer merely animal' life, this circumstance itself can only be owing to the fact that the conditions for the respects in which it is more than 'merely animal' are themselves prepared in the distinctive manner in which the constellation of our basic life-processes has developed. Human life is still but one of many forms of life, animal even if no longer merely so. This has

237

important implications not only for the understanding of human life, however, but also for the interpretation of life more generally. For even though the latter cannot be supposed to incorporate all of the specific features of the former (any more than the former can be supposed to reduce completely to the common features of the latter), results attained in the course of analyzing the former may serve to shed light upon the latter. The location of human life within the larger domain of organic nature, in short, is a two-way street; and thus it is by no means illegitimate and inappropriate 'to employ man as an analogy to this end,' as Nietzsche proposes doing, even though it is obviously imperative to employ caution in doing so.

The caution he recognizes to be necessary is reflected in the second of the general guiding considerations requiring to be noted here. It is clear that human life does differ markedly from other forms of life, both in the (quantitative) complexity and in the (qualitative) character of many of the patterns of activity and interaction it involves. Its difference is most apparent when these patterns are considered not with regard to the basic functions they perform and the origins from which they derive, but rather in terms of their specific emergent features. Consequently, however, it is to the former rather than the latter that attention is best directed if one's aim is to find indications of the existence of tendencies suitable to the purpose of 'employing man as an analogy,' and reasonably generalizable where other forms of life are concerned. Care must thus be taken to focus upon what is most basic in human life, and to guard against falling victim to the distorting influence of any predilections one may have for certain of its elaboration and modifications.

X

It has already been indicated that the 'formula' Nietzsche employs to express the theme on which all such forms are variations is that 'life is will to power' (*WP* 254). In the section in *Beyond Good and Evil* in which he sets out his 'hypothesis' concerning the nature of both life and the world in its most general and comprehensive form, he suggests that 'all organic functions,' and with them 'our entire instinctive life' as well as all those activities subsumable under the heading of 'thinking,' are to be both explained and understood as instances of the 'development and ramification' of the 'one basic form' of disposition indicated by the expression 'will to power' (*BGE* 36). He elsewhere advances this interpretation more straightforwardly, as when he writes that 'the organic functions' may be 'translated back to the basic will, the will to power — and understood as offshoots,' and likewise 'thinking, feeling, willing in all living beings,' together with 'the spiritual functions' (*WP* 658).

All of these things, Nietzsche contends, are 'not explained mechanistically' at all adequately and properly; and they likewise are not to be construed as the expressions or derivations of any rational or spiritual principle. He takes it to be self-evident that they cannot be supposed to originate and consist in the merely random congregation of dispositionless dynamic quanta; and thus he holds that they require to be explained in terms of the operation of some disposition intrinsic to the forces involved in the unfolding of these life-processes. But he argues that this disposition cannot be held to consist either in a Hegelian impulse to self-conscious knowledge, or in a Spinozistic or Schopenhauerian impulse to self-preservation. The former view is held to be too blatantly anthropomorphic to warrant serious consideration; and in any event it is ruled out by the fact that the various forms of life do not admit of the kind of monolinear hierarchical ordering (culminating in the Absolute Knowing of Hegelian *Geist*) which its tenability requires of them. And the latter is likewise to be rejected, owing to the inadequate explanatory power of the hypothesis in terms of which it is framed. Perhaps because of its association with a form of naturalism from which he considers it imperative to disassociate his own, he repeatedly attacks this hypothesis, insisting upon the merely derivative status of self-preservation in the realm of life.

Nietzsche's main argument here is quite simple. The most durable organic units or systems are the simplest ones. If the dominant theme in the realm of life were self-preservation, therefore, the development of life-forms would never have gone beyond the emergence of very simple ones. In point of fact, however, it has not stopped with them, but rather has issued in the existence of a great variety of forms of varying degrees of complexity, whose conditions of existence are comparably complex and therefore insecure. 'The richest and most complex forms,' which represent 'a greater sum of coordinated elements,' tend to 'perish more easily' than the simplest; for their very complexity renders their 'disintegration . . . incomparably more likely' (*WP* 684).

Organic units and kinds do endure through time, even if not indefinitely or unchangingly. So Nietzsche suggests that 'life' could be 'defined as an enduring form of processes' involving the establishment and maintenance of power-relationships, 'in which the contenders grow unequally' (*WP* 642). The manner of their development, however, not to mention the character of their behavior, indicates that their endurance is a consequence of the operation of some other tendency at work in them, rather than itself being that which they are most fundamentally disposed to accomplish. Nietzsche sometimes puts this point by saying that it would be more accurate to conceive of them as striving to *surpass* rather than to preserve themselves — even though this formulation is only a provisional one, which points in the right direction but ultimately requires to be recast.

He thus considers the postulation of a disposition of the latter sort to be incapable of accounting for the emergence of complex forms of life, whose ability to ensure the continuation of their existence both as units and as kinds is inferior to that of the simpler forms out of which they have evolved. Indeed, it cannot even account for 'the most basic and primeval activities of proto-plasm,' which 'takes into itself absurdly more than would be required to preserve it,' and which moreover 'does not thereby "preserve itself," it falls apart.' And 'the drive that rules here has to explain precisely this absence of desire for self-preservation' (*WP* 651). An adequate conception of the nature of the basic disposition operative in all life-forms, on his view, must yield an explanation not only of the relative durability (and limiting vulnerability) they exhibit, but also of the fact of their evolution along these lines. And he feels that his conception of 'will to power' does both, whereas the rival view under consideration does not. Thus he writes:

> The wish to preserve oneself is the symptom of a condition of distress, of a limitation of the really fundamental instinct of life which aims at *the expansion of power*, and, wishing for that frequently risks and even sacrifices self-preservation . . . . In nature it is not conditions of distress that are *dominant* but overflow and squandering, even to the point of absurdity. The struggle for existence is only an *exception*, a temporary restriction of the will to life. The great and small struggle always revolves around superiority, around growth and expansion, around power — in accordance with the will to power which is the will of life (*GS* 349).

One should not allow Nietzsche's predilection, in this and other such passages, for such terms as 'wish,' 'want,' 'desire' and 'will' to distract and mislead one; for his use of such terms in this context is only figurative. He draws upon them as a fund of convenient terminological shorthand; but they are one and all to be understood dispositionally, and interpreted in the light of his critical treatment of their conventional (ordinary and traditional philosophical) employment. His main contention here is that life-processes basically tend to unfold along lines involving an assertiveness which is restricted to self-preservation only in marginal cases of diminished vitality, even though it often serves at least temporarily to produce this result in other cases as well. Fundamentally, however, it is a matter of an expanding-expending transformation that he calls a struggle for power, in which self-preservation is as commonly endangered and even undermined as it is secured and prolonged.

This disposition *can* manifest itself in the form of a struggle for self-preservation, as well as both securing and endangering it derivatively in the course of taking other forms, on Nietzsche's view, because the nature of this assertive tendency determines only that it must be expressed in some sort of transformative activity or other commensurate with the transformative capacity of the system in question; and where this capacity is modest, this may represent the limit of its self-assertive potential. But that is only one possibility among many; and the development and present character of life suggest to him that it is the exception rather than the norm. So he also observes that one should 'think before putting down the instinct of self-preservation as the cardinal instinct of organic being.' For, he contends, 'a living thing seeks above all to *discharge* its strength — life itself is *will to power*; self-preservation is only one of the indirect and most frequent results' (*BGE* 13).

It is important to observe that 'discharge' here is not to be understood in a one-sidedly narrow way, as a matter of nothing more than the mere using up or random expending of disposable energy. Thus, in a related note, Nietzsche writes: 'It can be shown most clearly that every living thing does everything it can not to preserve itself but to become *more* —' (*WP* 688). And it is of further interest, with respect to the manner in which he develops his case, that in the previous passage he goes on to say: 'Here as elsewhere, let us beware of *superfluous* teleological principles — one of which is the instinct of self-preservation.' The hypothesis which recognizes no other basic disposition than this not only is held to compare unfavourably with Nietzsche's own in explanatory power; it also is suggested to suffer from the defect of postulating a teleological principle where none is called for in order to explain the phenomena under consideration. This is something he holds his own hypothesis does not do, and shows to be unnecessary.

The former is teleological (though the end or goal in question may seem very modest compared with those postulated in most teleologies), because it involves the attribution, to each living creature as such, of a long-term aim (self-preservation) in relation to which its various forms of behavior are then conceived to stand as means to governing end. Nietzsche is critical of teleological principles in general, because of the dubiousness of the notion of final causality; and he considers '*superfluous* teleological principles' to be doubly objectionable, on grounds of 'method, which must be essentially economy of principles' (*BGE* 13). His own hypothesis renders this one superfluous by explaining everything it can and more. And it avoids the pitfall of teleology, because (appearances to the contrary notwithstanding) what he calls 'will to power' is not a teleological principle, identifying some state of affairs describable in terms of 'power' as a goal to which all forms of behavior of living creatures are instrumentally related. Rather, it is a dispositional principle indicating the general character of the mutually tranformative interactions of functional unities in which 'each power draws its ultimate consequences at every moment' (*WP* 634).

'Power-struggle' and 'power,' in short, are not conceived by Nietzsche to stand in a means—end relationship; for the reality of the latter is taken to be entirely a matter of the kinds of transformative activities involved in the former. And 'will to power' does not designate an inclination imputed to all living things to work out and maintain a pattern of internal organization and external relationships conducive to the attainment of a certain sort of overall result. It refers instead to a tendency purported to be manifested immediately and in a sense completely at every moment in the unfolding of the processes in which their life and reality consist; and it thereby serves merely to indicate the general character of the 'relations of tension' between the 'dynamic quanta' involved, which in essence (and existence) are a matter of nothing other than 'their relation to all other quanta' (*WP* 635). Thus when Nietzsche goes on to refer to 'will to power' as 'not a being, but a becoming, but a *pathos*,' he might well have gone on to add that this *pathos* neither is itself (or reflects) a *telos*, nor stands as a *nomos* to which all organic (and other) units are constrained to conform as they organize and comport themselves.

XI

Perhaps the most fundamental consideration underlying Nietzsche's contention that the interpretation of life in terms of 'will to power' is superior to that cast in terms of an impulse to self-preservation, however, is a good deal more concrete. His characterization of

242

organisms (along with all other functional unities) as 'systems' and his emphasis upon organization notwithstanding, he holds that the most salient feature of life through time is not the perpetuation or gradual stabilization of established networks of processes and relationships. Rather, it is *change*, and more specifically the ebb and flow of construction and destruction, growth and decline. 'Stasis' and equilibrium occur, but only occasionally and temporarily, arising through a momentary offsetting of forces in tension, and invariably being disrupted as the interplay of these forces proceeds. On Nietzsche's hypothesis, this is just what one would expect; whereas it does not square at all well with the alternative hypothesis under consideration.

To be sure, reactive adaptations and accommodations conducive to self-preservation may be discerned among the changes which thus occur. Nietzsche considers it absurd to imagine, however, that it is possible to account for all actual sorts of changes in the realm of life entirely or even largely in terms of some such reactive tendency alone. And he further argues that it is erroneous to suppose that responses of this sort are made only along lines serving to bring about the (re-)establishment of internal and external equilibrium, and to ensure self-preservation to the extent that they do occur. They are more appropriately regarded simply as special cases or partial aspects of those more comprehensive forms of activity and interaction which collectively render the processes of life a matter of growth and decline. The transformative assertion and counter-assertion they involve is destructive as well as productive of order and stability; and their general tendency is toward the transcendence rather than the perpetuation of existing patterns. This sometimes preserves and strengthens, and sometimes weakens and destroys, but invariably changes the organisms and ultimately the forms of life involved, along with the relations among them.

There is much more to life than the self-perpetuation of organic individuals and kinds, and much more to their alteration than adaptive accommodation to external circumstances. To say 'more' here is to some extent misleading, however; for what Nietzsche has in mind is neither something else presupposing and added on to this, nor something of which self-preservation and effective accommodation are invariably derivative results. What life fundamentally and generally involves, he contends, is this: 'Not merely conservation of energy, but maximal energy in use, so the only reality is the will to grow stronger of every center of force — not self-preservation' (*WP* 689). And it is in this light that he suggests the emergence of complex life forms is to be understood:

> Greater complexity, sharp differentiation, the contiguity of
> developed organs and functions with the disappearance of
> the intermediate members — if that is perfection, then there
> is a will to power in the organic process by virtue of which
> dominant, shaping, commanding forces continually extend
> these bounds of their power and continually simplify within
> these bounds: the imperative grows (*WP* 644).

It further by no means suffices, Nietzsche argues, to construe
the nature of the fundamental disposition accounting for the
developmental (transcending rather than conserving) character of
life in terms of anything like 'hunger,' which might be supposed to
lead to ceaseless encroachments resulting in expansion when more
is assimilated than is required for preservation — even though he is
prepared to allow that, on a certain level of consideration, 'life'
may be conceived in terms of 'a multiplicity of forces connected
by a common mode of nutrition' (*WP* 641). There may be such a
potentially overreaching drive; but if so, it is merely a derivative
one. The generalized hypothesis cast in terms of it must thus be
rejected as a candidate for the position also to be denied to that
formulated in terms of self-preservation: ' "hunger" is an interpretation based on far more complicated organisms (— hunger is a
specialized and later form of the drive, an expression of a division
of labor in the service of a higher drive that rules over it)' (ibid.).
In short: 'It is not possible to take hunger as the *primum mobile*,
any more than self-preservation' (*WP* 652).

The same is true in the case of the other alternative hypothesis
most commonly encountered in this context, which accords
primacy in the realm of life to a *procreative* impulse. For it suffers
from the same double defect as does the self-preservation hypothesis, of attributing ultimacy to a principle that is at once
teleological and superfluous. And in addition, Nietzsche argues,
while this impulse is cogently ascribable to various higher forms of
life as a convenient way of designating certain specialized aspects
of their activity, it too (insofar as it is appropriate to speak of it at
all) must be recognized to be an offshoot or emergent refinement
and elaboration of a more basic tendency. Thus he writes: ' "Procreation" — only derivative.' Originally, he suggests, it was but a
consequence of the problem arising as simple organisms continually
appropriated more than they could assimilate; their inability 'to
organize the entire appropriated material' resulted in the emergence
of a process involving the dissolution of a single 'center of
organization' and its replacement by several of them (*WP* 657). In
other words: 'A protoplasm divides in two when its power is no

longer adequate to control what it has appropriated: procreation is the consequence of an impotency' (*WP* 654). At this level, therefore, it is not even appropriate to speak of an impulse to procreation or reproduction; for the process to which these terms are applicable may thus be seen to be but a side-effect of another. And the development and modifications of the former in the course of the emergence of more complex forms of life are to be understood not as determinative of the general and specific lines along which these forms take shape and unfold, but rather as supplementary adaptations of this secondary process.

Finally, Nietzsche also dismisses the idea that the various general features of life might be accounted for in terms of a tendency to react accommodatively or adaptively to environmental conditions. It is relatively easy to see why he does so, given his view that the development and present reality of life shows it to be characterized by a continuing transcendence of established organizational forms and relational patterns, in the direction of an increasing profusion and complexity of both, accompanied by an intensification of the tensions which both sustain and serve to disrupt their ever more intricate structures. For while changes of various sorts would undoubtedly occur in and among a multiplicity of organisms whose functions and interactions all were informed ultimately by a tendency of this sort, one would expect their general drift to be in precisely the opposite direction, toward standardization, simplification, harmonious integration, and stable equilibrium. To account for the very different reality of life, he concludes, it is necessary to relegate this tendency to a subordinate role, and to conceive the basic tendency operative in both its development and the processes in which it consists along quite different lines. So he writes: 'Life is not the adaptation of inner circumstances to outer ones, but will to power, which, working from within, incorporates and subdues more and more of that which is "outside" ' (*WP* 681). And, along similar lines but more fully:

> The influence of 'external circumstances' is overestimated
> by Darwin to a ridiculous extent: the essential thing in the
> life process is precisely the tremendous shaping, form-creating
> force working from within which *utilizes* and *exploits*
> 'external circumstances' — The new forms molded from
> within are not formed with an end in view; but in the struggle
> of the parts a new form is not left long without being related
> to a partial usefulness and then, according to its use, develops
> itself more and more completely (*WP* 647).

245

The reference to Darwin here is not particularly important; nor is the question of whether Nietzsche's criticism of him, if well taken in its own right, is actually applicable to him. What matters for present purposes is the light these remarks shed on his reason for construing life in terms of 'will to power' rather than a tendency to reactive adjustment or adaptation. They also are revealing of his meaning in doing so. It is necessary, however, to guard against misunderstanding his references to 'utility' as indicative of a fundamental acceptance on his part of the 'self-preservation' hypothesis after all. As he observes, ' "useful" in respect of acceleration of the tempo of evolution is a different kind of "useful" from that in respect of the greatest possible stability and durability of that which is evolved' (*WP* 648). Nor are these the only relevant sorts of utility; and even when the list is complete, it does not follow that the impetus to change characteristic of life is a matter of a disposition to maximize any of them.

It may be that some sort of 'natural selection' occurs with respect to the results of the operation of 'the tremendous shaping, form-creating force working from within' of which Nietzsche speaks, in relation to which a comprehensive notion of 'utility' might retrospectively (and rather abstractly) be identified and defined, involving reference to or embracing a number of narrower kinds of usefulness including those just mentioned. But it would be an error to suppose that this 'shaping, form-creating force' itself consists in a tendency to move in the direction of enhanced 'natural selectibility' through modifications effecting the requisite adjustments along these lines. 'Will to power' is conceived as a disposition rendering the fact of evolution comprehensible, but not as a 'will to evolution' (and thereby also to whatever is necessary to achieve it) as such. The latter principle would be either blatantly teleological or vacuous, depending upon its construal; and so in either event it is not to be taken seriously.

Indeed, Nietzsche is inclined to think that the relation between 'will to power' and both natural selection and evolution is a rather ambiguous one. In the absence of the transformations in which he takes the former to issue, to be sure, there would be no continuing generation of alternatives among which such selection could go on, and no development of the sort the actual evolution of life constitutes. But these transformations as often as not — and perhaps even much more often than not — fail to survive such selection and play no part in the long-term evolution of life, even when they result in the temporary emergence of forms of life possessed of the most exceptional 'potency.' Thus he remarks: 'Higher types are indeed attained, but they do not last . . . . The richest and most complex forms — for the expression "higher types" means no more than this — perish more easily: only the lowest preserve an apparent indestructibility' (*WP* 684).

This view has a number of important applications and implications. For present purposes, however, its significance is simply that it makes clear that 'will to power' for Nietzsche is a disposition that is both conceptually and actually distinct from the promotion of the kind of utility associated either with natural selection or with the emergence of successively 'higher' forms of life. It also is to be distinguished from the idea of a purely indeterminate and irreducible *chance*-factor in organic processes resulting in the occurrence of random mutations, which then serve as grist for the mill of natural selection. Nietzsche is prepared to allow that the notion of 'chance' has a kind of provisional applicability here, particularly in view of the inapplicability of conceptions of mechanical or logical necessity and of nomologicality (other than as shorthand ways of referring to merely statistical regularities). He maintains, however, that it is imperative 'to recognize the active force, the creative force in the chance event: — chance itself is only the clash of creative impulses' (*WP* 673).

'Will to power' is essentially transformative, but in no specific direction. The only sort of 'utility' which may be said to be directly associated with it, and that which Nietzsche has in mind in the passage cited above, is that which relates to the transformative capacity of the organic unit, as this is concretely manifested in the context of the relationships in which it stands. Here it is appropriate to speak of it, just as (and just insofar as) it is appropriate to speak of 'will to power' as a disposition on the part of a dynamic quantum or system to extend its sway. But such utility is exclusively a function of activity in accordance with this disposition, and neither refers conceptually nor relates instrumentally to any further end or development.

XII

'Life,' Nietzsche contends, 'is the expression of forms of the growth of power' (*WP* 706). It has a double character both elements of which require to be taken into consideration if its nature is to be properly understood; for rather than representing merely the persistence of an arrangement of forces, it further fundamentally involves both an expanding and an expending. Thus he observes that, on the one hand, it 'is specifically a will to the accumulation of force . . . , essentially a striving for more power' (*WP* 689); and that, on the other, 'a living thing wants above all to *discharge* its force' (*WP* 650). These are simply different 'moments' or aspects of the phenomenon of 'growth,' which he takes to be the primary characteristic of all life that is flourishing rather than declining: 'To have and to want more — *growth*, in one word, that is life itself' (*WP* 244).

Growth is not a process which even in principle can occur independently of interaction. It essentially involves a dialectic of assertion and assimilation, according to Nietzsche, having the character of a 'struggle.' And whether one looks at the simpler forms of organic existence, or reflects upon 'where and how the plant "man" has so far grown most vigorously to a height' (*BGE* 44), or turns one's attention to human societies, he contends that this struggle 'always revolves around superiority,' and so concludes that 'the really fundamental instinct of life . . . aims at the expansion of power' (*GS* 349).

If this is so, however, it should be observed that there is for Nietzsche a distinction as well as an intimate connection between the notions of 'life' and 'growth'; and that 'will to power' is to be understood neither as meaning 'will to growth' nor as a derivative disposition in a means—end functional relationship to some sort of more fundamental growth-imperative. As his own contrast between 'ascending' and 'declining' life also implies, a system may cease to grow without thereby ceasing to constitute an instance of a form of life. And as his attribution of 'will to power' to all such instances regardless of their relative 'strength' or 'weakness' indicates, the existence of this disposition neither entails nor presupposes an actual ability to grow in any appreciable way.

Growth further is to be conceived neither simply in terms of the quantitative expansion of a system, nor merely in terms of an elaboration of its structural complexity. As Nietzsche understands it, it is rather to be construed in terms of the enhancement of its transformative capacity in the context of its actual relationships to other systems. It is thus a possible outcome of the 'power-struggle,' but requires to be viewed as a function of it rather than a principle governing it. Nietzsche's reason for fixing upon it is that he supposes growth, even more than health, to characterize life in its fullest vigor, and so to draw attention to cases in which it is reasonable to suppose that the basic features of life are most clearly exhibited. This reasoning might appear circular; but while he does indeed ultimately construe growth in terms of 'power,' his conception of the latter is elaborated in terms of an analysis of what is involved in a rather broad range of developments in the realm of life which undeniably stand out as paradigm cases of vitality, precisely by virtue of the fact that the flourishing life with which they confront us involves not merely tenacity but also a kind of change most readily describable as growth.

In short, one can identify cases of growth even in the absence of a clear and adequate understanding of what growth actually involves; and through their analysis one can achieve an insight into the underlying character of life when (we may suppose) it is at its fullest stride, as it were. Here one can discern the basic tendencies informing it with greater clarity than when attention is distracted by complications associated with their inhibition or frustration. Having done so, one is then in a better position both to deal with the latter and to comprehend 'growth' itself more precisely and adequately. Thus life is viewed in the perspective of growth, and growth then is reconsidered in the perspective of life as it is thereby illuminated. This approach, while in a sense circular, is at any rate not viciously so.

Nietzsche nowhere better summarizes his position than in a long section in *Beyond Good and Evil*, in which his immediate concern is with forms of society, but in the course of which he elaborates upon the more general version of the hypothesis he is advancing concerning the nature of life. He writes:

> Here we must beware of superficiality and get to the bottom of the matter, resisting all sentimental weakness: life itself is *essentially* appropriation, injury, overpowering of what is alien and weaker; suppression, hardness, imposition of one's own forms, incorporation and at least, at its mildest, exploitation — but why should one always use those words in which a slanderous intent has been imprinted for ages? . . .
> [Anything which] is a living and not a dying body . . . will have to be an incarnate will to power, it will strive to grow, spread, seize, become predominant — not from any morality or immorality but because it is *living* and because life simply *is* will to power . . . . 'Exploitation' . . . belongs to the *essence* of what lives, as a basic organic function; it is a consequence of the will to power, which is after all the will of life (*BGE* 259).

In short: the realm of life confronts one concerned to develop a comprehensive 'philosophy of life' with a broad range of phenomena which are at once manifestations of and clues to its nature, and at the same time 'problems' demanding not only description but also 'solution.' The task Nietzsche sets for himself here is to develop an account satisfying this demand and further establishing a framework within which these phenomena can be integrated with each other. These phenomena include 'procreation and nourishment,' and also various other, more specialized 'organic functions' (e.g., perception and movement), as well as such more general phenomena as 'growth.' And Nietzsche contends that reflection upon them, once freed of 'all sentimental weakness' and metaphysical preconceptions, both suggests and tends to confirm a hypothesis of the sort he advances. One can 'find in it the solution' to all of these 'problems,' he maintains, and can 'trace back' all these phenomena to the single underlying disposition he calls 'will to power' (BGE 36).

It is beyond the scope of this discussion to determine whether Nietzsche's proposed treatment of these phenomena can be borne out in terms of ongoing biological inquiry. Two points, however, should be remarked. First, he clearly invites evaluation based on considerations of this sort. But second, he undoubtedly would insist upon the necessity of distinguishing between the import of the findings of working biologists (which is in principle considerable), and that of the theories prevailing among biologists and the conceptual schemes they happen to employ (which may be highly problematical, and may adversely affect both their statements of their findings and what they make of them).

Most biologists might well feel that what Nietzsche has to say cannot be regarded as sound biological theory, because it goes beyond anything it is of concern to them to try to establish, and indeed beyond anything it is *possible* to establish, given the methods and criteria of theory formation and confirmation with which they find it necessary or most fruitful to operate. He would be quite willing to concede as much himself, however, and to acknowledge that he ventures beyond the limits set by such procedural and programmatic constraints. But he does so from design rather than indiscretion. For he takes the development of a philosophy of life to be a different if related enterprise, in the context of which it is permitted and indeed required to raise further kinds of questions.

Nietzsche undoubtedly would consider it distressing, and perhaps fatal to his position, if it could be shown that certain fundamental developments in biological theory had implications incompatible with what he is saying, even after allowances were made for the philosophical shortcomings of the conceptual schemes employed in their articulation. It would be of little concern to him, however, if it were merely to be pointed out that few biologists subscribe to anything like his interpretation of life, or even that the weight of current biological-theoretical opinion would seem to be against it. Biologists might favor, e.g., the idea that life is ultimately a mechanistic affair to be conceived in terms of physiochemical processes; but this, to his way of thinking, would only make them bedfellows of the physical scientists he discusses, whose favored mode of interpretation he considers both super-ficial and highly problematical.

It must be allowed that Nietzsche does not demonstrate the validity of his interpretation in any clearly compelling and decisive way. Yet he does at least succeed in making a case for its viability, and for the necessity of giving it serious consideration as a philosophy of life. For he satisfies the general conditions which any attempt along these lines must meet to be tenable, and also the further, broader methodological requirements indicated earlier. He sets forth — in outline if not in detail — a scheme in terms of which the various biological phenomena mentioned become comprehensible and integratable, and which further is capable of performing the same function in the specific domain of human existence, as shall be seen in the following chapter. And it may also be said in its favor that it has the double advantage of featuring a principle which neither requires life to be regarded and treated as an anomaly in the world, nor exceeds the limits of plausibility.

XIII

In conclusion, I shall draw upon the foregoing discussion to shed further light on one issue in his philosophical cosmology dealt with above, and to introduce a concluding examination of another of his best known but most perplexing ideas: that of the 'eternal recurrence.' In this way, as it were, the present chapter will fittingly come full circle.

The first-mentioned issue is that of whether the world is to be conceived as a chaotic flux, given that it constitutes no essentially and timelessly ordered cosmos. It has been observed that Nietzsche avails himself of the former characterization of it to indicate his rejection of the latter construal of it; but that he nonetheless is quite prepared to concede — indeed, he insists — that there is order in the world, which while contingent and mutable is no less characteristic of it than is change. His reflections on the nature of life and the living are of no little relevance in this connection; for they afford one the clearest indication of how far he is prepared to go here, and of what he more specifically has in mind. Life, on his view, is not something distinct from or merely apparent in relation to 'the actual world,' but rather is very much a part of it. As has been seen, he even goes so far as to suggest that 'the so-called mechanistic (or "material") world' may be considered 'a pre-form of life' (BGE 36). In any event, he clearly and very reasonably supposes that, because life occurs in and is a part of the world, account must be taken of the nature of the former in framing and elaborating an interpretation of the latter.

Organisms or living creatures, for Nietzsche, are organizations, or organized systems of dynamic quanta, which at least for a time preserve their integrity despite the changes they undergo. The 'determination of degrees and relations of force' they represent is held to be characterizable not only 'as a *struggle*' among unequal contenders for power, but also as 'an ordering process'; for, though it is 'not intentional,' it nonetheless happens that 'as soon as dominion is established over a lesser power and the latter operates as a function of the greater power, an order of rank, of organization' results (*WP* 552).

Notwithstanding their individual uniqueness, moreover, organisms exhibit similarities as well as differences in the manner of their organization and functioning, which show them to be instances of relatively fixed if slowly changing types or forms of life. Change may be among life's most salient features, both in the long run and more immediately; but in neither case is it change so radical and irregular as to render life a chaotic flux in any strict sense. Were this to obtain, something would indeed exist, but it would not and could not be anything on the order of life. A world in which there is life is a world in which there is order, even if the world might once have been or become devoid of both. Nietzsche's cosmology incorporates this latter possibility, but is not confined to it; and his conception of the world as it exists excludes it in favor of the former.

Thus while there may be no eternal and immutable world-order of any kind, as he repeatedly insists, life bears witness to the obtaining of order in the world, in a threefold way: it presupposes a certain degree of order in the world, as a condition of its possibility; it itself is a part of the world representing another kind of order; and it imposes further order upon the world as it establishes and extends its domain in it. To be sure, the kinds of order life-forms constitute and impose not only are rather untidy, but also may wane as well as wax; nothing in the world's nature determines them to be as they are, and they cannot be supposed to amount to any permanent achievement. Nonetheless life paradigmatically exemplifies what Nietzsche has in mind when he speaks of 'the world as a work of art that gives birth to itself' (*WP* 796). And the enhancement of life by the same token is the extension of order in the world in which it occurs.

The order to be found in the world, most clearly and extensively elaborated in the realm of life but prefigured also in inorganic processes, may not conform to models derived from the more abstract and artificial domains (e.g., mathematics) in which our reason can most easily move, and to which it is prejudiced. To the extent that we are wedded to such models and the associated criteria of order, we will find life a most disorderly affair, and the world largely devoid of anything conforming to them. In this respect it will seem and be a chaos. This recognition, however, is no more than an intermediary and transitional stage on the way to its more adequate comprehension, the achievement of which involves the revision of one's conception of order along lines adjusted to a new model derived from reflection on the nature of life. The notion of chaos retains a meaning — signifying the absence of such order and 'pre-forms' of it — and also an application to the world, but only selectively, to certain of its aspects and possible or periodically recurring states.

The eternal recurrence

XIV

So Nietzsche speaks of 'this, my *Dionysian* world,' as one which tends alternately toward extremes of order and disorder, 'with an ebb and a flood of its forms; out of the simplest forms striving toward the most complex . . . , and then returning home again out of this abundance,' this alternation repeating itself 'with tremendous years of recurrence' (*WP* 1067). And here we come upon one of the variants of his idea of the 'eternal recurrence.' This is not, to be sure, that formulation of this idea upon which commentators generally focus their attention. It is of considerable importance to observe, however, that on different occasions he both makes a variety of different suggestions with respect to what it is that is to be thought of as 'recurring eternally,' and also accords the idea differing sorts of status and import. There can be no doubt that he took it to be of great significance, and believed that there was much to be said for it, in all of the forms he gives it. But what he took its significance to be, and what he thought could be said for it, go well beyond the confines of his cosmology, and in the case of his most extreme formulation stand in a highly problematic relation to it. Indeed, it is arguable that in this case his main motive for advancing it derives from considerations of a very different sort, and that it is as something of an afterthought that he makes a few tentative attempts to incorporate it into his cosmology and to argue for it accordingly.

Commenting upon *Zarathustra* in *Ecce Homo*, Nietzsche terms 'the idea of the eternal recurrence' the entire work's 'fundamental conception' (*EH* III:6:1). At the end of *Twilight*, moreover, he characterizes himself as 'the teacher of eternal recurrence' (*TI* X:5). The idea is indeed introduced with much fanfare in *Zarathustra*, and figures very centrally in it; and he subsequently recurs to it repeatedly. There also is at least an anticipation of it in his early manuscript on *Philosophy in the Tragic Age of the Greeks*, which is worth noting. In it he makes much of Heraclitus' belief 'in a periodically repeating end of the world, and in an ever renewed emergence of another world out of the all-consuming world-conflagration,' through a 'world-forming' impulse which 'calls other worlds to life' in a manner at once 'playful' and repetitious. 'This is the game the aeon plays with itself,' he writes of Heraclitus' view, 'building and destroying, without moral overtones, in ever equal innocence'; and so the world goes endlessly. 'From time to time it begins the game over again' — and 'as soon as it starts to build, it links, arranges and shapes regularly and in accordance with inner patterns' (*PTA* 6, 7). Nietzsche parts company with Heraclitus on this last point, concerning the conformity of events to 'inner patterns' of the world; but in other respects he follows him rather closely — as one might expect he would, given his concluding contention that 'the world ever needs the truth, and thus it ever needs Heraclitus,' who 'raised the curtain on this greatest of plays' (*PTA* 8).

In his development of the idea of the eternal recurrence, Nietzsche seeks to recapture and elaborate what he takes to be the truth in this Heraclitean vision, if also to put the idea to further uses in certain of the forms he gives it. One reason why he seizes upon this idea is that it enables him at a stroke to express his complete rejection of all views according to which the world develops in some sort of linear, teleological manner, proceeding toward some pre-established final goal or end-state. 'Becoming is not a merely *apparent state*,' and 'does not aim at a *final state*,' he was earlier observed to argue, adding: 'I seek a conception of the world that takes this fact into account' (*WP* 708). In his idea of the eternal recurrence, this conception is given vivid expression.

But this idea conveys and is intended to convey more than this as well. In the first place (and this is perhaps the most basic and general of its formulations), it makes the sort of point Nietzsche has in mind when he insists upon 'the homogeneity of all events,' maintaining more specifically that 'all "purposes," "aims," "meaning" are only modes of expression and metamorphoses of one will that is inherent in all events: the will to power' (*WP* 675). Here his point may be taken to be that in all that transpires in the world, it is the same basic story everywhere and always: at bottom all events and all structurings and restructurings manifest a single fundamental disposition that is ever at work in them. What recurs eternally is the manifestation of this 'one will that is inherent in all events.' On this level of consideration, all events are ultimately the same; and so one may likewise speak of the eternal recurrence of the same (sort of) events.

In the second place, however, there is something further that Nietzsche takes to recur eternally, which he also avails himself of this notion to convey. In another of its formulations it may be understood to refer to a sequence of basic world-states, in which at one extreme 'the simplest forms' are the rule, while at the other 'the most complex' emerge in profusion. Here the suggestion being made is that the world oscillates between these extremes in a never-ending cycle, the former gradually giving way to the latter only to resolve itself at length into the former again, 'with tremendous years of recurrence' (WP 1067). This version of the idea echoes the view Nietzsche ascribes to Heraclitus: the cosmic 'fire,' as the origin and essence of all things and 'world-forming force,' is held to 'pass through the course of becoming in innumerable transformations,' which 'transformation-courses of fire perpetually run upward and downward, back and forth,' in an endless alternation (PTA 6).

To be sure, Nietzsche does not follow Heraclitus in his characterization of the various states through which this cycle passes, substituting the language of dynamic quanta and their manner of organization for the language of elements. The similarity of the basic pattern he has in mind to that which he here discovers in Heraclitus, however, should be obvious. Quantitatively considered, he contends, 'the energy of the totality of becoming remains constant; regarded economically, it rises to a high point and sinks down again in an eternal circle.' At what he here thinks of as the bottom of the cycle it is dispersed and chaotic; but it does not remain so, achieving degrees of organization eventuating in the 'tranformation of energy into life,' with 'life at its highest potency' representing the world's 'climactic condition' — a condition, however, which 'is not a condition of equilibrium,' but rather is only a transient stage of extensive but unstable organization, gradually giving way to further stages marked by its dissolution (WP 639).

In this same passage, it may be noted, Nietzsche speaks of 'the absolute necessity of similar events occurring in the course of one world [and] in all others,' and yet states that what this signifies is 'not a determinism ruling events,' but rather only the 'impossibility' of events following a different course in any successor (or prior) world. And it should also be observed that what counts as 'an event' here is left unspecified. It could be, therefore, that on this version of the idea of the eternal recurrence it is on the macro-level of the general course of the world, rather than on the micro-level of what specifically transpires within each successive stage in the 'eternal circle,' that he means to suggest that there is an 'absolute necessity of similar events occurring.' Even if 'event' is construed as having a narrower and more local as well as a broader and more macrocosmic application, moreover, the fact that Nietzsche speaks only of 'similar' events allows for different interpretations of the position he is advancing. And on one permissible construal of what he is saying, he may be taken to be allowing that at least within certain limits variations may occur on general themes, which only as such are the same across all successive world-formations.

Another important point relating to this version of the idea concerns its compatibility with the reality of development. Far from ruling out the possibility of any sort of real development in the world, the occurrence of transformations Nietzsche supposes to represent a most important kind of development is one of its basic features, characterizing the entire half of the great cycle through which the world repeatedly passes during which increasingly complex forms of 'higher potency' emerge. To be sure, one of the basic suggestions this general picture is intended to convey is that such development does not continue indefinitely. It is held instead to reach a 'high point' and then to give way to a broad-scale movement in the opposite direction, thus characterizing only a part of the cycle and constituting no permanent attainment. But this means only that its reality is periodic rather than unceasing, and not that it is merely apparent and unreal.

This development likewise may involve the mere retracing of the same basic course the world always takes; but that too does not count against its reality during a significant part of the world's recurring course. It further may not conform to conceptions and criteria of development associated with various metaphysical, religious and moral modes of interpretation and evaluation; but it is a kind of development nonetheless, the significance of which is not to be underestimated. What Nietzsche terms 'the highest types' — those forms of existence of the greatest complexity and highest potency — also, by virtue of their very complexity and accumulated energy, may be the most fragile and unstable and therefore the least durable, and so indeed may tend to precipitate the reversal of the very development of which they are the culmination. But these too are circumstances he does not take to affect the legitimacy of conceiving of their emergence as the outcome and high point of a long-term and genuine developmental process. Rather than mandating the abandonment of the view that it is appropriate to speak of the occurrence of genuine development in the world, they simply serve to oblige us to reconsider and recast our conception of development, bringing it into line with this understanding of what transpires in the world.

Nietzsche's case for his contention that the version of his idea of the eternal recurrence presently under consideration applies to the world is rather different from his case for the soundness of that version indicated previously, which boils down simply to the case he makes for construing all that obtains and transpires in the world as 'modes of expression and metamorphoses' of a single basic principle, 'will to power.' The former version is not implied by the latter, and so can be established only by means of the introduction of considerations of a further sort. The most important of these have already been indicated earlier in this discussion. First, he takes it to be beyond dispute that 'the world is not striving toward a stable condition' (WP 639), whether of some fixed and abiding order or of complete and final dissolution; for 'if the world could in any way become rigid, dry, dead, *nothing*, or if it could reach a state of equilibrium, or if it had any kind of goal' that were a 'once-and-for-all' affair, 'then this state must have been reached. But it has not been reached' (WP 1066) — and so the world must be otherwise conceived. Second, however, he supposes this world to be a world not only of change but of 'becoming' and of the 'passing away' of that which 'becomes,' neither of which is 'a merely *apparent state*' (WP 709). And more specifically, he considers it appropriate to speak here of both the emergence and the dissolution of complex systems and patterns of relations among them, resulting in the obtaining of comparable states of order and disorder not only locally but in the world more generally.

Third, Nietzsche draws upon a pair of principles which express what he takes to be limits on movements in both directions. One is a consequence of his ascription of the disposition he terms 'will to power' to all dynamic quanta: the collapse of previously established power-relationships among them immediately occasions the establishment — first locally, and then more broadly — of new power-relationships among them, and thus of their gradual reorganization into new systems of increasing complexity and potency. The other is a consequence of the tensions both within and between such systems, and of the increasing strains to which they are thus subject as this development proceeds: greater

257

complexity is attended by greater instability and vulnerability, which eventually lead to collapse — not only of the over-extended systems, but also of the wider network of relationships among them constituting a particular world-order.

It is these suppositions upon which Nietzsche bases his case for the hypothesis that the world eternally retraces the general sequence of states he describes in the passage cited above. They may not strictly entail this version of the idea of the eternal recurrence, but he does not claim they do. His aim is rather the more modest one of attempting to develop a 'conception of the world' which takes them into account, weaving them together into a coherent interpretation for which they provide support. In this he succeeds. It must be allowed, however, that there are other conceptions of it which would do so just as well; and that he takes a large and rather problematic step when he extends to the world as a whole his characterization of a cyclical pattern of transformation derived from a consideration of what may reasonably enough be supposed to occur throughout it on a local scale. This cycle might well be repeated endlessly within the world in regions of varying compass, without ever being described by the world in its entirety. Such a world could still be said to be a 'Dionysian world of the eternally self-creating, the eternally self-destroying' (*WP* 1067); but it would not be the 'circle' or 'ring' Nietzsche goes on to suggest 'this world' to be.

XV

If he has a reason for taking this further step, it would seem to have less to do with any considerations bearing directly on the matter as a cosmological hypothesis than with a very different sort of concern, which also leads him to advance the more radical version of the idea of the eternal recurrence to the effect that all events recur eternally, down to the last detail. This version goes far beyond either of those considered previously, and involves much more than 'the eternal recurrence of war and peace' to the thought of which he restricts himself in his first explicit reference to the notion (*GS* 285). It is instructive in considering what to make of it, however, that here as so often subsequently, his chief interest is in the question of whether one would have (or might be able to acquire) 'the strength' to be able to 'will' this, and to 'resist' longing for 'any ultimate peace' (ibid.). The thought of the eternal recurrence of all events without addition, subtraction or alteration would, on his view, present an even more formidable challenge and test of one's 'strength' and ability to affirm life as it exists. And

258

it is in the first instance this function that his 'doctrine' to this effect is intended to serve. Thus it is clearly *as a test* that he first sets it forth, in the penultimate section of the fourth book of *The Gay Science*. (The following, final section, it may be noted, introduces the figure of Zarathustra, and in effect announces the work bearing his name, in which this version of the idea of the recurrence looms large.)

> *The greatest weight.* — What, if some day or night a demon
> were to steal after you into your loneliest loneliness and say
> to you: 'This life as you now live it and have lived it, you will
> have to live once more and innumerable times more; and
> there will be nothing new in it, but every pain and every joy
> and every thought and sigh and everything unutterably small
> or great in your life will have to return to you, all in the same
> succession and sequence — even this spider and this moon-
> light between the trees, and even this moment and I myself.
> The eternal hourglass of existence is turned upside down
> again and again, and you with it, speck of dust!'
> Would you not throw yourself down and gnash your teeth
> and curse the demon who spoke thus? . . . Or how well
> disposed would you have to become to yourself and to life
> *to crave nothing more fervently* than this ultimate eternal
> confirmation and seal? (*GS* 341).

In *Zarathustra*, the literary form of which allows Nietzsche to take many liberties in his manner of expression, he has Zarathustra recount essentially the same picture (even down to the spider and the moonlight), presenting it as a 'vision,' and concluding with the question — his 'most abysmal thought,' which however he comes to celebrate — 'must we not eternally return?' (Z III:2:2). Indeed, this idea is subsequently represented as one of Zarathustra's most important 'teachings.' Throughout the work, however, it functions fundamentally in the same manner as it does in the section from *The Gay Science*: as a test, and more generally, as a touchstone of strength and affirmativeness. It is a challenge, the ability to meet which is also the ability to live joyfully without any hope that life and the world will ever have a significantly different character than they do. Thus Nietzsche elsewhere refers to it as 'the great *cultivating* idea' (*WP* 1053, 1056), and speaks of 'the idea of recurrence as a *selective* principle,' which operates 'in the service of strength' (*WP* 1058). What matters here is not the *truth* of the idea; it is rather the emergence of human beings capable not only of enduring it (were it to be true), but moreover of embracing it without qualm, and indeed of 'craving nothing more fervently.'

For the qualities they would have to possess in order to be able to do so are taken to be characteristic of that higher humanity of which the *Übermensch* stands as Nietzsche's symbol.

Once having hit upon the idea of employing the thought of the eternal recurrence as this sort of device, it is not surprising that Nietzsche should have been led to consider whether it might be true as well. Before turning to his reflections along these lines, however, it is worth pausing to take note of the fact that, in the Fourth Book of *The World as Will and Idea*, Schopenhauer had in effect thrown down a gauntlet which Nietzsche is picking up here. Schopenhauer envisions the possibility of a kind of person no longer impelled to live on (as he believes most people are) either by a blind and unthinking 'will to live' or by a fear of death, 'who had thoroughly assimilated the truths we have already advanced' save only that he 'had not come to know . . . that constant suffering is essential to life,' and 'whose love of life was so great that he willingly and gladly accepted all the hardships to which it is exposed for the sake of its pleasures.' Such a person, he writes, 'could calmly and deliberately desire that his life, as he had hitherto known it, should endure forever or repeat itself ever anew' (Arthur Schopenhauer, *The World as Will and Idea*, trans. R. B. Haldane and J. Kemp (London: Routledge & Kegan Paul, 1964), § 54 — henceforth *WWI*). He contends, however, that with the attainment and 'thorough assimilation' of this additional piece of knowledge, the attitude of a reflective person must undergo drastic alteration, any such disposition to a 'love of life' he may initially have notwithstanding: 'at the end of life, if a man is sincere and in full possession of his faculties, he will never wish to have it over again, but rather than this, he will much prefer absolute annihilation' (*WWI* 59).

Schopenhauer thus could well have been the inspiration of Nietzsche's story of the demon with the message and of Zarathustra's vision. In any event the parallel is as clear as is Nietzsche's determination to contest the inescapability of the conclusion Schopenhauer draws, even while conceding his basic premises. Quite significantly, for him as well as for Schopenhauer it is one's own life the recurrence of which is immediately contemplated. In expanding the scope of the thought of that which is to recur as he does, Nietzsche is merely raising the ante, to make it clear that his radical departure from Schopenhauer does not depend in the least upon the facts of any particular case. He is quite prepared to concede that the natural reaction to the prospect presented would indeed be rather like Schopenhauer's; hence his references to Zarathustra's thought as 'abysmal' and dismaying, and to the

260

demon's message as 'the greatest weight,' likely to prompt curses and the gnashing of teeth. But he is no less determined to vindicate a completely different response, and to suggest that at least some successor to the sort of person Schopenhauer speaks of might know the worst and still preserve his 'love of life.' And it is this possibility he means to evoke through the presentation of the idea of the eternal recurrence considered above, as a prospect which such a human being (if no lesser type) might be able not only to endure but to relish and 'will.'

Nietzsche's motivation for introducing this idea and making so much of it in *Zarathustra* is thus inseparable from two of his most basic concerns: with the idea and possibility of a total 'affirmation of life' and of the world (as they are, rather than merely as one might wish them to be), and with the emergence of an enhanced form of life strong and rich enough to stand as a 'justification of life' (so that, in the language of *Zarathustra*, 'the earth shall have a meaning,' and may warrant affirmation). No greater affirmation of life is (actually) *possible*, on his view, than one that would take the form of an affirmation of the world conceived as an affair in which everything that happens recurs eternally; although the possibility of this affirmation (in the absence of all forms of metaphysical comfort) would appear to depend for him upon the supposition that the appearance of such an enhanced form of life, no less than the prevalence of lesser forms of existence, is included in what comes to pass. (Were the latter not accompanied by the former, he seems to feel, the world and life would constitute too bleak a spectacle for anyone of any discernment to be well disposed toward it, and Schopenhauer would carry the day.) On the other hand, the truth of the thought that 'everything becomes and recurs eternally' aside, what Nietzsche terms the 'ripeness of man for this idea' — 'as *selective* principle' (*WP* 1058) and '*cultivating* idea' (*WP* 1054) and 'the *hardest* idea' (*WP* 1059) — is associated by him with the emergence of this enhanced form of life, both as a symptom of the fact that a relatively highly enhanced form of it has been attained, and as a condition of the possibility of its further enhancement. And in this context the thought itself would serve as a means of testing it, stimulating it, and reorienting it evaluatively — almost in the manner of a 'regulative' idea.

XVI

Nietzsche might well have left it at that; but he did not. He was further moved to wonder whether a different sort of case might also be made, for according the idea the status of a constitutive principle as well; and in several notes he embraces it as an actual cosmological hypothesis, for which he thinks it would be possible to argue. Thus he contemplated writing a book in which he would have dealt not only with the 'probable consequences of its being *believed*,' but also with the 'proof of the doctrine' and with 'its *theoretical* presuppositions and consequences' (*WP* 1057). And in another note he distinguishes the topic of the 'means of *enduring* it' from that of 'the presuppositions that would have to be true if it were true' (*WP* 1059). Here he speaks tentatively; but elsewhere he goes further than this. So, for example, after mentioning the idea of 'existence as it is, without any meaning or aim, yet recurring inevitably without any finale of nothingness: the eternal recurrence,' he maintains that 'the energy of knowledge and strength compels this belief. It is the most *scientific* of all possible hypotheses' concerning the world's course (*WP* 55). And he indicates at least part of what he has in mind here when he asserts: 'The law of the conservation of energy demands *eternal recurrence*' (*WP* 1063).

In such passages as these it is not clearly indicated *which version* of the idea is intended. In neither of those just cited is reference made to particular sequences of specific events; and indeed the picture in the former would seem to be a much more general one, while in the case of the latter it is hard to see how anything more might follow from 'the law of the conservation of energy' than the conclusion that the energy of which the world consists must (as it were) continually recycle itself. Likewise when Nietzsche argues on the one hand that 'the world has no goal, no final state, and is incapable of being,' and on the other that 'the world also lacks the capacity for eternal novelty,' he does no more with these points than to offer them as grounds for abandoning the idea that the world 'keeps itself from entering into a circular course,' 'prevents itself from returning to any of its old forms,' and 'avoids any repetition' (*WP* 1062). And even if this is supposed at least to endow with plausibility the contrary view that the world *does* follow a 'circular course' in which there is *some* sort of degree of 'repetition' and a 'return to' certain 'old forms,' this view may be spelled out further in a number of different ways, only one of which is the strong version of the idea of the eternal recurrence. These points do not suffice to establish the soundness of the latter doctrine; and nothing Nietzsche says in this passage implies that he means them to or thinks they do.

Yet he does at least on occasion go further, embracing this doctrine and setting out an argument for it. To be sure, it is no argument when he observes that 'a certain emperor always bore in mind the transitoriness of all things so as not to take them too seriously and to live at peace among them,' and then remarks: 'To me, on the contrary, everything seems far too valuable to be so fleeting; I seek an eternity for everything.' For while he does go on to assert that 'my consolation is that everything that has been is eternal: the sea will cast it up again,' his desire that this should be so obviously does not lend any weight to the hypothesis (*WP* 1065). His only attempt to work out a line of reasoning that *would* count as an argument for this version of the idea is to be found in a note bearing the heading 'The new world-conception,' in which he begins by rehearsing his reasons for supposing that the world involves ceaseless 'becoming' and 'passing away,' never reaching any 'state of equilibrium' or resolving itself once and for all 'into being or into nothingness.' These considerations by themselves neither amount to nor entail the desired conclusion. Nietzsche then proceeds, however, to argue as follows:

> If the world may be thought of as a certain definite quantity of force and as a certain definite number of centers of force — and every other representation remains indefinite and therefore uselessness — it follows that, in the great dice game of existence, it must pass through a calculable number of combinations. In infinite time, every possible combination would at some time or another be realized; more: it would be realized an infinite number of times. And since between every combination and its next recurrence all other possible combinations would have to take place, and each of these combinations conditions the entire sequence of combinations in the same series, a circular movement of absolutely identical series is thus demonstrated: the world as a circular movement that has already repeated itself infinitely often and plays its game in infinitum (*WP* 1066).

In this way Nietzsche attempts to demonstrate the 'eternity for everything' he says he seeks (if not in the form of the endless duration of 'everything,' at least through its recurrence infinitely many times in 'a circular movement of absolutely identical cases' repeating itself endlessly). This attempt, however, fails completely. And it does not fail owing simply to the fact pointed out by Georg Simmel, in his celebrated 'refutation' of this proposed proof, that it would at least be possible for a world so constituted to contain an analog of a relatively simple model (involving marked wheels of equal size revolving at specified rates of n, 2n, and n/π), of which it can be shown mathematically that a certain state of the model (the original alignment of the marked points) will never be repeated

263

(Simmel, *Schopenhauer und Nietzsche* (Leipzig, 1907), pp. 250–1). One can readily imagine Nietzsche dismissing this purported refutation rather derisively, remarking that if no more serious objection than this could be brought forward, he would have nothing to worry about.

Much more troublesome, however, are a number of the steps in his reasoning, even if his initial assumptions are granted. Even if we suppose the world to be composed of a finite and definite number of discrete units ('centers of force'), which preserve their identity through all time, and that it has the character of a 'great dice game' in which they are continually combined and recombined through an infinity of time, these suppositions by themselves entail neither that 'every possible combination' would occur 'an infinite number of times,' nor even that 'every possible combination' would actually occur. For either conclusion to follow, one would have to introduce certain further assumptions pertaining to possibility and probability, the justifiability (not to mention the applicability in this context) of which are problematical.

It likewise neither follows nor is intrinsically necessary that 'between every combination and its next recurrence all other possible combinations would have to take place.' That is either an arbitrary stipulation or a point requiring strong independent argument, the very possibility of which is highly dubious. Even if this could be established, moreover, nothing would directly follow about the *order* in which the combinations would occur. The last point is at least addressed when Nietzsche asserts that 'each of these combinations conditions the entire sequence of combinations in the same series' (and presumably is to be thought of as conditioned by it as well); but this is yet another assumption for which he here provides no independent justification, rather than an inference warranted by any previous point. And it is also an assumption it would seem hard to square with the idea that it is rather in the manner of a 'great dice game' that these combinations are formed. This raises the further problem of the internal consistency of the argument; for it is not at all easy to see how the 'dice game' model (upon which hinges the legitimacy of introducing the probabilistic assumptions Nietzsche needs for the earlier part of it) can be reconciled with the invocation of a picture of a sequence of events characterized by this 'conditioning' relation.

Worst of all, however, one of the assumptions Nietzsche makes at the outset of the argument (and must make in order even to get it going) is forbidden to him by certain of his own basic tenets concerning that of which the world consists. He consistently adheres to the position that the world is comprised of an enormous

264

but finite and fixed quantity of energy or force, ceaselessly transforming itself but neither increasing nor decreasing in magnitude. Elsewhere, however, as was seen earlier in this and the previous chapters, he repeatedly criticizes and emphatically rejects the idea that it has the character of anything like an aggregation of discrete units preserving their identities through all changes — whether these units be conceived as substances or bits of matter or dynamic atoms. He does often speak of dynamic quanta and of 'centers of force'; but he is at pains to make clear that they undergo ceaseless alteration, come to be and pass away, and constitute unities (for a time) only in a functional sense. Indeed, he has been observed to hold that even at a given point in the course of the world there is no one correct answer to the questions of how many of them there are and how their identities are to be determined; for on different levels of analysis and from different perspectives these questions admit of appropriate but differing answers.

If in a sense 'the world may be thought of' as consisting in 'a certain definite number of centers of force,' therefore, it is not open to Nietzsche consistently to suppose them to be anything on the order of the irreducible, immutable, extra-perspectivally specifiable elements of the world which this argument requires them to be taken to be, preserving their identities throughout all of the combinations and permutations through which they are here suggested to pass in the course of 'the great dice game of existence.' If the 'centers,' fields, quanta and systems of force of which the world consists are construed as he generally insists they must be, and the error of falling back into a quasi-atomistic or -mechanistic way of construing them (against which he so often warns) is avoided, the argument he gives here cannot get off the ground. Nietzsche insists in vain, therefore, that 'this conception is not simply a mechanistic conception.' Or rather: while it may not be *'simply* a mechanistic conception,' it shares certain features with mechanism which his critique of the latter rules out, and for which there is no room in his own cosmology as he elsewhere elaborates it.

For a variety of reasons, therefore, this argument must be considered one of Nietzsche's thought-experiments which fails. Its failure is no great disaster; for even though it does mean that he is not entitled to console himself with the idea that 'everything that has been is eternal' at least in the sense of recurring eternally, little else is affected by it. His cosmology as a whole neither stands nor falls with it; and the same is true of the rest of his philosophy, from his anthropology to his theory of value. Indeed, even the idea of the eternal recurrence itself survives, in its other and more general versions if not in that presently under consideration. And in its other versions it retains enough of its impact to be able to serve — as well or even better — at least some of the extra-cosmological functions he would have it serve; for it is arguable that their greater generality renders them much more effective stimuli to endeavor conducive to the enhancement of life than is this one, with its fatalistic overtones.

Moreover, an admission that truth cannot be claimed for this version of it is no obstacle to its employment as the sort of test of one's strength and disposition toward life discussed above. Such an admission would not, for example, require Nietzsche to change a word of the 'demon' passage from *The Gay Science*. In contexts of that kind and for purposes such as his there (and also in *Zarathustra*), fictions have their uses and are entirely appropriate. They also are suggestive of hypotheses; and Nietzsche is not to be faulted for making the experiment of turning his demon's story into an hypothesis, and considering how an attempt to prove it might go and what would have to be the case for it to be true. Fault may be found with what he comes up with, on both of the latter counts. But this merely requires of him that he return and restrict the idea of 'everything recurring eternally' to its original role of depicting a hypothetical state of affairs for the purpose of making a very different sort of experiment, where what is at stake is not the world's actual nature but rather something having to do with our human nature and the enhancement of human life. These are his paramount concerns, here as elsewhere; and it is to his treatment of them that I now shall turn.

V

Man and Men

On the map of Nietzsche's philosophical interests and concerns, the domain of inquiry which lies at its center is what might be called philosophical anthropology; for it is above all upon 'man' — upon human nature, human life, and human possibility — that his attention focusses. His interest in other matters and the extensiveness of his treatment of them are for the most part almost directly proportional to the significance he takes them to have for philosophical anthropology so conceived. A preoccupation with questions relating in one way or another to problems concerning man's nature, existence and future informs his writings from first to last; and his incomplete and often sketchy handling of many other issues (e.g., in epistemology and cosmology) is at least in part a consequence of his tendency to pursue them far enough to allow their anthropological import to emerge, and then to set them aside in favor of others which also have some such bearing. His treatments of the evaluative and normative matters to be considered in the following chapters likewise unfold in the context of his understanding of human nature and human life more generally, and reflect it in a number of important respects. And this, on his view, is entirely appropriate; for he holds that the phenomena to which they pertain will inevitably be misunderstood if they are abstracted from their basic human setting.

The characterization of this domain of inquiry as 'philosophical anthropology' is not only fitting but more appropriate than the employment in this connection of such commonplace designations as the philosophy of 'mind' or 'spirit,' and 'philosophical psychology' in both the traditional and contemporary senses of the latter term. For it is one of Nietzsche's most fundamental contentions that the proper object of investigation here is not the 'mind' or 'spirit,' the 'soul' or 'psyche,' or the 'ego' or 'consciousness,' but rather *man* in the generic sense (*der Mensch*) — a kind of creature whose existence is animate, bodily, active, social and historical, and involves a variety of forms of experience and processes. In relation to this complex totality in which human life and our human reality consists, he regards all such mentalistic notions as artificial abstractions at best, which adversely affect the attempt to comprehend ourselves and even those phenomena with which they are associated.

Toward a philosophical anthropology

I

Whatever we may more specifically be, Nietzsche constantly reminds us, we are in the first instance human beings — living creatures of 'the type "man."' And a human being, as such a creature, is properly to be construed neither as *res cogitans* nor as *res extensa*, nor yet again as some hybrid or compound of the two. Human beings are rather to be thought of as instances of a general type of animate existence, the complex nature of which it is the task of philosophical anthropology to comprehend. Nietzsche's frequent references to man as 'a kind of animal' are intended to underscore this basic point. On the other hand, this is not the only important point he seeks to make in this connection. Another is indicated when he writes: 'Man is beast and superbeast; the higher man is inhuman and superhuman: these belong together' (*WP* 1027).

In what follows, I shall attempt to make clear what Nietzsche has in mind in making these and related claims. And I would suggest at the outset that in interpreting him it is crucial to take note of both of the things he says in the passage just cited, about man and about the higher man. To focus exclusively upon the former characterization he gives in each case, or to understand the latter term in each coupling merely in terms of the former, is to misunderstand him seriously. Thus he neither intends his 'higher man' to be construed as one who departs from the 'human, all-too-human' only to descend to the depths of dehumanized barbarity, nor means to suggest that man is but a creature whose basic animal nature and origins constitute an unalterable destiny. To be sure, he does propose 'to translate man back into nature.' Indeed, he takes it to be a 'task' incumbent upon anyone who would 'seek knowledge at all' to do so, and thus

> to become master over the many vain and overly enthusiastic
> interpretations and connotations that have so far been scrawled
> and painted over that eternal basic text of *homo natura*; to

268

see to it that man henceforth stands before man as even today,
hardened in the discipline of science, he stands before the rest
of nature . . . , deaf to the siren songs of old metaphysical
bird catchers who have been piping at him all too long, 'you
are more, you are higher, you are of a different origin!'
(*BGE* 230).

His denial of the notion that man has a supernatural origin and
thus an extra-natural essential nature, however, should not be
taken to commit him to the view that our human existence
constitutes but a variation on the theme of animal life, differing
in no significant respect from other instances of it. On the contrary,
it is one of his central concerns to show that and how the former
has undergone a profound transformation, and differs radically
from the latter as a result — so radically, in fact, that he feels
justified in asserting that, with this development, 'the aspect of the
earth was essentially altered, (*GM* II:16). This is a strong and
important claim, and should be borne in mind — even if one also
should not read too much into it. So Nietzsche attempts to
counter the latter tendency even as he draws attention to the
distinctiveness of human life:

We have become more modest in every way. We no longer
derive man from 'the spirit' or 'the deity'; we have placed
him back among the animals. We consider him the strongest
animal because he is the most cunning: his spirituality is a
consequence of this. On the other hand, we oppose the vanity
that would raise its head again here too — as if man had been
the great hidden purpose of the evolution of the animals
(*A* 14).

Indeed, Nietzsche goes even further, suggesting that man actually
contrasts unfavorably with other forms of life, at least when viewed
in a certain light: he must be recognized to be 'the most bungled
of all the animals, the sickliest,' in that 'not one has strayed more
dangerously from its instincts.' Yet 'for all that,' Nietzsche adds,
man 'is of course the most *interesting*' (ibid.). And this is because
our very 'sickliness' not only is itself quite unique, but moreover is
directly associated with a variety of processes and activities serving
to set us importantly apart from the rest of nature, as shall be seen.
This may accord our human reality a more 'modest' place in the
scheme of things than that attributed to it in traditional religious
and metaphysical thought; but it is a special one nonetheless. And
it poses a most intriguing challenge to the philosophical 'lover of
the "great hunt," ' whose 'predestined hunting ground' Nietzsche

suggests to be 'the human soul and its limits, the range of inner human experiences reached so far, the heights, depths, and distances of these experiences, the whole history of the soul *so far* and its as yet unexhausted possibilities' (*BGE* 45). It is in this spirit that his philosophical anthropology is developed.

Nietzsche's employment of the term 'soul' in this context may at first sight seem odd, in light of his emphatic repudiation of the 'soul-hypothesis.' As was noted in that connection, however, he is quite prepared to countenance its use, as long as it is understood to refer to a dimension of human life and experience transcending that of strictly physiological processes, rather than to a hypostatized 'soul-entity.' When he remarks, e.g., that the fact that man 'has a nervous system (but no "soul")' is still the secret of the best informed' (*WP* 229), he is construing the notion along traditional lines, and dismissing it. And when he has Zarathustra proclaim, against the ordinary way of speaking of ourselves as 'body and soul,' that 'the awakened and knowing say: body am I entirely and nothing else; and soul is only a word for something about the body' (Z I:4), he is making one of his most basic points concerning our human nature. But, on the other hand, he frequently styles himself a psychologist, whose business it is to investigate the human 'soul'; and he would not have it conceived merely in behavioristic terms. 'Man's growing inwardness' (*WP* 376) is one of his main themes; and he is no less intent upon making clear the radical transformation of our previously merely animal nature which this involves, than he is upon insisting that 'the *internalization* of man,' through which 'man first developed what was later called his "soul" ' (*GM* II:16), is to be accounted for naturalistically.

Care must also be taken not to read too much into Nietzsche's talk about 'the body.' He does write that, compared to consciousness, 'the phenomenon of the body is the richer, clearer, more tangible phenomenon'; but he immediately adds that it is merely 'to be discussed first, methodologically, without coming to any [immediate] decision about its ultimate significance' (*WP* 489). He proposes to take 'the body and physiology' as 'the starting point,' since he believes that one thereby can 'gain the correct idea of the nature of our subject-unity, namely as regents at the head of a community (not as "souls" or "life-forces"),' and of 'how living unities continually arise and die and how the "subject" is not eternal' (*WP* 492). But this is simply to suggest that we make use of what we can observe about the body, in the course of developing an account of our nature going well beyond characterizations cast in purely physiological terms.

Nietzsche thus would have us learn to understand ourselves and

270

what we call our 'minds' or 'souls' in the light of a consideration of our bodily, organic existence as 'living unities' of a certain complex sort. Yet he also would have us guard against taking for granted the validity and adequacy of those conceptions of our bodies and our physiological nature suggested to us by ordinary language and biological science. He most certainly is not prepared to accept any simple-mindedly materialistic conception of the body, as is indicated most strikingly when he does an about-face and suggests that 'our body is but a social structure composed of many souls' (*BGE* 19). The 'souls' of which he here speaks are by no means to be thought of as 'things' or substances of some sort; but the point he is making is that the body is not to be so thought of either. 'The body is a more astonishing idea than the old "soul," ' he remarks (*WP* 659); and one of the reasons it is so astonishing is precisely that we here have to do with a complex of organic processes which no longer constitutes a merely biological phenomenon. For it has undergone a profound transformation, resulting in the emergence of a broad range of activities constituting our human spiritual life, and having a psychological (and socio-cultural) rather than a strictly physiological character. So while suggesting that 'perhaps the entire evolution of the spirit is a question of the body,' he goes on to say: 'it is the history of the development of a higher body that emerges into our sensibility. The organic is rising to yet higher levels' (*WP* 676).

While it may be appropriate to identify and distinguish 'physical' and 'psychical' phenomena when considering our form of existence, moreover, he considers it an error either to hypostatize them or to regard them as aspects of the nature of some kind of 'being' we are purported fundamentally to be. 'Nothing is more erroneous,' he writes, 'than to make of psychical and physical phenomena the two faces, as it were, the two revelations of one and the same substance. Nothing is explained thereby: the concept "substance" is perfectly useless as an explanation' (*WP* 523). While he rejects dualism, therefore, he does not do so in the name either of classical materialistic or idealistic reductionism, or of some such Spinozistic double-aspect monism. He seeks instead to develop a naturalistic conception of human reality which takes as its point of departure our status as instances of a certain form of life among others, holds to this perspective in dealing with all aspects of our experience and activity, and shuns both the 'soul-hypothesis' *and* the 'thing-hypothesis' in doing so. Nietzsche's frequent employment of terminology relating to 'the body' thus is no less provisional and merely a matter of temporary convenience than is his talk of 'the soul.' Both are to be regarded as terminological and conceptual

271

shorthand, requiring ultimately to be replaced by different and more adequate concepts. The same also holds true of other pairs of contrasting and juxtaposed notions in terms of which it is both common and (at least for certain purposes) convenient to characterize ourselves: e.g., mind and matter, consciousness and object, thought and thing, spirit and flesh. On his view they all express abstract and artificial distinctions, which may have some basis in human reality, but are merely provisional at best; and these distinctions can be seriously misleading if this is not recognized, and if they are not ultimately superseded by a more adequate conception of our fundamental nature.

II

Human existence, for Nietzsche, is fundamentally to be construed along the lines of his general account of all forms of organic existence and the world itself: it is a matter of the occurrence of instances of a certain type of organized quanta of force — a type of system of systems of dynamic quanta — characterizable in terms of the manner of their internal constitution and external relations with the world of other such systems encroaching upon and encroached upon by them. His characterization of human existence in terms of drives and affects is only a second-order description, superseding the language of bodily functions and spiritual activities alike, but in its turn superseded by this more fundamental schema. In the final analysis we cannot properly be said to *be* a certain structure of drives and affects, any more than the world in general can be said actually to *consist* in that disposition which he calls 'will to power.' In both instances, what we are in fact dealing with is what he terms a 'multiplicity of forces,' the behavior of which is what is so characterized.

In his philosophical anthropology, it is thus with the general nature of the multiplicity of forces and related processes characteristic of 'the type "man," ' and with certain major variations of them occurring within the limits of this 'type,' that Nietzsche is concerned. His point of departure is that our human nature requires to be understood in terms of what has become of our basic animal nature in the course of the development of our species, and must be comprehended in terms of the kinds of processes constitutive of human life as it goes on in a world everywhere characterized by interaction, striving, change and challenge. And while he considers it appropriate to speak of the human 'species,' he does not think of this 'type' as being either fixed and immutable or entirely homogeneous. Both the relation of the individual to the species and the similarity of human individuals to each other, on his view, are matters requiring to be considered.

One other preliminary point should be noted. As has already been seen in a number of other contexts, Nietzsche's estimation of the significance of 'errors' in our thought is not entirely negative, and is not confined solely to his concern to expose and improve upon them. He is likewise convinced that what he takes to be some of the basic errors that have long been made with respect to our human nature have, despite their erroneousness, played an important role in the developmental process through which our nature has come to be what it is. No little of what qualitatively distinguishes human from merely animal life, he suggests, derives from the influence of the long acceptance of these erroneous beliefs. Thus he writes:

> *The four errors.* — Man has been educated by his errors. First he always saw himself only incompletely; second, he endowed himself with fictitious attributes; third, he placed himself in a false order of rank in relation to animals and nature; fourth, he invented ever new tables of goods and always accepted them for a time as eternal and unconditional: as a result of this, now one and now another human impulse and state held first place and was ennobled because it was esteemed so highly. If we removed the effects of these four errors, we should also remove humanity, humaneness, and 'human dignity' (*GS* 115).

More generally, it is not much of an overstatement to say that on Nietzsche's view virtually the whole complex affair of the human, in contrast to the merely animal, is a multifaceted result of a variety of things having *gone wrong* in different ways. And where things that have 'gone wrong' in human life (by reference to the standard of 'healthy animality') are concerned, he would not have them 'corrected' in the sense of restoring life to conformity to that standard. For even if that were possible (contrary, in all probability, to fact), it would remove the conditions of the very possibility both of all that makes us human and of that 'higher humanity' to the emergence of which he attaches such importance. It is the *Übermensch*, after all, rather than the 'beast of prey,' which he has Zarathustra proclaim to be 'the meaning of the earth' (Z P:3); and 'man is a rope, tied between beast and *Übermensch*' (Z P:4). And while he considers it appropriate to characterize man not only as 'the most endangered animal' (*GS* 354) but also as 'the sickliest' and 'most bungled of all the animals' (*A* 14), he regards the condition to which he here refers as the admittedly dangerous

273

but nonetheless indispensable precondition of all higher development, and in particular of 'the entire evolution of the spirit.' To be sure, he does look beyond this 'sickness' to the attainment of a new 'great health.' It is a different sort of 'health,' however, from that which he takes to have preceded the onset of this sickness that set man apart from the rest of animate nature, as shall be seen.

III

It will be helpful at this juncture to consider more closely what Nietzsche has in mind in suggesting that an initial characterization of our human nature is to be given in such pathological terms. One indication of his meaning is to be found in his explanation of his conception of what he terms 'the corruption of man.' He writes: 'I call an animal, a species, or an individual corrupt when it loses its instincts' (A 6). He goes on to observe that when this happens, such 'corruption' not only jeopardizes the creature or species, but moreover easily leads to its 'decline' — or, as he more commonly puts it, to its becoming 'decadent.' This is not, however, invariably the case. A general breakdown of the previously established instinct-structure of a form of life also has the significance of liberating it from the constraints imposed upon it by that structure; and while its survival is thereby certainly endangered, developmental possibilities open up for it which it would not otherwise have. In this situation, several different things can happen, in addition to the (perhaps all too likely) one Nietzsche here characterizes in terms of 'decline.' A further possibility is that a new instinct-structure may emerge in place of the old. And another is that the place of the latter may be taken by something other than an instinct-structure, which nonetheless suffices to perform the basic life-preserving and -enhancing function that is generally performed in nature by such structures.

It is Nietzsche's view that, while the eventual outcome is still very much in doubt, nature is making a unique experiment of the latter sort in the case of man. In our social and conscious life, a complex alternative to the general kind of instinct-structure operative in other forms of life has at least partially emerged. Indeed, he considers certain aspects of the conditions imposed upon us by our social life to have played an important role in the breakdown of our former instinct-structure, as well as in the filling of the void left upon the occurrence of this development. This may be seen, for example, in his discussion relating to the emergence of 'the bad conscience' in *Genealogy*. He takes this phenomenon

274

to be a 'serious illness' marking the onset of man's larger 'sickness,' which

> man was bound to contract under the stress of the most
> fundamental change he ever experienced — that change which
> occurred when he found himself finally enclosed within the
> walls of society and of peace. The situation that faced sea
> animals when they were compelled to become land animals
> or perish was the same as that which faced these semi-animals,
> well adapted to their wilderness, to war, to prowling, to
> adventure: suddenly all their instincts were disvalued and
> 'suspended.' From now on they had to walk on their feet
> and 'bear themselves' whereas hitherto they had been borne
> by the water: a dreadful heaviness lay upon them . . . . In this
> new world [men] no longer possessed their former guides,
> their regulating, unconscious and infallible drives: they
> were reduced to thinking, inferring, reckoning, co-ordinating
> cause and effect, these unfortunate creatures; they were
> reduced to their 'consciousness,' their weakest and most
> fallible organ! (*GM* II:16).

Nietzsche goes on to refer to this department of man's instinctive 'former guides,' in favor of conscious processes better attuned to the different and variable circumstances of social life, as 'a forcible sundering from his animal past, as it were a leap and plunge into new surroundings and conditions of existence,' involving a departure from and 'declaration of war against the old instincts upon which his strength, joy and terribleness had rested hitherto.' Given this picture of what thus took place as man left his merely 'animal past' behind him and began upon his human career, it is small wonder that Nietzsche should have availed himself of the notion of 'sickness' to characterize the initial result and lingering effects. At the same time, however, he is quick to draw attention to the potentiality and promise implicit in this development. Thus he considers it important to 'add at once' that this spectacle of 'an animal soul turned against itself,' departing from the life its old instincts marked out for it, and having to oppose and disengage them by means of and in favor of a very different sort of life-regulating and guiding process, 'was something so new, profound, unheard of, enigmatic, contradictory, *and pregnant with a future* that the aspect of the earth was essentially altered' (*GM* II:16).

As these remarks indicate, it is not Nietzsche's intention to suggest that, either at this point in human development or subsequently, man's old instincts simply vanished altogether and without residue, leaving the field entirely to the socially conditioned conscious processes which thus came to the fore. On the contrary, he contends that in the circumstances thus described, even while no longer possessing their former sovereignty, 'the old instincts had not suddenly ceased to make their usual demands!' And although with the breaking of their hold upon the course of life their structure too is suggested gradually to have broken down, he holds that the basic drives once finely articulated in this structure can by no means be supposed to have disappeared. They may in a sense be said to have been 'reduced' from the highly differentiated and specialized state characteristic of other complex forms of life, and presumably also of that which was ancestral to our own. The drive-reduction presumed thus to have occurred here, however, is suggested to be qualitative rather than quantitative, and to be far from a drive-*diminution* or -*elimination*.

Moreover, on Nietzsche's view, this drive-reduction has not been carried to completion in the interval. Strong residues of our old instinct-structure are held to have survived the 'fundamental change' he describes in the passage cited above, and to survive to some extent still. And their survival is purported to have played a profoundly important role in the specific direction taken in the development of major portions of our spiritual life, as well as serving (together with the more generalized forces 'released' through drive-reduction) to fuel and inform the whole range of our conscious processes and activities. Thus in this same context he advances one of his central ideas touched upon briefly above:

> All instincts that do not discharge themselves outwardly *turn inward* — this is what I call the *internalization* of man: thus it was that man first developed what was later called his 'soul.' The entire inner world, originally as thin as if it were stretched between two membranes, expanded and extended itself, acquired depth, breadth, and height, in the same measure as outward discharge was *inhibited* (*GM* II:16).

Instincts so inhibited by the pressure of circumstances from discharging themselves 'naturally' do not (as Freud was also to observe) simply dissipate. Rather, Nietzsche suggests, they 'seek new and, as it were, subterranean gratifications.' When they take such modified and sublimated forms as 'the bad conscience' or that broader class of phenomena with which he deals later in the same work under the rubric of 'ascetic ideals,' their impact upon human life is largely negative and even self-destructive. But this phenomenon can also take a very different turn. Thus he regards this process of 'internalization' and sublimation as the key to the emergence of all the life-enriching and -enhancing phenomena of human spiritual life as well, from the political to the emotional, artistic and intellectual. If he considers it appropriate to term this too a form of 'sickness' in relation to the 'healthy animality' of a kind of life governed by an undisrupted, smoothly functioning and comprehensive instinct-structure, he is far from supposing that the latter is inherently preferable to it. Thus he remarks that we would do well to consider whether 'the will to health alone is not a prejudice, cowardice, and perhaps a bit of very subtle barbarism and backwardness' (*GS* 120).

It should not be inferred from what has been said so far that Nietzsche considers *all* survival of our old complex of instincts to run counter to the modified conditions and requirements of our existence, and thus to require (and to have undergone) inhibition and redirection. And it likewise is not the case that he believes them no longer to be of more than marginal significance in the preservation and enhancement of human life. On the contrary, he holds that we still do and must depend very largely upon no small portion of what is left of them, notwithstanding the emergence of that form and degree of consciousness associated with the social transformation of the course and nature of human reality. So, for example, he writes:

> Consciousness is the last and latest development of the organic and hence also what is most unfinished and unstrong. Consciousness gives rise to countless errors that lead an animal or man to perish sooner than necessary . . . . If the conserving association of the instincts were not so very much more powerful, and if it did not serve the whole as a regulator, humanity would have to perish of its misjudgments and its fantasies with open eyes, of its lack of thoroughness and its credulity — in short, of its consciousness; rather, without the former, humanity would long have disappeared (*GS* 11).

He goes on to speak of the 'ridiculous overestimation and misunderstanding of consciousness' which has been the rule among interpreters of man's nature, and contends that even now we are still only beginning with 'the task of *incorporating* knowledge and making it instinctive,' developing our consciousness to the point that it would be extensive and accurate and deeply engrained enough to be relied upon to take over the life-sustaining role hitherto played by our old instincts. We are conceited enough to think that the general form and extent of the consciousness we now have, and with which we reckon what is useful to us, is already quite adequate in this connection. Nietzsche demurs, however, contending rather that by and large 'so far we have incorporated only errors,' and that 'all our consciousness relates to errors' (GS 11). And he further suggests that, notwithstanding a certain medium-range utility of many of these 'errors' in the conduct of our lives, it may be that 'even what is here called "utility" is ultimately . . . perhaps precisely that most calamitous stupidity of which we shall perish some day' (GS 354).

On the other hand, it is important to observe that Nietzsche contrasts the most prevalent sort of human consciousness — arising from and geared to the conditions of our ordinary social existence, and involving a variety of fundamentally 'erroneous' but 'useful' ways of thinking — with a relatively exceptional and almost untried kind of knowing which penetrates beyond such consciousness and transcends its narrower limitations. The conventions informing the first are suggested to perform a regulative function somewhat comparable to that of an articulated instinct-structure, and to have been developed in response to the need for something of this sort which arose when altered conditions of human existence rendered our old instinct-structure in part inadequate and in part dysfunctional. The second may be thought of as somewhat analogous to our basic drives in their reduced and generalized form — to which, indeed, Nietzsche goes on explicitly to link it. It stands to our ordinary consciousness rather as what he calls 'will to power' stands to a preoccupation with the means of ensuring survival. It affords a superior outlet and means of satisfaction for the former more fundamental form of affect, and has come to be possible as the process of drive reduction has freed us for it. Many other avenues are of course open for the expression of the 'quantum' of affect thus set free, and are in fact more commonly taken; but this, for Nietzsche, is at least a possible one. (As shall be seen, he further takes it to be among the 'highest,' most 'spiritualized' forms of expression available to it.) 'Thus knowledge,' he suggests,

> became a piece of life itself, and hence a continually growing
> power — until eventually knowledge collided with those
> primeval basic errors [of ordinary consciousness] : two lives,
> two powers, both in the same human being. A thinker is now
> that being in whom the impulse for truth and those life-
> preserving errors clash for their first fight, after the impulse
> for truth has proved to be also a life-preserving power.
> Compared to the significance of this fight, everything else is
> a matter of indifference: the ultimate question about the
> conditions of life has been posed here, and we confront the
> first attempt to answer this question by experiment. To what
> extent can truth endure incorporation? That is the question;
> that is the experiment (GS 110).

278

His recognition of the possibility of this 'fight' as important implications for his conception of human reality. It shows that he considers it necessary to take into account not merely a variety of features of our affective nature as such, nor in addition only the socially conditioned conscious processes to which certain basic aspects of the altered conditions of our existence have given rise, but also a further capacity for the transcendence of the latter that has come to be ours as well, if justice is to be done to our nature. One might ignore the latter and still develop an account of human existence incorporating most of what he has to say about it as it generally obtains; but one could not begin to give a fair accounting of his conception of 'higher men,' let alone of the 'new philosophers' he envisions. And his insistence upon the possibility of these 'human types' must be taken into consideration, no less than his remarks pertaining to the human norm, human development, and the fundamental features of human life.

Instinct, consciousness, and society

IV

The passages cited above serve to illustrate another important point as well. It concerns his meaning in speaking of 'instinct(s)' — as he very frequently does, in many different contexts. In these and other such passages, he both contrasts conscious thought and knowledge to them, and also refers to the possibility of an 'incorporation' of the former sufficient to render them 'instinctive.' He further employs the language of 'instinct' in discussing a great many other phenomena which clearly constitute acquired rather than innate traits. And while he holds that man's 'sundering from his animal past' through the disruption of 'his old instincts' and the assumption of a significant role of 'consciousness' was a decisive step in his emergence as human, he also suggests that 'genius resides in instinct,' and that 'one acts perfectly only when one acts instinctively' (WP 440).

In order even to begin to make sense of all of this, one must recognize that Nietzsche does not construe 'instinct' and 'instinctive' as narrowly as it is now customary to do, but rather employs such language in a much broader, dispositional sense. Its primary application may be to the 'regulating, unconscious and infallible drives' with some set of which members of each species of animal are innately endowed. In his hands, however, it has a further application (which in the case of human existence becomes the principal one), to all firmly established dispositions of any

279

significant degree of specificity, however acquired. As the qualification with respect to specificity is intended to indicate, the notion is to be understood to apply to ways in which that most fundamental of dispositions he calls 'will to power' is articulated and manifested, rather than to the latter itself in its undifferentiated universality. And it likewise does not comprehend the entire range of human activity; for it is intended to contrast with the many sorts of cases in which actions are arrived at in ways that neither are 'first nature' nor have become 'second nature' for us. In such cases actions ensue rather in consequence of the 'toil, tension, and strain' involved in our 'becoming conscious' (WP 440) and being 'reduced to thinking, inferring, reckoning, co-ordinating cause and effect' (GM II:16).

There *is*, on Nietzsche's view, a very real and important distinction to be drawn here. It is neither an absolute one, however, nor that which might first suggest itself. Thus, with regard to the former point, he warns against a 'misunderstanding of passion and reason, as if the latter were an independent entity and not rather a system of relations between various passions and desires'; and, on the other hand, 'as if every passion did not possess its quantum of reason' (WP 387). And, with regard to the latter, the 'unconsciousness' he ascribes to 'instinctive' action — which he contrasts with the labored, uncertain and fumbling 'consciousness' operative in non-instinctive action — is not to be construed as tantamount in all cases to the blank mindlessness of a mere automaton. On the contrary, 'becoming-instinctive' for Nietzsche is something that by no means need involve a reversion to the plane of smoothly proceeding but 'spiritless' and unwitting animality that was first transcended with the advent of such consciousness. It may also have the significance of an *advance beyond* that sort of consciousness, to a new and 'higher naturalness' in which the laboriousness, hesitancy and clumsiness — but *not* the intentionality and awareness — characteristic of it are overcome.

Here an analogy, which also is a minor case in point, will perhaps be helpful. Anyone who has ever become highly proficient at any of a wide variety of kinds of complicated activity (playing a musical instrument, skiing, typing, cycling, etc.) will be aware of the enormous difference between the character of one's performance of the activity when one's mastery of it is low or only moderate, and its character when one has mastered it to a high degree. One must learn how to do such things if one is ever to come to know how to do them, and one may be said to know how to do them once one has learned how to execute certain rudiments of them; but as long as one's mastery of them is only partial, one's performance will be halting, tentative, uncertain, and flawed. One is still in the position of *having to think about* how various procedures are supposed to be carried out; one's actions are and must be mediated by one's consciousness, and one has not reached the point of having 'incorporated' one's knowledge of what is to be done. The requisite repertoire of techniques is neither 'first nature' nor, at this point, truly 'second nature' for one. Proficiency is achieved only when one succeeds in making them 'second nature' and thoroughly 'incorporating' the principles appropriate to the activity, thus enabling one to dispense with the mediation of conscious deliberation and reckoning at each step of the way.

One's engagement in the activity then takes on the appearance of complete 'naturalness,' and is experienced similarly — to the extent that one is self-conscious at all. Typically, however, one who is doing something of this sort on this level of proficiency is too absorbed in doing it to carry on any such second-order reflection. Indeed, when this level is attained thinking about the particulars of what one is doing is more likely to impede than to facilitate one's performance of the activity. Yet a person in this situation is far from having 'lost consciousness' altogether. On the contrary, one rarely achieves any higher degree of psychic intensity and sensitivity than when one is absorbed in the performance of some such activity.

To be sure, one may also perform such activities absentmindedly and routinely; and some of them serve principally as means to the accomplishment of further ends and purposes (e.g., typing). But even then they do not involve an actual extinction of consciousness, for the latter would render one as incapable of performing them as of doing anything else at all. And in the more interesting kinds of cases (e.g., those of the accomplished musician, the creative artist, the fine athlete, etc.) the mastery of the form of activity attained hardly eclipses consciousness entirely. Rather, this serves to liberate it for objectives transcending the plane of technique, and thus to enable those in question to address themselves to the realization of larger and higher (interpretive, creative, competitive, etc.) intentions and values.

There is indeed a kind of 'perfection' that may be ascribed to the behavior of an animal governed entirely by a fixed set of innate, reliable instincts attuned exactly to its environment and its needs. This is not the model of 'perfection' Nietzsche has in mind, however, when he asserts that 'one acts perfectly only when one acts instinctively.' And it is not the attendant absence of all genuine consciousness in the instance of such animal life to which he means to accord preferability when he goes on to suggest that 'all

281

conscious thinking is merely tentative,' and reflects 'a discomfiture of the organism' (*WP* 440). Thus he writes: 'I too speak of a "return to nature," although it is really not a going back but an *ascent* — up into the high, free, even terrible nature and naturalness where great tasks are something one plays with, one *may* play with' (*TI* IX:48).

Once it is seen that Nietzsche uses the term 'instinctive' sufficiently broadly to render it applicable in the above sorts of cases as well as to a variety of more fundamental (innate as well as acquired, and general as well as specific) dispositions, and uses the term 'consciousness' sufficiently narrowly on some occasions to render it inapplicable in such cases, as well as more broadly on others (so that it may be applied to them on a different level of consideration), he may be seen to be making a point that is both intelligible and well taken. The task of interpreting him is indeed complicated by the fact that he does not mean the same things on all occasions on which he uses these and other such terms. But a recognition of this fact, and attention to the different things he intends them at different times to convey, enables one to sort them out, and avoid distorting oversimplifications of his construal of the human reality to which these notions apply.

V

More requires to be said than this, however, concerning Nietzsche's views with respect to consciousness. To begin with: while he does consider the role and status of consciousness in human life to have been 'absurdly overestimated' by most previous philosophers, he is far from denying that there are any events or processes to which the notion is properly applicable. Thus, on the one hand, he supposes it to be an error if (as is often done) 'one takes consciousness itself as the general sensorium and supreme court' of human existence (*WP* 524); and he makes much of the point that 'consciousness is present only to the extent that consciousness is useful' (*WP* 505). On the other hand, however, he *does* take it to *be* 'useful' in a very major way — and so to be 'present' — as shall be seen shortly. And even though he argues that 'we have no right whatever to posit this piece of consciousness as the aim and wherefore of this total phenomenon of life' (*WP* 707), he recognizes and indeed insists that it cannot be left out of account in characterizing the nature of human reality. It may be, as he also says here, that 'in relation to the vastness and multiplicity of collaboration and mutual opposition encountered in the life of [this type of] organism, the *conscious* world of feelings, intentions,

and valuations is a small section.' It likewise may be, as he urges
elsewhere, that the various 'animal functions are, as a matter of
principle, a million times more important than all our beautiful
moods and heights of consciousness: the latter are a surplus,
except when they have to serve as tools of these animal functions'
(*WP* 674). But this is to acknowledge the reality of consciousness
even while relegating it to a relatively minor and supporting role in
ordinary cases.

It should further be noted that, while when viewed in this
context consciousness may be deemed but a 'tool' and otherwise
a mere 'surplus,' it is precisely the existence of this surplus that
Nietzsche considers to have rendered possible the *qualitative*
enhancement of human existence beyond the level of all merely
'animal functions.' The kind of consciousness he associates with
the attainment of 'spiritual superiority' or 'high spirituality,'
however, is not to be regarded as fundamentally identical with
that which is characteristic of ordinary human existence. So he
speaks in this connection of a 'higher form of being,' to which this
'luxury surplus of mankind' attains or approaches to a greater or
lesser extent (*WP* 866). However 'small' the 'conscious world' may
be in relation to 'the tremendous multiplicity of events within an
organism' (*WP* 676) out of which the former (as well as the latter)
kind of consciousness emerges, he takes it to differ markedly from
anything of the sort attributable to other forms of life, its most
common 'human, all-too-human' form included.

Nietzsche further thinks of consciousness in different ways,
even when setting aside all concern with 'higher' transformations
of it. What he often has in mind in speaking of it is the broad
range of phenomena characterizable by such terms as perceiving,
thinking, feeling, intending, etc. Yet he also at times construes it
more narrowly, as when he addresses himself to what he terms 'the
problem of consciousness (more precisely, of becoming conscious
of something).' This problem, he suggests, comes into focus 'only
when we begin to comprehend how we could dispense with it.'
Referring to Leibniz in this connection, he goes on to maintain
that

> we could think, feel, will, and remember, and we could also
> 'act' in every sense of that word, and yet none of all this would
> have to 'enter our consciousness' (as one says metaphorically).
> The whole of life would be possible without, as it were, seeing
> itself in a mirror. Even now, for that matter, by far the greatest
> portion of our life actually takes place without this mirror
> effect: and this is true even of our thinking, feeling, and willing
> life (*GS* 354).

Nietzsche's point is that one can (and generally does) 'think,' 'feel,' 'will,' etc., without at the same time having a second-order awareness of doing so. And as he understands 'consciousness' here, the notion refers precisely to such second-order awareness (as his characterization of it as a kind of 'mirror effect' shows), rather than to the various first-order mental processes designated by these other terms. It thus is to be construed as a kind of *self-consciousness*, and is to be contrasted not only with merely biological processes and entirely unconscious or subconscious events, but also with a multitude of forms of *unselfconscious* experience which make up the great part of what he elsewhere terms 'the conscious world.'

It is a matter of no little importance, in the interpretation of a good deal of what Nietzsche has to say concerning the status and role of 'consciousness' in human life, to bear in mind that the term has both of these broader and narrower meanings for him. He acknowledges the reality of a broad range of mental phenomena which may or may not themselves be objects of awareness, and also recognizes the possibility of a reflective awareness with respect to them (which is to be distinguished from them). A human being, he contends, 'thinks continually without knowing it; the thinking that rises to *consciousness* is only the smallest part of all this.' And the fact that 'consciousness' here is to be understood in the sense of 'self-consciousness' is evident when he goes on to characterize it as a matter of coming 'to know ourselves,' and to analyze its relation to certain features of human social existence which are held to place a premium upon 'the human being who becomes ever more keenly conscious of himself.' Thus he continues: 'It was only as a social animal that man acquired self-consciousness — which he is still in the process of doing more and more' (*GS* 354).

What Nietzsche has to say along these lines is of considerable importance. The origins of that (self-) consciousness through which we come to some extent 'to know ourselves,' he contends, are social in character, and this is a circumstance he takes to have had (and to continue to have) a profound effect upon the general character of such consciousness. 'My idea is,' he says, that it 'does not really belong to man's individual existence, but rather to his social or herd nature; that, as follows from this, it has developed subtlety only insofar as this is acquired by social or herd utility' (*GS* 354). (From this, it should be observed, it follows that he does not consider such self-consciousness to be entirely inconsequential. More shall be said on this point subsequently.)

In taking this position, Nietzsche is not committing himself to the view that our self-consciousness and the various forms of thought and expression associated with it are limited exclusively and permanently to the performance of functions having such utility. On the contrary, he also discerns here the existence of a kind of 'surplus' at the disposal of the 'late born' who stand 'at the end of a long chain' of generations in whom it has developed — 'a capacity that has gradually been accumulated and now waits for an heir who might squander it,' in a manner transcending these social-utilitarian limitations and involving the transformation of the character of this consciousness. Indeed, he does not merely envision the future possibility of such 'heirs'; for he also suggests that various artists, writers and others already may be considered to number among them. These, however, are held to be exceptions to the general rule as well as 'late born'; and it is in the common case that he is here primarily interested. Concerning the foundation and point of departure of all further refinements and developments of human self-consciousness and spirituality, he writes:

> Now . . . it seems to me as if the subtlety and strength of consciousness always were proportionate to a man's . . . *capacity for communication*, and as if this capacity in turn were proportionate to the *need for communication* . . . , [at least] when we consider whole races and chains of generations . . . .
>
> Supposing that this observation is correct, I may now proceed to the surmise that *consciousness has developed only under the need for communication*; that from the start it was needed and useful only between human beings . . . ; and that it also developed only in proportion to the degree of this utility. Consciousness is really only a net of communication between human beings; it is only as such that it had to develop; a solitary human being who lived like a beast of prey would not have needed it. That our actions, thoughts, feelings, and movements enter our own consciousness — at least a part of them — that is the result of a 'must' that for a terribly long time lorded it over man. As the most endangered animal, he *needed* help and protection, he needed his peers, he had to learn to express his distress and to make himself understood; and for all this he needed 'consciousness' first of all, he needed to 'know' what distressed him, he needed to 'know' how he felt, he needed to 'know' what he thought . . . . [O]nly this conscious thinking *takes the form of words*, which is to say signs of communication, and this fact uncovers the origin of consciousness.
>
> In brief, the development of language and the development

of consciousness (*not* of reason but merely of the way reason
enters consciousness) go hand in hand . . . . The emergence
of our sense impressions into our own consciousness, the
ability to fix them and, as it were, exhibit them externally,
increased proportionately with the need to communicate
them to *others* by means of signs. The human being inventing
signs is at the same time the human being who becomes ever
more keenly conscious of himself (*GS* 354).

There can be no doubt that Nietzsche is right to stress the role
of language in the development of our ability not only to express
but also to apprehend reflectively what we feel and fear, desire
and discern, and to insist upon the fundamentally social rather
than 'private' character of language here, as a means of communication answering to pressing practical need. It should be observed
that all of the forms of our experience penetrated and informed
by language are thereby radically transformed, and become
amenable to further diverse and novel sorts of development. Much
of human experience along these lines, however, while thus
rendered both communicable and available for elevation into
reflective self-awareness, remains largely unremarked. While no
longer essentially 'pre-reflective,' it is in any event commonly
'unreflected,' only occasionally becoming the object of actual
self-consciousness. But the possibility of such self-consciousness is
thus established; and Nietzsche's point is that we owe this
possibility fundamentally to our acquisition of a body of language
answering to the requirements and purposes of social communication.

VI

This is not the only respect, however, in which he takes social
factors to have played a crucial role in the formation of our
mental life. It has already been noted that he links the change by
which man came to be 'enclosed within the walls of society and of
peace' to the disruption of our old instinct-structure, and thus to
a more extensive reliance upon and intensive development of our
nascent and initially rudimentary practical intelligence — our
powers of 'thinking, inferring, reckoning,' and the like. This suggests
a certain view of the status of our 'reason,' which warrants attention
and elaboration. The matter is an important one, not least because
it has long been common to attribute special importance to reason
in the interpretation of our nature as human beings. Nietzsche's
treatment of it, however, is complex, as well as revisionist on this
point; for while he does hold that social considerations have had a

286

good deal to do with its development and the place it has come to occupy in human life, he does not consider it to be as fully and fundamentally a social phenomenon as he takes many other aspects of our spiritual life in germ to be.

It is virtually axiomatic for Nietzsche that our reason cannot be construed as a special God-given (or otherwise supernaturally originating) faculty, owing to our possession of which we stand ontologically apart from all modifications of nature, as essentially rational beings. While not denying that we can and do reason, therefore, he considers it imperative to understand our capacity to do so (along with the results of our utilization of this capacity) as the outcome of a developmental process occurring entirely within the context of human life in this world. He considers the roots of reason to go deeper than the social conventions in which language consists, however, even though it is indeed in this medium that he takes it to have attained its fullest flower and greatest power (and also its highest artificiality). Thus he has been observed to suggest that while 'the development of language and the development of consciousness . . . go hand in hand,' this holds '*not* of reason but merely of the way reason enters consciousness' (*GS* 354). And he further rejects the radical opposition of reason to the 'passions,' maintaining both that the latter are at work in it, and that they themselves possess a 'quantum of reason' (*WP* 387). To speak of reason in this way is obviously to do so in a rather broadly extended sense of the term. But it is Nietzsche's conviction that reason more narrowly conceived represents only a highly refined, special case of a more fundamental and commonplace phenomenon. More specifically, he holds that the basic character of human reason is not to be located in the abstract and rigid forms and formulas of logic, but rather in practical intelligence.

Practical intelligence is fundamentally a very mundane affair. It is an instrument for the achievement of concrete results enhancing the position of the creature operating with it, often by means of artifices devised to circumvent obstacles barring their immediate attainment. And it is along these lines that Nietzsche proposes to deal with what might be called 'the problem of reason,' which he states in a relatively early work by asking, 'How did reason come into the world?' The answer he goes on to give is little more than a hint: 'As is fitting, in an irrational way, through an accident. One will have to guess at it, like a riddle' (*D* 123). This phenomenon did not long remain a 'riddle' for him, as the foregoing discussion will already have indicated; but his full solution to it has several distinct parts, which require sorting out. The most basic point upon which he insists is the necessity of avoiding what he judges

287

to be the 'mistake' of thinking: ' "We must once have been at home in a higher world (instead of a very much lower one, which would have been the truth); we must have been divine, *for* we have reason!" ' (*TI* III:5). As a corrective to this error, he suggests that in the case of our intellect as elsewhere, a basic naturalistic principle is to be supposed to apply: 'we would not have it if we did not need it, and we would not have it if we did not need to have it *as it is*, if we could live *otherwise*' (*WP* 498).

Practical intelligence is held to be fundamentally a matter of cunning, which ability gives those capable of it a compensatory advantage in relation to creatures endowed with natural powers and equipment they lack. Thus Nietzsche says: 'We consider [man] the strongest animal because he is the most cunning'; and he proceeds to identify this capacity as the basis of all further, 'higher' forms of human intellect, remarking that 'his spirituality is a consequence of this' (*A* 14). He has this same basic capacity in mind when he contrasts 'man' to 'other animals' as 'a manifold, mendacious, artificial, and opaque animal,' who stands apart from the rest 'less because of his [brute] strength than because of his cunning and shrewdness' (*BGE* 291).

This sort of intelligence is regarded by Nietzsche as pre-social in nature, originating 'as a means for the preservation of the individual' (*TL* p. 370), even if strongly furthered in its development and refinement by certain kinds of social conditions. (It is held to receive an additional powerful stimulus, for example, in the widespread occurrence of inter-human subjugation, placing the subjugated under the necessity of resorting to it to maintain and assert themselves in the face of superior and directly unanswerable force.) Reference to it alone, however, still leaves us a considerable distance from an adequate account of human reason. It is only when one takes into consideration that employment of it associated with certain further forms of calculation that its outlines can be completed. Such calculation involves the schematization of the world of our experience in such a way that, in the absence of fixed and reliable instinctive mechanisms governing our actions, we are nonetheless enabled to act and react effectively by means of it. Here, Nietzsche contends, 'there is no question of "subject" and "object," but of a particular species of animal that can prosper only through a certain relative rightness; above all, regularity of its perceptions (so that it can accumulate experience).' We are said to be a kind of creature which 'grasps a certain amount of reality in order to become master of it, in order to press it into service' (*WP* 480).

In this 'grasping' of 'a certain amount of reality,' however, and precisely in order to be able to render what is grasped serviceable, Nietzsche contends that an 'expedient falsification' occurs. The schematization required to render calculation possible involves 'posit[ing] unity, identity, permanence, substance, cause, thinghood, being' (*TI* III:5). And rational thinking is a matter of 'measuring the world according to magnitudes posited by itself' of this sort (*WP* 574). The practical necessity of rendering the world of our experience calculable through the 'reduction' of it to something conforming to such a 'manageable schema' may not be immediately evident to us, either as we think rationally or as we inquire into aspects of the framework of rationality and logic. It is to this necessity, however, that Nietzsche thinks the very existence and content of this framework must ultimately be referred. It does not reflect 'the *real world*,' but rather only our 'compulsion to arrange a world for ourselves in which our existence is made possible: — we thereby create a world which is calculable, simplified, comprehensible, etc., for us' (*WP* 521).

Nietzsche thus may be regarded as following Kant up to a point — but only up to a point. With Kant, he takes what the latter had termed the categories of the understanding and its operations, and also the ideas of reason and their uses (together with the principles of logic), to be functions of our mental constitution, and to be restricted in their legitimate employment to the confines of our experience. He departs from Kant, however, in proposing a naturalistic developmental account of that constitution, according to which the end it has been fashioned fundamentally to serve is to be conceived in terms of 'utility for life.' And he parts company here with Hegel as well; for this sort of development is far removed from the kind of thing Hegel had in mind in his conception of the 'becoming' of *Geist*, and is not conceived as tending toward anything on the order of Hegelian Absolute Knowledge — or indeed toward the attainment of any form of theoretical (or moral) knowledge.

> In the formation of reason, logic, the categories, it was need that was authoritative: the need, not 'to know,' but to subsume, to schematize, for the purpose of intelligibility and calculation — (The development of reason is adjustment, invention, with the aim of making similar, equal . . . .) No pre-existing 'idea' was here at work, but the utilitarian fact that only when we see things coarsely and made equal do they become calculable and usable to us (*WP* 515).

As will already have become apparent, however, Nietzsche conceives of the development into reason of this capacity to schematize and calculate in such a way that nothing more than its most rudimentary manifestation could be supposed to have been attainable prior to the emergence of certain social conditions. For its development is suggested to have gone hand in hand with that of *language*, to such an extent that he considers the nature of each to be fundamentally reflected in the other. Language is the medium in which reason must move if it is to achieve any degree of refinement, beyond the level of the crudest practical intelligence; for it is only by means of it that any significant schematization of experience can be achieved, and thus any genuine process of reckoning can be performed. The importance of language (and therefore of social considerations) in the development of reason beyond the level of rudimentary practical intelligence is something upon which Nietzsche remarks as early as his essay *On Truth and Lie*. There, however, he had been concerned primarily with the origin of various particular concepts, maintaining that 'language worked originally upon the construction of ideas' (*TL* p. 380), and arguing that the 'conventions of language' arose in consequence of man's coming 'to exist socially and in an organized manner' (*TL* p. 371). He recurs to the same theme in later writings, contending, e.g., that 'man's greatest labor so far has been to reach agreement about very many things and to submit to a *law of agreement* — regardless of whether these things are true or false.' Here, however, he takes this to apply not only to the meanings of words, but also to 'rationality.' Its cultivation, he maintains, is a 'discipline' without which 'humanity would have perished long ago' (*GS* 76).

The point Nietzsche thus seeks to make is that it is not merely with respect to the 'designation of things' that agreement and regularity had to be achieved in order to establish a framework conducive to the development of human social relations; for the same also had to occur with respect to the more fundamental 'schematism of things' on which the possibility of all such particular designations depends. It was an imperative deriving from circumstances relating to our social existence, on his view, which resulted in the transformation of our rudimentary practical intelligence from mere cunning into the capacity to reckon in accordance with a general schematization of our experience which gradually crystalized into 'logic and the categories of reason.' And so, while the deepest roots of reason are not social in character and origin, social circumstances are suggested to have played a crucial role in the development of human rationality, the existence of which in its present form would be inconceivable were it not for their guiding and constraining influence.

VII

Where many other major constituent features of our mental life are concerned, moreover, Nietzsche contends that they are to be understood as 'social phenomena' through and through, owing their very origins to our social existence. He is particularly concerned to establish that this is so with respect to those that have long been regarded as operations of special faculties of 'the mind' − of which, after 'reason,' two of the most prominent examples are memory and conscience. He identifies the context in which their development received the most powerful stimulus as the practical one of action. Thus he links the phenomenon of memory to that of *promising*; and his answer to the question 'How can one create a memory for the human animal?' is developed with reference to this social practice (*GM* II:3). He approaches the matter by rhetorically asking: 'To breed an animal *with the right to make promises* − is not this the paradoxical task that nature has set for itself in the case of man?' (*GM* II:2). The thought he expresses here is deserving of attention in its own right, owing to its implications for the issue of our human nature. What engages his attention is not the normative question of whether one is morally obligated to keep one's promises, but rather the larger and more fundamental one of what the possibility of promising (and keeping one's promises) presupposes, and the ramifications in human life of the establishment of this possibility.

The establishment of this possibility, Nietzsche contends, required the development of a kind of memory going beyond the (basically animal) capacity to absorb and retain things experienced. Where the latter alone is operative, such experience 'enters our consciousness as little while we are digesting it . . . as does the thousandfold process involved in physical nourishment' (*GM* II:1). For promising to be possible, a further sort of more explicit memory had to be developed, involving the partial abrogation of what he terms the overt 'forgetfulness' characteristic of this basic retentive capacity. 'A real *memory of the will*' had to be attained, enabling one to 'ordain the future in advance,' despite the intervention of many other events and the continuous alteration of circumstances (ibid.). And 'it was only with the aid of this kind of memory,' he suggests, 'that one came at least "to reason," ' i.e., to be capable of 'reason, seriousness, mastery over the affects, the whole somber thing called reflection, all those prerogatives and showpieces of man.' He goes on to observe, moreover, that 'they have been dearly bought,' at the price of 'much blood and cruelty.' ' "If something is to stay in the memory it must be burned in:

only that which never ceases to *hurt* stays in the memory" — this is a main clause of the oldest (unhappily also the most enduring) psychology on earth' (*GM* II:3). And it is only in a social context that the inculcation of this capacity in this way became possible.

This account is highly speculative, and its details may certainly be questioned; but all Nietzsche requires for his larger purposes is that some such social-psychological aetiology of the phenomenon of overt remembering is sound. And he would in any event seem to be on safe ground in identifying this sort of active memory as a precondition of the various forms of spirituality and conscious activity he indicates. His only really essential point here is that it was the social necessity of rendering human beings responsible and therefore reliable, and thus of so molding them that they can make and keep promises, which was the original and primary impetus to its development. Without this necessity there would and could never have emerged the phenomenon of a 'long chain of will' sufficing to override our natural condition of being 'attuned only to the passing moment.'

Nietzsche takes the consequences of this development to have been (and to continue to be) of the greatest importance, both for our manner of relating to our environing world and for our own identity. With regard to the former, our immersion in and preoccupation with the 'passing moment' is thereby at least partially broken; we are impelled to learn to 'see and anticipate distant eventualities,' to operate in terms of ends and means, to 'think causally,' and 'in general to be able to calculate and compute.' And with regard to the latter, Nietzsche observes that something of profound significance had to occur: 'Man himself must first of all have become *calculable, regular, necessary*, even in his own image of himself, if he is to be able to stand security for *his own future*, which is what one who promises does!' (*GM* II:1).

This is 'the long story of how *responsibility* originated'; but it is a good deal more as well. For it thus may be seen further to have direct and important bearing on the nature of *personal identity*, which is worth pausing to consider at this juncture — where, on Nietzsche's view, its consideration belongs. Personal identity is suggested by this account to be a function and consequence of this socially induced transformation, rather than attaching to some sort of substantial (and individual) 'self' each of us has or is innately and on our own. What is here at issue is not the sort of identity we each possess by virtue of the spatio-temporal continuity and discreteness of our bodily existence (which is equally attributable to animals generally, and thus falls short of personal identity or selfhood). Rather, it is what is purportedly characteristic of each

292

human being as a single *person* persisting as the same thinking, feeling, choosing, acting, responsible subject throughout the course of his life. Nietzsche does not dispute that there is something to this idea of personal identity. But he maintains that it requires to be fundamentally reinterpreted.

On a rather rudimentary level, a human being may be said to have (acquired) such an identity to the extent that he has come to have a relatively settled set of rather specific behavioral dispositions. This is a development which goes no little distance toward satisfying the social demand for regularity and calculability in the conduct of members of a social group; and it accordingly may be supposed to be strongly promoted and also guided by societal pressures. But such identity is insufficient by itself to ensure the degree and kind of regularity and calculability required in order for social institutions to develop and function. Assurance is needed of reliability in courses of action reaching far beyond the present, even if one's dispositions change or incline one otherwise, and independently of the desires one might have or come to have. It is only if one learns to think of oneself as having an identity transcending one's desires, dispositions, immediate circumstances and momentary condition, which remains the same even though all of these may vary and extends from the present back into the past and on into the future, that one becomes fit for social life.

As long as one's existence is little more than a succession of episodes in which one responds in an immediate way to situations with which one is confronted in accordance with whatever dispositions and desires are dominant at the moment, this social requirement is not met. If actions are viewed as having their source in nothing beyond so ephemeral a combination of external and internal circumstances, it would make little sense to suppose that anything done upon one occasion would ensure that something else of a particular sort would be done upon another. A kind of consciousness requires to be established which transcends the immediacy of absorption in these circumstances of the moment, bringing both past and future into view, and forging links of identification between episodes in one's life such that one can feel bound in the present by performances occurring in the past, and bound in the future by what one does in the present. One must learn to *think of oneself*, rather than merely acting and reacting as one is moved in the moment to do — and moreover to think of oneself as somehow being the *same* now as previously, and as being the same in the future as now, notwithstanding changes in one's states and situation.

The purpose of such self-consciousness and self-identification

293

becomes clear only when the idea of agency with respect to one's performances and actions is added to them. It is only with this addition that the social demand is satisfied, of rendering human beings reliable in their dealings with each other beyond the extent to which settled dispositions render them predictable. Our personal identity, according to Nietzsche, may thus be seen to originate in this socially-induced self-identification, as unitary agents in relation to our conduct through time. And while fundamentally a fiction, the acceptance of this idea (under the pressure of our being treated as though it were fact) has the consequence that we not only apprehend ourselves accordingly, but also to a considerable extent cease to *be* creatures of the moment, and *become* such 'selves' — at least in a functional sense, if not substantially. Thus Nietzsche concludes the passage cited previously by observing that, 'with the aid of the morality of mores and the social straitjacket, man was actually *made* calculable' (*GM* II:2). One is brought to *take on* the sort of identity 'even in his own image of himself' that is the basis of such calculability, and so is rendered fit for society.

But this is not all: one also becomes capable, in principle at least, of that more exceptional, extra-social sort of undertaking Nietzsche has in mind when he speaks of the 'great tasks' to which 'higher men' may apply themselves. Thus he suggests that, even though the process of transforming human beings in such a way that they may be said to come to have personal identities is a socialization-phenomenon in which the 'social straitjacket' is employed to render them reliable members of society, it prepares the way for a further development which transcends this result. For 'at the end of this tremendous process,' there emerges its 'ripest fruit,' which is 'the *sovereign individual*, like only to himself, liberated again from the morality of custom, autonomous and supramoral,' who 'has his own independent protracted will,' and whose 'mastery over himself also necessarily gives him mastery over circumstances, over nature, and over all more short-willed and unreliable creatures' (*GM* II:2).

In this way, Nietzsche seeks to show how the foundation is laid for the possibility of those he elsewhere calls 'higher men,' through a process he considers to have come about in response to certain very fundamental demands, and which initially has a considerably different sort of result. Even the personal identity of such a 'sovereign individual,' however, is not to be conceived as the 'being' of an unchanging spiritual substance. Yet it is no mere illusion either, but rather a genuine attainment. It radically transcends the merely spatio-temporal identity of a living creature;

294

and it further differs qualitatively from that which human beings typically develop under the circumstances described above.

The socially-induced development under consideration also has important implications for the nature of human action. The behavior of a mere creature of the moment, doing what it does in accordance with whatever impulses and dispositions happen to be dominant on any given occasion, may no more appropriately be considered *action* than such a creature may be ascribed personal identity. And the same sorts of social impositions which engender the latter also serve to establish the context in which the former emerges, through the disruption of this immediacy which occurs when one learns and is compelled to take the past and the future into account. Human action involves at least a minimal degree of what Nietzsche terms 'mastery over the affects' (*GM* II:3), even if it never occurs in their absence or without their influence; and it is by means of the 'social straitjacket' that a degree of such mastery is first achieved.

A fundamental distinction between human action and animal behavior is therefore clearly implied, and is held to be bound up with the development of this cluster of social practices and with the transformation of the individual's manner of comporting himself through his initiation into them. The acquisition of language is only the first step in this process, albeit an important and indispensable one. The decisive step is a matter of coming further to be able to operate in terms of promises, agreements, rules, values, and in general, to frame and act pursuant to *intentions*. The social character of the conditions of human action by no means implies that all such intentions are but the internal-ization of general social norms, and all human action but the expression of various social influences; this should be clear from Nietzsche's remarks about the possibility of 'the sovereign individ-ual.' But even the very 'autonomy' and 'independent protracted will' of which he speaks in characterizing an individual of this sort are represented as outgrowths of what is basically a social phenomenon, rather than attributes assignable to some special non-natural and extra-social faculty of the individual as such. He does not consider all human action to be completely determined by prevailing social institutions together with our general human and particular individual biological endowments, let alone by these latter endowments exclusively. But he does hold that it is grounded in the social transformation of our fundamental biological nature; and he takes the more exceptional forms of action to which autonomy and independence may legitimately be ascribed to be a matter of the individual transformation of a previously established social nature.

What has been said along these lines so far, however, serves merely as an introduction to Nietzsche's treatment of several of the most important and basic matters with which he deals in the course of working out his philosophical anthropology: the phenomena of consciousness, will, and the affects. I now shall examine his views with respect to them more closely, beginning with his discussion of 'will' and its relation to action.

Will and action

VIII

Few philosophers have even come close to employing the term 'will' as extensively and as centrally in their discussions of human nature and human action as Nietzsche does. Schopenhauer would seem to be his chief rival in this regard; and it is perhaps for this reason that both are often thought of as 'philosophers of the will,' with the chief difference supposedly being that, whereas Schopenhauer deplores it, he celebrates it. As has already been seen, however, while Nietzsche initially was persuaded by the Schopenhauerian case for the idea of 'will' as the sole ultimate metaphysical reality and 'thing-in-itself,' he subsequently attacked and repudiated this idea, and disassociated himself from Schopenhauer's construal of it in general. Thus he contends that in Schopenhauer one encounters the 'enthronement' of 'a primeval mythology,' according to which 'a will has to be at work in the background as a cause' wherever something is observed to happen, and 'willing' is taken to be 'something simple, a brute datum, underivable, and intelligible by itself.' He himself rejects the latter view of the nature of 'willing' (to the extent that there actually is something which may legitimately be so identified), and terms the former belief a 'faith in magically effective forces' (*GS* 127). Indeed, he maintains of Schopenhauer that 'what he calls "will" is a mere empty word.' And more generally, he states: 'My proposition is: that the will of psychology hitherto is an unjustified generalization, that this will *does not exist at all*' (*WP* 692).

Nietzsche makes this point repeatedly. 'There is no such thing as "will"; it is only a simplifying conception of understanding, as is "matter" ' (*WP* 671). And while he has nothing against the use of 'simplifying conceptions' in their proper place and as long as they are recognized to be such, he considers it imperative to expose and oppose their hypostatizing transformation in the hands of unwary and superficial thinkers. 'In the beginning,' he observes, 'there is that great calamity of an error that the will is something which is effective, that will is a capacity. Today we know that it is only a word' (*TI* III:5). Speaking of the traditional and still common view of the matter, he writes:

> We believed ourselves to be causal in the act of willing: we
> thought that here at least we caught causality in the act . . . .
> The causality of the will was firmly accepted as given, as
> *empirical*. Meanwhile we have thought better of it. Today
> we no longer believe a word of all this. The 'inner world' is
> full of phantoms and will-o'-the-wisps: the will is one of them.
> The will no longer moves anything, hence does not explain
> anything either — it merely accompanies events; it can also
> be absent (*TI* IV:3).

In addition to this 'bad habit' and this error, moreover, Nietzsche discerns a species of ulterior motivation at work in the promulgation of what might be termed 'the myth of the will' on the part of 'priestly' types bent upon being able 'to impute guilt' (and thereby justify punishment), and so upon 'making mankind "responsible" in their sense, that is, *dependent upon them*.' They wished people to be 'considered "free" so that they might be judged and punished'; and to this end 'every act had to be considered as willed' (*TI* VI:7). He recurs to the same theme in *The Antichrist*, observing that 'formerly man was given a "free will" as his dowry from a higher order,' while 'today we have taken his will away altogether, in the sense that we no longer admit the will as a faculty' (*A* 14).

While Nietzsche thus denies that there is some sort of faculty or entity to which the expression 'the will' properly refers, however, it does not follow that he holds there to be nothing at all with reference to which this notion may appropriately be employed. In the very passage just cited, for example, he goes on to say that 'the old word "will" ' may still be taken to have a legitimate use. He argues, however, that it 'serves only to denote a resultant, a kind of individual reaction.' It is thus to be conceived as something on the order of a function and manifestation of forces at work within one (rather than a faculty that ' "acts" or "moves," ' or the operations of such a faculty).

In considering what he has in mind, it is well to take notice of some of the characteristic ways in which he avails himself of the notion. They form two large clusters. One consists in the various things he has to say by way of providing an analysis and account of what is involved in the sort of phenomenon which 'willing' may still be taken to denote, and which requires to be dealt with anew once the 'myth of the will' in terms of which it formerly was interpreted has been rejected. The other consists in the many uses he makes of the notion of 'will' in his discussion of different human types, capacities and states, which are by no means restricted to cases in which phenomena of the sort just mentioned are understood to be occurring. It is something on the order of dispositions with which we have to do in both cases. Those he has in mind in the latter case are certain 'standing dispositions,' and in the former, certain 'episodic' ones.

Turning first to the latter, we find Nietzsche speaking not only of 'the will to power' as 'the basic form of will' of which our entire effective and spiritual life is 'the development and ramification' (*BGE* 36), but also of great differences among human beings with respect to their 'strength' and 'weakness' of will. So, for example, he contends that not only the 'free will,' but also the ' "unfree will" is mythology: in real life it is only a matter of *strong* and *weak* wills' (*BGE* 21). Several points emerge immediately from passages such as this one. In particular: notwithstanding his rejection of 'the will' as an entity or faculty, Nietzsche holds that there is something about human beings which is both legitimately and appropriately characterizable in terms of 'will'; and what he has in mind is something which can and does vary significantly among human beings. The situation here would thus appear to be somewhat similar to that which obtains in the case of 'intelligence,' of which one can continue to speak in characterizing human existence even if one denies that there is any such thing as 'the intellect,' and which further is attributable to some human beings in greater measure than to others.

An indication of the sort of thing he has in mind here is given when he writes that 'the weakness of the will — or, to speak more definitely, the inability *not* to respond to a stimulus — is itself merely another form of degeneration' (*TI* V:2). He thus contrasts 'what, unphilosophically speaking, is called a strong will,' with 'the inability to resist a stimulus: one *must* react, one follows every impulse.' The 'essential feature' of the former is 'to *be able* to suspend decision' in the face of such immediate stimuli and impulses, and to make and hold to 'long-range decisions' despite their promptings (*TI* VIII:6). Strength of will is a matter of fixing upon and resolutely pursuing 'ends' evaluatively selected (*WP* 260). Thus Nietzsche criticizes Schopenhauer, according to whom 'craving, instinct, drive were the *essence* of will,' on the ground that this is to treat as essential what is actually a 'symptom of the exhaustion or the weakness of the will: for the will is precisely that which treats cravings as their master and appoints them their

298

way and measure' (*WP* 84). He recognizes that this is a rather 'unphilosophical' way of speaking, however; and so remarks of this sort require to be construed in the light of his more cautious and careful elucidations of his meanings, as when he writes:

> *Weakness of will*: that is a metaphor that can prove misleading.
> For there is no will, and consequently neither a strong nor
> a weak will. The multitude and disintegration of impulses
> and the lack of any systematic order among them result in
> a 'weak will'; their coordination under a single predominant
> impulse results in a 'strong will': in the first case it is an
> oscillation and the lack of gravity; in the latter, the precision
> and clarity of the direction (*WP* 46).

In the course of his discussions of these matters, Nietzsche seeks to avoid the error he attributes to Schopenhauer (and the associated neglect of the role played by decision and evaluation where 'strength of will' is to be discerned). But he is even more concerned to combat the opposite errors of over-intellectualization and the underestimation of the importance of affective factors here, associated with 'the rudimentary psychology that considered only the *conscious* motives of men (as causes)' (*WP* 434). In order to understand the sort of balance he proposes to strike, however, it is necessary to turn to a consideration of the account he proposes of what is generally involved in the kind of thing commonly thought of as 'willing.'

IX

One of the main points Nietzsche is intent upon making in this connection is that, far from playing a major role in all human action, those episodes often referred to (at least by philosophers) as 'volitions' or 'acts of willing' are of little actual significance in relation to action, where they occur at all, and in general at least verge upon epiphenomenality. (Of this more shall be said subsequently.) It should not be inferred from this, however, either that he attributes the same marginal status to everything he characterizes in terms of 'will,' or that he means the analysis he gives of 'acts of willing' to apply to all such other phenomena as well. On the contrary, what he has to say along these lines must be recognized to be limited in its applicability, if his larger position is not to be misunderstood.

Indeed, it is precisely here that the following remark about what becomes of the notion of 'will' in the light of Schopenhauer's treatment of it has its main bearing: 'The reduction of the will to reflexes, the denial of the will as an "efficient cause"; finally — a real rechristening: one sees so little will that the word becomes free to designate something else' (*WP* 95) — something other, that is to say, than episodes of volition which are purported to be the causes of actions. Nietzsche considers it important, however, to give some attention to such 'acts of willing,' before going on to elaborate this alternative conception and associated account of action, in order both to justify relegating them to a position of relative insignificance, and to set the stage for further discussion. And he believes that, notwithstanding the importance they have long been attributed by many philosophers, they for the most part have been conceived very superficially and have not really been examined with any care even by those who have made most of them.

'Philosophers are accustomed to speak of the will as if it were the best-known thing in the world,' he says; but this, on his view, is by no means the case. 'Willing seems to me to be above all something *complicated*, something that is a unit only as a word — and it is precisely in this one word that the popular prejudice lurks, which has defeated the always inadequate caution of philosophers.' Proposing 'for once [to be] more cautious' in this connection, he goes on to make a number of points:

> in all willing there is, first, a plurality of sensations, namely,
> the sensation of the state *'away from which,'* the sensation
> of the state *'towards which,'* the sensations of this *'from'* and
> *'towards'* themselves, and then also an accompanying muscular
> sensation, which, even without our putting into motion 'arms
> and legs,' begins its action by force of habit as soon as we 'will'
> anything . . . .
> [Second,] in every act of the will there is a ruling thought
> — let us not imagine it possible to sever this thought from
> the 'willing,' as if any will would then remain over!
> Third, the will is not only a complex of sensation and
> thinking, but it is above all an *affect*, and specifically the
> affect of the command . . . . A man who *wills* commands
> something within himself that renders obedience, or that he
> believes renders obedience.
> But now let us notice what is strangest about the will — this
> manifold thing for which people have only one word . . . .
> [One] who wills believes sincerely that willing *suffices* for
> action . . . ; he ascribes the success, the carrying out of the
> willing, to the will itself, and thereby enjoys an increase of
> the sensation of power which accompanies all success (*BGE* 19).

Nietzsche takes this belief to rest upon 'a whole series of erroneous conclusions'; but it nonetheless serves, along with the other factors mentioned, to shape the sort of experience that has come to be designated an 'act of willing' or 'volition.' He does not deny or doubt that such experiences ever *occur*; but he does dispute the interpretation of them as a special type of inner 'act' which precedes and brings about overt actions, and further observes that they do not even invariably attend such actions. Volition 'merely accompanies events; it can also be absent' (*TI* VI:3). Thus Schopenhauer was in error not only in holding that 'all that has being is only a willing,' but even in believing there to be 'a willing' wherever there is action. He is further to be criticized in that 'he never even attempted an analysis of the will because, like everybody else, he had *faith* in the simplicity and immediacy of all willing — while willing is actually a mechanism that is so well practiced that it all but escapes the observing eye.' In short, he was basically no different from any 'thoughtless person' who fixes upon 'the feeling of will' and fails to 'see any problem' in the supposed connection between it and action (*GS* 127).

As has been noted, Nietzsche suggests that volitions involve the occurrence of certain sensations, and also thoughts of certain things which are to be done or achieved. He contends that we ought to stop and consider what sort of connection, if any, we are entitled to suppose there to be between either sort of constituent phenomenon and the actions which we perform; and he clearly considers it dubious to regard the latter as consequences of the former. Thus, for example, he observes: 'When we do something there arises a feeling of force, often even before the deed, occasioned by the idea of what is to be done.' And he stresses the point that 'it is always an accompanying feeling. We instinctively think that this feeling of force is the cause of the action, that it is "the force" . . . ; [but] the force we feel "does not set the muscles in motion" ' (*WP* 664).

Matters are no different, he maintains, with respect to the intentions we frame with which this 'force we feel' is conjoined in experiences of volition: 'I have the intention of raising my arm,' he writes; 'what could really be more vague, pale, uncertain than this intention, when compared with what follows upon it?' It is obvious that it makes no difference whether 'I know as little of the physiology of the human body . . . as the man in the street,' or instead am 'specially instructed in the formulas applicable here,' since possession of such knowledge does not render me 'able to raise my arm one whit the better or the worse.' And Nietzsche takes this to count strongly in favor of the idea that our thoughts with respect to our actions (our express intentions included) and our actions themselves 'lie coldly apart, as if in two different domains — ' (*WP* 665). It should not be forgotten, however, that what is here at issue is the status of a relatively narrow, special class of conscious events ('acts of willing') in relation to what we do, and in the ordinary sort of case at that, rather than the relation to all human action of anything that may transpire on what may loosely be called the psychological level in human life.

This qualification is also applicable to Nietzsche's suggestion of the epiphenomenality of the aims, purposes, reasons, and the like which are commonly taken to be instrumental in the origination and guidance of our actions generally. What he has to say along these lines requires careful interpretation. There can be no question that he believes that the role and importance of these 'subjective epiphenomena' have been vastly overestimated, in both the understanding and the evaluation of human action; and in his attempt to counter this error, he asserts that 'there are no mental causes at all' (*TI* VI:3), that 'an action is never caused by a purpose' (*WP* 666), and even that 'everything of which we become conscious is a terminal phenomenon' which 'causes nothing' (*WP* 478). He asks:

> Why could 'a purpose' not be an epiphenomenon in the series
> of changes in the activating forces that bring about the
> purposive action — a pale image sketched in consciousness
> beforehand that serves to orient us concerning events, even as
> a symptom of events, *not* as their cause? — But with this we
> have criticized the will itself: is it not an illusion to take for a
> cause that which rises to consciousness as an act of will?
> (*WP* 666).

Despite the categorical and sweeping character of these and other similar remarks, they clearly are intended primarily as correctives to a particular view, according to which actions are to be construed as causally determined by a special sort of autonomous mental event — an 'act of will' — in terms of which the setting of aims and purposes is understood. If these remarks are understood in this way, however, as an emphatic repudiation of this view, it remains an open question precisely what sort of position Nietzsche wishes to advance in place of it. A strict physiological-deterministic account of human action is not the only alternative to it; and it should not be inferred from the strong language he employs that he is committed to the acceptance of such an account. Indeed, it would be a drastic oversimplification and considerable distortion of his actual position to conclude, on the basis of these remarks, that he is simply an epiphenomenalist.

Thus, for example, in one of his most important and illuminating statements on this general topic, Nietzsche stops well short of full epiphenomenalism, reserving at least the possibility of a genuine and significant role for intentions in the genesis of human actions — even though a much more modest and occasional one than that which is commonly assigned to them. (His use of causal language here should not be regarded as anything more than a bit of conceptual shorthand.)

> *Two kinds of causes that are often confounded.* — this seems to me to be one of my most essential steps and advances: I have learned to distinguish the cause of acting from the cause of acting in a particular way, in a particular direction, with a particular goal. The first kind of cause is a quantum of dammed-up energy that is waiting to be used up somehow, for something, while the second kind is, compared to this energy, something quite insignificant, for the most part a little accident in accordance with which this quantum 'discharges' itself in one particular way — a match versus a ton of powder. Among these little accidents and 'matches' I include so-called 'purposes' . . . . They are relatively random, arbitrary, almost indifferent in relation to the tremendous quantum of energy that presses . . . to be used up somehow. The usual view is different. People are accustomed to consider the goal (purposes, volitions, etc.) as the *driving force*, in keeping with a very ancient error; but it is merely the *directing* force — one has mistaken the helmsman for the stream. And not even always the helmsman, the directing force (*GS* 360).

Since what Nietzsche is doing here is distinguishing between these 'two kinds of causes' or factors involved in human action, it clearly is not his intention to suggest that there really is only one to which reference need be made in a general account of it. To be sure, he does propose that the intentions we frame are 'not even always' the 'directing force' in our actions, but rather 'often enough' merely accompany and rationalize behavior that is to be explained by reference to the underlying 'driving force' to which he refers, in conjunction with various social and other circumstances impinging upon us. Yet his use of such qualifying phrases shows that he does not mean this to be taken to be the whole story in all cases. He does conclude the above passage with the remark that 'we still need a critique of the concept of "purpose." ' But he would still seem prepared to allow, and indeed to insist, that it is at least possible for intentions to perform a significant 'directing' function where human action is concerned. And if this is so, it follows that he would not have all human action thought of as determined invariably and exclusively by non-conscious forces and environmental factors.

Indeed, did Nietzsche not think otherwise, he could hardly attach as much importance as he elsewhere does to the ability to make and keep promises, to resist momentary impulses and set and pursue goals, and to internalize existing values and create new ones. And he likewise could not have accorded the significance he does to the possibility and power of ascetic ideals and differing moralities, to the impact of lies and self-deceptions, and to the teachings of Zarathustra, With such central themes as these in mind, it is obvious that on his view a very great deal indeed depends upon whether and how the quantitatively relatively insignificant 'directive' capacity to which he refers is brought to bear upon the potential for action he characterizes as a 'quantum of energy that presses to be used up somehow.'

X

We are now in a position to consider Nietzsche's treatment of a problem that commonly looms large in discussions of 'the will' and 'willing': the problem of freedom and determinism. Conceived as the problem of whether 'the will' is 'free' or 'determined,' this is for him a mere pseudo-problem, since he holds that there is no such entity or faculty the freedom or determination of which might be disputed. So he writes: 'Freedom of will or no freedom? − There is no such thing as "will"; it is only a simplifying conception of understanding, as is "matter" ' (*WP* 671). If one focusses only upon his denunciation of one or the other of these alternatives, it may appear to one that he must subscribe to the contrasting view. It is a misunderstanding of him to attribute either a libertarian or a deterministic position of a traditional sort to him, however; for his intention is to undermine both, and to transform the issue itself in a fundamental way.

Thus Nietzsche is not to be taken to be embracing determinism when, for example, in a passage with the heading 'The error of free will,' he declares himself to have no sympathy at all 'for the concept of "free will," ' asserting it at bottom to be 'the foulest of all theologians' artifices, aimed at making mankind "responsible" in their sense, that is, *dependent upon them*,' and suggesting that 'men are considered "free" so that they might be judged and punished − so that they might become *guilty*' (*TI* VI:7). And he likewise is not indicating a commitment to libertarianism when he associates subscription to the idea of 'the "unfreedom of will"' with a certain different but no less odious disposition on the part of those who 'do not wish to be answerable for anything, or blamed for anything, and owing to an inward self-contempt, seek to *lay the blame for themselves somewhere else*' (*BGE* 21). Rather, in passages of both sorts he is at once disassociating himself from *each* of the positions under consideration, and attempting at least to raise doubts about their tenability by exposing links between them and various all-too-human tendencies.

Nietzsche is well aware, however, that considerations of this sort alone do not suffice to establish the conclusion that we are dealing here with a pair of equally specious notions and unsound views. And he recognizes that more also requires to be said along these lines than simply that, since there is no such thing as 'the will,' there can *a fortiori* be neither a 'free will' nor an 'unfree will.' The former reasoning is not decisive; while the latter may seem too short, and therefore unpersuasive. In conjunction with both, however, certain further arguments he advances serve to render his position to this effect a rather convincing one. 'The *causa sui*,' he contends, 'is the best self-contradiction that has been conceived so far; it is a sort of rape and perversion of logic.' And he maintains that the notion of 'freedom of the will' is fundamentally entangled with 'just this nonsense.' For the 'desire for "freedom of the will"' is suggested in effect to be a 'desire to bear the entire and ultimate responsibility for one's actions oneself, and to absolve God, the world, ancestors, chance, and society' — and this would be 'nothing less than to be precisely this *causa sui*.' Nietzsche then continues:

> Suppose someone were thus to see through the boorish
> simplicity of this celebrated concept of 'free will' and put
> it out of his head altogether, I beg him to carry this
> 'enlightenment' a step further, and also put out of his head
> the contrary of this monstrous conception of 'free will': I
> mean 'unfree will,' which amounts to a misuse of cause and
> effect . . . . In the 'in itself' there is nothing of 'causal
> connections,' of 'necessity,' or of 'psychological non-freedom'
> (*BGE* 21).

To think otherwise, he holds, and to regard the concepts employed as anything more than mere 'conventional fictions for the purpose of designation and communication — *not* for explanation,' is to think '*mythologically*'; and thus, he concludes, 'the "unfree will" is mythology.' In short, he considers the notion of psychological necessity to which determinism characteristically appeals to be no more tenable than the notion of a form of autonomous self-determination tantamount to the generation of one's actions *ex nihilo*.

While Nietzsche considers it untenable either to accord or to deny 'freedom of the will' to human beings, however, he is quite prepared to allow that the notion does have some genuine experiential significance. Thus, for example, he writes:

> That which is termed 'freedom of the will' is essentially the affect of superiority in relation to him who must obey: 'I am free, "he" must obey' — this consciousness is inherent in every [act of] will . . . . 'Freedom of the will' — that is the expression for the complex state of delight of the person exercising volition, who commands and at the same time identifies with the executor of the order — who, as such, enjoys also the triumph over obstacles (*BGE* 19).

Nietzsche is thinking along similar lines when, in his discussion of the emergence of our ability to promise, he speaks of the 'emancipated individual, with the actual *right* to make promises, the master of a *free* will,' who has a 'proud awareness' of how his 'mastery over himself also necessarily gives him mastery over circumstances' (*GM* II:2). And in the same vein, he observes elsewhere that ' "peace of soul" can be . . . the expression of maturity and mastery in the midst of doing, creating, working, and willing — calm breathing, *attained* "freedom of will" ' (*TI* V:3). In all such passages, however, his underlying view is clear: to the extent that the notion of 'freedom of the will' remains a meaningful one, its meaning is not that of a sound metaphysical concept, but rather is to be understood in terms of the possibility and reality of the kinds of experience which he here describes. And while it may be that the occurrence of such experiences is itself of some philosophical-anthropological significance, caution must be exercised in its interpretation — and the error of hypostatization along the lines of the traditional notion of a 'free will' avoided.

In place of the notion of 'free will,' which traditionally has been supposed to be something every human being as such either possesses 'as his dowry from a higher order' (*A* 14) or else lacks with deterministic consequences, Nietzsche prefers to speak of 'free spirits.' This is an expression he uses to characterize some human beings as opposed to others, and to apply to them owing to their being the *sort* of human beings they are, rather than to some entity or faculty that is part of their basic human constitution. The contrast he thereby intends to mark, however, is taken by him to be a significant one. And if this is kept in mind, one is given a clear indication both of the fact that he does consider it proper to regard a certain sort of freedom as a genuine human possibility, and of the direction in which to look in order to grasp what his conception of this freedom involves.

In this connection it is worth noting that, in speaking of freedom, Nietzsche emphatically does *not* have in mind merely 'letting go' and giving free rein to one's impulses. Thus under the heading 'Freedom which I do *not* mean,' he writes: 'abandonment to one's instincts is one calamity more. Our instincts contradict, disturb, destroy each other,' when not subjected to rigorous controls (*TI* IX:41). Such a conception of freedom, he goes on to say, is itself a 'symptom of decadence,' from which he recoils; and the condition it describes, while only too prevalent in modern times, constitutes no genuine human freedom at all, but rather a kind of tyranny to which people may succumb. Freedom for Nietzsche is instead to be associated with the very opposite of this sort of state of affairs: not with having and blindly indulging the affects (this, he says, 'is the cause of the greatest evils'), but rather with 'having them under control' (*WP* 928).

This point connects with one of the recurrent themes in his remarks on freedom: its association with the assumption of responsibility for what one does. This association has already been touched upon in connection with the manner in which he elucidates the experiential basis of the idea of 'freedom of will.' And indeed the sort of person he has in mind in his discussion of the emergence of a capacity to make and keep promises is at least an anticipation of the 'higher type' of human being to whom his notion of the 'free spirit' applies. Nietzsche does deny that most human beings can ever be said to have anything more than an illusory feeling or conviction of responsibility for what they do; but once having made this point, it is one of his chief concerns to go on to suggest that it is possible to acquire at least a significant measure of such responsibility, and so of genuine freedom. To the extent that human freedom is a reality, it is an *achievement*, and a difficult and exceptional one at that. And one no more achieves it merely by coming to act self-consciously, or by learning to think of oneself as responsible for one's actions, than one is endowed with it as a part of one's human nature. Yet it is something one can achieve, if one 'has the will to assume responsibility for oneself,' and becomes master of oneself sufficiently to render this assumption of responsibility meaningful. Thus Nietzsche writes, in a section with the heading 'My conception of freedom':

For what is freedom? That one has the will to assume
responsibility for oneself. That one maintains the distance
which separates us. That one becomes more indifferent to
difficulties, hardships, privation, even to life itself . . . .

How is freedom measured in individuals and peoples?
According to the resistance which must be overcome, according
to the exertion required, to remain on top. The highest type
of free men should be sought where the highest resistance is
constantly overcome (*TI* IX:38).

In this passage Nietzsche also characterizes freedom in terms of
a disdain for both 'pleasure' and bourgeois 'well-being,' and a
disposition instead to 'delight in war and victory' in various forms.
Relatively few people may satisfy this description, and thus the
attainment of such freedom is far from common; but 'the human
being who has *become free*' is for him at least a genuine and
occasionally realized possibility. And the importance he attaches
to this possibility may be seen in the fact that he characterizes the
'higher man' in just such terms as these, saying that he measures
superiority by 'how far one can extend one's responsibility,' and
suggesting that 'the highest men' are those who can 'bear the
greatest responsibility and not collapse under it' (*WP* 975). Here
he is thinking of *genuine* responsibility, rather than the idea of it
which in the ordinary case is a mere illusion and requires to be
'unlearned.' 'The capacity for long-range decisions,' he writes,
'must belong to the concept of "greatness" ' (*BGE* 212).

In the passage from *Twilight* cited above, Nietzsche also speaks
of 'the *spirit* who has become free'; and he elsewhere develops the
notion of such a 'free spirit' in terms which provide a clearer
indication of what the sort of 'freedom' he has in mind amounts
to. One would do well to think here of his notions of 'slave
morality' and of the 'herd' mentality which he takes to be so
pervasive among mankind at large; for the freedom of which he
speaks may be conceived in part as contrasting to them, and as
involving their transcendence. Thus it is lacking in the case of one
who finds that 'he *must* be commanded,' and so 'becomes a
"believer." ' On the other hand, Nietzsche continues,

one could conceive of such a delight and power of self-
determination, such a *freedom* of the will that the spirit could
take leave of *all faith* and every wish for certainty, being
practiced in maintaining himself on insubstantial ropes and
possibilities and dancing even near abysses. Such a spirit would
be the *free spirit* par excellence (*GS* 347).

The contrast between the great majority of human beings who are incapable of 'becoming free' and those who are capable of doing so (although even they can do so only with difficulty) is one of the main themes of the chapter in *Beyond Good and Evil* entitled 'The Free Spirit.' 'Independence is for the very few,' Nietzsche there contends; 'it is a privilege of the strong.' And even 'the strong' are 'reckless' if they 'attempt it . . . without inner constraint' (*BGE* 29). The self-mastery involved in the achievement of such 'inner constraint' is an essential aspect of freedom as he conceives it; and it is with this sort of mastery in mind that he links freedom with struggle and conquest, and characterizes the 'free spirit' in terms of the complementary notions of 'independence and command' (*BGE* 41). He considers freedom rare and true 'free spirits' very few, regarding freedom as a distinctive attainment of exceptional human beings. But it is crucial to observe that for him such human beings can and do appear. They constitute at least partial exceptions to the generalizations he elsewhere makes, which might seem to suggest a much more strongly deterministic picture of human action. 'Freedom,' he suggests, should be 'understood as facility in self-direction' (*WP* 705); and such facility, which he regards as presupposing both 'fortunate organization' and the various forms of self-mastery discussed above, is a possibility which may be realized.

For the most part in ordinary human life, however, Nietzsche considers the notion of 'self-direction' to have little or no genuine applicability. It would be as misleading to focus exclusively on his remarks along the former lines, therefore, as it would be to take what he has to say about human action generally to express his complete and final position where freedom is concerned. Accordingly, I now shall return to the more general account he offers, expanding the scope of my previous discussion to comprehend the larger issue of the status of consciousness in relation to action.

XI

'The phase of modesty of consciousness' is now upon us, Nietzsche writes, in the sense that 'ultimately, we understand the conscious ego itself only as a tool in the service of a higher, comprehensive intellect,' which 'does not will and is unconscious.' Thus he considers it appropriate and necessary 'to ask whether all conscious willing, all conscious purposes, all evaluations are not perhaps only means through which something essentially different from what appears in consciousness is to be achieved,' and 'to what extent everything conscious remains on the surface' (*WP* 676). His answer

309

to these questions is that, at least to a very considerable extent, this is the case. And to the extent that this is so, a form of determinism would seem to be suggested. Observing that 'the direction or protection and care of the co-ordination of the bodily functions does *not* enter our consciousness,' he contends: 'that a higher court rules over these things cannot be doubted — a kind of directing committee on which the various chief desires make their votes and power felt.' Consciousness, he goes on to suggest, 'is not the directing agent, but an organ of the directing agent.' For 'it is only a means of communication: it is evolved through social intercourse and with a view to the interests of social intercourse' (*WP* 524).

Insofar as what transpires in consciousness and in human life more generally is thus conditioned by what goes on in these 'directing committees' within each of us, in conjunction with the social circumstances which constitute the framework of our inter-personal existence, therefore, it follows that events of both sorts are to be regarded as socially and psychophysiologically determined. This line of thought (or rather, the former part of it) is reflected in what Nietzsche has Zarathustra say in his speech, 'On the Despisers of the Body,' amplifying on his contention that 'the awakened and knowing say: body am I entirely, and nothing else; and soul is only a word for something about the body.'

> An instrument of your body is also your little reason . . .
> — a little instrument and toy of your great reason . . . .
> Behind your thoughts and feelings, my brother, there stands a mighty ruler, an unknown sage — whose name is self. In your body he dwells; he is your body . . . .
> Your self laughs at your ego and at its bold leaps. 'What are these leaps and flights of thought to me?' it says to itself. 'A detour to my end. I am the leading strings of the ego and the prompter of its concepts.' . . .
> The creative self created respect and contempt; it created pleasure and pain. The creative body created the spirit as a hand for its will (*Z* I:4).

Or, as Nietzsche elsewhere says much more prosaically and concisely, 'The entire *conscious* life, the spirit along with the soul . . . — in whose service do they labor? In the service of the greatest possible perfection of . . . the basic animal functions: above all, the enhancement of life.' Even the 'heights of conscious-ness,' he suggests, 'are a surplus, except when they have to serve as tools of these animal functions' (*WP* 674). In passages such as these, he passes over the overlaying 'social functions' (which are at least very nearly as important), perhaps simply because on his view they are only second-order functions deriving from those to which he here refers; but he amply compensates for this neglect elsewhere.

It is important to observe, however, that Nietzsche is not propounding a *strict* determinism here, even though he does represent consciousness as operating in the service of the 'animal functions.' For, first, it is the emergence and existence of various general forms of consciousness of which he is speaking, rather than of particular conscious events or episodes, in ascribing this status to them. It does not follow that all such episodes or events are to be understood as linked directly with some particular physiological (or social) requirement. And, second, he acknowledges at least the possibility of a partial emancipation of consciousness from the service of more basic needs, in allowing that it can be a kind of 'surplus' in relation to them. It may be *fundamentally* a 'means' in their service, which exists and is as it is (broadly considered) because of its utility in relation to them; but it does not follow that it is *exclusively* and inevitably this and no more.

It also should be noted that Nietzsche rejects the applicability of the notion of 'necessity' to the relation between actions and the associated psychophysical states, and thus clearly disassociates himself from determinism in its classical, 'hard' form. So he remarks that, 'from the fact that I do a certain thing, it by no means follows that I am compelled to do it'; for he argues that, even if 'something ensues regularly and ensues calculably, it does not follow that it ensues *necessarily*. That a quantum of force determines and conducts itself in every particular case in one way and manner does not make it into an "unfree will." ' A determinism construed in terms of such notions as compulsion and necessity is tied to a kind of 'causal' thinking and to a 'doer—deed' model of events which he rejects, and thus is to be repudiated along with them (*WP* 552).

On the other hand, the same sort of criticism is appropriate in the case of the libertarian view according to which causal efficacy is assigned to certain mental acts (decisions, choices, etc.) performed by an autonomous, self-determining, conscious subject, which issue in various (bodily) actions. Thus Nietzsche contends that 'one should take the doer back into the deed after having conceptually removed the doer and thus emptied the deed' (*WP* 675). He considers the notions of such a subject or self, of such inner or mental acts, and of such causal power all to be fundamentally untenable. Our actions are not caused by our thoughts; 'the "purpose" *usually* comes into the mind only after everything has been prepared for its execution' (*WP* 671), and is actually to be regarded as 'a condition that accompanies an event' which is erroneously 'projected as the "sufficient reason" for the event' (*WP* 689). Consequently, 'in regard to bodily motions and changes,' he sides with those who have 'long since abandoned the belief in an explanation by means of a consciousness that determines purposes' (*WP* 676). He does not deny that 'thoughts' may be said to occur; but he considers it telling that 'a thought comes when "it" wishes, and not when "I" wish' (*BGE* 17).

There is more to be said than this about what thus transpires in human thought and action, on Nietzsche's view; but the deeper account he proposes traces both to the workings of the same principle that is operative in all natural phenomena. Thus he contends that not only the 'organic functions' but also 'thinking, feeling, willing,' and all other 'spiritual functions' are to be traced 'back to the basic will, the will to power — and understood as offshoots' (*WP* 658). 'All "purposes," "aims," "meaning," ' he holds, 'are only modes of expression and metamorphoses' of this fundamental disposition (*WP* 675). What we do is not to be regarded as a function of what transpires in our consciousness. It is rather to be understood as the specific issue in particular circumstances of the organized and developed ensemble of forces which each of us is, and which has been molded through the impress of our heredity and the dialectic of our prior encounters with our environing natural, social and cultural world.

Nietzsche's position with respect to the question of epiphenomenalism is more difficult to discern. He hardly sounds like a thorough-going epiphenomenalist when he discusses the existence and nature of consciousness in terms of its 'utility for life,' when he elaborates upon what he takes to set the 'higher man' apart from ordinary human beings, and when he deals with many other matters ranging from morality to science. Yet he at times speaks of consciousness as though it were little more than an epiphenomenon in relation both to action and to the multiplicity of non-conscious processes human life involves. Thus he contrasts 'the action itself' with 'its epiphenomena in consciousness,' to which he also refers as 'its subjective epiphenomena' (*WP* 291). Here he is thinking specifically of intentions, aims and purposes; and he considers it important to 'understand that an action is never caused by a purpose,' since the purposes we formulate for ourselves 'are interpretations whereby certain points in an event are emphasized and selected at the expense of other points, which, indeed, form the majority.' Indeed, he suggests that one ought to go further and ask:

312

why could 'a purpose' not be an epiphenomenon in the series
of changes in the activating forces that bring about the
purposive action — a pale image sketched in consciousness
beforehand that serves to orient us concerning events, even
as a symptom of events, *not* as their cause? (*WP* 666).

Pursuing this line of thinking, he goes on to raise the more
general question: 'Are not all phenomena of consciousness merely
terminal phenomena, final links in a chain, but apparently
conditioning one another in their succession on one level of
consciousness? This could be an illusion — ' (ibid.). It should be
noted, however, that Nietzsche's manner of expression here
suggests that while he feels obliged to give serious consideration to
the epiphenomenalist position he sketches, he regards it only as a
possible interpretation of the status of purposes and of consciousness more generally, the soundness and extent of applicability of
which remain to be determined. On occasion he does express
himself less tentatively, as when he simply asserts that 'everything
of which we become conscious is a terminal phenomenon, an end
— and causes nothing' (*WP* 478). What he is objecting to here,
however, is above all the view that a *causal* role may be attributed
to conscious events, in relation both to other conscious events and
to actions.

For the most part Nietzsche not only is more guarded in his
reflections on this thesis of epiphenomenalism, but also tends to
introduce modifications of it even as he considers it. So, for
example, after urging against this 'causal' view that purposes cannot
by themselves be held to bring actions about (since 'all actions
must first be made possible mechanically,' and since the framing
of intentions cannot be held to accomplish this), he says: 'The end
is a "mere" stimulus — no more' (*WP* 671). But this is still to allot
at least some role, albeit a much more modest one, to the 'end' or
intention of the agent. One should recall, in this connection, the
'essential step and advance' he considers himself to have made and
describes in the section of *The Gay Science* cited previously, in
which he distinguishes the 'driving force' of an action from the
'goal' which may be (although it is 'not even always') 'the *directing*
force' (*GS* 360).

Similarly, in a long and important note mentioned above
(*WP* 676), Nietzsche dismisses 'the belief in an explanation by
means of a consciousness that determines purposes' where 'bodily
motions and changes' in general are concerned, and then raises the
question: 'Is the whole of conscious life perhaps only a reflected
image? . . . Only the faintest reflection of [a] natural expediency

313

in the organic but not different from it?' This might appear to indicate an endorsement of epiphenomenalism; but something short of it is actually being suggested. For it follows neither from his observation that most bodily motions and changes 'have nothing whatever to do with consciousness,' nor from his contention that 'sensations and thoughts are something extremely insignificant and rare in relation to the countless number of events that occur [in us] every moment.' And while he goes on to remark that 'we as conscious, purposive creatures, are only the smallest part of us,' this leaves open the question of whether this 'smallest part' — the reality of which is thus acknowledged — does or does not play a genuine role in the course of our lives.

Indeed, Nietzsche goes on to imply that it does, even while suggesting that this role is both more modest and quite different from what it usually is taken to be. For even if it is true that 'all conscious purposes' and the like are 'only means through which something essentially different from what appears in consciousness is to be achieved,' this would have an important consequence: namely, that while they themselves could not be regarded as the 'causes' of anything else that happens, they would still figure significantly in the 'achievement' of certain results in the lives of human agents. Thus he can also maintain that 'our opinions, valuations, and tables of what is good certainly belong among the most powerful levers in the involved mechanism of our actions,' although 'in any particular case the law of their mechanism is indemonstrable' (GS 335).

Similar observations are applicable to virtually all of the things Nietzsche says which at first glance appear to express an epiphenomenalist position. And thus they may be reconciled without great difficulty to the much more frequent passages in which he focusses on the question of the utility (and disutility) of human consciousness for human life. A balanced and careful consideration of his discussion of consciousness shows, therefore, that he is no more a true epiphenomenalist than he is a strict determinist. The occasional remarks he makes which are suggestive of the former position may both reasonably and most coherently be interpreted as somewhat overstated reactions on his part against the attribution of causality to certain sorts of conscious events in the explanation of human actions. He is in effect exclaiming: 'Causalism indeed! Epiphenomenalism is closer to the mark!' Once the former doctrine is disposed of, however, the occasion for the employment of such strong contrasting language as a needed corrective passes as well. And when one looks beyond it, one can see that the view he is actually advancing is somewhat less extreme, even though still quite radical in relation to traditional philosophical (and religious) thought.

XII

This view may be stated roughly as follows. Conscious events generally, and those we characterize as making decisions, framing intentions, and setting goals and purposes in particular, *by themselves and as such* do not suffice to accomplish anything in the domain of human action. They neither exist in and of themselves, nor unfold in an autonomous manner, nor even figure significantly in the explanation of much of what we do. Instead they typically reflect underlying dispositions, and merely announce in an anticipatory (and sporadic) way the lines along which these dispositions incline us to act; although on occasion they may serve to modify the manner in which certain of these dispositions enter into the larger interplay within us, in accordance with the character and strength of others and of various social realities. That is to say, they *may* perform a 'directing' function, though they by no means invariably do so; but even when they do, they do not do so in an entirely autonomous way. For their occurrence and specific character is closely bound up with both effective-dispositional and sociocultural factors, as well as with the character of the specific circumstances in which we find ourselves.

In short, human consciousness for Nietzsche requires to be understood as a phenomenon intimately connected with our underlying animate nature and constitution and our entanglement in a web of social relations. In abstraction and apart from these factors it can neither be understood nor attributed any genuine existence or concrete nature, and so amounts to nothing of any consequence. It is a function of human life more broadly conceived, which is neither completely reducible to nor entirely determined by either non-conscious psychophysiological processes and forces or extra-conscious sociocultural practices and forms, but which owes both its general character and much of its specific content and orientation for anyone at any time to their occurrence and interaction. Consciousness is capable of attaining at most a limited degree of semi-autonomy in relation to them. The importance of this possibility, for Nietzsche, is not to be underestimated. Even where it is realized, however, its realization is to be conceived as the rather inadvertent result of a long process of human development during which it was quite lacking, rather than as the result of one's employment of a special mental or spiritual faculty with which human beings are essentially equipped.

315

Nietzsche's general view of consciousness is thus that it is a social phenomenon, in which our affective nature is strongly at work as well. He holds that it constitutes a transformation of a certain portion of our affective life, rather than a domain radically distinct from it and autonomous in relation to it. It is only with our affective capital, as it were, that the enterprise of our conscious life can be funded. And the investment thereby made is to be regarded as a diversification of our affective portfolio, occurring 'in the service' of the 'preservation and enhancement' of human life in an intensely competitive world, rather than as a completely independent development motivated by altogether different (e.g., purely cognitive) concerns.

One may be said to be conscious, however, only if one's awareness of the world and of one's situation and needs is interrupted and mediated by thought — and more specifically by its vehicle, language. 'Becoming-conscious,' for Nietzsche, is thus a development which (at least beyond a very rudimentary level) proceeds apace with the linguisticization of awareness. In order to avoid making 'a mistake over the role of "consciousness,"' he writes, it must be recognized to be 'only a means of communication: it is evolved through social intercourse' (WP 524). It is with this point in mind that he suggests that 'consciousness does not really belong to man's individual existence but rather to his social or herd nature,' and goes on to maintain that it 'has developed subtlety only insofar as this is required by social or herd utility.' Generally speaking, he contends, 'the subtlety and strength of consciousness' are proportionate to the 'capacity for communication.' For 'conscious thinking *takes the form of words, which is to say signs of communication*, and this fact uncovers the origin of consciousness.' If this is right, it is undeniable that 'consciousness is really only a net of communication between human beings,' and thus is fundamentally a social phenomenon (GS 354).

Yet it must immediately be added, according to Nietzsche, that it is not entirely a social phenomenon; for he takes it also to require to be understood in terms of the relation of what transpires in conscious experience to underlying forces and dispositions within us, which our conscious processes reflect no less importantly than they do the character of the social relations indicated above. And this leads to the next large topic to be considered: Nietzsche's 'theory of affects.'

The theory of affects

XIII

It was earlier observed that, while Nietzsche rejects 'the soul-hypothesis' in its traditional form and subsequent disguises, he also suggests that 'the way is open for new versions' of this notion once they have been laid to rest (*BGE* 212). In this passage he specifically mentions 'such conceptions as . . . "soul as subjective multiplicity," and "soul as social structure of the drives and affects".' These conceptions, both of which he takes to have application on different levels of consideration of our human nature, provide an indication of the centrality of his theory of affects in his account of it. Here and elsewhere he employs such terms as 'affects,' 'drives' and 'instincts' more or less interchangeably. His 'theory of affects' embraces his views with respect to the range of phenomena they collectively subsume. Thus he takes one of his 'fundamental innovations' to be his development of what he calls 'a perspective theory of affects (to which belongs a hierarchy of the affects; the affects transfigured; their superior order, their "spirituality")' (*WP* 462).

It is a central part of this theory that all aspects of human 'spiritual' life and activity are to be understood as outgrowths and developments of 'the affects transfigured.' The importance of the results of this 'spiritualizing transfiguration' for Nietzsche can hardly be overstated. He considers no part or form of our mental existence and operations to be completely autonomous in relation to our affective constitution. The whole of the former, on his view, must be recognized to be conditioned by and expressive of the latter. As has previously been remarked, he argues that 'reason' is fundamentally 'a system of relations between various passions' (*WP* 387). And he takes the same position with respect to thought more generally, contending that 'thinking is merely a relation of [our] drives to each other' (*BGE* 36). He further maintains that the various forms of experience shaped by social and cultural institutions are at least indirectly related to the character of our affective natures, since he considers such institutions to be primarily geared to the control of the latter; thus he subsequently generalized one of his early insights with respect to the Greeks: 'I saw how all their institutions grew out of preventive measures taken to protect each other against their inner explosives' (*TI* X:3). Moreover, he holds that all 'high spirituality' that is humanly attainable (and which sets those attaining it apart from ordinary, merely social and 'moral' men) 'itself exists only as the ultimate product of moral qualities' (*BGE* 219) and of the 'preliminary schooling' of social-institutional discipline (*TI* VIII:6); and thus it too is to be understood as the issue of a complex transformation of elements of our affective nature.

Nietzsche's theory of affects is intimately connected with his conception of 'will to power.' It was observed in the last chapter that he holds that 'it is possible to trace all of [an animal's] drives to the will to power; likewise all the functions of organic life to this one source' (*WP* 619). And he believes that the same thing should be (and is) possible where all human affective phenomena are concerned. Thus he advocates undertaking the experiment of seeing whether one can succeed in 'explaining our entire instinctive life as the development and ramification of *one* basic form of the will,' or fundamental disposition, 'namely of the will to power, as *my* proposition has it' (*BGE* 36). He considers his efforts along these lines to warrant the conclusion that this hypothesis is correct. So he criticizes 'all psychology so far,' on the grounds that it 'has got stuck in moral prejudices and fears,' and proposes that one 'understand it as morphology and *the doctrine of the development of the will to power*, as I do.' And he then goes on to mention such subsidiary specific themes as 'the reciprocal dependence of the "good" and the "wicked" drives,' the original 'derivation of all good impulses from wicked ones,' and the status of 'even the affects of hatred, envy, covetousness, and the lust to rule' as 'fundamental and essential' to the nature of life, and to its preservation and enhancement (*BGE* 23).

The basic thesis of this theory is that 'the will to power is the primitive form of affect, all other affects are only developments of it' — to which he adds that there is no other 'psychic force' at work within us (*WP* 688). His reasoning in taking this to be so is indicated by his remarks relating to the evaluation of the hypothesis he advances in the section of *Beyond Good and Evil* cited previously: 'the reality of our drives' is indisputable; and thus if all psychological and behavioral phenomena can be explained in terms of them, and if they in turn can all be explained in terms of the one fundamental principle he calls 'will to power,' then since it is 'a moral of method' that one ought not to postulate more than one such explanatory principle if 'making do with a single one' is possible, one has 'gained the right' to assert the validity of the above conclusion (*BGE* 36).

At this point a note of caution is in order, and is supplied by Nietzsche himself. Terms for specific affects may mark significant differences among our dispositions. Such differing dispositions, however, are not the discrete irreducible entities which our manner of speaking makes them out to be; and they further can no more properly be construed in terms of the schematism of causality than they can legitimately be hypostatized. To the extent that the language we use to talk about them suggests that what we are dealing with here is a variety of such causal units, it relates to 'fictions,' here as elsewhere (*WP* 676). So Nietzsche says, with respect to ' *"The belief in affects"* ': 'Affects are a construction of the intellect, an invention of causes that do not exist' (*WP* 670). Affective phenomena are by no means fictitious; but we fictionalize them insofar as we conceive of them in the manner just indicated.

XIV

At times Nietzsche is very free in his enumeration of things he counts as affects, as when he observes that 'under the impress of the ascetic morality of depersonalization, it was precisely the affects of love, goodness, pity, even those of justice, magnanimity, heroism, that were necessarily misunderstood' (*WP* 388); or when he lists 'pride, joy, health, sexual love, enmity and war, reverence, beautiful gestures and manners, strong will, the discipline of high spirituality, will to power, gratitude toward earth and life' as being among 'the affirmative affects' (*WP* 1033). Not all of these things are even direct correlates or consequences of specific dispositions, let alone such dispositions themselves; it is only their general association with various affects more strictly construed, sublimated and transformed in certain directions, which warrants the mention of some. But Nietzsche does not always speak thus loosely; and from his more guarded designations of affective phenomena, one can put together a somewhat clearer picture of the range and nature of traits he means to include among them.

That which he mentions perhaps more often than any other, and regards as 'most fearful and fundamental,' is the 'drive for power' (*WP* 720). This most basic form of affect, taken by Nietzsche to reflect a tendency that is of the very essence of life itself, also appears as a specific affect alongside others which have emerged through its transmutations and developments in many different directions, and which have come to acquire their own specific character and relative autonomy in their manner of expression. The drive to obtain nourishment, for example, is one such 'derivative phenomenon' (*WP* 702). Derivative though it may be, however, he observes that it has come about that 'hunger' now has the status of a 'drive,' a feature of our 'instinctive life,' along with a variety of similar affects likewise linked with basic 'organic functions' and geared to the meeting of biological requirements (*BGE* 36; *WP* 658).

A further such function is that of procreation, with which another (also 'derivative') drive is associated: 'the sexual drive' (*WP* 697), which figures very prominently in Nietzsche's discussions of our basic affective constitution. Itself originally an 'offshoot' and 'specialization' of a more basic drive, it is held to have acquired a distinctive character and to have become one of the most powerful and pervasive forces at work within us. Indeed, its influence is suggested to reach into a great many regions of human 'spiritual' life; for it tends itself to a wide range of further transformations, the issues of which constitute yet another class of affective phenomena.

A different sort of affect upon which Nietzsche places considerable emphasis, and which he regards as an outgrowth of the will to power insofar as it is directed to conquest, is that which he characterizes in terms of 'covetousness' or 'greed' (broadly construed). This disposition to seek to acquire and appropriate may itself take many different forms, and is not to be thought of as having any particular sort of proper object, or as being essentially attuned to any specific type of appropriation. Like all basic human affects, as Nietzsche conceives them, it is highly plastic and adaptable in both respects; if frustrated along certain lines, it shifts to others. But in one form or other, he contends, it makes its influence felt throughout all human life that is possessed of any degree of vitality, and plays an indispensable role in all growth and development, enrichment and enhancement.

Another affect he frequently mentions consists in a disposition to engage in a more negative type of self-assertion in relation to what is other than and potentially threatening to oneself. It has the character of an inclination to 'hostility' and 'destruction.' This aggressive disposition, which is capable of being redirected away from others and toward oneself (a possibility the fateful realization of which Nietzsche explores at length in the *Genealogy*, in his discussion of the phenomenon of the 'bad conscience' and the origin of 'ascetic ideals'), also admits of a variety of 'healthier' expressions and sublimations. It is commonly taken to be a prime example of a ' "wicked" drive,' and may indeed require to be brought under the control of others if it is not to wreak wide havoc in human life. Nietzsche argues, however, that its weakening or extirpation would be most undesirable even if it were possible, since it is among the 'factors which, fundamentally and essentially, must be present in the general economy of life' if life is to flourish and 'is to be further enhanced' (*BGE* 23).

There are a great many other things which Nietzsche on various occasions terms affects, instincts, drives and passions, most of which have the status of further derivatives or modifications of these more basic dispositions. They include pride, envy, cruelty, pity, foolhardiness, cowardice, cunning, contempt, reverence, justice, magnanimity, and vengefulness. Tendencies to act, react, regard and treat in such relatively specific (and often culturally conditioned) ways cannot be thought of as the sorts of affects which warrant characterization as 'the mightiest natural powers' (*WP* 386) and 'the basic drives of man' (*BGE* 6). While others may at least arguably be so regarded, these can at most be thought of either as special cases of the latter or as certain of their outgrowths and spiritualized refinements or sublimations.

The same holds with respect to the various 'impulses' Nietzsche takes to be at work in such paradigmatically 'rational' intellectual activities as logical reasoning (*GS* 111) and 'scientific thinking': the latter, for example, being held to involve the interaction of 'many things' which 'had to be invented, practiced, and cultivated separately,' such as 'the impulse to doubt, to negate, to wait, to collect, to dissolve' (*GS* 113). These too are taken by Nietzsche to be instances of affective phenomena, and are the sorts of things he immediately has in mind when he asserts that 'thinking is merely a relation of these drives to each other' (*BGE* 36). But such impulses as these are themselves highly refined and developed rather than basic and irreducible forms of affect. Their existence is owing to their having been formed ('invented, practiced, and cultivated') on the basis and through the transformation of others of a more rudimentary nature.

It might at first seem objectionable of Nietzsche to subsume dispositions of such widely differing sorts and degrees of natural-ness and nurturedness under the same general heading. While there obviously are important differences among them, however, he is by no means oblivious to them. Some are purported to be features of our general human nature (and indeed to be by no means uniquely human, but rather traits shared with other forms of life). Others are taken to vary with the particular constitutions of different types of human beings; and others still are held to have the status of possibilities which may or may not be actualized in various human beings, depending upon the presence or absence of particular social and cultural conditions or upon the specific circumstances of their individual lives and the manner of their response to them. In using the same cluster of terms to refer to this whole broad range of phenomena, moreover, Nietzsche is not merely being careless and imprecise. On the contrary, this practice serves the purpose of underscoring the point that all of the higher-order dispositions associated with our collective and individual forms of life, experience and activity are ultimately rooted in lower-order or more primordial dispositions with which we are endowed; while the latter generally find expression through the former sorts of channels.

This point warrants brief elaboration. Human beings, Nietzsche argues, as they presently exist and have long existed, are not to be thought of as possessing two discrete and autonomous sets of dispositions, one biological or physiological and the other cultural or spiritual. Rather, all aspects of their lives are informed by complexes of dispositions representing diverse variations on general themes, in the elaboration of which both sociocultural and individual variables and also human-constitutional constants play important roles. A person's dispositional make-up admits of being viewed and analyzed on a number of different levels, and in terms of a variety of frames of reference — for which reason Nietzsche speaks of the desirability of 'a *perspective* theory of affects' (*WP* 462). Our affective life, having its foundation in our biological nature and the conditions of our existence, is thus the basis and encompassing context of all the 'spiritual functions' and process and experiences figuring in our conscious lives. These dearly bought 'showpieces of man' at once include 'mastery over the affects,' and also are held to constitute certain forms of their transformed manifestation to which the imposition of constraints upon them has given rise (*GM* II:3).

What is called 'the will,' for example, 'is above all an *affect*, and specifically the affect of the command' (*BGE* 19). Likewise 'reason' is 'a system of relations between various passions' (*WP* 387); and when a morality speaks in us with the voice of conscience as well, it is 'a sign language of the affects' with which we are confronted (*BGE* 187). Artistic activity and experience in their various forms involve the 'excitation' of the 'affective system' in specific ways (*TI* IX:10); and 'scientific thinking' is a matter of the operation of a variety of 'impulses' in coordination (*GS* 113). And differences in type of character and level of spirituality are functions of the relative strength, multiplicity and organization of the affects operative within different human beings; thus all 'high spirituality' is held to be a 'consequence of a dominating affect' establishing order among the rest.

In short: while granting and indeed insisting upon the diversity and complexity of human psychological phenomena, Nietzsche contends that they all are either affects or functions and manifestations of affects; while they in turn are to be referred ultimately to 'physiological systems and forces' (*WP* 229), and secondarily to the social circumstances which shape their direction and manner of expression. The idea that some part of human mental or spiritual life has some altogether different seat and source, and that there are certain states and operations which obtain and transpire quite independently of all factors of either sort (affective or social), must on his view be abandoned. The seeming autonomy of those phenomena we commonly construe as affairs of the intellect or will or spirit is only apparent; for the presuppositions of such autonomy are wanting, and so this interpretation of these phenomena cannot be sustained. While they are not directly reducible to states of the 'nervous system,' or completely explicable in terms of 'physiological systems and forces,' Nietzsche contends that the only remaining way of understanding the existence of the former and their relation to the latter is to suppose that something on the order of his 'affects' are associated with the latter, and that the former are their issue.

XV

Having made this basic point, one of Nietzsche's chief further concerns is to develop his account in such a way that an overly simplistic view of human mental and spiritual life is avoided, and justice is done to the richness and refinement it actually exhibits and is capable of attaining. He is well aware that the tenability of his own model is crucially affected by such considerations of adequacy; and that it depends in particular upon his ability to identify transformative processes consonant with its basic outlines, and yet sufficient to render the reality and possibility of such refinements comprehensible. To this end he nominates two main candidates, which he considers together to meet these requirements as well as may reasonably be expected. The first he terms 'internalization,' and the second, 'sublimation' or 'spiritualization.'

These notions refer to processes whereby various relatively simple affects (confined largely to the level of the accomplishment of basic organic functions) are untracked, diverted and diversified. When this occurs, *both* their degeneration into anarchical disarray or pathological reduction, *and* their refinement, reorganization and employment as means to the achievement of a 'higher' form of life, become possible. The former, it will be recalled, is linked by Nietzsche to the imposition upon human beings of social constraints. And it is his contention that the consequent *'internalization of man,'* involving the *'turning inward'* of 'instincts that do not discharge themselves outwardly,' was the occasion of the emergence of 'the entire inner world' of psychological states and associated forms of consciousness. This 'inner world,' he suggests, 'acquired depth, breadth and height, in the same measure as outward discharge was inhibited' (*GM* II:16). Such 'internalization' is taken to be both the basic condition of the possibility

323

of the development of dispositions departing in their specific manner of expression ('outwardly' again, as well as 'inwardly') from these 'old instincts,' and the impetus to the cultivation of certain of them as functional replacements for these 'former guides' better attuned to man's 'new surroundings and conditions of existence.' 'Thus it was,' Nietzsche writes, 'that man first developed what was later called his "soul" ' (ibid.).

All 'spirituality,' on his view, also derives ultimately from this turn of events. 'The ferocity and anarchy of the instincts,' in a human animal that could no longer comport itself as an animal, would long ago have spelled disaster, if they had merely been internalized ('turned backward *against man himself*'), and had not also been taught new employments. Their general 'ferocity and anarchy' served and serves as a stimulus ('to avoid perishing') to the development of 'shrewdness, clarity, severity and logicality' (*WP* 433), in all of which traits they also more subtly reassert themselves. And the many other diverse forms of human spiritual life, from the intellectual to the artistic to the emotional (and including the religious as well as the moral), likewise are suggested to represent the 'spiritualization' of various more rudimentary drives and impulses, the most 'natural' forms of expression of which have been checked and the course of which has been redirected. 'All passions have a phase when they are merely disastrous, when they drag down their victims with the weight of their stupidity − and a later, very much later phase when they wed the spirit, when they "spiritualize" themselves' (*TI* V:1).

Thus, for example, 'the spiritualization of sensuality is called *love*'; and 'another triumph is our spiritualization of *hostility*,' which takes the form of competitiveness and involves 'a profound appreciation of the value of having enemies' (*TI* V:3). Moral sentiments and attitudes are likewise to be construed as a kind of 'sign of language of the affects' (*BGE* 187), in which a variety of the latter assume sublimated forms under different social conditions. Further: 'All virtues are really refined *passions* and enhanced states'; the sense of 'justice,' for example, is a 'development of the drive to revenge,' and the sense of 'honor' is a derivative of 'recognition of the similar and equal-in-power' (*WP* 255). Artistic activity and aesthetic experience alike involve the operation of 'sensuality' in one of its 'disguises' (*WP* 806); here our sexual drive is transferred from its original objects, and transformed in its expression and the form of sensibility attendant upon it. And 'the so-called drive for knowledge can be traced back to a drive to appropriate and conquer' (*WP* 423); even though the forms of appropriation and conquest which the attainment of knowledge involves, as well as the means of effecting them, constitute highly spiritualized departures from the sorts of activity in which this drive finds its most basic expressions.

All such spiritualizations of the affects have as their general precondition the learning of restraint. 'That is the *first* preliminary schooling for spirituality: not to react at once to a stimulus'; for 'the inability to resist a stimulus,' and the tendency to 'follow every impulse,' are marks of 'unspirituality' (*TI* VIII:6). What has '*educated* the spirit,' and indeed has enabled it to become a reality, has always been, 'as opposed to *laisser aller*, a bit of tyranny against "nature" ' — and, Nietzsche adds, 'also against "reason." ' 'What is essential "in heaven and on earth," ' he contends, is 'that there should be obedience over a long period of time and in a *single* direction; given that, something always develops, and has developed, for whose sake it is worth while to live on earth . . . — something transfiguring, subtle, mad, and divine,' such as 'virtue, art, music, dance, reason,' or simply, in a word, 'spirituality' of one sort or another (*BGE* 188).

In the cases of those exceptional individuals whom Nietzsche takes to represent the emergence of a higher form of humanity, externally imposed constraints and enforced obedience give way to self-control, and experiments in the cultivation of forms of spirituality involving the enlistment of a multiplicity of strong affects are undertaken in many different directions. Here and there such 'great, fruitful, inventive spirits' have appeared, he observes, in whom a 'dominating spirituality' took shape 'whose demands prevailed against those of all the other instincts' (*GM* III:8). For the most part, however, he holds that such spiritualizations of the affects as have been achieved in the course of man's history have been rather fortuitous products of the subjection of human beings of various types to particular pressures under differing sorts of social conditions.

So he reflects upon the 'different degrees of development which the human impulses have attained' in 'different moral climates' (*GS* 7), as various social needs and circumstances have brought it about that 'certain affects and states' have been 'selected and reared at the expense of others' (*WP* 889). In some instances a 'high culture' has been achieved; and where this has happened, it came about because a selected multiplicity of strong affects have been organized, cultivated, and taught sublimated and creative forms of expression. Matters have turned out very differently, however, wherever the affects of those in question have been weak, or anarchic and unrestrained, or were given a self-destructive turn through their repression; or where they were so completely and severely subordinated to some single demand that their expressions were impoverished.

Thus, according to Nietzsche, 'to press everything terrible into *service*,' gradually and 'experimentally,' as the strength and discipline required to be able to do so are acquired, 'is what the task of culture demands'; for 'the greater and more terrible passions are that an age, a people, an individual can permit themselves as *means, the higher stands their culture*' (*WP* 1025). This proposed 'standard' affords a measure both of strength and of enhancement, by reference to which the 'order of rank' of which he so often speaks (among societies, groups, individuals and spiritual states) may be established. And his conception of the process of 'spiritual-ization,' which figures so prominently in it, is the final major element of his 'theory of the affects,' rendering it sufficiently comprehensive and sophisticated to endow his interpretation of human spiritual life in terms of it with plausibility.

The same may now be said of Nietzsche's philosophical anthropology more generally. If 'the reality of our drives' (*BGE* 36) is granted; if it is conceded that the independence of those states and events we identify as mental and spiritual in relation to them is by no means self-evident; if it is recognized that 'economy of principles' is an essential requirement of sound 'method' (*BGE* 13); and if the explanatory adequacy of the foregoing sort of account is allowed, then on his view the case for his hypothesis concerning the basic outlines of our human nature is strong enough to warrant its adoption. Alternative interpretations remain possible; and his own admittedly remains sketchy and provisional. These consider-ations, however, do not seriously affect its tenability. Unless reasons can be advanced either establishing that it is fundamentally flawed or making a stronger case for some other, his claim that it is at least an approximation of the truth of the matter must be allowed to have considerable force.

Human inequality and higher humanity

XVI

If the prominence Nietzsche accords to the affects in his conception of human nature will be found by many to be rather disconcerting, there is another topic, to which he devotes considerable attention in his elaboration of this conception, on which his position is commonly found to be even more so. Indeed, there is perhaps no view he advances for which he has been more vehemently attacked — and also with respect to which he has been more seriously misunderstood. I refer to the issue of human equality and inequality, or the matter of the respects in which human beings differ and what is to be made of the differences among them.

Speaking very generally, Nietzsche argues that while human beings may be allowed to have a common human nature, which sets them collectively apart from all forms of merely animal life, they differ in ways so substantial and significant that the doctrine of their essential equality requires to be adjudged a myth. Some, he holds, have it in them to surpass others in various respects, and so constitute at least potential exceptions to the human rule. He allows that a kind of actual equality among human beings generally is attainable; but he contends that its realization would mean the stultifying confinement of these potentially exceptional human beings to the level of the rule, fixed at a relatively low level by the inherent mediocrity and all-too-human limitations of the latter. Those endowed with certain capacities others lack (either relatively or entirely), on his view, represent potentially 'higher' types in relation to the rest; and to the extent that these capacities are cultivated, developed and manifested in their lives, they are held actually to be 'higher' than others (including those in whom these capacities remain unrealized).

Nietzsche thus discerns an 'order of rank' among human beings, reflecting the qualitative differences among the various 'types' of man and forms of humanity there have been and are and can be. And he considers it imperative, if human life is to flourish and develop, 'to maintain the *order of rank* in the world' (*BGE* 219), and indeed to widen the 'difference between strata' and intensify 'the pathos of *distance*' growing out of it. For he regards this as a condition of the possibility of the 'ever new widening of differences within the soul itself, the development of ever higher, rarer, more remote, further-stretching, more comprehensive states − in brief, simply the enhancement of the type "man," the continual "self-overcoming of man" ' (*BGE* 257). The alternative possibility he envisions, should this condition not be met, is that of the overall 'degeneration and diminution of man into the perfect herd animal ..., the dwarf animal of equal right and claims.' Thus he continues: 'Anyone who has once thought through this possibility to the end, no longer knows any other nausea than other men − but perhaps also a new *task*!' (*BGE* 203). Nietzsche's concern to drive home these points informs the greater part of his writings from *Zarathustra* onward. As he has Zarathustra say:

> thus blinks the mob − 'there are no higher men, we are all
> equal, man is man; before God we are all equal.'

Before God! But now this god has died. And before the
mob we do not want to be equal (Z IV:13).

Nietzsche here gives brief expression to one of the basic arguments by means of which he seeks to undermine the doctrine of
the basic equality of all men, and so to clear the way for the
development of his case to the effect that some not only differ
from but are superior to others. This argument involves drawing
attention to the fact that the doctrine referred to derives its main
support from a certain religious interpretation of man that cannot
any longer be considered tenable. The differences between human
beings are so readily apparent and considerable that they can be
discounted only by supposing there to be some metaphysical
respect in which all are to be considered equal in status or worth,
in relation to which their differences pale into insignificance. But
this supposition makes sense only within the context of a belief in
something on the order of the equality of all men before God,
their creation as somehow equal (their differences notwithstanding)
by God, or their endowment by God with souls of equal worth.

Beliefs of this sort have long been appealed to by proponents of
the idea of human equality. This idea may linger on among many
who no longer embrace religions of which such beliefs are a part.
It bears the stamp of its origin, however, and continues to
reverberate only as a kind of echo of this old faith, amplified and
sustained by the unwillingness of most people to face and accept
the consequences of abandoning it. Motivational factors of the
latter sort require to be recognized and reckoned with; but they
clearly do not affect the validity of the idea under consideration.
It stands — and falls — with the faith of which it is an article; for
there is no other, more viable interpretation of human nature onto
which it can successfully be grafted. Essential human equality is a
metaphysical-religious postulate requiring to be abandoned with
the recognition that it rests upon presuppositions which do not
obtain. Once one comes to appreciate that 'the belief in the
Christian God has become unbelievable' (GS 343), and learns to
ignore 'the siren songs of old metaphysical bird-catchers who have
been piping . . . all too long, "you are more, you are higher, you
are of a different origin" ' than all other forms of life (BGE 230),
one is compelled to take the various respects in which human
beings differ very seriously, and to refer the question of their
equality and inequality to considerations of this sort.

Nietzsche considers the notion that 'everyone has an "immortal
soul," has equal rank with everyone else' to be a groundless
conceit so *'impertinent'* that it 'cannot be branded with too much

328

contempt' (*A* 43). This view emerged and gained currency, he suggests, 'when Christian prejudice was a power,' and it was supposed that 'meaning lay in the salvation of the individual soul.' This 'optical magnification of one's own importance to the point of insanity — nothing but insanely important souls, revolving about themselves with a frightening fear — ' brought in its train the 'extremest form of equality of rights,' all souls being supposed to possess the same enormous importance. And even though 'this absurd self-inflation' may no longer be professed, he laments the fact that 'nevertheless, fundamentally, one [still] upholds the perspective of personalization as well as equality of rights before the ideal' (*WP* 339).

These notions are prime examples of what Nietzsche has in mind when he speaks of 'how much must collapse now that this faith has been undermined because it was built upon this faith, propped up by it, grown into it' (*GS* 343). For when one abandons the perspective generated by this faith, and looks at human beings with a colder and more discerning eye, one finds nothing warranting the accordance of such importance to each individual. And one further sees little beyond the fact that the vast majority exhibit only minor variations on a very mediocre general theme to support the supposition of their fundamental equality. When one directs one's attention not only to this general rule but also to various sorts of exceptions to it, however, instructed by other human possibilities realized at different times and places, one learns to think and estimate otherwise. One then discerns neither equal individuals nor basically identical members of a species, but rather 'an enchanting wealth of types, the abundance of a lavish play and change of forms' (*TI* V:6).

In this connection Nietzsche proposes to 'distinguish between a type of ascending life and another type of decay, disintegration, weakness,' contending that there can be no doubt about 'the relative rank of these two types' (*WP* 857). He also takes human beings generally to fall into one or the other of two radically different and widely disparate groups, one very numerous and occupying 'the human lowlands,' and the other, 'very small in number,' constituting 'a *higher, brighter* humanity' standing far 'above' the rest (*WP* 993). Thus he contrasts the general run of mankind, among whom 'sickliness' is purported to be the norm, with 'man's *lucky hits*' consisting of 'the rare cases of great power of soul and body' (*GM* III:1). On the one hand there is 'the domestic animal, the herd animal,' which is now and has long been the rule (*A* 3). On the other, there are the 'exceptions,' the 'fortunate accidents of great success,' which are 'encountered in the most widely different places and cultures: here we really do find a *higher type*, which is, in relation to mankind as a whole, a kind of *Übermensch'* (*A* 4).

This way of speaking, however, which Nietzsche often permits himself, is rather misleading and lends itself only too easily to an unfortuante over-simplification of his views; for it encourages the blurring of many important distinctions he draws when engaging in a more fine-grained analysis of human types. The same observation also applies with respect to his characterization of 'order of rank as order of power' (*WP* 856), and his occasional remarks to the effect that 'what determines your rank is the quantum of power you are' (*WP* 858). Though this way of putting the matter has the advantage of suggesting the idea of a continuum rather than a simple bifurcation, it is equally misleading if one forgets that 'power' for Nietzsche is not to be construed merely in terms of 'strength.' And it must be borne in mind that the 'mastery' of which he so often speaks is conceived as leading to fundamental transformations of the qualitative character of human life in those who carry it furthest, above all in what they make of themselves.

XVII

Nietzsche's notion of 'higher humanity' is actually a complex notion. It refers to a human possibility and an 'enhanced' form of human life requiring to be understood in terms of several related but distinct factors; and it therefore admits of a variety of contrasts with lesser forms of human life, in which certain things may either be lacking or improperly integrated. This 'luxury surplus of mankind,' consisting of 'a higher type that arises and preserves itself under different conditions from those of the average man,' is held to represent the emergence of a *'higher form of being'* in relation to human existence generally — Nietzsche's 'metaphor' for which, he remarks in passing, is 'the word *Übermensch'* (*WP* 866). This 'higher form of being' involves the attainment of a 'union of spiritual superiority with well-being and an excess of strength' (*WP* 899) that is not to be found in the more commonplace forms of humanity, which are wanting in various of these respects. And it further involves the achievement of a kind of 'wholeness' and 'completeness' that is lacking among the greater part of mankind. The latter, he holds, since they themselves are incapable of becoming such 'synthetic, summarizing, justifying' human beings, have a merely supporting role to play, as the 'precondition' and 'base' on which this exceptional type of man 'can invent his higher form of being' (*WP* 866).

330

The conditions which must obtain in order for this to occur are highly unusual. Thus most potentially 'higher' human beings have wound up, along with the rest, among the 'excess of failures' one everywhere encounters (*BGE* 62). Furthermore, actual 'higher types,' which Nietzsche characterizes as 'the richest and most complex forms' of human life, 'are indeed attained, but they do not last,' for they 'perish more easily'; they 'are achieved only rarely and maintain their superiority with difficulty,' while 'only the lowest preserve an apparent indestructability' (*WP* 684). So he writes:

> the higher the type of man that a man represents, the greater the improbability that he will turn out *well*. The accidental, the law of absurdity in the whole economy of mankind, manifests itself most horribly in its destructive effect on the higher men whose complicated conditions of life can only be calculated with great subtlety and difficulty (*BGE* 62).

These remarks should make clear the necessity of distinguishing Nietzsche's 'higher men' from 'the splendid *blond beast* prowling about avidly in search of spoil and victory,' no less than from the 'tamed' (and 'sickened') '*domestic animal*' to which civilization reduces it, as well as from the inherently weak, ill-constituted and mediocre type of man he calls the 'herd animal' (*GM* I:11). What sets his 'higher men' apart from and above the rest of humanity is not merely their possession of powerful drives, robust health, exceptional strength and overflowing vitality, even though he does insist that 'this is the essential thing in a well-constituted and complete man: the splendid "animal" must be given first — what could any "humanization" matter otherwise!' (*WP* 1045). Necessary conditions are not to be confused with sufficient ones. The attainment of their 'higher form of being' requires more: as has been observed, these resources of 'the splendid "animal"' must be 'controlled' (*WP* 966) and 'pressed into service' (*WP* 933).

On the other hand, their 'higher humanity' is not simply a function of the lengths to which their 'civilization' has been carried. To be sure, Nietzsche argues that 'high spirituality itself exists only as the ultimate product of moral qualities . . . , after they have been acquired through long discipline and exercise, perhaps through whole chains of generations' (*BGE* 219). He recognizes that the 'taming' process in which 'civilizing' essentially consists is a necessary precondition of the emergence of all higher forms of culture and spirituality, in the absence of which it could never have come about that there is in man not only 'creature' ('material, excess, clay, dirt, nonsense, chaos') but 'also creator, form-giver, hammer hardness, spectator divinity, and seventh day' (*BGE* 226). While he allows and indeed insists that 'every enhancement of the type "man" has so far been the work' of a certain type of 'society' (*BGE* 257), however, he contends that 'civilization has aims differing from those of culture,' owing to which there is an 'abysmal antagonism of culture and civilization' beyond a certain point in the development of both; for the civilizational imperatives center-ing upon 'the taming of the human animal' are also held to lead to the suppression of 'the boldest and most spiritual natures' (*WP* 121). Nietzsche's point here is that if 'civilization' is understood in terms of socialization, and if socialization is recognized to aim primarily at the transformation of human beings into a homo-geneous 'herd' on a plane reflecting their 'common' nature and the requirements of a smoothly functioning social order, then that which sets 'higher men' apart obviously cannot be a matter of their being more completely 'civilized' than others.

It is those who are at once the 'strongest' and the 'most spiritual' of men (*A* 57), possessed of 'great power of soul and body' (*GM* III:1) and of the 'richest and most complex' natures (*WP* 684), rather than those who are either the least or the most thoroughly civilized of human types, who are Nietzsche's 'higher men.' They are exceptional in being the 'strongest, richest, most independent, most courageous,' having at their disposal 'a great quantum of power to which one is able to give direction' (*WP* 776), and thus being capable of genuine creativity. Their 'higher form of being' thus translates into higher forms of 'culture' (*WP* 1025), transcend-ing the planes of merely natural and social existence and activity, and so opening a new chapter in the 'enhancement of life.' In them 'the spontaneous, aggressive, expansive, form-giving forces that give new interpretations and directions' (which Nietzsche refers to 'the essence of life, its *will to power*') are present in abundance (*GM* II:12), and are brought into a 'fortunate organ-ization' conducive to 'facility in self-direction' (*WP* 715) and 'self-elevation' (*WP* 403).

What Nietzsche has in mind is the attainment of a type of humanity the possibility of which was discerned by Goethe, who, he writes, 'conceived a human being who would be strong, highly educated, skillful in all bodily matters, self-controlled, reverent toward himself, and who might dare to afford the whole range and wealth of being natural,' because he is 'strong enough for such freedom,' and 'knows how to use to his advantage even that from which the average nature would perish.' Nietzsche conceives of the 'higher man' in the same way, as his explicit linking of this concep-tion with his own 'Dionsyian faith' indicates (*TI* IX:49). This 'higher man' is the type of 'the *sovereign individual*, like only to himself, liberated again from the morality of custom, autonomous and supramoral . . . , who has his own protracted will,' and whose 'mastery over himself also necessarily gives him mastery over circumstances, over nature,' and elevates him above 'all more short-willed and unreliable creatures' (*GM* II:2).

For a human being of this sort 'great ventures and over-all attempts of discipline and cultivation' are possible (*BGE* 203). Possessed of a 'great health' that is 'more seasoned, tougher, more audacious and gayer' than that of lesser men even under circumstances most favorable to them, Nietzsche's 'higher men' are 'argonauts of the ideal,' through whose 'overflowing power and abundance' the landscape of human existence is transformed, and 'the destiny of the soul changes' (*GS* 382). They possess 'creative powers' others lack, and stand apart from the rest both in terms of the 'strength' the measure of which is 'to what extent one can endure to live in a meaningless world *because one organizes a small portion of it oneself*' (*WP* 585). In terms of Nietzsche's conception of the 'enhancement of life,' his 'higher men' thus at once represent a highly 'enhanced' form of human life, and also are the primary instruments of its further enhancement.

It is owing above all to this circumstance that he considers it appropriate to term the sort of human being under consideration not merely 'different' but also 'higher' than others — not only exceptions to the general rule, but also 'exceptional' in the sense of 'superior.' He argues that, given the untenability of assigning intrinsic value to each and every human being as such, it is only in terms of something along the lines of his 'Dionysian value standard for existence' (*WP* 1041) that they can be attributed any value at all. And it is his contention that, when this perspective of evaluation is adopted, considerations pertaining to the 'enhancement of life' take on decisive importance, and the differences noted acquire differential evaluative significance. There is an 'order of rank of different kinds of life' (*WP* 592) because some constitute more 'enhanced' forms of it and figure more prominently and directly in its further enhancement than others, and because no considerations of any other sort carry any weight in the reckoning to be made. And that 'type of man' Nietzsche terms 'higher' is to be esteemed as being 'higher in value' than others accordingly, and is to be regarded as 'worthier of life' as well (*A* 3).

This is not to say that no value whatever is ascribable to all others, or that they are entirely 'unworthy of life'; but it is to relegate them to lower positions on the 'order of rank,' and does carry the implication that some may fare very poorly indeed. It is not, however, either as individuals or as members of any particular racial, national or other group as such that they are to be accorded greater or lesser value, but rather only as instances of 'different kinds of life' — which, it bears repeating, Nietzsche contends are to be 'encountered in the most widely differing places and cultures' (A 4).

> Every individual may be scrutinized to see whether he
> represents the ascending or the descending line of life . . . .
> If he represents the ascending line, then his worth is indeed
> extraordinary — and for the sake of life as a whole, which
> takes a step farther through him, the care for his preservation
> and for the creation of the best conditions for him may even
> be extreme . . . . If he represents the descending development,
> decay, chronic degeneration, and sickness . . . , then he has
> small worth, and the minimum of decency requires that he
> take away as little as possible from those who have turned out
> well (TI IX:33).

The only value human beings have thus relates to what they represent and may bring about, and is a function of characteristics they do not all possess in equal measure. The specific sorts of differences Nietzsche has in mind are less likely to be disputed than are his interpretation and assessment of them; but it must at least be conceded that he succeeds in placing the burden of proof upon egalitarians, who all too commonly pay such differences too little heed. One must recognize and come to terms with them; and if one is unable to adduce any considerations overriding them or warranting writing them off, one is left with abstention from taking any position on the matter of human equality as the only alternative to the general sort of line he takes. He does at least make a strong *prima facie* case for human inequality; and unless it can be countered (or the theory of value he goes on to invoke can be faulted in some relevant respect), even the more disconcerting consequences he draws cannot be dismissed out of hand. Our prejudices may incline us to do so, as he observes is only to be expected of the children of an ideologically democratic age; but philosophers who are content to be guided by mere prejudice in this or any other matter amply merit his charge that they 'are not honest enough in their work' (BGE 5).

XVIII

Perhaps the point at which Nietzsche is most vulnerable to criticism in this connection is in his subscription to a rather strong form of biological pre-determinism, one especially dubious feature of which is the Lamarckian notion of the biological heritability or transmission of acquired characteristics which he builds into it. That he accepts this notion (now in general disrepute among biologists), apparently supposing it simply to be an established biological fact, is beyond dispute. Thus he writes that 'one cannot erase from the soul of a human being what his ancestors liked most to do and did most constantly'; that 'it is simply not possible that a human being should *not* have the qualities and preferences of his parents and ancestors in his body'; and that 'with the aid of the best education one will at best *deceive* with regard to such heredity' (*BGE* 264).

Lest Nietzsche be misunderstood (as well as convicted of error), however, it should be observed that by the same token he takes comparable constitutional alterations to be achievable by so arranging things that successive generations are induced constantly to do, and so eventually to come to 'like most to do,' different sorts of things. (It is worth noting his remark in this connection that 'this is the problem of race', for this constitutes a very different understanding of 'race' and of the status of 'racial' differences than that generally associated with 'racism,' with which brush he is often but unfairly tarred.) Thus he constantly speaks of the importance of 'breeding,' conceived as a process operating not only within particular generations but through trains of them, involving the cultivation of certain traits, and in consequence of which they gradually come to be relatively fixed and strong. The prominence of this notion in his thinking renders it deserving of attention; and as shall be seen, he develops and employs it in a manner which loosens its link to his Lamarckianism sufficiently to warrant taking it seriously despite the fact that the latter requires to be rejected.

There is no substitute, Nietzsche maintains, for 'breeding,' which he contrasts emphatically and repeatedly to the strategy of 'taming' — shackling and weakening (and thus rendering relatively harmless) — those who otherwise would pose dangers to others obliged to live in proximity to them. 'Both the *taming* of the beast, man, and the *breeding* of a particular kind of man have been called "improvement," ' he writes; but these two sorts of transformation could not be more different. 'To call the taming of an animal its "improvement" sounds almost like a joke to our ears' (*TI* VII:2). 'Breeding,' on the other hand, while by no means invariably resulting in any enhancement of life, at least may do so, and indeed is held by Nietzsche to be essential to the emergence of any 'higher' type of man. Thus he urges that consideration be given to 'what, given a favorable accumulation and increase of forces and tasks, might *yet be made of man'* (*BGE* 203), and to the problem of 'what type of man shall be *bred'* which would be 'higher in value' than the 'herd animal' type that has most commonly been 'bred and *attained'* (*A* 3).

> All the virtues and efficiency of body and soul are acquired laboriously and little by little, through much industry, self-constraint, limitation, through much obstinate, faithful repetition of the same labors; but there are men who are the heirs and masters of this slowly acquired manifold treasure of virtue and efficiency (*WP* 995).

This, according to Nietzsche, is how some come to 'attain great strength,' and to have it in them to accomplish 'great tasks' (ibid.). While he thus accords considerable importance to the kind of 'breeding' (or lack of it) that has gone on in the course of the emergence of human beings of various types, however, he considers it to be but one part of a much larger complex of factors, from which it cannot be separated without distortion. Particular human beings, with their differing constitutions, are configurations reflecting the convergence and interaction of innumerable forces under widely varying conditions; and his notion of 'breeding' is to be understood as expressing what he takes to be one variable feature of this tangle of processes on a certain (provisional) level of description.

Nietzsche quite reasonably supposes that there are limits to the developmental potential of any human being; and that one can become only what one has it in one to be, as well as what one's circumstances permit and make possible. He further observes that some 'turn out' very differently from others; and that the ways they turn out correlate very imperfectly with externally obtaining conditions, even though he concedes to such conditions a homogenizing influence. His 'breeding-hypothesis' is advanced in an attempt to provide at least a part of an answer to the question of why this is so, as well as to that of why human life affords the spectacle of a 'wealth of types' (rather than exhibiting the basic homogeneity one might expect of creatures of the same biological kind). The untenability of this hypothesis as he formulates and employs it must, however, be conceded. It is neither required by the evidence nor justifiable on other grounds. Much of what Nietzsche ascribes to 'breeding' may more reasonably be accounted for by a transmission process operating on the cultural level rather than biologically. And to the extent that this is so, differences among human beings are acquired rather than innate, and cannot be taken to warrant any judgment concerning the inherent

336

superiority of some over others — even though they may warrant judgments of *attained* superiority.

On the other hand, quite apart from the fact that at least something of Nietzsche's 'breeding-hypothesis' would appear to be salvageable once it is recast in cultural terms, the abandonment of biological Lamarckianism by no means requires one to conclude that all human beings are initially endowed with the same capacities, and that they differ only in incidental respects or in ways attributable to the particular circumstances of their life-histories. Granting the difficulty of determining what is owing to nature as opposed to nurture, and conceding the crucial importance of many sorts of contingencies in the development and manifestation of all human capacities, it must still be admitted that many of the physiological differences human beings exhibit derive from constitutional differences. And it must further be allowed at least to be a strong possibility that constitutional differences also underlie and are at work in certain of the variations among them on other levels of their existence.

If our only 'essential nature' is our biological nature, of which all aspects of our distinctively human nature (our entire conscious and 'spiritual' life included) are expressions and developments; if this biological nature is not so *plastic* that all human beings admit of being shaped in the same ways; if our biological natures further are not so *uniform* that every capacity with which some come into the world endowed is initially possessed by all in roughly equal measure; if moreover some capacities which are not equally distributed admit of translation into creative forms of activity contributing to the enrichment and enhancement of human life to a significantly greater extent than most forms of human activity do; and if it is in such terms, and such terms alone, that value is ultimately to be understood, by reference to which standard the relative values of things are properly determinable — then sense can indeed be made of the idea that 'there are higher and lower men,' differing not only in nature but also in value. And it further would be naive to suppose that the 'higher humanity' of which Nietzsche speaks represents the manner of existence to which all human beings could attain if only various obstacles could be removed and the appropriate circumstances were to be arranged — even though it may well be that he underestimates what the 'average' and 'mediocre,' the ordinary run of mankind, have it in them to be.

In short: if Nietzsche is right in maintaining that all psychological and 'spiritual' phenomena are inextricably bound up with physiological forces, processes, systems and states, and that 'the soul is only a word for something about the body' (Z I:4), a qualified form of the biological determinism to which he subscribes would seem to have much to be said for it. Few would deny that our *general* human-biological nature at once enables us to do (and learn to do) and experience (and come to experience) various sorts of things, and also sets limits upon what we are able to do and experience. If this is so, however, it is reasonable to suppose that the same also applies with respect to our *particular* biological natures.

It may run counter to certain of our most cherished beliefs when Nietzsche writes that he is 'altogether convinced that, in spite of all, one will [or can] become only that which one is,' by nature, as it were, adding: 'in spite of all: that means education, instruction, milieu, chance, and accident' (*WP* 334). But our right to beliefs to the contrary is questionable at best. Factors of the latter sort certainly figure importantly in determining what becomes of 'that which one is'; but it is 'only that which one is' upon which they can have any influence, and which can be drawn upon as one's life unfolds. One's basic constitution may not itself determine very *definitely* how one will turn out, what particular course one's life will take, and what one's specific manner of existence will be; but it may be considered to set boundary conditions, rendering some sorts of things within the realm of possibility while precluding others. Even our most fundamental common features have been established only through an evolutionary process in which many contingencies have operated; and they may quite plausibly be taken to be affected in particular cases by variables in the natural processes of which they are the issue. Nietzsche may have been mistaken about how all of this works; but his general position would appear to survive his correction.

XIX

Let it be supposed, however, that it should prove impossible to reconstruct a case strong enough to render his position on the issue of human equality convincing. Indeed, let it even be supposed that, when all of the biological evidence is in, it turns out that the only human beings who are exceptions to the general human norm (in any constitutional respects having a significant bearing upon their capacity to attain to the sort of 'higher humanity' Nietzsche takes to be humanly possible) are the relative few who are genetically defective or otherwise developmentally disabled. In this case most human beings would not be constitutionally barred from achieving that 'higher form of being' he supposes only a few have it in them to reach. Yet his conception of 'higher humanity' would still remain of interest, and something like his differentiation of 'higher' and 'lower' men could still be made out. This distinction would have a rather different significance; for the difference between those possessed of the 'union of spiritual superiority with well-being and an excess of strength' (*WP* 899) he celebrates, and those lacking in these respects, would require to be accounted for entirely in terms of events transpiring in the course of their lives. Even so, however, it could well remain a useful distinction, serving to mark very important differences in the ways people turn out. The conditions which would have to obtain in order for any to 'turn out well' might (as Nietzsche suggests) be so special that few would do so; and thus those who come to be of 'great power of soul and body' would still be appropriately characterizable as 'man's lucky hits' (*GM* III:1). The 'diminution of man into the perfect herd animal' could still be recognized as an 'over-all danger,' and the thought of 'what, given a favorable accumulation and increase of forces and tasks, *might yet be made of man*' would retain its legitimacy and significance (*BGE* 203).

Nietzsche might be right or wrong to insist, where all qualitative enhancements of life are concerned, upon their inseparability from exploitation, and from the establishment of 'ever wider distances' between some human beings and others. These are separate matters, however, which do not in either event crucially affect the main points under consideration. What one must ask oneself, in the end, is whether he has succeeded in identifying a form of human existence which represents a genuine human possibility (however many or few those may be who might realize it, and whatever its realization might involve); and whether he is justified in his contention that it is more estimable than any other. These are questions which remain even if matters actually stand as they are here described, rather than as he supposes. An affirmative answer clearly seems to be warranted with respect to the first; for while his conception of the *Übermensch* may be based upon an extrapolation from actual human types, the 'higher humanity' of which he speaks is something he finds exemplified here and there throughout human history.

With respect to the second question, it would be difficult to fault Nietzsche's accordance of superiority to human life possessed of the characteristics he indicates over all alternatives to it, given the soundness of his general interpretation of human nature and the human condition. Life certainly can be — and usually is — a different sort of affair than that which he has in mind when he speaks of the type of man he terms 'higher.' One would be hard put, however, to say how the latter picture might be improved upon, or what might compensate for the deletion of any major feature he includes in it. Overflowing vitality and great health; powerful affects and the ability to control and direct them; high spirituality and refinement of sensibility and manners; independence of mind and action; the capacity to befriend and to respect and disdain and deal justly with others as they warrant; intellectual honesty and astuteness; the strength to be undaunted by suffering and disillusionment; persistence in self-overcoming; the resources to undertake and follow through on the most demanding of tasks; and the ability to love and esteem, and above all to create — this configuration of qualities well warrants identification as the consummation of human existence translated back into nature and then transformed beyond it. It represents the greatest and richest enhancement of life Nietzsche considers possible; and if any major injustice to our human potential is done here, it is not readily apparent.

If there is any attainable form of human life that requires no independent justification to be found worthy of affirmation, and that may be considered to 'redeem' mankind more generally as well, Nietzsche makes a strong case for taking it to be something of this sort. And if life on this earth, no longer admitting of interpretation in terms of metaphysical schemes and religious beliefs, is to be accorded any 'meaning' at all, then if one grants him his metaphor of the *Übermensch* as a way of designating the essence of his notion of such a 'higher humanity' transcending all that is merely animal and 'all-too-human,' this 'meaning' would indeed appear to be fairly expressed by means of it. It is thus with good reason that he has Zarathustra proclaim:

> Behold, I teach you the *Übermensch*. The *Übermensch* is the meaning of earth. Let your will say: the *Übermensch* shall *be* the meaning of earth! (Z P:3).

VI

Value and Values

No philosopher has been more intensely concerned with questions of value than Nietzsche was. Moreover, notwithstanding his radical critique and emphatic repudiation of much of what both traditionally and more recently has been taken to constitute morality, he devoted as much attention to it as almost any of the many philosophers before and after him who have viewed it more sympathetically. Indeed, it was his concerns along these lines, above all others, which supplied the main motivation for his explorations of the matters dealt with in previous chapters. His attention in his early works was drawn continually to evaluative questions posed but not resolved by the ancient and modern cultural phenomena with which he found himself confronted in his philological studies and in his own time. The investigations he went on to undertake, in the years prior to *Zarathustra*, were in effect efforts to place himself in a better position than either classical scholars or previous philosophers were to deal with these questions properly and adequately. The whole of *Zarathustra* revolves around evaluative and moral concerns; and the same is true of his subsequent *Beyond Good and Evil* and *On the Genealogy of Morals*.

To be sure, Nietzsche's further reflections on other matters had a significant impact upon his thinking with respect to values and morality. The centrality and prominence of the latter throughout the whole course of his intellectual life, however, should be clear. It may be seen in *The Birth of Tragedy*, in which he seeks to convince us that 'it is only as an aesthetic phenomenon that existence and the world are eternally *justified*' (*BT* 5). And it is also reflected in the title he gives for the projected 'work in progress' to which he refers in *Genealogy* — '*The Will to Power: Attempt at a Revaluation of All Values.*' Indeed, the 'First Book' of this projected work (namely, *The Antichrist*), which was among the last things he wrote, excoriates Christianity precisely on the ground that it 'has turned every value into an un-value' (*A* 62). I shall examine Nietzsche's views with respect to value and values in this chapter, turning to a consideration of his treatment of morality in the next.

Toward a revaluation of values

I

Account should be taken at the outset of a difficulty confronting many philosophical readers, which at the same time has some significance of a positive nature for the interpretation of Nietzsche. It was observed in the Introduction that, while he could and often did write in a cool, dry, measured way, he also frequently expresses himself very strongly and colorfully. And he nowhere waxes more rhetorical, or indulges himself more freely in vehement and extravagant language, than in connection with the matters presently at hand. While no doubt at least in part a deliberately chosen tactic, intended to startle and unsettle and command attention, this tendency also is unquestionably a manifestation of the intensity of his concern with questions relating to value and morality, and shows it to be deeply and prominently normative (rather than merely analytical) in character.

To be sure, Nietzsche was quite disdainful of mere 'moralizers' and value-advocates who 'do not dissect enough and preach all too much' (*WS* 19), and remain complacently oblivious to (if not simply ignorant of) the wealth of moralities and value-systems, their histories, and their relation to other (e.g., psychological and social) phenomena in human life. 'How remote from their clumsy pride,' he writes, 'was that task they considered insignificant and left in dust and must − the task of description − although the subtlest fingers and senses can scarcely be subtle enough for it' (*BGE* 186). He considered it necessary to undertake this task, from a variety of angles, and to refrain from mere preaching. Yet he considered it no less important, and in the end a great deal more so, to proceed well beyond such description. And the tasks lying beyond it for him include not only the thorough deflation of the pretentions of previously established and commonly accepted moralities and values, but also the development of an evaluative scheme by reference to which a 'revaluation' of the things they prescribed and proscribed and commended and condemned could be carried out, and a new general direction of human life could be charted.

342

Nietzsche's concern thus was above all to work out a new theory of value which would at once provide an interpretation and decisive reassessment of existing moral and evaluative schemes, and also fill the normative void which their mere 'devaluation' under critical scrutiny would otherwise leave. And it is worth stressing here, in view of the common supposition that Nietzsche ultimately was nothing more than a preacher after all in his normative moments, that he did aspire and lay claim to philosophical tenability in setting forth his theory of value and the fundamental standard of value and evaluation it incorporates. Thus he insists that his critique of moralities and his revaluation of values are mandated by 'intellectual conscience' and 'honesty' in philosophical thinking; and he at least means to measure up to the same standard when he goes on to develop the normative side of his theory of value and moral philosophy. He is no less concerned to work out a position on these matters that will stand up under critical examination, than he is to do so where the world, life, and human nature are concerned.

A number of considerations, pertaining both to things Nietzsche asserts and to the character of major portions of his philosophical activity, serve to reveal the fundamentally and strongly normative orientation of his value-theory. (They also should be borne in mind when one is considering what to make of the many passages in his writings in which he might appear to be saying or implying that all valuation has at most a social, psychological, or physiological significance.) This first is his oft-repeated contention that a 'genuine philosopher,' or at any rate the sort of 'new philosopher' he envisions, is one who does not simply 'press into formulas . . . some great data of [former] evaluations' (*BGE* 211), and is not merely a 'critic' either (*BGE* 210), but rather *establishes* values — which, at least in relation to previous values, will be 'new' ones. 'Fundamental thought,' he writes: 'the new values must first be created — we will not be spared this task! For us the philosopher must be a legislator' (*WP* 979). So he suggests that 'there are two distinct kinds of philosopher: 1. Those who want to ascertain a complex fact of evaluations (logical or moral); 2. Those who are legislators of such evaluations' (*WP* 972). The former, on his view, are mere 'philosophical laborers' (*BGE* 211) — or, if 'critics,' they are but 'instruments of the philosopher and for that very reason . . . a long ways from being philosophers themselves' (*BGE* 210). To be sure, Nietzsche's remarks along these lines raise a number of large and important questions, concerning the character of such 'legislation' or 'creation,' and the status of the values which are thereby established. Whatever problems they may pose for him,

343

however, they leave no doubt about his commitment to the idea that philosophy has a constructive as well as analytical and critical role to play in value inquiry.

Second, and on a much more general level, it is important to appreciate the fact that Nietzsche's thinking on the matter of value initially had the fundamental character of a profound reaction against and response to Schopenhauer's pessimism and radical condemnation of life; and that it developed as an intended counter to and supersession of what he came to see as the looming larger threat to mankind of the phenomenon he calls 'nihilism.' Thus in *The Birth of Tragedy* his basic concern was to try to understand how the Greeks could have found it possible to endure and indeed exuberantly embrace and affirm life, even though they shared Schopenhauer's recognition of the 'absurdity' and 'terror and horror of existence' (*BT* 3) — and so to discover how we, bereft of the consolations of faith, might be able to do so as well. This ran directly counter to Schopenhauer's inclination and intentions, as gradually dawned on Nietzsche. 'Around 1876,' he later wrote, 'I grasped that my instinct went into the opposite direction from Schopenhauer's: toward a *justification* of life, even at its most terrible, ambiguous and *mendacious*' (*WP* 1005). His central proposition in *The Birth of Tragedy* had been that 'it is only as an aesthetic phenomenon that existence and the world are eternally *justified*.' And while this was but his first approach to the general issue of value, posed here only in the broadest terms, the view he expresses is one which he may have modified but did not abandon.

II

Nietzsche likewise did not abandon his determination to meet the challenge posed by Schopenhauer in favor of a nihilistic devaluation of all values. That would have been in effect to concede everything to Schopenhauer except the righteousness of his indignation with respect to the character of existence. 'What does nihilism mean?' Nietzsche asks, and answers: '*That the highest values devaluate themselves*' (*WP* 2). His concern with nihilism and its overcoming loomed ever larger in his thinking in the course of the last decade of his productive life, as he came to regard 'pessimism as a pre-liminary form of nihilism' (*WP* 8), and nihilism as both a 'necessary' intellectual-historical development (*WP* P:4) and the gravest of dangers. He recognized that he himself had 'hitherto been a thoroughgoing nihilist' (*WP* 25), and speculates that 'it could be a sign of a crucial and most essential growth, of the transition to new conditions of existence, that the most extreme form of pessimism, genuine *nihilism*, would come into the world' (*WP* 112). But he came to see nihilism as 'only a *transitional stage*' (*WP* 7), and to view his philosophy as a step in the direction of a '*counter-movement*' to it, 'regarding both principle and task; a movement that in some future will *take the place* of this perfect nihilism.' He himself, he says, has 'even now lived through the whole of nihilism, to the end, leaving it behind, outside himself' (*WP* P:4).

'*Radical nihilism*,' as Nietzsche understands it, 'is the conviction of the absolute untenability of existence when it comes to the highest values one recognizes' (*WP* 3). And he suggests that it is not in some profound insight into the actual nature of existence, but rather 'in one particular interpretation, the Christian—moral one, that nihilism is rooted' (*WP* 1). Thus he refers to nihilism as a 'consequence of moral valuation,' which leaves us unprepared to 'confer any value on that other sphere in which we live,' while the 'truthfulness' it itself commands eventually dissipates 'the sphere in which we have placed our values' (*WP* 8). But this is a 'consequence' Nietzsche rejects. 'Nihilism represents a pathological transitional stage (what is pathological is the tremendous generalization, the inference that there is no meaning at all)' (*WP* 13). Thus he speaks of it as a 'rebound from "God is truth" to the fanatical "All is false"' (*WP* 1). The problem, he contends, is that 'we have measured the value of the world according to categories that refer to a purely fictitious world.' Nihilism is the consequence, historically and psychologically if not logically, of 'the realization that the overall character of existence may not be interpreted by means of . . . the categories "aim," "unity," "being" which we used to project some value into the world.' These have 'proved inapplicable'; and so, Nietzsche says, to those making this discovery 'the world looks valueless' (*WP* 12).

This leads him to remark that 'a nihilist is a man who judges of the world as it is that it ought *not* to be, and of the world as it ought to be that it does not exist' (*WP* 585A). And, in a more serious vein, it leads him to reflect, less with respect to his own newly won perspective than to 'our' situation prior to its super-session, that 'the time has come when we have to pay for having been Christian for two thousand years; we are losing the center of gravity by virtue of which we have lived; we are lost for a while' (*WP* 30). But Nietzsche is no less anxious to make the point, with respect to the above-mentioned interpretive categories, that 'the demonstration that they cannot be applied to the universe is no longer any reason for devaluating the universe' (*WP* 12). It may be that 'the world does not have the value we thought it had,' and that the 'initial result' is that 'it seems worth less.' But herein lies 'the pathos that impels us to seek *new values*,' rather than simply resigning ourselves to axiological nihilism. Indeed, he continues, 'the world might be far more valuable than we used to believe,' and we previously 'may not even have given our human existence a moderately fair value' (*WP* 32).

As shall be seen, Nietzsche holds that, strictly speaking, it is inappropriate to speak of and attempt to assess the value of life and the world in general; for he contends that there is no objective standard of value definable independently of their actual fundamental character by reference to which they can be evaluated. This reservation does not, however, lead him to halt merely with a critique of any sweeping negative value judgment pronounced upon 'this world' generally, and a typological inventory of forms of value-systems which have emerged in the course of human history. For he believes it possible to ground a certain conception of value and standard of evaluation in a consideration of the fundamental character of reality, by reference to which it turns out to make sense after all to assign value to 'our human existence' and the world in which we find ourselves, and to privilege their affirmation over both their repudiation and an attitude of indifference toward them.

This belief finds expression in a number of Nietzsche's most striking formulations. It is reflected, for example, in his embrace of the idea of the 'eternal recurrence,' and also in his proclamation of '*amor fati*' as his 'formula' for 'a Dionysian relationship to existence,' which he takes to be 'the highest state a philosopher can attain.' 'I want to cross over to the opposite of [a negation, a No] ,' he says, 'to a Dionysian affirmation of the world as it is.' He goes on to say of this 'highest state' that 'it is part of this state to perceive not merely the necessity of those sides of existence hitherto denied, but their desirability.' And what he has in mind here is their 'desirability' not merely as useful or indispensable means to the attainment of various traditionally and commonly valued ends, 'but for their own sake, as the more powerful, more fruitful, *truer* sides of existence, in which its will finds clearer expression' (*WP* 1041). In this connection he speaks of 'a Dionysian value standard for existence,' which is 'little obliged' to prevailing modes of valuation, deriving rather from the above-mentioned apprehension of fundamental aspects of 'existence' which the latter are held to overlook or 'deny' (ibid.). It is this basic value standard which he seeks to formulate and undertakes to elaborate, and in terms of which he carries out his 'revaluation of values.'

It is important to observe, however, that the value standard

Nietzsche here terms 'Dionysian' is not one which he supposes is to be arrived at simply by ascertaining the nature of the 'truer sides of existence' to which he refers in their simplest and most pervasive forms. On the contrary, he employs the term 'Dionysian' not only to indicate the relation of this standard to them, but also to convey the idea of what he sometimes calls their 'deification' or qualitative transformation, and culminating in the 'highest' of 'joys' thereby attainable, 'in which existence celebrates its own transfiguration' (*WP* 1051). The 'sides of existence' he has in mind thus are not incorporated into this value-standard in the form of their lowest common denominator; for the 'transfiguration' of which they are capable and to which he takes them to tend is an essential feature of it. Here too, however, he holds this standard to reflect an aspect of the world's actual character — 'this, my Dionysian world of the eternally self-creating, the eternally self-destroying, this mystery world of the twofold voluptuous delight' (*WP* 1067) — rather than to express a demand or preference of ours (or his) which is then imposed upon it.

Nietzsche's 'Dionysian value standard' is thus no mere elevation of regularities of the sort which generally pass for 'laws of nature,' biological or other, to the status of norms of evaluative judgment. But it is intended to reflect what goes on in the world, as it goes on independently of any evaluative schemes which the likes or dislikes, wishes or desires, and reasonings or errors of particular human beings may lead them to hatch. And, no less importantly, it is intended to serve as a basis for evaluative judgments. 'Dionysus is a *judge*!' Nietzsche exclaims; 'have I been understood?' (*WP* 1051). If one fails to see this, one fails to understand him. And more specifically, one fails to understand his much-heralded 'revaluation of values,' in its double character as both a critique of former values and traditional modes of valuation, and also a development of a substantive alternative to them.

In speaking of a 'revaluation of values,' Nietzsche is employing the term 'values' in a way that should by now be quite familiar, to refer to those things which have long been taken by philosophers and others to be its primary referents. It thus has a descriptive use, and when so used should not be taken to convey his own endorsement of the significance and preeminence long accorded to these things. Its generality likewise should not be supposed to signify any thought on his part that a complete inventory of them would exhaust the full range of possible candidates for acknowledgment as supreme or intrinsic values (with the corollary that their de-thronement would entail either complete relativism or axiological nihilism). A clearer restatement of his program of a 'revaluation of values' would thus be a 'revaluation of those things which, traditionally or commonly, are supposed to be of greatest value.' And in proposing such a 'revaluation,' Nietzsche takes himself to be expressing a 'new demand': that we cease to take received estimations of these things for granted, and that 'the value of these values themselves must be called into question' (*GM* P:6). We must ask, in short: 'what value do they themselves possess?' (*GM* P:3). No philosophical inquiry is of greater importance for him than this one, as he indicates (along with his conviction that it cannot be adequately carried out in a purely speculative or a priori or analytical manner) when he writes: '*All* the sciences have from now on to prepare the way for the future task of philosophers: this task understood as the solution to the *problem of value*, the determination of the *order of rank among* values' (*GM* I:17).

As Nietzsche's reference here to an 'order of rank among values' suggests, he by no means assumes from the outset that no value whatever (or a purely negative value) attaches to everything hitherto accorded the status of a high or intrinsic value. On the contrary, he is quite prepared to discover that at least some such things do properly deserve to be accorded some measure of value — even though it may turn out to be much more modest or quite different from that generally attributed to them. Thus, for example, he remarks:

> for all the value that the true, the truthful, the selfless may deserve, it would still be possible that . . . the value of these good and revered things is precisely that they are insidiously related, tied to, and involved with [other] seemingly opposite things (*BGE* 2).

In speaking of 'the value' of such 'revered things' as these, Nietzsche clearly is employing this term in a way different from that in which he employs it when he uses it descriptively (i.e., as determined by its conventional applications) to refer to them. And when he cites 'the problem of value' as 'the future task of philosophers,' he likewise has something more in mind than the mere identification and explication of received and established modes of evaluation. He is proposing to evaluate them by reference to a standard of valuation independent of them, from a perspective which transcends them. And the sort of 'value' of which he speaks when viewing them from this perspective is one which he considers, in contrast to them, to have a kind of validity which they lack. It is an actual value, which he readily affirms to be such, even though its apprehension is associated with the attainment of a certain perspective. For this perspective is a privileged one, which an understanding of the fundamental character of life and the world serves to define and establish.

It is for this reason that Nietzsche employs the double formula 'The Will to Power: Attempt at a Revaluation of Values' both in identifying a major 'work in progress' of which he speaks in *Genealogy* (*GM* III:27) and in formulating a 'title' for the 'gospel of the future' he announces, in which the 'countermovement [to nihilism] finds expression, regarding both principle and task' (*WP* P:4). (The 'revaluation' obviously is the 'task,' and 'will to power' the 'principle' to be employed in carrying it out.) The standard of value with which he operates in his 'revaluation of values' is for him neither conventional nor stipulative (nor, for that matter, merely symptomatic of his own constitution); it has the same status, on his view, as that which is to be accorded to his interpretation of the fundamental character of reality generally in terms of 'will to power.' It reflects and derives from the latter, and so is affirmed by Nietzsche with no more qualification than that which he allows to be appropriate in the case of the latter. 'Assuming that life itself is the will to power,' he states, 'there is nothing to life that has value, except the degree of power' (*WP* 55) — although he gets a great deal of mileage out of the deceptively simple notion of 'degree of power.'

Thus, for example, he elsewhere writes, with equal straight-forwardness but somewhat greater explicitness: 'What is the objective measure of value? Solely the quantum of enhanced and organized power' (*WP* 674). The enhancement and organization of power is further associated by Nietzsche with the notions of 'growth' ('that is life itself') and development — 'the morality of development' being termed 'the doctrine preached by life itself to all that has life' (*WP* 125). And these notions themselves receive further refinement, along lines which lead to the conception of an 'enhancement of life' conceived both quantitatively and qualit-atively (i.e., in terms of both heightened vitality and greater cultivation and creativity). Nietzsche's designation of some (actual or possible) human beings as 'higher' in relation to the general run of mankind is to be understood accordingly (as in his image of the *Übermensch*, who stands as its apotheosis). I shall elaborate upon these points subsequently.

III

Since Nietzsche's 'revaluation' involves the employment of a standard of value by reference to which the value of things taken to be 'values' can be assessed, it might seem most natural to undertake a fuller discussion of what he himself has to say on the matter of value before dealing with it. I find it more illuminating, however, to reverse the order, beginning with an examination of the latter (drawing upon the above provisional sketch of his basic standard and supplementing it as needed), and then turning to a closer consideration of his own efforts to develop a theory of value when the ground has thus been cleared.

There is no better point of departure for this discussion than the following passage, in which Nietzsche sounds one of his main themes:

> Man has repeated the same mistake over and over again: he has made a means to life into a standard of life; instead of discovering the standard in the highest enhancement of life itself . . . ., he has employed the means to a quite distinct kind of life to exclude all other forms of life, in short to criticize and select life. I.e., man finally loves the means for their own sake and forgets they are means: so that they enter his consciousness as aims, as standards for aims (*WP* 354).

This process itself may be considered a kind of 'revaluation of values' which has occurred in the course of human history, and which Nietzsche's own 'revaluation' is intended both to expose and to oppose. The former represents what he often speaks of as a 'denaturalization' of values, to which his attempted 'naturalization' of values is meant to be both the countermove and the corrective. Thus he declares 'war' upon ideals and valuations reflecting adversely upon life, and cites first among his *fundamental innovations* the replacement of prevailing denaturalized values with 'purely naturalistic values' (*WP* 462). He obviously does not think that the rejection of the former will leave one empty-handed, therefore, and even goes so far as to suggest that 'if the tyranny of former values is broken in this way,' and the idea of a 'real world' beyond the world of life and change is 'abolished' once and for all, 'then a new order of values must follow of its own accord' (*WP* 461). This may be to overstate the case, but it does help to clarify Nietzsche's intentions. And it should also be clear from the passages already cited that he by no means considers the revaluation associated with the 'denaturalization' of values to be on a par with that which he undertakes and associates with their 'naturalization.' For the former is held to be both 'mistaken' and 'dangerous' in ways which the latter is evidently thought not to be. And it is owing to both sorts of defect that the valuations under revaluation here are considered to warrant criticism.

Indeed, Nietzsche's revaluation of them consists primarily in their scrutiny with an eye to both of these possible defects. This bears stressing; for the character of the revaluation is misunderstood if it is taken to consist in either sort of assessment alone. (Nor, for that matter, is it identical with their history or their 'genealogy.') He considers it possible to speak of and inquire into both the mistakenness or soundness and also the dangerousness or beneficiality of such valuations – and he further insists upon the very real possibility that these different forms of assessment may yield differing results in particular cases: 'Something might be true while being harmful and dangerous in the highest degree' (*BGE* 39). (This point is to be borne in mind in connection with his revaluation of knowledge, as well as in considering what his revaluation more generally involves attending to.)

Next, notice should be taken of a number of different sorts of questions Nietzsche holds can and should be raised with respect to existing values in connection with the project of their revaluation, which facilitate it but do not as such constitute it. It will be recalled that he refers to 'the solution of the problem of value,' and with it the revaluation establishing 'the order of rank among values,' as 'the future task of the philosophers,' for which 'all the sciences have from now on to prepare the way' (*GM* I:17n.). It is to such 'preparatory' inquiries that I here refer; and the first to be mentioned are those the relevance of which, to the ascertainment of 'the value of existing valuations,' Nietzsche cites earlier in this same passage: linguistics and etymology, and physiology and medical science. The former, he suggests, may be especially illuminating in considering 'the history of the evolution of moral concepts' (ibid.). Questions concerning the evolution of existing valuations are not, of course, exclusively philological ones; and thus historical inquiry more generally is called for as well. So he elsewhere urges philosophers to ask: 'Why is it that the sun of one fundamental moral judgment and main standard of value shines here and another one there?' (*GS* 7).

This question, however, is not a purely historical one; and a recognition of this fact is what led Nietzsche to the idea of the sort of inquiry designated in the title of the work cited previously: *On the Genealogy of Morals*. The 'genealogical' inquiry exemplified in this work draws upon historical investigation but probes more deeply, with the assistance not only of sociological and psychological but also 'physiological investigation and interpretation' (*GM* I:17). Thus he considers it imperative to ask, 'under what conditions did man devise these value judgments' (*GM* P:5); and he contends that, in order to place ourselves in a position properly to carry out a revaluation of values, 'there is needed a knowledge

351

of the conditions and circumstances in which they grew, and under which they evolved and changed' (*GM* P:6).

This 'knowledge,' however, does not for Nietzsche settle the question of 'the value of these values.' The revaluation of values only begins, and does not end, with inquiry into their genealogy. It is only on this preliminary level that he is speaking when he says: 'Whenever we encounter a morality, we also encounter valuations and an order of rank of human impulses and actions. These valuations and orders of rank are always expressions of the needs of a community and a herd' (*GS* 116). And the same holds with respect to his oft-repeated contentions to the effect that 'in valuations are expressed conditions of preservation and growth' (*WP* 507), and that the 'valuations' which underlie 'all logic' are expressions of 'physiological demands for the preservation of a certain type of life' (*BGE* 3). To trace existing valuations to the requirements of certain communities and/or types of human beings is to learn something important about them, and to arrive at an appreciation of them differing significantly from that of those who 'reverence them' and fail to recognize their 'empirical and conditional' character (*WP* 460). But it is not yet to solve 'the problem of value' and 'determine the order of rank among values.' In short, it is not yet to carry through the most important part of their revaluation. Thus Nietzsche writes:

> The inquiry into the *origin of our evaluations* and tables of good is in absolutely no way identical with a critique of them, as is so often believed: even though an insight into some *pudenda origo* certainly brings with it a *feeling* of a diminution in value of the thing that originated thus and prepares the way to a critical mood and attitude toward it (*WP* 254).

Nietzsche holds two sorts of considerations to be of primary relevance when one turns from the investigation of the 'origin' of existing valuations (their genealogy) to the more philosophical task of their 'criticism' (their revaluation). The first pertains to the soundness or tenability of the presuppositions concerning the character of reality or human nature, upon which the estimation of some 'value' and its recognition as a value fundamentally and crucially depend. It is precisely because Nietzsche holds that 'the values we have had hitherto' rest upon such presuppositions, and because these presuppositions are now coming to be seen to be untenable, that he speaks of 'the advent of *nihilism*' as 'necessary,' pending the attainment of a reorientation enabling us to arrive at 'new values' by reference to which 'we can find out what value these [old] "values" really had' (*WP* P:4). The exposure of the untenability of these presuppositions thus is suggested to have important consequences for the critical assessment of various existing values, even if it does not have the exclusive and final word in their revaluation. So Nietzsche calls for 'the purification of our opinions and evaluations' (*GS* 335) of whatever depends upon its association with 'false and mendacious interpretations.' Any 'values' which derive their status from the supposition that a certain view of the world is sound are 'devaluated' if the categories employed in that interpretation turn out to 'refer to a purely fictitious world' (*WP* 12B).

Not all values depend in this way upon the tenability of characterizations of our own nature or that of reality; but Nietzsche evidently thinks that some do, and makes much of this point. What he takes to be at stake in the case of the God-hypothesis, for example, as was observed in earlier discussion, is not only the status of morality (i.e. both the content of morality and the importance of 'being moral') insofar as it depends upon divine sanction, but also a whole range of valuations pertaining to everything from political authority and organization to the world in which we find ourselves, and to the individual and various human qualities and capacities. Thus he observes that 'the world does not have the value we thought it had,' once we cease to conceive it to be God's creation — although he goes on to remark that 'the world might be far more valuable than we used to believe' on this interpretation of it (*WP* 32). It further was seen in the previous chapter that the value attributable to human beings is profoundly affected by the rejection of the presuppositions of the notions that all human beings are created equal (and in God's image), and that all are endowed by their creator with certain inalienable rights, and an immortal soul to boot. And with respect to our institutions, the following remarks suffice to make the point:

> Consider the damage all human institutions sustain if a divine and transcendent higher sphere is postulated that must first sanction these institutions. By growing accustomed to seeing their value in this sanction . . . one has reduced their natural dignity, in certain circumstances denied it (*WP* 245).

In the case of the 'being-hypothesis,' certain conceptions of truth, goodness and beauty — conceived in terms of a correspondence to or expression of some aspect of a 'true world' of 'being' — require to be abandoned, since the fictitiousness of the latter means that an essential condition of this very possibility is lacking. And when these conceptions are abandoned, value can no longer be attributed to their supposed referents. Taken by many

353

philosophers from Socrates and Plato onward to constitute supreme values greatly exceeding the worth of anything else which might be attained or experienced in the world of human life and action, these 'values' are 'devalued'; and indeed such valuations come to take on a negative significance, because of the manner in which they divert attention from and distort appreciation of everything actual and actually attainable.

What Nietzsche calls 'the fatefulness of a belief in God' thus has its philosophical counterpart in the postulation of such a 'true world': in both cases 'all actual values were therewith denied and systematically conceived as non-values' (*WP* 245). With the repudiation of the latter hypothesis along with the former, on the other hand, 'the value feelings that hitherto have been squandered on the world of being are again set free' (*WP* 585C). The 'values' in question — the attainment of certain states conceived in terms of metaphysical notions of truth, goodness, and beauty linked to the postulation of such a world — are dethroned, and thus the way is cleared for a reorientation of human aspirations.

IV

It remains to take account of another sort of consideration, which if anything is of even greater ultimate significance for Nietzsche in connection with this revaluation. To some extent, at least, it leads in a different direction, and often prompts him to place major qualifications on the judgments he makes with respect to the value of existing values on the basis of his assessment of the tenability of their presuppositions. An indication of the character of this sort of consideration is given in a passage in which he distinguishes sharply between 'inquiry into the origin of our evaluations' and 'a critique of them,' and then goes on to ask: 'What are our evaluations and moral tables really worth?' This question, he suggests, cannot be answered *in vacuo*, but rather becomes meaningful only if it is further asked, 'in relation to what?' And he does consider this question to have an answer, transcending all others of a narrowly perspectival character. He writes: 'Answer: for life.' The 'real worth' of these evaluations is a matter of their value 'for life.' He then continues: 'But *what is life*? Here we need a new, more definite formulation of the concept "life." My formula for it is: Life is will to power' (*WP* 254).

It is thus with reference to their value for life, conceived along these lines, that Nietzsche proposes to carry his revaluation beyond presuppositional criticism. The connection between the notions of value, valuation, and will to power is complex, and will be considered at length subsequently. For the moment, it will suffice to extract only this much from his elaboration of the concept of 'life' in this way: he has in mind more than mere survival, and certainly more than that of the individual organism or person. So, for example, in the opening sections of *Beyond Good and Evil*, where he again makes the point that 'value' ultimately requires to be understood as 'value for life' (*BGE* 2), the notion of the value of something for life is glossed in terms of the extent to which 'it is life-promoting, life-preserving, species-preserving, perhaps even species-cultivating' (*BGE* 4).

Here as so often elsewhere, that in relation to which Nietzsche speaks of value thus transcends individuals and their subjective states. And he further thinks of value as attaching fundamentally not only to what *preserves* 'life' and 'species' of life but also to what *promotes* and *cultivates* them. 'Will to power,' as has earlier been seen, is for him a fundamentally *transformative* principle. This is reflected in his constant emphasis upon 'growth' and 'development,' and also in the great importance he accords to the idea of *overcoming* (as opposed to mere *enduring*) in this connection — as, for example, when he has Zarathustra say: 'And life itself confided this secret to me: "Behold," it said, "I am *that which must always overcome itself.*" ' And when he goes on to say that the will of life is thus not a 'will to life but . . . will to power,' it is clear that he intends the distinction between these two notions to be understood above all in terms of such 'overcoming' (*Z* II:12).

The same point is meant to be conveyed in his repeated references to *enhancement* as well as preservation in speaking of value, as when he writes: 'the standpoint of "value" is the standpoint of conditions of preservation and enhancement for complex forms of relative life-duration within the flux of becoming' (*WP* 715). And the possibility of a divergence between the two is never far from his mind. Thus, for example, while recognizing the important role that morality has played and continues to play in the preservation of human life, he also contends that there is a 'contradiction between "becoming more moral" and the elevation and strengthening of the type man'; and it is the latter which he takes to be the basic 'standard by which the value of moral evaluations is to be determined' (*WP* 391).

Nietzsche often speaks of 'preservation and enhancement of life' when glossing what he means by 'value for life'; but this should not be taken to indicate that he supposes the two invariably to go together, or that they are one and the same thing expressed in different words. Together they may serve to mark out the general

355

frame of reference within which value is to be understood and discussed and his revaluation of values is to be undertaken; and for certain purposes they may be considered together. But the difference between them is the basis of the crucial distinction he ultimately seeks to draw between values associated with 'abundance' and those associated with 'want' (*WP* 1009) — between genuinely 'creative' and merely 'utilitarian' modes of evaluation — and by the same token between values which are to be accorded high and low standing in terms of the 'order of rank' which he considers to apply to them as well as to 'different kinds of life' (*WP* 592).

Once one rids oneself of religious and metaphysical illusions concerning the status of values, therefore, and recovers from the nihilistic reaction to this disillusionment which denies any objectivity to all values and evaluation, the 'problem of value' reemerges, now in its proper, 'naturalistic' light. 'Life' becomes its focus; and considerations pertaining to what is and is not conducive to the 'preservation and enhancement' of life in its various actual and possible forms consequently come to the fore. These, however, are two different matters, to which Nietzsche is attentive in his earlier as well as later writings. So, for example, in *On the Use and Abuse of History*, he argues that history may be 'useful to life' (as well as harmful to it) in either of these ways, depending upon the manner in which history is appropriated. And so also, in *Dawn*, he writes, with reference to the aim of 'the preservation and furtherance of humanity,' that it makes a great deal of difference whether this is understood to mean that 'one must be concerned with the longest possible existence of mankind,' or on the other hand with 'the greatest possible dis-animalizing of mankind' (*D* 106).

Nietzsche accords primacy to a modified version of the latter notion in his subsequent attempts to revalue a wide variety of received and putative values, positive and negative. The fact that he does not collapse the two, however, but rather draws upon both ideas, is one of the reasons why his revaluation is such an untidy affair. Its basic outlines may be stated simply enough; but matters often become very complicated when some particular value is viewed in this double perspective. And they become even more complicated when it is recalled that his revaluation also involves subjecting any such 'value' to assessment in terms of the soundness of the presuppositions and associated interpretation on which it depends.

Religious, moral, and psychological 'values'

V

In turning to the various matters with which Nietzsche deals in this way, I shall first take up that which is the main subject of Nietzsche's 'First Book' of his 'Revaluation of All Values,' *The Antichrist*: Judeo-Christianity, and more generally any such other-worldly religion and faith. He repeatedly recurs to the idea that, even though the 'death of God' is at hand, 'everywhere the Christian—nihilistic value standard still has to be pulled up and fought under every mask' (*WP* 51). The 'value' which he calls 'the "Christian ideal" ' requires to be accorded a profoundly negative significance, he maintains, in that it involves the 'attempt to make the virtues through which happiness is possible for the lowliest into the standard ideal of all values' (*WP* 185). For this is a development he considers to be most detrimental to the enhancement of human life, and even to its general prospects for preservation in the long run. It represents as 'something exalted' a 'petty, peaceful mediocrity' and an 'equilibrium of a soul that knows nothing of the mighty motivation of great accumulations of strength' (*WP* 249). And, on the other hand, 'what "the true Christian" does with all that which his instinct opposes' is to subject it to a radical negative devaluation: 'he sullies and suspects the beautiful, the splendid, the rich, the proud, the self-reliant, the knowledgeable, the powerful – in summa, the whole of culture' (*WP* 250).

It is this thought which animates *The Antichrist*, in which Nietzsche proclaims that he views 'what has been revered as God, not as "godlike," but as miserable, as absurd, as harmful, not merely as an error but as a *crime against life*' (*A* 47). 'I *condemn* Christianity,' he writes, because 'the Christian church . . . has turned every value into an un-value,' with its 'subterranean conspiracy . . . against health, beauty, whatever has turned out well, courage, spirit, *graciousness* of the soul, *against life itself*' (*A* 62). He observes that there is no 'necessity in the direction of elevation, enhancement and strength' in the historical course of events (*A* 4); and it is precisely this absence of historical necessity which renders human development susceptible to influence, for better or worse, by 'ideals' both of the Christian sort and of the sort he wishes to see replace it. Christianity is to be condemned, on his view, not only because it fails to promote development in the above-mentioned direction, nor simply because it is an erroneous doctrine, but rather because – in addition to both being the case – it is fundamentally and profoundly 'decadent' in character, and

357

'corruptive' in influence, with respect to this standard. It 'has made an ideal of whatever *contradicts* the instinct of the strong life to preserve itself' (*A* 5), and in various ways hobbles and subverts 'those instincts which aim at the preservation of life and at the enhancement of its value' (*A* 7). Here, Nietzsche claims, *'value judgments* have been stood on their heads,' and 'whatever is most harmful to life is called "true"; whatever elevates it, enhances, affirms, justifies it, and makes it triumphant, is called "false" ' (*A* 9). He sums up his position in the following passage:

One should never cease from combating just this in Christianity: its will to break precisely the strongest and noblest souls. One should never rest as long as this one thing has not been utterly and completely destroyed: the ideal of man invented by Christianity, its demands upon men, its Yes and No with regard to men. The whole absurd residue of Christian fable, conceptual cobweb-spinning and theology does not concern us; it could be a thousand times more absurd and we would not lift a finger against it. But we do combat the ideal that, with its morbid beauty and feminine seductiveness, with its furtive slanderous eloquence appeals to all the cowardices and vanities of wearied souls . . . as if all that might, in such states, seem most useful and desirable — trust, guilelessness, modesty, patience, love of one's fellows, resignation, submission to God, a sort of unharnessing and abdication of one's whole ego — were also the most useful and desirable as such; as if the petty, modest abortion of a soul, the virtuous average-and-herd man . . . provided nothing less than the ideal, the goal, the measure, the highest desideratum for mankind in general. To erect *this* idea was the most sinister temptation ever placed before mankind: for with it, the most strongly constituted exceptions and fortunate cases among men, in whom the will to power and to the growth of the whole type 'man' took a step forward, were threatened with destruction; with the values of this idea, the growth of these higher men . . . would be attacked at the roots. What is it we combat in Christianity? That it wants to break the strong . . ., exploit their bad hours and their occasional weariness . . ., that it knows how to poison and sicken the noble instincts until their strength, their will to power turns backward, against itself (*WP* 252).

It is arguable that neither the humble piety nor the harsh asceticism which Nietzsche takes to be the two faces of 'the Christian ideal' is actually properly so identifiable. It must be allowed, however, that they are clearly recognizable phenomena, and that they have indeed figured prominently in the history of Christianity — and also in the history of what he takes to be the other great 'world religion,' Buddhism, as he elsewhere repeatedly observes. And so he is at least to that extent justified in speaking as though, in revaluing them, he were carrying out a revaluation of 'religious values'. They may not be the only things to have been elevated to the status of 'values' within the context of religious thought, as even he is prepared to allow. Whether or not they occupy the position of centrality in relation to others which he believes them to have, however, they may at least reasonably be considered cases in point. And his treatment of them provides one with a fairly clear indication of the kinds of considerations by reference to which he carries out his revaluation.

Nietzsche's assessment of them thus turns out to be much more cogent than some of his more vitriolic rhetoric might initially lead one to suppose. For he is by no means simply and violently ill-disposed toward Christianity (and any other religion at all similar to it). He styles himself 'antichrist,' as he also styles himself 'immoralist,' because — in contrast to those who advocate both Christianity and morality as he understands them — he takes 'life' in this world to be the sole locus of value, and its preservation, flourishing, and above all its enhancement to be ultimately decisive for determinations of value. And this provides him with strong reasons to take radical exception to the high estimation of a number of things which have come to be commonly regarded (with some justification) as what Christianity stands for.

VI

Nietzsche takes the same dim view of what he calls 'moral values.' Part of his reason for doing so is that he takes them to be genealogically linked to those considered above. A more important reason, however, is that his analysis of them reveals them to be *of the same sort* as these 'religious values,' symptomatic of the same basic deficiencies, and tending in the same general direction. A comprehensive examination of his treatment of morality will be undertaken in the next chapter. For the moment, I shall simply mention two of the 'moral values' he considers to be prime candidates for 'revaluation,' and briefly indicate what he suggests is to be made of them, anticipating the fuller discussion each will receive in due course. The two cases in point are *pity* and *selflessness*, both of which are commonly accorded high moral honors.

Each involves attending to something about *others* — in the former instance, their sufferings, in the latter, their desires and interests; and their elevation to the status of primary virtues is associated with the view that these matters take precedence over other considerations where right conduct is concerned.

As was earlier observed, Nietzsche suggests that 'for all the value that . . . the selfless may deserve,' a 'higher and more fundamental value for life might have to be ascribed to . . . selfishness' (*BGE* 2). And for this reason, he argues, the 'value' consisting in the ideal of 'self-sacrifice for one's neighbor,' and more generally 'the whole morality of self-denial' for the sake of others, requires to be 'questioned mercilessly and taken to court' (*BGE* 33). He strongly objects to the high estimation of such selflessness, even though he finds it very understandable that it should have come to be so regarded. His main contention is that the general tendency to which this value is *opposed*, and which it seeks to eliminate, is too essential to life and too crucial to its development for its suppression to be desirable. 'We think,' he says, 'that everything evil, terrible, tyrannical in man . . . serves the enhancement of the species "man" as much as its opposite does. Indeed, we do not even say enough when we say only that much' (*BGE* 44). He does not oppose the unqualified valuation of selflessness in the name of idiosyncratic self-assertion. Rather, he takes it to be detrimental to the development of certain creative human powers and capacities, the potentiality for the strengthening and unfolding of which is shared by relatively few, and is actualizable only if those happening to possess it are not induced to restrict themselves to actions agreeable to others generally. (His thinking along these lines requires elaboration; but I shall postpone further discussion of it until the following chapter.)

The other example to be considered here of a 'moral value' Nietzsche proposes to 'revalue' is 'pity' (*Mitleid*, also commonly rendered as 'sympathy' or 'compassion'). It too will be dealt with only briefly for the moment. Nietzsche contends that modern morality represents 'a veritable cult of suffering'; and that 'what is baptized as "pity" in the circles of such enthusiasts,' as the appropriate and commendable response to suffering, has come to be regarded as the epitome of moral sensitivity (*BGE* 293). He takes the contemporary high estimation of pity or compassion to be the culmination of a very widespread and longstanding preoccupation with suffering, with which pity is fundamentally linked (as the German terms *Mitleid* and *Leid* indicate). Its inescapability has long been held to constitute a powerful objection to and withering blight upon human existence. In the philosophy of Schopenhauer, however, which loomed so large in Nietzsche's thinking, this theme found what may still be its most radical expression and extensive elaboration. And the morality he proceeded to espouse may appropriately be characterized as a morality of pity, so centrally does pity figure in it.

Supposing all suffering to be both ultimately pointless and intrinsically abhorrent, Schopenhauer considered its elimination to be supremely desirable. He insisted, however, that suffering is inseparable from life, and thus that our human lot is a sorry one, even if sorrier for some than for others. Pity establishes a community of sufferers; one suffers with them (as the term *Mitleid* suggests), their sufferings thereby coming to be added to one's own. Schopenhauer's valorization of pity is clearly linked with, and indeed is a function of, his strong negative valuation of suffering.

Because he so deeply abhorred the suffering which is inseparable from life, Nietzsche observes, 'Schopenhauer was hostile to life.' And thus, he continues, 'pity became a virtue for him.' The elevation of pity to the status of a 'moral value' of prime importance, on the other hand, serves to focus attention upon that for which people are to be pitied, and so to contribute to the strength of the emphasis placed upon it in relation to other considerations. In this way, 'pity persuades men to *nothingness*,' for it fastens upon 'all that is miserable,' and 'multiplies misery' in that it 'makes suffering contagious.' So, he writes, 'Schopenhauer was consistent enough: pity negates life and renders it *more deserving of negation*.' Thus he remarks that 'pity is the *practice* of nihilism'; for it 'crosses those instincts which aim at the preservation of life and at the enhancement of its value,' encouraging us to see only suffering and feel only distress and nausea when we consider the consequences of the strengthening and expression of such 'emotions.' Nor is this all: 'Quite in general, pity crosses the law of development, which is the law of *selection*,' in that it 'conserves all that is miserable' even while lamenting its misery and condemning life therefor (*A* 7).

It is with this thought in mind that Nietzsche opens his discussion by asking, 'What is more harmful than any vice?' and answering: 'Active pity for all the failures and all the weak' (*A* 2). And the same line of thought leads him to conclude that, from the standpoint of what life involves and what is requisite if it is to flourish and to be enhanced, 'a remedy certainly seems necessary for such a pathological and dangerous accumulation of pity as is represented by the case of Schopenhauer,' and by the prevalence of the high estimation of pity for 'all that suffers' in conventional moral thinking more generally. 'To be physicians *here*,' he says, 'to be inexorable *here*, to wield the scalpel *here* — that is *our* part, that is *our* love of man, that is how *we* are philosophers' (*A* 7).

VII

A further part of Nietzsche's program of revaluing prevailing 'values' focusses upon various *feelings* or 'subjective states' which are commonly accorded considerable importance. It is generally thought to matter a great deal *how people feel*, and in particular whether they are happy or unhappy, and whether it comes about that they experience pleasure or pain. For Nietzsche, however, this way of thinking is small-minded, to say the least.

> Whether it is hedonism or pessimism, utilitarianism or eudaimonism — all these ways of thinking that measure the value of things in accordance with *pleasure* and *pain*, which are mere epiphenomena and wholly secondary, are ways of thinking that stay in the foreground and naivetés on which everyone conscious of creative powers and an artistic conscience will look down not without derision, nor without pity (*BGE* 225).

On the other hand, there are certain feelings and states of which he himself speaks very highly indeed. 'The feeling of power' is one of them; and he also cites (evidently with laudatory intent) a whole list of 'affirmative affects,' ranging from 'pride' and 'erotic love' to 'reverence' and 'gratitude toward earth and life' (*WP* 1033). It thus is necessary to take a closer look at what he has to say about the various 'subjective states' he singles out for attention, in order to understand the character of his revaluation of them, and the basis for his differing assessments of their significance.

'Happiness,' Nietzsche contends, is 'no argument' in favor of something; and 'making unhappy' is 'no counter-argument' (*BGE* 39), where either truth or value is concerned. Something might have 'value for life' without occasioning personal happiness, even when recognized to have such value by those affected, or while at the same time engendering considerable unhappiness and suffering on their part. Happiness is an independent variable in relation to 'the strengthening and elevation of the type man,' and is neither characteristic of this process nor its ultimate aim. We may desire happiness, and may occasionally attain it, and can so adjust what we do as to pursue it and increase it for a time. Neither our desire for it nor our attainment of it has any general significance, however; and the assignment of priority to its pursuit and extension is no less dangerous and misguided than is the abhorrence of

362

suffering which would seek its elimination everywhere possible. If what matters most (as Nietzsche supposes) is 'what becomes of man,' then whether individuals feel happy or unhappy will matter little — except insofar as 'what becomes of man' is affected by such feelings, and by the effects differing sorts of concern with them have upon what people do. And in this light the importance of our present happiness, and especially the happiness of the greatest number, appears as very problematical indeed; for in *that* direction lies stultifying ministration to the 'creaturely' in man, rather than the selection and cultivation of 'creative powers,' which is a hard and painful process. So Zarathustra is made to urge that one ask 'What matters my happiness?' and recognize that it is nothing which could 'justify existence itself' (Z P:3).

Nietzsche regards all 'ways of thinking,' which ultimately come down to the assignment of values to things 'in accordance with pleasure and pain,' as reflections of mediocrity and weakness. When 'no ultimate meaning is posited except the appearance of pleasure or displeasure,' he observes, 'that is how a kind of man speaks that no longer dares to posit a will, a purpose, a meaning: for any healthier kind of man the value of life is certainly not to be measured by the standard of these trifles' (WP 35). In short, 'pleasure and displeasure' are 'value judgments of the second rank' (WP 701). Their adoption as the fundamental standard of evaluation is to be 'looked down upon' with 'derision' owing to the marginal vitality and insensitivity to creativity it reflects (BGE 225); and a concern with such reactive phenomena is indicative of weakness on the part of those who posit them as primary values, in that they thereby show themselves to lack the capacity to operate on any higher and more demanding level.

The most fundamental point Nietzsche seeks to make in this connection, however, is to be found in his suggestion that such states as pleasure and pain are 'mere epiphenomena and wholly secondary,' in relation to something else of a very different nature — as he takes all 'value feelings' to be. 'Can one think of a madder extravagance of vanity,' he asks, than 'to measure whether existence has value according to the pleasant or unpleasant feelings aroused in this consciousness? For it is only a means!' (WP 674). They are 'accidentals, not causes,' in that they are 'derived from a ruling value — "useful," "harmful," speaking in the form of feelings, and consequently absolutely sketchy and dependent' (WP 701). He does not deny the meaningfulness of considering whether some action will be attended by these or other such 'value feelings.' 'Obviously value feelings accompany it,' he writes; 'but does the value of an action lie in its subjective epiphenomena?' (WP 291).

He considers this to be out of the question, remarking: 'the "conscious world" cannot serve as the starting point for values'; and he goes on to suggest that we consequently are faced with a 'need for an *"objective"* positing of values' which does not make reference to it (*WP* 707). He indicates the direction in which he looks to meet this need when he writes: 'What is the objective measure of value? Solely the quantum of enhanced and organized power' (*WP* 674). What he has in mind here requires to be gone into in more detail, and will receive extended discussion subsequently. If this idea can be made out and is adopted, however, it follows that any value attaching to such phenomena as pleasure and pain is indeed secondary and derivative. 'The enhancement of power' is held to be 'the aim' — although Nietzsche does go on to say that 'in this enhancement the utility of consciousness is included; the same applies to pleasure and displeasure' (*WP* 711).

Phenomena of the latter sort thus are held to be of value only insofar as they betoken 'usefulness' and 'harmfulness,' which here register 'in the form of feelings' — and moreover, only insofar as the latter have not been rendered inappropriate by changing conditions and forms of life. Indeed, they further matter only to the extent that these feelings come to be *more* than mere feelings, making a difference in the conduct of life that is conducive to such enhancement rather than remaining mere experiences. Nietzsche's characterizations of them as generally 'epiphenomenal' suggests that he believes this last condition to be met much less often than one might suppose. They must be given their due: they have some significance in the general 'economy of life,' owing to their utility in relation to the establishment and maintenance of the 'healthy consolidated mediocrity' upon which Nietzsche takes all 'higher culture' to depend (*WP* 864). But it is only as 'means' in this context that these 'values' are actually of value; their value is only instrumental, and is indirect and rather marginal at that. It pales in comparison with that of factors contributing more directly and strongly to the enhancement of life, of which the 'higher humanity' finding expression in such 'higher culture' is the issue.

The overestimation of the importance of these phenomena not only represents an error, but moreover itself can be detrimental to the enhancement of life; and in this way they can actually come to have a negative value in this perspective of evaluation. The feelings of pleasure and pain and the experiences of happiness and unhappiness we have may be mere 'subjective epiphenomena' which as such are 'accidentals, not causes.' Our estimation of them, however, can endow them with greater weight. So Nietzsche observes that 'our opinions, valuations, and tables of what is good

364

certainly belong among the most powerful levers in the involved mechanism of our actions' (GS 335). And when these feelings are accorded an exaggerated importance, they may come to disrupt the general 'economy of life,' and more specifically to displace other concerns in the instance of potentially exceptional human beings. They thus may impede the strengthening and cultivation of 'truly active affects' in the latter (without which there can be no enhancement of life), with results no less unfortunate than when the sorts of religious or moral values considered previously achieve general sway. This is one of the greatest dangers Nietzsche discerns as he looks not only back but ahead, beyond the 'death of God' and the nihilistic reaction to it. And the strong language he uses is indicative of how real and how serious he considers this danger to be.

Nietzsche accords very different and much more favorable treatment to the 'feeling of power' — and also to the 'joy' which stands to this feeling as contentment stands to pleasure and the absence of pain. At first glance it might seem odd, in view of Nietzsche's relegation of feelings generally to the status of mere 'subjective epiphenomena' which 'cannot serve as a starting point for values,' that he should accord the significance he does to this feeling. For if it is allowed that 'the objective measure of value' is 'solely the quantum of enhanced and organized power' (WP 674), his very insistence upon the 'need for an "*objective*" positing of values' (WP 707) would seem to render inappropriate his inclusion of reference to 'the feeling of power' (along with 'power itself') when, for example, he asks 'What is good?' and answers: 'Everything that heightens the feeling of power in man, the will to power, power itself' (A 2). Yet this is what he does, linking the former closely to the latter even if not collapsing the distinction between them. 'Whether benefiting or hurting others involves sacrifices for us does not affect the ultimate values of our actions,' he writes, then going on to remark that 'even if we offer our lives . . ., this is a sacrifice that is offered for *our* desire for power or for the purpose of preserving our feeling of power' (GS 13). And he refers to both as 'expedient, species-preserving, and indispensable' in relation to the flourishing or our 'species' to the highest degree, thus contending that both are of greater 'ultimate value' than any immediate impact they may have upon our own or others' happiness and well-being (GS 4).

The solution to this apparent problem is to be found in Nietzsche's construal of feelings of this sort as 'means' in the service of life as well as 'expressions' of underlying processes and conditions. Considered merely as subjective epiphenomena which may reflect and may also exaggerate what is actually the case, feelings of power no more add to the 'quanta of enhanced and organized power' of those having such feelings than does a 'will to power' on their part, regarded simply as a standing disposition. But a disposition of this sort obviously may make a significant contribution to the growth of 'power itself,' by prompting a search for strategies and the adoption of corresponding courses of action resulting in an 'accumulation of strength' and a marshaling of resources thus accumulated. Indeed, so indispensable does Nietzsche suppose this disposition to be in this connection that he takes the attainment of power generally to be inseparable from it, and to be comprehensible only by reference to it.

It is for this reason that he brackets the two together in passages like those cited above. And it is for similar reasons that he includes 'the feeling of power' along with them. The feeling of power may not be an entirely reliable indicator of the possession of power, but if it is at least frequently an even partially adequate reflection of the latter, it is of no little value in relation to the increase of 'power itself,' in the case of creatures like ourselves in whom the 'will to power' is whetted by what we feel with respect to the things we do. The value of such feelings resides not in the feelings themselves (any more than does that of feelings of pleasure and pain) but rather in their instrumental value for life, and more specifically for the heightening of power which the enhancement of life essentially involves. They are virtually indispensable if our 'will to power' is to be able to get its proper bearing, and issue in this result.

On the other hand, such feelings *may* for Nietzsche take on a negative significance, if they are mere illusions of power, the cultivation of which is given precedence over its actual enhancement to the detriment of the latter. This is something he considers to have happened time and again throughout the history of both religion and philosophy, it may be noted, sometimes with the excuse of weakness, and in other instances as great and lamentable folly. He discerns a 'will to power' in them as well as in other domains of human endeavor, even though in them it takes more rarefied forms than it does elsewhere. And in metaphysical thought and religious belief he sees the elaboration of stances in relation to reality which afford those who adopt them feelings of power far surpassing any they might attain in the world of action. Spurious though these feelings may be, however, and notwithstanding the negative significance attaching to their preference to the actual attainment of more mundane but substantial forms of power, their evident attraction provides a further instance and confirmation of

Nietzsche's point concerning the significance of feelings of power as a factor in the direction of human life.

The affects, art, and truth revalued

VIII

If in this revaluation Nietzsche thus accords a significantly different and higher value to feelings of power than that commonly attributed to them, his treatment of a broad range of human drives and impulses departs even more radically from the customary estimation of them. The most important case in point is that general disposition which he takes to be fundamental to all of them: the 'will to power' itself (here understood in psychological terms). From what has already been said, it will be obvious that his revaluation of it involves what amounts to a complete inversion of the long-standing assessment of it as utterly deplorable. It is above all with a view to effecting a critique and reversal of this assessment of it that his efforts are directed in *Beyond Good and Evil* and in many of his other later writings.

His main argument is stated simply enough. Life, as he construes it, *is* 'will to power' in various forms — an array of processes all of which are 'developments and ramifications' of this basic tendency; and there is nothing external to it by reference to which its value might be measured or its character weighed and found wanting. In the last analysis, value can only be 'value for life,' and can only be understood in terms of what life essentially involves. The sole 'objective' standard of value recognizes only 'quanta of enhanced and organized power,' and assesses them exclusively in terms of the extent and manner of their enhancement and organization. 'Will to power' generally is precisely the fundamental disposition to such enhancement and organization, and is the basic condition of their possibility. As a constitutive principle it is the ultimate basis of all value; while as a fundamental psychological trait it is of unsurpassable instrumental value. It is only owing to their derivation from and manifestation of it that the various more specific functions, drives and processes that may be distinguished from it in its more overt forms may also be considered to be of value. And this holds for those which are generally despised no less than for those which are usually prized.

Nietzsche by no means wishes to suggest that the value of any human tendency is a function of the extent to which it approximates to the lust to overpower and either dominate or destroy (which is commonly enough to be observed in human life, and is with good reason condemned). He does contend, however, that 'the good and revered things' in the name of which such judgment is usually passed are 'insidiously related, tied to, and involved with' such 'wicked, seemingly opposite things – maybe even one with them in essence.' And he further argues that 'a higher and more fundamental value for life might have to be ascribed' to the latter than to the former, and certainly a far greater one than the representation of them as unmitigated evils allows for (*BGE* 2).

It is of great importance to observe that Nietzsche's basically positive evaluation of various putatively evil tendencies is by no means unqualified. (This will become clear shortly.) He considers them to have been so long and so greatly maligned, however, that as a corrective measure they require to be acclaimed and affirmed, before the necessary reservations are entered. The prevailing over-whelmingly negative valuation of them is blind to the kind of consideration he takes to be decisive, of 'value for life' not merely where the preservation and interests of the individual or the majority of people or society are concerned, but rather in the broader setting of the flourishing and enhancement of 'the type man.' When priority is given to the social or moral or religious 'values,' however, or where pleasure and pain or the well-being and happiness of each (or even of all) is taken to be of primary importance, then such 'strong drives' as 'an enterprising spirit, foolhardiness, vengefulness, craftiness, rapacity, and the lust to rule' are 'experienced as dangerous' and so 'abandoned to slander' (*BGE* 201).

Nietzsche concedes the 'dangerousness' of the latter, especially in relation to such commonplace concerns. He nonetheless seeks to rescue them from slander; for he rejects the assignment of primacy to these concerns. He holds that an understanding of the actual character of 'life' and what its flourishing and enhancement involve and require, in conjunction with the 'naturalization' of criteria of evaluation along these lines which alone can supply it with an 'objective' basis, reveals them not only to be dangerous (often leaving suffering, destruction and disorder in their wake) but also indispensable and even commendable. Thus he contends that 'in truth,' our supposedly 'evil instincts are expedient, species-preserving, and indispensable to as high a degree as the [supposedly] good ones; their function is merely different' (*GS* 4). And with the enhancement as well as the preservation of life in mind, he likewise speaks of the 'greater biological value' of 'the truly *active* affects, such as lust for power, avarice, and the like' (in contrast to that of all merely 'reactive affects'), owing to which they are more deserving to be 'esteemed' (*GM* II:11).

Nietzsche considers it imperative 'to give men back the courage to their natural drives' (WP 124); for their negation or repression runs counter to such enhancement, and further weakens and so imperils the life supposedly protected thereby. Thus he has Zarathustra 'place the three most evil things on the scales and weigh them humanly well,' and maintain that they deserve to be 'blessed' even though 'these three have so far been best cursed and worst reputed and lied about': namely, 'sex, the lust to rule, selfishness.' For these provide the 'compulsion' at work in the origin of everything 'higher,' and are 'what bids even the highest grow still higher' (Z III:10). They are prime examples of what Nietzsche has in mind when he writes: 'My insight: all the forces and drives by virtue of which life and growth exist lie under the ban of morality,' which must be lifted 'if one is to liberate life' (WP 343).

His estimation of them, however, is not unqualifiedly positive; and he would by no means have the 'liberation of life' of which he speaks to be understood merely in the sense of a regressive unleashing of these drives. Thus he is very nearly as disdainful and disapproving of any such 'letting go' as he is of the crude and harmful strategy of repression directed against them. He may champion the idea of 'Homo natura,' of the 'translation of man back into nature' (BGE 230), and of a 'restoration of nature: moraline-free' (WP 401); but the last thing he has in mind is a reversion to the level of the 'beast of prey,' our transcendence of which is something for which he expresses gratitude to morality and other such constraints. He writes: 'I too speak of a "return to nature," although it is really not a going back but an ascent' (TI IX:48). One misunderstands him completely if one fails to appreciate this point. So also he maintains that 'blind indulgence of an affect is the cause of the greatest evils' — and here he is not using the term 'evils' merely in a conventional moralistic or herd-social sense (WP 928).

'Greatness of character,' as he conceives it, 'does not consist in not possessing these affects — on the contrary, one possesses them to the highest degree — but in having them under control' (ibid.). Control of them is taken by Nietzsche to be crucial to their evaluation, and matters on his way of thinking no less than does their strengthening. 'The affects are one and all useful,' he remarks; but 'in regard to utility it is quite impossible to fix any scale of values' by reference to which one could decide which has the greatest 'value for life' — except in quantitative terms, and by reference to the potentiality they thus represent for deployment: 'The most one could say is that the most powerful affects are the

most valuable, in as much as there are no greater sources of strength'
(*WP* 931). They are *sources of strength*, and as such enormously
important; but how such strength is used is crucial. Thus in a
note entitled 'Standard,' Nietzsche writes: 'The greater and more
terrible the passions are that an age, a people, an individual can
permit themselves, because they are capable of employing them as
means, the higher stands their culture' (*WP* 1025). 'Higher culture'
is the qualitative attainment in relation to which this quantitative
factor takes on significance, as the most fundamental condition of
its possibility, and as an indispensable means to it.

It is in this context that Nietzsche is to be understood when he
contends that 'from a superior point of view one desires . . . the
growing emancipation of man from the narrow and fear-ridden
bonds of morality, the increase of force, in order to press the
mightiest natural powers — the affects — into service' (*WP* 386).
So he had earlier written, in the concluding section of *The
Wanderer and His Shadow* (which sheds considerable light on his
general intentions and position in his revaluation of the 'values'
under consideration):

> Many chains have been placed upon man, that he might unlearn
> behaving as an animal; and in point of fact he has become
> milder, more spiritual, more joyful, and more circumspect than
> any animal. But now he still suffers from having borne his
> chains so long. . . . It is only when the chain-sickness is over-
> come that the first great goal is entirely attained: the separation
> of man from the animals. — Now we stand in the middle of our
> work, of removing these chains, and in doing so must take the
> greatest care. *Only the ennobled man may be given freedom of
> spirit* (*WS* 350).

While Nietzsche attributes great value to a variety of drives the
more immediate and uncontrolled expressions of which are often
destructive and seemingly far removed from any sort of 'higher
humanity,' therefore, he does not do so because he supposes the
enhancement of life to be furthered by such actions, or because he
relishes their consequences. Rather, he does so because he takes
these drives to be so fundamental to life that honesty and consistency require one who regards it affirmatively to affirm them
along with it; because he considers their strengthening or weakening
to be that which the raising or lowering of the basic vitality on
which all else depends ultimately comes down to; and because he
believes them to constitute the resources through the sublimation
of which all creativity and all qualitative enhancement of life alone
are possible. In their more basic forms they do indeed constitute

dangers which require to be dealt with; but this is not the way to deal with them.

> All passions have a phase when they are merely disastrous, when they drag down their victims with the weight of their stupidity — and a later, very much later phase when they wed the spirit, when they 'spiritualize' themselves. Formerly, in view of the element of stupidity in passion, war was declared on passion itself, its destruction was plotted. . . . *Destroying* the passions and cravings, merely as a preventive measure against their stupidity and the unpleasant consequences of this stupidity — today this itself strikes us as merely another acute form of stupidity (*TI* V:1).

Nietzsche takes what he calls the 'spiritualization of passion' to be the healthier and wiser alternative course, which avoids both sorts of 'stupidity,' and is life-affirming and -enhancing rather than hostile and harmful to it. As long as they are strong, however, our drives remain potentially dangerous; and the consequences of their expression in action may be distressing for many in various ways, not only when they are uncontrolled but also when they are channeled into certain 'higher' and more creative forms of action. But Nietzsche contends that this is a circumstance which simply must be faced. The value attaching to the vitality and creativity of flourishing and ascending life and to the development of higher culture requires one to accord a correspondingly high (though instrumental) value to these drives and their strengthening, upon which the former draw and depend. Thus Zarathustra is made to say, to an imagined audience of 'higher men':

> Once you suffered passions and called them evil. But now you have only your virtues left: they grew out of your passions.
> . . . Once you had wild dogs in your cellar, but in the end they turned into birds and lovely singers. . . .
> And nothing evil grows out of you henceforth, unless it be the evil that grows out of the fight among your virtues (Z I:5).

IX

The metamorphosis of these 'wild dogs' of the cellar of man's animality into 'birds and lovely singers' of the air of man's attainable higher humanity would seem to have no more paradigmatic exemplification for Nietzsche than the sublimation of basic drives which issues in *art*. One might suppose, therefore, that he must regard art as a primary locus of realized value. In fact, however, he rejects this estimation of art, terming 'art for art's sake' a 'dangerous principle' on a par with the assignment of 'ultimate value' to morality. Art no less than morality requires revaluation, and like the latter is held to have value only as a *'means,'* and only insofar as it serves 'the aim of enhancing life' (*WP* 298). His reassessment of art is one of the instances of his revaluation of values to which he devotes the most attention and attaches the greatest importance. Although his views concerning art will be considered at length in a later chapter, therefore, his revaluation of it requires to be discussed briefly here.

'Every art,' Nietzsche maintains, 'may be viewed as a remedy and an aid in the service of growing and struggling life' (*GS* 382). It performs this service in various specific ways; and he takes it to be a matter of great importance to identify and distinguish them, for this has important evaluative consequences where different sorts of art are concerned. At its best, on his general view of it, he holds that 'art is the great stimulus to life' — and so, he asks, 'how could one understand it as purposeless, as aimless, as *l'art pour l'art*?' (*TI* IX:24). Its roots in human nature and life are much deeper than the advocates of *l'art pour l'art* suppose. And far from being essentially purposeless and detached from life more generally, it is 'sublimely expedient' in relation to life, even if transcending the plane of the sort of immediately purposive activities which make up much of ordinary existence. Its value thus does not reside principally in its serving as a source of 'disinterested pleasure,' but rather derives above all from its life-promoting powers.

With this in mind, Nietzsche dismisses the idea that the value of art is a function of its cognitive import. Its value for life is not a matter of any sorts of truths it conveys, for he holds that it by and large conveys no such truths. Rather, as he likes to say in his more provocative moments, it 'lies' and 'deceives'; or, somewhat more moderately put, it is the 'cult of appearance,' and deals in 'illusions.' Its 'value for life' *is* in a sense a function of its relation to truth — but it is an *inverse* function. 'Truth is ugly,' he writes. 'We possess *art* lest we *perish of the truth*' (*WP* 822). There is more to be said with respect to its value than this; but this, for Nietzsche, is among the first things to be said about it, and he says it repeatedly. When he looks beyond the function art is capable of performing (in the service of life) rendering life endurable (where strength sufficient to confront 'the truth' about ourselves and the world is wanting), he conceives its further significance and value in terms of its non-cognitive, *creative* character. It is as the expression and development of 'creative powers' that he considers art to be of the highest value.

'Creation' is at the center of a cluster of notions – affirmation, overcoming, higher humanity and *Übermensch*, and value – around which Nietzsche's *Zarathustra* revolves. 'Creation,' he has Zarathustra say: 'that is the great redemption from suffering, and life's growing light' (Z II:2). 'He who creates,' Zarathustra proclaims, 'creates man's goal and gives the earth its meaning and its future' (Z III:12:2). Life is 'that which must always overcome itself' (Z II:12), and it does so through creation. Creators render things valuable through their creative transformations, and thereby 'write new values on new tablets' (Z P:9). 'Change of values – that is a change of creators' (Z I:15). Higher men are such creators; they are 'higher' by virtue of their creativity, not owing to their exceptional vitality and strength alone. And the *Übermensch*, who is 'the meaning of the earth,' is the personification of creativity (Z P:3).

In art, Nietzsche sees all of this intimated, anticipated, and at least partially instantiated – but only partially, not universally or uniformly, and somewhat questionably, too, in that art tends to become separated from the rest of life to the detriment of both. Thus while he later observed that in *The Birth of Tragedy* he had given expression to the 'knowledge' and 'experience' of the fundamental fact that 'art is *worth more* than truth' (*WP* 853), he also came to recognize and insist upon the further point that 'life' is worth more than art. But to the extent that art involves the development of man's 'creative powers,' promotes their strengthening and cultivation, expands the range of possibilities for their expression, and in doing so not only 'embellishes' and 'glorifies' life but also enhances it, its value is very great indeed – greater by far than the very marginal value it may have in so far as it serves as an immediate and temporary remedy for various forms of distress associated with spiritual poverty and weakness (a need to be tranquilized or relaxed, or to be stimulated or excited, or to be entertained or amused).

Of the several types of art Nietzsche distinguishes which operate 'in the service of life' in more positive and important ways, one is linked much more closely to *need* (if not 'impoverishment') than to the 'overfullness' which finds expression in the other. It is this need which he has in mind in saying, for example, that 'we possess *art* lest we *perish of the* truth' (*WP* 822). Such art is transfigurative and celebrative of 'appearance' out of a '*need* of the cult of surfaces' as a means of avoiding the 'disastrous results' of 'reaching *beneath* them,' and owes its existence to an ability to 'find enjoyment in life only in the intention of *falsifying* its image' (*BGE* 59). It is thus to be contrasted with art which transfigures and delights in appearance out of no such need, but rather out of overflowing strength and the associated gratitude for and glorification of life Nietzsche takes to characterize 'all of *great* art' (*CW* Epilogue). The former sort of art may be of value insofar as it is life-sustaining; but its value is held to be subject to serious qualification, in that it may lead to a negation rather than an affirmation of life, and work to its detriment rather than serve 'the aim of enhancing life.' For 'if one severs an ideal from reality one debases the real, one impoverishes it, one defames it' (*WP* 298).

Nietzsche does not take the value of the latter sort of art to require to be qualified in this respect, but he nonetheless considers it too ultimately to be limited, in that 'the artist hitherto, as a perfecter on a small scale, working on material,' merely anticipates in a restricted domain and preliminary manner a 'higher concept of art' (*WP* 795). Here 'creative powers' and an 'artistic conscience' are conceived as being brought to bear upon human life and the world more generally insofar as they admit of transformation at our hands, rather than merely upon the media and material of which artists typically avail themselves. Art as the production of 'works of art' thus gives way to what Nietzsche calls 'the great conception of man, that man becomes the transfigurer of existence when he learns to transfigure himself' (*WP* 820). Insofar as art shows the way to this higher, healthier and richer humanity, however, the contribution it makes to the enhancement of life is unsurpassed by any of the other 'means' to which Nietzsche directs his attention. To the extent that it has this character and effect, its value not only survives his revaluation but is exalted. (In the final chapter certain of these points will be developed and examined in greater detail.)

X

Since Nietzsche has been seen to attribute a certain (lesser but still considerable) value to art insofar as it serves as an antidote to 'truths' the full glare of which would be unbearable, it will be obvious that the value of *truth* (or knowledge) emerges from his revaluation greatly diminished; and if 'art is *worth more* than truth,' this certainly constitutes a major change in the customary rank-ordering of values. It should by no means be supposed, however, that he takes as dim a view of truth and knowledge generally as he does of the various moral and religious 'values' he singles out for attention, or even that he assesses all truths and forms of knowledge in the same way. There is perhaps no 'value' toward which he is more ambivalent, or at any rate with respect to which his revaluation yields a more complex and variously qualified conclusion; and there is none concerning which it is more important to arrive at an appropriate assessment. One of Nietzsche's central concerns in his early writings was with the question of the extent to which knowledge might turn out to be a dangerous thing, and even seriously harmful or fatal to creatures like ourselves, while illusion and error might be needful and beneficial. He took the Enlightenment faith that knowledge and human well-being go hand in hand, and that any increase in knowledge must be a boon for mankind, to require to be reconsidered, and to be problematical at best. (This may well have been owing at least initially and in part to the early impact of Schopenhauer upon him. Schopenhauer had argued, and apparently convinced the young Nietzsche, that a clear knowledge of the general character of life in this world and of the individual's lot in it would lead any reasonable person to abhor it and seek release from it; and that only the blindness and illusion which nature cunningly fosters in us renders us willing grist for the mill.)

Thus, for example, in his early *On Truth and Lie*, Nietzsche undertakes an 'extra-moral' reflection upon these matters, questioning the assignation of negative value to all 'lies,' errors and fictions, and of positive value only to 'truth,' and proceeding to suggest that the former are not only unavoidable but useful and indeed indispensable in our relations both to the world and with each other. And in *The Birth of Tragedy* he likewise maintains that the 'knowledge gained' when one has 'once looked truly into the essence of things' results in 'nausea,' which 'inhibits' and 'kills action,' since one 'sees everywhere only the horror or absurdity of existence' (*BT* 7). This reassessment of knowledge was carried on in his subsequent essay *On the Use and Abuse of History*, and more specifically with its utility and disutility 'for life.' Historical knowledge, he argues, may be either conducive or detrimental to the flourishing and development of life; and it is in these terms that he there suggests this or any other sort of human endeavor should be measured. Thus he urges that one learn 'to pursue history for the purpose of life!' (*UAH* p. 253: page references locating citations from this work are to pages in part III, vol. 1 of the *Kritische Gesamtausgabe*); and although it is often 'triumphantly proclaimed that "science is now beginning to rule life",' he contends that 'life ruled in this manner is not worth much,' and is of doubtful future promise (*UAH* p. 294).

As Nietzsche later recognized, that with which he had actually been grappling from the outset was '*the problem of science* itself,' and indeed of all rigorous cognitive endeavor. The 'problem' here indicated is that of the significance to be accorded to such endeavor and its results (*BT* S-C:2). This concern was one of the origins of his subsequently explicitly attempted 'revaluation'; thus he remarks that '*The Birth of Tragedy* was my first revaluation of all values' (*TI* X:5). Throughout his subsequent writings, Nietzsche continued to stress that it is the height of naiveté and folly to suppose the actual value of this 'value' to be unproblematic and unqualified, and to deny value (or attribute negative value) to all beliefs and aspects of our experience which are found to be at variance with it. For if certain of the latter turn out to be among the conditions of the preservation and enhancement of life, while the former and exclusive devotion to its pursuit tend to endanger and obstruct them, something approaching an inversion of their respective customary valuations is required by the adoption of 'value for life' as the basic standard of evaluation.

This in fact is Nietzsche's general view of the matter. '*We have need of lies,*' he later saw himself as having maintained in *The Birth of Tragedy*, 'in order to live' (*WP* 853). And he continued to regard this as being the case. It must be allowed, he argues, that 'truth is ugly' at least as often as not (*WP* 822). Moreover, he contends that it must be admitted that 'there would be no life at all if not on the basis of perspective estimates and appearances' (*BGE* 34), and realized that 'delusion and error are conditions of human knowledge and sensation' (*GS* 107). Thus he suggests that 'for all the value that the true . . . may deserve,' it would seem that 'a higher and more fundamental value for life' attaches to 'appearance' (*BGE* 2). And this being the case, he maintains that 'it is no more than a moral prejudice that truth is worth more than mere appearance' (*BGE* 34). Indeed, he considers the likelihood of 'disastrous results' — if one should 'get ahold of the truth *too soon*, before [one] has become strong enough, hard enough, artist enough' (*BGE* 59) — to require the attribution of value to 'ideas by which one could live better, that is to say, more vigorously and cheerfully' (*BGE* 10), independently of their veracity. In short, he writes:

> we are fundamentally inclined to claim that the falsest judgments . . . are those most indispensable for us . . . — that renouncing false judgments would mean renouncing life and a denial of life. To recognize untruth as a condition of life — that certainly means resisting accustomed value feelings in a dangerous way (*BGE* 4).

Nietzsche here has in mind (among other things) the interpretive judgments of natural science, the formal propositions of mathematics, Kant's synthetic *a priori* judgments, the 'immediate certainties' upon which other philosophers have sought to build, the notion of persisting substances, and the principles of logic and the categories of reason generally. While these are commonly taken to be fundamental 'truths,' they are on his view only more or less useful or practically indispensable falsehoods. As was earlier seen, he considers them all to involve artificial and distorting simplifications and erroneous schematizations of the actual character of life and the world. They are merely instances of 'the kind of error without which a certain species of life could not live'; and he adds that, here as elsewhere, 'the value for *life* is ultimately decisive' (*WP* 493). But precisely because he takes 'the value for life' to *be* decisive, in assessing them as features of our thought which have become 'part of the conditions of [our] existence' (*WP* 496), he by no means intends their 'erroneousness' to warrant their repudiation and negative evaluation. On the contrary, he is prepared to accord them a very considerable general value — and indeed a greater value than that which a more accurate apprehension of reality and our existence would have, at least in most contexts. But it is *as useful* (though 'erroneous') *means of life*, relative to the needs and limitations of a certain form of life, that they are to be accorded such value — and not, as philosophers and others long have supposed, as genuine truths the possession of which is of value for its own sake.

This indeed constitutes a 'revaluation' of the 'value' in which the attainment of such putative 'knowledge' has commonly been taken to consist. But it is not a radical *devaluation* of the kinds of notions and judgments indicated. If it is part of Nietzsche's purpose to expose and consider the harmful effects of the error involved in taking such 'expedient falsifications' to be ultimate truths, it is also part of it to combat the 'moral' prejudice which casts aspersions upon all deception and falsification, and therefore stands in the way of the attainment of a proper appreciation of the value of these forms of them. He writes: 'I keep in reserve at least a couple of jostles for the blind rage with which the philosophers resist being deceived. Why *not*?' For, as he goes on to ask, 'Why couldn't the world *that concerns us* — be a fiction?' (*BGE* 34). If it is the case that we for the most part do better to think and act in terms of the 'perspective estimates and appearances' which structure this world of ordinary experience, then carrying the demand for truth and truthfulness to the point of disdaining them would be worse than pointless.

Science, Nietzsche suggests, tends in this direction; and it is for this reason that he considers it to be covertly in league with life-endangering asceticism. Thus he says: 'No! Don't come to me with science when I ask for the natural antagonist to the ascetic ideal'; that, on his view, is art (*GM* III:25). Yet he contends that scientific thinking also has a positive 'value for life.' It takes account of certain actual features of the world with which we must deal, and facilitates our dealings with it, enabling us not only to preserve ourselves in it but also to achieve a degree of control and mastery of it. As a 'means' thus employable in the service of 'life,' it is to be accorded a value which, while instrumental rather than intrinsic, is nonetheless considerable. And so, despite its superficiality, narrowness, and susceptibility to being given an ascetic turn, it may be seen amply to satisfy Nietzsche's stricture that, 'if the morality of "thou shalt not lie" is rejected, the "sense for truth" will have to legitimize itself before another tribunal: — as a means of the preservation of man, as *will to power*' (*WP* 495).

The same sort of mixed verdict is reached by Nietzsche where that fuller and more adequate sort of comprehension of ourselves and the world is concerned which he takes to supplement such cognition (and to be at least in some measure achieved in his own account of reality). On the one hand, he repeatedly insists upon the hazardousness of insights into the actual nature of things, and that those capable of living (let alone living 'joyfully') with such knowledge are and always will be few. On the other, however, he is a strong partisan of 'truthfulness.' He terms 'honesty' in all intellectual matters 'our virtue from which we cannot get away, we free spirits,' going on to say: 'Well, let us work on it with all our malice and love and not weary of "perfecting" ourselves in *our* virtue, the only one left us' (*BGE* 227). And he roundly rejects the view (sometimes attributed to *him*) that 'it does not matter whether a thing is true, but only what effect it produces,' saying that this reflects an 'absolute lack of intellectual integrity' (*WP* 172). The effects produced by the adoption of an interpretation do indeed matter, on his view, and are accorded great weight in his revaluation; but as this passage shows, he holds that there are *some* special contexts in which it *does* 'matter whether a thing is true,' and where its truth is not to be conceived merely as a function of the 'effect it produces.' At least in those among whom 'honesty' is a 'virtue' and an acute and lively 'intellectual conscience' has come to exist, 'whether a thing is true' will figure importantly in the 'effect it produces'; and this effect may well be very different from that which does or would obtain in the case of others having no such scruples.

The later Nietzsche cannot be said to have sustained the enthusiasm for knowledge he expresses in some of his relatively early writings, as when he asserts that, where 'the knowledge of truth' is concerned, 'no sacrifice is too great' (*D* 45). But he continued to associate the attainment of knowledge with the 'elevation of man' and the enhancement of life, even while also underscoring the dangerousness of its attainment in this same perspective of evaluation. This is not only because he holds that 'the impulse for truth' has become 'a piece of life,' and 'a life-preserving power' at that, in conflict with our old 'life-preserving errors.' For the question now is: 'To what extent can truth endure incorporation?' (*GS* 110). And his interest extends beyond the question of the extent to which such knowledge may facilitate the preservation and enhancement of human life, to that of the possibility of an enhanced form of life the very character of which itself is to be conceived (in part at least) precisely in terms of its attainment. He does consider the 'unconditional will to truth,' and the associated conviction that 'in relation to it everything else has only second-rate value,' to be manifestations of a categorical 'moral' imperative not to deceive which, in addition to being 'quixotic,' is 'a principle that is hostile to life and destructive' (*GS* 344). But he regards a less consuming concern with truth, modified in the nature of its demands and expectations, and complemented by the development and expression of 'creative powers,' as an important feature of the sort of life he terms 'higher,' attesting to both the 'greater strength' and the 'spiritual superiority' which characterize it.

Thus Nietzsche takes the ability to apprehend and endure 'the "truth" ' to be something in terms of which 'the strength of a spirit should be measured' (*BGE* 39). He likewise conceives of 'the most spiritual men' as lovers of 'knowledge,' to whom 'difficult tasks are a privilege' — that of the attainment of knowledge and the associated 'self-conquest' and self-overcoming most of all (*A* 57). And he has Zarathustra proclaim: 'With knowledge, the body purifies itself; making experiments with knowledge, it elevates itself; in the lover of knowledge all instincts become holy; in the elevated, the soul becomes gay' (*Z* I:22:2). The attainment of a penetrating comprehension of ourselves and the character of reality is not all that Nietzsche takes to matter, either in philosophy or in life more generally. But he does take it to matter, not only as a means to the preservation and enhancement of life (which it may also threaten), but also as partially constitutive of enhanced life. He considers it to be intimately linked — even if not identical — with the strength and also the creativity of which he makes so much in this connection. To this extent and for this reason, however, it is a consequence of Nietzsche's revaluation that it is to be accorded a very high value indeed.

379

Human beings and their value

XI

The final instance of Nietzsche's revaluation I shall consider, which lies at the very heart of his concerns, has as its object something quite different from any of the sorts of things dealt with above. We ourselves are this object; and the question at issue is that of the value ascribable to us, as individuals, as a general 'type,' and also as various 'types.' The revaluation of the value we are supposed to possess is for him a task of the greatest importance and urgency. It is important because he believes that the consequences of whatever view of this matter is taken are invariably profound and far-reaching. And it is urgent because he at once considers the principal traditional valuations of man and men to be fundamentally erroneous and untenable, and also regards the imminent prospect of a nihilistic rebound from them which would halt with a radical and total devaluation of human existence as a most dismaying and equally misguided likelihood.

Nietzsche's revaluation here thus has the twofold aim of demolishing the former while at the same time countering the latter, thereby reorienting our thinking about the value of human life (both in particular sorts of cases and more generally) along lines that are fundamentally sound and adequate. An indication both of the centrality of this concern in his larger enterprise, and of the direction his revaluation leads him to take, is provided by several of the very first things he has Zarathustra proclaim: 'Man is something that shall be overcome. . . . The *Übermensch* is the meaning of the earth' (Z P:3). 'Man is a rope, tied between beast and *Übermensch* — a rope over an abyss. . . . What is great in man is that he is a bridge and not an end: what can be loved in man is that he is an *overture* and a *going under*' (Z P:4). Much of what he has to say with respect to the values human beings under various descriptions do or can come to have may be regarded as an explication, elaboration and defense of these contentions.

The meaning of such assertions, however, is far from evident, and is easily misconstrued. It would be an error, for example, to take them to warrant imputing to Nietzsche a crudely evolutionistic picture, according to which we possess a certain derivative value as a biological species out of which another is to arise that will realize some essential aim or purpose of the evolutionary process. 'The problem I thus pose,' he writes, 'is not what shall succeed mankind in the sequence of living beings' (A 3); for on his view, 'mankind does *not* represent a development towards something better or stronger or higher in the sense accepted today' (*A* 4). His concern rather is with the question of 'what type of man' is or would be 'higher in value, worthier of life, more certain of a future' (*A* 3). And while he rejects all forms of teleological thinking which make reference to any sort of preestablished purpose of human existence, aim of evolution, or human essence to be actualized, he does consider it appropriate to characterize and assess human 'types' evaluatively. This may be seen in his frequent employment of the terms 'higher' and 'lower' in referring to them, and in many of his other ways of speaking (as when he contrasts those who have 'turned out well' and those who have not) — as well as in his preoccupation with '*the problem of rank-order*, of which we may say that it is *our* problem' (*HH* I:P:7).

Indeed, Nietzsche even goes so far as to avail himself of quasi-teleological language in this connection. When he does so, however, it is neither with reference to the individual as such nor to 'man' in general; for 'man' is to be 'overcome.' 'Not "mankind" but *Übermensch* is the goal!' (*WP* 1001). Insofar as it is possible to speak of a 'goal' here at all, however, this is possible only evaluatively, and not metaphysically. 'When one moves toward a goal it seems impossible that "goal-lessness as such" is the principle of our faith' (*WP* 25). Yet that, for Nietzsche, is precisely the case. The 'seeming impossibility' of affirming both this principle and a 'goal' serving to orient evaluation and human life is removed when one 'unlearns the habit' of thinking of goals in this context in a metaphysical way, as deriving from some source transcending life and the world; or as reflecting the character of a culminating state of affairs to which some law inherent in the very nature of things directs the general course of events. It is against the supposition of goals of this sort that the principle of 'goal-lessness' is directed. The 'goal' of which Nietzsche speaks, on the other hand, is of a different kind, and is to be conceived in terms of the idea of what he calls 'life raised to the highest degree of potency,' which translates into the idea of a 'union of spiritual superiority with well-being and an excess of strength' (*WP* 899).

Although Nietzsche speculates a good deal on the topic, he is far from confident that it can be ascertained how this enhancement of life can be brought about. But he feels quite capable of identifying many of the conditions and influences which contribute to 'the diminution of man, making him mediocre and lowering his value' (*BGE* 203). And he is especially concerned with the consequences of the 'extreme overvaluation of man' associated with Christian and kindred metaphysical and moral interpretations of ourselves and the world, and in particular with the abrupt nihilistic 'plunge into the opposite valuations' or radical devaluation of human life (and all else along with it) when we 'lose the center of gravity by virtue of which we have lived' (*WP* 30). He seeks to 'check' our 'self-underestimation' which is glaring in the latter case (*WP* 124), and suggests that in the former case too, 'while we thought that we had accorded it the highest value, we may not even have given our human existence a moderately fair value' (*WP* 32).

The first step in the direction of ascertaining what this 'fair value' is, for Nietzsche, involves clearing away those obstacles to it posed by certain longstanding tendencies to construe it in mis-guided and untenable ways. One such tendency involves positing something transcending ourselves as supremely valuable, to which we are then conceived to be related — be it God, a world of 'true being,' or some sort of 'world-process' or grand historical develop-ment. So he observes that man often has 'conceived such a whole in order to be able to believe in his own value,' and then 'has lost the faith in his own value' upon coming to the recognition that 'no infinitely valuable whole works through him' (*WP* 12A). Whatever a fair estimate of our value may involve, it cannot for Nietzsche be a value predicated upon the supposition of anything of this sort.

It also is not to be conceived in the related way of taking our-selves to have some sort of special essence which sets us radically apart from other forms of life in origin and status. As was earlier observed, Nietzsche considers it imperative to 'translate man back into nature,' ignoring 'the siren songs of old metaphysical bird-catchers who have been piping at him all too long, "you are more, you are higher, you are of a different origin!" ' (*BGE* 230). Our value has long been taken to be a matter of our having a mental or spiritual as well as a corporal and animal nature, and to depend upon the distinctness of the former from the latter. Thus he observes that, 'formerly, the proof of man's higher origin, or his divinity, was found in his consciousness, in his "spirit," ' the body being a mere 'mortal shroud,' while 'his essence' is 'the "pure spirit." ' On his view, however, nothing could be further from the truth: 'The "pure spirit" is a pure stupidity; if we subtract the nervous system and the senses — the "mortal shroud" — *then we miscalculate* — that is all!' The upshot of these reflections is that a 'more modest' position requires to be taken:

> We no longer derive man from 'the spirit' or 'the deity'; we
> have placed him back among the animals. We consider him the
> strongest animal because he is the most cunning; his spirituality
> is a consequence of this. On the other hand, we oppose the

382

vanity that would raise its head again here too — as if man had been the great hidden purpose of the evolution of the animals. Man is by no means the crown of creation; every living being stands beside him on the same level of perfection (*A* 14).

Indeed, Nietzsche goes on to suggest that, in a sense, 'even this is saying too much'; for other animals compare favorably with man in that no other 'has strayed more dangerously from its instincts' — although for reasons directly related to this fact, he adds, man is 'of course the most *interesting*' (ibid.). And more importantly, he contends, man is for the same reasons at least potentially the most promising as well. He terms man '*the* sick animal,' 'more sick, uncertain, changeable, undeterminate than any other animal' (*GM* III:13), who still suffers from 'the gravest and uncanniest illness' resulting from his 'forcible sundering from his animal past' with the advent of the constraints of social existence. At the same time, however, he also suggests that 'the existence on earth of an animal soul turned against itself' and thus unsettled in its constitution 'was something so new, profound, unheard of, enigmatic, contradictory, *and pregnant with a future* that the aspect of the earth was essentially altered' (*GM* II:16).

This only means, however, that conditions were thus established rendering *possible* a new and greater sort of enhancement of life, and the emergence of 'creatures of the highest value.' What we are as human beings does not as such constitute the realization of this possibility. On the contrary, Nietzsche holds, that occurs in any appreciable measure only in relatively few instances; while for the most part nothing of the sort comes about. The 'human, all-too-human' prevails, and the general run of mankind ('the herd') lives in a manner which reflects the weaknesses and disadvantages associated with this departure from the norm of healthy animality. While importantly and interestingly *different* from other forms of life, therefore, human life as such is not to be regarded as radically superior to them; and human beings generally are not to be considered 'creatures of the highest value' merely by virtue of their existence as tokens of 'the type "man." ' Thus while 'the first problem' for Nietzsche is that of 'the *order of rank* of different kinds of life' (*WP* 592), the rank-ordering he discerns is not one of biological species, with ours at the top. Rather, it distinguishes different 'kinds of life' in terms of the 'quanta of enhanced and organized power' they represent (*WP* 674), and so draws distinctions serving to divide 'mankind' into 'higher' and 'lower' sub-types. His '*first proposition*' is that 'man as a species is not progressing. Higher types are indeed attained, but they do not last. The level of the species is *not* raised' (*WP* 684). And he argues that 'mankind is not a whole: it is an inextricable multiplicity of ascending and descending life-processes' (*WP* 339). Indeed, he writes:

> 'Mankind' does not advance, it does not even exist. The overall aspect is that of a tremendous experimental laboratory in which a few successes are scored, scattered throughout all ages, while there are untold failures, and all order, logic, union, and obligingness are lacking (*WP* 90).

XII

A different sort of obstacle to the attainment of a proper estimate of the value of 'our human existence,' which Nietzsche is equally concerned to clear away, consists in the supposition that each and every human being has an intrinsic and absolute value *as an individual*, and that all human beings possess this value in equal measure. As was seen in the previous chapter, he argues that this supposition is profoundly erroneous and quite absurd; and he considers it to be highly dangerous as well, owing to the detrimental impact upon the enhancement of life it has when it achieves sway in human affairs. It has come to be one of the most basic articles of faith of the supposedly enlightened modern world. It is taken to be indisputable, and scarcely in need of any sort of justification; and anyone who questions or challenges it is suspected either of harboring insidious motives, or at least of being the victim of benighted prejudice.

A major element of the legacy of Christianity, Nietzsche observes that this supposition has if anything acquired even greater prominence as Christian faith has begun to recede, supplanting belief in God as the lynchpin of the 'humanistic' mode of interpretation and evaluation which is the offspring of and successor to that which he calls the 'Christian–moral' one. What is seldom recognized, however, is that it is in fact not thus separable from the latter, but rather stands and falls with it, having no tenability independently of it. His basic point here, once again, is that the idea that every human being possesses an intrinsic and absolute value equal to that of every other derives from the belief that, in creating us, God endows all of us with immortal souls of supreme and identical worth, in relation to which all differences they exhibit are insignificant; that this idea further makes no sense unless something of this sort is supposed to be the case; and that nothing of this sort may reasonably be supposed to *be* the case. He

384

concedes that it might come about that none would possess qualities of any kind or to any degree which would set them apart from the rest. Were this to transpire, all human beings would be basically equal — on the level of mediocrity which is presently the rule among them. The value which then would be ascribable to each would thus likewise be equal — but it would also be negligible.

This is a prospect before which Nietzsche recoils. 'This degeneration and diminution of man,' he writes, 'into the dwarf animal of equal rights and claims, is *possible*, there is no doubt of it.' He views this possibility with 'an anxiety that is past all comparisons,' suggesting that one who recognizes its implications 'no longer knows any other nausea than other men — but perhaps also a new *task*!' And this task is that of prompting precisely the opposite sort of development, so that life may be enhanced in the only way it can be: through 'a favorable accumulation and increase of forces' and a cultivation of 'the greatest possibilities' among the few who have it in them to be exceptions to the rule (*BGE* 203). Thus Nietzsche takes the 'mission' of 'high spirituality' to be to establish and maintain not equality but an *'order of rank* in the world' (*BGE* 219).

The accomplishment of this 'mission,' however, will be frustrated not only by the natural resistance of the 'herd' to the accordance of superiority to the exceptions and to any deviance from its norms, but also by a misguided acceptance on the part of potential exceptions themselves of the ideology of the equal and intrinsic value of all human beings as individuals. And while Nietzsche regards the former as a very understandable circumstance which must simply be expected and reckoned with, he seeks to remove the latter obstacle by exposing the untenability of this ideology. If both the God-hypothesis and the soul-hypothesis are to be rejected, then no greater value (or equality of value) can be accorded to human beings than can be explicated and justified in terms of their natural constitutions, abilities, potentialities, and attainments. These vary considerably, and so human beings differ considerably; and if neither of the above-mentioned hypotheses can be appealed to, these differences must be allowed to be relevant to the determination of any value they might have. There remains no reason to ascribe value to each individual as such, regardless of what he is and can do and does. This is done often enough; but Nietzsche sees here only a generalized manifestation of vanity, given a good conscience first by Christianity and then by humanistic morality. 'In fact,' he contends, 'it was Christianity that first invented the individual to play the judge of everyone and everything.'

385

Christianity has accustomed us to the superstitious concept of
the 'soul,' the 'immortal soul,' soul-monads that really are at
home somewhere else and have . . . become 'flesh'; but their
essence is held not to be affected. . . . With this idea the
individual is made transcendent; as a result, he can attribute
a senseless importance to himself (*WP* 765).

In philosophical discussion, of course, the old notions of the
'soul' and of the 'equality of souls before God' have long since
given way to different language; but, Nietzsche observes, 'fundamentally, one upholds the perspective of personalization as well as
equality of rights before the ideal' (*WP* 339). Thus one now finds
philosophers speaking of the individual as a *person*, of all persons
as being equally deserving of respect, and of each person as
warranting consideration and treatment as an 'end' possessing
value simply by virtue of *being* 'a person.' This designation is
supposed to convey more than the mere fact that one so denomin-
ated is a member of our species and a biological individual. If it is
to do so, however, and yet is to have a more legitimate employment than does the old 'soul'-concept (that is, if 'person-hood' is
to be something other than a kind of metaphysical status attributed
unjustifiably to all human beings as such), it must be understood
to apply to certain of the qualities and capacities human beings
actually exhibit. The most obvious candidates are those pertaining
to their 'spiritual' (rather than merely biological) natures by virtue
of which they may be considered to have 'personal identities.' It
will immediately be evident, however, that so construed, this
notion cannot bear the weight formerly borne by that of the
'soul'; for it is as obvious as anything can be that people differ
greatly, not only as particular persons but also with respect to the
extent to which they may be said to *have* personal identities — and
further, in terms of the kinds of traits comprising whatever
personal identities they may have, the significance of which varies
considerably.

Nietzsche does appear to conceive of the 'higher men' of whom
he so often speaks in such a way that the idea of a 'person' as one
with a distinctive identity, and who 'possesses his value apart'
rather than merely by virtue of 'conforming to a pattern' or being
a member of a group, is applicable to them. Indeed, he seems to
regard what thus qualifies them as 'persons' as being at least
related to that which makes them 'higher,' maintaining that the
'virtuous man' or solid herd type is both 'lower' and 'not a
"person" ' precisely because this cannot be said of him (*WP* 319).
It is not *qua* 'persons,' however, that the former are considered by

Nietzsche to be worthy of esteem. Their estimability, on his view, is rather a matter of the 'enhancement of life' they represent and to which they contribute, in relation to which their 'person-hood' is but a secondary affair, mattering only to the extent that it figures in the cultivation and creative employment of their powers and abilities (as in the case, e.g., of the artist, which case Nietzsche here as so often elsewhere would appear to regard as paradigmatic).

Even this indirect link between being a 'person' and possessing a measure of worth thus does not suffice to endow individuals generally with value, let alone equal value; indeed, the weight of these considerations is if anything to the contrary. The notion of what it is to be a 'person' may in this way be rendered more meaningful than it is when loosely taken to apply to each and every human being. If it is so elaborated, however, it applies only selectively: 'One should not assume in any case that many men are "persons,"' Nietzsche writes; for in fact, 'most are *none*,' while on the other hand 'some are *several*' (*WP* 886). Most people have it in them to be little more than tokens of the type 'man' and members of whatever sociocultural order they happen to be born into, with their individuality amounting to but minor variations on general biological and societal themes; as such, they are 'persons' in name only. Some, however, have it in them to be more than this, and thus to become 'persons' in a more significant sense – although generally not simply one specific 'person'; for it 'is often the case' that such an individual is actually 'a multiplicity of persons, [or] at least the embryos of persons,' owing to the range of possibilities his greater potentialities opens up (*WP* 394). Moreover, what Nietzsche takes to matter is neither this richer potential as such nor the emergence of some definite personality or other out of it, but rather the *use made* of these potentialities; and this is something he assesses by a standard which transcends the level of individuality and the 'person' altogether.

To be sure, he does say that 'we want to *become those we are* – human beings who are new, unique, incomparable, who give themselves laws, who create themselves' (*GS* 335); that the 'first question concerning order or rank' is 'how solitary or how gregarious one is' (*WP* 886); that 'value is the highest quantum of power that a man is able to incorporate – a man: not mankind' (*WP* 713); and that a 'single individual can under certain circumstances justify the existence of whole millennia – that is a full, rich, great, whole human being' (*WP* 997). In such remarks prominence appears to be given to a certain sort of individuality, and the locus of value seems to be those in whom it is attained. But it is only owing to their significance in relation to the enhancement

387

of life that he accords individuals of this 'higher type' special status; everything hinges upon the sort of development they represent and to which they contribute (cf. *TI* IX:33).

XIII

It does not follow, however, that Nietzsche considers value to be ascribable only to those he calls 'higher men.' Differences in rank and greater and lesser worth are relative notions; and he is far from considering even those he calls 'the herd' to have no significance (let alone negative significance) according to his revaluation. On the contrary, he insists upon the value of the human 'herd' — instrumental, to be sure, but substantial nonetheless — in this same connection, insofar as it is indispensable to the preservation and enhancement of life, as their precondition. It may be that on Nietzsche's view 'every enhancement of the type "man" has so far been the work of an aristocratic society,' i.e., of a society in which there is a recognition of 'the long ladder of an order of rank and differences in value between man and man,' and that 'it will be so again and again' (*BGE* 257). Even if this is the case, however, and indeed precisely because it *is* the case, the presence of the herd no less than that of 'higher men' is held to be required for such enhancement to occur and continue. 'Viewed from a height, both are necessary; their antagonism is also necessary' (*WP* 886).

The herd ensures that life goes on, and establishes conditions through the exploitation of which the qualitative enhancement of life may occur. The exceptions, on the other hand, should they manage to escape its rule and develop their greater powers and abilities, may bring about this enhancement — but only on the condition that their separation from the herd is sufficiently great to establish a 'pathos of *distance*,' a disdain for the concerns of the herd; for without it, Nietzsche contends, 'that other, more mysterious pathos could not have grown up either — the craving for an ever new widening of distances within the soul itself, the development of ever higher, rarer, more remote, further-stretching, more comprehensive states,' which is the hallmark of 'the enhancement of the type "man," the continual "self-overcoming of man" ' (*BGE* 257). This makes it clear, however, that for him a proper consideration of the value human beings do or may possess requires shifting attention away from 'the individual' as well as from 'mankind' generally, and focussing it upon the various human types which may be distinguished with respect to their 'value for life.'

It is these types to which Nietzsche's 'order of rank' fundamentally applies; and this 'rank-ordering' is not to be made in terms of the sorts of superiority philosophers have been most willing to acknowledge, and indeed most eager to proclaim in differentiating among human beings. In particular, it is not the more 'moral,' or the more civilized, or the more conscious or rational or sapient, who by virtue of these traits are to be deemed higher human types — even though Nietzsche by no means considers possession of most of them to be incompatible with high ranking, and indeed takes some to be associated with it. Thus, for example, while he contends that 'the moral man is a lower species [i.e., type] than the immoral,' both because he is 'weaker' and because 'the measure of his value lies outside him,' it is above all of those capable of living 'beyond good and evil' — rather than of the merely brutal or unscrupulous — that he is thinking in speaking of a 'higher type' of man. The contrast he intends is between those whose worth is a function of their usefulness to others and those who amount to something themselves; between those requiring to be led, and those capable of independence. One who attains spiritual superiority transcends conventional morality, but does not simply revert to a pre-moral level. Indeed, on Nietzsche's view the former would never have come to be a possibility in the absence of the latter:

> High spirituality itself exists only as the ultimate product of moral qualities . . .; it is a synthesis of all those states which are attributed to 'merely moral' men, after they have been acquired singly through long discipline and exercise, perhaps through whole chains of generations (*BGE* 219).

The same sort of contrast and relation is to be seen between that spiritual superiority which characterizes this 'higher type' and renders it 'higher' in rank and value, and that attainment which consists in being 'civilized.' Being thoroughly 'civilized,' for Nietzsche, does not as such endow human beings with high status on his scheme of revaluation; for by itself it means only that they have been well tamed and socially integrated, and thus turned into good 'herd animals.' So he suggests that 'the *meaning of all culture* is the reduction of the beast of prey "man" to a tame and civilized animal, a *domestic animal*,' and contends that those subdued 'represent the *regression* of mankind,' rather than its elevation to the highest rank attainable (*GM* I:11). He insists upon a distinction between 'the *taming* of the beast, man, and the *breeding* of a particular kind of man,' and says: 'To call the taming of an animal its "improvement" sounds almost like a joke to our ears' (*TI* VII:2).

The tendency he ascribes to 'culture' in the previous passage is one which he for the most part holds to be characteristic of 'civilization' *in contrast to* 'culture' in a narrower and rather different sense; and this contrast is crucial, for the attainment of a high level of cultural development of the latter sort is likewise an aspect of spiritual superiority as he intends it to be understood. Thus he sees a 'basic contradiction' between 'civilization and the enhancement of man,' owing to the fact that the former primarily involves the imposition of constraints favoring the herd and securing it against the disruptive influence of those who are not integrated into it; whereas the latter is possible only under 'the conditions of every enhancement of culture (making possible a *selection* at the expense of a mass) . . .' (*WP* 134). And he likewise contends that 'civilization has aims different from those of culture,' and that as a general rule 'the periods when the taming of the human animal ("civilization") was desired and enforced were times of intolerance against the boldest and most spiritual natures' (*WP* 121).

Even though Nietzsche thus seeks to draw attention to 'the abysmal antagonism of culture and civilization,' however, he is far from supposing that culture and the high spirituality associated with its development could ever have been attained or can exist in the absence of 'civilization.' The attainment of spiritual superiority on the part of potential exceptions to the human rule involves a transcendence of their merely 'civilized' second nature; but this transcendence is not even a possibility and a task prior to their previous attainment of this second nature, through their transcendence of their merely 'animal' first nature — by means of the 'civilizing process' which may also be their ruin. Spiritual superiority as Nietzsche conceives of it is not a matter of being highly 'civilized' (or 'socialized'); but it certainly is not a matter of being 'uncivilized' either. It involves being much more than civilized, and not being so *completely* civilized that all else is subordinated to the norms of civil life; but what more there is to it is attainable only on the basis of it. And this includes the attainment of a high level of culture which Nietzsche contrasts with it.

It also incorporates something else: intellectual conscience, and the mind — and stomach — for knowledge. Thus Nietzsche has been observed to suggest that 'the strength of a spirit should be measured according to how much of the "truth" one could still barely endure,' as opposed to *'requiring* it to be thinned down, shrouded, sweetened, blunted, falsified' (*BGE* 39). And in a similar vein, he writes in *Ecce Homo*: 'How much truth [can] a spirit *endure,* how much truth does it *dare*? More and more that became for me the real measure of value' (*EH* P:3). A further

indication of the importance he attaches to this sort of consideration is provided in the same work when he singles it out in characterizing the sort of human being he intended to have Zarathustra
seek and celebrate. 'What Zarathustra wants,' he writes, 'this type
of man that he conceives, conceives reality *as it is*, being strong
enough to do so' (*EH* IV:5).

There is more to the picture than this, however. Thus for
Nietzsche it is 'a sign that will and strength are small' if people
become nothing more than 'men of knowledge, who leave everything as it is,' and 'who desire only to ascertain what is,' rather
than to 'alter and transform.' It is a further 'measure of the degree
of strength' one possesses, he holds, 'to what extent one can
endure to live in a meaningless world *because one organizes a small
portion of it oneself*' (*WP* 585A). While the ability to attain a
comprehension of reality and to dispense with erroneous interpretations of it is clearly a mark of his higher humanity, it thus is
not simply *qua* 'man of knowledge' that the 'higher man' is held to
have the special status Nietzsche attributes to him. Knowledge
thus attained merely serves to set the stage for this further and
more crucial development. 'To impose upon becoming the character
of being — that is the supreme will to power' (*WP* 617), and the
step beyond all objectivity he considers to be required if this
status is to be achieved. Here creation takes precedence over even
that comprehension which surpasses cognition; and to underscore
this point Nietzsche speaks of 'the *artist*-philosopher' (*WP* 795),
the 'Caesarian cultivator and cultural dynamo' (*BGE* 207), the one
who '*determines* values,' as 'the *highest* man' on his 'order of rank'
(*WP* 999). The spiritual superiority of such human beings is thus
conceived as involving, but not being confined to, the attainment
of knowledge, employing it in the service of the creative transformation of human life: 'all knowledge is for them only a means
for creation' (*WP* 972).

What warrants according them the highest rank and value, for
Nietzsche, is that they are capable of effecting the greatest possible
quantitative and qualitative enhancement of life, and embody that
enhancement most fully. It is not, however, their achievement of
results of any particular kind of magnitude. 'The "higher nature"
of the great man,' he contends, has nothing to do with his
producing 'an effect of any kind — even if he made the whole
globe tremble' (*WP* 876). It is 'his *higher form of being*,' as 'a
synthetic, summarizing, justifying man' (*WP* 866) in contrast to
'the tremendous majority' who 'represent pieces and fragments of
man' (*WP* 881), and the relation Nietzsche conceives to obtain
between that 'higher form of being' and the fundamental nature of
life, which renders him 'higher in value.'

It is further not because they belong to a certain race or derive from certain stock that those Nietzsche terms 'higher men' have the higher status he attributes to them. His criteria of higher humanity are defined independently of considerations of this sort; and it is only if his 'higher type' is itself defined (in a clearly *ad hoc* manner) as a 'race' set off from the rest of mankind, notwithstanding its scattering across 'the most widely different places and cultures,' that he may be said to champion any 'race' above the rest. He does suggest that not only individuals here and there but 'even whole families, tribes, or peoples may occasionally represent such a *bull's eye*' (*A* 4); but he does not have in mind 'the European of today,' let alone Germans as opposed to Jews (the former faring considerably worse at his hands than the latter, whom he rather admires). What matters for him is the kind of humanity one is capable of attaining and does attain. Higher humanity of the sort he envisions never has been and in principle is not the monopoly of any biological race or ethnic sub-set of mankind. It is limited in its attainability, however, to those (of whatever such sub-set) who happen to be endowed with exceptional powers and abilities, and in its attainment to the few of these few in whom both are cultivated and developed.

Finally, while is should by now be obvious, it is nonetheless worth stressing that Nietzsche's emphasis on the possession of 'an excess of strength' and an abundance of powerful drives should not be taken to imply that their possession and unfettered expression is what he takes to be definitive of the 'higher humanity' to which he accords evaluative primacy. He does take the position that 'what determines your rank is the quantum of power you are' (*WP* 858); but the 'quantum of power one is,' on his view, is not merely a matter of the magnitude of the forces and drives present within one. Rather, it is a function of their magnitude together with their organization and the manner in which this renders them disposable.

Thus he terms 'all fitness the result of fortunate organization' (*WP* 705), and contends that 'man, in comparison with pre-man, represents a tremendous quantum of *power*,' in that he has become 'master over his own savagery and licentiousness' as well as 'over the forces of nature' (*WP* 704). 'To press everything terrible into *service*, one by one, step by step . . . .: this is what the task of culture demands' (*WP* 1025); and this is what the emergence of the 'higher man' involves, no less than the 'capital accumulation of strength' (*WP* 969). The ability to do this — the yet greater power that knows how to press these 'magnificent monsters into service' (*WP* 933) — is crucial to the attainment of higher humanity, and is quite lacking in the case of mere 'beasts of prey,' in whom 'these magnificent monsters' run rampant.

> The highest man would have the greatest multiplicity of drives, in the relatively greatest strength that can be endured. Indeed, when the plant 'man' shows himself strongest one finds instincts that conflict powerfully . . ., but are controlled (*WP* 966).

This is the sort of human being Nietzsche takes to represent the 'ascending line' of life most unambiguously, to contribute most strongly and directly to its enhancement, and to represent it in its most highly enhanced form. This is what he has in mind when he speaks of someone not only having great promise, but 'turning out well.' It is along these lines that he conceives the 'higher form of being' to which he holds the 'luxury surplus of mankind' may attain. Neither those who belong to the herd nor those who are but 'splendid animals' and 'beasts of prey' have a value comparable to those who attain it; they are of significance only instrumentally, as its preconditions. Here it may be recalled that Nietzsche has Zarathustra proclaim man to be 'a rope, tied between beast and *Übermensch*' — an image which requires that beast and *Übermensch*, and with them barbarian and higher man, be sharply distinguished and conceived as separated by a chasm wide enough to have to be bridged by an intermediate form of life.

Given Nietzsche's contention that 'the *Übermensch* is the meaning of the earth,' it is not at all surprising that his concern with the 'order of rank of different kinds of life' should loom so large in his 'revaluation of values.' I have dwelt at length upon that which he does and does not consider to warrant the assignment of high rank and value to human beings, because there is no better way of bringing out the insight which underlies and informs his more general reflections on the matter of value, and because it is here that they find their ultimate focus. It is 'only to the rarest and best-constituted men,' he holds, that it falls to experience 'the highest and most illustrious human joys, in which existence celebrates its own transfiguration' — 'that height of joy where man feels himself to be altogether a deified form and self-justification of nature' (*WP* 1051), and moreover *attains* this elevated status. In this way he thinks of human life as coming to be the sort of 'aesthetic phenomenon' in terms of which (as he had put it in *The Birth of Tragedy*) 'existence and the world' alone admit of 'justification' (*BT* 24).

Thus it is the 'full, rich, great, whole human being' whose emergence is said to 'justify the existence of whole millennia'

(*WP* 997), and to whom Nietzsche looks to provide the '*justification of life*, even at its most terrible, ambiguous, and mendacious,' which he says he sought from the outset in response to Schopenhauer's indictment of it (*WP* 1005). Representing a transformation of life beyond the level of healthy and robust but insipid animality, and also beyond that of sickened and weakened (though more interesting) all-too-human humanity, and themselves thus representing a kind of artistic creation and triumph without an artist, such exceptional human beings are held to have an extraordinary and very singular sort of value. It is 'underrated, almost overlooked, almost denied' by that 'obtuseness of judgment' involved in those 'moral' and 'social' modes of evaluation in which one 'measures men exclusively accordingly to the effects they produce' (*WP* 878); and it is missed entirely in that nihilistic way of thinking according to which human life along with everything else is valueless and meaningless.

A new theory of value

XIV

Nietzsche's initially rather intuitive but lively appreciation of the value of human beings of this sort, it would seem, was what led him to attempt to work out a conception and standard of value differing from and superseding those involved in various prevailing modes of evaluation. It is to an elaboration of the main elements of his theory of value that I now turn. An important clue to the nature of his thinking along these lines is to be found in his enumeration of what he takes to be 'the real achievements of philosophical thinking that one owes to Germans' (but which he argues are by no means attributable to anything specifically 'German' about them): he lists '*Leibniz's* incomparable insight . . . that consciousness is merely an *accident* of experience . . ., *Kant's* tremendous question mark that he placed after the concept of "causality" . . ., the astonishing stroke of *Hegel*, who . . . first introduced the decisive concept of "development" into science' — and then adds '*Schopenhauer*, too,' with his discernment of 'the problem of the *value of existence*' (*GS* 357).

Nietzsche shows himself to be their heir by himself making much of each of the matters mentioned; and what is of particular relevance in the present context is his related remark that 'the two greatest philosophical points of view,' namely, 'that of *becoming*, of *development*' and that which focusses upon 'the *value of existence*,' are 'brought together by me in a *decisive* way' (*WP*

1058). The last thing his own position represents, however, is a mere synthesis of Hegel and Schopenhauer. Thus he goes on to say that 'the wretched form of German pessimism must first be over-come' in recasting the latter problematic; and he considers Hegel's understanding of development in the world as the unfolding and actualization of the Absolute Idea to be quite unacceptable. But he does bring each of these 'points of view' in revised form to bear upon the other, and considers the recognition of a fundamental connection between the nature and standard of value and the character of 'becoming' to be of the greatest importance in the understanding of both.

Notice should also be taken of Nietzsche's contention — seemingly quite at odds with the above endorsement of something like the Schopenhauerian problematic — that 'for a philosopher to see a problem in the value of life is . . . an objection to him' — and further, that 'judgments of value, concerning life, for it or against it, can, in the end, never be true,' since *the value of life cannot be estimated*.' This is a point, he says, which 'one must by all means stretch out one's fingers and make the attempt to grasp' (*TI* II:2). But it is also a point which may easily be misinterpreted. For what he says here should *not* be taken to imply that it is fundamentally inappropriate to suppose that 'life' and 'value' have anything to do with each other. The relation he conceives to exist between them goes further and deeper than that which he indicates when he contends that 'life itself forces us to posit values; life itself values through us when we posit values' (*TI* V:5). And it also does not consist merely in the 'symptomatic' significance of the 'judgments of value concerning life' people may often be found to make. (He does, however, consider them to have this significance (*TI* II:2), and to be very revealing indications of the sort of stuff those who make them are made of.)

In considering Nietzsche's view on this matter, account must be taken of his insistence upon the 'absurdity' of the 'posture of judging existence' (*WP* 675). His claim is that such judgments are fundamentally meaningless, lacking any truth-value (even when positive) when that to which they are applied is reality generally; and his reason for taking this position is that no standard of value can be established independently of a consideration of the nature of 'existence,' by reference to which its value might be assessed. This is his point in asserting that 'the value of life cannot be estimated,' and that judgments concerning its value 'can never be true.' Judgments of the sort he has in mind are those which state that life (or the world) possesses value *because* it happens to contain certain features to which a conceptually distinct standard of value accords importance; and he maintains that they cannot be true because he denies the tenability or objective validity of any such external standard of value.

In short, if by 'life' (or 'the world') one understands the fundamental and all-encompassing reality of which our existence is a part, it is not something the value of which can be judged or determined by reference to any independent criteria. On the other hand, in suggesting it to be objectionable if a philosopher should 'see a problem in the value of life,' Nietzsche is implying that he considers it a mistake to regard the value of life as *problematical* — something which remains an open question after the basic character of 'life' has been comprehended. This, he holds, is not the case; but it is not the case for a reason which goes beyond that indicated above, and which in a sense renders it appropriate to speak of value with reference to life and the world. For on his view there is an ultimate standard of value, which is to be conceived in terms deriving directly from a consideration of the essential nature of reality generally — and so of life and the world — the character of which he indicates by means of his notion of 'will to power.' And if the former is given and determined by the latter, then once this is seen, and life (along with 'the existing world') is apprehended as 'the expression of forms of the growth of power' (*WP* 706), reference to its value at once becomes intelligible and ceases to be problematical.

This standard is not external to life and the world, deriving instead from a consideration of what they fundamentally are. And when they are viewed in the light of this standard, they take on the value Nietzsche elsewhere proclaims them to have — in opposition both to the 'prejudice of prejudices' that 'only a "true" world [of "being"] can be valuable in itself' (*WP* 583A), and also to the 'radical nihilism' which consists in 'the conviction of the absolute untenability of existence' evaluatively speaking (*WP* 3). Thus he urges the repudiation of all versions of the idea of a 'real world' which have so long been employed 'against partisanship in favor of life,' and contends that once 'we have abolished the "real" world, then a new order of values must follow of its own accord' (*WP* 461) — though only after an 'intermediary period of nihilism: before there is yet present the strength to reverse values and to deify becoming and the apparent world as the only world, and to call them good' (*WP* 585A).

It is important to observe that, understandable though this 'transitional stage' may be, Nietzsche takes it to be merely that, and 'pathological' as well (*WP* 13). So he opens the second volume of *Human, All-too-Human* by upbraiding 'the disillusioned in philosophy,' saying: 'If you formerly believed in the highest value of life and now find yourselves disillusioned, must you immediately dispose of it at the lowest price?' (*HH* II:1). This is something he is by no means prepared to do. He readily allows it to be the case that 'the world is *not* worth what we thought it was'; but, he continues, 'we are far from claiming that the world is worth *less*,' and 'have turned our backs' on all postulations of 'values that were supposed to *excel* the value of the actual world' which might lead to any such depreciation of it. 'The whole pose of "man against the world," ' he says, 'of man as the measure of the value of things, as judge of the world who in the end places existence itself upon his scales and finds it wanting,' is a piece of 'monstrous insipidity' which 'has finally come home to us and we are sick of it' (*GS* 346). What he would have replace this 'insipidity,' however, is a different sort of stance, and a different sort of judgment, rather than the cessation of all judgment with respect to life and the world. This is a point on which he is quite emphatic. 'Dionysus is a *judge*! Have I been understood?' (*WP* 1051).

Nietzsche thus advocates the adoption of what he calls 'a Dionysian value standard for existence,' which does not 'halt at a negation' of traditional forms of assessment of life, let alone of life itself, but rather proceeds to 'a Dionysian affirmation of the world as it is,' for which his 'formula' is '*amor fati*.' And the fact that he regards this stance not *merely* as symptomatic of a particular type of psychosomatic constitution, but *also* as superior to any other philosophically, is clear from his contention in this same passage that 'to stand in a Dionysian relationship to existence' is 'the highest state a philosopher can attain' (*WP* 1041). From *Zarathustra* onward, he repeatedly recurs to the idea of such an 'affirmation,' and takes it to be of the utmost importance. It marks the point of his transcendence of nihilism; and, in conjuction with his comprehension of the 'total character' of existence that is thus affirmed, it yields the ultimate standard of value he identifies and proceeds to employ.

An affirmation is neither true nor false — although that which is affirmed may be a state of affairs under a description or interpretation to which questions of truth, or at least relative adequacy, may be pertinent. Moreover, in the context established by an affirmation, judgments not only may be adduced but also admit of assessment. It is not to them, however, that the strictures Nietzsche lays down in the passage from *Twilight* cited above apply. What he has in mind there is the status of that special sort of 'judgment' in which basic affirmations (or negations) consist. As has already been seen, he is quite prepared to make second-order judgments of value even with respect to such broad-scale phenomena as 'life' and 'the world' as they happen to exist. Making them is part of what he feels both impelled and enabled to do from the philosophical standpoint at which he arrives, upon coming to conceive reality as he does, and in consequence of his affirmation of what he thus takes to be its basic character. And he further considers no evasion of the taking of some such stance to be permitted on the part of the genuine philosopher: 'a philosopher,' he says, 'demands of himself a judgment, a Yes or No, not about the sciences but about life and the value of life' (*BGE* 205), even though this means going beyond the limits of analysis and demonstration. For this is the only way in which one can come to grips with the most fundamental of concerns; and it is only with such a decision or value-determination that one can begin to address oneself to specific substantive issues of value, as the philosopher as Nietzsche understands him must.

Such 'affirmation' is by no means merely arbitrary, even if it is not simply a matter of recognizing what is the case or making a warranted inference. Indeed, it not only is *permitted* and *demanded*, but also admits of a certain sort of *justification*. Human life, for Nietzsche, is ultimately a part of a kind of vast game in which reality generally consists, the basic rules of which allow of innumerable variations but are unalterable in their general outlines. It is, so to speak, the only game in town. Once its nature is discerned, and the impossibility of getting outside of it is recognized, its affirmation presents itself as the only alternative to a rejection leading nowhere but to nihilism. No categorical imperative applies to this stark choice; but whereas the former course accords with the only reality there is, the latter may be considered a kind of absurdity – albeit one which may beckon to those weary of the game or unsuited to its rigors. Nietzsche's way of justifying the basic affirmation which is the point of departure for all that he goes on to say with respect to value is thus in effect to suggest that one consider the alternative.

As an argument, this may be inconclusive. Nietzsche considers it neither possible nor necessary, however, to say more. And he supposes this to be enough to go on. The nature of the game, he holds, establishes a standard for the evaluation of everything falling within its compass. The availability of this standard places evaluation on footing that is as firm as that on which the comprehension of life and the world stands. And he is persuaded that this footing is quite firm enough to banish the spectres of both radical nihilism and mere subjectivism in the theory of value.

398

XV

Nietzsche characterizes his position on the matter of value in two different ways, each of which is misleading if seized upon by itself, and requires to be understood in light of the other: as he commonly puts it, along both 'naturalistic' and 'artistic' lines. These notions may seem difficult to square with each other. Actually, however, they are complementary rather than contradictory, each serving to bring out an important and fundamental aspect of his view of value. They come together in his conception of 'the artistic basic phenomenon that is called "life" ' (*WP* 1046), and in his underlying interpretation of 'the world' (and 'life') as 'will to power,' understood at once 'as force throughout, as a play of forces' and as 'eternally self-creating, eternally self-destroying' (*WP* 1067).

In citing his 'fundamental innovations,' Nietzsche writes: 'In place of "moral values, purely naturalistic values" ' (*WP* 462). It is of values thus 'naturalistically' conceived that he is thinking when he remarks upon 'the fatefulness of a belief in God' and the attendant belief that divine 'sanction' is required to endow anything with value, in consequence of which 'all actual values were therewith denied and systematically conceived as non-values' (*WP* 245). He inveighs against the former in part precisely because he seeks to gain recognition for the latter, maintaining that 'the standpoint of "value" is the standpoint of conditions of preservation and enhancement for complex forms of relative life-duration within the flux of becoming' (*WP* 715). Thus he proposes 'enhanced and organized power' as the sole 'objective measure of value' (*WP* 674).

If in this respect Nietzsche's conception of value is fundamentally and emphatically 'naturalistic,' however, it accords great importance to qualitative no less than to quantitative considerations — as indeed is indicated even in passages of the sort just cited, in which reference is made to complexity, organization and enhancement as well as to quantity. So he writes that what he espouses is 'an anti-metaphysical view of the world — yes, but an artistic one' (*WP* 1048), and speaks of 'the world as a work of art that gives birth to itself' (*WP* 796). In *The Birth of Tragedy* he had maintained that 'we have our highest dignity in our significance as works of art' (*BT* 5); and he observes that the 'instinct' by which he then as subsequently was guided, which 'aligned itself with life,' led him to the 'discovery' of 'a fundamentally opposite doctrine and valuation of life' to that which had prevailed for so long — a 'purely artistic' one (*BT* S-C:2). And the 'artistic' character of his conception of value is reflected in his disdain for any merely

399

quantitative or ' "scientific" interpretation of the world,' on the grounds that it would be as shallow and blind to what matters in it as would be a purely ' "scientific" estimation of music' (*GS* 373).

Certain things Nietzsche elsewhere says might appear to stand in direct conflict with the judgment he here delivers, and indeed to involve the adoption of precisely that orientation with respect to values which is here held to be so woefully inadequate. It has been noted that he maintains that 'the "conscious world" cannot serve as a starting point for values,' and goes on to speak of 'the need for an *"objective"* positing of values' (*WP* 707). He suggests how he proposes to go about meeting this need when he writes: 'What is the objective measure of value? Solely the quantum of enhanced and organized power' (*WP* 674). And he carries this line of thought even further, in an attempt to establish at least a 'starting point for values' the 'objectivity' of which is as complete as might possibly be imagined or desired, thereby providing assessments of value with a firm footing in the very nature of reality as he conceives of it. He writes:

> The attempt should be made to see whether a scientific order of values could be constructed simply on a numerical and mensural scale of force — All other 'values' are prejudices, naivetés, misunderstandings. — They are everywhere *reducible* to this numerical and mensural scale of force. The ascent on this scale represents every rise in value; the descent on this scale represents diminution in value (*WP* 710).

The 'quanta of enhanced and organized power' which such a 'scale of force' would differentiate and rank-order are the realities of which alone values are ultimately predicable, for Nietzsche, because there are no other realities of which they could possibly be predicated. And he considers an 'objective' evaluative differentiation of them to be possible, at least in principle, in terms of the differences in incorporated and disposable force they represent. The fact that he considers this (and this alone) to be the 'objective measure of value,' however, does not necessitate the conclusion that value and value-differences are properly and adequately explicable exclusively in such quantitative terms; nor does this even follow from the suggestion that 'all *other* "values" ' are 'naivetés' which, if not entirely spurious, are 'reducible' to values so identified. His 'naturalism' with respect to value is here clearly to be seen; but what he says leaves ample room for its supplementation by reference to considerations of the sort suggested by his remarks concerning its 'artistic' dimension.

Something possessing value, on Nietzsche's view, does so owing

400

fundamentally to its constitution along lines to which the sort of 'objective measure' he has in mind would be sensitive. Its value is not to be thought of as consisting in some entirely non-natural property the presence of which would by all 'objective' criteria be undiscernable from its absence. Rather, the value properly attributable to it is essentially bound up with features of it which admit of objective characterization and even quantitative assessment; and all *other* value-predictions either are misguided and naive, or else require to be given an analysis and a revaluation in terms of this sort of value, if the question of their status is pursued beyond their immediate contexts. This is what Nietzsche has in mind in speaking of their reducibility. When attention is turned from putative values generally — such as 'moral values,' which 'are only apparent values compared with physiological values' (*WP* 710) — to those which satisfy the demand of 'objectivity,' however, it then becomes important to proceed beyond the mere 'starting point for values' thus established. In particular, it is necessary to take account of differences associated with variously organized systems of power-quanta which do not admit of adequate characterization in purely quantitative terms.

Thus Nietzsche does not stop with the suggestion that 'the most powerful affects are the most valuable, in as much as there is no greater sources of strength' (*WP* 931), and the contention that 'value is the highest quantum of power that a man is able to incorporate' (*WP* 713). Rather, as has been observed, he goes on to attribute great further importance not only to 'possessing these affects' but also to 'having them under control' (*WP* 928), and to the transfiguration of their possessors and their expressions which results from their sublimation. He does not accord equal status to all human beings 'incorporating' quantitatively comparable 'quanta of power.' On the contrary, he singles out 'a certain strong kind of man of the highest spirituality and strength of will' in the 'reversal of values' he proposes (*WP* 958), and attributes 'the highest value' to 'the sublime man' in whom 'an abundance of very difficult and rare things' has been cultivated (*WP* 996).

In short, the 'objective measure of value' of creatures like ourselves may be the magnitude of the 'quantum of power' we incorporate and express; but the *full standard* of value Nietzsche advances further discriminates with respect to its expressions, for which his inclusion of reference to organization as well as enhancement prepares the way. Quality here is thought of as depending crucially upon quantity, but not as being directly reducible to or simply identical with it. The first of the things Nietzsche mentions under the heading 'Point of view for *my* values' is: 'whether out of

401

abundance is out of want?' (*WP* 1009). It is only out of such 'abundance' that 'the whole force of *transfiguring* virtues,' which 'replenishes and gilds and immortalizes and deifies life' (*WP* 1033), can issue. It is to such transfiguration, however, coming about through the creative sublimation of an abundance of energy where the latter has been brought under control and suitably organized and channeled, rather than to this abundance as such, that Nietzsche attaches greatest significance. And in doing so, he takes himself *not* to be imposing upon reality a standard that is alien to it, but rather to be elaborating a standard consonant with and indicated by 'the artistic basic phenomenon that is called "life"' (*WP* 1046).

Nietzsche's naturalistic construal of the fundamental nature of value thus turns out to have a strongly 'artistic' cast because the 'will to power' in terms of which he understands life and the world — and thus also value as they determine it — is a fundamentally artistic affair. His 'Dionysian world of the eternally self-creating' and 'self-destroying' (*WP* 1067), in which 'life' is *that which must always overcome itself* (*Z* II:12), sets the context for his positing of a naturalistic-artistic 'Dionysian value standard for existence' (*WP* 1041) involving the essential association of value on this most basic level of consideration with what he terms 'the enhancement of life.' It is within the larger framework thus established that he proceeds to identify what might be termed several lower-order, more concrete sorts of 'values.' This basic understanding of value, however, is neither superseded by nor in conflict with the accounts he gives of them. (As in the case of 'truth,' there is no surer way to misinterpret him here than to take certain of his remarks about values as though they were meant to apply without qualification across the board and on all levels of analysis.)

One such lower-order sort of value pertains to specific conditions of preservation and growth of various forms of life, by reference to which they are fixed and may be considered mandated. Another is that relatively more unusual sort the posssibility of which is established only by the emergence of a quite distinctive form of life capable of development in diverse directions, and in connection with which Nietzsche considers it appropriate to employ such terms as 'legislation' and 'creation.' While the foregoing analysis of value transcends both and does not reduce to either of them, it does not suffice by itself to do justice to the manner in which values can and do emerge *among* the forms of life with which we are confronted. Nietzsche offers an account of the latter, therefore, in an attempt to flesh out his theory of value along these lines.

402

XVI

To begin with, he makes much of the fact that different kinds of creature — different species, and also different intra-specific types — have different requirements which must be met if they are to survive, flourish and develop. These requirements, or the 'conditions of life' (and 'health' and 'growth') of the type, serve to establish a set of 'values' for it. For obvious reasons, he frequently terms such values 'physiological.' They have a reality which he takes to be as genuine as the creature's constitution. They possess an objectivity which is not diminished by the fact that they exist as values only relative to (or in the 'perspective' of) that type of creature's constitution and requirements. They do not reduce to value-feelings or beliefs or positings on anyone's part, any more than do its physiological functions. Such values admit neither of absolutization nor of generalization; they are only conditional, and of limited applicability. But in the context appropriate to them, there is nothing arbitrary about them; and the perspective in which they are constituted is by no means merely that of the interpreting observer. This applies, for Nietzsche, to ourselves as human beings, and to human beings of various types, as well as to other sorts of living creatures.

Consequently, values of this sort require to be distinguished from the kind of values consisting in the 'opinions, valuations, and tables of what is good' which we encounter when we survey different societies; and they also differ from those of the sort Nietzsche has in mind when he speaks of the 'creation' of 'new tables of what is good' which would be 'their own' by exceptional human beings who are able to 'give themselves laws' and thereby to 'create themselves' (*GS* 335). The last-mentioned obviously are not identical with such 'physiological' values — even though the latter pertain to conditions which set the stage for any such value-creation, and so are of no little relevance to it. And their difference from values of the other sort, of which prevailing 'moral values' are examples, is indicated quite clearly when Nietzsche observes, e.g., that 'moral values are only apparent values compared with physiological values' (*WP* 710). The two are by no means unconnected, on his view; but the connection he recognizes between them does not suffice to ensure that they remain in accord, and in fact is sufficiently loose that they can come to be strongly at variance with each other. Indeed, it is precisely his discernment of the emergence of such a discrepancy which underlies Nietzsche's characterization of certain moral and religious values as 'decadence-values.' These 'Christian-moral' values, he contends, which have

403

come to be 'the supreme values of mankind,' involve the valorization of 'what is disadvantageous for it' (A 6); while 'every demand
inspired by the instinct of life – in short, everything that contains
its value in itself is made altogether valueless, *anti*-valuable' (A 26).
Here, therefore, *'value judgments* have been stood on their heads'
(A 9); and it is his aim to set them right side up.

To do this, however, it is necessary to begin by sorting out the
different kinds of values encountered here. And this involves
distinguishing between that fundamental order of values relating
to 'the conditions of a creature's life,' on the one hand, and on the
other that secondary order of values representing the identification
by some population of certain things as estimable (of which such
'Christian-moral' values are examples). The latter, which might be
termed 'explicit values,' may either accord or conflict with the
former, which transcend the level of all collective or individual
value-determinations. They are not functions of attributions of
value or 'esteeming' and 'condemning,' but rather have an objective
basis independent of any such evaluations, in the constitution of
the type of creature in question and its circumstances.

It is true that for Nietzsche 'estimating' and 'preferring' are
basic features of 'living' (*BGE* 9). Thus evaluation of the sort
which issues in the establishment of such second-order 'explicit
values' is no mere accidental occurrence in human life, on his view,
but rather is part and parcel of it, rooted in its very nature. This
does not detract, however, from the importance of drawing the
distinction presently under discussion, and certainly should not be
taken to imply that it is meaningful to speak of values only in
relation to such value-determinations. Beyond the question of
what various people value and why they do so is another question,
of what the values of different things for various people *are*, and
why they are. And Nietzsche suggests that the answers to these
questions may differ very considerably.

Moreover, he holds that just as the first set of questions does
not have the same answers for all human beings, the second set
also may have quite different answers for various human types,
which can and do differ sufficiently to require the discrimination
of values of this order as they pertain to them. 'What serves the
higher type of man as nourishment or delectation,' he observes,
'must almost be poison for a very different and inferior type'
(*BGE* 30). And, on the other hand, certain things required by the
latter if they are to survive and flourish may be stultifying and
even dangerous for the former, detrimental not only to their
development but even to their endurance. If all human beings had
more or less the same psychosomatic constitution, whatever had

value (conceived as 'value for life') for any would have the same value for all; but if (as Nietzsche supposes) our constitutions differ, these differences will be reflected in differences along the latter lines.

The fact that values of this sort are thus conditional, exhibiting not only inter-specific but also (at least in our case) intra-specific variability, means that in dealing with this order of values all value-attributions must be strongly qualified. There are additional reasons, however, for which they must be qualified even further, thus making evaluation of this sort very complicated indeed, and rendering a great deal of that which admits of such evaluation of highly equivocal significance. The situation obtaining here is rather like that encountered in evolutionary theory, with respect to the significance of various structural and behavioral traits and environmental features in relation to the prospects of different biological types and populations. The significance of particular such traits and features not only varies from one type or species to another, but also often differs in cases of different types. For something advantageous to a type at one point in its development may come to be detrimental to it subsequently (or vice versa); and something of positive significance for it in some respects may affect its prospects negatively in others.

The same applies with respect to the 'conditions of life' and related values of which Nietzsche speaks. And the situation is further complicated by the fact that he considers it necessary to go on to distinguish between conditions of the mere (short-term and long-term) *preservation* of a type, those of its health or *flourishing*, and those of its growth or *development*. The conditions of each may differ considerably from type to type, even among human beings — as Nietzsche indicates, for example, when he observes that 'there is no health as such,' and thus suggests that '*your* virtue is the health of *your* soul' (*GS* 120). And they also may differ significantly from each other in the case of a single type, as he points out in objecting to the 'formula' according to which 'the aim of morals' is defined as 'the preservation and furtherance of humanity': 'How different in each case the means, i.e., the practical morals, would have to be,' he exclaims, depending on whether the object is the longest possible survival or rather the greatest 'dis-animalizing' of mankind (*D* 106). The conditions under which 'the highest power and splendor actually possible to the type man' are attainable, and the requirements of its attainment, coincide neither with the measures best suited to the *survival* either of human beings generally or of the exceptions to the general rule among them, nor with those which are most

405

favorable to their attainment of those states consisting in the forms of greatest possible *health* of which each is capable. For each of the latter involves the minimization of risks the running of which is required by the former.

This order of values, therefore, is a very complex affair; and it is with its complexity in mind that Nietzsche stresses the importance of reflection upon 'the problem *"value for what?"* '; and he observes that things may have different values in relation to 'the survival of a race,' 'the enhancement of its power of adaptation' to some environmental circumstance, 'the preservation of the greatest number,' and 'the well-being of the few' as well as 'producing a higher type' (*GM* I:17n.). One may speak of value as generally being a matter of 'value for life' in all such cases; but the cases require to be distinguished, and the sort of value for the sort of 'life' specified, in the elaboration and application of this conception of value.

XVII

Value-assessments of this sort may be made with respect to a great many things, and by no means only to the sorts of things conventionally considered to have the status of values. They do *include* 'existing evaluations,' however; thus in the above passage Nietzsche poses the question of 'the *value* of this or that table of values and "morals." ' These may be termed 'second-order values'; and more requires to be said about them at this point, even though they have already been dealt with to some extent in the discussion of his 'revaluation' earlier in the chapter. They 'exist,' as phenomena of human life which play no small part in it; and Nietzsche is no less concerned to understand them as such than he is to get 'beyond' them in undertaking to place evaluation on a different footing. His interpretation of them thus constitutes a further, different but important, part of his theory of value.

Generally speaking, for Nietzsche, there is a strong connection between schemes of 'existing evaluations' and first-order values of the sort discussed above, the former constituting expressions of certain of the latter and devices whereby the fulfillment of the 'conditions of life' in question is promoted. It is *only* certain instances of the latter which typically are thus expressed and promoted, however; and these may not be the most crucial of them, or even those presently obtaining for all members of a population. The above-mentioned strong connection suggests the lines along which an answer may be found to the question: 'Why is it that the sun of one fundamental moral judgment and main standard of value shines here and another one there?' (*GS* 7). For the reasons indicated, however, the existence of this connection is quite compatible with the possibility — which according to Nietzsche turns out to be a reality — that the *fit* of particular existing evaluations to the actual conditions of life of a population or portion of it may be only partial, or even very poor indeed.

Human beings have 'invented ever new tables of good,' imagining them to be 'eternal and unconditional,' and thereby elevating 'now one and now another human impulse and state' above the rest (*GS* 115), in accordance with various needs they have come to have. And it is one of Nietzsche's basic contentions that investigation of 'tables of good' which have thus been established reveals that they are primarily responses to the needs of *groups* rather than individuals, and of those who constitute the general rule in human populations rather than of the exceptions to it. 'These valuations and orders of rank are always expressions of the needs of a community and herd: whatever benefits it most — and second most, and third most — that is also considered the first standard for the value of all individuals' (*GS* 116).

Existing evaluations of the sort which presently prevail and have long prevailed among human beings — informing their assessments and guiding their conduct to the extent that they transcend the plane of natural inclination — are thus fundamentally *social* phenomena, the social-utilitarian basic character of which is concealed beneath the fine garments of transcendent justification or authorization fashioned to fit them. Nietzsche undertakes to strip them of these garments and expose their 'natural,' social-functional origin. His intention in doing so, however, is not simply to demolish them, but rather at once to enable us to achieve a better (more modest but fair) appreciation of them, and also to limit their sway and point beyond them to the possibility of a different sort of evaluation, of an extra-social character. Such second-order values, on his analysis, are linked to certain interests of groups or similarly constituted and situated human beings, which interests they promote as these groups attempt to come to terms with various problems they face. They might be thought of as strategies devised to enable groups exposed to certain dangers to surmount them. These dangers may be of a number of different kinds, some taking the form of external threats, others arising from internal deficiencies, and others still pertaining to the general requirements of social existence; and for this reason values of this sort exhibit considerable diversity.

'During the longest part of human history,' Nietzsche observes, 'the value or disvalue of an action was derived from its consequences.' Subsequently this way of thinking came to be modified, 'in a few large regions of the earth,' along lines which made the focus of attention not the particular consequences of specific actions but rather 'the intention' with which actions were undertaken (*BGE* 32). The interest and importance of this shift notwithstanding, however, 'the utility reigning' in such 'value judgments' is still fundamentally 'the utility of the herd,' centering on 'the preservation of the community,' and directed against 'what seems dangerous to the survival of the community' (*BGE* 201). For if it is in the interest of the community that the consequences of people's actions should be conducive to its preservation rather than dangerous for its survival, it is even more in its interest that they should have the sorts of intentions and general dispositions which would regularly issue in actions to the same effect. 'A man's virtues,' Nietzsche thus contends, 'are called good depending on their probable consequences not for him but for us and society' (*GS* 21).

Under different conditions, however, different sorts of actions and dispositions have the greatest utility for societies, while the same sorts have relatively differing or even opposite utilities. Prior to the point at which 'the structure of society is fixed on the whole and seems secure against external dangers,' for example, Nietzsche suggests that 'certain strong and dangerous drives . . . had to be trained and cultivated to make them great.' Because 'they were socially useful,' they were 'honored' and encouraged — 'under different names, to be sure,' from those he uses here and often elsewhere to designate them; e.g., 'foolhardiness, vengefulness, craftiness, rapacity, and the lust to rule.' But once this point was reached, these dispositions were 'experienced as doubly dangerous,' having no longer any useful employment. Consequently they were 'abandoned to slander'; while 'the opposite drives and inclinations,' such as 'the fair, modest, submissive, conforming mentality,' and 'the *mediocrity* of desires' associated with it, were valorized and cultivated, owing to the great utility *they* came to have in these altered conditions in relation to the maintenance of the society (*BGE* 201).

This is not the only sort of group interest, however, which Nietzsche takes to be reflected in the establishment of such second-order schemes of values. He discerns another, of a related but different kind, in the instance of that 'discrimination of values' associated with what he calls 'slave morality.' In this case it is the circumstances of a 'ruled group' under the heel of a 'ruling group,' and the interests and needs of those constituting the former under these circumstances, which are reflected in the valorization of different qualities. 'Slave morality is essentially a morality of utility,' in that the dispositions and actions which it values negatively are those associated with the 'power and dangerousness' of the 'ruling group' in relation to the 'ruled group,' whereby the latter is adversely affected; while 'those qualities are brought out and flooded with light which serve to ease existence for those who suffer.' These are 'the most useful qualities' for the latter group, since for it they are 'almost the only means for enduring the pressure of existence' (*BGE* 260).

It might appear that, since Nietzsche draws attention to the 'utility' for the 'ruled group' which finds expression in the 'value-discriminations' it makes, and since he contrasts the latter with those originating 'among a ruling group whose consciousness of its difference from the ruled group was accompanied by delight,' he means to suggest that considerations of utility play no significant role in their establishment (and in the 'master morality' elaborated around them). And indeed he considers no collective reaction of the same utilitarian character to be at work in this contrasting case, contending that 'when the ruling group determines what is "good" ' it is *value-creating* in a more positive and direct way, by 'honoring' 'everything it knows as part of itself.' He characterizes its way of 'determining values,' however, in terms which indicate that he takes it too to have a utilitarian dimension of a kind. For that in which it delights and to which it accords honor is in the first instance suggested to be that about itself which sets it apart from the 'ruled group,' and by means of which it maintains its ascendency over (i.e., both mastery of and superiority to) the latter; while, on the other hand, it negatively values 'what is harmful' to it as well as what is beneath it (*BGE* 260). Here too, it should also be observed, we are confronted with a fundamentally *social* mode of valuation, reflecting the character of one sort of group and bound up with its relation to another. (Thus while it to some extent anticipates the order of values emerging with Zarathustra's 'creators' who 'write new values on new tablets' (*Z* III: 12:26), this is one respect in which it differs from the latter.)

These two fundamental and 'opposing' types of second-order, explicit value-schemata, Nietzsche contends in the *Genealogy*, 'have been engaged in a fearful struggle on earth for thousands of years' (*GM* I:16). He begins his examination of them in this work by posing the question: 'Under what conditions did man devise these value judgments?' (*GM* P:3); and he then goes on to elaborate upon the above general picture of the contrasting forms of 'value-positing' they involve. That which he here calls 'the noble mode of valuation' is held to be first and foremost self-affirmative: 'it acts and grows spontaneously, it seeks its opposite only so as to affirm itself more gratefully and triumphantly.' On the other hand, he discerns an 'inversion of the value-positing eye' in the case of the 'slave'-mentality, whose 'creative deed' is its resentful 'No' to 'what is "different," what is "not itself," ' what it lacks and what is apprehended as threatening to it (*GM* I:10). Both, however, have a social character. This will be obvious in the latter instance; and it is also to be recognized in the former case, as Nietzsche indicates in terming it 'knightly-aristocratic,' and contending that it was out of a 'pathos of distance' that 'the noble, powerful, high-stationed and high-minded' came to posit their values (*GM* I:2).

Nietzsche further suggests that considerations of utility are reflected in the former in a way that is quite alien to the latter, maintaining that here 'the viewpoint of utility is as remote and inappropriate as it possibly could be in the face of such a burning eruption of the highest rank-ordering, rank-defining value judgments' (*GM* I:2). Once again, however, it turns out that the contrast he actually has in mind on this point pertains to the *sort* of utility involved and the manner in which it manifests itself in the two cases. Thus he goes on to link 'knightly-aristocratic value judgments' not only to 'a powerful physicality, a flourishing, abundant, even over-flowing health,' but also to 'that which serves to preserve it' — namely, 'all that involves vigorous, free, joyful activity' (*GM* I:7).

The reason Nietzsche often speaks as though the latter mode of valuation has nothing to do with utility is that he associates 'the viewpoint of utility' with a concern for self-preservation (on the part of either individuals or groups), and holds that the pre-dominance of a 'wish to preserve oneself is the symptom of a condition of distress,' in which 'the really fundamental instinct of life which aims at *the expansion of power*' is curtailed. Where this 'instinct' is subject to no such limitation, one 'risks and even sacrifices self-preservation' — and so, in that respect, transcends utilitarian considerations relating to self-preservation (*GS* 349). But utilitarian considerations — albeit of a different sort — still come into play where 'the expansion of power' is concerned. For that which is experienced as enhancing it as well as flowing from it is esteemed, according to Nietzsche, at least by those who have not yet been taught otherwise; and it is such esteeming which is held to be reflected in the 'noble mode of valuation.'

The 'insight' Nietzsche considers himself to have hit upon through his examination of existing valuations, to the effect that 'valuation is always from a perspective' that is more or less 'definite'

— which may be 'that of the preservation of the individual, a community, a race, a state, a church, a faith, a culture' (*WP* 259) — carries with it the recognition that among the '*many* tablets of value [which] have existed,' a great variety of interests find expression. 'Analysis of individual tables of value revealed that their erection was the erection of the conditions — often erroneous — of existence of a limited group — for its preservation' (*WP* 260). Their 'conditionality' and even their frequent 'erroneousness' notwithstanding, 'one must grasp the need for their existence: they are a consequence of causes which have nothing to do with reasons' (*WP* 262). In the most common sort of case certain '*social values* were erected over man,' as 'the supreme values in whose service man *should* live' (*WP* 7). It is Nietzsche's contention, however, that 'all these values are, psychologically considered, the results of certain perspectives of utility, designed to maintain and increase human constructs of domination' (*WP* 12B) — or, on a different functional level, 'to render the world estimable for ourselves,' or to render ourselves estimable in our own eyes.

His 'inquiry into the *origin of our evaluations* and tables of good,' which is also an examination of the character of such existing evaluations, further leads Nietzsche to remark upon their *symptomatic* significance. He asks: 'What is the meaning of the act of evaluation itself?' And in answer to this question he proposes that the sort of evaluation of which conventional 'moral evaluation' is an example 'is an exegesis, a way of interpreting,' which 'itself is a symptom of certain physiological conditions, likewise of a particular spiritual level of prevalent judgments,' adding: 'who interprets? — our affects' (*WP* 254). On his account, therefore, this sort of evaluation is not only a valorization on the part of 'the community' of 'that which made possible its continued existence,' and a defensive tactic directed against threats both to the well-being and the self-esteem of the 'herd' posed by the stronger and by 'that which set apart the higher man from the lower' (*WP* 32). There is more to it as well. It is also an expression of 'a merely physiological value judgment' — or, 'more clearly: the feeling of impotence . . ., translated into a moral or religious judgment.' Thus Nietzsche suggests that an intimation of the fact that one is 'ill-constituted' underlies a 'preponderance of an altruistic mode of valuation' (*WP* 373). All of this, of course, is by no means explicitly present in the value judgments under consideration. They are rather the 'consequences' of such factors (*WP* 675), through which the latter make themselves felt, but by which they are masked.

Existing evaluations are thus viewed by Nietzsche as expressions

411

of factors of a variety of sorts — social, psychological, and physiological — which conspire in different ways and to different effects. They often accord poorly with 'conditions of preservation and growth,' since long-established 'feelings about values are always behind the times,' and 'resist new conditions of existence with which they cannot cope and which they necessarily misunderstand' (WP 110). They also invariably reflect some aggregation of such factors to the exclusion of others, commonly in a way injurious to the prospects of at least a portion of the population in which they come to prevail. And more often than not they are manifestations of something 'human, all-too-human.'

While Nietzsche considers the once-established but now largely eclipsed variations of the mode of valuation characteristic of 'the noble races' to reflect a different state of affairs (both constitutional and situational), he does not propose to revert to this mode of valuation, or take it as his model of 'value creation.' Like the 'barbarian' types whose self-affirmation it represents, it is a historical phenomenon requiring to be recognized, for which moreover he feels a certain admiration, and of which he stands somewhat in awe. He maintains the same distance in relation to it, however, that is indicated in his observation that one is 'quite justified in continuing to fear the blond beast at the core of all noble races and in being on one's guard against it,' no less than in feeling a deep 'antipathy' to 'the "tame man," the hopelessly mediocre and insipid man' (GM I:11). He advocates the super-session of both, and the modes of valuation he associates with each.

This is reflected in his contention that 'morality in Europe today,' which he takes to be 'herd animal morality,' is 'merely one type of human morality beside which, before which, and after which other types, and above all higher moralities, are, or ought to be, possible' (BGE 202). For since he considers morality to embody and express modes of valuation, the same point applies in respect to the latter. And while he clearly regards the mode of valuation just indicated as an instance of the 'other types' of valuation to the possibility of which he seeks to draw attention (in contrast to that which he considers currently to prevail), it is by no means the only one he has in mind. It may be that of which he is chiefly thinking in speaking of others 'before' and perhaps also 'beside' this one; but in conceiving of others 'after' the latter — and 'above all higher' ones — which 'are, or ought to be, possible,' he quite obviously is envisioning something differing from the former as well.

412

XVIII

In looking beyond presently and previously established evaluations to a form of 'value-creation' transcending both of these modes of valuation, each of which is bound up with a configuration of dispositions and circumstances from which it naturally and understandably issues, Nietzsche also looks to a different such configuration, and to the emergence of human beings in whom both 'herd animal' and 'beast of prey' have been overcome. Indeed, their 'overcoming' is an important aspect of such value-creation as he construes it. Here neither self-preservation nor even self-assertion and self-affirmation (as the sort of creature one initially is) is the dominant theme. For what Nietzsche has in mind is rather that self-overcoming and self-transformation through which alone we can be said to '*become* those we are'. (potentially, though not actually at the outset), as only those can who 'create themselves' – and, inseparably from doing so, only as we 'create our own new tables of what is good' (*GS* 335). This in turn is held, first of all, to involve the selection and 'production' of 'virtues' which will serve 'as conditions of precisely *our own* existence and growth, which we recognize and acknowledge independently of whether other men grow with us under similar or different conditions' (*WP* 326). And here as elsewhere, the greatest emphasis is to be placed on the second of the pair 'existence and growth.' For while the first may be a condition of the possibility of the second, the second is essential to the endowment of the first with any significance.

There is more to the 'value creation' Nietzsche has in mind than this, however. It goes beyond the establishment of certain of the conditions under which such development can best occur through the cultivation of an appropriate set of dispositions as virtues, and relates more directly to the course of this development. Thus he contends, in the course of elaborating upon his suggestion that the 'task' of the 'true philosopher' is to '*create values*,' that the latter is a matter of determining 'Whither and For What,' and so is analogous to the activity of the 'legislator' (and not merely to that of the husbandman). And it is of interest, in this connection, that he expressly contrasts such value-creation with the philosopher's attainment of a sensitivity to 'the whole range of human values and value feelings' (both first- and second-order, in terms of the foregoing analysis), suggesting their ascertainment and exploration to be 'merely preconditions of his task' (*BGE* 211).

The same also applies, moreover, with respect to the 'conscience for the over-all development of man,' which Nietzsche likewise

413

takes to characterize 'the philosopher as *we* understand him' (*BGE* 61). For even this 'conscience,' by itself, cannot be expected to do more than draw attention to the necessity of the establishing of '*new* values' (*WP* P:4) and the fixing of new 'goals' by exceptions to the human rule. 'Goals are lacking,' he writes, 'and these must be individuals' ' (*WP* 269). Thus he has Zarathustra reject the idea that it is possible to specify any particular course that would be appropriate and best for all, and any 'good for all, evil for all': ' "This is *my* way; where is yours?" — thus I answered those who asked me "the way." For *the* way — that does not exist' (Z III:11:2).

In speaking of 'creating values,' Nietzsche is thinking of the endowment of various things with value through 'esteeming' them. We do not discover that they happen to *be* valuable, and esteem them accordingly; rather, he contends, man has 'placed values in things' by coming to esteem them — and in this respect, he observes, 'to esteem is to create.' So Zarathustra is made to say: 'Esteeming itself is of all esteemed things the most estimable treasure. Through esteeming alone is there value: and without esteeming, the nut of existence would be hollow' (Z I:15). It is 'he who creates' in this sense, and so brings it about 'that anything at all is good and evil,' who 'creates man's goal and gives the earth its meaning and its future' (Z III:12:2) — not by fixing any particular values once and for all, but rather by generating esteem and so enriching and stimulating human life. 'Whatever has *value* in our world now does not have value in itself, according to its nature'; rather, it 'has been *given* value at some time . . . — and it was *we* who gave and bestowed it' (*GS* 301). Fundamentally considered, on Nietzsche's view, this bestowal of value upon things is intimately connected with 'will to power' — 'valuation itself is only this will to power' (*WP* 675) — in a twofold way: it is both an expression of it and a means whereby the power of those in question is actually enhanced. 'We have invested things with ends and values: therefore we have in us an enormous fund of latent force' (*WP* 270).

As things presently stand, however, it seems to Nietzsche that new commitments of this sort are called for, at least on the part of exceptional human beings. 'Observation of contemporary man reveals that we employ very diverse value judgments and that they no longer have any creative force,' he writes. And he sees no reason for the exceptions to continue to follow the lead of the rule; for from their quarter no answer is any longer to be looked for to the question 'who creates *the goal* that stands above mankind and above the individual?' Moreover, the only answer to the question of what such a goal might be which Nietzsche is prepared to countenance — the *Übermensch* conceived as the apotheosis of the idea of the enhancement of life — is one which, far from supplying one with definite direction, is brought closer to realization only through the creative positing and pursuit of specific goals transcending mere preservation and well-being. 'Therefore an *experimental morality*,' he continues: 'to *give* oneself a goal' (*WP* 260).

In this way there can come to be goals (and 'new values'), even though in a purely objective and absolute sense 'goals are lacking,' and previously established goals are no longer experienced as estimable. It is to this possibility that Nietzsche looks in envisioning 'a development toward a greater fullness of life' (*WP* 272) for which the symbol of the *Übermensch* stands. A part of what he calls 'my final proposition' is that 'man's abililty to posit values has hitherto been too little developed for him to be just . . . to the real values of man' (*WP* 390). And this is the ability, unharnessed from its subordination to the requirements and promptings of the merely 'creaturely' in man, which underlies his 'ideal of a spirit who plays naively — that is, not deliberately but from overflowing power and abundance — with all that was hitherto called holy, good, untouchable, divine' (*GS* 382). This is the 'antichrist and antinihilist' whose advent Nietzsche anticipates, 'the *redeeming* man of great love and contempt, the creative spirit whose compelling strength will not let him rest in any aloofness or any beyond,' capable of the sort of 'great decision that liberates the will again and restores its goal to the earth and hope to man' (*GM* II:24). It may be that 'previous interpretations have been perspective valuations by virtue of which we can survive in life'; but here the 'strengthening and increase in power opens up new perspectives' (*WP* 616), and 'the value feelings that hitherto have been squandered on the world of being are again set free' (*WP* 585C).

Nietzsche thus goes beyond the general observation that 'the existing world . . . appears as it does' owing to the ways in which 'all earthly living things have worked' upon it, and that 'our valuations are a part of this building' (*WP* 1046). And he further is not content simply to make the point that 'we have to realize to what degree we are the *creators* of our value feelings — and thus capable of projecting "meaning" into history' (*WP* 1011). Celebrating 'the continually creative' rather than dwelling upon the fact that such values are only our creations, the attitude he considers appropriate is 'no longer the humble expression, "everything is *merely* subjective," but "it is also *our* work! — Let us be proud of it!" ' (*WP* 1059). The sort of value-creation and state of mind of which he here is thinking is inseparable, on his view, from 'the type of a well-constituted and ecstatically over-flowing spirit,' which thereby 'takes into itself and *redeems* the contradictions and questionable aspects of existence' (*WP* 1052). And conversely, he takes such value-creation to figure fundamentally in the attainment, by 'the rarest and best-constituted men' who may be so described, of 'the highest and most illustrious human joys, in which existence celebrates its own transfiguration. . . .' (*WP* 1051). It is a general proposition of Nietzsche's that 'life itself values through us when we posit values' (*TI* V:5); and it is life raised to its highest potency, expressing itself at once self-affirmatively and self-transformatively, which he conceives to be at work here.

The creation of values thus takes its place with the notions of strength, spiritual superiority, affirmation, and joy in terms of which Nietzsche understands the higher humanity he envisions, and the culmination of the enhancement of life he projects. Each of these notions adds something important to the others; and value-creation, as the expression of the greatest strength and spiritual superiority, is their unifying link. It is a task to which only those who are both 'strongest' and 'highest' are equal, in rising to which alone they attain their full stature on both counts. And it is only through such creation that they are enabled to experience the joy surpassing all woe of which Zarathustra speaks, and mount to the general embrace of life notwithstanding all that is problematic about it. For it is attended by a transformation of their own existence, which is no mere illusion or ephemeral episode, but rather is a genuine metamorphosis. And such metamorphoses have as their issue that higher humanity which translates the idea of the *Übermensch* as the meaning of the earth into reality.

The value with which human existence and 'the earth' thus come to be endowed, through the emergence of this higher humanity, may itself thereby be said to be 'created,' and is nothing apart from its life and creative activity; but it is no merely apparent value in Nietzsche's eyes, and no small one either. It is as real as this higher humanity itself is (or may come to be); and it is great enough to move him to an affirmation of life and the world so strong that he required the notions of *amor fati* and the 'eternal recurrence' in order to be able to express it. The creation of values is more than the bestowal of value upon something one appropriates, establishes or pursues; for it is even more importantly an *attainment* of value. And the imbuing of life and the world with value in this manner is for Nietzsche the highest of all forms of the will to power. Nor does it matter that particular value-creations, like particular existences, are but momentary attainments, swept away almost as soon as they make their appearance. It is enough that they come to be, and always will.

416

Morals and Morality

Nietzsche was preoccupied with moral matters throughout the whole of his philosophical life. His stance in relation to them is complex, to say the least. For these matters themselves are very diverse (as he is at pains to make clear); and in addition his treatment of them is multifaceted, and his assessment of them mixed. In *Ecce Homo* he styles himself an 'immoralist'; but this label is misleading at best, inviting a drastically oversimplifying and distorting understanding of his position even as it indicates one feature of it — namely, his relentless and uncompromising hostility to a certain type of morality and moral mode of valuation and interpretation, which he considers to have achieved ascendency in the Western world (and elsewhere as well). His favorite name for it is 'herd animal morality'; and it is his contention that *'morality in Europe today is herd animal morality.'* To this specification, however, he immediately adds something of no less importance in his thinking on this matter: 'In other words, as we understand it,' he writes, it is 'merely *one* type of human morality beside which, before which and after which many other types, above all *higher* moralities, are, or ought to be, possible' (*BGE* 202).

Bringing moralities into focus

I

It clearly is thus necessary to proceed with caution in characterizing Nietzsche's views on this topic. There is no case among all of the matters he discusses in which it is more important to recognize that on various occasions he has different things in mind, and thus that there are implicit scope restrictions on many of the claims he makes. To anticipate: on some occasions he is thinking of what commonly passes (e.g., 'in Europe today') as 'morality'; on others, of certain philosophical variants and developments of this sort of 'morality'; on others, of a variety of historical forms of 'morality'; on others, of 'morality' in a broader sense, relating to the conditions of social existence, or more broadly still, to the 'conditions of life' of creatures like ourselves; and on yet others, of what 'morality' might be in the case of human beings capable of attaining a higher form of humanity than that which is the general rule. If these differences of reference are not marked, and what Nietzsche says with respect to any or each of the above is taken to be applicable across the board, confusion and misunderstanding are bound to result.

Even when these differences are noted, care must be taken in each instance to discern precisely what Nietzsche means by 'morality' and related expressions. It will not do, for example, simply to observe that, in advancing certain claims, he is referring to conventional morality of the sort he takes to predominate in the modern Western world, and to draw either upon one's intuitions or upon information pertaining to moral convictions and attitudes prevalent in Nietzsche's Europe to fill in the blanks. For neither may square very closely with what he specifically has in mind; and the only way to arrive at a proper construal and appreciation of what he is saying is to attend to the manner in which he identifies and characterizes the particular referents of the general terms he employs. What he says is meant at least in the first instance to apply to *them*; and it should not be assumed that he intends what he says to apply to other possible referents of these terms as well.

(It should be noted in passing that, while Nietzsche avails himself of a considerable number of German expressions and coinages in the course of his discussions of these matters — e.g., *die Moral, Moralität, Moralismus, moralisch, moralistisch,* and also *Sittlichkeit* and *sittlich* — he neither distinguishes systematically between them nor uses them in specified ways to mark the many distinctions he wishes to draw. I have occasionally rendered the latter pair of terms (which he uses relatively infrequently, and primarily in his earlier writings) as 'ethics' or 'ethic' and 'ethical'; but since he for the most part uses them interchangeably with the others, even referring to the phenomenon he calls '*die Sittlichkeit der Sitte*' as a 'species of morals' (*Art Moral*) (*GM* P:4), there would seem to be no good reason to make much of their occurrence in certain passages, or even always so to render them. He likewise uses the term '(*die*) *Moralität*' far less frequently than '(*die*) *Moral*'; but

418

no particular significance is to be read into this fact, 'morality,' 'morals' and 'moralities' all being appropriate renderings of the latter. It is to what he says, rather than to his particular choices from among these terms in saying it, that one must look to discover the points and distinctions he is making.)

A further observation requiring to be made at the outset concerns the meaning of certain claims he makes with respect to the status of moral matters. On the one hand, he is quite emphatic in his repeated insistence, early and late, that 'there are no absolute morals' (*D* 139); indeed that 'moral judgment' is an 'illusion,' and that '*there are altogether no moral facts*' (*TI* VII:1); and ('my chief proposition') that '*there are no moral phenomena*,' but rather only 'a moral interpretation' of certain phenomena which 'itself is of extra-moral origin' (*WP* 258). On the other hand, however, he allows that there can and do exist various moralities, devoting a great deal of attention to them; and he grants and makes much of the fact that they have long played a very significant role in human affairs and the course of human development.

Indeed, Nietzsche is prepared to go further still, remarking that 'there are, e.g., moral truths,' although philosophers generally have lacked the 'intellectual integrity' to recognize them for what they are, and have all too often failed to see that 'a faith in morals is not a proof of morality' (*WP* 445). And what is more, he holds that once morality is 'naturalized,' restored to its proper role as a 'means of life' and of 'the enhancement of life' (*WP* 298), and adjusted so as to take account of the differing 'conditions of preservation and development' of different types of human beings, it ceases to be a harmful 'lie' and dangerous 'illusion,' and acquires legitimacy and significance in the light of his philosophical anthropology and value theory.

The reconciliation of his remarks along the lines first mentioned with the admissions he makes and claims he advances of the latter sorts may seem to pose problems. These problems, however, are not as serious as they might appear to be; for the former do not actually conflict with the latter. They are not intended to have the force of a denial of the reality of moralities as features of human life, or even of the possibility of justifying all forms of morality. Rather, they are meant as rejections of claims for moral principles and values of a different kind, to the effect that they possess unconditional validity in their own right and are binding independently of any and all extra-moral circumstances and considerations. Nietzsche's basic point here is that all moralities are of extra-moral origin, and derive whatever force and standing they may have from factors and considerations which themselves

419

are quite other than 'moral' in nature; that no actual or possible morality is 'absolute,' none being anything more than a contingent, conditioned set of rules of limited applicability; and that there are no *underivatively* 'moral' values, and no *intrinsically* 'moral' phenomena.

Even supposing this to be the case, however, actual moralities remain to be dealt with, and possible alternatives to them remain to be considered. Moreover, on Nietzsche's view the justifiability of instances of both — on extra-moral but nonetheless evaluative grounds — is at least conceivable. Thus he applies himself to the task of attempting to determine what is to be made of the former, and what is to be said concerning the latter. Indeed, it is only at this point that he takes the profoundly problematic character of past and present moralities to become fully evident, and the fundamental 'problem of morality' to come clearly into view.

Nietzsche prides himself on being an exception to the rule among his philosophical predecessors and contemporaries, in recognizing how very problematic such moralities actually are in a variety of basic respects. He considers himself to differ from them in taking morality to *be* a 'problem' to be critically investigated, rather than something to be embraced and vindicated more or less as it is received. 'To see and to demonstrate the problem of morality,' he writes: 'that seems to me the new principal task. I deny that it has been done in previous moral philosophy' (*WP* 263). 'It is evident,' he contends, 'that up to now morality was no problem at all'; for 'I see nobody who ventured a *critique* of moral valuations,' and only 'a few meagre preliminary efforts to explore the *history of the origins* of these feelings and valuations' (*GS* 345). Philosophers of course have long concerned themselves with morality very extensively, and in some cases have even made bold to undertake to establish a 'science of morals.' On Nietzsche's view, however, what they in the main have wanted basically to do was 'to supply a *rational foundation* for morality.' This morality itself, on the other hand, which actually was only 'the morality of their environment, their class, their church, the spirit of their time, their climate and part of the world,' was 'accepted as "given." ' Thus

> they never laid eyes on the real problems of morality; for these emerge only when we compare many moralities. In all 'science of morals' so far one thing was *lacking*, strange as it may sound: the problem of morality itself; what was lacking was any suspicion that there was something problematic here (*BGE* 186).

This suspicion occurred to Nietzsche very early on, and deepened into strong conviction as he pursued his inquiries into moral matters. So he observes, in his later preface to *Dawn*, that in that work 'I began to investigate and excavate an old *confidence*, on which we philosophers have been accustomed to build for several thousand years, as though it were the most secure of foundations. . . . I began to undermine our *confidence in morals*' (*D* P:2). And in this connection he remarks: 'to criticise morals, to regard morals as a problem, as problematic: What! was that not — *is* that not — unmoral?' (*D* P:3). He allows that, in a certain important respect, this was and is not entirely so; for here 'confidence in morals is withdrawn — but why? *Out of morality*.' For 'here, if anywhere, we too are still *men of conscience*, in that we do not want to go back again to that which we regard as outlived and decayed' (*D* P:4).

Apart from this important vestige of 'morality,' however, Nietzsche considers a suspension of commitment to any form and part of it to be one basic prerequisite of any adequate treatment of it. Another, on his view, is the attainment of a vantage point upon its variations which transcends them, along with careful attention to them. ' "Thoughts about moral prejudices," ' he contends, availing himself of the subtitle of his earlier *Human, All-Too-Human*, 'if they are not meant to be prejudices about prejudices, presuppose a position *outside* morality, some point beyond good and evil to which one has to rise, climb, or fly,' having 'liberated oneself from many things that oppress, inhibit, hold down, and make heavy precisely us Europeans today' (*GS* 380). He takes this to be possible as well as imperative for the genuine 'moral philosopher,' and proceeds to 'articulate this *new demand*: we need a *critique* of moral values; *the value of these values themselves must first be called in question*.' And he goes on to say that 'for this there is needed a knowledge of the conditions and circumstances in which they grew, under which they evolved and changed' (*GM* P:6), even though such knowledge only sets the stage for this critique.

'My problem,' he writes, is this: 'under what conditions did man devise these value judgments good and evil? *and what value do they themselves possess*?' (*GM* P:3). This, his professed 'real concern' from the time of *Human, All-Too-Human* to that of the *Genealogy* and beyond, 'was something much more important than hypothesis-mongering . . . on the origin of morality.' The issue to which he addresses himself is that of 'the *value* of morality,' to the treatment of which such reflections were 'only one means among many' (*GM* P:5). Nietzsche represents his ideas along the latter lines as having remained 'in essentials the same' throughout this entire period, and says:

> *That* I still cleave to them today . . . strengthens my joyful assurance that they might have arisen in me from the first . . . from a common root, from a *fundamental will* of knowledge, pointing imperiously into the depths, speaking more and more precisely, demanding greater and greater precision. For this alone is fitting for a philosopher (*GM* P:2).

Speaking very generally, Nietzsche's preliminary aim is to arrive at a knowledge of the nature of morality in its various actual and possible forms that will serve to render possible an adequate appraisal of it (and them) along the lines of his larger project of a 'revaluation of values,' with a view not only to the criticism and overcoming of all 'merely moral' modes of thought and evaluation, but moreover to a subsequent reorientation and new grounding of normative thinking. He is well aware that much work of a preparatory nature must be done before this program can be carried out. In this connection, he maintains that philosophers must restrain their impatience to establish anything as grandiose as a 'science of morals,' let alone something along the lines of 'a rational foundation of morality,' and must first of all direct their attention to 'the facts of morality' to be found in human history and present-day life, with all the care they can muster and as much detachment and descriptive and analytical acumen as possible.

> One should own up in all strictness to what is still necessary here for a long time to come: to collect material, to conceptualize and arrange a vast realm of subtle feelings of value and differences of value which are alive, grow, beget, and perish . . . — all to prepare a typology of morals (*BGE* 186).

While he might easily have done so, Nietzsche did not lose himself in the preliminary, necessary, and potentially endless tasks of description and genealogy, nor confine himself entirely to the subsequent but nonetheless still only intermediary tasks of interpretation and critical and revaluative analysis. He came to believe that he had done enough along the former lines to proceed further, and had developed a standpoint from which he not only could carry out the latter tasks, but could also venture beyond them to undertake to work out the beginnings of a new form of normative theory. To anticipate: the latter involves what he takes to be the 'fundamental innovation' of a 'naturalization of morality' (*WP* 462); and it further involves the elaboration of the implications for morality of his view that considerations pertaining to 'the preservation and enhancement of life' are decisive for all value-determinations (from which in turn all norms of action derive the only sort of justification of which they admit).

One other remark of a preliminary nature is also in order. It is unfortunate, according to Nietzsche, but a circumstance to be reckoned with, that the 'moralist' or moral philosopher is commonly confused with the 'preacher of morality,' owing to the fact that 'the older moralists did not dissect enough and preached all too much' (WS 19). One consequence of this is that people expect moral philosophers to be 'preachers of morality,' while those who refrain from advocating some recognizable morality and instead 'dissect morals' in an analytical and critical way must 'now put up with being rated as immoralists.' This is something he is prepared to live with, as his subsequent embrace of this label amply demonstrates; but as these remarks suggest, the reality behind the label is by no means as startling as it might be taken to be. And it is of further interest that Nietzsche goes on to say: 'Whoever would dissect must kill; but only thereby to promote better knowing, judging, and living — and not that all the world might dissect' (ibid.). This leaves the door open, beyond all 'dissection,' to normative-valuational theorizing, even as it affirms the centrality of such 'dissection' in moral philosophy. Such theorizing may be expected to lead the normative thinker no less than the dissecter of morals 'beyond good and evil' as these notions are generally understood and applied. As Nietzsche states with respect to 'the aim of that dangerous slogan,' however, 'this does not mean "Beyond Good and Bad" ' (GM I:17).

II

Turning first to Nietzsche's preliminary treatment of morality in the forms it has long taken and as it has come to be generally understood, notice must be taken of the various ways in which he undertakes to approach and think about it. His point of departure is the observation that, both at the present time and throughout human history, what he calls 'moral prejudices' of one sort or another have prevailed, finding expression in 'sentiments,' 'valuations,' 'attitudes,' 'beliefs,' 'convictions' and the disposition to pass 'judgments' concerning various qualities, tendencies, actions and intentions. Certain of the latter are commended, encouraged, or prescribed, while others are condemned, discouraged, or proscribed. This is sometimes done by means of precepts laying down laws, duties, rights and obligations, and sometimes takes the form

423

of the erection of ideals and their negative counterparts, expressing conceptions of the sort of person one ought or ought not to be.

Nietzsche has a special interest in what he often refers to as 'our morality' (and 'our moral prejudices'); but he holds that one cannot even begin to achieve an adequate understanding and fair assessment of it unless one broadens one's view to include others, both independent of and ancestral to it. The moral philosopher's first order of business, therefore, is the task of description, both cross-cultural and historical; for, as has been seen, he holds that it is 'only when we compare *many* moralities' that 'the real problems of morality emerge' (*BGE* 186). Such investigations are required as a corrective to the 'armchair moralizing' which pronounces 'the criterion of a moral action' to be, for example, '(1) its disinterestedness, (2) its universal validity, etc.' 'One must study peoples,' he contends, 'to see what the criterion is in every case' (*WP* 261).

This sort of inquiry, however, serves only to put moral philosophy on the right track. It is merely the beginning and not the end of its task. Once having looked into 'the *origin* of our moral prejudices,' according to Nietzsche, we are in a position to go on to see them for what they are (*GM* P:2) — but have not thereby settled the questions of their tenability and value. So he observes, for example, that 'the history of the origins of these feelings and valuations' is 'something quite different from a critique and again different from a history of ethical systems,' and that 'even if a morality has grown out of an error, the realization of this fact would not so much as touch the problem of its value' (*GS* 345).

As this passage also suggests, the 'critique' of moral views, inquiring into their philosophical tenability, is a task Nietzsche takes to be identical neither with their 'genealogy' nor with the assessment of their 'value.' And it is a further problem to determine the sorts of social functions various moralities perform and social requirements or needs to which they answer. It is yet another, moreover, to uncover the psychological factors at work in the motivation of individuals of differing constitutions to embrace or reject different forms of morality. In short:

Anyone who now wishes to make a study of moral matters opens up for himself an immense field of work. All kinds of individual passions have to be thought through and pursued through different ages, peoples, and great and small individuals; all their reason and all their evaluations and perspectives on things have to be brought into the light. . . . It would require whole generations, and generations of scholars who would collaborate systematically, to exhaust the points of view and the material. The same applies to the demonstration of the reasons for the differences between moral climates. . . . And it would be yet another job to determine the erroneousness of all these reasons and the whole nature of moral judgments to date (*GS* 7).

Nietzsche obviously neither had at his disposal the results of the vast labors for which he here merely recognizes the need, nor was able to carry them out himself. He did attempt to make a beginning on all of these points, but recognized that any conclusions he reached could only be tentative and provisional at best. This pertains, however, more to his 'hypothesis-mongering . . . on the origin of morality' (*GM* P:5) than to his critique and evaluation of 'our moral prejudices,' with respect to which he felt entitled to considerable confidence. And it is with comparable assurance that he addresses himself to questions relating to the psychological motivation and social functions of a fair range of forms of morality, including but not confined entirely to those of present currency. For he believes it possible to penetrate rather deeply into such matters by drawing upon the sorts of larger philosophical resources at his disposal even in the absence of as much historical and cross-cultural knowledge as might in principle be desirable.

It bears stressing, however, that Nietzsche considers the 'gathering of material' of this sort to be indispensable to his sort of 'moral philosophy.' And he likewise places great emphasis upon the importance of cultivating the art of its psychological and socio-logical analysis. Thus as early as *Human, All-Too-Human* he urges that in order for any 'reckoning and counter-reckoning' to proceed,

the awakening of moral observation has become necessary, and mankind cannot continue to be spared the gruesome sight of the psychological dissecting table and its knives and forceps. For here reigns that science which inquires into the origin and history of the so-called moral sentiments, and which upon proceeding further must pose and resolve complex sociological problems (*HH* I:37).

It follows from this view of the matter that Nietzsche thereby lays himself open at least to some extent to the possibility of criticism and correction of his interpretation and assessment of morality in its various forms on a number of different grounds, should his historical claims or his psychological or sociological analyses be found inaccurate or inadequate. This is a consequence, however, which his conception of the enterprise of moral philos-

425

ophy as an essentially interdisciplinary undertaking (and his understanding of philosophical inquiry generally as an interpretive and tentative affair) would undoubtedly lead him to embrace.

Even if what he has to say along these lines were to prove wanting in certain respects, moreover, this would by no means invalidate his entire position; for he also brings to bear a variety of other sorts of considerations, the force of which would not thereby be significantly affected. Chief among these, to anticipate, are his reflections on what might be termed the conditions of the possibility of the applicability of moral judgments to human beings and their actions; on the presuppositions of the validity of various moral precepts; and on the values of those qualities and types of conduct subsumed under positive and negative moral categories. These are matters he takes to be of far greater ultimate importance than those indicated above taken by themselves.

III

Moralities, once again, are regarded by Nietzsche as a species of valuations, which commonly find articulation and expression in precepts prescribing and proscribing various courses of conduct and advocating or condemning certain possible types or traits of human beings, and which are reflected in attitudes their adherents have and assessments they are disposed to make with respect to such matters. Thus he speaks of 'moral valuations,' 'moral laws,' 'moral sentiments' and 'feelings,' and 'moral judgments.' He generally employs these notions descriptively and noncommittally, to refer to instances of things of this sort which have acquired currency among human beings at different times and places, rather than to affirm their content. He does not reserve the term 'moral' (and related expressions) to cases of principles the soundness and binding character of which he is prepared to endorse, as is the practice of many philosophers for whom the only proper use of such language is in connection with what they take to be 'true morality.' Rather, he refrains from placing upon it any such honorific restrictions, applies it wherever he considers there to be historical or conventional justification or analytical reasons for doing so, and adopts an 'extra-moral' standpoint with respect to all that it thus designates.

These policies are essential, on his view, if a 'moral philosophy' deserving of the name is to supplant the mere 'preaching of morals' of some sort, and justice is to be done to the phenomena with which it is its business to deal. As long as one thinks of morality as consisting objectively in whatever precepts and standards one (along with everyone else) ought actually to strive to adhere to and measure up to, and subjectively in the disposition or determination to live and judge accordingly, one remains *within* morality, and indeed in all likelihood within some particular morality; and thus one lacks the distance from it which must be achieved if its nature and significance are to be comprehended. The acquaintance with it that such an internal relationship to it can afford one is not without relevance to its comprehension; but it is only when the spell generated by an immediate relationship of this sort is broken, and the kind of experience such acquaintance yields is itself transformed into a phenomenon to be taken into consideration and interpreted, that its relevance can be properly assessed. If one remains in its grip, the intuitive 'certainties' it yields will only lead one astray philosophically.

The fundamental step which must be taken if one is ever to arrive at a sound understanding of morality, for Nietzsche, involves viewing moralities from *without* (GS 380) — and more specifically, recognizing them to be devices whereby modifications of the attitudes and actions of human beings living together are brought about. These modifications may be of diverse kinds; but he contends that they generally are related to the establishment or maintenance of *advantages* of some sort (accruing either to certain segments of the populations of various societies or to these societies themselves as ongoing enterprises), and have the basic character of *direction*, which in most cases reduces to that of *control*.

'Advantages' must not be taken too narrowly here; it is to be understood as embracing a broad range of respects in which the position of such groups in relation to others and to other forms of life may be secured and enhanced. In the first instance they pertain to the preservation of the group. Thus Nietzsche contends that an analysis of various moralities reveals that 'their erection was the erection of the conditions — often erroneous — of existence of a limited group — for its preservation' (WP 260). Their basic common feature, he suggests, is the 'belief that "such a schema of behavior is one of the first conditions of our existence" ' (WP 261). He takes 'life' reduced to the state in which preservation alone is the issue, however, to be an impoverishment of the sort of affair it more fundamentally is, which he indicates by characterizing 'life' as 'will to power' (WP 254); and so he places considerable emphasis upon the notion of 'relations of supremacy' mentioned above as well. Moralities may or may not promote 'the enhancement and strengthening of the type "man," ' and indeed may in many cases work against it; but they generally perform the function of strengthening the hand of the groups which develop them in their dealings with others, or at least of heightening their sense of their superiority in relation to others.

The notion of 'direction' likewise is to be understood rather broadly in this connection. What moralities fundamentally convey, on Nietzsche's view, are norms of human life. They distinguish among purported human possibilities, identifying certain ways one might be or act as better or worse than others, and endowing these discriminations with normative force. They thus perform a directive role, encouraging and discouraging ways of living, thinking and choosing to which those concerned may or may not have any prior inclination. In the latter case they may at least initially bear the aspect of constraint, while in the former they serve more to refine and intensify; but in both they educate and transform the consciousness and conduct of those who come under their influence.

This will be obvious enough in the case of that sort of morality which Nietzsche (as early as *Human, All-Too-Human*) takes to have originated among 'the oppressed and powerless,' in their fear both of those in whose power they find themselves, and of each other. 'Here every *other* man is taken to be hostile, ruthless, predatory, cruel, cunning'; and all that makes others appear thus threatening is denounced and proscribed, man's basic nature therewith being regarded as 'evil' and as requiring to be reformed. The inability — or, failing that, the unwillingness — to act in ways affecting one adversely, on the other hand, emerges as the ideal; and norms are devised with a view to rendering everyone harmless and helpful to everyone else (*HH* I:45).

The basic phenomenon of the provision of direction may also be seen, however, in the contrasting case of the genesis of that type of morality Nietzsche associates with 'ruling tribes and castes' for whom threats posed by others are not of major concern, and among whom it is possible for each to 'practice requital' and be both 'grateful and revengeful' to others. Here whoever has such 'power' is esteemed in his own and his peers' eyes, as is the exercise of such power. They are 'called good,' while 'whoever is impotent and unable to requite is considered bad,' along with the related forms of conduct (*HH* I:45). And in this way an ethos emerges which accentuates this difference and guides those in question both in their understanding of themselves and in their dealings with others, establishing norms of action contrasting markedly with those typical of moralities of the former sort. The former moreover commonly turn out to be at least as demanding as the latter, and are only in the most rudimentary cases tantamount merely to giving free reign to one's immediate impulses. Of this distinction, to which Nietzsche repeatedly recurs, more shall be said subsequently.

Analytical investigations

IV

As the foregoing remarks suggest, moralities generally are taken by Nietzsche to be fundamentally (although by no means purely) *social* phenomena. In making this observation he means more than merely that they pertain chiefly to interpersonal relationships, even though he does make much of the extent to which they are other-regarding. His larger point is that moralities as a rule are primarily the moralities of certain societies, peoples or groups, and are only secondarily the moralities of individuals. The idea that morality is essentially an affair of solitary individuals and their consciences, or their consciousness of the requirements of some absolute moral standard, is on his view an error born of the fictitious picture of individuals standing alone before God. 'The ground for all morality can only be properly prepared,' he contends, when some human agency, 'for instance society or the State, subdues separate individuals, thus draws them out of their separateness, and forms them into a group.' And whatever morality emerges and comes to prevail among them is initially a function of the character of that association; while the modifications it may undergo are the consequences of subsequent shifts in the relations among those who are thus linked together. The general pattern Nietzsche sees here is this:

> Morality is preceded by *compulsion*; indeed, it itself remains compulsion for some time, to which one submits to avoid disagreeable consequences. Later it becomes custom, later still free obedience, and finally almost becomes instinct: then, like everything long customary and natural, it is linked with gratification — and now is called *virtue* (*HH* I:99).

It is the intimate connection between custom or ethos (*Sitte*) and morality or an ethic (*Moralität* or *Sittlichkeit*), wherever anything of the sort may be observed to have attained currency and taken root in people's lives, which Nietzsche regards as the necessary point of departure for the philosopher who would understand the actual nature of the latter; and he takes this connection to reveal its basically social nature. 'To be moral or ethical is to be obedient to a long-established law or tradition,' he writes, in a passage bearing the heading '*Sitte und sittlich*' (*HH* I:96). And in

429

another in which he takes up the same point (*Begriff der Sittlichkeit der Sitte*, 'Concept of the Morality of Mores'), he contends that we should not be misled by the 'refined' character of our modern 'sense of morality.' We must recognize that, fundamentally considered, morality (*Sittlichkeit*) 'is nothing other (and thus in particular *nothing more*) than obedience to customs, of whatever kind these may be; customs, however, are but the *traditional* way of acting and esteeming.' And, Nietzsche continues: 'In things where no tradition reigns, there is no morality' of this sort (*D* 9). He further observes that 'how the tradition has *arisen* does not matter' to 'the distinction between ethical and unethical,' having nothing to do with the attainment of insight with respect to what is intrinsically 'good and evil or any immanent categorical imperative.' It is rather 'above all for the sake of the preservation of a *community*, a people' that it is established (*HH* I:96).

In short, it is 'society,' on Nietzsche's view, which is the source of 'all morality and all celebration of moral action' (*WS* 40). The social unit in any given case, however, need not be inclusive of the entire set of individuals coexisting and interacting with each other in some part of the world and historical period. It may instead consist in some relatively cohesive group within a larger social totality, existing alongside or in conflict with others. In such cases differing moralities may emerge, and eventually encroach upon and even mix with each other. 'Wandering through the many subtler and coarser moralities which have so far been prevalent on earth,' he writes, 'I finally discovered two basic types and one basic difference.' The two types are '*master morality* and *slave morality*' — and, he continues, 'I add immediately that in all the higher and more mixed cultures there also appear attempts at mediation between these two moralities' (*BGE* 260).

Whatever the case may be in any particular instance, however, all such moralities for Nietzsche are to be regarded as social formations, and referred to the character of the social groups, structures and processes of which they are the issue. The moral sensibilities of individuals (the moral views of philosophers most definitely included) are not to be thought of as somehow originating and developing within each of them independently of these social formations, any more than their religious beliefs may be supposed to take shape through their autonomous employment of their own intellectual and spiritual resources. Rather, they are primarily the effects of the internalization of initially external social norms, together with the operation of a variety of psychological factors rooted in the individual's particular constitution and history. Thus Nietzsche maintains that conscience, far from

430

being 'God's voice in man's breast,' is merely 'the voice of some men in man' (*WS* 52); and that 'your judgment "this is right" has a pre-history in your instincts, likes, dislikes, experiences, and lack of experiences' (*GS* 335).

He is thinking here specifically of deliverances of the conscience associated with that type of morality he terms 'herd instinct in the individual,' which 'trains the individual to be a function of the herd and to ascribe value to himself only as a function' (*GS* 116). His point applies with equal force, however, in the case of those which might be experienced by people in whom any other sort of morality has been inculcated — 'master moralities' included. For 'wherever we encounter a morality, we also encounter valuations and an order of rank of human impulses and actions,' which 'are always expressions of the needs of a community' and reflect 'whatever benefits it most — and second most, and third most' (ibid.). The mistake would be to suppose that all 'communities' or social groups have essentially the same 'needs,' and that the same sorts of things would 'benefit' all kinds of groups to the same extent. In point of fact, Nietzsche contends, 'the conditions of life' of different types of human beings vary, as do the policies contributing to its enhancement in different cases. And these differences find expression not only in different moralities but also in different 'consciences' which they engender.

Both of the two basic types of moralities Nietzsche discerns ('master' or 'noble' moralities and 'slave' or 'herd' moralities), along with their various historical admixtures, are thus in this respect fundamentally akin to the very ancient phenomenon he calls the 'morality of mores.' And he further suggests that 'the labor performed by man upon himself during the greater part of the existence of the human race' by means of it, in its different forms, 'finds its meaning, its great justification, notwithstanding the severity, tyranny, stupidity, and idiocy involved in it,' in the fact that 'with the aid of the morality of mores and the social straitjacket, man was actually *made* calculable' (*GM* II:2). Human beings thereby ceased to be creatures of the moment (*HH* I:94), and of untutored instinct (*GM* II:17). Without it, in short, 'man would have remained an animal' (*HH* I:40).

This is a point to which Nietzsche often returns. It is with morality in particular in mind that he observes that 'many chains have been laid upon man, that he might unlearn behaving like an animal,' even though we now suffer from them (*WS* 350). These relatively early remarks are echoed in his later reflections on the 'evolution of man,' to the effect that 'morality was needed that man might prevail in his struggle with nature and the "wild animal" ' in himself (*WP* 403). 'Profoundest gratitude for that which morality has achieved hitherto,' he exclaims, then adding: 'but now it is only a burden which may become a fatality!' (*WP* 404). This is a judgment he proceeds to qualify, as shall be seen; but it should already be apparent that his conception of 'custom as the true "morality" (*Sittlichkeit*)' (*WP* 283), or of morality as fundamentally a matter of the establishment of certain sorts of customs binding and regulating the members of social collectivities, is accompanied by an estimation of it that is by no means entirely negative.

Nietzsche places considerable emphasis upon the point, however, that such moralities may be and have been of significantly different sorts and origins. In particular, they can have the character of an aristocratic code, embodying 'aristocratic value judgments' reflecting the self-affirmative self-consciousness of 'the noble, powerful, high-stationed and high-minded, who felt and established themselves and their actions as good, that is, of the first rank, in contradistinction to all the low, low-minded, common and plebian.' On the other hand, they may have the character of the expression of the 'herd instinct' of the latter, which 'at last gets its word (and its *words*) in,' proscribing what the 'herd' finds threatening and prescribing what seems advantageous to it (*GM* I:2). Or, somewhat differently, they can take shape in more direct and insidious reaction to the former, 'when *ressentiment* itself becomes creative and gives birth to values' and to opposing conceptions of 'good' and 'evil' (*GM* I:10).

These are among Nietzsche's prime examples of 'revolutions that have already occurred in moral judgments.' And while he goes on to link the expression 'morality of custom' with 'one of these displacements' in particular (*WP* 265) — clearly the second type is meant — it also has a broader application, wherever adherence to some code of conduct is the touchstone of judgment. What he terms the 'morality of intentions,' which represents yet another 'revolution' and constitutes a different sort of case, shall be considered shortly. Custom looms large, however, not only where the 'herd instinct' holds sway, and the principle that 'the community is of greater worth than the individual' has found expression in norms of behavior (*HH* II:89), but also where 'the principle of *honor*' prevails, bound up with a different sort of standard. Thus Nietzsche writes of the latter case that here one 'brings oneself into line, and submits to common sentiments; and this elevates one far beyond the stage in which one is guided only by personally conceived utility: one respects, and wants to be respected' (*HH* I:94). And it is further to be discerned in the instance of the 'slave morality' that is born of *ressentiment*. For its emergence involves

432

nothing less than the establishment of a counter-culture, the cornerstones of which are contrasting norms of conduct in which new content is provided for the basic formula: 'thus and thus does one act among us' (*WP* 346).

V

While Nietzsche considers it important to bear in mind that moralities other than those he terms 'herd' and 'slave' moralities have on occasion prevailed and remain possible, much of what he has to say pertains to these types. He focusses his attention upon them not only because he takes them long to have been the rule in most human societies, but also because he regards modern-day Western morality as a late and dangerous case in point. They (and 'our morality' along with them) most emphatically are not *his* sort of morality — 'morality as constantly practiced self-control and self-overcoming in the greatest and smallest matters' (*WS* 45), a morality 'which desires to train men for the heights' and so promotes 'the elevation of the type man' (*WP* 957). He readily allows, however, that they are prominent features of human life past and present, which require to be reckoned with in any treatment of morality.

Reflecting on 'the oldest moral judgments,' Nietzsche suggests that they had their origin in the tendency to suppose that ' "whatever harms me is something evil . . ., whatever benefits me is something good" ' (*D* 102), and in the subsequent shift of the frame of reference from the individual to the group, so that 'preserving the community generally and protecting it from destruction' became its primary emphasis, and after that 'preserving the community on a certain level' (*WS* 44). These circumstances are reflected in the fact that 'the person whose conduct is sympathetic, disinterested, commonly useful, and social is now regarded as the *moral* one' (*D* 132). Nietzsche allows this to be a *fait accompli*, but contends that it is 'only a narrow and petty-bourgeois morality' that focusses upon 'the most direct and immediate consequences of our actions for others' and 'choosing accordingly' (*D* 146). This refinement of 'herd morality' is commonly considered to represent the essence of 'true morality,' and a high point of enlightenment; but he takes a very different view of it:

> Behind the basic principle of current moral fashion: 'moral actions are actions of sympathy for others,' I see a social impulse of fearfulness at work, which dresses itself up intellectually in this way. This impulse has as its highest, most import-

ant and immediate aim the removal from life of everything *dangerous* which was earlier associated with it, to which end *everyone* is supposed to contribute and make every effort: consequently only actions conducive to the common security and feeling of security are permitted to be accorded the predicate 'good'! (*D* 174).

Nietzsche recurs to and elaborates upon this point on many other occasions, as for example in *Beyond Good and Evil*, where he argues that, 'in the last analysis, "love of the neighbor" is always something secondary, partly conventional and arbitrary-illusory in relation to *fear of the neighbor*.' In the beginning he considers a different sort of fear to have been primary in the establishment of 'moral value judgments': fear of whatever 'external dangers' threaten 'the survival of the community.' This fear, he suggests, initially prompted the accordance of 'moral honors' to those human types and qualities best serving to promote the preservation of the community in the face of such peril. With the subsidence of threats from without, however, attention shifted to the dangers posed to 'the herd' from within the community by the very types and qualities which previously had been most needful. Thus it is 'fear of the neighbor,' he writes, that at this juncture 'creates new perspectives of moral evaluation.' What 'now constitutes the moral perspective' is the different question of what is conducive or threatening to the sense of security and well-being of those who are the rule within the community. The type of morality which emerges may be dressed up and presented as a 'morality of "neighbor love" '; but Nietzsche contends that 'here, too, fear is again the mother of morals' (*BGE* 201).

'Herd morality' may thus be seen to be 'malice spiritualized,' the subtle and 'favorite revenge of the spiritually limited against those less limited' (*BGE* 219). Indeed, it is more than this: it constitutes a form of 'slander in the service of a will to power' — namely, that of the 'herd,' which 'rebels against the human beings who are stronger' (*WP* 125) through the 'reinterpretation as vices' of their 'natural drives' (*WP* 150). So Nietzsche answers his question 'Whose will to power is morality?' by asserting it to be that of 'the herd,' 'the suffering' and 'the mediocre.' And it is held to be directed not only toward the establishment of the conditions of their preservation and flourishing, but also 'against the strong and independent,' 'against the fortunate,' and 'against the exceptional,' in relation to all of whom they feel themselves and their sense of themselves to be imperiled (*WP* 274).

Thus the negative side of this sort of morality is taken by

Nietzsche to be the working out of a general tendency the formula for which is that *'the more dangerous a quality seems to the herd, the more thoroughly it is proscribed'* (WP 276). Its positive side, on the other hand, is the expression of 'all the herd thinks desirable,' combining the celebration of the very qualities constitutive of its 'mediocrity' with the promotion of conditions conducive to its 'comfort' (WP 957). So he remarks that 'the herd animal thus glorifies the herd nature,' and 'with fair words' masks its 'judgment of comfort' − and 'thus "morality" arises' (WP 285).

Nietzsche finds both sides of this morality quite dismaying, when he considers the consequences for 'the enhancement of life' of the extension of its sway to potentially 'higher' as well as intractably mediocre human beings. He is more than willing that 'the ideas of the herd should rule in the herd'; but he is very much concerned that they should 'not reach out beyond it' (WP 287). His reasons, very briefly put, are that, where its negative side is concerned, 'all the forces and drives by virtue of which life and growth exist lie under the ban of morality' (WP 343). And, with respect to the values it promotes, he contends that 'the elevation of the type man' requires that one 'train men for the heights, not for comfort and mediocrity.' Human life which remains within the confines of what 'the herd thinks desirable,' on his view, is a rather pathetic spectacle (WP 957). Thus he speaks of 'the fundamental fact' of a 'contradiction between "becoming more moral" and the elevation and strengthening of the type man' (WP 391). The latter requires that one 'increase' and 'press the mightiest natural powers − the affects − into service' (WP 386); but 'the moralist's madness . . . demands, instead of restraining the passions, their extirpation. Its conclusion is always: only the castrated man is a good man' (WP 383).

I shall have more to say concerning Nietzsche's views along these lines shortly. But first it is necessary to expand the scope of the discussion by turning briefly once again to his conception of a significant variation on the general theme of herd morality, which he calls 'slave morality.' As has been observed, he considers this form of morality to have had a significant influence upon the development of modern morality beyond its origins in more primitive stages of 'herd morality.' And it is worth noting that a morality suited to the convenience, limitations and conceit of the 'herd' need not be a 'slave morality,' since it may or may not be the case that the 'mediocre' and 'ill-constituted' find themselves in circumstances to which 'slave morality' is a response. 'Thus in the history of morality,' Nietzsche writes, 'a will to power finds expression, through which now the slaves and oppressed, now the ill-constituted and those who suffer from themselves, now the mediocre attempt to make those value judgments prevail that are favorable to *them*' (*WP* 400).

It may be that these 'value judgments' exhibit strong affinities, as indeed Nietzsche would appear to suppose. But this does not mean that there are no differences among the forms of morality associated with them. So, for example, he remarks that 'the weakness of the herd animal produces a morality very similar to that produced by the weakness of the decadent' (*WP* 281); but he also allows for the possibility of an at least marginally healthy and flourishing type of 'herd animal' with a morality well suited to its needs, urging that 'two types of morality must not be confused: the morality with which the healthy instinct defends itself against incipient decadence — and another morality with which this very decadence defines and justifies itself and leads downwards' (*WP* 268). Indeed, he actually considers even more fine-grained discriminations within this 'basic type' of morality to be required; thus he enumerates and distinguishes the following four possibilities, under the heading of morality's 'usefulness for life':

1. Morality as the principle that preserves the general whole, as a limitation upon its members: 'the *instrument*.'
2. Morality as the principle that preserves man from the inner peril of his passions: 'the *mediocre*.'
3. Morality as the principle that preserves man from the life-destroying effects of profound misery and atrophy: 'the *suffering*.'
4. Morality as the principle that opposes the fearful outbursts of the powerful: 'the *lowly*' (*WP* 266).

It is the last-mentioned of these possibilities to which his notion of 'slave morality' specifically refers; although the situation is complicated by the fact that, since the subjugated often happen to be mediocre, ill-constituted or both as well, the moralities they develop may represent combinations of these 'principles' at work. What gives 'slave morality' proper its distinctive flavor and orientation, however, is taken by Nietzsche to be its *reactive* character in relation to the qualities possessed by those to whom the population among whom it originates are in thrall, which appear to the latter to be linked to the ascendance of the former over them and so to threaten them. And this means that it is at least initially bound up with the obtaining of a rather specific sort of *social situation*. This situation is one in which there is 'a ruling group' and a 'ruled group,' and in which the former further is both strikingly different from and quite indifferent to the latter. It

436

blithely exploits the latter as it pursues its own course and celebrates, cultivates and gives expression to 'everything it knows as part of itself' that sets it apart from and enables it to dominate the population over which it holds sway (*BGE* 260).

These might seem to be rather special circumstances; but Nietzsche would appear to think they once rather widely obtained. In any event, the phenomenon he calls 'slave morality' is the mode of moral value- and norm-determination with which he suggests such a subjugated population might respond to their plight. 'Suppose the violated, oppressed, suffering, unfree, who are uncertain of themselves and weary, mobilize,' he writes; 'what will their moral valuations have in common?' His answer is that they are likely to take a dim view of 'the whole condition of man,' and perhaps 'of man along with his condition' (*BGE* 260). In short, their valuations will tend generally to reflect unfavorably upon the basic character of human nature and human existence, and so to express what Nietzsche elsewhere terms a fundamental 'hostility to life.'

Next, since 'the slave's eye is not favorable to the virtues of the powerful,' but rather associates them with his own distress, a notion of 'evil' is devised into which 'one's feelings project power and dangerousness,' and under which all of these attendant 'virtues' are subsumed. Whatever the ascendant group 'knows as part of itself' and 'honors' thus receives an opposite valuation. Finally, and 'conversely, those qualities are brought out and flooded with light which serve to ease existence for those who suffer.' These, Nietzsche says, include 'pity, the complaisant and obliging hand, the warm heart, patience, industry, humility and friendliness.' For such a population, in such circumstances, 'these are the most useful qualities and almost the only means for enduring the pressure of existence' (*BGE* 260).

In all of these respects, 'slave morality' stands in marked contrast to the sort of ('noble') morality which 'develops from a triumphant affirmation of itself' on the part of a dominating group which feels itself to be on top of the world. They collectively indicate what Nietzsche has in mind when he contends that 'its action is fundamentally reaction,' and that its positive valuations are secondary in relation to certain negative ones, of which the former are direct or indirect reflections and consequences. If a morality does not have this character, it is not a 'slave morality' (even though it may be a 'herd morality'); for Nietzsche lays it down that 'in order to exist, slave morality always first needs a hostile external world,' and, more specifically, this sort of adverse social-relational backdrop (*GM* I:10).

Social conditions of course may change; the erstwhile 'ruled group' may achieve ascendency, and its morality may eclipse all rivals, without this morality being altered in its essentials. The morality prevailing in a society thus may continue to be of the type Nietzsche calls 'slave morality' even though it is no longer the morality of one segment of the population that is ruled by another. Indeed, he considers something like this situation presently to obtain in much of the Western world, and contends that this very morality was one of the chief instruments by means of which the 'ruled group' came to prevail, as they succeeded in converting their former rulers to it. But to the extent that it perpetuates the modes of valuation and judgment shaped under the conditions he describes, it remains a morality fitting only for 'slaves.' Moreover, and more seriously, it works to instill in those induced to adopt it the slave's 'evil eye' for human nature and the conditions of human life generally, and in particular for the qualities of those who held sway when it was fashioned, along with all they stood for. In it the old *ressentiment* lingers on, casting a pall over human life and poisoning the wellsprings of human growth and development.

It is this sort of morality Nietzsche has in mind when he links it with 'pessimism' and contends that 'insofar as we believe in morality we pass sentence on existence' (*WP* 6); when he holds it to be 'detrimental to life' — to the 'enjoyment' and also the 'beautifying and ennobling of life,' and further 'to the development of life,' in that 'it sought to set the highest phenomena of life at variance with life itself' (*WP* 266); and when he speaks of 'morality as the instinct to deny life' owing to its hostility to 'all the forces and drives by virtue of which life and growth exist' (*WP* 343). It constitutes one of the fateful 'metamorphoses of slavery,' the 'transfiguration through morality' of which has the effect of elevating the slave's distorted perspective to the status of the last and highest word with respect to human life and conduct (*WP* 357). And this is something to which Nietzsche objects in the strongest possible terms.

VI

The details of Nietzsche's 'typology of morals' could be explored at greater length; but enough has been said about it to warrant turning to certain further matters it serves principally to introduce. There are a variety of human (and all-too-human) needs, vulnerabilities, limitations, and drives and dispositions to which moralities may answer, on Nietzsche's view; and he suggests that the remedies moralities provide and the satisfactions they afford in relation to

438

them may or may not be adequate to them, and also may be more or less costly in the toll they exact. None, however, originates either fortuitously or immaculately. All, he contends, are of extra-moral and indeed extra-rational origin, and maintain and extend their sway by extra-moral and extra-rational means. All admit of some sort of explanation in terms of one or more of the sorts of factors just indicated — which explanation, while not amounting to a vindication, does at least confer upon them a kind of under-standability, and even a measure of appropriateness, in relation to the human situations in question. These points warrant brief elaboration.

However the attempts of philosophers to devise or reconstruct and purify moralities along rationally defensible lines might be judged to fare, it can hardly be supposed that anything of the sort is what gave birth and direction to the moralities one encounters when one looks beyond the results of these attempts to human societies past and present. Indeed, Nietzsche contends that the moral theories presented and argued for by moralizing philosophers generally have only been pale and dressed-up versions and selections of such more deeply entrenched and widely accepted evaluative and normative schemes — or, more bluntly put, 'moral prejudices.' He takes the idea that they could have been of supernatural origin or inspiration to be unworthy of serious consideration, owing to the untenability of the sorts of hypotheses which would be required to sustain such an interpretation of them. He likewise considers naive and indefensible the view that any of them is the issue of the operation of some special faculty of moral intuition, or the expression of the exercise of a properly developed moral sensibility. And he therefore concludes that their appearance requires to be understood in purely naturalistic terms (understood sufficiently broadly to embrace social and psychological as well as biological considerations).

This applies not only to 'every naturalism in morality,' in which 'some commandment of life is fulfilled by a determinate canon of "shalt" and "shalt not," ' but also to every 'anti-natural morality — that is, almost every morality which has so far been taught, revered, and preached,' even though the latter involve a turning 'against the instincts of life' (TI V:4). Thus he goes on to observe that 'even that anti-natural morality which conceives of God as the counter-concept and condemnation of life is only a value judgment of life' — albeit 'of declining, weakened, weary, condemned life' (TI V:5). And by the same token he takes 'the ascetic ideal,' not-withstanding its overt hostility to all natural drives, actually to be 'an artifice for the preservation of life' that 'springs' from the

439

protective instinct of a degenerating life which tries by all means to sustain itself and fight for its existence' (*GM* III:13).

These are but special instances of Nietzsche's more general construal of 'morality as the work of immorality.' By this he means that 'the origin of moral values is the work of immoral affects and considerations,' and that 'for moral values to gain domination' they require the assistance of a variety of 'immoral forces and affects' (*WP* 266). The term 'immoral' in these and other remarks to this effect is to be understood primarily in the sense of 'non-moral' or 'extra-moral,' and secondarily in the sense of being contrary to principles associated with (what is commonly accepted as) morality. 'My purpose,' he writes, is 'to demonstrate how everything praised as moral is identical in essence with everything immoral and was made possible, as in every development of morality, with immoral means and for immoral ends.' And in this connection he seeks to establish that 'the application of moral distinctions' is invariably 'conditioned by perspective,' rather than dictated by insight into the existence and nature of moral absolutes or irreducible and unconditioned moral truths (*WP* 272).

Thus Nietzsche links his contention that '*there are altogether no moral facts*' of the latter sort with the suggestion that, 'semeiotically' considered, moral judgments 'remain invaluable,' in that 'they reveal, at least for those who know, the most valuable realities of cultures and inwardnesses which did not know enough to "understand" themselves' (*TI* VII:1). This is a point to which he frequently returns. Thus he suggests that moralities are 'merely *a sign language of the affects*' (*BGE* 187). And he regards 'moral judgments as symptoms and sign languages which betray the processes of physiological prosperity or failure,' and which also reflect and express 'the conditions for preservation and growth' of various 'communities' and types and groups of human beings. This is what he has in mind when he writes: 'My chief proposition: there are no moral phenomena, there is only a moral interpretation of these phenomena. This interpretation itself is of extra-moral origin' (*WP* 258).

This is the essence of what Nietzsche terms 'moralistic naturalism: the tracing back of apparently emancipated, supranatural moral values to their "nature": i.e., to natural immorality, to natural "utility," etc.' And this is an undertaking he calls 'my task' (*WP* 299). There is nothing intrinsically 'moral,' he argues, about the ends moralities serve and the functions they perform. The establishment of conditions conducive to preservation and growth, the allaying of dangers from without and within, the attainment of mastery over nature, others and oneself, the achievement of self-esteem, and the obtaining of revenge, are the sorts of purposes in terms of which he contends that the emergence of various moralities can and should be understood; and they are simply pieces of life, to which no moral categories may properly and justifiably be applied.

In short, extra-moral considerations set the stage upon which moralities merely play particular roles. And 'the victory of a moral ideal is achieved by the same "immoral" means as every victory: force, lies, slander, injustice' (*WP* 306). Nietzsche elsewhere extends this list, most notably to include on it appeals to and subtle manipulations of various basic and paradigmatically 'immoral' affects, from *ressentiment* and cruelty to pride and selfishness to the desire for power. The details may differ as one turns from 'master' and 'noble' moralities and the manner of their establishment to 'slave' and 'herd' moralities, and from cruder to more refined variants and combinations of them; but he contends and attempts to show that when one digs and probes deeply enough, one invariably finds such factors at work.

Supposing this to be the case, he proceeds to develop what he takes to be a strong argument against certain claims commonly made for moralities, and in particular against 'the assertion that moral values are the supreme values.' For he holds that 'the supremacy of moral valuations would be refuted if it could be shown to be the consequence of an immoral valuation,' and thus 'a special case of immorality' (*WP* 583). 'To abolish the supreme value hitherto, morality,' he maintains, 'it suffices to demonstrate that even morality is immoral, in the sense in which immorality has always been condemned' (*WP* 461). For if (or to the extent that) moralities legislate against the very conditions of their own establishment, the legitimacy of such proscriptions is subverted by insight into the nature of the phenomenon of moral valuation itself. Where this is so, morality in effect 'contradicts itself' (*WP* 266), and thus stands shorn of its lofty pretentions. This point applies wherever 'apparently emancipated, supranatural moral values' are juxtaposed to the 'natural' ends and means characteristic of human life generally (*WP* 299), with the latter being relegated to the status of ancillary or even negative values in relation to them. And Nietzsche believes that this has happened so frequently that it may fairly be considered the rule in the history of morals.

Presuppositional criticisms

VII

This argument, however, does not go nearly far enough. Morality further is held by Nietzsche to be 'the work of error' (*WP* 266); and his attempts to expose it as such constitute a broad critique, for which the kinds of investigation and analysis considered above prepare the way. (It in turn requires to be supplemented by a *revaluation* of moral values, to which I shall turn subsequently.) In a sense, this larger critique is the counterpart of the foregoing argument; for whereas in the latter case it is the actual nature of morality which is taken to belie its basic principles and so subvert them, here morality in its supposedly more sophisticated as well as cruder forms is held to fall at the hands of one of its own principal demands — namely, that of truthfulness or honesty. 'But among the forces cultivated by morality was *truthfulness*: this eventually turned against morality, discovered its teleology, its partial perspective,' and revealed the 'needs for untruth' and forms of 'untruth' that have arisen in the course of 'centuries of moral interpretation' (*WP* 5).

Thus Nietzsche remarks: 'In us (supposing that you would like a formula) *the self-supersession of morality* is accomplished,' since it is in this respect *'out of morality'* that 'confidence in morals is withdrawn' (*D* P:4). By proscribing lying, whether to others or to oneself, and prescribing truthfulness, regardless of the disadvantages with which it might be attended, morality contains within itself the seeds of its own destruction. For it provided the initial impetus to the development of an intellectual conscience which, when turned back upon it and informed by insight into various matters pertaining to it, bars the way to the retention of 'our *confidence in morals*' (*D* P:2). The same fate is thus held to be in store for 'Christianity *as morality*' as that which has befallen 'Christianity *as a dogma*'; for it likewise is in this way 'destroyed by its own morality.' Nor is the morality directly associated with Christianity the only one that is to fall. 'As the will to truth thus gains self-consciousness — there can be no doubt of that — morality will gradually perish now,' at least as it has long been construed (*GM* III:27). So Nietzsche concludes: 'The entire old morality concerns us no more: there is not a concept in it that still deserves respect' (*WP* 459).

The critique he develops, which leads him to this conclusion, has a number of different parts. Most pertain to what he takes to be the presuppositions of moralities of a non-'naturalistic' character, and to the consequences for the latter of the untenability of these presuppositions. 'To deny morality,' he writes (here using the terms *Sittlichkeit* and *sittlich*), 'may first of all mean to deny that the moral motives people *profess* actually move them to their actions.' He admits to supposing that, at least 'in very many cases,'

442

a suspicion to this effect is well warranted. But he goes on to say that it also 'may mean to deny that moral judgments rest on truths.' 'This is *my* point of view,' he continues: 'I deny morality as I deny alchemy — that is to say, I deny its presuppositions; but *not* that there have been alchemists, who believed in these presuppositions and acted upon them' (*D* 103).

What Nietzsche has in mind here requires elaboration. In the first instance, he argues that the situation of such moralities with respect to their justifiability is hopeless. They cannot stand *in the absence* of an other-worldly, religious or metaphysical grounding and sanctioning; but they also cannot be defended *by reference to* any such set of beliefs, since the latter do not survive critical examination. Thus he maintains that 'the whole of our European morality' is a part of 'what must now collapse,' with the recognition that 'the belief in the Christian God' is 'unbelievable' and requires to be abandoned; for the former 'was built upon this faith' and 'propped up by it' (*GS* 343). 'When one gives up the Christian faith, one pulls the right to Christian morality out from under one's feet,' he writes; 'it stands and falls with faith in God.' For it 'is by no means self-evident,' even though, owing to the long 'dominion of the Christian value judgment . . ., the very conditional character of its right to existence is no longer felt,' and it is now reflected in people's 'intuitions' of 'what is good and evil.' Fundamentally it has the status of 'a command,' which 'has truth only if God is the truth' (*TI* IX:5).

A morality of this sort 'no longer has any sanction after it has tried to escape into some beyond,' and this 'beyond' is discovered to be a fiction (*WP* 1). And the attempt 'to get along with a morality without religious background,' or without comparable metaphysical underpinnings, is an exercise in futility, which 'necessarily leads to nihilism' (*WP* 19) — at least in the absence of a radical reorientation of one's entire approach to normative and evaluative matters along 'naturalistic' lines. 'Naiveté!' Nietzsche exclaims; 'as if morality could survive when the *God* who sanctions it is missing! The "beyond" [is] absolutely necessary if faith in morality is to be maintained' (*WP* 253). A morality from the perspective of which 'life, nature, and history are "not moral"' can be defended only on the condition that one is prepared to '*affirm another world* than the world of life, nature, and history' (*GS* 344). And once the erroneousness of supposing any such 'other world' to exist is recognized, no morality of this sort can be saved. One may embrace it without any explicit awareness that one is presupposing anything along these lines, and even without being at all prepared to affirm anything of the sort. One's 'right to it,' however, upon examination turns out to be dependent upon the soundness of positing some such higher reality to which it can be referred; and consequently, Nietzsche holds, it cannot be sustained.

He further observes that 'when the English actually believe that they know "intuitively" what is good and evil,' and 'therefore suppose that they no longer require Christianity as the guarantee of morality,' they err and deceive themselves. For they thereby take as an intuitive apprehension of moral truths what is merely the experience of sentiments which are among 'the *effects* of the Christian value judgment and an expression of the strength and depth of this dominion' (*TI* IX:5). He similarly denies that any other morality can be legitimately deemed self-evident, or considered to require no justification beyond one's moral intuitions or the deliverances of one's conscience. Experiences of this sort cannot be supposed to fill the justificatory void left by the abandonment of the religious beliefs or metaphysical schemes in terms of which moralities of the sort under consideration may formerly have been supported, because they are inherently problematic. 'The assent of the conscience,' Nietzsche contends, 'proves nothing at all.' It may echo long-established moral norms; but it is no source of knowledge of moral truths: 'It merely repeats' (*WP* 294). And an understanding of the manner in which such 'subjective value feelings' are shaped and acquired should undermine any confidence one might have been inclined to repose in it (*GS* 335).

If a morality has nothing more going for it than certain 'intuitions' and deliverances of conscience on the part of its adherents, therefore, it has no claim to tenability. Once 'this world' comes to be understood exclusively in terms of what is found to obtain and transpire throughout 'nature, life, and history,' the supposition that moral 'truths' of the sort we are purportedly capable of intuiting are somehow written into it likewise becomes unintelligible. This interpretation is rendered untenable by the irreconcilability of certain of its basic presuppositions with the consequences of eschewing any religious or metaphysical recourse to a transcendent reality. And thus whatever other significance our 'moral intuitions' might have, they lend no support to the sorts of judgments and evaluations associated with them. Indeed, the more closely the latter are linked with the former, according to Nietzsche, the more suspicious we ought to be with respect to any grand claims made with respect to them. For this association should serve to alert us to the likelihood that our confidence in the latter is but a function of the operation of the same basic and very 'human' factors which conspire to generate these 'intuitions' and deliverances of our conscience.

VIII

The erroneous interpretation of such 'subjective value feelings' as the immediate apprehension of 'moral truths' is not the only thing Nietzsche has in mind when he contends that morality up to now has rested upon a 'dreadful *forgery of the psychology of man*' (*WP* 786). What he terms 'the erroneousness of . . . the whole nature of moral judgments to date' (*GS* 7) is also held to be related to a further set of mistaken suppositions pertaining to human actions. 'The error of free will' (*TI* VI:7) is one; the explanation of actions in terms of 'intentions,' and the attribution to human beings generally of a significant measure of 'responsibility' for their actions, are others related to it; and the myth of the possibility of genuine 'altruism' is yet another. Nietzsche sees 'a tremendous rat's tail of errors' here (*WP* 705), and holds that their exposure leaves little of morality as it has for the most part been understood still standing. 'Owing to these errors,' he writes, 'we have up to now accorded certain actions a higher value than they possess' (*D* 148). There are actions to which the predicates 'moral' and 'immoral' are commonly applied; but he maintains that as these notions are *conceived*, in point of fact '*there are neither moral nor immoral actions.*'

> This entire distinction 'moral' and 'immoral' proceeds from the idea that moral as well as immoral actions are acts arising from free spontaneity — in short, that such a spontaneity exists, or in other words: that moral judgments in general relate only to one species of intuitions and actions, those that are *free*. But this whole species of intentions and actions is purely imaginary (*WP* 786).

In sum: 'If only those actions are moral . . . which are performed out of freedom of will, then there are no moral actions' (*D* 148). For the doctrine that each human being possesses a 'free will' is an 'error,' motivated by a desire to be able 'to impute guilt,' justify punishment, and influence behavior (*TI* VI:7). While Nietzsche likewise takes 'the "unfree will" ' to be a piece of 'mythology' (*BGE* 21), the subtler 'psychology of man' he considers to be required in place of both does not accord to human beings the sort of freedom presupposed by any morality imputing complete responsibility to them for their actions, to the extent of holding them answerable as self-moving initiators of whatever courses of action in which they engage.

'During the longest part of human history,' Nietzsche writes, which he terms 'the *pre-moral* period of mankind,' it was 'its consequences . . . that led men to think well or ill of an action.' But in the course of 'the last ten thousand years' this gradually changed. 'A reversal of perspective' occurred, ushering in 'a period that one may call *moral* in the narrower sense,' in which 'it is no longer the consequences but the origin of an action' that was the focus of attention and the object of assessment. And with this shift 'a calamitous new superstition . . . became dominant: the origin of an action was interpreted in the most definite sense as an origin in an *intention*,' supposed to be determined upon by an autonomous subject capable no less of disregarding than of yielding to all promptings of a merely 'human' nature. 'But today,' Nietzsche continues, 'owing to another self-examination of man, another growth in profundity,' this superstition requires to be abandoned. He takes this to be a consequence of the recognition that 'everything about [an action] that is intentional, everything about it that can be seen, known, "conscious," still belongs to its surface and skin,' and of the realization that the notion of an autonomous subject transcending our affective nature is a fiction. And so he contends that 'morality in the traditional sense, the morality of intentions, was a prejudice, precipitate and perhaps provisional — something on the order of astrology and alchemy — but in any case something that must be overcome' (*BGE* 32). It rests on a fundamental error: 'Through a psychological misunderstanding, one has invented an *antithesis* to the motivating forces, and believes one has described another kind of force: one has imagined a *primum mobilum* that does not exist at all' (*WP* 786).

It should be borne in mind, however, that Nietzsche is very much concerned to distinguish between several different human possibilities. There are, on the one hand, those who are unable to 'resist reacting to a stimulus' (*WP* 334) and are impelled to act by whatever impulses, dispositions and needs or fears happen to come to the fore and override all others. But there also are those who achieve at least a degree of 'mastery over the affects' and of 'facility in self-direction,' and are capable of keeping promises, honoring commitments, and pursuing long-term projects. In the case of the latter, he considers it appropriate to speak of the attainment of a real measure of autonomy and responsibility, holding this to be one of the marks of a 'higher nature.' And while he objects strongly to the postulation of a special, peculiarly 'moral' (or even intrinsically 'rational') type of motive or 'will' apart from and fundamentally antithetical to the 'motivating forces' associated with our basic 'natural' human constitution, he allows for the possibility of the emergence (through the transformation of certain of the latter) of qualitatively differing 'motivating forces,' which

446

can serve to restrain and further redirect their more rudimentary relatives. This is the key to all human 'self-overcoming,' to which theme he repeatedly recurs and attaches the greatest importance in connection with the 'enhancement of life.' Still, Nietzsche contends that what is actually attained along these lines by all but the more exceptional of human beings does not amount to very much. And more importantly, he holds that these possibilities do not suffice to vindicate moralities predicated upon the existence within all human agents of a species of motive entirely different from and contrasting with all natural 'motivating forces' and their derivatives. For they refer only to derivatives of the latter rather than to confirming instances of the former.

Nietzsche thus argues that human beings simply are not the sort of creature they would have to be for morality as it is usually understood to be defensible. They cannot be held responsible for their 'nature,' for that is something they do not determine, being shaped by forces transcending their own apparent agency. And the same holds for actions: one 'can admire their strength, beauty, richness, but may find nothing meritorious in these things.' As in the case of the former, one 'may neither praise nor blame any longer, for it is absurd to praise and blame nature and necessity' (*HH* I:107). Nietzsche is quite prepared to allow that human beings perform actions from a variety of motives, and that the former may (at least on a certain level of description) be explained in terms of the latter. But he argues that they cannot be held accountable for the particular character and relative strength of the various motives from which their actions issue; for these reflect the operation of the same forces within and without the individual through which his nature is fashioned. They are but particular facets of that nature for which he cannot be supposed to be responsible, and which makes him who he is.

Thus while value judgments may be appropriate in connection with what people are and do, moral judgments are not — even though they of course may be and long have been *made*, and are by no means incapable of altering the motivational structure and actions of those whose lives they touch. To be sure, nothing is more common, or of greater consequence, than moral indoctrination. But the frequent success of such indoctrination, and the fact of its great impact upon the course of people's lives, are circumstances which do not necessitate or warrant any revision in Nietzsche's construal of the basic character of human nature and human action. They may mark the opening of a relatively new chapter in human history (though not, he thinks and hopes, its final one); but while they give a different twist to human life, they

447

do not signify that human beings have come to be 'moral agents' of the sort traditional moralities presuppose. People may be altered by this means, but there is no reason to suppose that they are thereby radically reconstituted along those lines.

IX

Nietzsche further maintains that those who thus become 'moral men' are no more truly 'moral' than the rest of mankind in their basic manner of conduct. What he here has in mind is *altruism*, the reality and indeed the very possibility of which he disputes, even while conceding the important influence the idea and level of altruism have had in human affairs. I shall pass over his psychological reflections on the phenomenon of the *espousal* of altruistic principles and values (the upshot of which is that it is more likely to be symptomatic of a well-warranted lack of self-esteem than indicative of an elevated state of mind) to concentrate upon his critique of what he might have called 'the myth of altruism.'

Nietzsche does not consider 'our morality' to be confined to the celebration and advocacy of altruism; but he does suppose the latter to be so central to the former that its abandonment would in effect spell the end of morality as we know it. And he contends that 'the antithetical concepts "moral" and "immoral"' are rooted in the 'psychological error' which consists in the interpretation of certain human actions and motives as ' "selfless," "unegoistic," "self-denying" – all unreal, imaginary' (*WP* 786). He finds it possible at least to make some sense of the 'apparently crazy idea' that the welfare of my neighbor *ought* to possess for me a higher value than my own . . . [while] my neighbor himself *ought* to . . . subordinate [his] to *my* welfare,' by supposing that a certain sort of 'social' interest is thereby expressed, fostering 'a perspective that seeks to make it impossible to see oneself' (*WP* 269). But he denies both that this idea answers to any genuinely altruistic strand in the basic fabric of human nature, and also that human nature admits of being so transformed that a strand of this sort does or may come to appear in it.

Nietzsche by no means thinks that human beings never do anything that is not in their own interest. On the contrary, he recognizes and indeed makes much of the fact that they can be and often are induced to act in ways which are at variance with it. Thus he remarks that society commonly manages at least in part to restrain and subdue 'the selfishness and willfulness of the individual' (*WS* 40), and to bring it about that in what people do 'the long-term advantage of the community' is promoted at the expense of both the immediate 'advantage of the individual, namely his momentary well-being, and also his long-term advantage and even his continued existence' (*HH* II:89). He takes it to be obvious, however, that this represents no triumph of 'disinterestedness' over the pursuit of 'advantages' in human affairs. Moreover, he suggests that this result is obtained chiefly through the subtle (and sometimes not so subtle) exploitation of the fears, anxieties, resentments, needs, aspirations, conceits and other such self-centered and advantage-seeking motives of those in question, and through their conversion to alternative forms of self-identification giving different direction to their basic self-interestedness.

Even when acting contrary to their own actual best interest, therefore, Nietzsche argues that people do so in direct and indirect consequence of the operation of motivating forces geared to the securing of advantages and the avoidance of disadvantages. And the same applies with respect to actions serving to benefit others rather than oneself, even when they are performed with this as one's avowed aim and in the belief that one is morally obligated so to act. If anything like a disposition to benefit others is exhibited by some, he maintains, it is only a derivative one, in the formation of which self-interested motives have been enlisted and are covertly operative. Thus, he writes, 'if only those actions are moral, as the usual definition has it, which are done for the sake of others and for their sake alone, then there are no moral actions!' And he goes on to suggest that it is only as a result of 'a few intellectual mis-conceptions' in the interpretation of certain phenomena that some actions have been 'separated from "egoistic" actions' and so understood and valorized (*D* 148).

If 'moral actions' are construed as actions *serving* primarily to benefit others (either individually or generally), and only secondarily if at all to benefit the agent, then of course *there are* such actions. But if it is further laid down that only those actions of this sort qualify as 'moral' the determining ground of which is a 'moral will' existing and operating independently of all forms and mani-festations of self-interest, and having the good of others as its inherent object, Nietzsche takes objection to the supposition that anything human beings ever do answers to this description. He finds it quite understandable that actions benefiting others, and those who perform them to their own disadvantage, should be *praised*; but he contends that 'this praise certainly was not born from the spirit of selflessness,' and 'has always been far from "selfless," far from "unegoistic," ' since it is fundamentally tied to estimations of the 'probable consequences' of such actions 'for us and society.' Acting in a 'selfless' and 'self-sacrificial' manner

449

earns praise *'because it brings advantages'* (*GS* 21). He further allows that human beings respond to such praise and encouragement, as well as to the prospect of the imposition of negative sanctions if they fail to act in the prescribed manner, and thus may gradually come to be disposed to do so. But while such influences may join with their basic susceptibilities to create the semblance of a 'moral will,' it is in terms of them rather than the possession of any such faculty operating independently of them that the phenomenon variously described in terms of 'selflessness,' 'benevolence' and 'altruism' is to be understood.

Thus if 'the spirit of selflessness' is conceived essentially as the outcome of the process which 'trains the individual to be a function of the herd,' and altruism is construed as 'herd instinct in the individual' (*GS* 116), their possibility and reality may readily be granted, and the morality centering upon them may be allowed to play a significant role in human life and have a genuine basis in fact. But if larger claims are made for them, and they are taken to involve the radical transcendence of all more mundane elements of human nature and conditions of human existence, they turn out to be among the grand illusions and errors by means of which human life has been sustained and transformed, but which cannot be philosophically countenanced. They have long been misinterpreted in this way, and associated with what Nietzsche terms a 'dreadful forgery of the psychology of man.' Once one discerns the 'psychological error' it involves, however, 'one grasps that altruistic actions are only a species of egoistic actions.' Nietzsche's guiding thought here is 'the derivation of all affects from the one will to power: the same essence'; and it leads him to conclude that *irreducibly* 'altruistic' actions are 'altogether impossible.' For if this hypothesis is correct, the possibility of anything as different from this type of 'motivating force' as a purely other-regarding will is precluded (*WP* 786).

Thus for Nietzsche the lofty language of 'altruism' and 'selflessness' is only misleading rhetoric, serving as a kind of 'moral disguise' of which 'the herd animal with its profound mediocrity, timidity, and boredom with itself' avails itself in order 'to look nobler, more important, more respectable, "divine" ' (*GS* 352). Those who embrace such a morality thus have not transcended egoism at all; they have only substituted a subtler, perhaps more 'enlightened' but also rather dishonest form of it for a more blatant (and possibly less advantageous) one. The existence of moralities of this sort should by no means be taken to demonstrate that human beings are actually capable of achieving a complete transcendence of egoism, and of adopting an entirely selfless and disinterested

450

standpoint in their deliberations. To leap to this conclusion is to interpret this phenomenon superficially and erroneously, or at least very questionably. And if it is indeed the case that one only 'praises selflessness *because it brings him advantages*,' Nietzsche adds that this reveals a 'fundamental and fatal contradiction in the morality that is very prestigious nowadays: the *motives* of this morality stand opposed to its *principle*' (GS 21).

Nietzsche's position with respect to the possibility of altruism rests heavily upon his more general account of human nature, action, and social existence. His case is essentially that the actual 'evidence' afforded by the performance of apparently altruistic actions, the profession of altruistic intentions and the prevalence in many societies of altruistic ideals can be handled quite well by the sort of account he provides, on which they are all derivative of fundamentally non-altruistic features of human life; and that, on the other hand, the sort of philosophical anthropology which would have to be assumed in order to accord these phenomena independent status in relation to the latter would be at once less 'economical' and much more dubious in its principles than is his own. Human beings may not lose the character of being very complicated creatures when they are 'translated back into nature,' as he is convinced they must be; but once they are, their complicated nature assumes a different aspect. And one casualty of the translation is the idea that they are capable of putting the 'motivating forces' rooted in their fundamental natural constitution out of play, and judging and acting instead in a purely 'selfless' and 'disinterested' manner, directed by motives of an altogether different sort.

Moralities at the bar of judgment

X

It bears repeating, however, that the adoption of the account of human nature Nietzsche advances does not deny to moralities the power to exert a significant influence upon the course and character of human life. 'Law-giving moralities are the principal means of fashioning men' in various particular ways, he writes, when they achieve concrete embodiment 'in the form of laws, religions, and customs.' So, for example, the 'herd-animal morality' aiming at 'a universal green-pasture happiness on earth' is suggested to have exerted a profound influence in recent human history, and to stand 'malignantly in the way of [the] rise and evolution' of 'men of great creativity' through whom human life might be further enhanced (*WP* 957).

Moralities thus are taken by Nietzsche not only to be symptomatic of the affective constitutions of those who embrace them, and expressive of the conditions of the preservation and flourishing of the human communities in which they appear, but also to promote the adoption of certain valuations by those whose lives they touch. Under the spell of such 'moral values,' people come to live differently than they otherwise would or might, were they to come to adopt differing sets of values. What Nietzsche takes to be the dominant morality of the present time is marked by a number of these value-determinations. And his most fundamental objections to it concern the detrimental impact he considers them to have had and to continue to have upon the quality of human life. 'Even if a morality has grown out of an error,' he writes, 'the realization of this fact would not as much as touch the problem of its value' (*GS* 345). The latter, on his view, ultimately comes down to its 'value for life'; and when assessed in this light, he argues that present-day morality fares very badly indeed.

This is a topic on which Nietzsche waxed increasingly vehement. His strongest polemics are reserved for Christianity and for Wagner. The 'herd-animal morality' aiming at the happiness and well-being of all and championing selflessness, 'equal rights' and 'sympathy with all that suffers' (*WP* 957), however, is not far behind. His opposition to it derives from his conviction that 'a tendency hostile to life' — to its enhancement, if not to its mere preservation — is 'characteristic of morality' of this sort. 'Whoever reflects upon the way in which the type man can be raised to his greatest splendor and power,' he writes, and on the other hand considers the nature of this morality and the consequences of its ascendency, must recognize that 'morality has been essentially directed to the opposite end: to obstruct or destroy that splendid evolution wherever it has been going on' (*WP* 987).

This may not be its overt aim and express intent; but it is its general effect, for 'all the forces and drives by virtue of which life and growth exist lie under the ban of morality,' while the dispositions it cultivates have a stultifying impact upon human development. It is for this reason that Nietzsche contends that 'One must destroy morality if one is to liberate life' (*WP* 343), even though it may have long been 'a useful error' (*WP* 402), which 'was needed that man might prevail in his struggle with nature and the "wild animal"' in himself (*WP* 403). 'From a superior point of view,' he writes, what is required and to be desired is the 'emancipation of man from the narrow and fear-ridden bonds of morality' (*WP* 386).

A new and different sort of look at 'moral values' is called for; and the 'standard by which the value of moral evaluations is to be determined' is that of 'the elevation and strengthening of the type man' (*WP* 391).

Nietzsche arrived at this position after having earlier considered, and dismissed, the idea that these 'evaluations' and the precepts deriving from them might be justified by reference to considerations pertaining to the 'greatest happiness.' In the first place, he observes that it is not clear whether this is supposed to mean 'the greatest amount that particular individuals might eventually achieve, or an ultimately achievable (but in no way calculable) average-happiness of all' (*D* 106). And he then suggests that the desired justification is not forthcoming in either case. For, with respect to the former, he contends that 'the precepts one calls "moral" are in truth directed against individuals and by no means promote their happiness' — except, perhaps, in the event that they have been so thoroughly schooled by morality that they know no form of felicity other than that which they derive from adherence to it. And with respect to the latter, he reflects: 'These precepts have equally little relation to the "happiness and well-being of mankind" — which words cannot even be given any strict meaning, much less be used as guiding stars on the dark ocean of moral endeavor' (*D* 108).

In the second place, and more fundamentally, Nietzsche takes a very dim view of the preoccupation with 'happiness' which underlies this entire approach to morality. Thus he derides 'the indefatigable, inevitable British utilitarians,' who promote '*English* morality' with great zeal, out of the conviction that 'it serves humanity best, or "the general utility," or "the happiness of the greatest number" — no, the happiness of *England*.' For in addition to being afflicted with this odd enthusiasm, he holds that 'none of these ponderous herd animals' recognizes 'that "the general welfare" is no ideal, no goal, no remotely intelligible concept, but only an emetic' (*BGE* 228). And he further suggests that their 'morality of utility' reflects the stunted aspirations of 'the violated, oppressed, suffering, unfree, who are uncertain of themselves and weary' and are preoccupied with merely 'enduring the pressure of existence' (*BGE* 260), knowing nothing of 'creative powers and an artistic conscience' (*BGE* 225).

It is at least a step in the right direction, on Nietzsche's view, when attention is shifted from human happiness to the flourishing of mankind; but this is only a first step, which he still finds far from sufficient to enable one to view morality in the proper light. 'Everywhere one now hears the aim of morality put roughly thus,'

453

he remarks: 'it is the preservation and advancement of mankind. But this means only that a formula is wanted, and nothing more.' For this formula provides no answer to the questions of what sort of life is to be preserved, and what sort of advancement is to be achieved. 'Can one tell sufficiently from it whether one is supposed to be concerned with the longest possible endurance of mankind? Or with the greatest possible dis-animalizing of mankind?' This is left unspecified, though it makes a great deal of difference. Thus Nietzsche exclaims: 'How different the means — that is, the practical morals — would have to be in each of these cases!' (D 106).

He further is not prepared to accord intrinsic value either to the perpetuation of the human race or to its 'dis-animalization' as such. They too stand in need of justification; and thus morality cannot be justified in terms of its utility in relation to either eventuality. One must look beyond both, he holds, to find the broader standard by reference to which they may be conceived to possess significance, and in terms of which 'our' or any other sort of morality is ultimately to be assessed. As has been seen, the standard he proposes — derived from his reflections on the fundamental nature of life and the world as 'will to power' — focuses upon the idea of the quantitative and qualitative enhancement or 'strengthening and elevation' of life. And this is a development which is by no means guaranteed by the 'dis-animalization' of human life, by its indefinite preservation, or by the ascendency of the type of morality under consideration. Indeed, it is purported to be endangered by certain turns the first may take, by the subordination of all other concerns to the second, and by the effects of the third.

The examination of 'the *value* of that most famous of all medicines which is called morality' in this larger perspective is what Nietzsche calls 'our task' (GS 345). It will be obvious why, in this perspective, he considers the sort of ascetic morality which '*condemns* for its own sake, and *not* out of regard for the concerns, considerations, and contrivances of life' to be 'a specific error with which one ought to have no pity.' In brief, it 'causes immeasurable harm' to all those who are induced to embrace it (TI V:6). It is 'the very *instinct of decadence*, which makes an imperative of itself' (TI V:5); and as such it is only the most extreme form of '*anti-natural* morality' generally, which essentially is directed '*against* the instincts of life: it is *condemnation* of these instincts, now secret, now outspoken and impudent' (TI V:4).

It should also be clear why Nietzsche extends this harshly negative verdict to the seemingly more humane sort of morality which places a premium upon happiness, and promotes selflessness and pity (or 'sympathy with all that suffers') as central virtues. It is upon the question of the value of this sort of morality in particular that he focuses his attention, remarking that this is where his 'real concern' lay, since it is 'precisely here that I saw the great *danger* to mankind' (*GM* P:5). His point, in brief, is that 'a symptom of regression' is 'inherent in the "good" [so construed], likewise a danger, a seduction, a poison, a narcotic, through which the present was possibly living *at the expense of the future*' — and thus that 'precisely morality would be to blame if the *highest power and splendor* actually possible for the type man was never in fact attained' (*GM* P:6). It is worth noting, however, that he also takes this sort of morality to have a place in the larger economy of human life. For he regards it as the type of morality best suited both to the needs of the great majority of them ('the herd'), and to their adaptation to a supporting role in the emergence of an enhanced form of human life.

Thus Nietzsche would by no means have everyone abandon the 'herd morality' he so frequently excoriates. On the contrary, he considers it to be entirely fitting, and hardly capable of being improved upon (at least in its milder, non-ascetic form) where all those who do not have it in them to be *more* than the 'herd type' of human being are concerned. What he objects to is rather its inculcation in the potential exceptions to the human rule; *that* is where he takes it to be so seriously detrimental to the enhancement of human life. 'The ideas of the herd,' he writes, 'should rule in the herd — but not reach out beyond it' (*WP* 287). His critique of the 'evaluations' he takes to be central to this type of morality thus must be understood as subject to these qualifications if its force and its limits are to be properly understood.

It is in part owing to considerations of this sort that Nietzsche arrives at conclusions with respect to the value of these 'moral values' which are not as simply and completely negative as one might initially suppose, and indeed as some of his less guarded and more polemical remarks might seem to suggest. Their evaluative status, on his view, like that of many other 'values' considered in the previous chapter, is fundamentally ambiguous, even if emphatically negative in certain contexts and more negative than positive on balance. Perhaps the best way to see this is to turn again to his assessment of what he considers to be two of the most important instances of these 'values,' namely, 'selflessness' and 'pity,' amplifying upon what was earlier said with respect to them in the context of discussion of his 'revaluation of values.' I shall deal with the former first.

455

XI

The idealization of selflessness, it will be recalled, is suggested by Nietzsche fundamentally to have the significance of a reaction to (and defensive strategy directed against) those in whom basic human 'drives' are strongest and therefore most threatening, on the part of those in whom they are relatively weak and the capacity to assert themselves directly is wanting. It is the culmination of a development involving the denigration of 'everything that elevates an individual above the herd and intimidates the neighbor,' while only the 'modest, submissive, conforming mentality, the *mediocrity* of desires attains moral designation and honors' (*BGE* 201). This development may be understandable; but it also poses a danger, since the strongest of the 'forces and drives by virtue of which life and growth exist' are thus given a negative valuation, and those who possess them are given a bad conscience with respect to them. And to the extent that the latter are induced by an altruistic morality to make that sort of self-sacrifice on behalf of others which consists in checking and repressing these 'forces and drives' in order not to risk harming or offending them, human life is diminished both in vigor and in quality.

It is in this way that Nietzsche sees selflessness as linked with 'decadence' and 'decline.' 'Life itself is to my mind the instinct for growth,' he writes, and 'for an accumulation of forces, for *power*,' rather than a condition of stability in which none poses any threat to anyone else; 'where the will to power is lacking there is decline' (*A* 6). And he regards the 'value' of selflessness both as expressive of a relative lack of 'will to power' (or rather, of a deficient modality of it which aims merely at preservation), and as suppressive of it where it is to be found in any greater measure. A morality which makes selflessness a value and condemns any form of self-assertion adversely affecting others thus may be seen to have a fundamentally negative relation to life and value for it.

The self-assertiveness against which Nietzsche takes the valuation of selflessness to be detrimentally directed, however, should not be confused with the mere selfishness and impulsive self-indulgence of which everyone is capable. Indeed, where the latter are concerned, he is more than willing to concede value to self-control and self-denial, not only for the 'herd' but for all. For he regards such 'self-overcoming' not only as a means to the harmonization of ordinary social relations, but moreover as indispensable to the achievement of significant forms of self-assertion on the part of those who have it in them to rise to them. In this context he thus takes the morality of selflessness to have something to be said for it, notwithstanding its underlying twofold connection with 'weakness.' As a *general rule* he considers it to be preferable to an 'egoistic' morality or to mere egoism; and the exceptions to it, upon the desirability and importance of which he lays great stress, are better handled by being allowed for *beyond* it, on his view, rather than by being generally prescribed in place of it or incorporated into it.

Nietzsche's 'beyond good and evil' thus has the character more of a 'teleological suspension of the ethical' than of either its utter repudiation or its piecemeal modification — with the proviso, however, that it is only as a 'means' that a morality of selflessness has any value whatever. This counter-reckoning with respect to it first involves recognizing that the associated form of morality serves to enable one to attain 'a certain power over oneself'; and that, once attained, 'one can employ this power in the further free development of oneself: will to power as self-elevation and strengthening' (*WP* 403). And, second, it involves drawing an important distinction in the consideration of 'the natural value of egoism' and of selflessness: in the case of many, the valuation of the latter is quite appropriate; while in the case of some, the former (provided that it is distinguished from mere self-indulgence) is warranted instead.

> Self-interest is worth as much as the person who has it: it can
> be worth a great deal, and it can be unworthy and contemptible.
> Every individual may be scrutinized to see whether he represents
> the ascending or the descending line of life. . . . If he represents
> the ascending line, then his worth is indeed extraordinary — and
> for the sake of life as a whole, which takes a step farther
> through him, the care for his preservation and for the creation
> of the best conditions for him may even be extreme (*TI* IX:33).

On the other hand, Nietzsche goes on to say, 'if he represents the descending development,' it matters not at all that he too is 'an individual.' For 'the single one, the "individual," as hitherto understood by the people and philosophers alike, is an error after all: he is nothing by himself.' What matters is only which sort of development a person represents. And if it is the 'descending' one, 'then he has small worth,' and ought to 'take away as little as possible from those who have turned out well.' This, Nietzsche asserts, is 'required' by 'the minimum of decency'; and if so, egoism would certainly have a negative value in such cases, while selflessness would be entirely commendable (*TI* IX:33).

Nietzsche's revaluation of this 'moral value' thus does not stop with the critique which reveals it to be a 'false valuation,' nor with

457

a 'genealogical' and psychological analysis which renders it even less palatable (although more understandable). It also extends beyond a historical-evolutionary reconsideration which prompts 'profoundest gratitude for that which morality has achieved hitherto,' and further still beyond a reflection on the nature of life and what is conducive to the enhancement of life which leads to the judgment that it is 'a burden which may become a fatality' (*WP* 404). For it involves the additional subjection of it to a differentiating assessment in various more specific human contexts, in the light of the 'order of rank' applying to them and their place in the larger economy of human life and development.

XII

Turning next to Nietzsche's examination of the value of pity as a 'moral value,' a few preliminary remarks are in order. As was seen in the previous chapter, he is harshly critical of the common accordance of great importance to it in the conduct of human affairs. Lest it be supposed, however, to his discredit, that he was simply callous or utterly heedless of human suffering, it should be recalled that he certainly was no stranger to personal distress. Indeed, what he had to endure along these lines was far more than most of us ever even approach. The 'hardness' toward suffering and the 'cheerfulness' in the face of it, which he commends in contrast to pity, by no means came easily to him. Rather, they were something he had to strive for, against the grain of the self-pity to which it would have been only too natural and easy for him to succumb. His conception of 'self-overcoming' had no more poignant application in his own case than with respect to the suffering he knew so well.

Suffering and life thus went hand in hand for Nietzsche. It was their very inseparability, in his eyes, which led him to stress the necessity of coming to terms with suffering rather than avoiding the issue in one's philosophical moments. And the 'joy' he repeatedly celebrates is not characterized by obliviousness to suffering, but rather by a strength and vitality great enough to enable one to take it in stride. This notion, which one encounters from his early account of the Greeks' triumph over suffering through their art in *The Birth of Tragedy* to his last writings, is given its most striking expression in the 'Drunken Song' near the end of the last book of *Zarathustra* (Z IV:19:12):

> The world is deep.
> Deeper than day had been aware.

> Deep is its woe;
> Joy — deeper yet than agony:
> Woe implores: go!
> But all joy wants eternity —
> Wants deep, wants deep eternity.

Nietzsche's critique of pity is above all an attack upon the tendency sufferers have (as he well knew) to be overwhelmed by their own suffering and the similar sufferings of others, and in their preoccupation with it to take it to matter more than anything else. And he inveighs against this tendency all the more vigorously in view of the widespread success of those moved by it in extending the sway of this essentially negative perspective of evaluation to those who at least have it in them to avoid adopting it and the pessimism it engenders, and to think and live more affirmatively. The issue is not whether suffering is an eradicable and pervasive feature of life, or whether it is onerous, but rather *how much it matters*, and what attitudes with respect to it are detrimental and conducive to the flourishing and enhancement of life.

Nietzsche is prepared to concede that it *does* matter, by no means regarding it positively or even with complete indifference *per se*. What he denies is that it matters more than anything which might cause or increase it. Indeed, he even allows that, within certain limits, pity is appropriate with respect to it. Thus he says of one who is strong and 'by nature a *master*' that 'when such a man has pity, well, *this* pity has some value.' For such a person is not so blinkered by suffering and so hobbled by his own weakness and distress that they frame his manner of seeing himself and others and set the tone of his thought and action. 'But what good is the pity of those who suffer,' Nietzsche continues, or of 'those who, worse, *preach* pity'; for in them it is only an expression of weakness, or at any rate of a dangerous subordination of other concerns to this fundamentally negative one (*BGE* 260).

'Noble and courageous human beings,' he thus contends, 'are furthest removed from that morality which finds the distinction of morality precisely in pity,' even though 'the noble human being, too, helps the unfortunate.' For that morality is the sort of 'slave morality' in which he suggests that, characteristically, 'a pessimistic suspicion about the whole condition of man will find expression, perhaps a condemnation of man along with his condition.' The 'noble human being' who helps the unfortunate does so 'not, or almost not, from pity, but prompted more by an urge begotten by excess of power' (*BGE* 260). Here pity, while not absent, is

459

not primary, for the abhorrence of suffering is not the central operative principle. It is generosity proceeding from strength, rather than commiseration issuing from weakness, which is the dominant theme in this case.

'Where pity is preached today,' on the other hand, Nietzsche contends that one with a good psychological ear 'will hear a hoarse, groaning, genuine sound of *self-contempt*' (*BGE* 222). One who 'preaches pity,' he suggests, is thereby covertly asking that pity be felt not only for others but also for himself. In calling attention to the sufferings of others along with himself, and implying that their and his sufferings are what are most deserving of attention and concern about them, one gives expression to what may indeed be called 'self-contempt,' along with contempt for others. For if what matters most about people is the grievousness of their sufferings, then they must be admitted to be a contemptible lot, unworthy of any genuine esteem.

This might seem to be Nietzsche's own view; but it is important to see that it is not. It is rather the implicit upshot of the 'morality of pity,' which he extracts from the latter precisely in order to show how far it is from being an expression of the 'love of man' its advocates profess it to be. It *belittles* man, in a way to which he takes strong objection — even while conceding that it unfortunately comes very close indeed to the truth where the great majority of human beings are concerned. He was convinced that, great though his own sufferings were, they were not what mattered most about *him*; this, he believed, was rather what he had it in him to become and to do, with his sufferings requiring to be turned to advantage, transcended, or in any event endured as best he could. And he took the same to be true of others — of some, at any rate, if not of all. He had neither patience nor respect for the self-pitying, and for those whose idea of love for their fellow man reached no further than commiseration with them.

Thus Nietzsche refers disparagingly to the prevalent 'faith in the morality of *shared* pity, as if that were morality in itself, being the height, the *attained* height of man.' On his view it actually is the opposite of this: a 'new Buddhism' running counter to the attainment of such 'higher states' and even to the preservation of the vitality this presupposes. It is expressive of a 'deadly hatred of suffering generally' (*BGE* 202), born of weakness, and unheeding of the fact that avoidable suffering is a part of the price requiring to be paid if life is to flourish, 'higher cultures' are to be created, and a higher humanity is to be attained. 'A morality . . . which desires to train man for the heights,' Nietzsche holds, will of necessity have 'reverse intentions' from those of this morality,

460

which combines the 'doctrine' of 'sympathy with all that suffers' with the view that 'suffering itself [is] something that must absolutely be absolished' (*WP* 957). Indeed, he writes: '*You* want, if possible — and there is no more insane "if possible" — *to abolish suffering*. And we? It really seems that *we* would rather have it higher and worse than ever' (*BGE* 225). His point here is that the avoidance of all 'needless suffering' would preclude attainment of the level of activity and experience he has in mind. For its achievement is arduous, and the employment of creative powers it involves is disruptive. Thus he has Zarathustra exclaim: 'Alas, where in the world has there been more folly than among the pitying? . . . Thus be warned of pity.' And:

> But mark this too: all great love is even above all of its pity;
> for it still wants to create the beloved.
>   'Myself I sacrifice to my love, *and my neighbor as myself*'
> — thus runs the speech of all creators. But all creators are
> hard (*Z* II:3).

Suffering, in short, is inseparable from the qualitative enhancement of life; and instead of taking the former to warrant repudiation of the latter, Nietzsche takes the latter to sanction the former, and so to require a reversal of the basic intention of the morality of pity.

Beyond good and evil

XIII

This sort of assessment of moral values might appear to be the culmination of Nietzsche's thinking with respect to morality. And in a sense it is, at least where moralities past and present are concerned; for he takes there to be little more of any philosophical significance to be said about them, once this assessment has been carried out in conjunction with those forms of analysis of it considered previously. In another sense, however, what he has to say along these lines is but the conclusion of an investigation that is merely a long preliminary in relation to a further part of his treatment of morality. For he is concerned not merely to come to terms with such moralities, but moreover to look beyond them, and to achieve a reorientation of the manner in which morality is understood that would serve to place it on a new footing and enable it to acquire new substance.

Here as so often elsewhere (e.g., in his discussions of truth and knowledge, of the soul and consciousness, and even of philosophy

461

itself), Nietzsche is not content to allow the notion to remain the exclusive possession of those whose construal and application of it draw his fire upon it, and to disassociate himself from it as completely as he repudiates their views. Rather, he proceeds to appropriate it and recast it along lines he considers more tenable, thereby giving it a new lease on life and a positive role in his own thinking. Moral philosophy takes (or should take) a new turn, on Nietzsche's view, and is provided with new tasks, when its subservience to prevailing modes of moral interpretation is ended. It is one of his main purposes to set it upon this different course.

But he seeks to do more than this as well. For he desires further to revolutionize moral thinking, and help usher in a new 'period which should be designated negatively, to begin with, as *extra-moral*' (*BGE* 32) — but which also may no less appropriately be thought of, in a broader sense of the term, as involving the *reformation* of morality, and thus as a new chapter in its (as well as mankind's) history. 'The overcoming of morality' — that is, 'morality in the traditional sense' — may be the initial task confronting 'the finest and most honed . . . consciences of today' (*BGE* 32). But with the accomplishment of this preliminary task another takes its place, 'morals' or moral theory now being transformed into the elaboration of 'the doctrine of the relations of supremacy under which the phenomenon of "life" comes to be,' and may flourish and admit of enhancement (*BGE* 19).

This, at any rate, is the perspective in which Nietzsche proposes to reinterpret and resurrect the notion of morality, thereby abolishing the longstanding opposition between the 'moral' and the 'natural.' His formula for this is the 'naturalization of morality' — by which he has in mind not only the establishment of the status of all putatively 'moral phenomena' as 'natural phenomena,' but also the recasting of morality along 'naturalistic lines,' with 'purely naturalistic values' replacing distinctively and irreducibly 'moral values' as its basic principles. This he proclaims to be one of his 'fundamental innovations' (*WP* 462). He insists that it is not his intention to 'promote any morality' (*GS* 292); for on his view there is no *one* morality which alone answers to and expresses ultimate truths of some sort written into the fundamental nature of reality or of man, or which even would be best for all to embrace and follow. This does not mean, however, that he considers there to be nothing to be said concerning the appropriateness of various types of moralities in particular human contexts. So, for example, he contends that the 'herd animal morality' he finds to predominate at present is at once well suited to the conditions of existence and constitutions of many human beings, and also highly detrimental to others. If, as he urges, 'moralities must be forced to bow first of all before the order of rank' (*BGE* 221) in consequence of the recognition that 'the demand of one morality for all is detrimental for the higher man' (*BGE* 228), he also holds that 'the order of rank between man and man' mandates the establishment of comparably differing moralities adjusted to their divergent requirements and capabilities.

'Every morality,' Nietzsche writes, is in one sense 'a bit of tyranny against "nature," ' not only standing 'opposed to *laisser aller*' but also constituting 'a long compulsion' in some 'single direction,' which does not leave those subject to it as it finds them (*BGE* 188). In another sense, however, this accords with a fundamental imperative which he takes to be rooted in the basic character of life (although it can and not infrequently does take a pathological turn); for he considers 'the morality of development' to be 'the doctrine preached by life itself to all that has life' (*WP* 125). In the language of *Zarathustra*, 'self-overcoming' is of the very essence of life, and moralities of the sort presently under consideration are instruments of such 'self-overcoming' — strictures under the constraint and discipline of which human developmental potentialities become actualizable.

'Every naturalism in morality — that is, every healthy morality — is dominated by an instinct of life; some commandment of life is fulfilled by a determinate canon of "shalt" and "shalt not" ' (*TI* V:4). Owing to the constitutional differences among human beings, however, different manners of life are properly prescribable for various human 'types,' in the form of differing moralities. For if these constitutional differences translate into different 'conditions of life,' and if one thinks of a 'morality' as 'a system of evaluations that partially coincides with the conditions of a creature's life' (*WP* 256), as Nietzsche proposes to do, the result is a form of moral pluralism when this general conception of morality is applied more concretely to human life, according to which different moralities are warranted in different human contexts, while being undesirable in others.

While this moral pluralism may be regarded as a kind of relativism, it is not a *cultural* relativism, let alone a subjective one. It does not involve the denial that there are any objective considerations transcending cultural formations or subjective determinations by reference to which particular moralities may be justified and assessed, even though it does deny unconditional validity to any of them. It links them to the contingently obtaining and varying — but nonetheless definite — psycho-physiologically grounded 'conditions of life' of human beings. None is or can be absolute;

but moralities answering to this description are not merely conventional either, and clearly cannot be considered arbitrary. They are indeed 'relative'; but what they are relative *to* are circumstances pertaining to the actual constitutions of human beings of different sorts. Nietzsche's 'naturalization of morality' thus involves the incorporation of moral theory into philosophical anthropology, in the context of which it loses its autonomy but acquires legitimacy.

Nietzsche's meta-level 'morality of development,' however, reflects his conviction of the possibility of carrying the matter a step further. It represents a broadening of the context in which moral theory is situated, through the introduction of considerations deriving from his more comprehensive interpretation of 'life' and his associated general theory of value. Moralities, in his naturalistic perspective, when they are what they should be, are 'means' serving 'the aim of enhancing life' (*WP* 298); and for him this is not simply a matter of enabling each particular form of life, as it is, to flourish. He requires more of moralities than that they answer to the 'conditions of life' of various types of human beings, and thus within such contexts may be deemed 'healthy.' Rather, it is to 'life' more generally that they require to be referred — human life as a broader phenomenon, the strengthening and enhancement of which they are to serve, indirectly if not directly.

Nietzsche takes this position because he considers the health of a particular form of life as such to be no end or intrinsic value. It derives its only significance, on his view, from its relation to the emergence of 'life at its highest potency.' The significance it may thus possess, moreover, is taken to be limited as well as conditional, owing to the circumstance that certain kinds of 'sickness' are likewise conditions of the possibility of the long-term enhancement of life. A particular sort of morality may be indicated for human beings of some type not simply because it answers to their needs, and not because it is the version of the broader 'morality of development' best suited to them (for it may be nothing of the kind), but rather, more fundamentally, because it serves to maximize the merely indirect contribution of their existence to the 'elevation of the type "man." '

It is not owing primarily to its benefits for the general run of mankind, for example, that Nietzsche would have 'herd animal morality' cultivated among them. His reason is rather that the attainment of 'a high culture,' and thus of an enhanced form of human life, is possible 'only upon a broad base, upon a strong and healthily consolidated mediocrity' (*WP* 864). And it is likewise not owing to its advantages for exceptional individuals *themselves* that he considers a strongly self-assertive and rather

464

'egoistic' morality to be warranted in their case; nor yet again because he takes such a morality to *be* what the 'morality of development' of which he speaks comes down to in concrete terms. Rather, his advocacy of the former in their case derives from his conviction that, in the long run (though by no means in each instance and directly), the prospects for the enhancement of life will thereby be brightened, and will otherwise be virtually nil.

Both kinds of morality thus have the status of means to the same larger end; but they are no more than means. And they are means of very different sorts, adapted to the differing roles human beings endowed with varying capacities are suited to play in the attainment of this end. His 'morality of development' is a meta-level morality, in the sense that it is not a morality for everyone or anyone to live by, but rather a higher-order principle of moral theory by reference to which particular moralities people can live by may be arrived at and endowed with significance. It derives its meaning from his interpretation of 'life' in terms of 'will to power' and its transformations, and its force from the standard of value he extracts therefrom. And its implications vary with the human contexts and possibilities obtaining at different junctures in human history and in the cases of different human types.

Working all of this out is a task beyond that of elaborating a 'typology' and 'genealogy' of morals past and present, and further beyond that of subjecting them to 'revaluation.' It is undoubtedly at least in part with it in mind that he calls upon philosophers to be 'legislators,' and to do more than merely elaborate, analyze and assess existing evaluative and normative schemes. As one who is able to look beyond the forms of human life which have hitherto and presently been attained, and to discern 'what might yet be made of man' (*BGE* 203) and what sort of humanity is 'higher in value' (*A* 3), the 'genuine philosopher' is in a position to ascertain what sorts of moral 'legislation' along these lines are called for. And as one who ought to have a 'conscience for the overall development of man' (*BGE* 61), it is incumbent upon him to press for them.

Moral philosophy for Nietzsche thus is ultimately a strongly prescriptive as well as analytical and critical affair, notwithstanding his insistence upon the necessity of 'naturalizing' moral theory. It must take account of the links between moralities and the affective phenomena and social circumstances which tend to shape them and impose constraints upon their modifiability; but it should also be sensitive to the extent to which they nonetheless admit of modification, and concerned with the respects in which this may be desirable. It further must be appreciative of the fact that human beings differ in respects which are relevant to the determination of the sorts of morality appropriate for them. It therefore must deal with the possibility and desirability of differing moralities in different human contexts; and, recognizing that the morality prevailing 'in Europe today' is 'merely *one* type of human morality beside which . . . many other types, above all *higher* moralities, are, or ought to be, possible' (*BGE* 202), it should proceed from an examination of the former to the exploration and elaboration of the latter.

XIV

In speaking here and elsewhere of possible 'higher moralities' and contrasting them with 'herd animal morality,' Nietzsche does not merely have in mind the sort of thing he takes to have been its most notable historical rival, which he terms 'noble' or 'master morality.' He does indeed regard the latter as a type of 'higher morality' in relation to the former. The kind of higher morality with the possibility of which he is above all concerned, however, and for the preferability of which he argues in the case of the potentially 'higher man,' is by no means simply 'master morality' resurrected. It may be akin to the latter in certain respects; but it differs importantly from it as well, reflecting the fact that Nietzsche takes the 'higher humanity' this exceptional sort of human being is capable of attaining to differ markedly from the sort of existence he supposes to have been characteristic of these 'master races.'

While he considers the *kind* of morality he has in mind to be appropriate for 'higher men' generally, he does not conceive of it as having the same specific content for them all. By its very nature it requires to be supplied with content reflecting not only the exceptional affective resources and creative power with which he takes potentially higher men generally to be endowed, but also the specific direction they may come to be given in particular cases. Thus he urges that, in place of seeking to establish some 'universal law' or 'categorical imperative,' we 'limit ourselves' to something quite different, at once less 'selfish' and more important: 'to the *creation of our own new tables of what is good*,' as 'human beings who are new, unique, incomparable, who give themselves laws, who create themselves,' and so *'become those we are'* (GS 335). The 'laws' potentially higher men are here spoken of as giving to themselves, and the 'tables of what is good' they are depicted as creating for themselves, are to be thought of as the concrete realizations of the 'higher morality' by means of which the higher humanity they have it in them to attain can be developed. And

466

while these concrete instances of it may have certain common characteristics worth noting, they clearly are likely to diverge very considerably.

One might object that it is inappropriate to continue to speak of 'morality' in this context, on the ground that the notion is properly applicable only where what Nietzsche terms 'laws of life and action' with at least a semblance of universality are concerned. Nietzsche undoubtedly would concede that he is certainly stretching the notion. On the other hand, a precedent can be found for its application in connection with such laws which one gives to oneself in none other than Kant, whom Nietzsche may be viewed as echoing here, albeit in a radically relativized manner. And it may further be said in his defense that once the notion of morality ceases to be regarded as having any legitimate application as it has traditionally been construed, one is at liberty to put it to a different use, adapting it as may be required. Nietzsche sometimes seems disposed simply to repudiate it along with the burden of erroneous interpretation and misguided evaluation it has come to carry. This course, however, is not the only one someone determined to dispense with the latter may reasonably take; nor does he invariably do so, frequently choosing instead to avail himself of the notion. And his appropriation of it for his purposes in the present context is actually but an instance of a rather common philosophical practice, which he follows on many other occasions as well.

Nietzsche's conception of a type of morality 'higher' than the other moralities he catalogs, and more appropriate than they in the case of 'higher men,' also draws upon another recognizable (though relatively unpopular) current of moral thought, according to which what one ought to do is related to how one ought to be. Advocates of this way of understanding morality have generally supposed that there is some one way all human beings ought to be, and therefore that all ought to do the same sorts of things to this end. While Nietzsche ultimately parts company with them on this point, he views and construes his 'higher morality' along the same basic lines.

In his relatively early remarks in this connection he does not concern himself with the differences among human beings affecting what they can be (and therefore how they ought to be), which figure so prominently in his later thinking. Rather, he focusses upon the possibility of modifying the prevailing notion of morality in such a way that 'the impersonal' would no longer be 'considered the true identifying mark of moral action,' and suggests replacing it with the idea of a type of 'personal action.' Thus he contrasts what he terms 'the morality of the mature individual' with the various forms of 'previous morality,' the latest and heretofore 'highest' of which seeks to induce one to 'live and act as a collective individual'; and he holds the basic principle of the former to be: 'to make a whole *person* of oneself, and in all one does to be concerned with one's *highest well-being* as such.' This, he continues, 'may take one further than those sympathetic impulses and actions for the benefit of others' to which the latter accords primary importance (*HH* I:94–5). If he subsequently abandoned the notion of a 'whole person' as a satisfactory specification of the nature of that 'higher humanity' to the attainment of which his higher type of morality would serve as a means (in favor of a broader notion stressing spiritual superiority and creativity), he retained this view of the sort of thing morality can be, and should be in this special human context.

Nietzsche often stresses the function of this kind of morality as a form of *discipline* indispensable to the potentially higher man's realization of his potential. Thus he speaks of it as serving 'to train men for the heights' (*WP* 957), and to enable one to 'transfigure himself and place himself way up, at a distance,' in contrast to others which answer to various all-too-human desires and interests (*BGE* 187). And in the same vein he writes:

> All those who do not have themselves well under control, and do not know morality as self-mastery and self-overcoming constantly practiced in the greatest and smallest matters, come naturally to exalt the good, sympathetic, benevolent sentiments of that instinctive morality which has no head, but rather seems simply to be all heart and helping hands (*WS* 45).

Such a morality of 'self-mastery and self-overcoming' involves restraint, resistance to impulse, negation and proscription no less than do other forms of morality. Moralities of this type too have their 'shall nots' as well as their 'shalls,' as does 'every healthy morality' along with all 'anti-natural morality' (*TI* V:4). If anything they are even more severely opposed to the principle of *laisser aller* than are other forms of morality. The restrictions and prohibitions they impose, however, have the significance of conditions of the possibility of attainment of states representing an enriched, strengthened, refined and more creative form of life. 'Morality, insofar as it *condemns* [otherwise than] out of regard for the concerns, considerations, and contrivances of life,' may 'cause immeasurable harm,' Nietzsche writes (*TI* V:6); but the qualification he attaches to this negative assessment is of great importance and should not be overlooked. When a morality 'condemns' in such a way that one living accordingly is thereby enabled to achieve that combination of 'spiritual superiority' and heightened vitality Nietzsche associates with the enhancement of life, his estimation of it is very different. Indeed, in this case it is something which he holds the 'higher man' cannot do — and cannot actually come to be — without. The capacity for self-control it cultivates represents a 'power' one may employ 'in the further free development of oneself'; and the very possibility of this development depends upon it (*WP* 403).

While morality in its more commonplace forms is to be superseded, therefore, he holds that if their supersession is not accompanied by the adoption of something along these lines, nothing on the order of an enhancement of life can be expected to result. And it too may also be considered a 'morality,' at least in an extended sense of the term. Nietzsche suggests that what is required is 'to *give* oneself a goal,' and to work out the means whereby it may be attained; and in this connection he takes 'an *experimental morality*' to be called for (*WP* 260). The 'laws of life and action' appropriate to the attaining of a goal one has fixed upon are what one's particular morality here would consist in; and they may be said to have an 'experimental' character, in that they require to be worked out through the exploration of alternative ways of pursuing it.

XV

A morality of this sort, like the kind of goal one may give oneself, is not conceived by Nietzsche to be inherently idiosyncratic, let alone essentially self-promoting. Both might appropriately be termed self-assertive, at least in a broad sense, and by way of contrasting them to those which are essentially other-regarding. They are no more self-centered, however, than are the tasks and efforts of the genuine artist, and involve self-sacrifice and self-overcoming no less than a kind of self-realization. Indeed, it is misleading even to speak of 'self-realization' here; for that is by no means the dominant theme of Nietzsche's remarks in this connection, either in the sense of the actualization of some 'true' but initially merely potential 'self,' or in the sense of the attainment of a type of 'selfhood' involving the acquisition of a distinct personal identity. The individuality he does suppose to be characteristic of his 'higher men' may be a mark of their higher humanity, but it is not that in terms of which the latter is to be conceived; nor, for that matter, does he take it to be a *desideratum* which it is the function of the positing and pursuit of goals to bring about. A measure of individuality may likewise in point of fact be indispensable to creativity,

469

and a symptom of highly developed spirituality; but it has no further significance than this on his view.

Indifference to oneself rather than preoccupation with oneself, and hardness toward oneself for the sake of goals which transcend one's own limited existence, are essential features of spiritual superiority as Nietzsche understands it. One might therefore think of the type of morality he has in mind here, together with the higher humanity with which he associates it, as *supra-individualistic*. It may be that the kinds of 'goals' through the positing and pursuit of which human life can alone be further enhanced can *only* be posited and pursued by exceptional human beings who have emancipated themselves from the anonymity and regimentation of the 'herd,' and the common, all-too-human concerns of the vast majority. If they are to lead in this direction, however, it is likewise the case for Nietzsche that they must extend beyond the mere self-preservation, self-affirmation and self-expression of those in question. Thus he takes exception to the idea that 'true morality' has as its object merely the promotion of the well-being *either* of 'other people' *or* of oneself, urging that it would be 'higher and freer' to '*look beyond*' all considerations of this sort and to 'pursue more distant purposes even under circumstances involving the suffering of others,' and one's own suffering as well. For 'through such sacrifice — meaning both ours *and our neighbors*' — we would strengthen and elevate the general sense of human *power*,' even though we might 'achieve nothing more' (*D* 146).

It is of some interest that, in this relatively early passage, the case in point Nietzsche mentions is that of 'advancing knowledge,' notwithstanding the 'doubt, grief and worse' by which the pursuit of knowledge may be attended (ibid.). It is difficult to imagine a goal one might set for oneself which would be further removed from a preoccupation with one's own well-being or selfhood; and yet this is clearly intended to exemplify the sort of undertaking through which Nietzsche supposes life may be enhanced. To be sure, he supposes the advancement of knowledge to require thinkers who are not merely highly self-disciplined and well-trained 'objective men' but also independently-minded, strong-willed, creative investigators and interpreters — and thus human beings who may stand out as individuals no less than as intellects. Indeed, it may be characteristic of them that they comport themselves in what might appear to others as an egoistic (or at any rate self-absorbed) manner; and it even could well be that markedly egoistic tendencies will as a rule be a part of the 'spiritual' make-up of those capable of significant endeavor along these lines. But what *matters* about them in the long run (which, for Nietzsche, is what far and away matters most) is what they are able to *do*, rather than their individualism and egoism; these are to be 'overcome' (as they themselves are to 'go under'), and are of significance only as material conditions of the former — even though, as such, they do take on a certain derivative significance.

The same may be said with respect to exceptional human types other than 'men of knowledge,' who operate in other domains of human endeavor with different sorts of goals. Artists, for example, are often mentioned by Nietzsche in this connection, as are men of action whose 'more distant purposes' have a political cast. They set different sorts of tasks for themselves, to which different means are appropriate; and by pursuing them they also may contribute to the broader enhancement of human life, enriching and transforming it. This is more often than not at some expense both to themselves and to others; but the payment of this price is of no ultimate significance, any more than is the measure of individuality without which such activity likewise would not be possible.

The higher type of morality Nietzsche conceives would seem to be modeled on the sort of thing involved in the idea of the 'morality' of the artist, which has a variety of analogs in cases ranging from that of the 'man of knowledge' to that of the statesman and even to that of the athlete. The apparently very disparate character of the aims discernable in this broad range of cases notwithstanding, these forms of endeavor all admit of a significant measure of creativity or innovativeness, and of the attainment thereby of varying forms and degrees of excellence. And what is meant in speaking of the 'moralities' of those who devote themselves to them is the particular sorts of discipline, selection and application necessary for the cultivation and fullest utilization of their powers along these lines. Different moralities are called for in different cases, and may further be called for in various instances of each; but on a general level of consideration they have a fundamentally similar character. They are dictated by the nature of that to which one aspires and the requirements of the specific tasks one determines upon; and they have to do with channeling one's efforts in certain ways, prescribing and proscribing various things affecting one's endeavor.

It is this sort of morality that Nietzsche considers to be appropriate to the 'higher man.' It is essentially the morality of the creator, whose only law is that to which the task he sets for himself requires that he submit. If he is subject to any higher imperative, it is only that which demands of him that he determine upon *some* way of being the creator he has it in him to be. It is as creators that human beings achieve the only sort of self-realization to

471

which Nietzsche attaches importance. Thus he holds that 'in man *creature* and *creator* are united' (*BGE* 225), and that the key to the enhancement and justification of life is the ascendence of the latter element over the former. 'Creation,' it will be recalled, is what he has Zarathustra proclaim to be 'the great redemption from suffering, and life's growing light.' Creators are the 'justifiers of all impermanence'; only the 'fervent will to create' which finds expression in the setting and pursuing of new and consuming tasks can endow human existence with worth. So Nietzsche has Zarathustra exclaim: 'Willing no more and esteeming no more and creating no more — oh, that this great weariness might always remain far from me!' (*Z* II:2).

This is the context in which his notion of a higher sort of morality appropriate to higher men is to be viewed. Broadly conceived, it has the basic general character of a dual demand. It requires of those capable of doing so that they strive at once to achieve a radical 'self-overcoming' with respect to all those 'all-too-human' tendencies which would weaken them and dissipate their energies, and also to engage in the most intensive possible cultivation and exercise of their creative powers. Thus Nietzsche writes: 'I teach the No to all that makes weak — that exhausts. I teach the Yes to all that strengthens, that stores up strength, that justifies the feeling of strength' (*WP* 54).

Maintaining that 'society must *not* exist for society's sake but only as the foundation and scaffolding on which a choice type of being is able to raise itself to its higher task and to a higher state of *being*' (*BGE* 258), Nietzsche conceives of this morality as an imperative pointing beyond the requirements of social life. It directs any such 'choice type of being' so to 'raise itself,' and thus to transform itself along the lines he indicates when he speaks of 'the development of ever higher, rarer, more remote, further-stretching, more comprehensive states' with which he associates 'the enhancement of the type "man"' (*BGE* 257). If this self-transformation is a privilege of such exceptional 'choice types,' it is also their responsibility; for he takes 'counting one's privileges and their exercise among one's *duties*' to be one of the basic 'signs of nobility' — along with 'never thinking of degrading our duties into duties for everybody' (*BGE* 272). Self-overcoming, self-mastery, self-cultivation, and self-direction in the employment of one's powers, along with the '*loftiness* of soul' they make possible, characterize both his higher type of human being and his higher type of morality.

Here 'the greater, more manifold, more comprehensive life transcends and *lives beyond* the old morality; the "individual"

472

appears, obliged to give himself laws and to develop his own arts and wiles for self-preservation, self-enhancement, self-redemption' (*BGE* 262). On this level of consideration, however, Nietzsche's higher morality assumes a somewhat different aspect; for as it is implemented it takes on a multiplicity of concrete forms, to which there is in principle no limit. Thus in a section entitled 'On the Way of the Creator,' he has Zarathustra ask: 'Can you give yourself your own evil and your own good and hang your own will over yourself as a law?' (*Z* I:17). Here he clearly implies that he takes precisely this to be an essential part of 'the way of the creator,' and to be required of one by the kind of morality he has in mind in its broader form. The latter can be followed only by devising such a more specific morality for oneself. There is nothing either in the idea of the enhancement of life or in the general notion of a higher morality of this sort from which one can infer what one's particular good — and therefore the content of one's concrete morality — ought to be; and the same applies with reference to anything which inquiry into the general nature of life or man might discover. So Nietzsche observes that 'to establish anew the laws of life and action' is a task for which 'our sciences' do not suffice. While 'it is only from them that one can get the foundation-stones for new ideals,' he contends, we cannot hope to extract from them 'the new ideals themselves.' These we must construct for ourselves; and thus we must 'do our best' in the absence of any guidelines 'to be our own *regis*, and set up little *experimental states*. We are experiments: and that is also what we want to be!' (*D* 453).

This view is the point of departure for Nietzsche's subsequent ringing affirmation of the possibility to which he here seems simply to resign himself, in his celebration of 'the creator' who 'breaks tablets and old values' and 'writes new values on new tablets' (*Z* III:12:26), adding to the store of 'good inventions on earth' for the sake of which 'the earth is to be loved' (*Z* III:12:17). This sort of creator stands in contrast to 'all rabble' and 'all that is despotic' as the type of '*a new nobility*,' whose 'new honor' lies in its representatives' 'will to go over and beyond themselves' as 'procreators and cultivators and sowers of the future' — in which connection 'many who are noble are needed, and noble men of many kinds' (*Z* III:12:11—12). What is most needful to this type of human being is summed up by Nietzsche in the formula: 'a Yes, a No, a straight line, a *goal*' (*A* 1). The 'straight line' is the path to the goal, whatever it may be; and the course thus determined is the law of life and action — the concrete morality — by which alone such a person is properly restrained and guided.

Whether this sort of law is one to which the term 'morality' may be considered legitimately applicable is in the end of little consequence to Nietzsche. What matters to him is that one see what is meant, rather than what one chooses to call it. Concern for others and their well-being admittedly does not figure directly in it (although the same applies with respect to concern for one's own preservation and well-being); and some may take this consideration alone to weigh decisively against the employment of the term in this connection. To Nietzsche's way of thinking, however, that would be a mere prejudice, even if one deeply entrenched in popular and philosophical usage. It is worth observing that others actually are not left entirely out of account, since he considers mankind generally to have a stake in the larger development to which exceptional human beings contribute by conducting themselves in the manner he indicates. But he does not rest his case for the construal of this kind of way of comporting oneself as a certain (higher) type of morality on this point. He would frankly concede that he is simply breaking with the traditional way of conceiving of morality in this respect, in the interest of giving the notion a new use which acquires great importance in the aftermath of the collapse of traditional modes of interpretation and evaluation, and in the light of those he proposes in place of them.

Notice remains to be taken of but one further aspect of Nietzsche's higher type of morality. It is relatively concrete, but does not relate directly to the specific laws of life and action associated with particular tasks exceptional human beings might set for themselves. It pertains rather to the general manner in which he supposes them to be prompted to live their lives by that sensibility engendered through their attainment and appreciation of their own high spirituality and spiritual superiority, which are of the essence of his 'new nobility.' He gives expression to it most fully in a passage in the last part of *Beyond Good and Evil*, which deals with 'What is Noble.' There he writes:

> To live with tremendous and proud composure; alsways beyond — . To have and not to have one's affects, one's pro and con, at will; to condescend to them, for a few hours; to seat oneself on them as on a horse, often as on an ass — for one must know how to make use of their stupidity as much as of their fire. To reserve one's three hundred foregrounds; also the dark glasses; for there are cases when nobody may look into our eyes, still less into our 'grounds.' And to choose for company that impish and cheerful vice, courtesy. And to remain master of one's four virtues: of courage, insight, sympathy, and solitude (*BGE* 284).

In a sense this is description rather than prescription; for Nietzsche takes himself here and in other such passages to be laying down or articulating no 'law,' either for all human beings or even for any particular set or type of them, but rather to be characterizing a certain distinctive manner of existence, which some may be or become capable of attaining and sustaining. This is a kind of description, however, which is intended to have normative import, for the latter if not for everyone. It expresses aspects of the nature of that 'higher humanity' which he considers not merely to be a human possibility, but moreover to be highly estimable and superior to any other; and it sets forth a standard preeminently worthy of adoption by those who have it in them to measure up to it. The higher morality of which it is the final part may be no morality for everyman, and no morality of any conventional sort; but Nietzsche never pretended or supposed that it is. Whether one chooses to call it a morality of a different kind or something else altogether, it is what he would have both exclude *laisser aller* and supplant all more commonplace moralities among those capable of doing without them. It may be 'beyond good and evil'; but it amply warrants his insistence that 'at least this does *not* mean "beyond good and bad" ' (*GM* I:17).

VIII

Art and Artists

No higher significance could be assigned to art than that which Nietzsche assigns to it in the opening section of *The Birth of Tragedy*: 'The arts generally' are said to 'make life possible and worth living' (*BT* 1). Art is never far from his mind, even when he is dealing with matters seemingly far removed from it. Thus, for example, as was earlier observed, he later characterized his 'view of the world' not only as 'anti-metaphysical' but also as 'an artistic one' (*WP* 1048), and suggested the world to be something on the order of 'a work of art which gives birth to itself' (*WP* 796). He also includes a number of artists among the 'higher men' whom he takes to stand out from the greater part of mankind hitherto, and likens to artists both the 'philosophers of the future' he envisions and the *Übermensch* he declares to be 'the meaning of the earth.' Indeed, he even aspired to art himself, investing much effort and a good deal of himself in poetic (and, in his early years, also musical) composition.

His views with respect to art and artists underwent a number of changes; but he never lost his concern with it, or abandoned the whole of his initial understanding and estimation of it. It would be an error to take the position set forth in *The Birth of Tragedy* to be 'Nietzsche's philosophy of art'; but it is with this book (purporting in the very first sentence to make a major contribution to 'the science of aesthetics') that his efforts along these lines began. It amply warrants extended discussion; for while it constitutes his first word about art rather than his last, it is a most remarkable one, long recognized as a classic contribution to the philosophical literature on art. I therefore shall devote the first half of this chapter to it, and then shall turn to his subsequent modifications of his views relating to art.

476

Art in The Birth of Tragedy

I

In a foreword entitled 'Attempt at a Self-Criticism' (*BT* S-C below), written some fourteen years after the book's publication, Nietzsche shows himself to be his own best critic — both severe and insightful. He readily acknowledges that 'this questionable book' has many faults, not the least of which is that it is so obviously 'a first book.' It would be hard to imagine any fair-minded reviewer speaking more harshly of it than he does, when he writes:

> today I find it an impossible book: I consider it badly written, ponderous, embarrassing, image-mad and image-confused, sentimental, in places saccharine . . ., uneven in tempo, without the will to logical cleanliness, very convinced and therefore disdainful of proof (*BT* S-C:3).

He recognizes the seriousness of the defects resulting from his having been under both the spell of Wagner and the sway of Schopenhauer, and scornfully brands the book's author a romantic, a pessimist and an 'art-deifier' (*BT* S-C:7). Yet he also observes that the book poses a number of questions of the utmost importance, and moves at least some distance toward a proper treatment of them. 'The problem of science,' 'the significance of morality,' and indeed 'the value of existence' are among the 'whole cluster of grave questions with which the book burdened itself' (*BT* S-C:4). But the question in the foreground of this cluster, which guides and structures his treatment of these others, concerns the nature of art and its significance in human life — Greek art in particular, but by no means exclusively. Thus he refers to 'the task which this audacious book dared to tackle for the first time: *to look at science in the perspective of the artist, but at art in that of life*' (*BT* S-C:2).

Nietzsche's interest in art was by no means either exclusively academic or merely personal; and the urgency he felt with respect to the task to which he refers was not at all simply a function of his belief that Greek art and art generally had not previously been adequately understood by his fellow classical philologists and aestheticians. In his original preface to the book, he speaks disparagingly of readers who may 'find it offensive that an aesthetic problem should be taken so seriously,' and who are unable to consider art more than a pleasant sideline, 'a readily dispensable tinkling of bells that accompanies the "seriousness of life".' Against them, he advances the startling contention that 'art represents the highest task and the truly metaphysical activity of this life' (*BT* P). And as has been observed, he goes on to maintain that 'the arts generally' serve to 'make life possible and worth living' (*BT* 1). It remains to be seen what he has in mind in so speaking of art. But these remarks provide ample indication of the centrality of art in his consideration of the set of issues he deals with here.

Nietzsche makes no attempt to conceal the influence of Schopenhauer on both his conception of reality and his thinking about the arts in *The Birth of Tragedy*. Schopenhauer may fairly be said to have been Nietzsche's primary philosophical inspiration, in a twofold way. On the one hand, he was initially convinced of the soundness of much of what Schopenhauer had to say about the world, life and the arts. But on the other, he was deeply unsettled by Schopenhauer's grim conclusions with respect to 'the value of existence' and the worth of living. He felt obliged to grant that Schopenhauer had a *prima facie* case, and had placed the burden of proof upon anyone who would make a different assessment of them. Rather than agreeing with him to the bitter end, however, he accepted the challenge Schopenhauer had thus posed. Much of his own thought may be regarded as an attempt to meet this challenge, and to establish a viable alternative verdict. And both in *The Birth of Tragedy* and subsequently, art figures centrally in his efforts to accomplish this task, as has been seen. Thus it is one of his central contentions that 'it is only as an *aesthetic phenomenon* that existence and the world are eternally justified' (*BT* 5). It is to art that he turns, in discussing the comparably dangerous predicament of 'the profound Hellene' upon 'having looked boldly right into the terrible destructiveness of so-called world history as well as the cruelty of nature,' saying: 'Art saves him, and through art — life' (*BT* 7).

The world 'in itself' for Schopenhauer, while not in principle unknowable, is not identical with phenomena as we experience them; and it neither contains nor consists in matter in motion, irreducible mental substances, or fundamental rational structures. Rather, it has the character of a formless, aimless, turbulent principle he elected to call 'will.' He conceived the world as a profusion of processes, in which this single basic principle manifests itself in many different ways; and for him the phenomena of nature as we experience them are appearances of certain instances of it. Each form of existence (such as man), on his view, is one possible *type* (or 'grade') of manifestation of this dynamic principle, analogous to a Platonic 'Idea' — a notion taken over by Schopenhauer and employed in this connection, to designate the blue-prints

478

(as it were) followed by his demi-urgic 'will' in its concrete articulation (Schopenhauer, *WWI*, § 26).

Schopenhauer conceived the plastic arts as having to do essentially with the discernment and representation of these Ideas; while music for him had the essentially different function of reflecting the nature of the underlying 'will' itself. To tragedy, on the other hand, he attributed yet another kind of function — to reveal the fate inexorably awaiting all specific manifestations of this 'will,' and the hopelessness of the plight of even the greatest in this essentially irrational world of ceaseless strife and destruction. This recognition was for him the deepest wisdom that either art or philosophy can yield, rendering insignificant not only the concerns with which we ordinarily are preoccupied, but also all knowledge — whether consisting in the cognition of relations among phenomena attainable through scientific investigation, or in the relatively higher-order discernment of the Ideas to which all existence conforms, or in the still higher knowledge of the nature of the 'world-will.'

Schopenhauer's basic reason for taking this darkly pessimistic position was that on his view all existence and life generally are characterized by ceaseless struggle and striving, inevitably resulting in destruction, and (among sentient forms of life) involving incessant suffering of one sort or another. The whole affair, to him, is quite pointless, since nothing of any value is thereby attained (the perpetuation of life merely continuing the striving and suffering). No transcendent purposes are thereby served; no pleasures, enjoyments or satisfactions attainable can suffice to overbalance the sufferings life involves, thus excluding a hedonic justification of living; and so life stands condemned at the bar of evaluative judgment. It is, in a word, absurd. There is nothing to it but ceaseless striving, inescapable suffering, inevitable destruction — all pointless, with no meaning and no justification, no redemption or afterworldly restitution, and with the only deliverance being that of death and oblivion (cf. *WWI* §71). Thus the pre-Christian and pre-Socratic apprehension of life attributed by Nietzsche in *The Birth of Tragedy* to the early Greeks recurs again in the modern world, as Christianity enters its death-throes.

Nietzsche does not question the soundness of this picture; and even though he later rejected the Schopenhauerian metaphysics which he here accepts, he continued to concur with this general account of the circumstances attending life in the world. To live is to struggle, suffer, and die; and while there is more to living than that, no amount of 'progress' in any field of human enterprise can succeed in altering these basic parameters of individual human existence. And even more significantly, for Nietzsche as well as for Schopenhauer and Nietzsche's Greeks, it is not possible to discern any teleological *justification* of what the individual is thus fated to undergo, either historically or supernaturally. We can look neither to a future utopia nor to a life hereafter that might serve to render endurable and meaningful 'the terror and horror of existence' (*BT* 3).

II

How can one manage to endure life in a world of the sort described by Schopenhauer, once one recognizes it for what it is — endure it, and beyond that *affirm* it as desirable and worth living *despite* the terrors and horrors that are inseparable from it? 'Suppose a human being has thus put his ear, as it were, to the heart chamber of the world will,' Nietzsche writes; 'how could he fail to *break*?' (*BT* 21). He terms this general recognition of the world's nature, and of the fate of the individual within it, 'Dionysian wisdom'; and he compares the situation of the Greek who attained it to that of Hamlet — and implicitly, to that of modern man (with a Schopenhauerian-existentialist world-view) as well:

> In this sense the Dionysian man resembles Hamlet: both have once looked truly into the essence of things, they have *gained knowledge*, and nausea inhibits action; for their action could not change anything in the external nature of things. . . .
>
> Now no comfort avails any more. . . . Conscious of the truth he has once seen, man now sees everywhere only the horror or absurdity of existence. . .: he is nauseated (*BT* 7).

Nietzsche desperately wanted to find some sort of solution to this predicament — though he cloaked his longing in the guise of a more detached interest in the question of how it has been possible for 'life' to manage to 'detain its creatures in existence' even when the erroneous beliefs which commonly shield them are no longer in operation. For this reason his attention was drawn to a people who were already very much on his mind owing to his professional concerns, and who constituted a perfect subject for a case study along these lines: the early Greeks. They were no brute savages, mindlessly and insensitively propelled through life by blind instinctive urges; rather, they were highly intelligent, sensitive, and cognizant of the ways of the world. And what is more, they were sustained neither by anything like Judeo-Christian religious belief nor by any myth of historical progress and human perfectibility. Yet they did not succumb to Schopenhauerian pessimism; on the

480

contrary, they were perhaps the most vigorous, creative, life-affirming people the world has known. And thus Nietzsche looked to them, asking of them: How did they do it? What was the secret of their liberation from the action- and affirmation-inhibiting nausea which seemingly ought to have been the result of their own Dionysian wisdom?

The answer, he believed, lay in that which was the most striking and glorious achievement of their culture: their art. Thus the passage cited above continues:

> Here, where the danger to [the] will is greatest, *art* approaches as a saving sorceress, expert at healing. She alone knows how to turn these nauseous thoughts about the horror or absurdity of existence into notions with which one can live (*BT* 7).

This is the guiding idea of Nietzsche's whole treatment of art in general, as well as of tragedy in particular. The main themes of this work are summarized in the following lines from its concluding section, which expand upon this idea by making reference to the key concepts of the 'Dionysian' and 'Apollinian,' and bring to the fore the most central and crucial notions in his entire philosophy of art — the notions of *overcoming* and *transfiguration*:

> Thus the Dionysian is seen to be, compared to the Apollinian, the eternal and original artistic power that first calls the whole world of phenomena into existence — and it is only in the midst of this world that a new transfiguring illusion becomes necessary in order to keep the animated world of individuation alive.
>
> If we could imagine dissonance became man — and what else is man? — this dissonance, to be able to live, would need a splendid illusion that would cover dissonance with a veil of beauty. This is the true artistic aim of Apollo in whose name we comprehend all those countless illusions of the beauty of mere appearance that at every moment make life worth living at all and prompt the desire to live on in order to experience the next moment.
>
> Of this foundation of all existence — the Dionysian basic ground of the world — not one whit more may enter the consciousness of the human individual than can be overcome again by this Apollinian power of transfiguration (*BT* 25).

Before turning to a closer consideration of these notions, a fundamental ambivalence in Nietzsche's conception of the relation between art and life in *The Birth of Tragedy* must be noted. And in this connection I shall refer briefly to his thinking about art

481

after as well as in this work. From first to last, he was deeply convinced that art requires to be understood not as a self-contained and self-enclosed sphere of activity and experience detached from the rest of life, but rather as intimately bound up with life, and as having the greatest significance in and for it. This is reflected in his later observation (in his 'Self-Criticism') that art in *The Birth of Tragedy* is viewed 'in the perspective of life' — a circumstance he regards as one of the signal merits of the work. And it is one of the most decisive and distinctive features of his general philosophical position that its development is characterized by a kind of dialectic between his understanding of life and the world and his understanding of art — each affecting the other, and bringing about changes in the other as the other worked changes upon it.

The underlying unity of the notions of art and life in Nietzsche's thinking is to be seen in *The Birth of Tragedy* in his treatment of the basic impulses operative in art — the 'Dionysian' and the 'Apollinian' — as manifestations of basic tendencies discernable in man and nature alike. And the consequences of his conviction of the existence of this unity are apparent in the subsequent development of the two notions which gradually moved to the center of his discussions of man, life and the world in his later writings: the *Übermensch* and the 'will to power.' For as was suggested earlier, the latter may be understood as an outgrowth of the dual notions of the Dionysian and Apollinian 'art impulses of nature,' in which they are transmuted in a manner lending itself to a further union with Nietzsche's successor-conception to Schopenhauer's 'world will,' his world of 'energy-quanta.' And the figure of the *Übermensch* may likewise be construed as a symbol of human life raised to the level of art, in which crude self-assertive struggle is sublimated into creativity that is no longer in thrall to the demands and limitations associated with the 'human, all-too-human.'

The overcoming of the initial meaningless and repugnant character of existence, through the creative transformation of the existing, cardinally characterizes both art and life as Nietzsche ultimately came to understand them. And this means for him both that life is essentially artistic, and that art is an expression of the fundamental nature of life. 'Will to power' is properly understood only if it is conceived as a disposition to effect such creatively transformative overcoming, in nature, human life generally, and art alike. And the *Übermensch* is the apotheosis of this fundamental disposition — the ultimate incarnation of the basic character of reality generally to which all existence, life and art are owing.

In *The Birth of Tragedy*, of course, neither 'will to power' nor

482

Übermensch makes an appearance; and the relation between art and life is discussed in other terms. One of the most notable features of the discussion, however, is Nietzsche's readiness to employ the term 'art' not only to refer in a conventional manner to sculpture, music and the other standard 'art forms,' but also in a broader, extended sense. For example, he suggests that 'every man is truly an artist' to the extent that everyone engages in the 'creation' of 'the beautiful illusion' of 'dream worlds,' even though no 'works of art' in the usual sense are thereby produced. Furthermore, turning his attention from such (Apollinian) 'dreaming' to the experience of what he calls 'Dionysian ecstasies,' he speaks of the Dionysian throng as *being* 'works of art' themselves: here 'man . . . is no longer an artist, he has become a work of art. . . . The noblest clay, the costliest marble, man, is here kneaded and cut' (*BT* 1).

Most strikingly of all, Nietzsche refers constantly to 'nature' herself as 'artistic,' and terms both the 'Apollinian' and the 'Dionysian' tendencies 'art-impulses' *of nature*. Thus he initially presents them 'as artistic energies which burst forth from nature herself, without the mediation of the human artist,' and goes on to say: 'With reference to these immediate art-states of nature every artist is an "imitator" ' (*BT* 2). And he contends that these two 'art-states of nature' are 'the only two art impulses' (*BT* 12). He even goes so far as to attribute the true authorship of *all* art to 'nature' rather than to human agency considered in its own right. 'One thing above all must be clear to us. The entire comedy of art is neither performed for our betterment or education, nor are we the true authors of this art world.' The human artist is said to be merely 'the medium through which the one truly existent subject celebrates his release in appearance.' Artists and the rest of us alike are 'merely images and artistic projections for the true author,' which is the fundamental principle of reality — the 'world-will' — itself; and we 'have our highest dignity in our significance as works of art,' as creations of this ultimate 'artist' (*BT* 5).

Yet Nietzsche also speaks of art very differently, and in a way that suggests a much less direct and even contrasting relation between it and the world. Thus, for example, he writes that 'the highest, and indeed the truly serious task of art' is 'to save the eye from gazing into the horrors of night and to deliver the subject by the healing balm of illusion from the spasms of the agitations of the will' (*BT* 19). Art spreads a 'veil of beauty' over a harsh reality — and when Nietzsche speaks of it as a 'transfiguring mirror' (*BT* 3), the emphasis belongs not on the latter term but rather on the former, which does away with any accurate reflection. Thus he writes that 'art is not merely imitation of the reality of nature but rather a metaphysical supplement of the reality of nature, placed beside it for its overcoming' (*BT* 24).

Here one should also recall the concluding passage of the entire work, in which Nietzsche returns to this theme of the necessity of overcoming whatever consciousness of the world's nature is attained by means of an art of 'transfiguration' capable of covering over what has been glimpsed with a 'splendid illusion' (*BT* 25). It was the 'terror and horror of existence' from which the Greeks needed to be saved; and 'it was in order to be able to live' that they developed their art: 'all this was again and again overcome by the Greeks with the aid of the Olympian *middle world* of art; or at any rate it was veiled and withdrawn from sight' (*BT* 3). And Nietzsche asserts that 'the tragic myth too, insofar as it belongs to art at all, participates fully in this metaphysical intention of art to transfigure' (*BT* 24).

Even while thinking along these lines, however, he supposes there to be a fundamental link between 'art' and 'life,' in that the latter is held to have been the source of the Greek's salvation from the desperate situation in which it also placed him: 'Art saves him, and through art — life' (*BT* 7). 'Life' thus is cast in a dual role, with the consequence that the relation of art to it is also a dual one. It is difficult to conceive of this dual relation coherently and faithfully to Nietzsche's representations of each aspect of it, however, without the two sides of it falling irreparably apart. Can the world of art in the narrower sense be thought of as a world 'supplementing the reality of nature, placed beside it for its overcoming,' and therefore distinct from it and contrasting to it — and at the same time as the creation of this very nature itself, expressing its own basic 'artistic impulses,' and therefore fundamentally homogeneous and identical with it? In *The Birth of Tragedy* Nietzsche tries to have it both ways; but it is far from clear that it is possible to do so.

Apollinian and Dionysian art

III

In any event, it should by now be clear that Nietzsche thinks of what art *is* in terms of *what art does* and *how art does it*; and that for him the answers to these two questions are to be given in terms of the notions of *overcoming* (*Überwindung*) and *transfiguration* (*Verklärung*). These two notions recur repeatedly throughout the work, and figure centrally in most of his major pronouncements about art. It should further be evident that they are to be understood in relation to certain human needs which he regards as fundamental and profoundly compelling, thereby endowing art with an importance transcending that of mere enjoyment or satisfaction derived from self-expression.

His interpretation of art in terms of the second of these two notions involves him in a fundamental break with Schopenhauer and all other cognitivist philosophers of art. For if art is essentially a matter of transfiguration, its ministrations to our needs will necessarily proceed otherwise than by heightening our powers of insight and understanding. Nietzsche's frequent references to 'illusions' in this connection make this obvious; but the point holds even where he does not consider this term to apply (notably in the case of music). Otherwise put: even where some sort of 'truth' about reality is purported to come through in art, he takes it to be essential to the artistic character of the expression that a transfiguration of the 'true' content has occurred in its artistic treatment — and its artistic character and quality attaches entirely to the element of transfiguration, rather than to this content and its transmission. (On this point more shall be said below.)

It is important to bear in mind the general applicability of the notions of overcoming and transfiguration when turning to Nietzsche's discussion of the art-impulses and art forms he is intent upon distinguishing, both in order properly to interpret what he says about them individually, and in order to avoid the error of supposing that he takes them to be entirely different phenomena. To be sure, when he introduces his idea of 'the *Apollinian* and *Dionysian* duality,' he asserts that 'art' is but a 'common term' until the two are 'coupled with each other' (*BT* 1); and he does go on to analyze them along very different lines — even to the point of maintaining that these notions represent '*two* worlds of art differing in their intrinsic essence and in their highest aims' (*BT* 16). These 'art impulses' and 'worlds of art,' however, while very different for Nietzsche, are nonetheless both '*art* impulses' and 'worlds *of art*,' with more than merely this same denomination in common — as the fact that their 'coupling' had a fruitful artistic issue (tragedy) itself suggests.

Schopenhauer had suggested that music is to be understood in terms fundamentally different from those appropriate to the plastic arts — the latter being concerned with the representation of the Ideas to which the manifestations of 'will' in the realm of appearances conform, and the former mirroring the underlying essential nature of this 'will' itself. Nietzsche believed that Schopenhauer had put his finger on an important difference here. He further

485

accepted the suggestion that the distinction between these art forms was linked to the distinction between the 'world-will' in itself and the world of appearances. Yet he by no means simply took over Schopenhauer's views along these lines, merely introducing the labels 'Apollinian' and 'Dionysian' in the course of restating them. He qualifies his endorsement of the idea that music 'copies' the world-will even as he gives it. For he holds that in music the nature of this ultimate reality is expressed *symbolically*, with the consequence that music neither *is* 'will' nor is a 'true' copy of it. Even here, he contends, transfiguration occurs; and it is upon the nature of this transfiguration, rather than upon the 'mirroring' relation as such, that he focusses his attention.

Even more radical is his departure from Schopenhauer with respect to the plastic arts. Gone is all reference to anything metaphysically comparable to the latter's 'Ideas,' and with it, any suggestion that here too a kind of cognitive function is performed. The forms fashioned by the plastic artist are construed not as representations of types to which existing particulars do and must more or less adequately conform, but rather as *idealizing transfigurations* of experienced phenomena — 'beautiful illusions' making up a 'dream world' that departs radically from the 'real world' of ordinary experience, 'placed alongside it for its overcoming' (*BT* 24).

Thus according to Nietzsche, neither in Apollinian nor in Dionysian art do we encounter unvarnished representations of the world, either as it presents itself to us in experience, or as it is in itself (or as it might be conceived by a thinker concerned with the natures of the types to which all existing things belong). The impulses to the creation of art for him are not cognitive impulses of any sort. Rather, if they stand in any relation at all to knowledge, he holds that this relation may best be conceived as an *antidotal* one. And it is undoubtedly in part to stress the extent of his departure from any cognitively oriented interpretation of art that he introduces his discussion of the Apollinian and the Dionysian by dwelling on their connection with the phenomena of dreaming and intoxication. Each of these phenomena, he maintains, manifests a deeply rooted and profoundly important aspect of our human nature; each answers to a powerful need — and the strength of the hold art exerts upon us can be understood only if it is recognized that the different art forms have their origins in these basic impulses, and emerge in answer to these strong needs. Nietzsche's discussion of 'the Apollinian and Dionysian duality' in *The Birth of Tragedy* is intended to bring out both the radical difference between what he thus takes to be the

486

two basic life-serving and art-generating impulses these names designate, and also the possibility of their interpenetration — and further, the great importance (for 'life' and art alike) of the results when this occurs. Thus he asserts that in tragic art 'Dionysus speaks the language of Apollo; and Apollo finally the language of Dionysus; and so the highest goal of tragedy and of all art is attained' (*BT* 21). And again:

> Where the Apollinian receives wings from the spirit of music
> and soars, we [find] the highest intensification of its powers,
> and in this fraternal union of Apollo and Dionysus we . . .
> recognize the apex of the Apollinian as well as the Dionysian
> forms of art (*BT* 24).

IV

At the outset of his discussion of 'the Apollinian and Dionysian duality,' Nietzsche singles out two art-forms as paradigms of each — 'the Apollinian art of sculpture and the non-imagistic, Dionysian art of music' (*BT* 1) — but then moves immediately to a consideration of the more fundamental experiential 'states' (also termed 'Apollinian' and 'Dionysian') to which he takes all such art-forms to be related: dreaming and intoxication. As has been observed, he contends that human beings are so constituted as to be impelled to each by deeply rooted dispositions, and to respond to each with powerful but differing positive feelings. Thus he suggests that there is something in 'our innermost being' which 'experiences dreams with profound delight and joyous necessity'; while it is likewise the case that 'paroxysms of intoxication' are accompanied by a 'blissful ecstasy that wells up from the innermost depths of man, indeed of nature' (*BT* 1).

It is these feelings of 'profound delight' on the one hand, and of 'blissful ecstasy' on the other, which are held to characterize the experience of the art-forms akin to and developing out of these two more basic forms of experience, and to render each so engaging. They touch the same deep chords in our nature, and so produce the same sort of response; and this is taken to be the key to understanding how it is that they are able to perform their life-sustaining functions (to the extent that they manage to do so). Thus Nietzsche explains his use of the name of Apollo in terms of its association with 'all those countless illusions of the beauty of mere appearances that at every moment make life worth living at all and prompt the desire to live on in order to experience the next moment' (*BT* 25) — whether in 'dreams' or in the 'imagistic' art which is a refinement and elevation to a higher plane of development of the 'creation' of the 'beautiful illusion of the dream worlds' (*BT* 1). And he likewise suggests that 'Dionysian art, too, wishes to convince us of the eternal joy of existence: only we are to seek this joy not in phenomena, but behind them,' through being ecstatically transported into a state of momentary identification with 'primordial being itself, feeling its raging desire for existence and joy in existence; the struggle, the pain, the destruction of phenomena now appear necessary for us' (*BT* 17).

As Nietzsche views them, dreaming and intoxication are not merely analogs to art, or pre-forms of art, or even experiential sources of artistic activity. Rather, there is an important sense in which they themselves *are* artistic phenomena — only the 'artist' in these cases is no human being, but rather 'nature,' working in the medium of human life. It is his contention that human artistic activities are to be regarded as of a piece with these more basic life-processes. They represent developments of them, to be sure, but are outgrowths sufficiently linked to them to warrant regarding 'every artist as an "imitator" ' in relation to 'these immediate art-states of nature' (*BT* 2). It is in this respect alone, for Nietzsche, that art may properly be conceived as involving 'the imitation of nature.' That is, art imitates nature in that the same sort of thing goes on in the former instance as goes on (among other things) in the latter. But precisely because creative transformation is involved in the former no less than in the latter (as part of the very 'imitation' in question), true art no more involves the attempt exactly to represent nature as it confronts us, than dreaming and intoxication faithfully record it; nor yet again does true art merely give expression to the contents of experiences had while in these states.

This last point is of particular importance. It is true that Nietzsche takes these states to be the point of departure and inspiration for artistic creation; and he does consider it appropriate to speak of 'every artist' as 'either an Apollinian artist in dreams, or a Dionysian artist in ecstasies,' or both at once (*BT* 2). But here the terms 'dreams' and 'ecstasies' are being used metaphorically; for it is no less central to his analysis of both types of (human) art that they involve the *further* transfiguration of what is experienced in these 'art-states of nature.' And what is more, they transfigure the already dissimilar contents of the visions associated with the two kinds of state in quite different ways.

It is with this difference in mind that Nietzsche speaks of the emergence of 'two worlds of art differing in their intrinsic essence' (*BT* 16). The basic contrast between them may be expressed in terms of the distinction between *images* and *symbols*; and the

488

difference just mentioned bears importantly upon it. In the case of Apollinian art, the chaotic play of crude and ephemeral appearances associated with such basic Apollinian experiential states as dreaming and imagination undergoes a transformative process, issuing in the creation of enduring, idealized images. They are 'beautiful illusions' — illusory because nothing either in the flux of appearance or beyond it corresponds to them, and of greater beauty than the haphazardly constituted contents of this flux. Transfigurations of appearances, they are images akin to the stuff of dreams, but also contrasting markedly with them.

In the case of Dionysian art, on the other hand, the transformation from which it issues is of the experience of the inexhaustible, dynamic 'primal unity' that is 'beyond all phenomena and despite all annihilation,' associated with such basic Dionysian states as intoxication and orgiastic revelry. What *this* transformation gives rise to is 'a new world of symbols,' in which 'the essence of nature is now . . . expressed symbolically' (*BT* 2); and it is the resulting *symbolic forms* in which Dionysian art consists. These symbolic forms are transfigurations of ecstatic states — expressions akin to immediate Dionysian ecstasy, but again, differing significantly from it, no less than from the underlying reality glimpsed in it. Thus Nietzsche holds that 'Dionysian art . . . gives expression to the will in its omnipotence, as it were, behind the *principium individuationis*' (*BT* 16) — and yet insists that even so paradigmatic a case of such art as music is not to be thought of as identical with this 'will.' 'Music,' he writes, 'according to its essence, cannot possibly be will. To be will it would have to be wholly banished from the realm of art' (*BT* 6). For were it the same as 'will,' it would lack the transfigured character constitutive of all art.

It is in terms of the difference between the kinds of transfiguration involved, rather than in terms of a division of the various art-forms into the 'plastic arts' on the one hand and the 'musical arts' on the other, that Nietzsche's 'Apollinian-Dionysian duality' in art is to be understood. In one sort of art the works produced have a symbolically expressive character; while in another they do not, having instead the character of idealized images. And it is one of the seemingly curious but important points of his analysis that the kinds of art generally regarded as most clearly 'representational' fall largely into the *latter* category, while those generally thought of as primarily 'non-representational' belong in the *former*. The idealized images of Apollinian art are not to be thought of as having the function either of faithfully representing or of symbolically expressing *anything at all*. They are rather to be thought of as 'beautiful illusions' to be contemplated simply for what they are in themselves, and to be enjoyed solely on account of their intrinsic beauty. They are, as Nietzsche says, a 'supplement of the reality of nature, placed beside it for its overcoming' (*BT* 24).

If there is any significant relation between them and this 'reality,' on his view, it does not consist in their linkage to the experiential phenomena of which they are transfigurations, but rather in their ability to lead us to think better of the world of ordinary experience by regarding it in the 'transfiguring mirror' they constitute, 'surrounded with a higher glory' (*BT* 3). Through Apollinian art, the world of ordinary experience is not actually transformed and its harshness eliminated. But to the extent that the idealized images created through the transformative activity of the Apollinian artist admit of association with what we encounter in this world, our attitude toward the latter benefits from this association, as our delight in these images carries over into our general disposition toward anything resembling them. Once again, however, it is not *knowledge* that we thereby attain, but rather only an altered state of mind, brought about by 'recourse to the most forceful and pleasurable illusions,' and 'seducing one to a continuation of life' (*BT* 3). Those works of art he terms 'Apollinian' are creations which neither represent nor symbolize, but rather delight precisely by virtue of the transfiguration accomplished in their production.

V

In the case of Dionysian art, matters stand quite differently. The Dionysian artist too is creative, and not merely someone with insight and the ability to communicate it. It may be that there is a kind of 're-echoing' of the fundamental nature of reality in instances of Dionysian art. In terms of this metaphor, however, such art is no less a 'transfiguring echo-chamber' than Apollinian art is a 'transfiguring mirror.' For the artistic 're-echoing' does not stand in the same near-immediate relation of identity to this 'primal unity' as does the more basic Dionysian phenomenon of intoxication. It rather comes back in an altered form, the creative production of which involves 'the greatest exaltation of all [man's] symbolic faculties.' Thus, Nietzsche continues, 'the essence of nature is now to be expressed symbolically; we need a new world of symbols' (*BT* 2); and it is this 'new world of symbols' which constitutes both the language and the substance of Dionysian art.

The symbolism of which he speaks here, however, is of a rather special sort. At least in its origins, it is neither conventional nor intentional, and is far removed from the use of words to formulate and express thoughts. So, in discussing the 'Dionysian dithyramb' (which he takes to be the proto-form of Dionysian art), he writes that, in order to develop the 'new world of symbols' needed to be able to express 'the essence of nature' symbolically,

> the entire symbolism of the body is called into play . . ., the whole pantomime of dancing, forcing every member into rhythmic movement. Then the other symbolic powers suddenly press forward, particularly those of music, in rhythmics, dynamics, and harmony (*BT* 5).

Nietzsche regards the 'symbolic powers' involved in such music and dancing as sublimations of deeper and darker natural impulses, and considers the symbolism to which they give rise to be *natural* in a significant sense; even though he also conceives it to be more than *merely* natural. The latter point is important: we have to do here with a transformation in which 'nature for the first time attains her artistic jubilee,' and 'days of transfiguration' supplant the nights of the 'horrible "witches' brew" of sensuality and cruelty' of pre-Dionysian savagery (*BT* 2). But the former point is no less important: the expressions in which such music and dancing consist, while symbolic, have a natural affinity with the reality they symbolize. And this reality is deeper than that of all individual thought, all social conventions and all 'appearance'; for its expression involves 'the destruction of the *principium individuationis*' (ibid.), and the 'height of self-abnegation' on the part of those through whom this expression is achieved. The Dionysian artist does not employ symbols to express some specific thought or emotion he happens to have had, or some particular feature of the cultural life and experience he shares with other members of his society. 'He has identified himself with the primal unity,' in all its 'pain and contradiction' and also its inexhaustible and indestructible vitality — and, thus 'released from his individual will,' he gives symbolic expression to the nature of the fundamental reality with which he identifies (*BT* 5). Some sorts and even some instances of (Dionysian) music and dance may be superior to others in terms of the adequacy with which they perform this expressive function; but it is essentially the character of these art-forms itself that accounts for their symbolic significance and their ability to perform this function.

In these arts the world's nature is expressed in a form that attracts rather than repels us — a symbolic form, the attractiveness of which is bound up with the transfiguration involved in this symbolization and made possible by the character of the 'new world of symbols' under consideration. Dionysian art does not have the character of a 'veil of illusion' radically different from the reality of nature and 'placed alongside it for its overcoming,' as does Apollinian art for Nietzsche. Yet it does have a somewhat analogous character and function, in that it expresses the reality of nature in a manner enabling us to overcome our abhorrence of it and to derive 'joy in existence' from identification with it, by means of a quasi-'illusory' *medium* of transfiguring symbolic forms.

VI

Nietzsche does not take the notions of transfiguration and illusion to apply only to works of Apollinian and Dionysian art conceived as object of aesthetic experience, but rather also to the *subjects* of such experience insofar as they become absorbed in them. This point is of great importance in connection with his treatment of tragic art, as well as in his analysis of these two art-forms, and so warrants close attention. The entire significance of art is missed, for him, if one does not recognize that the consciousness of those experiencing these art-forms undergoes a transformation analogous to that occurring in their creation; and that the experiencing subject's very psychological identity thereby is in a sense trans-figured, even if only temporarily and in a way that does not alter the basic reality of the subject's human nature and existence in the world. This happens in very different ways in the two general sorts of cases under consideration, however, representing what Nietzsche takes to be two fundamentally distinct stratagems by means of which 'the insatiable will' at the heart of nature conspires to 'detain its creatures in life and compel them to live on' (*BT* 18). He discusses them in terms of what occurs in the case of the 'Dionysian man' and in the case of the 'Apollinian man' (these expressions referring primarily to contrasting psychological possi-bilities rather than to distinct groups of human beings).

That an inward transformation occurs in the course of the kind of experience appropriate to Dionysian art is a point which has already been intimated, in Nietzsche's observation that one in the grip of the 'paroxysms of intoxication' in which the Dionysian impulse primordially manifests itself 'has become a work of art' (*BT* 1). And it has further been suggested in noting that he takes Dionysian art to mediate an identification of the individual with the reality underlying appearances. It is a common observation that art has the remarkable power to *transport* us out of our ordinary selves and everyday lives. Nietzsche seizes upon this idea and elaborates it, in a manner influenced significantly by Schopen-hauer.

Schopenhauer had contrasted our normal condition as creatures and captives of 'will,' absorbed in the constant struggle for existence characterizing all life in the world, with a radically different condition purported to be temporarily attainable through aesthetic experience. 'He who is sunk in this perception is no longer individual,' Schopenhauer had written, but rather 'is pure, will-less, painless, timeless subject of knowledge' (*WWI* §34). Nietzsche modifies this suggestion, and expands it so that it applies both to the contemplation of idealized images that elevates one above the world of ordinary experience and action, and to the experience of enrapturing symbolic expressions of the reality underlying this phenomenal world that carries one beyond it. Yet in either event, he agrees with Schopenhauer that one so affected is 'no longer individual,' or at any rate ceases for the moment to have the psychological identity associated with his ordinary individual existence. The transformation undergone by the Apollinian man (which is most akin to that indicated by Schopenhauer) will be considered shortly. That undergone by the Dionysian man was not envisioned by Schopenhauer, at least in connection with art; for it involves not the attainment of contemplative will-lessness, but rather the effecting of a deeper psychological union with the 'world-will.'

The Dionysian man does not exchange his physiological and sociocultural identity and situation in the world for another, or escape them altogether in the course of the 'destruction of the *principium individuationis*' of which Nietzsche speaks. As an experiental phenomenon, however, this destruction is very real: the Dionysian man is psychologically transformed into one for whom the only reality of which he is aware — and therefore that with which he himself identifies — is that which is expressed in the movements, tonalities or other symbolic forms in which he is immersed. Thus Nietzsche contends that, through the experience of Dionysian art, 'we are really for a brief moment primordial being itself' (*BT* 16). As one in a state of intoxication may be said not to 'be himself,' one immersed in the surge and flow of an instance of this type of aesthetic experience 'loses himself' in it. His consciousness is caught up in it, and his self-consciousness is altered accordingly — whether this transformation manifests itself behaviorally in an enraptured cessation of ordinary activity (outward inaction masking inward tumult), or in entrance into overt participation in the event as well. Such experience is fundamentally ecstatic, not only in the now ordinary but derivative sense of being blissful, but also in the original and literal sense of the term *ekstasis*, which denotes a displacement of oneself.

493

To the extent that one's own existence is discovered to be a moment of the reality expressed in Dionysian art, with which one thus comes to feel at one through the mediation of the latter, this transformation may be said to have the significance of a dispelling of the illusion involved in one's ordinary consciousness of oneself as something distinct from it and to be characterized in other terms. But to the extent that such experience leads one to identify oneself so completely with this reality that one takes oneself to have even those of its features that actually characterize it only as a whole, with which one is not truly identical, this transformation may also be said to have the significance of the fostering of another, different illusion. Thus Nietzsche suggests that, here no less than in the case of Apollinian art, we are dealing with a way in which, 'by means of an illusion,' life conspires 'to detain its creatures in existence' despite the harshness of the conditions it imposes upon them: in this instance, through 'the metaphysical comfort that beneath the whirl of phenomena eternal life flows on indestructibly' (*BT* 18).

The illusion in question is not that 'life flows on indestructibly' despite the ephemerality of all phenomena — for it does. We may be 'comforted' (and more) through the transformation of our psychological identity enabling us to achieve a sense of unity with this indestructible and inexhaustible underlying reality, of which we are truly manifestations. But while such comfort may be termed 'metaphysical,' this transfiguration is not; for it leaves our actual status in the world unchanged, and the basic conditions of our human existence unaltered. This we discover when the moment passes, the Dionysian aesthetic experience comes to an end, and we 'return to ourselves,' our psychological identities being transformed back again into their mundane non-Dionysian state. The only enduring 'comfort' is the recollection of the rapture of the Dionysian experience, and the knowledge that it remains available to us. But a profound danger attends this kind of 'overcoming,' of which Nietzsche is acutely aware. For the let-down may be great, the disparity between Dionysian states and ordinary life distressing, the illusion discerned, and its recognition found disconcerting; and thus the long-term effect of such experience may be detrimental rather than conducive to life (*BT* 7). It is for this reason, more than any other, that he has reservations about Dionysian art and experience generally, despite the evident fascination they have for him.

Nietzsche's Apollinian man constitutes a very different case, being the product of quite another kind of psychological transformation. As has already been observed, he conceives of this type in terms rather similar to those employed by Schopenhauer. For Nietzsche, one cannot appropriately speak here of 'knowledge,' since that with which we are confronted in the 'images' of Apollinian art are not representations of anything like Schopenhauer's 'Ideas,' but rather 'beautiful illusions.' Yet he does conceive of the subject of Apollinian aesthetic experience as transformed (through the contemplation of these idealized images) from an individual caught in the web of the world, into something like Schopenhauer's pure subject of knowledge — transcending time and will, and his own particular individuality and circumstances along with them. As in the previous case, however, this transcendence is held to be not only merely temporary but also fundamentally illusory, and the resulting transformation only psychological rather than genuinely ontological. And here too Nietzsche sees the cunning hand of nature at work, in this instance 'detaining its creatures in life' through 'ensnaring' the Apollinian man 'by art's seductive veil of beauty fluttering before his eyes' (*BT* 18).

The realm of Apollinian art is a kind of 'dream world, an Olympian *middle world* of art' (*BT* 3). It is neither the 'everyday world' nor the underlying world of 'will,' but rather a created world by means of which the latter is 'veiled and withdrawn from sight,' and the former is supplanted as the focus of concern. And entrance into this world is possible, Nietzsche holds, only for a kind of dreamer, or Olympian spectator, detached from the kinds of involvements and concerns that both characterize the everyday world and endow us with our ordinary psychological identities. Indeed, it requires that one *become* such a 'pure spectator' — or rather, the images presented are such that they induce a kind of contemplative consciousness through which one's psychological identity is transformed into that of such a subject. They stand outside of time and change, need and strife; and to become absorbed in them is for Nietzsche to have one's consciousness comparably transformed. If in the experience of Dionysian art one is enraptured, one may be said here to be entranced; and in a state of such entrancement, it is as if one had become a part of this world of images — not as one of them, but as a placeless, disembodied center of awareness, a subject fit for such objects and answering to their nature.

Schopenhauer had spoken of the occurrence of a significant release and liberation from the 'world of will' (however temporary and incomplete it might be) in aesthetic experience of this sort, as a result of which one effectively ceases to be a creature and captive of this 'will' for its duration. And for Nietzsche too, while Apollinian art involves 'the arousing of delight in beautiful forms,' it serves to effect an overcoming of the distress associated with our human condition through what is felt to be a kind of redemption from it. 'Here Apollo overcomes the suffering of the individual by the radiant glorification of the *eternity of the phenomenon*; here beauty triumphs over the suffering inherent in life' (*BT* 16). For one 'is absorbed in the pure contemplation of images' (*BT* 5), and seemingly becomes nothing but the delighted awareness of them. This psychological transformation is real — even though on a more fundamental level both the objects of such consciousness and this self-consciousness are merely two aspects of the 'Apollinian illusion,' which is but 'one of those illusions which nature so frequently employs to achieve her own ends' (*BT* 3).

If it is the case, however, that Apollinian art is thus 'called into being as the complement and consummation of existence' (ibid.), it follows that we have here to do with no *mere* illusion which leaves the reality of human life unaffected. It may not fundamentally alter the human condition; but if it is in some significant sense the 'consummation of existence,' it may be truly said to effect a significant transformation of 'existence,' or at least that portion of it which is the reality of human life. Art may be created by man, but man is also recreated or transfigured by art. This kind of experience and spirituality which become attainable in relation to the idealized images of Apollinian art may not constitute an elevation of those who attain to them entirely beyond the reach of the entanglements of ordinary life, and beyond the deeper harsh realities of existence in this world. Yet they do render the existence of those attaining to them qualitatively different from that of those who remain entirely immersed in the former, or who further succeed only in finding occasional respite through Dionysian experience. It is Nietzsche's appreciation of the magnitude of this qualitative difference that accounts for his celebration of the achievement of the archaic Greeks in their creation of Apollinian art.

Life cannot in the end be lived merely on the plane of Apollinian aesthetic experience, or even simply in the radiation of the reflected glory with which Apollinian art is capable of lighting the world of ordinary experience. The human condition is too recalcitrant, and the undercurrent of the 'Dionysian ground of existence' too strong, for the psychological transformation involved in the ascent into the realm of Apollinian art to prevail indefinitely. Absorbing and delightful as such experience is, it suffers from the fatal weakness of failing to come to terms with basic aspects of human life in the world that do not disappear when veiled. Yet Nietzsche is by no means disposed to conclude that what might be termed 'the

496

Apollinian experiment' is to be regarded as a mere blind alley, to be abandoned in favor of the Dionysian alternative. There remains another, which he associates with the phenomenon of tragic art. And the kind of transfiguration Apollinian art involves — both of the objects and the subjects of experience — is of the utmost importance in the emergence alike of tragic art and of the more viable form of human existence he associates with it.

Tragic art

VII

So, notwithstanding the full original title: *The Birth of Tragedy, Out of the Spirit of Music*, Nietzsche conceives tragic art to be no less Apollinian than Dionysian in origin and nature. At a certain point in Greek art the tendencies associated with each are said to 'appear coupled with each other, and through this coupling ultimately generate an equally Dionysian and Apollinian form of art — Attic tragedy' (*BT* 1). The burden of his entire discussion of it is that its emergence presupposed not only the prior development of the art of Dionysian transfiguration, but also the *re-transfiguration* of the latter under the influence of the likewise previously developed art of Apollinian transfiguration.

The birth of tragedy for Nietzsche was an event of the greatest significance; for it did not merely involve the appearance of a new art-form, thus opening another chapter in the development of art. It also made possible a further transformation of human life, which he conceives to have been and to be of far greater moment than is generally recognized. He does not regard tragic art as a phenomenon the significance of which is confined to but a single sphere of human experience and cultural life. Rather, he views it as the potential foundation and guiding force of an entire form of culture and human existence, which alone is capable of filling the void left by the collapse of 'optimistic' life-sustaining myths (both religious and philosophical-scientific). And he looks to it to assume anew the function of 'making life possible and worth living,' which neither Apollinian nor Dionysian art as such is capable any longer of performing. The former may still entrance and delight us, and the latter enrapture and excite us; and both may continue to transport and transform us in their respective fashions. But the power of the illusions they involve to sustain us has been lost.

In light of some of Nietzsche's remarks, one could be forgiven for supposing that his understanding of the psychological effect of tragedy is not very different from Aristotle's. Aristotle had maintained that this effect is basically one of catharsis; the tragedian constructs a dramatic means of enabling us to be purged of the feelings of fear and pity arising in connection with our recognition of our own plight in this world and threatening to paralyze us, by arousing such feelings directed toward a tragic figure and discharging them upon this figure. In this way, our capacity to feel them for ourselves is held to be diminished (at least for a time), thus enabling us to return to the world of action temporarily unimpaired by them.

Nietzsche says something of a similar nature. One who 'sees everywhere only the horror or absurdity of existence' may be beyond the reach of the consolations of lesser art-forms; but art can take other forms, in which it is able to 'turn these nauseous thoughts . . . into notions with which one can live: These are the *sublime* as the artistic taming of the horrible, and the *comic* as the artistic discharge of absurdity.' And Nietzsche is close to Aristotle when he concludes that the effect of this 'saving deed of Greek art' was that 'the feelings described here exhausted themselves' (*BT* 7).

However, to say this much is not to say enough. For if one confines one's attention to this aspect of the experience of tragic art alone, one misses something of even greater significance than the discharge or exhaustion of such negative feelings: namely, the powerful *positive* feelings generated at the same time, which are akin to those associated with Dionysian aesthetic experience. In a word, what is absent from the above account is reference to the *exhilaration* tragic art serves to inspire, notwithstanding the distressing fate of the central tragic figures. This exhilaration is much more than a mere feeling of relief from the torment occasioned by the negative feelings of which one is purged. And it is also different in both magnitude and kind from the delight associated with Apollinian aesthetic experience. Thus Nietzsche contends that 'the drama . . . attains as a whole an effect that transcends *all Apollinian* effects' (*BT* 21). There may be those whom tragedy does not affect in this way (Schopenhauer would appear to have been one); but that, for him, says something about *them* rather than about the nature of tragic art. Exhilaration is on his view an essential feature of the proper effect such art should have; and this phenomenon both renders comprehensible why he attaches such great significance to tragic art, and guides his interpretation of it.

In tragedy, according to Nietzsche, we find elements of both Apollinian and Dionysian art — not, however, merely externally combined, but rather employed in a subtle interplay. Moreover,

498

these elements do not retain their entire original character; for here 'Dionysus speaks the language of Apollo; and Apollo, finally, the language of Dionysus' (*BT* 21). Thus Nietzsche suggests that 'in this fraternal union of Apollo and Dionysus,' we find that 'an Apollinian *illusion*' is employed to admit the Dionysian 'spirit of music' into our experience, while at the same time protecting against an 'immediate unity with Dionysian music' by requiring it to be expressed 'in an Apollinian field.' And we also find that 'the Apollinian receives wings from the spirit and soars,' surpassing all 'weaker degrees of Apollinian art' by being 'illuminated from the inside by music' to an extent that 'in all other Apollinian art remains unattained' (*BT* 24).

In this connection it is both crucial and illuminating to bear in mind the passage cited earlier from the last section of the book, in which Nietzsche contends — clearly with tragic art specifically in mind — that, with respect to the underlying nature and character of the world and existence in it, 'not one whit more may enter the consciousness of the human individual than can be overcome again by [the] Apollinian power of transfiguration' (*BT* 25). To be able to endure the consciousness of them of which we are capable and which cannot in the long run be prevented from emerging, and to be able further to embrace and affirm life despite the attainment of such an awareness, a transformation of this consciousness is necessary. For in its starkest, simplest and most vivid form it would be overwhelmingly horrible, 'nauseating,' paralyzing and unendurable.

Tragic art alone, for Nietzsche in *The Birth of Tragedy*, is truly equal to this task. It enables us to experience the terrible not as merely terrible, but rather as sublime; and it achieves something akin to a Dionysian effect upon us, which however is not identical with it. For it does not take the kind of life-endangering toll Dionysian intoxication does, rather inducing an experiential state that differs as significantly from such intoxication as it does from Apollinian dreaming. In the long run it has the character of a tonic rather than a depressant; its aftermath is held to be exhilaration, rather than either the overall exhaustion which follows upon Dionysian excitement, or the exasperation which Apollinian exaltation leaves in its train. And considered more immediately, it might be said to enthrall, rather than to entrance *or* enrapture.

Tragic art too, for him, may be said to constitute a kind of 'transfiguring mirror.' It is a mirror, however, in which we see reflected neither 'appearances' idealizingly transfigured, nor the character of the reality underlying them symbolically expressed. We are confronted instead with 'images of life' — reflections of the (and our) human condition, highlighting both the individuation it involves and the fate bound up with the latter. What we encounter, however, is not a stark and brutally 'realistic' portrayal of this condition as such. We see it in transfigured form — even though this transfiguration of it does not consist in its radical transmutation into a merely imaginary, idealized condition *contrasting* with the actual human condition on these counts. And it likewise does not involve the effective obliteration of the salient features of human life through the diversion of attention from the entire domain of individuation to the collective, the impersonal, the merely vital and the enduring aspects of life underlying it. The kind of transfiguration occurring here is rather one which pertains to our perception of individual human existence — *as* existence that is individual rather than merely a part of an inexhaustible and indestructible flow of life, and that is human rather than above and beyond the conditions to which man is subject.

This transfiguration pertains first of all to the character of the dramatic figures with which we are confronted — or rather it comes about first in the context of our confrontation with them. Yet it does not remain confined to this encounter; for it further serves to alter our apprehension of the human condition more generally. It is in this sense above all that tragic art may be said to function as a transfiguring mirror: it works a transformation upon our consciousness of the human reality that is also our own, at the same time as it reflects that reality for us to behold. The fate of the tragic figure takes on the aspect of something sublime rather than merely horrible; and thus, without being denied or glossed over, it ceases to inspire mere 'nausea' and moves us instead to fascination and awe. The life of the tragic figure is endowed with a significance that entirely alters its aspect; and what might seem from a simple recitation of the brute facts of the matter to be a merely wretched and distressing tale emerges as an enthralling and moving spectacle.

Tragic art presents us neither with an ideal to be admired and emulated, nor with an avenue by means of which to escape all thought of the hard realities of life. The latter are very much in evidence; and the tragic figure caught up in them is one with whom, as an individual, we empathize, but with whom as a character we do not identify. Yet the manner of presentation of such figures, which renders them tragic and not merely pathetic, does much more than merely purge us of our self-directed feelings of fear and pity through an empathic discharge. It can have a powerful positive impact upon the way in which we perceive our human condition and experience the reality of our own lives, by revealing them to us in a very different light from that in which we would otherwise tend to view them. The point might be put by saying that the tragic artist, not through the persona of the tragic figure *per se* but rather in the larger structure of the tragic drama, interposes a medium between us and the reality of human existence which does more than simply give expression to this reality. For this medium further shapes and colors our consciousness of it, and is able to help us attain an affirmative attitude toward it precisely by virtue of doing so.

In short, tragic art provides us with a way of apprehending this reality that enables us to come to terms with it — and not only to endure but also to affirm what we see, as we thereby learn to see it. In this way it resembles Dionysian art; and for Nietzsche this similarity of tragic art to the Dionysian arts is by no means merely fortuitous. In tragic myth, as in music and dance, something transcending mere appearances is symbolically expressed — and in being so expressed, is transformed for our consciousness. Here, however, the symbolic forms employed are not primarily those characteristic of these Dionysian art-forms, but rather are drawn from the initially non-symbolic domain of Apollinian art.

VIII

In tragic art attention is focused upon individual figures who are no mere ordinary human beings, but rather 'great and sublime forms.' By means of them it both 'satisfies our sense of beauty' which delights in such images, and also 'incites us to comprehend in thought the core of life they contain' (*BT* 21). In the former respect it has an 'Apollinian artistic effect'; yet its effect is by no means simply Apollinian. For to the extent that it does the latter, these images have the significance of *symbols*, whose interest for us is further in part a matter of what they convey about the 'life' they symbolize, in which both they and we participate.

It is a basic feature of tragic art, according to Nietzsche, that 'at the most essential point this Apollinian illusion is broken and annihilated.' The central figures are destroyed, succumbing to forces which shatter their individual existence and give the lie to the appearance of self-contained and impervious reality of these 'great and sublime forms.' And yet the impact of tragic art upon us is by no means merely that of depression and despair, for we respond to the dramatic expression of the inexhaustible and indestructible power of the forces of life in relation to which all individual existence is merely ephemeral. What Nietzsche calls 'the spirit of music' speaks above the relation of what befalls the tragic figures, with the result that 'in the total effect of the tragedy, the Dionysian predominates once again,' and we are exhilarated rather than merely mortified (*BT* 21).

This 'total effect,' however, is not a purely Dionysian one. And the difference is crucial both with respect to the understanding of tragic art and where its 'value for life' is concerned. A discernment of and identification with the larger and deeper reality transcending the existence of the tragic figures and all individuals is attained — but not through an enraptured ascent into a state of consciousness in which the former alone absorbs us. Rather, this occurs in a manner which at the same time not only leaves us very much aware of individuals and the conditions of their existence, but moreover actually heightens this awareness. And the attendant exhilaration, while akin to Dionysian excitement, neither depends upon the attainment of such Dionysian transport, nor endures only as long as our consciousness remains thus transformed. On the contrary, it is wedded to a vivid recognition of the plight of particular individuals, and carries over after the event when our own lives once again come to the fore. A fundamentally Dionysian chord is sounded, and our responsiveness to it is tapped; but this is done to an importantly different effect. For what occurs, Nietzsche suggests, is not a transformation of our consciousness along lines rendering us oblivious to our individual existence, but rather a transfiguration of the character of our consciousness with respect to such existence.

Life regarded as tragic is no longer life seen as merely wretched and pathetic; and the 'displeasure' associated with 'the weight and burden of existence' is overshadowed and forgotten when the latter takes on the aspect of tragic fate rather than mere senseless suffering and annihilation. The fate of the tragic figure, when nobly met rather than basely suffered, enhances rather than detracts from his stature; and this figure serves as a symbolic medium through which individual existence more generally is dignified for us. The apparent oddity of the idea that exhilaration attends the attainment of a tragic sense of life disappears once it is recognized that this view of life is not a grim pessimism to which one is driven once the tenability of all forms of religious and secular 'optimism' is discerned. For it is no mere stark and unavoidable conclusion, but rather a signal accomplishment; and Nietzsche takes it to contrast in an incomparably more appealing and satisfying way with the much starker, utterly bleak conception of individual existence as the unmitigated and unadorned tale of mere ceaseless striving, senseless suffering and inevitable destruction it was proclaimed to be by Schopenhauer and ancient wisdom alike.

As has been noted, Nietzsche contends that tragic art 'participates fully in [the] metaphysical intention of art to transfigure.' He further maintains, however, that it does so differently from both Apollinian and Dionysian art. Thus he writes: 'But what does it transfigure when it presents the world of appearance in the image of the suffering hero? Least of all the "reality" of this world of appearance' (*BT* 24). It has to do with human existence in this world; and in the tragic figure we encounter a personified transfiguration of human existence, in which such existence is neither transmuted into idealized imagery purged of all conflict, pain, blemish, and vulnerability, nor reduced to the status of anonymous and individually insignificant instantiations of life. In contrast to what occurs in both of these cases, it is here ennobled within the very conditions imposed upon it. And it is by means of this transfiguration that tragic art works its distinctive transformation of our consciousness of ourselves. Thus Nietzsche goes on to contend that 'it is precisely the tragic myth that has to convince us that even the ugly and disharmonic are part of an artistic game that the will in the eternal amplitude of its pleasure plays with itself' (*BT* 24).

The unique achievement of tragic art is thus held to be that it fundamentally alters our apprehension of human existence and the circumstances associated with it, which result in the suffering and destruction of even the most extraordinary individuals. Through it these circumstances cease to stand as *objections* to human life and its worth, and emerge instead as features of it which — as part of the larger whole human lives are and can be — actually contribute to its overall significance and attractiveness. And thus, Nietzsche suggests, it serves to bring it about that 'existence' can 'seem justified' *aesthetically* — 'only as an aesthetic phenomenon' (*BT* 24). Nietzsche's use of the term 'only' here is highly important; for his general point is that it is *only* in this way, in the last analysis, that it is possible for us to find human life and our own existence endurable and worth while, without recourse to illusions which radically misrepresent the actual nature of our human reality and the world more generally.

IX

At the same time, however, Nietzsche maintains that this transfiguration of our consciousness of ourselves itself involves a kind of illusion. Thus he considers it appropriate to refer to it and the tragic art which brings it about as one of 'the stages of illusion' — albeit one 'designed . . . for the more nobly formed natures.' And given that this is so, one might well wonder why he considers it to be at all superior to 'the more vulgar and almost more powerful illusions which the will always has at hand' (*BT* 18), and how he can suppose it to be any less subject in the long run than they are to the disillusionment which eventually undermines the latter and renders them ineffective.

Nietzsche contends that 'it is precisely the tragic myth that has to convince us that even the ugly and the disharmonic are part of an artistic game' (*BT* 24) in terms of which reality in general is to be conceived, and human life along with it. Dionysian art is held to convey to us a sense that things of this sort do not fatally flaw this macrocosmic 'game' as a whole, but rather contribute to its fundamentally positive 'artistic' character. But here it is suggested that tragic art goes a step further, persuading us that they likewise may be accepted and affirmed as features of our own human lives, which even on the microcosmic scale of individual existence can thus be experienced as having an 'aesthetic' justification. And, very importantly for Nietzsche, this alteration of their aspect is not achieved by means of a resort to religious or metaphysical fictions. It is instead accomplished through their artistic incorporation into an aesthetically appealing and satisfying vision of life. If this involves no resort to any such fiction, however, wherein lies the 'illusion'?

This 'illusion' has to do with the status of the 'image of life' with which Nietzsche takes us to be confronted in the tragic figure (*BT* 21). While such figures are neither simply realistically drawn, fictitious but true-to-life individuals, nor representatives of the elemental characteristics of 'Dionysian universality' (as is the chorus), they are no mere Apollinian 'beautiful illusions' either. Like Apollinian idealized images, however, they constitute something on the order of a 'supplement of the reality of nature,' and of that of ordinary human existence along with it. The 'core of life they contain' is the same as our own (ibid.); but this core is artistically transformed into 'images of life' expressing possibilities which differ markedly from the commonplace, in ways moreover answering to no predetermined human essence or foreordained human ideal. They thus can in no sense be said to confront us with the 'truth' of human existence. And since what they confront us with is something other than 'truth,' they may be said to present us with a kind of 'illusion.' It is in this way that Nietzsche's remarks to this effect are to be understood.

Yet this illusion is no *mere* illusion; and the transformed consciousness of ourselves which emerges, when we view our own lives in the light of the manner of those of these tragic figures, is not *merely* illusory. For the creations in which they consist are not distorted or erroneous representations of something that has a fixed and immutable character and cannot be otherwise. And they also are not simply imaginary substitutes temporarily usurping a position in our consciousness that is normally and more properly occupied by our ordinary conception of our own mundane reality. Rather, they are symbols of *human possibility*. And as such they serve to carry us beyond the mere acknowledgment of intractable aspects of the human condition, enabling us to discern ways in which the latter may be confronted and transformed into occasions for the endowment of life with grandeur and dignity.

By means of these symbols, human life thus may come to take on an aesthetic significance sufficing to overcome the distressing character of its harsh basic features. It stands revealed as a potentially aesthetic phenomenon, 'justifiable' accordingly in our estimation even in the face of its hardest circumstances. And of paramount importance for Nietzsche is the fact that tragic art does not confine this perception to the tragic figures themselves, while precluding its application to our lives. For these figures stand as symbols serving to facilitate our apprehension of the possibilities they express (together with 'the core of life they contain') *as our own* — and so to alter the aspect of our own lives. To say that this is all 'illusion,' as Nietzsche does, is neither to deny the reality of this alteration nor to downplay its significance. It is rather to make the point that our lives thus acquire an experiential character which is no part of their fundamental objective nature; and that this occurs through the transforming mediation of created images enabling us to discern aesthetic significance in human existence, notwithstanding that its basic circumstances as such warrant the attribution to our existence of no significance whatsoever.

X

In the attainment of a tragic sense of life the 'terror and horror of existence' are surmounted, through the remarkable alchemy of tragic art which transmutes the terrible and horrible into the sublime and magnificent. And the key to this transmutation is not the quickening of that sense of 'metaphysical comfort' that 'beneath the whirl of phenomena eternal life flows on indestructibly' — though this too occurs. It is rather the 'Apollinian power of transfiguration,' which alone enables us to endure and affirm the existence that is ours as parts of this 'whirl' — not only in moments of Dionysian rapture, self-abnegation and obliviousness to the human condition, but also when we acknowledge our individuality and confront the circumstances of human life.

Nietzsche may often seem to be more concerned with what might be termed the ecstatic component of the experience of tragic art than with this companion feature of it. Yet it is the latter that he finally stresses, when he concludes his discussion by emphasizing that 'of this foundation of all existence — the Dionysian basic ground of the world — not one whit more may enter the consciousness of the human individual than can be overcome again by this Apollinian power of transfiguration' (*BT* 25). This power must be brought to bear upon our consciousness of our existence as 'human individuals,' and not merely upon our awareness of 'the Dionysian basic ground of the world' as such, if we are to be able to find our lives 'endurable and worth living.' It would avail us little to regard 'the world' generally as 'justified' if no comparable 'justification' were discernable when we turned to a consideration of our own existence. And for Nietzsche in *The Birth of Tragedy* this is something which tragic myth alone can provide. It transforms what might otherwise be taken to be life at its worst into life at its best, endowing even suffering and destruction with aesthetic quality — not as such, to be sure, but as central elements of an aesthetically charged whole, into which are interwoven the tragic figure's life, circumstances, flaws, strivings, sufferings and destruction.

What is thus transformed is not tragedy; for the accomplishment of tragic art is not the transformation of tragedy into something else. Tragedy rather is the *issue* of this artistic transformation, through which existence comes to be experienced as tragic. This is indeed an artistic accomplishment, since tragedy no less than beauty may be said to exist only in the eye of the beholder, whose sensibility has been formed and cultivated by art. It is no brute fact of human existence, but rather an acquired aspect it may come to bear through the transfiguring agency of the tragic artist.

There is 'illusion' in the apprehension of existence as bearing the aspect of tragedy, since its tragic character is a matter of the imposition of significant form upon its given sundry features, rather than of the intrinsic nature of any or all of the latter. And there is a further 'illusion' involved in what Nietzsche terms the 'noble deception' generated to the effect that something more than this is encountered here. For tragic art does not merely transform our manner of regarding existence by means of its elaboration of 'a sublime parable, the myth.' It also 'deceives the listener into feeling that the music' — that is, the symbolic expression of the undercurrent of life that is manifested both in the tragic figure

506

and in the forces to which this figure succumbs — 'is merely the highest means to bring life into the vivid world of myth' (*BT* 21).

It is in this way that the tragic myth comes to be endowed with what Nietzsche terms its 'intense and convincing metaphysical significance' (ibid.) — and also its most profoundly 'illusory' character. For it leads us to feel something to be the deepest and highest 'truth' of human existence — the tragic character it is capable of coming to bear, with all the sublimity and majesty devolving upon it therefrom — which is no part of its fundamental nature. Yet according to Nietzsche, tragic art requires ultimately to be conceived as working in the service of life. Here too, what we are said to be dealing with is simply another means (even if also the most exalted one) through which 'the insatiable will' manages to 'detain its creatures in life and compel them to live on' — in this case, by employing tragic myth to lend human existence an aspect endowing it with an aesthetic justifiability. But it does this in such a way that we are led to view life as though it were a means to the end of actualizing the aesthetic values associated with human experience as it is revealed in the transfiguring mirror of tragic myth.

In *The Birth of Tragedy* Nietzsche places his hope for a revitalization of Western civilization, in the face of the collapse of both other-worldly religiousness and rationalistic-scientific optimism, in a re-emergence of a tragic sense of life. But as he readily acknowledges, such a view of life cannot be sustained in the absence of tragic myth and an acceptance of the understanding of human existence associated with some instance of it. It is for this reason that he devotes so much discussion in this work to the importance of myth and to the need for a new and compelling form of tragic myth in the modern Western world. He ventures to hope that the ground for a 'rebirth of tragedy' and a new 'tragic culture' is being prepared by science itself, as it 'speeds irresistibly toward its limits where its optimism, concealed in the essence of logic, suffers shipwreck' (*BT* 15). But he recognizes that the 'shipwreck' of which he speaks, consisting in the collapse of the belief that scientific or other rational modes of inquiry will lead to the discovery of truths establishing the meaning and justifiability of existence, is only a negative condition of such a rebirth and renewal, and by no means suffices to accomplish it. Tragic myth alone is held to be capable of doing this, by means of tragic art. It is for this reason that he speaks of art as 'even a necessary correlative of and supplement for science' (*BT* 14).

Nietzsche obviously thought, when he wrote this book, that Wagner was well on the way to accomplishing the task he thus conceived. The details of his discussion of this and related matters, however, are of relatively little intrinsic interest — especially since he soon after both lost his enthusiasm for Wagner and abandoned his commitment to the ultimacy and indispensability of that form of art he associates here with tragic myth. He further came to be convinced that art generally has a significance in relation to life, and also a variety of features, to which his analysis of it in *The Birth of Tragedy* does not do justice. And indeed there are a number of respects in which his later thinking concerning it is clearly superior to his early treatment of it (owing both to his self-emancipation from Schopenhauer and Wagner, and to his stylistic and philosophical maturation).

Yet however unsatisfactory, questionable and excessive some of what Nietzsche says in *The Birth of Tragedy* may be, he is to be credited with a number of extremely valuable insights in this early effort, concerning such things as the relation between art and life, the transfigurative character of art, the nature of artistic creation, the distinction between imagistic and symbolically expressive art forms, and the distinctive character and impact of tragic art. It may be that few classics in the literature of the philosophy of art are as flawed in as many particular respects as is this; but it is also the case that few so richly reward patience with their flaws and close attention to their substance.

Second thoughts about art

XI

Nietzsche's enthusiasm for art in *The Birth of Tragedy* was so great that further reflection could only have tempered it — as it in fact did. The Nietzsche of the subsequently attached 'Self-Criticism' is no longer the ardent 'art-deifier' he sees himself as having been at that time, as his self-critical remarks make clear. And as he indicates in a note from the same later period concerning 'Art in *The Birth of Tragedy*,' he likewise ceased to embrace the gospel of 'Art and nothing but art!' according to which art is 'the only superior counterforce to all will to denial of life' (*WP* 853). Something of this attitude endures in his later thinking, but only in considerably modified form, as shall be seen. Moreover, obviously thinking of this early work, he writes in the contemporaneous Fifth Book of *The Gay Science* that 'initially I approached the modern world with a few crude errors and overestimations' (*GS* 370), the latter most especially applying to Wagner, and the former at least including certain of his views with respect to art generally.

Nietzsche remained persuaded, however, of the validity and usefulness of 'the conceptual opposites which I have introduced into aesthetics, *Apollinian* and *Dionysian*' (*TI* IX:10). He makes use of these notions on a number of occasions in his later writings, and explicates them in language differing little from that which he initially employed (at least when pairing them). Thus he observes that they are to be understood as referring to 'two conditions in which art appears in man like a force of nature,' both of which 'release artistic powers in us, but different ones' (*WP* 799). And in another late note, in which he makes clear their enduring centrality in his understanding of art, he writes:

> The word 'Dionysian' means: an urge to unity, a reaching out beyond personality, the everyday, society, reality, across the abyss of transitoriness: a passionate-painful overflowing into darker, fuller, more floating states. . . .
> The word 'Apollinian' means: the urge to perfect self-sufficiency, to the typical 'individual,' to all that simplifies, distinguishes, makes strong, clear, unambiguous, typical: freedom under law.
> The further development of art is as necessarily tied to these two natural artistic powers as the further development of man is to that between the sexes. Plenitude of power and moderation (*WP* 1050).

He also continued to view art, as he observes in his 'Self-Criticism,' 'in the perspective of life.' Thus in his subsequent writings he gives considerable attention to the sources of art in human nature, and to certain general human tendencies which frequently manifest themselves in it; and he likewise is very much concerned with the various functions art can and does perform in human life, and with the light it sheds upon our human nature and possibilities. If he modified his thinking along these lines, he did so by deepening and elaborating his account of the character of these forces, giving greater prominence, e.g., to sexuality and its sublimation; and by broadening his analysis to take into consideration the influence of such secondary, social rather than 'natural' factors as prevailing forms of moral and religious conviction. So he argues that, in dealing with art, 'one must examine the artist himself, and his psychology,' and consider not only the products of his efforts but 'what drives he sublimates' (*WP* 677). And he contends that 'the phenomenon "artist," ' when so approached, is 'the most transparent: — to see through it to the basic instincts of power, nature, etc.!' (*WP* 797). (I shall have more to say along these lines subsequently.)

509

Nietzsche likewise continued to echo — even if not simply to reiterate without qualification — a central theme of this early work, to the effect that art performs the signal function of rendering life endurable and worth living, by sufficiently transfiguring its aspect or supplementing its basic character that we are enabled to endure and affirm it. He does not consider it to be the *only* means of achieving this result, either in *The Birth of Tragedy* or subsequently; but the manner in which art achieves it seems to him to have much to recommend it. And this leads him to accord it a much larger role in human life throughout his writings than most philosophers and people generally seem prepared to do. 'It is the great means of making life possible, the great seduction to life, the great stimulant of life': so Nietzsche retrospectively sees himself as having maintained in that book (*WP* 853). And this idea recurs in various forms throughout his later writings.

To be sure, he also came to have reservations about art on this point. Thus, for example, he observes that such 'means of easing life' have certain defects: 'they soothe and heal only temporarily, only for the moment; they even deter men from working toward a genuine improvement in their conditions, in that they eliminate and palliatively discharge the very passion of the discontented which impels to action' (*HH* I:148). Moreover, he sees a danger in the growth of a dependence upon the products of the artist's idealizing transfigurations of reality, and of an increasing preference of them to real life and the real world. This may lead to adherence to the 'dangerous principle' of 'art for art's sake,' and to a divorce of art from life which 'introduces a false principle into things'; and the tendency in this direction he discerns is held to 'culminate in a defamation of reality,' at which point art ceases to be a *'means'* serving 'the aim of enhancing life,' and instead becomes antithetical and detrimental to it. And this is something to which he objects in the strongest terms.

Further, in his later writings Nietzsche becomes increasingly less solicitous of those who require much protection from any clear awareness of the actual character of life and the world in order to find existence endurable and worth while, and who are incapable of finding anything to be of value that is not pleasing to them. Thus, while making much of the point that 'we possess *art* lest *we perish of the truth*,' which is 'ugly' (*WP* 822), it is clearly with derisive intent that he remarks that 'an artist cannot endure reality, he looks away from it' (*WP* 572). And only somewhat more charitably, he terms artists 'an intermediary species,' in that while they 'actually alter and transform,' they merely 'fix an image of that which ought to be,' and so are still relatively lacking in 'will and strength' of the sort necessary to be able to 'endure to live in a meaningless world *because one organizes a small portion of it oneself*' (*WP* 585A).

XII

Nietzsche does not, however, abandon the non-cognitivism which found expression in *The Birth of Tragedy* in his insistence upon the centrality of 'illusion' in the various forms art takes. Indeed, in his later writings this theme becomes if anything even more strongly pronounced, most notably in his frequent association of art with 'lying.' Thus in a relatively early aphorism with the heading '*The Muses as Liars*' he states: 'If one for once conceives of the artist as deceiver, this leads to fundamental discoveries' (*HH* II:188).

His employment of such language invites misunderstanding, and care must be taken in interpreting his meaning. This is an instance of something one encounters time and again in Nietzsche's discussions of many different matters — his provisional adoption of language used by philosophers with whom he is in radical disagreement, as he takes up the gauntlet they have thrown down. In the present case he elects to concur with Plato's characterization of the poets as 'liars,' and of art as a kind of 'lying,' but with an intent that runs directly counter to Plato's. For while he is prepared to insist, with Plato, that art stands at a considerable remove from 'truth,' he urges against Plato that this is by no means a telling objection against it.

The burden of what Nietzsche has to say along these lines is twofold. First, he argues that art is *not* to be thought of as having to do basically with the revelation of fundamental truths about reality. And second, he maintains that this is to its credit rather than discredit, since what it *does* involve is not only to be conceived in other terms altogether, but also is of the utmost importance. He concedes that it is commonly supposed, both by many artists and by others who hold art in high esteem, that in artistic vision 'the true essence of the world' is approached; but he denies that this is actually the case. The arts, he writes,

are to be sure flowers of the world, but are certainly not
closer to the root of the world than the stalk: one can by no
means understand the nature of things better through them,
although this is believed by almost everyone. *Error* has made
man so deep, sensitive and inventive that he has produced such
flowers as religions and arts (*HH* I:29).

511

It is necessary to rid ourselves of the idea that art can and does have major cognitive significance, and that both its nature and its importance are to be conceived accordingly, he argues, if we are to be able to proceed to a reconsideration of it that will do justice to it. And for the later as well as for the early Nietzsche, this does not mean shifting attention merely to the pleasure art is capable of affording to those possessing a sensibility attuned to it. Rather, it involves recognizing the *transfiguring* character of artistic creativity, and the role it is thereby capable of performing in the service of human life. In *The Birth of Tragedy*, in which he later observed he took the position that 'man must be a liar by nature, he must above all be an *artist*,' since *'we have need of lies* in order to conquer this reality, this "truth," that is, in order to live' (*WP* 853), he had achieved this recognition, but in a form he subsequently found to be too narrow.

What Nietzsche here and elsewhere calls the 'lying' in which art traffics is actually only the aspect borne by artistic creations when they are viewed in terms of their cognitive import. They cease to bear this aspect when that perspective of assessment is abandoned, and art comes to be construed in terms of the creativity it involves, rather than the (failing) attempt to apprehend the nature of reality and the way things actually (and merely) happen to be. The cognitivist interpretation of art seemed to him to be so deeply entrenched, however, that it could not simply be ignored in favor of an immediate modification of the terms in which it is conceived along these a-cognitive lines. And so he employs the language of a defiant anti-cognitivism on many occasions, even though the entire preoccupation with the issue of the cognitive status of art is something he is ultimately concerned to lay to rest.

A further strand of continuity is to be found in Nietzsche's frequent recurrence throughout his writings to art as a basic metaphor in his characterizations of human life at its fullest, life more generally, and even the world itself. Or rather, both in *The Birth of Tragedy* and subsequently, he takes the former and latter to be intimately related, and frequently draws upon his understanding of each in discussing the character of the other. So, as was earlier observed, he characterizes 'the world as a work of art that gives birth to itself.' He goes on to suggest that both biological organisms and social systems may be conceived along these lines, speaking of 'the work of art where it appears without an artist, e.g., as body, as organization' (*WP* 796). And in a similar vein he writes: 'One must understand the artistic basic phenomenon that is called "life" — the building spirit that builds under the most unfavorable conditions' (*WP* 1046).

512

He also often avails himself of the image of art in his characterizations of many aspects of human life, not only as it might be
and occasionally is lived by exceptional human beings, but also as
it commonly proceeds. For example, he holds that 'one is much
more of an artist than one knows' even with respect to the events
which constitute our ordinary experience (*BGE* 192). Further, he
observes that when people are constrained to immerse themselves
completely in some 'particular role' in society, 'the role has actually
become character; and art, nature.' On the other hand, he continues, when one is freed from such constraint, discovers that one
'can manage almost any role,' and 'experiments with himself,
improvises, makes new experiments,' one becomes something
quite different, and 'all nature ceases and becomes art' (*GS* 356).
This latter possibility points to the new 'ideal' Nietzsche goes on
to formulate, of a type of human being capable of 'playing,' out
of an 'overflowing power and abundance' and on a plane of high
spirituality, with all those things which once were solemnly 'called
holy, good, untouchable, divine' (*GS* 382). And this form of higher
humanity which he envisions is the new 'artistic humanity' of
which his *Übermensch* is the symbol. In these and a variety of
other ways he thus continued to find it appropriate and illuminating to extend the employment of the notion of art beyond the
context to which it is customarily restricted.

One other matter warrants comment in this general connection.
In Nietzsche's discussion of art in *The Birth of Tragedy, tragic* art
not only receives more attention by far than any other art form
(as might be considered quite reasonable), but also is elevated
above all others in terms of its significance. In his subsequent
writings he continued to give it a special place. So, for example,
he remarks:

> The profundity of the tragic artist lies in this, that his
> aesthetic instinct surveys the more remote consequences, that
> he does not halt shortsightedly at what is closest at hand, that
> he affirms the large-scale economy which justifies the terrifying,
> the evil, the questionable — and more than merely justifies
> them (*WP* 852).

As this passage itself shows, however, Nietzsche's understanding
of the nature of tragic art underwent certain modifications — most
notably, perhaps, with respect to the matter of 'illusion.' No
reference is made to anything of the sort here; his emphasis is
instead upon the idea of 'strength' sufficient to enable one to do
without it (ibid.). Similarly, he links an 'over-fullness of life' with
'a tragic view of life, a tragic insight,' in that those possessed of

the former can 'afford the sight of the terrible and questionable.' To them, he continues, 'what is evil, absurd, and ugly seems, as it were, permissible, owing to an excess of procreating, fertilizing energies that can turn any desert into lush farmland' (*GS* 370).

Notwithstanding the special place tragic art continued to have in Nietzsche's thinking, however, it ceased to preoccupy him. The other arts loom much larger and receive much more attention in his later writings. It is perhaps only to be expected that they would, once he turned from the Greeks (and away from Wagner) and began to take a broader view of art in its historical and contemporary reality. But there was more to the change than this. Tragic art is a very special case; and he would appear to have come to recognize that to view the various arts from the perspective of this special case, as he had in *The Birth of Tragedy*, is both to distort one's understanding of their actual character, and to impoverish one's appreciation of art's place and promise in human life.

Types of art and life

XIII

Perhaps the most glaring departure of the later Nietzsche from the Nietzsche of *The Birth of Tragedy* with respect to art is the complete turnabout he makes in his assessment of Wagner, whom he criticizes at first indirectly and cautiously and then directly and with ever greater vehemence, culminating in the scathing denunciation of him, his art and his effect upon art in *The Case of Wagner*. There he depicts Wagner as the supreme 'artist of decadence' — and only as such as '*the modern artist par excellence.*' He is 'decadent,' and more than that a virulent and contagious 'sickness,' who 'makes sick whatever he touches'; he not only 'has made music sick,' but also 'increases exhaustion' (*CW* 5). His entire art is 'sick'; it represents and promotes 'a decay of art; a decay of the artist as well.' And it is notable that Nietzsche characterizes this 'sickness' not only in terms of 'the over-all change of art into histrionics,' but also in terms of the development of art 'more and more as a talent to *lie*' (*CW* 7).

In making the 'demand' that 'music should not become an art of lying' (*CW* 12), he evinces a very different appraisal (or at least a far more restricted endorsement) of that in art which might be characterized as 'lying' and illusion than he had initially proposed. Art for him might still be properly and importantly contrasted to 'truth'; but he now insists that there is or should be more to it than the sort of 'lying' — and also more than the 'over-excitement of the nervous mechanism' — paradigmatically exemplified for him in Wagnerian art. Neither, he argues, contributes to any real enhancement of life. On the contrary, they work in the opposite direction; and he takes the need for them to be symptomatic of a dangerous weakness. Thus he goes on to invoke his basic distinction between 'ascending life' and 'declining life'; and he employs it to distinguish between an art and 'an aesthetics of *decadence*' (to which he sets himself in opposition) and another, which he links to the 'self-affirmation, self-glorification of life.' Neither 'lies' nor artificial 'stimulants' have any place in it; for it proceeds and 'justifies itself solely out of abundance, out of the overflowing riches of strength.' And he adds: 'All of *beautiful*, all of *great* art belongs here: the essence of both is gratitude (*CW* Epilogue).

What is much more important than Nietzsche's change of heart with reference to Wagner and his art in their own right, however, is the fundamental modification in his view of the relation of art to life which underlies it, and the distinctions between different types of art or artistic tendencies (cutting across the recognition of different art forms and the Dionysian—Apollinian contrast) which he comes to make in conjunction with it. The character of this modification is suggested by his emphatic repudiation of the desirability of anything on the order of an 'art of metaphysical comfort,' and his advocacy instead of an 'art of *this-worldly* comfort,' which might enable one 'some day [to] dispatch all metaphysical comforts to the devil' (*BT* S-C:7).

The true 'sense of art,' for the later Nietzsche, is 'life.' 'Art is the great stimulus to life' (*TI* IX:24). It is fundamentally not merely a 'means of easing life' (*HH* I:148), but rather a 'means' with 'the aim of enhancing life' (*WP* 298). He recognizes that art *may* be 'a consequence of dissatisfaction with reality,' and often has been; but it may also be 'an expression of gratitude for happiness enjoyed' (*WP* 845). And it further can establish the conditions sufficing to elicit that gratitude and occasion that happiness, through the transformation of the aspect of the reality that concerns us. 'What is essential in art remains its perfection of existence, its production of perfection and plenitude; art is essentially *affirmation, blessing, deification of existence*' (*WP* 821). Existence so transformed ceases to be something 'the truth' of which would be so unendurable that we would perish of its apprehension. *Its* 'truth' can be affirmed; and 'art affirms' — affirms its 'perfection and plenitude,' and therewith also the life of which it is the issue. Its role in the 'enhancement of life' thus extends beyond the preservation of life's endangered children, to the alteration of the character of their existence.

This leads to a basic distinction figuring importantly in Nietzsche's later thought, mentioned previously but warranting further attention. 'Every art,' he writes, 'may be viewed as a remedy and an aid in the service of growing and struggling life.' But it performs *different* services in the case of 'those who suffer from the *over-fullness of life*,' and in the case of 'those who suffer from the *impoverishment of life*.' So he goes on to say: 'Regarding all aesthetic values I now avail myself of this main distinction: I ask in every instance, "is it hunger or super-abundance that has here become creative?" ' (*GS* 370). And he considers this distinction to be crucial to the understanding and assessment of certain artistic phenomena which can be and often are confused and mistakenly identified. Indeed, this would appear to be one of the 'crude errors' of which he here speaks of himself as having initially been guilty. It might be thought that the basic distinction requiring to be drawn is that between cases in which 'the desire for *being* prompted creation' (leading to the attempt 'to fix, to immortalize'), and those in which the desire for '*becoming*' (embracing 'destruction' and 'change') is predominant. In fact, however, Nietzsche argues that 'both of these kinds of desire are seen to be ambiguous when one considers them more closely,' and views them in the light of the foregoing distinction.

Thus he contends that the latter desire *may* be 'an expression of an overflowing energy that is pregnant with a future'; but it may instead be merely an expression of 'hatred' on the part of 'the ill-constituted,' who seek to 'destroy, because what exists, indeed all existence . . ., outrages and provokes them.' And similarly, he observes, the former desire 'can be prompted . . . by gratitude and love; art with this origin will always be an art of apotheosis.' But it may on the other hand be only an expression of 'the tyrannic will' of one who is 'tormented,' and seeks to turn 'the idiosyncrasy of his suffering into a binding law and compulsion' (*GS* 370). In this way Nietzsche seeks to give a more discriminating answer to the question 'What is romanticism?' than it commonly receives; and he also draws attention to an ambiguity he sees in art more generally, owing to which his later discussions of it are marked by an ambivalence not to be found in *The Birth of Tragedy*.

It should be observed that, as the above passage itself suggests, the distinction upon which Nietzsche there insists does not obliterate the differentiation of those basic artistic tendencies he initially baptized and on occasion continued to refer to as 'Apollinian' and 'Dionysian.' And it would be an error to suppose that he means to identify the latter alone with 'super-abundance that has become creative,' and to relegate the former to the status of 'hunger' that

516

has taken this creative turn in its desperation. He does expressly state, of the 'overflowing energy' which expresses itself as 'the desire for destruction, change and becoming,' that 'my term for this is, as is known, "Dionysian."' But in this passage the (Apollinian) 'desire for being' and 'will to immortalize' is *also*, in its affirmative form, linked to this same 'super-abundance,' by which the 'gratitude and love' characteristic of it are 'prompted' and which makes them possible.

In short, the *healthy* forms of *both* of these 'desires' are here suggested to be alternative — different but each estimable — expressions of the same 'over-fullness of life,' and are the proper referents of the two denominations. 'Art affirms' in both cases; both involve the 'self-affirmation, self-glorification of life' to which, as has been remarked, Nietzsche holds that 'all of *great* art belongs' (*CW* Epilogue). Only they manifest it in different ways — one might say, in different moods. And the importance of this is not only that it enables one to understand his celebration of 'art of apotheosis,' nor yet again simply that it shows that he accords 'Apollinian' art a much higher status than one might think in view of his revision of the interpretive framework within which he initially identified it. For it further serves to indicate that the idea of a fundamental diversity of forms of artistic expression carries over into his view of what art at its best is and would be.

The art-forms to which Nietzsche here draws attention are those he somewhat earlier had characterized as 'the genuine species of art, those of great repose and great movement,' *both* of which he contrasts with its 'degenerate types — tired, blasé art and agitated art' (*HH* II:115). The first pair, he insists, should not be confused with the second; and he is particularly concerned that one should not stop after marking the difference between the latter two types. Of these, he is utterly disdainful of the first, and somewhat more appreciative of the second, referring to it as 'that barbaric, if also still so charming, outpouring of hot and colorful things from an untamed chaotic soul.' This is 'an art of overstrain, of excitement, of aversion to the orderly,' for which there may indeed be a need 'which artists *must* meet,' for the sake of those who suffer from it, and also for the sake of others who might otherwise suffer from *them*. But he contrasts it with 'the true art,' which represents 'the overflow of a wise and harmonious manner of life' (*HH* III:173).

Art of *this* sort is characterized by the achievement of what Nietzsche calls 'the grand style,' of which he writes: 'The grand style emerges when the beautiful is victorious over the monstrous' (*WS* 96). Much of what now passes for 'great art' surpasses 'petty art, the art of recreation, of delightful diversion' only in that it employs 'the most powerful excitants,' by means of which it manages to 'overwhelm the exhausted and bring them into a night's overanimation' (*WS* 170). But this, he contends, is merely 'aping the high tide of the soul,' and should by no means be confused with attaining it (*GS* 86). Such art is at the furthest remove from an art of the 'grand style.' And it also is anything but conducive to the emergence of an enhanced form of human existence to which this character could likewise be attributed. It is in these terms, however, that Nietzsche conceives of 'the hardest and final task of the artist,' even though he recognizes that the achievement of such style in art is difficult and rare (*HH* II:177).

The 'grand style,' as he understands it, relates to a combination of elements, among which are the greatest strength, the strictest discipline, and the highest cultivation; and it answers to a type of spirituality that is 'neither a Dionysian nor an Apollinian state,' but rather transcends both, incorporating features of each even as it supersedes them.

> The highest feeling of power and sureness finds expression in a *grand style*. The power which no longer needs any proof, which spurns pleasing, which does not answer lightly, which feels no witness near, which lives oblivious of all opposition to it, which reposes within itself, fatalistically, a law among laws — that speaks of itself as a grand style (*TI* IX:11).

In passing, it may be noted that, through his reference here to obliviousness to any 'witness,' Nietzsche links his distinction between art in which the 'grand style' is and is not attained to what he elsewhere terms 'the first distinction to be made regarding works of art': namely, that between 'monological art' and 'art before witnesses.' 'I do not know of any more profound difference in the whole orientation of an artist than this,' he writes, 'whether he looks at his work in progress (at "himself") from the point of view of the witness, or whether he has "forgotten the world,"' and is concerned only with what he is doing (*GS* 367). Not all 'monological art' is as such possessed of 'grand style,' of course; but it would appear that for Nietzsche all art in which this style is achieved is essentially 'monological' in its creation.

'Art as the will to overcome becoming' finds its highest expression in art of 'grand style,' which transcends the flux of becoming by introducing order into it. Thus it manifests what Nietzsche terms 'the supreme will to power,' which is 'to impose upon becoming the character of being.' In 'the new desert' that has been made by 'the destruction of ideals,' it is to it above all that he looks in speaking of 'new arts by means of which we can endure it, we

518

amphibians' (*WP* 617). Much more is at stake here than mere 'artistic formulas,' according to Nietzsche. It will not be easy for us to be able to carry on in this altered landscape of human life; and such art is taken by him to prefigure a new manner of existence appropriate to it: 'one should remodel life so that afterward it *has* to remodel itself' (*WP* 849). The great significance of art possessed of such style is that it foreshadows this development and awakens us to its possibility.

It is undoubtedly in no small measure for this reason that Nietzsche returns repeatedly to the idea of such art, and esteems it so highly. Thus the terms in which he characterizes it also point beyond it, and show him to be thinking beyond it as well. 'The greatness of an artist,' he writes, 'cannot be measured by the "beautiful feelings" he arouses,' but rather only 'according to the degree to which he approaches to the grand style, to which he is capable of the grand style.' And here, he continues, one 'disdains to please' and 'forgets to persuade.' Instead, one 'commands' and 'wills,' in the following sense: 'To become master of the chaos one is; to compel one's chaos to become form' is the fundamental nature of 'the grand ambition here' (*WP* 842). This style is what he sees as the ultimate artistic issue of the 'antagonism of [the] two natural artistic powers' he calls by the names 'Apollinian' and 'Dionysian,' when they interact most felicitously. It incorporates 'plenitude of power and moderation, the highest form of self-affirmation in a cool, noble, severe beauty,' which 'the further development of art' can do no more than amplify, and human life can do no better than to emulate (*WP* 1050).

XIV

But Nietzsche is acutely aware that arts and artists for the most part fall far short of this sort of excellence and greatness; and to balance the picture it is well worth pausing to consider briefly what he regards as some of their typical limitations and shortcomings. Even when they transcend the mediocrity and avoid the decadence he discerns and laments, they are held often to exhibit certain 'all-too-human' tendencies, owing to which he finds them wanting. In particular, he writes, they

> do not stand nearly independently enough in the world and
> *against* the world for their changing valuations to deserve
> attention *in themselves*! They have at all times been valets of
> some morality, philosophy, or religion: quite apart from the
> fact that they have unfortunately often been all-too-pliable

courtiers of their own followers and patrons, and winning flatterers of ancient or newly arrived powers. They always need at the very least protection, a prop, and established authority: artists never stand apart; standing alone is contrary to their deepest instincts (*GM* III:5).

In the same work, Nietzsche goes on to observe that 'nothing is more easily corrupted than an artist' — even though, in the very same section, he also presents art in a very favorable light, saying that it 'is much more fundamentally opposed to the ascetic ideal than is science,' and implying that it is the closest thing to a 'natural antagonist of the ascetic ideal' to be found (*GM* III:25). The artist is thus regarded as typically constituting a mixed case. On the one hand, if he is an artist at all, then at least to some extent Nietzsche's answer to the question 'What does all art do?' applies to him: 'Does it not praise? glorify? choose? prefer? With all this it strengthens or weakens certain valuations,' and so enhances 'the desirability of life' (*TI* IX:24). But on the other, the direction his efforts take is suspect: 'An artist cannot endure reality,' and 'seriously believes that the value of a thing lies in that shadowy residue one derives from colors, form, sound, ideas,' in effect subscribing to the principle: 'the less real, the more valuable' (*WP* 572).

A different perspective on the artist and artistic activity is developed by Nietzsche through his attempt to understand the more elemental facets of human nature of which art is a manifestation and development. Here he might be thought of as carrying his demythologizing of them a step further. He does so, however, not merely with a view to stripping them of their unwarranted aura of sublimity, but also (and more importantly) in order to enhance our appreciation of the intimate relation between the phenomenon of art and human life. In artistic activity and experience, he contends, we do not transcend and leave behind our human nature, escaping the human condition and temporarily attaining a status contrasting with that of human life in the world. The phenomenon of art may constitute a special case in relation to many other phenomena which commonly or occasionally characterize human life; but it by no means involves the sort of radical departure from it that certain advocates and interpreters of it have suggested. Thus he denounces the idea of 'art for art's sake' not only as a 'dangerous principle' owing to the 'defamation of reality' implicit in it (*WP* 298), but also as involving a fundamentally erroneous understanding of the very nature of art: it ignores its basic character 'as an organic function,' in which, euphemistically speaking, 'the most angelic instinct, "love" ' is operative. 'If we subtracted all traces of this intestinal fever from lyricism in sound and work, what would be left of lyrical poetry and music?' Nothing, Nietzsche answers, save 'the virtuoso croaking of shivering frogs, despairing in their swamp.' To this the notion of *'l'art pour l'art'* might perhaps be applicable; but 'all the rest was created by love (*WP* 808).

Nietzsche inveighs equally strongly against the idea of 'disinterestedness' as definitively characteristic of aesthetic experience and the pleasure appropriate to it, of which both Kant and Schopenhauer had made much. He discerns a 'fat worm of error' at the core of the Kantian characterization of 'the aesthetic condition' in terms of the 'disinterestedness' of the pleasure appropriate to it and afforded by it. Here, he contends, Kant compounded the common philosopher's 'mistake' he made when, 'instead of envisaging the aesthetic problem from the point of view of the artist (the creator), [he] considered art and the beautiful purely from that of a "spectator" ' (*GM* III:6). No one who has known 'an abundance of vivid aesthetic experiences, desires, surprises, and delights from the realm of the beautiful,' he remarks, could possibly arrive at anything like 'Kant's famous definition of the beautiful' as that which 'gives us pleasure *without interest.*' Thus he juxtaposes to it another definition, 'framed by a genuine "spectator" and artist — Stendhal,' of the beautiful as *'une promesse de bonheur.'* This definition is held to be a much more appropriate one; and it runs directly counter to Kant's dictum. Nietzsche subjects Schopenhauer to similar criticism, for having followed Kant on this point despire the fact that he 'stood much closer to the arts than Kant' (*GM* III:6).

He takes Kant and Schopenhauer to have gone most fundamentally astray, however, in making the first mistake indicated. It is what led them to give insufficient attention to the creative side of art, and to ignore the sorts of 'interest' — the basic human states and drives — to which it answers and of which it is the sublimated expression. And he contends that one of the most salient of these drives is the very one *against* which Schopenhauer conceives the experience of art to work: human sexuality. 'If there is to be art,' he writes, 'if there is to be any aesthetic doing and seeing, one physiological condition is indispensable: frenzy.' And the 'most ancient and original form of frenzy' is 'the frenzy of sexual excitement'; although there are others as well, which may likewise perform the indispensable function of enhancing 'the excitability of the whole machine.' Such 'excitation,' according to Nietzsche, engenders a 'feeling of increased strength and fullness,' out of

521

which 'one lends to things, one *forces* them to accept from us, one violates them,' in a manner essential to the phenomenon of art (*TI* IX:8). 'In this state one enriches everything out of one's own fullness,' he writes, and 'transforms things until they mirror his power — until they are reflections of his perfection. This *having to* transform into perfection is — art' (*TI* IX:9). Art for him is thus to be conceived as the transforming expression of 'a fever that has good reason to transfigure itself.' For 'one *is* more perfect' when it does so; 'we should do wrong if we stopped at its power to lie; it does more than merely imagine; it even transposes values' (*WP* 808).

It is not only in the instance of the sort of art Nietzsche terms 'Dionysian' that he takes this sublimation of erotic impulses to be at work, but in others as well. 'In the Dionysian intoxication there is sexuality and voluptuousness: they are not lacking in the Apollinian.' What distinguishes them in this respect is a certain 'difference of tempo,' which is reflected in different forms of their expression (*WP* 799). He repeatedly returns to this conception of 'art as the "embellishing" power,' as 'sensuality' in one of 'its disguises' (*WP* 806). So, for example, in a note 'On the Genesis of Art,' he contends that 'the demand for art and beauty is an indirect demand for the ecstasies of sexuality' in a spiritualized form. 'That making perfect, seeing as perfect, which characterizes the cerebral system bursting with sexual energy,' may manifest itself not only immediately and directly, but also in artistic activity; while, 'on the other hand, everything perfect and beautiful works as an unconscious reminder of that enamored condition and its way of seeing' (*WP* 805). Thus art

> is on the one hand an excess and overflow of blooming physicality into the world of images and desires: on the other, an excitation of the animal functions through the images and desires of intensified life (*WP* 802).

It is not sexuality *per se*, however, but rather the sexually charged state as a cardinal instance of a human state in which a high level of vitality and strength are attained, to which Nietzsche attaches importance here. And he supposes this state neither to be the only one satisfying this description, nor the primordial one of which all others are derivative. Thus he cites '*three* elements principally: *sexuality, intoxication, cruelty* — all belonging to the oldest *festal joys* of mankind, all also preponderate in the early "artist."' This precursor of the artist proper is suggested to have been possessed of those 'states in which we infuse a transfiguration and fullness into things and poetize about them until they reflect back our fullness and joy in life,' while not yet sublimating them to the degree and in the manner of his more recognizably artistic off-spring. 'Conversely,' Nietzsche continues, 'when we encounter things that display this transfiguration and fullness, the animal responds with an excitation of those spheres in which all these pleasurable states are situated.' And it is a refinement of this basic phenomenon in which aesthetic experience fundamentally consists: 'a blending of these very delicate nuances of animal well-being and desires constitutes the *aesthetic state*' (*WP* 801).

Sexuality for Nietzsche is thus but one of the 'states of animal vigor' (albeit an important one) which spill over into the 'world of images,' and also are stimulated by the images thus produced, in art and aesthetic experience (*WP* 802). In art, however, this occurs in a manner mediated and so rendered subtler by the employment of a variety of established forms of expression: 'Every mature art has a host of conventions as its basis.' Thus he disassociates himself from those who regard conventions as impediments to artistic creativity. 'Convention is the condition of great art, *not* an obstacle' (*WP* 809); and thus the distinction between art proper and these proto-artistic processes and states is not to be collapsed.

The significance of art

XV

A subject upon which Nietzsche dwells at much greater length, and which is in the final analysis of much greater importance to him, is what might be called *our debt to art*. He considers this debt to be very great indeed, even though quite different from what most of its admirers and philosophical interpreters have supposed it to be. And his mature assessment of it also differs from that which he initially gave of it in *The Birth of Tragedy*. One might put the latter difference in terms of a shift from an emphasis upon the life-*sustaining* function of art to an emphasis upon its contributions to the *enhancement* of life. These contributions, on his view, are several.

One of them has already been touched upon briefly above. It relates to the metamorphosis of the basic impulses Nietzsche considers to underlie and figure crucially in artistic activity and experience. These proto-artistic forces not only are naturally transfiguring, he holds, but moreover themselves become increasingly transfigured as they learn artistic employment. Art manifests them and further stimulates them; but it also involves their sublimation and transforming redirection. In art they are not merely repressed, nor is their weakening and extirpation attempted. Rather, they are humanized and 'spiritualized' in the manner of their expression, and so are able to be enlisted in the service of the enhancement of life. Thus if (in the language of Zarathustra) man may be said to be a 'bridge' between 'beast' and *Übermensch*, art has played a major role in the construction of the bridge; and it can be taken as paradigmatic in exhibiting the nature of the crossing, and in indicating what lies on the other side. It exemplifies his conception of 'man's self-overcoming' — in a restricted sphere, to be sure, but in a way that points to a larger and more comprehensive human 'self-overcoming.' Essential to it is a self-mastery, discipline, and rigorous control exercised in relation to the 'passions' which perhaps differ in kind from those associated with the devices of 'civilization,' but are not surpassed by them in rigor. And it is only because he considers art to constitute an advance, rather than to be regressive in this regard, that Nietzsche views it not merely as a 'stimulus to life' but also as a phenomenon representing its qualitative enhancement, and exhibiting the character of such enhancement.

Art thus has served as a kind of special schooling of the spirit, in which capacities of expression other than those characteristic of merely vital existence have been cultivated, and a form of self-mastery contrasting with that taught in the obedience-school of society has been learned. The distinction Nietzsche draws between 'taming' and 'breeding' here finds application, with art giving substance to the latter notion and standing as its best exemplification thus far. Both involve the transformation of the 'human animal,' but along importantly different lines and in very different ways. The sort of spiritual 'breeding' involved in the emergence of the phenomenon of art in human life may leave much to be desired, as he suggests in remarking upon its merely 'preliminary' status (*WP* 796). But as an initial great experiment along these lines, providing an indication of 'what might yet be made of man' (*BGE* 203) and a sense of direction with respect to the attainment of a 'higher humanity,' he considers that we owe it very much indeed.

We also are indebted to art, according to Nietzsche, for the 'idealizing' manner of addressing ourselves to things which it cultivates, and which when well learned is of the greatest importance in enabling us to attain a fundamentally affirmative stance in relation to existence. This may be regarded as a modification of one of the central ideas advanced in *The Birth of Tragedy*. There the artistic generation of 'illusion' had been taken to be essential to the phenomenon of 'idealizing,' which he had associated with 'Apollinian' art in particular. In latter works such as *Twilight*, on the other hand, it is in terms of the 'perfecting transformation' of things that he conceives of art and its affirmation-inducing power

(*TI* IX:9); and his understanding of 'idealization' as it applies to art is altered accordingly.

'Let us get rid of a prejudice here,' Nietzsche writes; 'idealizing does not consist, as is commonly held, in discounting the petty and inconsequential.' And neither, it may be added, does it consist in the substitution for the real of beautiful but unreal images. 'What is decisive,' he continues, 'is rather a tremendous drive to bring out the main features so that the others disappear in the process.' And what come to *be* the 'main features' are themselves not merely *found* characteristics; for, as he observes in this connection, the 'process' of 'idealizing' is one in which 'one lends to things, one *forces* them to accept from us, one violates them' (*TI* IX:8). So conceived, 'idealizing' neither leaves everything as it is nor turns away from everything as it is, but rather involves imposing a construction upon what one encounters that alters its aspect and its character as well. Thus it serves and teaches how to 'embellish life,' not by diverting attention entirely away from 'everything ugly' (which can be neither eliminated from it nor ignored for long in any event), but rather by 'allowing the *significant* to shine through unavoidable or insuperable ugliness' (*HH* II:174). Another variation on this theme is sounded in a section in *The Gay Science*, which bears the heading 'What should win our gratitude.' Here Nietzsche writes: 'Only artists . . . have taught us the art of viewing ourselves as heroes — from a distance and, as it were, simplified and transfigured.' And the significance of this is considerable:

> Only in this way we deal with some base details in ourselves. Without this art we would be nothing but foreground and live entirely in the spell of that perspective which makes what is closest at hand and most vulgar appear as if it were vast, and reality itself (*GS* 78).

In this passage Nietzsche obviously has in mind 'artists of the theater' in particular; but later in the same work, in a section on 'What one should learn from artists,' he puts the point in more general terms, which are meant to embrace other sorts of artists as well. Beginning by asking, 'How can one make things beautiful, attractive, and desirable for us when they are not?' he suggests that we can 'learn something . . . from artists who are continually trying to bring off such inventions and feats,' through such devices as 'moving away from things until there is a good deal that one no longer sees and there is much that our eye has to add if we are still to see them at all.' While we owe much to art for the development of this capacity to 'idealize,' however, Nietzsche considers it a limitation of artists that 'with them this subtle power usually comes to an end where art ends and life begins.' For the real importance he attaches to it lies in its further extension: 'we want to be the poets of our life — first of all in the smallest, most everyday matters' (*GS* 299).

This leads to a final point concerning our debt to art. In another section in *The Gay Science*, dealing with '*Our ultimate gratitude to art*,' Nietzsche suggests that art consists in a 'kind of cult of the untrue,' which has served to cultivate a '*good* will to appearance' that now proves to be of the utmost importance by enabling us to live with 'the realization that delusion and error are conditions of human knowledge and sensation.' If art had not taught us to be well disposed to 'appearance' notwithstanding its ultimate 'untruth,' he submits, and if instead 'honesty' were our only concern, this realization would be 'utterly unbearable.' Without a sensibility enabling us to take satisfaction in that which we ourselves have created, we could not but be deeply dismayed upon recognizing the extent to which everything transpiring in our lives is and inescapably will continue to be a merely contingently established human affair, answering to nothing written into the fundamental nature of reality. It may be a mere prejudice we were better to dispense with (as Nietzsche elsewhere urges) to think of human reality and experience as mere 'appearance' for this reason. Given certain of our deep-seated intellectual predilections, however, the grip of this prejudice upon us is not easily broken. The emergence of 'art as the good will to appearance' constitutes an important step in that direction, and points the way to a reassessment of what we have made and might further make of ourselves. 'As an aesthetic phenomenon existence is still *bearable* for us, and art furnishes us with eyes and hands and above all a good conscience to be *able* to turn ourselves into such a phenomenon' (*GS* 107).

So also, in considering 'What remains of art,' Nietzsche writes: 'Above all it has taught us over thousands of years to look upon life in every form with interest and enjoyment, and to carry our sensibility to the point that we finally exclaim, "However life may be, it is good." ' And he goes on to observe that 'this teaching has grown into us,' to the point that 'one could give art up, but would not thereby lose this ability learned from it' (*HH* I:222). The suggestion that this involves the cultivation of a 'good will to appearance' is likewise echoed in his contention that art 'is much more fundamentally opposed to the ascetic ideal than science,' and so is much more closely aligned with 'the *opposing ideal*' of a 'value-creating' relation to existence, by virtue of the fact that in art 'the *will* to *deception* has a good conscience' (*GM* III:25). Artistic creativity transfigures, heedless of the way things may happen to be. 'Unlike men of knowledge, who leave everything as it is,' artists 'are productive, to the extent that they actually alter and transform' (*WP* 585). What they produce are not so much representations as *re-presentations* of life, which depart from it, thereby in a sense 'falsifying its image' (*BGE* 59). And they have no qualms about doing so, discovering and teaching us that there is no contradiction between relishing and embellishing life, and that more is gained than is lost by altering its aspect. We are indebted to art because it constitutes a crucial step in the larger process of the transformation of human life, in such a way that 'all nature ceases and becomes art' (*GS* 356).

In sum: beyond all it has been and has meant in peoples' lives and has done to sustain and stimulate life, and notwithstanding all that may be rudimentarily human in it and all-too-human about it, art has fostered and continues to promote the cultivation of human abilities and possibilities reaching beyond the confines of its established sphere of activity and experience. And in so doing it prepares the way for the emergence of this higher form of human life, which would be at once its supersession and its consummation. If artists are for Nietzsche only an 'intermediate' type, and art but a 'preliminary' state in relation to this 'higher concept of art' (which is also a conception of a higher type of human being and state of human existence), that is not only their limitation; it is also their great significance and their glory.

XVI

In light of the foregoing it is quite understandable that Nietzsche found a very warm reception in many artistic and literary circles around the turn of the century, and at least to some extent has continued to do so. Philosophers of art, however, have given him relatively little heed, beyond taking passing notice of certain of his views in *The Birth of Tragedy* and his subsequent repudiation of the art of Wagner which he there had lionized. This is unfortunate; for as the above discussion should have made clear, he has a good deal more to say about art than is contained in his early panegyric to the Greeks and Wagner and in his later polemics against the latter, much of which is of considerable interest. And what is more, I would suggest, philosophers would do well to follow his lead in a number of respects in thinking about art. I shall conclude this discussion with several remarks on this head.

In the first place, Nietzsche is surely right to insist upon the importance of thinking about art as much in terms of the activity of the artist as in terms of the experience of the observer. To be sure, it would be artificial to suppose that the former can be understood in isolation from the latter, both because art is a cultural phenomenon of which both are interdependent moments, and because they are interrelated in the case of the artists themselves. But he does not propose to do so, making much of this very point. He does, however, seek to counter the relatively widespread tendency among philosophers to develop their accounts of art from the perspective in which they most commonly encounter it, as observers rather than creators (or performers), and to assimilate them to more generalized analyses of aesthetic experience. Even if it should be the case that art for most people (and philosophers) is something on the order of a spectator sport, it does not and should not be taken to follow that it is to be construed as though this were its fundamental nature. On Nietzsche's view it requires to be recognized as a form of activity first of all, *engagement in* which (rather than the observation of which) is primary; and this means that it is above all the artist upon whom attention ought to be centered (even if not to the exclusion of all other parties to the affair).

There would also appear to be much to be said for his contention that art should be considered (as he puts it) 'in the perspective of life' more generally, rather than in abstraction and isolation from the larger context of human life within which it occurs and out of which it emerges. As has been seen, he means this in several respects; and in each of them his point is well taken. First, he has in mind the importance of inquiring into what might be termed the sources and springs of artistic activity and experience in our human nature. He further is suggesting the desirability of viewing art in the context of the larger social, cultural and intellectual setting in which it exists at any particular historical juncture, which can and often does have a significant influence upon the forms and directions it takes. And finally, he is proposing that art fundamentally is to be conceived and assessed by reference to the larger question of its significance for the preservation, flourishing and 'enhancement' of human life. To be sure, the merit of this proposal depends upon the cogency of the latter notions, and upon the possibility of elaborating them in such a way that sense may be made of the idea of art (and various sorts of art) being either conducive or detrimental to the attainment of the ends they specify. But even if one finds what Nietzsche has to say along these lines to be questionable, it must be allowed that the kind of thing he tries to do is something well worth trying.

One of the most important gains of thinking about art in the perspective of life extends beyond the enhancement of our understanding of art. For it is not only art that comes thereby to be better understood, but life as well — as it is, and also as it can be. Nietzsche's insistence upon the continuity of life and art is worth taking seriously in both directions; and of all the points he seeks to make none is of greater interest and importance than his contention that art is the clue and key to the possibility of discovering a way beyond nihilism, and a new 'center of gravity' — a new respect for ourselves and estimation of life, 'redeeming existence' in the aftermath of the collapse of old illusions. He disassociates himself from those who would have art as standardly delineated *be* the meaning of life and the locus of all value, and indeed suggests that art in its traditional forms may not be long for this world except as a kind of relic and marginal phenomenon. But he attaches his highest hopes to the emergence of a form of humanity that is heir to art hitherto, and becomes pervasively and continuingly artistic — concretely and richly manifesting the character he ascribes to the world fundamentally, of 'a work of art that gives birth to itself.'

Whether or not one is prepared to follow Nietzsche this far, and can here discern suggestions which are worth pursuing, one should at least find it possible to appreciate certain of the more specific points he makes along the way, and to recognize their fruitfulness for further reflection on art more narrowly conceived. He makes clear, for example, the utter inadequacy of the idea of art as serving to *please* in a disinterested sort of way, and the need to develop notions more adequate than those of 'pleasing' and 'disinterestedness' to be able to do justice to its experience (not to mention its creation). He further makes a strong case for the disassociation of art from the enterprise of the attainment and communication of knowledge, and more generally from the model of *representation*, suggesting that what is 'art' in art must be conceived along quite different lines. And while he is better disposed toward the notion of *expression*, to which many philosophers persuaded of this point have turned in its stead, he is quite convincing in his insistence upon according centrality and primacy to the idea of the *transfiguring* character of art. This most suggestive idea, pertaining not only to the creative activity of the artist and its immediate issue in the art work but also to the experience and indeed the manner of existence of artist and partaker alike, has yet to be fully appreciated; and it could in the end prove to be Nietzsche's most fruitful contribution to the philosophy of art.

Afterword

Alas, what are you after all, my written and painted thoughts!
It was not long ago that you were still so colorful, young, and
malicious, full of thorns and secret spices — you made me
sneeze and laugh — and now? You have already taken off your
novelty, and some of you are ready, I fear, to become truths:
they already look so immortal, so pathetically decent, so dull!
. . . And it is only your *afternoon* . . . for which alone I have
colors, many colors perhaps, many motley caresses and fifty
yellows and browns and greens and reds: but nobody will guess
from that how you looked in your morning, you sudden
sparks and wonders of my solitude, you my old beloved —
wicked thoughts! (*BGE* 296).

With these reflections Nietzsche concludes *Beyond Good and
Evil*. And if his own expressions of his thoughts were already paler
than the latter were for him upon their conception, something
similar must be allowed to apply with even greater force to whatever might be said about them in any study such as this one. This
progressive paling has a certain inevitability; and the loss it represents is not to be gainsaid. One minded to do so, however, may
learn to appropriate what one reads in such a way that at least
something of Nietzsche's thinking is captured and revived in one's
own, rendering one's philosophical palette the richer thereby.
Moreover, something is gained as well as lost in the process to
which he refers, as he indicates in suggesting, with seeming chagrin,
that (at least) some of his thoughts are 'ready to become truths.'
This is not only something Nietzsche 'fears'; it is also something
(if certainly not the only thing) he *desires* — and he undoubtedly
would have been very much more distressed were he to have

suspected otherwise. Some of his thoughts likewise are ready to be found wanting in this respect — misguided, ill-informed, outlived and outgrown, or simply erroneous — even as he found many ideas of others to be; and this too is a judgment he neither sought to avoid nor deemed irrelevant to his enterprise. More importantly, many of his interpretations are perhaps ready to be accorded superiority to their rivals, even as others may not fare so well; and more fundamentally still, his ways of dealing with various matters are at least in some cases ready to complement and even displace those previously and presently preferred. The present study has been intended to contribute to this sort of reckoning with him; and while his thinking admits of many forms of treatment, as was observed at the outset, this is not only one of those possible, but moreover one of those it expressly invites.

I have sought both to do justice to Nietzsche's philosophical thinking and to carry forward the process he recognizes already to have been occurring in his own writings, of turning his sparkling thoughts into more prosaic points, interpretations and procedures the soundness and merit of which may be considered. If nothing else, it should at least have become clear that his treatment of most of the issues he addresses is much subtler and more interesting than is commonly supposed, not only by his detractors but also by his popularizers and those who have seized upon him for their own ulterior purposes. Provocative and disconcerting though many of his views may be, they are far from simplistic, and require to be taken seriously. Certain of his self-styled followers may be deserving of contempt; but he himself cannot be dismissed so easily.

It also should be obvious that his claim to philosophical respectability and significance is by no means (as is commonly supposed) exclusively a matter of his anticipation of certain themes of existentialism, his affinity with which is in any event greatly exaggerated. What is living (and dead) in Nietzsche is by no means simply that in his thought which did (and did not) find an echo and amplification in existential philosophy. Indeed, a considerable step will have been made toward a just philosophical reckoning with him when he is no longer bracketed with the central figures associated with this subsequent philosophical development. It would be both more appropriate and more illuminating to regard him (as he commonly is in Europe) as one of the inaugurators of what has come to be known as *Lebensphilosophie*, and a progenitor of the 'philosophical anthropology' which developed out of it in Central Europe in the second quarter of this century.

The appropriateness (with qualifications) of Danto's characterization of him as a precursor of the 'analytic movement' in philosophy, however, must also be borne in mind — as should the fact that proponents of both 'critical theory' in Germany and 'poststructuralism' in France have deemed him one of their own (or at least a kindred spirit). He actually does not fit nicely into any of these niches in the recent history of philosophy. Yet it is some measure of the richness of his philosophical thought and of his philosophical importance that it is tempting and possible to view him in all of these ways; and that philosophers associated with all of these developments (and others as well) could find much in him to draw upon — or at any rate (as in the case of someone like Danto), upon discovering him, to resonate to.

It would be impossible in a short space to sum up those of Nietzsche's many 'thoughts' on the various matters dealt with in this book which do and do not appear to belong among the 'truths' he suggests at least some to be ready to become, or which are and are not sufficiently plausible and persuasive interpretations to be reckoned superior to others that have been and might be advanced. In many cases, moreover, the jury is still out, and a final verdict may never be able to be delivered. His treatment of most of these matters, however, both requires and will reward serious attention as consideration of them proceeds. His approach to and reflections upon matters as diverse as truth and knowledge, science and art, human nature and human possibility, values and morals, and philosophy itself as well, place large and important question-marks beside received ways of dealing with and thinking about them, even if what he himself has to say about them might be deemed problematical. And problematical though many of his views may be, his thinking is frequently both illuminating and suggestive of lines which warrant further trying.

By the circuitous routes philosophy has taken between his time and ours, it may be that the conditions have been established in which philosophy as Nietzsche conceived and practiced it both can be discovered to be called for and can take root and develop — neither in imitation of his style nor in adherence to the letter of his elaboration of his positions, perhaps, but at least in tune with the spirit and general direction of his philosophical enterprise. The linguistic-analytic and existential-phenomenological movements in philosophy alike would seem to have run their course, leaving their mark upon the sensibilities of philosophers of the present day even as a growing recognition of their limitations renders increasingly apparent the necessity of superseding them. Philosophers further at length have learned to overcome both their longstanding indifference, disdain or mistrust, and also their alternative awe and obeisance, toward the natural and human sciences. And Nietzsche stands available to us as one who has a good deal to say about where and how we might go on from here.

Nietzsche sought first and foremost to make clear that genuinely philosophical thinking requires an intellectual conscience sharp and demanding enough to shake and challenge our every old and new faith, not only in 'the old God,' but also in science, language, logic, perception, our moral sense, and traditional and prevailing modes of valuation, as well as in all social conventions and conceptions of historical progress. He was no less insistent that it requires sophistication along many different lines — historical, linguistic, natural-scientific, physiological, sociological, and above all psychological. And he further never tired of stressing its fundamentally interpretive character, and the indispensability of the development and employment of 'creative powers' in all interpretation which is more than a mere reflection of established ways of thinking. In all of these respects Nietzsche forces us to reconsider both the significance of the thought and efforts of philosophers past and present, and also the nature and future course of the philosophical enterprise.

He also insisted upon the inclusion of a number of large and important problems high on philosophy's agenda. They center upon the necessity of exploring and working out the full range of consequences of what he calls 'the death of God' — from the 'de-deification of nature,' to the naturalistic reinterpretation of human nature, human life and human knowledge and morality, to the 'revaluation of values.' If philosophy's first order of business must be to assess prevailing modes of interpretation, and if these are found wanting, its next and main task must be to reinterpret the matters which thus are no longer to be construed as they have been, chief among which are those just indicated.

Whatever one may make of Nietzsche's particular views and purported insights, and however one may assess the results of his specific attempts to reorient our thinking, his greatest contribution to philosophy consists (echoing the title of his early essay on Schopenhauer) in the service he is capable of performing as a philosophical 'educator,' for anyone prepared to encounter him seriously. One who does so might in the end differ with him on many points, but is bound to emerge with an altered philosophical sensibility. Philosophers and philosophy past and present cannot but appear to one in a different light once one has seen them through his eyes; and a broad range of metaphysical, evaluative and moral schemes which have long dominated philosophical thinking in one guise or another are discovered to be vulnerable in ways seldom suspected. Science and art too are approached and dealt with in a manner raising different sorts of questions about them than those usually considered, and so acquire an altered aspect as one continues to reflect upon them.

Further, the multi-level analysis of truth and knowledge Nietzsche undertakes, and the kinds of considerations he brings to bear in doing so, must lead one to have second thoughts about the adequacy of the kind of treatment they are usually accorded. The necessity of subjecting scientific accounts of life and the world to further interpretation in order to do justice to them is a suggestion one recognizes one must at least entertain. Our thinking about ourselves cannot but be affected by Nietzsche's way of framing and carrying out such inquiry; and he forces a confrontation with certain hard questions in this context which are seldom posed or seriously addressed. And his approach to matters of value and morality must be reckoned with by anyone whose concerns with them transcend those of the kind of thinker he calls the mere 'philosophical laborer.'

The subtitle of Nietzsche's *Beyond Good and Evil* is: *Prelude to a Philosophy of the Future*. His mature thought generally may be considered to constitute such a 'prelude,' rather than anything approaching (or intended to stand as) the full development of such a philosophy. Indeed, it is part of his purpose to make it clear that that genuinely philosophical thinking of the sort he envisions and attempts to practice can never achieve complete and final form. The task of philosophical interpretation will never be done — owing both to the nature of that which is to be interpreted, and to the nature of such interpretation. But it is not for either reason to be considered a futile or pointless affair. Our understanding of ourselves and our world may always be improved upon, and the manner of our human existence as well. Neither in what we think, nor in what we are, will we ever *have arrived*, once and for all, at some state of knowledge or spirituality or humanity that may properly be styled 'absolute.' Rather than signifying the end or the bankruptcy of the philosophical (and human) enterprise, however, this is taken by Nietzsche precisely in the opposite way — as underscoring the need for his 'new philosophers,' who will take the lead in new ventures of interpretation and enhancement as both 'men of knowledge' and 'creators,' quickened rather than daunted by the prospect of the 'open sea' without fixed horizon or final port that confronts them. With the assimilation of 'the news that "the old god is dead," ' and having banished the long philosophical shadow of this old faith and recovered from the nihilistic rebound initially attending its renunciation, 'our heart overflows with gratitude, amazement, premonitions, expectation' in the 'new dawn' which thus breaks:

> all the daring of the lover of knowledge is permitted again; the sea, *our* sea, lies open again; perhaps there has never yet been such an 'open sea' — (GS 343).

Bibliography

Some editions of Nietzsche's Collected Works

Werke: Kritische Gesamtausgabe, eds Giorgio Colli and Mazzino Montinari, 30 vols (Berlin: de Gruyter, 1967–78).

Werke: Musarionausgabe, 23 vols (Munich: Musarion, 1920–9).

Werke in drei Banden, ed. Karl Schlechta, 3 vols (Munich: Carl Hanser, 1954–6); with an Index in a fourth volume (1965).

The Complete Works of Friedrich Nietzsche, ed. Oscar Levy,18 vols (New York: Macmillan, 1909–11; reissued New York, Russell & Russell, 1964).

Some English translations of specific works

Some of Nietzsche's works and writings are available in English only in the Levy *Complete Works*. Some have been translated both by Walter Kaufmann and by R.J. Hollingdale (in several instances in collaboration) and by others as well; and some have been translated only by Kaufmann (and Hollingdale), or only by others. The translations listed below are those made by the two of them, or else those made by others in the cases of works they have not translated. (See the Reference Key following the Preface for German titles.)

The Birth of Tragedy (1872), trans. Kaufmann, with *The Case of Wagner* (New York: Vintage, 1966).

Philosophy in the Tragic Age of the Greeks (1870–3), trans. Marianne Cowan (South Bend, Ind.: Gateway, 1962).

David Strauss, the Confessor and Writer (1873) and *Richard Wagner in Bayreuth* (1876), trans. A. Ludovici, *Complete Works*, vol. IV.

On the Use and Abuse of History (1873), trans. Adrian Collins (New York: Bobbs-Merrill, 1957).

Schopenhauer as Educator (1874), trans. J.W. Hillesheim and Malcolm R. Simpson (South Bend, Ind.: Gateway, 1965).

Human, All Too Human (I) (1878), trans. H. Zimmern and Paul V. Cohn, *Complete Works*, vol. VI.

Mixed Opinions and Aphorisms (*Human, All Too Human*, II) (1879), trans. Paul V. Cohn, *Complete Works*, vol. VII.

The Wanderer and His Shadow (*Human, All Too Human*, II) (1880), trans. Paul V. Cohn, *Complete Works*, vol. VII.

Dawn [*of Day*] (1881), trans. J.M. Kennedy, *Complete Works*, vol. IX.

The Gay Science (1882), trans. Kaufmann (New York: Vintage, 1974).

Thus Spoke Zarathustra (1883–5), trans. Kaufmann (New York: Viking, 1966); also in *The Portable Nietzsche* (New York: Viking, 1954); trans. Hollingdale (Harmondsworth and Baltimore: Penguin, 1967).

Beyond Good and Evil (1886), trans. Kaufmann (New York: Vintage, 1966); trans. Hollingdale (Harmondsworth and Baltimore: Penguin, 1973).

On the Genealogy of Morals (1887), trans. Kaufmann and Hollingdale, with *Ecce Homo* (New York: Vintage, 1968).

The Case of Wagner (1888); see *The Birth of Tragedy*.

Twilight of the Idols (1888), trans. Kuafmann, in *The Portable Nietzsche* (New York: Viking, 1954); trans. Hollingdale, with *Antichrist* (Harmondsworth and Baltimore: Penguin, 1968).

The Antichrist (1888), trans. Kaufmann, in *The Portable Nietzsche* (New York: Viking, 1954); trans. Hollingdale, with *Twilight* (Harmondsworth and Baltimore: Penguin, 1968).

Nietzsche contra Wagner (1888), trans. Kaufmann, in *The Portable Nietzsche* (New York: Viking, 1954).

Ecce Homo (1888), trans. Kaufmann, with *Genealogy* (New York: Vintage, 1968); trans. Hollingdale (Harmondsworth and Baltimore: Penguin, 1979).

The Will to Power (1883–8), trans. Kaufmann and Hollingdale (New York: Vintage, 1968).

Selected Letters of Friedrich Nietzsche, trans. and ed. Christopher Middleton (Chicago: University of Chicago Press, 1969).

Nietzsche: A Self-Portrait from His Letters, trans. and ed. Peter Fuss and Henry Shapiro (Cambridge, Mass.: Harvard University Press, 1971).

Other useful volumes

Nietzsche, *Der Wille zur Macht*, selected and arranged by Peter Gast with the cooperation of Elizabeth Forster-Nietzsche (Stuttgart: A. Kroner, 1964).

Nietzsche, *Erkenntnistheoretische Schriften*, eds Hans Blumenberg *et al.* (Frankfurt a.M.: Suhrkamp, 1968).

Selected studies of Nietzsche

Alderman, Harold G., *Nietzsche's Gift* (Columbus, Ohio: Ohio University Press, 1977).

Allison, David B., ed., *The New Nietzsche: Contemporary Styles of Interpretation* (New York: Dell, 1977).

Baroni, Charles, *Nietzsche, educateur de l'homme au surhomme* (Paris: Buchet, 1961).

Bataille, Georges, *Sur Nietzsche, volonte de chance* (Paris: Gallimard, 1945).

Brandes, Georg, *Friedrich Nietzsche*, trans. A.G. Chater (London: Heinemann, 1914).

Brinton, Crane, *Nietzsche*, 2nd edn (New York: Harper, 1965).

Bueb, Bernard, *Nietzsches Kritik der praktischen Vernunft* (Stuttgart: Ernst Klett, 1972).

Copleston, Frederick, *Friedrich Nietzsche: Philosopher of Culture* (London: Burns, Oates & Washburn, 1942).

Danto, Arthur C., *Nietzsche as Philosopher* (New York: Macmillan, 1965).

Deleuze, Gilles, *Nietzsche* (Paris: Presses Universitaires de France, 1965).

Deleuze, Gilles, *Nietzsche et la philosophie* (Paris: Presses Universitaires de France, 1962).

Derrida, Jacques, *The Question of Style* (Venice: Corbo e Fiore, 1976).

Fink, Eugen, *Nietzsches Philosophie* (Stuttgart: Kohlhammer, 1960).

Granier, Jean, *Le Problème de la vérité dans la philosophie de Nietzsche* (Paris: Editions du Seuil, 1966).

Grimm, Ruediger Hermann, *Nietzsche's Theory of Knowledge* (Berlin/New York: de Gruyter, 1977).

Harper, Ralph, *The Seventh Solitude* (Baltimore: Johns Hopkins University Press, 1965).

Hayman, Ronald, *Nietzsche: A Critical Life* (New York: Oxford University Press, 1980).

Heidegger, Martin, *Nietzsche*, 2 vols (Pfullingen: Neske, 1961).

Heidegger, Martin, *Nietzsche*, vol. I: *The Will to Power as Art*, trans. David Krell (New York: Harper & Row, 1979).

Hollingdale, R. J., *Nietzsche* (London: Routledge & Kegan Paul, 1973).

Hollingdale, R. J., *Nietzsche: The Man and His Philosophy* (Baton Rouge, La.: Louisiana State University Press, 1965).

Jaspers, Karl, *Nietzsche: An Introduction to the Understanding of His Philosophical Activity*, trans. Charles F. Wallraff and Frederick J. Schmitz (Chicago: Regnery, 1965).

Jaspers, Karl, *Nietzsche and Christianity*, trans. E. B. Ashton (Chicago: Regnery, 1961).

Kaufmann, Walter, *Nietzsche: Philosopher, Psychologist, Antichrist*, 4th edn (Princeton: Princeton University Press, 1974).

Klages, Ludwig, *Die psychologischen Errungenschaften Nietzsches* (Leipzig: Barth, 1926).

Klossowski, Pierre, *Nietzsche et le cercle vicieux* (Paris: Mercure de France, 1969).

Kofman, Sarah, *Nietzsche et la Métaphore* (Paris: Editions Payot, 1972).

Lea, Frank A., *The Tragic Philosopher: A Study of Friedrich Nietzsche* (London: Methuen, 1957).

Love, Frederick, *The Young Nietzsche and the Wagnerian Experience* (Chapel Hill: University of North Carolina Press, 1963).

Löwith, Karl, *From Hegel to Nietzsche*, trans. David Green (Garden City, NY: Doubleday Anchor, 1967).

Löwith, Karl, *Kierkegaard und Nietzsche, oder Philosophische und Theologische Überwindung des Nihilismus* (Frankfurt a.M.: Klostermann, 1933).

Löwith, Karl, *Nietzsches Philosophie der Ewigen Wiederkunft des Gleichen*, 2nd edn (Stuttgart: Kohlhammer, 1956).

Magnus, Bernd, *Nietzsche's Existential Imperative* (Bloomington, Ind.: Indiana University Press, 1978).

Manthey-Zorn, Otto, *Dionysus: The Tragedy of Nietzsche* (Amherst, Mass.: University of Massachusetts Press, 1956).

Morel, Georges, *Nietzsche*, 3 vols (Paris: Aubier-Montaigne, 1970).

Morgan, George, A., Jr., *What Nietzsche Means* (Cambridge, Mass.: Harvard University Press, 1941; New York: Harper & Row, 1965).

Müller-Lauter, Wolfgang, *Nietzsche: seine Philosophie der Gegensätze und die Gegensätze seiner Philosophie* (Berlin: de Gruyter, 1971).

Schlechta, Karl, *Der Fall Nietzsche: Aufsätze und Vorträge* (Munich: Carl Hanser, 1958).

Simmel, Georg, *Schopenhauer und Nietzsche: Ein Vortragszyklus* (Leipzig: Duncker & Humblot, 1907).

Solomon, Robert C., ed., *Nietzsche: A Collection of Critical Essays* (Garden City, NY: Doubleday Anchor, 1973).

Stambaugh, Joan, *Nietzsche's Thought of Eternal Return* (Baltimore: Johns Hopkins University Press, 1972).

Stern, J. P., *A Study of Nietzsche* (Cambridge: Cambridge University Press, 1979).

Strong, Tracy, *Friedrich Nietzsche and the Politics of Transfiguration* (Berkeley: University of California Press, 1975).

Ulmer, Karl, *Nietzsche: Einheit und Sinn seines Werkes* (Bern and Munich: Francke, 1962).

Vaihinger, Hans, *Nietzsche als Philosoph* (Berlin: Reuther & Reichard, 1902).

Vaihinger, Hans, *The Philosophy of 'As If'*, trans. C. K. Ogden (New York: Harcourt Brace, 1924).

Valadier, Paul, *Nietzsche et la critique du christianisme* (Paris: Editions du Cerf, 1974).

Wahl, Jean André, *L'avant-dernière pensée de Nietzsche* (Paris: Centre de documentation universitaire, 1961).

Wahl, Jean André, *La pensée philosophique de Nietzsche des années 1885–88* (Paris: Centre de documentation universitaire, 1959).

Wilcox, John T., *Truth and Value in Nietzsche* (Ann Arbor, Mich.: University of Michigan Press, 1974).

Williams, W. D., *Nietzsche and the French* (Oxford: Clarendon Press, 1952).

Index